EXTENDING EDUCATIONAL CHANGE

This volume is part of a set of four. These volumes together form the *International Handbook of Educational Change,* which was originally published in 1998 as volume 5 in the Springer International Handbooks of Education series (formerly known as Kluwer International Handbooks of Education series), and edited by Andy Hargreaves, Ann Lieberman, Michael Fullan and David Hopkins.

The Table of Contents of the entire *International Handbook of Educational Change* has been printed at the end of this volume.

Extending Educational Change

International Handbook of Educational Change

Edited by:

Andy Hargreaves

Department of Teacher Education, Curriculum and Instruction Lynch School of Education, Boston College, MA, U.S.A.

 Springer

A C.I.P. Catalogue record for this book is available from the Library of Congress.

The Roots of Educational Change: ISBN-10 1-4020-3289-7
Extending Educational Change: ISBN-10 1-4020-3291-9
Fundamental Change: ISBN-10 1-4020-3292-7
The Practice and Theory of School Improvement: ISBN-10 1-4020-3290-0
Set: ISBN-10 1-4020-3423-7
The Roots of Educational Change: ISBN-13 978-1-4020-3289-9
Extending Educational Change: ISBN-13 978-1-4020-3291-2
Fundamental Change: ISBN-13 978-1-4020-3292-9
The Practice and Theory of School Improvement: ISBN-13 978-1-4020-3290-5
Set: ISBN-13 978-1-4020-3423-7
Springer Dordrecht, Berlin, Heidelberg, New York

The volumes can be purchased separately and as a set.

Published by Springer,
P.O. Box 17, 3300 AA Dordrecht, The Netherlands.

Printed on acid-free paper

springeronline.com

Printed in the Netherlands.

Table of Contents

II. Challenges

International Handbook of Educational Change - Introduction

ANDY HARGREAVES
Department of Teacher Education, Curriculum and Instruction Lynch School of Education, Boston College, MA, U.S.A.

ANN LIEBERMAN
Carnegie Foundation for the Advancement of Teaching, Stanford, CA, U.S.A.

MICHAEL FULLAN
Ontario Institute for Studies in Education, University of Toronto, Canada

DAVID HOPKINS
Department for Education and Skills, London, U.K.

This set of four volumes on *Educational Change* brings together evidence and insights on educational change issues from leading writers and researchers in the field from across the world. Many of these writers, whose chapters have been specially written for these books, have been investigating, helping initiate and implementing educational change, for most or all of their lengthy careers. Others are working on the cutting edge of theory and practice in educational change, taking the field in new or even more challenging directions. And some are more skeptical about the literature of educational change and the assumptions on which it rests. They help us to approach projects of understanding or initiating educational change more deeply, reflectively and realistically.

Educational change and reform have rarely had so much prominence within public policy, in so many different places. Educational change is ubiquitous. It figures large in Presidential and Prime Ministerial speeches. It is at or near the top of many National policy agendas. Everywhere, educational change is not only a policy priority but also major public news. Yet action to bring about educational change usually exceeds people's understanding of how to do so effectively.

The sheer number and range of changes which schools are now confronting is staggering.

Educators have always had to engage with educational changes of one sort or another. But other than in the last three decades or so, these changes were infrequent and episodic and they never really affected or even addressed the core of how teachers taught (Cuban, 1984). The changes were in things like how subjects were organized, how grade levels were clustered together into different school types, or how groups of students were divided between different schools or integrated within them according to ability, gender or race. Thus when educational

A. Hargreaves (ed.), Extending Educational Change, vii-xi.
© 2005 *Springer. Printed in the Netherlands.*

historians chastise contemporary change advocates for ignoring the existence of educational change in the past and for exaggerating current crises and change demands "as a marketing device to promote the new possibilities of education in a new century, designed to appeal to consumers of different kinds who are grown weary of the old familiar product" (McCulloch, 1997), they are only partially right. While educational change has always been with us in some sense or other (as also, of course, has educational continuity), many of the changes are very different now, in both their substance and their form.

Since the 1960s, educational change has became a familiar part of teachers' work, and has more directly addressed issues of what teachers teach and how they should teach it. Following the launch of Sputnik and the emergence of post-war egalitarian ideals, public education has been treated as a crucible of technological and economic advancement and as a creator of greater social justice. In the 1960s and 70s, teachers in many countries had to deal with the rhetoric and sometimes the reality of curriculum innovation in mathematics, science and the humanities. They saw students stay in school longer, the ability ranges of their classes grow wider and the walls of their classrooms come down and then go up again just a few years later. Successive waves of different approaches to reading or mathematical learning swept through their classrooms, each one washing away the marks left by its predecessors.

It was in these times of educational expansion and optimism that educational change really began in earnest - as also did the study of it. From the late 1960s and early 1970s, researchers like Matt Miles, Per Dalin, Lou Smith, Neil Gross, Lawrence Stenhouse and Seymour Sarason studied the growing phenomenon of educational innovation - whether in the shape of large-scale curriculum projects and packages, or in the form of newly-created innovative schools. They showed how and why large-scale curriculum innovations rarely progressed beyond the phase of having their packages purchased or "adopted" to the point where they were implemented fully and faithfully, and could bring about real changes in classroom practice. At the same time, they also revealed how the promise of exceptional innovative schools usually faded over time as their staffs grew older, their charismatic leaders left, and the system withdrew permission for them to break the rules.

As the limitations of large-scale curriculum innovations became apparent, educators began to treat the individual school as the centre or focal point of educational change efforts. School-based curriculum development, and school-based staff development initiatives proliferated in many places, instead of development being imposed or initiated from faraway.

Research on what made teachers effective in their classrooms also expanded to address what made schools effective or ineffective as a whole, and as lists of effective schools characteristics were discovered (such as creating a safe and orderly environment for learning, or setting and checking homework regularly), these were sometimes then used as administrative blueprints to try and make particular schools become more effective over time. Many districts or other administrative authorities initiated "effective schools" projects on this basis. Some schools and districts supplemented and sometimes supplanted this science of school effectiveness with a more loosely defined and humanistically interpreted art of school improvement - the process of how to help schools and their staffs become more effective through setting clear goals, creating staff involvement, measuring progress over time and so forth.

Ironically, this approach to school improvement was then translated back into a rational science by many educational systems. It was treated as a process of planned or managed change that schools could be moved through step-by-step, stage-by-stage, guided by the school's improvement team that its region or district mandated it to have.

When these various school-centred changes and improvements didn't work well enough or fast enough (and sometimes even when they did), impatient educational administrators (and American urban school superintendents with an average job tenure of less than two years can be very impatient indeed), imposed their own reform requirements instead. So too did ideologically driven politicians, whose agendas of educational reform have often been shaped by the desire to create public indignation (which they promise their measures will then answer), or by the private idiosyncrasies of their own educational pasts, (which their reforms are meant to cherish or purge).

This quarter century or more of educational change processes and initiatives that have been meant to alter learning and teaching in our schools, has left us with a mixed legacy. On the one hand, studies of what works and what doesn't across all the different change strategies have created a truly powerful knowledge base about the processes, practices and consequences of educational change. During this period, research studies have shown, for example, how educational change moves through distinctive stages of initiation, implementation and institutionalization; how people who encounter changes go through successive "stages of concern" about how those changes will affect them; and how people respond very differently to educational change initiatives depending on what point they have reached in their own lives and careers.

Some of the research findings on educational change have even been accorded the status of generalizable rules or 'lessons' of change. These include the maxims that practice changes before beliefs, that successful change is a product of both pressure and support, that evolutionary planning works better than linear planning and so forth (these 'lessons' have been synthesized especially effectively by Michael Fullan, 1991, 1993).

So extensive is the current knowledge base of educational change that it has come to constitute a field of study in its own right - drawing on and transcending the disciplines of sociology, psychology, history and philosophy, as well as the fields of curriculum and educational administration. In a way, educational change has now really come of age - but while this is a significant academic achievement, it is also where the problems of the field - the second part of its legacy - also begin.

Our experience of educational change today is stretching far beyond our experience, knowledge and investigations of it in times gone by. While the existing knowledge-base of educational change is impressive, it is no longer really sufficient to address the unique change problems and challenges that educators confront today.

Contemporary patterns of educational change present educators with changes that are multiple, complex and sometimes contradictory. And the change demands with which educators have to deal, seem to follow one another at an increasingly frenetic speed. A typical primary or elementary school these days may be considering a new reading program, developing cooperative learning strategies, thinking about how to implement new computers, designing a better parent newsletter, and trialling portfolio assessments all at the same time. The portfolio assessments favoured by the region or the district may have to be reconciled with imposed standardized test requirements by the nation or the state. A push to develop a more integrated curriculum and to recognize children's multiple intelligences may be reversed by a newly elected government's commitments to more conventionally defined learning standards within existing academic subjects.

All this can make teachers and administrators feel that the systems in which they are working aren't just complex but downright chaotic. This chaos is partly inherent in societies and organizations where information circulates and decisions are made with increasing speed. It is also the result of educational policy constantly being shaped and altered by different and competing interest groups in an ideological battle for the minds of the young. And sometimes it even results from a kind of *manufactured uncertainty* that more than a few governments wilfully create to arouse panic, to set pretexts for their policy interventions and to keep educators and everyone else off-balance.

Few of the existing theories and strategies of educational change equip educators to cope effectively with these complex, chaotic and contradictory environments

- Rational theories of planned change that move through predictable stages of implementation or 'growth' are poorly suited to schools where unexpected twists and turns are the norm rather than the exception in the ways they operate.
- The conventional academic and behavioural outcomes that defined the core of what an effective school should produce in the past are outdated in an age where many people now clamour for schools to develop higher-order thinking skills, problem-solving capacities, and the habits of collaboration and teamwork. Complex as the world of education is, people expect more and more from it, and the effective schools of the past cannot deliver what many expect of schools today.
- Theories and models that helped educators know how (and how not) to implement single curriculum innovations are of little use to schools where innovations are multiple and priorities compete.

While we have learned a lot about how to improve individual schools or small clusters of schools with additional resources, exceptional leaders, the ability to attract or shed particular kinds of staff members, and discretion to break the rules; we are only just beginning to understand the challenges of scaling reform up from small samples of improving schools, to entire school systems. The existing knowledge base of school improvement has shown us how to create islands of improvement, but has been less helpful in assisting people to make archipelagoes from islands, and still less in showing them how to build entire continents of change.

It is time, therefore, to reflect at some length about what we already know and have learned about educational change and to explore how the field can and should be pushed further, to help educators understand and deal effectively with the immensely complex change problems that are customary today. Each of the four volumes on *Educational Change* addresses these fundamental issues in its own distinctive way.

REFERENCES

Cuban, L. (1984). *How teachers taught: Constancy and change in American classrooms, 1890-1980.* New York: Longman.

Fullan, M. (1991). *The new meaning of educational change.* New York: Teachers College Press.

Fullan, M. (1993). *Change forces.* London: Falmer Press.

McCulloch, G. (1997). Marketing the millennium: Education for the twenty-first century. In A. Hargreaves, & R. Evans (Eds.), *Beyond educational reform.* Buckingham: Open University Press.

Introduction

Pushing the Boundaries of Educational Change

ANDY HARGREAVES

Department of Teacher Education, Curriculum and Instruction Lynch School of Education, Boston College, MA, U.S.A.

INTRODUCTION

This section of the Handbook deals with the idea and necessity of extending educational change — conceptually and in action. Extending educational change matters for getting existing approaches to educational change to work more effectively in more places, and for deepening our understandings of and sensitivity to whose interests are at stake in educational change. Who benefits and who loses? How do these interests and how we address them affect what kinds of changes we pursue? What challenges does all this pose for the change process itself?

THE DIFFICULTY OF EDUCATIONAL CHANGE

There are many reasons why educational change is so difficult, why getting it to take in many places, for more than brief periods, can be so hard. Among them are that:

- the reason for the change is poorly conceptualized or not clearly demonstrated. It is not obvious who will benefit and how. What the change will achieve for students in particular is not spelled out;
- the change is too broad and ambitious so that teachers have to work on too many fronts, or it is too limited and specific so that little real change occurs at all;
- the change is too fast for people to cope with, or too slow so that they become impatient or bored and move on to something else;
- the change is poorly resourced or resources are withdrawn once the first flush of innovation is over. There is not enough money for materials or time for teachers to plan. The change is built on the backs of teachers, who cannot bear it for long without additional support;
- there is no long-term commitment to the change to carry people through the anxiety, frustration and despair of early experimentation and unavoidable setbacks;

1

A. Hargreaves (ed.), Extending Educational Change, 1-14.
© 2005 *Springer. Printed in the Netherlands.*

- key staff who can contribute to the change, or might be affected by it, are not committed. Conversely, key staff might become overinvolved as an administrative or innovative elite, from which other teachers feel excluded. Resistance and resentment are the consequences in either case;
- students are not involved in the change, or do to have it explained to them, so they yearn for and cling to ways of learning that are familiar to them and become the school's most powerful protectors of the past;
- parents oppose the change because they are kept at a distance from it. Alternatively, influential groups or individuals among the parents can negotiate special deals with the school that protect their own children from the effects of innovation (for example, by placing them in 'gifted classes' or allocating the best teachers to them);
- leaders are either too controlling, too ineffectual, or cash in on the early success of the innovation to move on to higher things;
- the change is pursued in isolation and gets undermined by other unchanged structures (for example, when cross curricular learning standards comes are juxtaposed with subject-based report cards or standardized tests); conversely, the change may be poorly coordinated with and engulfed by a tidal wave of parallel changes that make it hard for teachers to focus their efforts.

These common causes of failure to bring about educational change have been well documented in the change literature, from the foundational period of educational change research and beyond (e.g., Sarason, 1971, 1990; Berman & McLaughlin, 1977; Fullan, 1991, 1993; Louis & Miles, 1990; Rudduck, 1991; Miles & Huberman, 1984; Stoll & Fink, 1996). As a *strategic* process of proper planning, design and structural alignment, and as a *cultural* process of building effective relationships of collaboration and consultation, educational change is something we now understand much better than a decade or more ago. Yet even with this impressive knowledge base and expertise about the strategic and cultural aspects of educational change, too many change efforts remain disappointing and ineffective. We create isolated islands of change much more than we build great continents of them. Successful school change on a widespread basis continues to be infuriatingly elusive. Why?

One reason is that educational change is not just a technical process of managerial efficiency, or a cultural one of understanding and involvement. It is political and paradoxical process as well (Handy, 1994). People fear change not just because it presents them with something new, uncertain or unclear — because it has no obvious or common meaning for them. The agenda of educational change is also contested. Education is the greatest gatekeeper of opportunity and a powerful distributor of life chances. In a socially divided and culturally diverse society, what education is and how it is defined, will always tend to favour some groups and interests over others. So attempts to change education in fundamental ways are ultimately political acts. They are attempts to redistribute power and opportunity within the wider culture. Educational change is not just a strategic puzzle. It is, and should be a moral and political struggle. Generalized theories of educational change which concentrate on its strategic and cultural aspects tend to ignore these essentially political elements of the change process. This is a pity. For it is the social and political dimensions of educational change which cause it to flounder most.

Second, significant educational change can no longer be achieved, (if it ever really could!) in a step-by-step, linear process. School improvement processes are not implemented smoothly through locked-in five year development plans. Schools do not have the luxury of being able to focus on a singular goal and to go through stages of achieving it over several years while the rest of their world stands still. Change today does not proceed through clear discrete stages of awareness, initiation, implementation and institutionalization. It is much more messy than that.

This lack or loss of predictability in the educational change process is due not only to the fact that the environment in which educational change takes place is increasingly complex and turbulent, but also because of the multi-dimensional nature of educational change itself. As Fullan (1991) has pointed out, schools today work in contexts of multiple rather than singular innovation, having to manage, coordinate and integrate numerous changes (some self-initiated, some externally imposed) all at once. Moreover, each change is itself also multi-dimensional in nature. And while the change literature (and change management practices) tend to focus on two or three of these dimensions only — especially cultural, structural and strategic ones — there are many more which demand equivalent attention: especially moral, political and emotional ones.

One of the major challenges of educational change today, therefore, is how to define and manage change in a politically contested and multi-dimensional environment. It is because of the urgency of these problems that there is a need to extend our approach to both the theory and practice of educational change.

There are four areas where extending and deepening our understanding of educational change beyond the boundaries of what is usually addressed in the field, can really strengthen how we think about change and deal with it in action. These are:

1. educational change in a world of chaos and complexity, and as a process that is complex and chaotic itself.
2. the societal change forces which drive educational change, and the ways that educators understand and respond to them.
3. the political factors that shape the purposes and processes of educational change.
4. the emotional aspects of learning, teaching and leading and how these can guide or divert educational change agendas.

1. Chaos and complexity

Managing organizations, including educational ones, is difficult work these days. Most problems that organizations face are not predictable or easy to control. Mintzberg's (1994) cryptically titled book on *The Rise and Fall of Strategic Planning*, discredits the capacity of strategic planning to address problems that elude being treated in logic, linear, step-by-step ways. The world in which schools, colleges and other organizations operate is manifestly complex, uncertain, paradoxical and chaotic. Leaders trying to focus on one initiative find themselves repeatedly sideswiped by another. Competing mandates pull them in opposite directions.

Some of the most recent writing in educational and organizational change theory, urges readers not only to accept the existence of chaos, complexity and paradox in their organizational worlds, but embrace and capitalize on it. In the most extreme cases, what are often deeply painful contradictions for practitioners (be integrated and subject based, be individualized and standardized, or be professionals while blindly complying with government demands), are celebrated in an academic ecstasy of change theory and advocacy that promotes living on the edge of chaos (Stacey, 1996).

In their book on *The Leadership Paradox*, Deal and Peterson (1995) urge their readers to accept "the seemingly contradictory approaches" to school leadership which emphasize its technical and expressive aspects respectively, "as a paradox to be embraced and creatively addressed" (p. 9). Similarly, Handy (1994, p. 18) argues that:

> Paradoxes are like the weather, something to be lived with, not solved, the worst aspects mitigated, the best enjoyed and used as clues to the way forward. Paradox has to be accepted, coped with and made sense of, in life, in work, in community and among the nations.

Senge (1990) points to dynamic complexity being a normal state of affairs in contemporary organizations. This complexity amounts to difficulties of tracing cause and effect when the consequences of our actions may not become evident until they are far removed in space and time. The existence of this dynamic complexity, argues Senge, is one of the fundamental reasons why we need to develop our organizations so that they have improved capacity to learn from and to solve ongoing problems. Taking up Senge's argument, one of Fullan's influential texts on educational change contends that "as the scale of complexity accelerates in post-modern society, our ability to synthesize polar opposites where possible, and work with their co-existence where necessary, is absolutely critical to success" (Fullan, 1993, p. 41).

Some theorists have turned to a new science of chaos and complexity theory to explain the uncertainties and unpredictabilities of organizational life. They argue that relationships between cause and effect are increasingly hard to trace, that systems are highly complex; and that patterns of change are non-linear in nature. They also point out that within the chaos, there is chaos (but unpredictable) order as well. There are boundaries to the instability. The task of leadership, under these circumstances is to learn from living on the edge of chaos; to realize that "you are not necessarily out of control if you are not in control" (Gunter, 1997, p. 96); to lead by empowering people, releasing their creativity, and finding different ways to bring them together so they can learn to improve continously, scan the environment and solve problems as effectively as they emerge.

One of the most influential writers on leadership in conditions of chaos argues that we often limit the potential of leaders

> because we circumscribe them with rules or chains of command or give them narrow mandates or restrict their access to information. But if we liberate them from these confines and allow them greater autonomy, constrained more by purpose than by rules or preset expectations, then their potential for generating information is great.
>
> (Wheatley, 1992, p. 115)

Another influential chaos theorist warns that

> The creative process in human systems . . . is inevitably messy: it involves difference, conflict, fantasy, and emotion; it stirs up anger, envy, depression, and many other feelings. To remove the mess by inspiring us to follow some common vision, share the same culture, and pull together is to remove the mess that is the very raw material of creative activity.
>
> (Stacey, 1996, p. 15)

Some of the implications of understanding educational change as a complex, paradoxical and chaotic phenomenon are important and challenging. Managing change becomes a collective process, not an individual one. Initiative and creativity come out of the shadows of coordination and control. Leadership calls for the ability to create underlying senses of basic personal safety and emotional security, in which risk and creativity can flourish. Efforts are coordinated and new directions set by learning, information gathering and dialogue rather than through administrative regulation and hierarchical control.

Despite its promise, this significant approach to extending educational change theory and practice has a number of important limitations though. Two of these are especially noteworthy. First, is that the euphoria of thriving on and living on the edge of chaos (in which change theorists and change instigators are inclined to revel) under-values the existence and desirability of incredible degrees of order, continuity and tradition in our schools. While the world of educational change does seem chaotic in some respects, many schools remain impervious to much of it. They are permeated by enduring regularities of subjects, classes, timetables, cyclical festivals, behaviour codes, graduation ceremonies, examinations, yearbooks, vacations, homeworks, seatwork, concerts and sports games (Sarason, 1990). Such things make many aspects of schools resoundingly familiar to all those who visit them. Schools may be assailed by change but they are also places of great historical continuity (McCulloch, 1997). Indeed, one of the recurring complaints about public education is that in anything more than isolated and episodic instances, it seems unable to break free of its basic "grammar" of classes, subjects, isolated teaching, etc. that was laid down many decades ago. In schools, there is chaos *and* order, complexity *and* regularity. Chaos theory has a point; but it's important not to overstate it.

Perhaps we should even actively embrace this order as much as we do the chaos.

Some teachers are, in their nature, pioneers. Living on the edge of chaos is the way they like to live their lives. Other teachers are settlers; they plant roots, form relationships and celebrate the rhythms of life. Schools today are in danger of rewarding only their pioneers, those who truly thrive on chaos. But schools, just like society, need their settlers as well as their pioneers — to water the horses, ensure the food supply, and maintain the secure base from which others can take their risks. In schools, it is usually the settlers who maintain order, coach the sports teams, coordinate the programmes and ensure that everything keeps running on time while change is going on all around them. Schools, therefore, do not only already have strong elements of continuity; these should also be actively cultivated and maintained. Knowing how to balance chaos with order, change with continuity, is one of the areas in which educational change theory and practice need to be extended further.

A second objection to chaos theory and its application to organizational change concerns how it explains the *sources* of the chaos. Interestingly though chaos theory may be as an analogy for understanding human organizations, its straight and uncritical application from the natural and physical world, with few social and political modifications, makes it vulnerable to the *naturalistic fallacy*. The naturalistic fallacy involves transposing explanations of the natural world straight into the human world — without any consideration of the distinctive way that humans interact, have language, make meaning and organize into highly complex social groups. Treating human behaviour as directly analogous to other animal behaviour is one example of the naturalistic fallacy. In the 1950s & 1960s, theories of functionalism which argued that biological systems were ordered and harmonious with all parts functioning to keep the whole in equilibrium, were applied to organizations that were then treated in the same way — as systems of interconnected, functionally integrated parts.

While chaos theory offers more radical explanations of the natural world than functionalism, its direct transposition to social organizations suffers from the same fallacy. The chaos in organizations, as in the physical world is presented as natural and inevitable. The challenge, therefore, is how to live and work with it.

This kind of chaos theory has no theory of agency, will, power or responsibility. The chaos is natural. Nobody wills it or is responsible for it. The management imperative is to adjust to and even enjoy the chaos; not to fight those who are responsible for creating it. What appears to be a highly radical theory of organizations and schools therefore has some deeply conservative components underneath.

Now even in the social world, it is fair to say that not all chaos that educators experience is wilful. Much of it is a result of a combination of social changes within a rapidly changing postmodern world. Elsewhere, I have argued that the pervasive social and moral uncertainty which afflicts contemporary culture is part of a postmodern condition driven by changes in the technological circulation of information, ideas and entertainment; by multicultural migration and international travel and by international economic restructuring (Hargreaves, 1994; Kenway, 1995). These forces create increased moral uncertainty as ideas, information and belief systems come into greater contact, they produce greater scientific uncertainty as information-flow is accelerated and knowledge is disconfirmed at an ever-increasing rate; and they help create contrary impulses to reinvent ideas of community and national identity (not least through education) in order to counter these trends toward globalization (Hargreaves, 1994; Harvey, 1989; Slattery, 1995). Most advocates of chaos theory in organizations also acknowledge these sorts of trends. But there are other, more wilful sources of organizational chaos as well.

Perhaps the most disturbing aspect of the advent of social and moral uncertainty is what Giddens (1995) calls *manufactured uncertainty*. This is a condition where postmodern chaos and complexity to some extent result from wilful attempts by governmental, corporate and financial powers to maximize their interests of profitability and control by opening up as much of social life as possible to the free play of the market, and by discrediting and disinvesting in the public sphere to boost the influence of the market by keeping labour forces flexible, interest groups fragmented, and everyone off-balance (also Jameson, 1990; Barlow & Robertson, 1994).

When organizations outsource their contracts, opt to use more temporary labour and fire their employees only to rehire them again as consultants (but without pensions or other benefits), it is not coping with complexity or becoming a learning organization that is uppermost in their priorities, but making the labour force more exploitable and manipulable to reduce costs and achieve other management ends. The loss or reassignment of teachers' jobs similarly creates individual career uncertainties that are the product of states with shrinking budgets seeking higher control over their expensive professional labour costs. Lastly, the worldwide assault on educational standards and the accompanying flurries of educational initiatives in response to it, are often a sign of governments seeking to discredit the public sphere to gain more control over what is left of it. Make no bones about it, the origins of some of our present educational uncertainties are manufactured and malevolent and should not be causes for celebration but for fundamental critique. The literature of educational change has largely avoided this challenge.

Another source of chaos and complexity is to be found in the struggles for power and in the conflicting visions of what educational change is for and who will benefit from it. For example, conflicts between making learning more sensitive to multiple intelligences while judging schools and teachers by standardized test scores that privilege only one or two kinds of intelligence above all others is not a consequence of accident or muddle, but of conflicting social and political values being played out in the classrooms of our nations. In an effort to acknowledge all interests, governments often will not arbitrate on these competing directions, leaving classroom teachers to deal with the contradictions instead.

In summary, one way in which the field of educational change is being extended is in terms of recognizing the complex and chaotic nature of educational change processes in the postmodern era. Where educational change theory needs to be pushed even further is in acknowledging that the source of that chaos is not all a natural or spontaneous effect of contingent events, but that part of it also has a clear and identifiable political basis.

2. Context

Until recently, educational change theory has taken little account of the context in which school-level change takes place — or has done so in relatively unsophisticated ways. Most large-scale reforms are usually a political response to economic or technological crises of some kind, and were once more attentive to issues like poverty and racism as well. More recently, the educational change literature has acknowledged, indeed highlighted a broader sense of wide-ranging societal changes that are pushing and should push transformations in the educational system.

In his presidential inaugural speech in January 1977, U.S. President Bill Clinton spoke of building a bridge to the twenty-first century. Philip Schlechty (1990) authored an influential book on *Schooling for the Twenty First Century* for which Bill Clinton wrote the foreword. This stated that schools in the twenty-first century would produce "knowledge workers", with children doing "knowledge work". In England, the National Commission on Education (1993) wrote a report, *Learning to Succeed* which spoke challengingly and motivationally about "twenty-first century" teachers. Twenty-first century discourse pervades the policy language and governmental pronouncements of many other countries too. Everywhere, there is a sense that schooling and society are changing drastically and that they will and perhaps should change more drastically still in the century to come.

Some educational writers, especially historians, are less convinced. McCulloch (1997), for example, casts serious doubts on much of the millennial thinking that runs through contemporary educational discourse.

A powerful and cogent metaphor for change is involved in the idea of turning over a new leaf to meet the fresh needs of the twenty-first century, and it is attractive to believe in the notion of developing a rational and comprehensive blueprint that will serve this purpose. The transformative impact of the new technologies and the image of the dawn of a new 'post-modernist' epoch tend strongly to underline these possibilities for the future in a way that can be used constructively in order to develop coherent and inspiring visions for radical, holistic reform. At the same time, however, they often suffer from two characteristic problems. First, they are prone to idealize the future, to build castles in the air that contrast starkly with the intractable dilemmas of the imperfect present. They involve a quasi-utopian discourse that generates high expectations for radical and fundamental change. It seems likely that this tendency may lead in turn to disappointment and alienation if there is a failure to deliver or benefit from reform. Secondly, they tend to overlook or ignore the continuities inherited from the past, or else to 'telescope' the past in order to draw simple and finished conclusions to particular problems that need to be resolved. In both respects they serve as a marketing device to promote the new possibilities of education in a new century, designed to appeal to consumers of different kinds who are grown weary of the old familiar product.

(McCulloch, 1997, pp.19–20)

Literature on educational and social change in the twenty-first century does indeed indulge in euphoric excess. It speaks of new economics, more dynamic forms of work and production, more self-conscious and self-reflexive approaches to lifestyle choices, greater representation of women in leadership and an overall "triumph of the individual". Those who cast doubt on these demonstrably positive benefits of the new age are swiftly dismissed as mere "doomsayers" (Naisbitt & Aberdene, 1990). There are other twenty-first century scenarios as well as heroic and optimistic ones that should be acknowledged and engaged with. More critical and considered responses to the social forces which are reshaping the world of education and educational change are urgently needed in the change literature.

At the same time, there is evidence that administrators within the educational system who are responsible for initiating and implementing change, have limited understanding of the forces bearing down on their schools and do not really know how to respond. Levin and Riffel (1997) studied how administrators in five school districts interpreted and responded to a selected range of social issues: the changing labour market, information technology, child poverty, and changing patterns of family life. They found that administrators:

- were usually unclear about how best to respond.
- were not "sufficiently oriented towards learning about the nature and implications of social change". They had no systematic strategies to scan the external environment, so they could anticipate the changes coming their way and assess their implications (p. 162).
- often misdiagnosed particular change forces that were affecting them (for example, problems that they perceived as resulting from increasing numbers of single present families, were really more to do with child poverty — with which single parenthood is closely associated).
- adopted change strategies that were "limited and unimaginative" (p. 163). These were often made around the edges of teaching and learning rather than affecting the classroom itself (e.g., non-instructional uses of new technology; or winter clothing drives and breakfast programmes to deal with child poverty but not ones that also focussed on improving teaching and learning for these students).

The theory and practice of educational change needs to be extended so that administrators such as those at school and district level, can make a more critical, considered and coordinated responses to the societal changes beyond the walls of their school. The walls of the school are already breaking down because of the access to information that new technologies provide, the changing patterns of cultural diversity in many teachers' classrooms, and so on (Hargreaves & Fullan, 1998). It is time that educational change took account of its changing context so that teachers and administrators can engage with it with greater thought and imagination.

Educational change theorists and administrators responsible for educational change both, therefore, tend to have rather generalized, uncritical and under-developed conceptions of the context of change. Some change theorists and practitioners — especially those in the field of school improvement — pay little or no attention to the context of improvement at all. They separate school-level change processes from analyses of policy change and reform efforts at the macro level. They treat school improvement in isolation from the contexts which advocate and promote it. One might, for instance, reasonably regard the advocacy of school improvement in a context of economic retrenchment, reduced preparation time for teachers to learn and plan together, and the imposition of narrow goals and standards that benefit only student elites as not improvement at all, but intensification and exploitation of the teaching force. Some nationally sponsored school improvement processes might also be regarded as ways of displacing blame for school failure from those who design policies and create unsupportive contexts, to teachers themselves, who have little option but to implement and work within them.

School improvement research and educational policy analysis must be integrated more rather than kept in separate sub-fields (Hargreaves & Evans, 1997). School improvement processes are affected very much by the policy contexts in which they operate — policies which can build or destroy confidence, trust and motivation among the teaching force, for example. Another way to extend educational change contextually is to bring these two areas of work more closely together.

Part 1 of this section of the Handbook addresses some of the key aspects of the changing social context of schooling in the postmodern age, and examines the ways these changes are impacting on schools and challenging them to change still further in years to come. It is these changes, in combination, that account for much of the chaos and complexity that educators are increasingly encountering within their work. These contextual changes include

- greater cultural and linguistic diversity
- changing patterns of family and community life
- increased economic uncertainty and the growth of the corporate agenda in the policies and practices of schooling
- the advent and spread of new technologies
- the rise of market influences on education (especially in relation to school image and school choice)
- the emergence of gender equity issues in classroom learning, teacher careers and leadership practices.

Some of the implications of these multifaceted societal changes include greater complexity of educational change; increasing speed of change; intensification of work for teachers and leaders; greater emphasis on image, appearance and accountability; stronger pull of competing and contradictory priorities; confusions about purpose and mission; mounting pressures to bring about fundamental changes in teaching and learning to accommodate cultural diversity and technological sophistication; and so on. To study the context of educational change, therefore, does not just mean adding colour to how we understand change processes at school level, but it leads us to see the process of educational change at every level in a fundamentally different light.

3. Politics

A third area in which the field of educational change would benefit from some extension is the politics of educational change. Some might argue that this is an unnecessary move. Politics has been one of the key preoccupations of many leading change theorists for a long time. In 1971, Seymour Sarason warned that

> Introducing, sustaining, and assessing an educational change are political processes because they inevitably alter or threaten to alter existing power relationships, especially if that process implies, as it almost always does, a reallocation of resources. Few myths have been as resistant to change as that which assumes that the culture of the school is a non-political one, and few myths have contributed as much to the failure of the change efforts
>
> (Sarason, 19971, p. 71)

More recently, Sarason (1990) has argued that educational reform efforts are doomed to failure unless they transform the power relationships of the classroom between teachers and students. Others have looked closely at the micropolitical conflicts that take place between teachers and principals and among teachers themselves in terms of subject departmental conflicts, relationships between 'insiders' and 'outsiders' in the innovation process, and so on (Ball, 1987; Siskin & Little, 1995; Hargreaves, 1994). Blase and Anderson (1995) have also addressed the more constructive aspects of school micropolitics, explaining how educators and others can engage in creating positive politics together, searching for common ground and finding ways to empower each other in ways that will benefit students' interests.

The issue is not *whether* educational change theory attends to political questions. Clearly, it does. It is *how* political issues are addressed that matters. In the main, educational change theorists address political questions in terms of conflict and representation among multiple interest groups. There is much talk of stakeholders, partnerships, collaboration and alliances. Until very recently, within the change field, there has been little attention to how systemic social inequalities and power imbalances do not just surround the school and its community as part of the change context, but permeate the politics of change within the school itself.

Datnow (1998), for example, describes how, in the schools she studied, innovative groups of female teachers were "resisted" by mid-to-late career male colleagues in their change efforts — to the point where, in one instance, legal action was taken. Teacher resistance which is variously seen as a symptom of a generalized fear of change; as a generational problem of mid-career teachers; or as great perspicacity among teachers who see through the smoke and mirrors of educational reform, is viewed by Datnow as a fundamentally political issue where pervasive social inequities are ingrained into the change process itself.

Oakes and her colleagues (1997) show how in American multiracial settings the school change processes is not easily shielded from racial politics and inequities either. Schools attempting to detrack (destream) frequently met with resistance from middle class white parents who argued against detracking, and won compromises which would benefit their own children such as retaining gifted classes, honours programmes, etc. Oakes and her colleagues' study makes clear how the politics of detracking is not just a politics of addressing and reconciling multiple interests, but of confronting and taking sides on major questions of social justice inside and outside the school. It is in this deep sense, of confronting pervasive power inequalities that the political dimension of educational change could add much of great value to the field.

4. Emotions

A fourth area in which educational change theory would benefit from some development is that of the emotions. I attend to this aspect more fully in my own chapter later.

A welter of excessively rationalist approaches to improvement and change have presented a view of learning, teaching, leadership, and change that is overwhelmingly cognitive, calculative, managerial and stereotypically masculine in nature. Higher order thinking skills, situated cognition, reflective practice, problem-based learning, cognitive leadership and even organizational learning presume the separation of head and heart, and privilege the first over the second.

Yet, the emotional dimensions of education are not distractions from the tough world of higher order thinking and academic results, but an integral part of academic learning and reasoning itself. Teachers, with clear emotional goals for and strong emotional bonds with their students for example, take very different approaches to their work and changes in it than many of their colleagues (see my own chapter later).

Emotions are important as ends of educational change, in the development of emotional as well as other kinds of intelligence — the capacity to cultivate feelings, express them, manage them and empathize with the feelings of others (Goleman, 1995). Emotional learning is integral to intellectual learning — adding value to the conventional kinds of achievement by which students are usually assessed.

Care too, is an important end of education, not just in setting safe and orderly climates for learning as in the school effectiveness literature. It is about infusing more passion into the classroom, reorganizing school structures so that *all* teachers can provide effective care for students, and creating conditions in schools that spark feelings of hope and senses of efficacy among teachers which benefit themselves and their students.

The emotional dimension of educational change also draws attention to the necessity of avoiding reform strategies, leadership styles and work conditions which create conditions of hopelessness, feelings of guilt (through being overwhelmed), (Blackmore, 1996) and of shame (by being blamed for failure or being placed at the bottom of league tables of performance) (Jeffrey & Woods, 1996). These sorts of emotional conditions in schooling reduce teachers' senses of efficacy and their ability to provide quality education for students. The emotional dimension of educational change, is not a frill but a fundamental of improvement, and deserves increased attention in the educational change literature.

Part 2 of this section of the Handbook takes up the political and emotional dimensions of educational change as ones that merit particular attention in the complex and turbulent postmodern world in which schools now operate. A number of other distinctive dimensions of change that may merit especially close attention in the complex times within which we live and work are also addressed in this second part: restructuring, reculturing, organizational learning, authenticity, community and different approaches to policy. These are not the only ways in which the field of educational change is being extended, and might be extended further — but they represent the beginnings of a quest to do so that is critical, contextual and suitably complex.

CONCLUSION

Educational change theory has taught us much over the past quarter century or more about how to manage and not to manage the change process. But as our knowledge deepens and our world inside and outside schools become more turbulent, it is time to revisit some of the fundamental issues in the field, extend our analysis of them further, and connect with sociological and political forms of inquiry that are attuned to the highly contested terrain that schooling comprises in the postmodern age.

REFERENCES

Ball, S. (1987). A subject of privilege: English and the school curriculum: 1906–35. In M. Hammersley, & A. Hargreaves (Eds.), *Curriculum practice: Some sociological case studies.* New York and Philadelphia: Falmer Press.

Barlow, M. and Robertson, H-j. (1994) *Class warfare: The assault on Canada's schools.* Toronto: Key Porter Books.

Berman, P. and McLaughlin, M. (1977). *Federal programs supporting educational change, Vol. VII, Factors affecting implementation and continuation.* Santa Monica, CA: Rand Corporation.

Blackmore, J. (1996). Doing emotional labour in the educational market: Stories from the field of women in management. *Discourse,* 17(3), 301–314.

Blase, J. C., & Anderson, G. (1996). *The micropolitics of educational leadership: From control to empowerment.* New York: Teachers' College Press.

Deal, T. & Peterson, K. (1995). *The leadership paradox.* San Francisco: Jossey Bass.

Fullan, M. (1991). *The new meaning of educational change.* with S. Stiegelbauer, New York: Teachers College Press.

Fullan, M. (1993). *Change forces: Probing the depths of educational reform* New York: Falmer Press.

Giddens, A. (1995). *Beyond left and right.* Stanford: Stanford University Press.

Goleman, D. (1995). *Emotional intelligence.* New York: Bantam Books.

Gunter, H. (1997). *Rethinking education: The consequences of Jurassic management.* London: Cassell.

Handy, C. (1994). *The age of paradox.* Cambridge, MA: Harvard Business Press.

Hargreaves, A. (1994). *Changing teachers, changing times.* London: Cassell, New York: Teachers College Press, Toronto: University of Toronto Press.

Hargreaves, A., & Evans, R. (Eds.). (1997). *Beyond educational reform.* Buckingham: Open University Press.

Hargreaves, A., & Fullan, M. (1998). *What's worth fighting for out there?* Toronto: Ontario Public School Teachers' Federation.

Harvey, D. (1989). *The condition of postmodernity.* Oxford: Basil Blackwell.

Huberman, M. and Miles, M. (1984). *Innovation up close.* New York: Plenum.

Jameson, F. (1990). *Postmodernism: Or the cultural logic of late capitalism.* London & New York: Verso.

Jeffrey, B., & Woods, P. (1996). Feeling deprofessionalized: The social construction of emotions during an OFSTEP inspection. *Cambridge Journal of Education,* November.

Kenway, J. (1995). *Reality bytes.* Unpublished paper, Faculty of Education, Deakin University, Australia.

Levin, B., & Riffel, P. (1997). *Schools in a changing world: Struggling toward the future.* London and New York: Falmer Press.

Louis K. S., & Miles, M. B. (1990). *Improving the urban high school: What works and why.* New York: Teachers College Press.

McCulloch, G. (1997). Marketing the millennium: Education for the twenty-first century. In Hargreaves, A. & Evans, R. (Eds.), *Beyond educational reform,* pp.19–28. Buckingham: Open University Press.

Mintzberg, H. ((1994). *The rise and fall of strategic planning.* New York: Free Press.

Naisbitt, J. & Aberdene, P. (1990). *Megatrends 2000: Ten new directions for the 1990s.* New York: Avon Books.

National Commission on Education. (1993). *Learning to succeed.* London: Heinemann.

Rudduck, J. (1991) *Innovation and change: Developing Involvement and Understanding.* Philadelphia: Open University Press.

Sarason, S. (1971). *The culture of the school and the problem of change.* Boston: Allyn and Bacon.

Sarason, S. (1990). *The predictable failure of educational reform.* San Francisco: Jossey-Bass.

Schlechty, P. (1990). *Schools for the twenty-first century: leadership imperatives for educational reform.* San Francisco: Jossey-Bass.

Senge, P. (1990). *The fifth discipline: The art and practice of the learning organization.* New York: Doubleday.

Siskin, L., & Little, J. (Eds.). (1995). *The subjects in question.* New York: Teachers' College Press.

Slattery, P. (1995). A postmodern vision of time and learning: A response to the National Education Commission Report Prisoners of time. *Harvard Educational Review,* **65**(4), Winter, 612–633.

Stacey, R. (1996). *Complexity and creativity in organizations.* San Francisco, CA: Berrett Koehler.

Stoll, L., & Fink, D. (1996). *Changing our schools.* Milton Keynes: Open University Press.

Wheatley, M. J. (1992). *Leadership and the new science*: San Francisco, CA: Berrett Koehler.

I: Contexts

Educational Change: Easier Said than Done

DEAN FINK

Educational Development Consultant, Dean Fink Consulting Associates

LOUISE STOLL

Institute of Education, University of London

In the opening chapter to this section of the Handbook, Fink and Stoll review the contemporary field of educational change and ask why educational change is so difficult to understand and achieve in present times. They begin by discussing the historical, social and organizational forces that create continuity in education; which sustain structures and practices that in many cases may be outliving their usefulness. They then discuss four common and widely used approaches to bringing about educational change in the face of such continuity: school effectiveness, school improvement, school restructuring, and more recent orientations to school reculturing. Each of these approaches is examined clearly and also critically.

Finally, Fink and Stoll turn to a number of agendas which they argue will continue to challenge the theory and practice of educational change in years to come – the need for a tighter connection between organizational change and developing better approaches to teaching and learning; the problem of motivating students in contexts of economic uncertainty; the difficulty of determining what kinds of leadership work best and are most practical in contexts of great complexity; the perennial problem of assessment and accountability; the relationship of change to teachers' lives, and the importance of micropolitics. Reculturing, they propose, offers one of the most hopeful ways of providing an integrated solution to these many different challenges.

A while back, the Minister of Education and Training for the Canadian province of Ontario was videotaped telling the senior officials of his department that they must spread the word that the educational scene in Ontario is much worse than it actually is. "Creating a useful crisis is part of what this will be about" (Brennan 1995, p.1), he said. By orchestrating a crisis of confidence he declared, his government's reform package could proceed more smoothly. Educators in many countries, states, and provinces will recognize the tactic. While few officials are foolish enough to admit publicly that their criticism of schools is a precondition to implementing educational reform, a fairly common governmental change strategy is to attempt to undermine the public's confidence in its schools and their teachers, and then to mandate a series of policies which effectively deskill teachers and undermine their judgments (Barlow & Robertson, 1994; Berliner & Biddle, 1995).

These reform policies have certain common features. Important decisions about

17

A. Hargreaves (ed.), Extending Educational Change, 17-41.
© 2005 *Springer. Printed in the Netherlands.*

students' learning, such as what they are to learn, when they are to learn it, and how students are to demonstrate their learning have been removed from local settings and assumed by bureaucrats in distant offices. Conversely, resources have been devolved directly to schools to make local 'site based' decisions, usually accompanied by a reduction in support. In most situations, increased parental involvement has been mandated in the form of school governors or school councils. What is remarkable, is the similarity of these change strategies throughout the world and the agreement among policy makers, business communities and large segments of the various publics that education is in dire need of reform. These forces for educational change, however, are merely reflection of much more pervasive trends in society.

"Social forces are human energies which, originating in individual motivations, coalesce into collective manifestations of power" (Gustavson, 1955, p. 28). Economic forces, technological forces and political forces among others, shape our daily existence. At certain points in history, combinations of these forces merge to produce dramatic, indeed, revolutionary social changes. The Enlightenment of the 18th century is an example. With its focus on reason, science, and progress, it impacted all aspects of society and accelerated the industrial revolution, which in turn brought revolutionary economic, social and ultimately political changes to western societies. Some commentators have suggested that western societies are presently in the midst of another such period in their histories. Institutions, political, economic and social structures and indeed value systems world-wide appear to be changing or under pressure to do so. It would seem that our societies are passengers in time between a passing 'modern' age and a new complex, diverse, confusing and (some have argued) chaotic post-modern era (Stacey, 1995). The problem for educators is how to create organizations which prepare our children to engage with this changing and uncertain world and shape it for the better, while preserving their basic humanity in the midst of potentially dehumanizing principles and practices.

The forces for change are discussed in considerable detail in this 'Handbook'. In all the pressure for change, however, those forces which contribute to the maintenance of continuity in schools are often forgotten. In this chapter, therefore, we examine the forces for continuity, then describe and critique the strategies for change; and finally address some of the continuing challenges of educational change.

FORCES OF CONTINUITY

In spite of the convergence of powerful forces for change, schools appear remarkably untouched, and exhibit many structures, policies and practices of years gone by. One may well argue that without continuity with the past, positive change cannot occur. Maintaining some degree of stability or organizational equilibrium is fundamental to effective management of schools and classrooms. Unfortunately, in many situations the quest for stability has become an excuse for immobility (see

Mulford's chapter in this book). Even many of the 'best' schools are "good schools – if this were 1965" (Stoll & Fink, 1996). Such 'cruising' schools appear to be effective but have ceased to grow and develop. These are schools in which the forces of continuity coalesce to prevent significant changes in the schools' structures or culture (Stoll & Fink, 1998). Why does such stability prevail? Cuban (1990) describes the resilience of the 'deep structures' of schooling; for example, subjects, grades, departments, department heads, streaming and selective schools.

Teacher 'resistance'

As Gustavson (1955) explains, people are "afraid of drastic innovations, partly because they prefer the familiar, and partly because the vested interests of most people are normally bound up with the existing set-up" (p. 72). Over the past 15 years, teachers have been swamped by innovations. Since teachers have largely been left out of policy discussions, they have resisted often ill-designed and poorly implemented change projects. Resistance is a natural and predictable response. For teachers who subscribe to the 'practicality ethic' – that is, "it has to be relevant to me in my classroom with these students" – change has usually been something 'done to' teachers as opposed to something 'done with' them (Doyle & Ponder, 1977). Richardson (1990) suggests that in recent years the change literature has moved from "viewing teachers as recalcitrant and resistant to change to examining the structure of the organization and personal attributes of teachers that affect whether or not they implement new programs" (p. 11).

A particular dilemma for those who are trying to bring about change in schools is the issue of overload (Fullan & Hargreaves, 1991). Taking one such example, in England, the 1988 Education Act heralded an enormous number of changes that impacted directly on the work of teachers. Many of those related to the National Curriculum were not even embedded in practice before they were amended. With the best will in the world, teachers who have been bombarded by an unrelenting plethora of changes over a short time period tend to be exhausted, and find it hard to keep up their energy, enthusiasm and, ultimately, willingness for change (Helsby & McCulloch, in press). It is, therefore, not necessarily the characteristics of teachers, per se, that cause resistance and the continuity it perpetuates, but the pressures on them and the limits placed on their involvement in making the decision to change.

Contextual constraints

Classrooms are part of a larger contextual network or 'nested system' (Smith, Dwyer, Prunty, & Kleine, 1987) of institutions – a school, a district, a province, state or nation – and are influenced by community organizations and teachers' unions, among other formal and informal organizations. Organizations generally tend to be influenced by "a proneness to keep the machinery running as in the past unless strong pressure for change materializes" (Gustavson, 1955).

Tyack and Tobin (1994) have demonstrated the difficulty of effecting change in 'real schools'. Often parents support "good schools – if this were 1965" because this is what they know. 'Real schools' (Metz, 1990) are what schools should be like based on their own experience. Many attempts at innovation have failed because the professionals' idea of a 'good school' has outstripped the community's conception of a 'real school' (Smith, Dwyer, Prunty, & Kleine, 1987). Innovations often fail because of the educators' inability or unwillingness to involve parents in meaningful ways in their development and implementation. At the same time, schools which deviate too far from conventional educational models often find themselves at odds with their community's conceptions of what schools should look like. The important message here is that a school's community can often serve as a powerful brake on authentic change in schools.

In recent years, the role of a school's community has become increasingly important in the change literature (Morgan & Morgan, 1992; Epstein, 1995). The mandating of school councils or school governors has heightened this interest. In some cases this is due to a change in role, for example in the United Kingdom where there has been a significant increase in the powers of school boards and governing bodies related to strategic decision-making and accountability (MacBeath, McCaig, & Thomson, 1992; Earley, 1994).

Looking further afield within the nested layers, Rosenholtz (1989) found that districts with strongly bureaucratic structures were considerably less effective in encouraging change in schools. As Fullan (1991) indicates, schools cannot redesign themselves without assistance and support:

> The role of the district is crucial. Individual schools can become highly innovative for short periods of time without the district, but they cannot *stay* innovative without the district action to establish the conditions for continuous and long term improvement (p. 209).

Although teachers' unions play an important role in change efforts, there is not a substantial literature on the role of unions in the life of schools and school reform. Unions are usually torn between their economic and political priorities and active involvement in professional issues (McDonnell & Pascal, 1988). While there are examples of unions which participate actively in educational reform efforts (Bascia, 1994; Barber, 1992), the general picture is one of vigilant union neutrality or in some situations, opposition. Change efforts which ignore union interests, however, do so at their peril.

Schools and districts are also influenced by national or state assessment policies which tend to reinforce the status quo. Teachers in the United Kingdom, for example, who want to teach interdisciplinary units have told us that they are inhibited by the subject specificity of the National Curriculum and testing practices. University requirements which tend to specify traditional subjects and conventional grading schemes, when combined with the expectations of various subject communities to which most secondary teachers owe some loyalty, contribute to the maintenance of 'tried and true' practices (Siskin, 1994; Grossman & Stodolsky, 1994).

A time for maintenance

Change for change's sake is a related issue that can be a cause of overload. Quite simply, not all change is improvement and the pace, timing and appropriateness of each particular change needs to be considered carefully. Maintenance of existing policies, practices and structures is an important part of schools' development (Hargreaves & Hopkins, 1991; MacGilchrist, Mortimore, Savage, & Beresford, 1995). Too much change can sometimes be more harmful than no change. Many innovative schools 'overreach' and fail to attend to basic organizational and structural issues. A number of innovative schools have been attacked, not because of academic problems, but rather because of poor discipline, vandalism and theft of resources (Fletcher, Caron, & Williams, 1985). Schools must attend to both forces of change and continuity simultaneously.

When forces for change, such as government mandate, economic pressures and technological issues are countered by such equally strong forces for continuity as teacher reluctance about and distrust of the purposes of change, inertia and resistance can ensue. Reform efforts, therefore, have developed within a context of competing forces of change and continuity. In parallel, however, from the late 1970s, research-based reformers have responded to these forces by developing and disseminating 'solutions' to schools and school systems to assist their change efforts. While these have taken many routes, four basic patterns have emerged in the literature: the school effectiveness movement, school improvement processes, restructuring, and a less widely known approach called reculturing (Hargreaves, 1994; Fullan, 1996a). The following discussion describes each approach as well as its inherent problems.

APPROACHES TO CHANGE

School Effectiveness

School effectiveness research was a response to the work of Coleman, Campbell, Hobson, McPartland, Mood, Weinfeld, and York (1966) and Jencks, Smith, Acland, Bane, Cohen, Gintis, Heyns, and Micholson (1972) challenged the efficacy of schools by producing research that was generally interpreted as demonstrating that a student's socio-economic background determined success. Schools, therefore, merely confirmed or reconfirmed the relative advantage or disadvantage of each child. Simply stated, schools did not make much difference to students. This raised the very large research question: "Do schools make a difference to students regardless of socio-economic (SES) background"?

Contributions of school effectiveness research to change in schools

International researchers (for a detailed discussion of school effectiveness, see Mortimore's chapter in Volume 1 of this Handbook) challenged the Coleman-Jencks thesis and made a number of significant contributions to our understanding of what needed to be considered when attempting to bring about change in schools. Among the more important are:

- a focus on outcomes. In an age of accountability, schools must demonstrate to themselves and the wider community that what they do makes a difference to student outcomes (Mortimore, Sammons, Stoll, Lewis, & Ecob, 1988).
- an emphasis on equity. Edmonds (1979) and others (for example Murphy, 1992) have argued that all students regardless of socio-economic background can achieve acceptable levels of achievement. Research on differential effectiveness demonstrates that some schools are more effective for girls or boys, more or less able students, older students, and students of certain socio-economic or ethnic backgrounds (Nuttall, Goldstein, Prosser, & Rasbash, 1989).
- the concept of progress. An effective school is one "in which pupils progress further than might be expected from consideration of its intake" (Mortimore, 1991, p. 9). This definition refers to the 'value added' by the school (Goldstein & Thomas, 1996). This term 'value added', describes the boost given by the school to students' achievement over and above what they bring in terms of prior attainment and background factors.
- consistency. Some departments or divisions within schools are more effective for some students than others (Sammons, Thomas, & Mortimore, 1996). This raises the question about whether it is possible to talk in terms of school effectiveness or whether this needs to be adapted to school, department and teacher effectiveness.

Researchers in many countries have attempted to identify characteristics of effective schools and to develop ways to define and measure the results of schooling more accurately. Influenced by this expanding area of research, many school jurisdictions throughout the 1980s introduced effective schools projects. Relatively few have survived. Those that have, have metamorphosed into something more than effective schools projects per se. We would suggest that this limited impact is the result of some fundamental difficulties with the school effectiveness approach to change.

An unclear definition of school effectiveness

The definition of school effectiveness as it has developed to date, the articulation of effectiveness characteristics, and more importantly, their application in real schools, with real students, have failed to evolve sufficiently because of two fundamental methodological problems. First, effective schools research is in danger of becoming dated. Key studies carried out in the 1970s and 1980s and even those underway now are largely based on what makes schools effective in the 'here and now', not what is necessary in a fast changing world as we move to the millennium (Elliott, 1996; Stoll & Fink, 1996). Despite this, governments of the 1990s uncritically use effective schools findings from the 1970s and 1980s as devices to coerce school improvement (Brown, 1995; Hamilton, 1996). This political 'hijacking' of research findings and their use to suit other agendas leaves schools asking the question: "Towards whose definition of effectiveness are we working"?

Equally important, school effectiveness research in some countries, by its tacit acceptance of such questionable tools as decontextualized standardized tests, I.Q. scores, and relatively narrow measures of educational purposes has colluded in perpetuating instruments of social inequity and educational reductionism. The adoption of policies based on the effective schools characteristics has in some jurisdictions reduced schools to checklists of the measurable parts, and has ignored, or conveniently forgotten, the connections, relationships and emotions which make schools human institutions (Elliott, 1996). School effectiveness literature to date has said very little about the moral purposes of schooling (Stoll & Fink, 1996). This is not to suggest that school effectiveness has ignored ethical issues. Certainly school effectiveness research has demonstrated that schools can and do make a difference regardless of students' socio-economic status. But unfortunately, not enough policies based on the effective schools research reflect its focus on the concepts of equity, differential effectiveness, and student progress.

School effectiveness research also provides few answers regarding approaches to teaching and learning which help to prepare students for a changing world (see Stoll & Fink, 1996 for a more detailed discussion). The reason for this may be related to the fairly narrow choice of outcome measures selected. Different outcomes are correlated with different teaching strategies (Mortimore, Sammons, Stoll, Lewis, & Ecob, 1986). Current outcome measures pay attention to a relatively small proportion of children's skills and ability. In this changing world, many new employees will need to demonstrate flexibility, creativity, problem-solving skills, confidence with information technology and be able to co-operate in the workplace. As global citizens, other ecological skills and understandings are also increasingly vital. If school effectiveness studies are to reflect this reality of the 1990s and beyond, it is essential that researchers use a broad range of outcome measures.

Schools will need to look very different from the ones which exist today. Unfortunately, tradition, politics and the preoccupation with standardization, measurement and rationality have resulted in a lack of imagination and creativity in many approaches to change which are influenced by school effectiveness research. Most 'reform' projects recycle old ideas. For example, the celebrated American 'Break-the Mold' initiative resulted in the choice of 11 projects which Mechlenburg (1992) describes as "not remarkably novel" (p. 282).

Present research on effective schools has, to date, not addressed these apparently non-rational aspects of education in the 1990s and beyond. We need, therefore, very rich, multidisciplinary, multi-leveled descriptions of schools and their communities as complex, interrelated non-linear systems that can help inform educational change efforts. Since this is a real 'mouthful', let us elaborate. Schools have unique cultures, contexts, macro and micro-politics. Schools are perceived differently by students, teachers, principals, parents and communities. Effective schools are the result of the interactions of innumerable individuals and groups. When a school is effective or ineffective, what are the teachers doing, how are the students involved, how does the principal (head) contribute, what are the roles of parents and the communities? How do the individuals and groups relate to each other, to school policies and procedures and to external organizations and agencies? Since schools' layered contexts are interconnected and interrelated, how do these relationships affect schools, and conversely how do schools affect their larger contexts? Studies which reduce people to numbers, miss the non-rational, non-linear aspects of schooling. It is difficult to quantify feelings, intuition, humour, tradition, memory, chance and many of the effects of social advantage or deprivation.

The neglect of context

Studies of school effectiveness have been carried out in many different contexts. This makes generalizability of research findings an issue, particularly in a changing world with different economic, cultural, technological and political patterns. It has become increasingly clear that 'what works' in one context may lack relevance for another. For example, do the same strategies have the same impact in the inner city compared to a rural school? Can an effective strategy found in research carried out in a small number of Taiwanese schools really be applied to schools in Britain (Reynolds & Farrell, 1996)? Studies of schools serving students from different social class backgrounds have shown that students' socio-economic status (SES) affects the success of strategies used to make schools more effective (Hallinger & Murphy, 1986; Teddlie, Stringfield, Wimpelberg, & Kirby, 1989), and international attempts to replicate one country's' findings elsewhere or examine the same factors have also faced difficulties. This could be because research instruments do not translate well from one cultural context to another, and interpretations of concepts may also differ from country to country (Reynolds, Creemers, Nesselrodt, Schaffer, Stringfield, & Teddlie, 1994).

Similarly uncertainty has been expressed about the relevance of the characteristics identified in effective elementary schools to secondary settings (Levine & Lezotte, 1990). Further study is needed to understand the precise nature of elementary and secondary school differences, and context in terms of students' social class background and school location (inner city, suburban or rural). Just knowing what the generic characteristics of effectiveness are, has proven insufficient to bring about change in particular settings. Increasingly, researchers and practitioners with a school effectiveness background have concluded that to achieve the outcomes of an effective school, change strategies need to be tied to a second avenue of research, 'school improvement' (Reynolds, Hopkins, & Stoll, 1993).

School Improvement

The school improvement research knowledge base largely resulted from reflection on failed change efforts in the 1960s and 1970s, when a wide variety of changes were adopted by schools with little lasting effect (Fullan, 1991). In her revisit to the Rand Change Agent Study of the 1970s in the United States, McLaughlin (1990) concluded that "the net return to the general investment was the adoption of many innovations, the successful implementation of a few, and the long-run continuation of still fewer" (p. 12). The failure of 'top-down' approaches to educational change led to 'bottom-up' approaches that involved practitioner rather than external knowledge, and the emphasis shifted from educational management as the focus for change to changes in educational processes (Reynolds, 1988). This process oriented approach, however, did not often lead to improvement in students' performance (Reynolds, Hopkins, & Stoll, 1993). By the 1990s, therefore, scholars were suggesting that change occurred best with a 'top-down, bottom-up' approach in which the larger system provided direction and support and the actual change process was left to schools through school-based decision making and school development planning. Among the school improvement literature's more significant contributions are the following:

- a focus on process. If school effectiveness focused on what to change to make schools more effective, then school improvement has offered guidance on how to effect change. We now have a very clear understanding of the process of initiating, implementing and institutionalizing change.
- an orientation towards action and on-going development. Schools do not stand still and wait to be measured by researchers. They are dynamic institutions subject to frequent change. Only by studying this process of change and its impact can we really understand schools (Stoll, 1996).
- an emphasis on school-selected priorities for development. School improvement emphasizes the importance of teacher involvement in change efforts, and ownership of the process. This is a fundamental principle of school development planning processes (Caldwell & Spinks, 1988; Hopkins, 1996).
- a view that the school is the centre of change (van Velzen, Miles, Eckholm, Hameyer, & Robin, 1985). School improvement not only views schools as the focus of change but also the centre of change because it cannot be separated

from the context around it. Schools need to be part of a wider system, networking with other schools as well as the school district, community, higher education, and business.

- an understanding of the importance of culture. There has been increased acknowledgment within the school improvement literature of the power of school culture and the importance of teacher collegiality to promote or obstruct change (Rosenholtz, 1989; Fullan & Hargreaves, 1991; Hargreaves, 1994; Hopkins, Ainscow, & West, 1994; Stoll & Fink, 1996).

The international work on school improvement has produced innumerable school projects. Governments such as those in parts of Australia and in many states in the United States, for example, have included a requirement for school improvement planning among their reforms. Our own efforts to use both the school effectiveness and school improvement literatures to effect change in schools has been well documented (Stoll & Fink, 1992, 1994, 1996). Our experience alone with our observations of the struggles of other school districts and schools to launch school improvement projects, have led us to see a number of limitations in the school improvement literature as it has evolved to date.

Process looking for purpose

Perhaps the central criticism of the school improvement literature is its relative neutrality on the purposes of school improvement. As governments attempt to change schools through technicist approaches which drive change through top-down mandates such as centralized curricula and standardized testing and site-based management, critics have suggested that collegiality as developed through 'site-based' management and collaborative school development plans is just another way to cajole teachers into accepting external mandates. As Smyth (1991) explains, "the widespread interest in teacher collaboration is neither incidental nor accidental, but it is part of a broader strategy (deliberate or otherwise), to harness teachers more effectively to the work of economic reconstruction" (p. 324).

While there is evidence to suggest that 'successful' schools in disadvantaged areas can often 'colonize' external reforms for their own benefit (National Commission, 1996), Smyth (1991) cautions that, in general, school leaders should be very suspicious of school improvement strategies which are initiated by corporatist governments that pander to the powerful groups who underwrite their elections. Reforms such as those in the United Kingdom, Victoria in Australia and in Alberta in Canada have effected a profound transformation by decentralizing business and maintenance decisions to the schools, and centralizing such professional issues as curriculum and student assessment. The irony is that the educational decisions for which school personnel are trained have been taken over by bureaucrats far removed from the students, and the schools' personnel have been left with items for which they have little training – ensuring building maintenance, organizing transportation, and juggling budgets. The 'catch 22' is that schools have often bought the rhetoric of empowerment and local initiative only to find themselves isolated, powerless and blamed for the failures of government policies. As Hargreaves (1996) suggests:

> A fundamental irony of educational change in the postmodern world, therefore, is that externally imposed problems are being accompanied by discourses and practices of interior solutions, such as stress management, individual wellness, reflective practice, personal narrative and school-level change (p. 10).

The managerial approach to change

With its focus on organizational planning, school improvement literature imputes a certain rationality and predictability to the change process. Like school effectiveness, school improvement has offered a range of organizational strategies to support change in classroom practice. School development planning, which has proven useful for schools who want to prioritize initiatives, assumes that change is linear – that cause and effect are not only knowable but manageable. Shifting enrolments resulting from market competition, changing political composition of school governors or school councils, the vicissitudes of national and/or local politics, new technologies, teachers' strikes, shrinking budgets, the loss of key personnel, are but a few of the unforeseen and often unpredictable issues to which schools must respond. The reality is that schools often have to plan on two levels, one for the predictable and linear, the other, for the non-rational and non-linear (Wallace, 1994).

Context and school improvement

How to address contextual differences between schools is one of the greatest challenges for school improvement. Currently there is insufficient detail about variations in improvement conditions and strategies as they apply to different types of schools, and yet one size clearly does not fit all (Stoll & Fink, 1996). Different change strategies, leadership styles and communications networks may be required to effect change in a school that is struggling from one that is already relatively effective but wants to become even more so (Hopkins, 1996), and even in two ostensibly 'similar' schools in terms of their effectiveness. This is seen only too clearly when a principal moves to a new school, tries what worked well for her in her previous school and finds because of different culture, community, and micropolitics, the same strategy is ineffective. It has also become clear that attempts to improve schools using the characteristics of effective schools have usually proven unsuccessful (Reynolds, 1991). It is, however, insufficient to assume that ineffective schools are the mirror opposite of effective schools – they may not be just devoid of 'effective' characteristics, but actively possess pathologies of their own.

(Stoll & Myers, 1998; Reynolds, 1996). In our work, school development planning also took on different guises in different contexts (Stoll & Fink, 1996). Since no two schools are the same, there would appear to be no one best way to approach school improvement. This can be terribly frustrating for those who seek simple solutions.

Restructuring/Reform

In recent years, many change agents, internationally, have advocated the restructuring or reform of schools as a vehicle for school improvement. The notion of changing the use of time, space, roles and relationships in schools to improve learning makes a great deal of sense. The term restructuring is seductively attractive. Sizer (1992), for example, suggests that the voluntary restructuring of his Essential Schools is intended for each student "to learn to use one's mind well". Unfortunately the terms 'restructuring' or 'reform' have many different and often conflicting meanings for different people. Although neither term has a stable meaning over different contexts – each one can refer to changes that are professionally empowering and self-regulated, or to ones that are externally imposed. It all depends on the context. For purposes of the following discussion we have used the words restructuring and reform interchangeably to describe a pattern of events and activities in which governments have mandated change through 'top-down' directives. These initiatives have tended to operate at two levels: the first directly involves the classroom, and the second, the larger contexts of the school, the district, and its larger jurisdiction. Discretionary reform efforts, such as our Halton Effective Schools' Project (Stoll & Fink, 1992, 1994), are essentially extensions of the school improvement process. The following discussion refers to mandated change initiatives.

Restructuring and teaching

At the classroom level, the pattern is consistent across many countries: design a centralized curriculum that more clearly prepares students for the changing economy, and support it with accountability testing (and in some countries external inspection) to ensure compliance. While there are notable exceptions, such as Kentucky, the effect of these initiatives has been to limit teachers' professional judgement and reinforce the existing "grammar" of schooling (Helsby & McCulloch, in press). Course coverage and test preparation replace innovation and risk-taking. Such solutions are exceedingly rational but they deny the individuality of both teachers and students. It is as though someone has decided that all eight year olds should all have the same shoe size, the same interests, or the same needs. It suggests that there are absolute scientific rules of teaching and learning which supersede the professional judgements of teachers in classrooms. The concept of the 'professional' teacher has been replaced by the image of the teacher as a skilled tradesperson. Robertson (1996), using Australia as an example, suggests that teachers have lost ideological control of the change agenda because they have been scarcely consulted before change was initiated. They have also failed to maintain technical control because they must now conform in their classrooms to the requirements of superordinates. Using the rhetoric of business efficiency, government reformers contend that one must define clear and useful learning outcomes for all students, align teaching strategies to meet these goals, and ensure their achievement through proper governance and accountability procedures. Students in this model have been reduced to commodities. Elmore (1995) offers three reasons for this line of logic:

- since structures are visible and malleable, changing them symbolizes that the reformers are serious;
- it is easier to change structures than other aspects of schooling;
- structural changes can remove barriers to learning for students and encourage alternative approaches to teaching.

There is ample evidence that changing organizational structures such as streaming or tracking (Oakes, 1985), the use of time and space (Hargreaves, 1994) and organizational roles (Schlechty, 1990), have the potential to assist change in teaching and learning. This is not to suggest that restructuring is unnecessary, nor that all changes initiated in the name of restructuring or reform are inappropriate. There are, of course, many significant and, in our view, required changes underway internationally; among these are efforts to destream schools, provide greater access to schools for parents, build rigour into curriculum, monitor school performance, and upgrade teacher skills. Unfortunately, most of these changes have proceeded as though teachers were a problem to be finessed or coerced. As Fullan (1991) has stated, "change in education depends upon what teachers do and think – it's as simple and complex as that" (p. 117). Until reformers and their academic advisors begin to look at school change in more ecological, holistic ways and recognize that schools are complex, non-linear organizations and that teachers can and should be professional partners in school improvement, then contemporary reform efforts will predictably wither and disappear, as many have in the past (McLaughlin, 1990).

A question of equity

At a second level, classroom practices in many countries have been influenced by significant alterations in governance, support service delivery and accountability procedures. Brouilette (1996) has summarized the four most common ways of viewing the purposes of education as humanist, social efficiency, developmentalist, and social meliorist. To the *humanist,* the purpose of education is to prepare students for citizenship so that they understand the values, and traditions embodied in their societies' institutions. To this end, students must be sufficiently literate to communicate with their fellow citizens and have the knowledge necessary to comprehend current issues and cast their vote appropriately. In practice this has tended to mean an emphasis on the teaching of the liberal arts with an emphasis on the 'basics' – grammar, spelling, and an understanding of western values and traditions. To those who advocate *social efficiency*, the purpose of schools is to prepare students for jobs, and to contribute to the economic well-being of society as a whole. The concept of students as 'human capital' evolves from this point of view.

The *developmentalist* position holds that education should help individual students to develop their personal potential "so that they are prepared to be crea- tive, self-motivated lifelong learners who are effective problem-solvers, able to com- municate and collaborate with others, and to meet the varied challenges they will encounter in their adult lives" (p. 224). Conversely, the purpose of education to the *social meliorist* is to bring about a more just society, "through using the schools to help those children whose background puts them at risk, to get the resources they need to succeed, and through teaching all students about diverse cultures and ethnic heritages, thus helping them to grow into open-minded, tolerant adults" (p. 224). It would appear that in the 1990s, in many countries, the social efficiency and humanist views have replaced the developmentalist and social meliorist purposes at policy-making level. Both the social efficiency and humanist perspec- tives imply a social Darwinist attitude – the survival of the fittest. What better device, therefore, to encourage competition, and winners and losers, than the application of the market to education.

Restructuring and reform as they have been interpreted in many jurisdictions have meant that the market rather than the public service determines educational practice. Market principles have already brought significant structural changes to education such as voucher systems, charter schools and selective grant maintained schools, which threaten the very existence of public education by allowing more affluent and influential segments of society to opt to remove their children from association with the less advantaged and with them, their support for public educa- tion. These policies tend to place individual self-interest above the public good. As the 19th century industrialist Robert Owens (1991) said, public education is "the most powerful instrument of good that has ever yet been placed in the hands of man" (p. 84). Polices such as school choice and vouchers and selective schools have produced competition where co-operation should prevail (Reynolds & Packer, 1992). They have promoted disparities in educational opportunities and outcomes and overt and covert resistance to structural changes (Tanner, 1993; Barlow & Robertson, 1994). As Gerwitz and colleagues (1995) argue, "The education market (like all markets) is intended to be driven by self-interest"(p. 2). Key to this market strategy is to empower smaller units such as schools. One might cynically suggest that strategically, individual schools are easier to influence and oblige compliance.

Restructuring or reform agendas have, therefore, usually included some version of site-based management. School improvers in the 1980s saw decentralization as a way to ensure more involvement in decision making at the school level. By mandating this reform, however, governments have undermined the ability of many school systems to ensure some degree of equity among schools. When one adds the market mechanism as a quality control device, then schools must compete for students, and indeed departments and teachers within schools, must compete to keep programmes alive (Siskin, 1994). As Reynolds and Packer (1992) explain, this contributes to variability in schools " because of the ways in which the schools will differ markedly in their ability to cope with rapid externally induced changes, a variability that is likely to be more marked than when the rate of external change was slow" (p. 172).

While the rhetoric of equity is still heard, the reality for marginalized students is different. The dream of more inclusionary approaches for special education students for example, is beginning to fade in some jurisdictions like Ontario where arbitrary budget cuts and more elitist educational policies like the reaffirmation of streaming means special classes for those who do not 'fit'. Similarly, there is evidence that the goal of comprehensive education in the United Kingdom is being undermined by government policies (Benn & Chitty, 1996). As a report of the National Commission on Education (1995) states:

> Too much reliance has been placed on introducing the philosophy of the market into education. Competition plays a useful part when its effect is to improve learning. There is, however, little to be said for stimulating competition which is either unfair or which enables some schools to flourish only by making it more difficult for other schools to offer education of good quality (p. 6).

Questionable impact

With all this reform activity, there is little evidence that ideologically-driven, 'top-down' change strategies are substantially altering life in classrooms (McLaughlin, 1990) any more than they did in the 1970s. Elmore (1995) has concluded that changes "in structure are weakly related to changes in teaching practice, and therefore structural change does not necessarily lead to changes in teaching, learning, and student performance" (p. 25).

While restructuring has brought short-term movement in educational practice, such as destreaming in Ontario, more uniformity of curriculum in the United Kingdom, ungraded primary classrooms in Kentucky and British Columbia, it would appear that the quantum shift required in educational practice to deal with rapidly changing societal forces will not result from restructuring alone (Elmore, 1995; Corcoran & Goetz, 1995). The 'grammar of schooling' remains fundamentally unchanged (Tyack & Tobin, 1994). If anything, content-coverage, subject content, teaching for the test, and didactic teaching have been reinforced (Helsby & McCulloch, 1996). Similarly the power of the timetable and examination schedules seems to prevail. If anything, teachers' work has intensified through larger class sizes, more paper work, and the pressure to be entrepreneurial (Robertson, 1996). Elmore has concluded from his studies on restructuring that the relationship of structure to teaching practice is mediated by "relatively powerful forces such as the shared norms, knowledge and skills of teachers" (p. 26). Increasingly, academics and practitioners are looking at these non-structural aspects of schooling for 'doors' to educational change (Joyce, 1991). Restructuring, therefore, needs to be balanced by reculturing (Hargreaves, 1994; Fullan 1996a).

Reculturing

Over the past few years the school improvement literature has evolved from an emphasis on structures and formal processes such as school development planning to a focus on the less tangible and ultimately more impactful aspects of schools such as school culture (Fullan, 1993; Hargreaves, 1994; D. Hargreaves, 1995a). This shift in focus has been described as reculturing (Hargreaves, 1994). Reculturing is "the process of developing new values, beliefs and norms. For systematic reform it involves building new conceptions about instruction . . . and new forms of professionalism for teachers" (Fullan, 1996a). The origins of reculturing lie within the school improvement tradition, but school improvement is also concerned with other issues like planning and restructuring as well. We have separated it here to place it in the foreground and to discuss what happens when beliefs, relationships and the like are made the focus of change efforts, rather than programmes and procedures.

Schools are complex networks of interrelated and interconnected forces which help to define each school's uniqueness. These forces are often unseen and intangible but are knowable by their results. Anyone who has sat in the wrong chair in a staff room, or used the wrong coffee cup will have encountered a microcosm of a school's culture. Culture is not easily defined because it is largely implicit. Schein (1985) notes various interpretations of the content and forms of culture – among these are observed behavioral regularities, including language and rituals; norms that evolve in working groups; dominant values espoused by an organization; the philosophy that guides an organization's policy; and the feeling or climate conveyed in an organization. More simply, organizational culture can be viewed as "the way we do things around here" (Deal & Kennedy, 1983).

As we have suggested in some detail elsewhere, improving schools are characterized by a teaching staff which has shared goals, collegiality as defined by joint work, continuous improvement and learning, risk-taking and mutual support, among other cultural norms (Stoll & Fink, 1996). In addition, leadership in improving schools is pervasive and does not just reside with the principal or other formal leaders, but is a shared activity (Barth, 1990). Reculturing also requires schools to attend to the micro-politics that influence every institution (Ball, 1987; Blase, 1988). Different departments often have different goals, communications networks, and educational purposes (Grossman & Stodolsky, 1994). Class teachers and teachers without specific class assignments often have alternative perspectives. Principals and teachers, of necessity, see aspects of the school differently. Improving schools are able to recognize these perspectives and turn micro-politics into positive forces

(Stacey, 1995). Schools which reculture successfully develop educational meaning. This is more than a commitment to specific goals. It is the shared sense that staff members know where they are going and is present throughout the school.

If schools are to be effective in the future for all students and build structures which promote interrelationships and interconnections, then cultures must be developed which simultaneously promote collegiality and individuality (Hargreaves, 1994). As paradoxical as it sounds, not only must the school's culture promote group learning to enhance the knowledge and skills of teachers but it also must honour the individual, the 'maverick', because creativity and novelty will be required to deal with an unknowable future and prevent 'groupthink' (Janis, 1972). In effect, cultures and counter-cultures must interact to find innovative solutions to complex and unpredictable circumstances. Reculturing goes beyond redefining the content and forms of *teacher* cultures. It must include *student* and *community* cultures as well. Students can be a conservative force when teachers attempt to change their practice (Rudduck, 1991; McLaughlin & Talbert, 1993) because they find change from usual practice threatening. Similarly, as many studies reveal, communities are also often resistant to educational change (Fletcher et al., 1985; Smith Dwyer et al., 1987).

So far we have attempted to describe some of the forces which perpetuate continuity and have described and analysed four rather broad currents of activity intended to promote change in schools. We then, described and analyzed four rather broad currents of activity intended to promoting change in schools – school effectiveness, school improvement, restructuring and reculturing. School effectiveness, with its focus on equity and student results, has had a significant impact on the course of educational change by showing what makes a contemporary school effective. This is a useful starting point. School improvement has provided 'rational' tools like school development planning to promote school growth. It too has identified non-rational aspects of schools as areas worthy of investigation. Restructuring or reform has attempted to influence or, the more cynical might suggest, coerce or shame teachers into altering their teaching-learning processes. To date, however, none of these approaches have proved sufficient to change the fundamental 'grammar' of schooling. Attending to the non-rational, non-linear aspects of change holds more promise for meaningful and lasting change for students in classrooms. If, however, reculturing is 'the way of the future', then the following problems must be addressed.

PERVASIVE CHANGE ISSUES

Alternative views on teaching and learning

We have been critical of paths to change which are silent on the purposes of change. This suggests that one of the key challenges to more successful change is to focus on teaching and learning for our changing world. Elsewhere, we have critiqued in detail traditional approaches to teaching and learning and suggested that a more holistic concept of teaching and learning is emerging which already manifests itself in many settings (Stoll & Fink, 1996). It is based on the premise that each student has a mind, each mind works differently, has strengths and weaknesses, and should be developed to its fullest possible potential (Gardner, 1983). Furthermore, intelligence is learnable (Perkins, 1995). Truly democratic education may be seen as idealistic, especially in the present political climate, but in democratic societies in which quality and equity co-exist uneasily, to do less wastes our most important national resources in an information age, the minds of all people.

Learning for an uncertain future

An equally difficult question to answer is the one asked by older students, "Where do I go after school?". The old rules do not apply any longer. The 'job for life' is a thing of the past (Handy, 1994). Already, friends and colleagues all around us are experiencing the uncertainty of redundancy, short-term contracts, part-time work and unemployment. And whereas university graduation used to be an almost certain guarantee of a job, this is no longer the case. Several problems, therefore, arise. How do teachers convince their students of the importance of learning when students perceive the future to be very uncertain. If, as the school effectiveness literature attests (Cotton, 1995; Sammons, Hillman, & Mortimore, 1995), high expectations are extremely important to student outcomes, how do teachers keep students motivated to learn?

Conceptions of leadership

If schools are to be viewed holistically, and if, as we have suggested, human organizations are non-linear, complex webs of relationships and connections, then formal leaders not only need to foster coherence through organizational meaning but also initiate, nurture, develop and preserve the kinds of relationships which promote organizational learning. Leadership as we know it, with its power, perks, and monopoly on defining purpose, places inordinate pressure on a few leaders in a crisis. The concept of visionary leaders propounded by the management literature requires a few to have extraordinary foresight (Stacey, 1995)

We suggest, therefore, that schools need a conception of leadership which recognizes the complexity of formal educational leadership roles while at the same time ensuring that schools have the type of leadership necessary to face an unknowable future. These changing conditions will require the intuition, creativity and reasoning power of everyone on a school staff, not just its formal leaders (Fullan, 1996b). This suggests that 'moving' schools which can confront complexity and confusion will be led by 'leaders of leaders' (Barth, 1990) who lead less, and disperse power, control, and resources, to enable staff, students, parents, school governors to lead more. Such leaders would communicate 'invitational' messages to people to inform them that they are able, responsible and worthwhile (Fink, 1992; Stoll &

Fink, 1996). To change current conceptions of leadership, particularly when principals throughout the world have been overwhelmed with the demands of various forms of site-based management, is a major challenge.

Assessment of Change

In our own work, assessing the results of change efforts proved to be the most significant hurdle (Stoll & Fink, 1992, 1994). We are not alone. There appears to be little agreement as to what to assess, how to assess it, and how to report the results. The effective schools' focus on conventional outputs has been adopted by many jurisdictions because it fits the 'bottom-line' mentality of the market ideology. Unfortunately such a direction tends to forget the equity origins of the effectiveness movement. Performance tables, or 'League Tables' as they are known in Britain, which rank order schools according to their raw examination results, is a well known example of this approach. The limitations of raw scores as a measure of school performance and as a vehicle for change have been well documented (Gray, Jesson, & Sime, 1986; Nuttall, 1992; Goldstein & Myers, 1996) and have resulted in attempts to develop 'value-added' measures which take account of a schools' intakes (Raudenbush & Bryk, 1986; Goldstein, 1995).

What will the future bring? Some talk of increased leisure. What does leisure mean? How do schools help students prepare for an uncertain future? One certainty is that the future will bring new children into the world but little attention has been paid in schools to key life skills such as parenting. One study has found that I.Q. scores among children born in very deprived areas rise 15 to 30 points if attention is focused on babies in the first year of life (Hawkes, 1996). After that the impact is dramatically reduced. Whatever one might say about I.Q. scores, there is a powerful cycle of disadvantage that works against what educators try to do in classrooms and schools. Ironically at a time when social issues consume huge amounts of teachers' time and get in the way of learning, governments, in the name of efficiency, are cutting the existing supports. It is the same mentality which solves problems of poverty by redefining what it means to be poor, demonizes people on welfare as malingerers and builds more and bigger prisons. Certainly support in parenting appears to be one vital step in breaking the cycle. The question remains however, who breaks the cycle and who pays for it? Not only will it be necessary to come up with new answers to old questions, but what is even more challenging is to know what questions to ask in an increasingly complex environment. In the present climate in which governments appeal to self interest and short term gains through tax cuts, creative solutions to public problems seem bereft of creative answers.

A related approach to assessing schools and change in schools is the inspection process. Preparation for an Office for Standards in Education (OFSTED) inspection in Britain has contributed to the identification of failing schools and, in some schools, appears to have motivated short-term change, especially during the period of preparation for the inspection (Earley, 1995). One has to question the expense of a process, "estimated to be over £100m per annum or about £30,000 for an average-sized secondary school" (Earley, 1995, p. 11), which can create short term activity in a school whose long-term impact is unproven. As yet, there is too little research to determine the impact of inspections and whether they lead to real improvement in students' learning and the motivation of staff to effect change (D. Hargreaves, 1995b).

While a number of other ways to monitor change have been identified, assessment and evaluation are crucial but often overlooked or superficial parts of the development planning process (Hargreaves & Hopkins, 1994; MacGilcrist et al., 1995; Stoll & Fink, 1996). Without some measures of results, however, process measures can tell us if things are working as intended, but not whether the improvement process is making any differences in students' learning. A balance of process and outcome measures is required, but the question which remains is what are the best measures to support positive change? Moreover, what are the best ways to promote assessment literacy (Stiggins, 1991) among practitioners?

Perhaps an equally important question is how do educators help key decision makers to support 'good' assessments. Unfortunately, present models which have been imposed by governments and supported by academics, reinforce dated and potentially damaging concepts of teaching and learning. The rationalist model is nowhere more in evidence than in the reductionist assessments which have multiplied in most western countries in recent years. The market ideology is pervasive in how reporting processes are designed and used in these large scale, high stakes assessments. Efforts to improve schools from within are certainly undermined by inadequate and inappropriate assessment strategies. If we want teachers to do a better job for students then one place to start is with the what, the how, and the why of assessment. Rather than using assessment to find weaknesses, place blame, and promote guilt, change agents need to work with teachers to find more appropriate ways to use assessments to promote students' learning.

Teachers' Lives

Attempts to coerce teachers into change through assessment systems or other policy initiatives have resulted in the intensification of teachers' work (Apple, 1986), the deskilling of teachers (Apple & Teitelbaum, 1986), guilt (Hargreaves, 1994), and 'burnout' (Byrne, 1994). Efforts to use school based management as a vehicle to deliver government policies have met with teacher indifference, cynicism (Smyth, 1991) and divided teachers and principals from each other (Bishop & Mulford, 1996). There appears to be little evidence to suggest that many of these efforts have brought much positive change to classrooms. Greater attention, therefore, might usefully be paid to the personal and biographical influences on teachers and what teachers do. Several writers argue that an understanding of how teachers' lives affect their work is necessary to grasp how teachers relate to educational change (Goodson, 1981; Ball & Goodson, 1985; Louden, 1991; Huberman, 1993).

Schools are human institutions, and as such non rational (not irrational). Change strategies that ignore the meanings, emotions and cultures of schools, we would submit, are doomed to failure.

Teachers and micro-politics

Teachers are also strategic. They make decisions on a daily basis as to what is ideal and what is possible in their context. Some teachers are ambitious, some want to influence school decisions, others just want to be left alone. Many secondary teachers tend to be more loyal to their departments than their school. Often, competition for students pits one department against another (Ball, 1981; Siskin, 1994). Declining enrolment also creates rivalries within departments and schools. Schools are micro-political organizations (Hoyle, 1986; Woods, 1986; Ball, 1987; Blase, 1988). We, therefore, need to know more about the micro-politics of schools. How can the natural political activities of people within schools contribute to the goals of the organization. How do schools promote positive politics (Blase, 1988)? How can schools promote the kinds of self-organizing networks which lead to creative solutions to complex problems (Stacey, 1995) without encouraging divisiveness? Answers to these questions will help change agents to promote change 'with' teachers, not apply change 'to' teachers.

CONCLUSION

The social forces for substantial change are compelling. There is an urgency to prepare students already in our schools for the changing world. Change in schools, however, is influenced by conflicting intellectual paradigms. One describes a world of predictability, stability and progress. It is a world which is knowable through rational, reasoned thought. If we just study its parts they will add up to a complete picture. This comforting, hopeful world, often described as 'modernity' is one which is difficult to abandon. This world view has contributed substantively to our understanding of the change process through school effectiveness, school improvement and restructuring. We have, however, suggested that the results of these approaches in terms of changed classroom practice, have been disappointing. We have, therefore, described a fourth approach, reculturing, which builds on previous models, but embraces a different conceptual framework which is more in tune with this age of discontinuity (Drucker, 1993). As we have suggested, each approach offers guidance on the change journey – school effectiveness with its emphasis on equity and value added results; school improvement's focus on process, careful planning and school-based change; and restructuring which addresses the 'grammar' of schooling by changing the structures of schools. When lessons learned from these approaches are combined with the emphasis on the non-rational and non-linear aspects of change identified within the reculturing approach, change agents have some powerful tools for school development.

This 'post-modern' world is a world of diversity, uncertainty and confusion. It is also a world open to human creativity, intuition and sensitivity. Reculturing as an approach to change, seeks to find the ecological connections among the purposes of education, the organizational values of schools, as well as its structures, cultures, leadership, and the work and lives of teachers. It is a promising avenue to change but one which is very much in its infancy, with many unanswered questions. For as our title suggests, change is indeed, 'easier said than done'.

REFERENCES

Apple, M. (1986). *Teachers and texts.* New York: Routledge and Kegan Paul.

Apple, M. & Teitelbaum, K. (1986). Are teachers losing control of their skills and curriculum. *Journal of Curriculum Studies*, **18**(2), 177–184.

Ball, S. (1987). *Micropolitics of the school.* London: Methuen/Routledge & Kegan Paul.

Ball, S. (1981). *Beachside comprehensive: A case-study of secondary schooling.* Cambridge: Cambridge University Press.

Ball, S., & Goodson, I. (1985). Understanding teachers: Concepts and contexts. In S. Ball and I. Goodson (Eds), *Teachers' lives and careers.* London: The Falmer Press.

Barber, M. (1992). *Education and the teacher unions.* London: Cassell

Barlow, M., & Robertson, H. (1994). *Class warfare.* Toronto: Key Porter.

Barth, R. (1990). *Improving schools from within: Teachers, parents and principals can make the difference.* San Francisco: Jossey Bass.

Bascia N. (1994). *Unions in teachers' lives: Social intellectual and practical concerns.* New York: Teachers' College.

Benn, C., & Chitty, C. (1996). *Thirty years on: Is comprehensive education alive and well or struggling to survive?* London: David Fulton.

Berliner, D., & Biddle, B. (1995). *The manufactured crisis: Myth, fraud, and the attack on America's schools.* New York: Addison-Wesley.

Bishop, P., & Mulford, W. (1996). Empowerment in four Australian primary schools: They don't really care. *International Journal of Educational Reform*, **5**(2), 193–204.

Blase, J. (1988). The teachers' political orientation vis a vis the princial: The micropolitics of the school. *Politics of Education Association Yearbook: 1988*, pp. 113–26.

Brennan, R. (1995). Minister called dishonest. *The Spectator*, 13 February, 1.

Brouilette, L. (1996). *A geology of school reform: The successive restructuring of a school district.* New York: State University of New York Press.

Brown, S. (1995). School effectiveness research: The policy-maker's tool for school improvement? *European Educational Research Association Bulletin*, **1**(1), 6–15.

Byrne, B. M. (1994). Burnout testing for the validity, replication, and invarience of causal structure across the elementary, intermediate, and secondary teachers. *American Educational Research Journal*, **31**(3), 645–673.

Caldwell, B., & Spinks, J. (1988). *The self-managing school.* Lewes: Falmer Press.

Coleman, J. S., Campbell, E., Hobson, C., McPartland, J., Mood, A., Weinfeld, F., & York, R. (1966). *Equality of Educational Opportunity.* Washington D. C.: National Center for Educational Statistics.

Corcoran, T., & Goetz, M. (1995). Instructional capacity and high performance schools. *Educational Researcher*, **24**(9), 27–31.

Cuban, L. (1990). Reforming again and again and again. *Educational Researcher*, **19**(1), 2–13.

Deal, T., & Kennedy, A. (1983). Culture and school performance. *Educational Leadership*, **40**(5), 140–1.

Doyle, W., & Ponder, G. A. (1977). The practicality ethic in teacher decision-making. *Interchange*, **8**(3), 1–12.

Drucker, P. (1993). *Post capitalist society.* New York: Harper Business.

Earley, P. (1995). School improvement and OFSTED inspection: The research evidence. In P. Earley, B. Fidler & J. Ouston (Eds), *Improvement through inspection?: Complementary approaches to school development.* London: David Fulton.

Earley, P. (1994). *School governing bodies: Making progress?* Slough: National Foundation for Educational Research.

Edmonds, R. (1979). Effective schools for the urban poor. *Educational Leadership*, 37(1), 15–27.

Elliott, J. (1996). School effectiveness research and its critics: Alternative visions of schooling. *Cambridge Journal of Education*, 26(2), 199–224.

Elmore, R. (1995). Structural reform in educational practice. *Educational Researcher*, 24(9), 23–26.

Epstein, J. L. (1995). School/family/partnerships: Caring for the children we share. *Phi Delta Kappan*, 76(9), 701–712.

Fink, D. (1992). Invitational leadership. In J. Novak (Ed.), *Advances in invitational theory*. San Francisco: Caddo Gap Press.

Fletcher, C., & Williams, W. (1985). *Schools on trial: The trials of the democratic comprehensives*. Milton Keynes: Open University Press.

Fullan, M. G. (1996a). Turning systematic thinking on its head. *Phi Delta Kappan*, 77(6), 420–423.

Fullan, M. G. (1996b). Broadening the concept of teacher leadership. In National Staff Development Council, *New directions*. Oxford, OH: NSDC.

Fullan, M. G. (1993) *Change forces: Probing the depths of educational reform*. London: Falmer Press.

Fullan, M. G. (1991). *The new meaning of educational change*. New York: Teachers' College Press.

Fullan, M., & Hargreaves, A. (1991). *What's worth fighting for in your school?* Toronto: Ontario Public School Teachers' Federation.

Gardner, H. (1983). *Frames of mind: The theory of multiple intelligences*. New York: Basic Books.

Gewirtz, S., Ball, S. J., & Bowe, R. (1995). *Markets, choice and equity in education*. Buckingham: Open University Press.

Goldstein, H. (1995). *Multilevel models in educational and social research* (2nd edition). London: Edward Arnold.

Goldstein, H., & Myers, K. (1996). Freedom of information: Towards a code of ethics for performance indicators. *Research Intelligence*: *British Educational Research Association Newsletter*, 57(July), 12–16.

Goldstein, H., & Thomas, S. (1996). Using examination results as indicators of school and college performance. *Journal of the Royal Statistical Society*, 159, 149–163.

Goodson, I. F. (1981). Life history and the study of schooling. *Interchange*, 11, 62–76.

Gray, J., Jesson, D., & Sime, N. (1986). The search for a fairer way of comparing schools' examination results. *Research Papers in Education*, 1(2), 91–122.

Grossman, P. L., & Stodolsky, S. S. (1994). Considerations of content and the circumstances of secondary school teaching. In L. Darling-Hammond (Ed.), *Review of research in education*. Washington, D.C.: American Educational Research Association.

Gustavson, C. G. (1955). *A preface to history*. Toronto: McGraw-Hill.

Hallinger, P., & Murphy, J. (1986). The social context of effective schools. *American Journal of Education*, 94(3), 328–355.

Hamilton, D. (1996). Peddling feel-good fictions. *Forum*, 38(2), 54–56.

Handy, C. (1994). *The empty rain coat: Making sense of the future*. London: Hutchinson.

Hargreaves, A. (1996). Cultures of teaching and educational change. In Biddle, B., Good, T., & Goodson, I. (Eds.), *International handbook of teachers and teaching*. The Netherlands: Kluwer Press.

Hargreaves, A. (1994). *Changing teachers, changing times*. London: Cassell.

Hargreaves, D. H., & Hopkins, D. (1991). *The empowered school: The management and practice of development planning*. London: Cassell.

Hargreaves, D. H. (1995). School culture, school effectiveness and school improvement. *School Effectiveness and School Improvement*, 6(1), 23–46.

Hawkes, N. (1996). Intensive pre-school: Key to higher I.Q. *Times Educational* Supplement, February 16, p.16.

Helsby, G., & McCulloch, G. (in press). *Teachers and the national curriculum*. London: Cassell.

Helsby, G., & McCulloch, G. (1996). Teacher professionalism and curriculum control. In I. F. Goodson, & A. Hargreaves (Eds.), *Teachers' professional lives*. London: Falmer.

Hopkins, D., Ainscow, M., & West, M. (1994). *School improvement in an era of change*. London: Cassell.

Hoyle, E. (1986). *The politics of school management*. London: Hodder and Stoughton.

Huberman, M. (1993). *The lives of teachers*. London: Cassell.

Jencks, C.S., Smith, M., Acland, H., Bane, M. J., Cohen, D., Gintis, H., Heyns, B., & Micholson, S. (1972). *Inequality: A reassessment of the effect of family and schooling in America*. New York: Basic Books.

Joyce, B. R. (1991). The doors to school improvement. *Educational Leadership*, 14(3), 10–12.

Levine, D. U., & Lezotte, L. (1990). *Unusually effective schools: A review and analysis of research and practice.* Madison, WI.: National Center for Effective Schools Research and Development.

Louden, W. (1991). *Understanding teaching.* London: Cassell.

MacBeath, J., McCaig, E., & Thomson, W. (1992). *Making school boards work.* Glasgow: SOED, Jordanhill College.

MacGilcrist, B., Mortimore, P., Savage, J., & Beresford, C. (1995). *Planning matters: The impact of development planning in primary schools.* London: Paul Chapman.

McDonnell, L. M., & Pascal, A. H. (1988). *Teachers' unions and educational reform.* Washington, D. C.: Rand Corporation.

McLaughlin, M. W., & Talbert, J. E. (1993). *Contexts that matter for teaching and learning.* Palo Alto: Center for Research on the Context of Secondary School Teaching.

McLaughlin, M. W. (1990). The Rand change agent study: Macro perspectives and micro realities. *Educational Researcher,* **19**(9),11–15.

Mechlenberg, J. A. (1992). The braking of the break-the-mold express. *Phi Delta Kappan,* **74**(4), 280–289.

Metz, M. H. (1990). Real school: A universal drama amid disparate experience. In D. E. Mitchell & M. E. Metz (Eds.), *Education politics for the new century.* New York: Falmer Press.

Morgan, G., & Morgan, K. (1992). *Beyond the glitterspeak.* Toronto: Ontario Teachers' Federation.

Mortimore, P. (1991). The nature and findings on school effectiveness in the primary sector. In S. Riddell & S. Brown (Eds), *School effectiveness research: Its message for school improvement.* Edinburgh: HMSO.

Mortimore, P., Sammons, P., Stoll, L., Lewis, D., & Ecob, R. (1988). *School matters: The junior years.* Somerset: Open Books (Reprinted 1994, London: Paul Chapman).

Mortimore, P., Sammons, P., Stoll, L., Lewis, D., & Ecob, R. (1986). *The junior school project: Main report.* London: Research and Statistics Branch, Inner London, Education Authority.

Murphy, J. (1992). School effectiveness and school restructuring: Contributions to educational improvement. *School Effectiveness and School Improvement,* **3**(2), 90–109.

Myers, K. (1995). *Intensive care for the chronically sick.* Paper presented to the European Conference on Educational Research, University of Bath.

National Commission on Education. (1996). *Success against the odds: Effective schools in disadvantaged areas.* London: Routledge.

National Commission on Education. (1995). *Learning to succeed: The way ahead.* London: National Commission on Education.

Nuttall, D. L. N. (1992). Add value to league tables. *The ISIS Magazine,* 4, Spring, 14.

Nuttall, D., Goldstein, H., Prosser, R., & Rasbash, J. (1989). Differential school effectiveness. *International Journal of Educational Research,* **13**(7), 769–776.

Oakes, J. (1985). *Keeping track: How schools structure social inequality.* New Haven: Yale University Press.

Owens, R. (1991). *A new view of society and other writings.* London: Penguin Classics

Perkins, D. (1995). *Outsmarting IQ: The Emerging science of learnable intelligence.* New York: The Free Press.

Raudenbush, S. W., & Bryk, A. S. (1986). A hierarchical model for studying school effects. *Sociology of Education,* **59**(January), 1–17.

Reynolds, D. (1996). Turning around ineffective schools: Some evidence and some speculations. In J. Gray, D. Reynolds, C. Fitz-Gibbon, & D. Jesson (Eds.), *Merging traditions: The future of research on school effectiveness and school improvement.* London: Cassell.

Reynolds, D. (1991). Changing ineffective schools. In M. Ainscow (Ed.), *Effective schools for all.* London: David Fulton.

Reynolds, D. (1988). British school improvement research: The contribution of qualitative studies. *International Journal of Qualitative Studies in Education,* **1**(2), 143–154.

Reynolds, D., Creemers, B. P. M., Nesselrodt, P. S., Schaffer, E. C., Stringfield, S., & Teddlie, C. (1994). *Advances in school effectiveness research and practice.* Oxford: Elsevier Science Ltd.

Reynolds D., Hopkins, D., & Stoll, L. (1993). Linking school effectiveness knowledge and school improvement practice: Towards a synergy. *School Effectiveness and School Improvement,* **4**(1), 37–58.

Reynolds, D., & Farrell, S. (1996). *World's apart?: A Review of international surveys of educational achivement involving England.* London: HMSO for the Office of Standards in Education.

Reynolds, D., & Packer, A. (1992). School effectiveness and school improvement in the 1990s'. In D. Reynolds, & P. Cuttance (Eds.), *School Effectiveness: Research Policy and Practice.* London: Cassell.

Richardson, V. (1990). Significant and worthwhile change in teaching practice. *Educational Researcher*, **19**(7), 10–18.

Robertson, S. (1996). Teachers' work, restructuring and post fordism: Constructing the new professionalism. In I. F. Goodson, & A. Hargreaves (Eds.), *Teachers' professional lives*. London: Falmer.

Rosenholtz, S. J. (1989). *Teacher workplace: The social organization of schools*. New York: Longmans.

Rudduck, J. (1991). *Innovation and change*. Milton Keynes: Open University Press.

Sammons, P., Thomas, S., & Mortimore, P. (1996). *Differential school effectiveness: Departmental variations in GCSE attainment*. Paper presented at the annual meeting of the American Educational Research Association, New York.

Schlechty, P. (1990). *Schools for the twenty first century: Leadership imperatives for educational reform*. San Francisco Ca.: Jossey Bass.

Schein, E. H. (1985). *Organizational culture and leadership*. San Francisco Ca.: Jossey Bass.

Siskin, L. (1994). *Realms of knowledge: Academic departments in secondary schools*. London: Falmer Press.

Sizer, T. (1992). *Horace's school: Redesigning the American high school*. Boston: Houghton Mifflin.

Smith, L. M. , Dwyer, D. C., Prunty, J. J., & Kleine, P. F. (1987). *The fate of an innovative school*. London: The Falmer Press.

Smyth, J. (1991). International perspectives on teacher collegiality: A labour process discussion based on the concept of teachers' work. *British Journal of Sociology in Education*, **12**(3), 323–346.

Stacey, R. (1995). *Managing chaos*. London: Kogan Page.

Stiggins, R. M. (1991). Assessment literacy. *Phi Delta Kappan*, **72**(7), 534–539.

Stoll, L. (1996). Linking school effectiveness and school improvement: Issues and possibilities. In J. Gray, D. Reynolds, C. Fitz-Gibbon, & D. Jessop (Eds.), *Merging traditions: The future of school effectiveness and school improvement*. London: Cassell.

Stoll, L., & Fink, D. (1998). The cruising school: The unidentified ineffective school. In L. Stoll, & K. Myers (Eds.), *Schools in difficulty: No quick fixes*. Chichester: Falmer Press.

Stoll L., & Fink, D. (1996). *Changing our schools: Linking school effectiveness and school improvement*. Buckingham: Open University Press.

Stoll, L., & Fink, D. (1994). Voices from the field. *School Effectiveness and School Improvement*, **5**(2), 149–177.

Stoll, L., & Fink, D. (1992). Effective school change: The Halton approach. *School Effectiveness and School Improvement*, **3**(1), 19–41.

Stoll, L., & Myers, K. (Eds.). (1998). *Schools in difficulty: No quick fixes*. London: Falmer Press.

Tanner, D. (1993). A nation truly at risk. *Phi Delta Kappan*, **75**(4), 297.

Teddlie, C., Stringfield, S., Wimpelberg, R., & Kirby, P. (1989). Contextual differences in models for effective schooling. In B. P. M. Creemers, T. Peters, & D. Hopkins (Eds.), *School effectiveness and school improvement*. Proceedings of the second international congress, Rotterdam. Amsterdam: Swets and Zeitlinger.

Tyack, D., & Tobin, W. (1994). The grammer of schooling: Why has it been so hard to change? *American Educational Research Journal*, **31**(3), 453–479.

van Velzen, W., Miles, M., Eckholm, M., Hameyer, U., & Robin, D. (1985). *Making school improvement work*. Leuven, Belgium: ACCO.

Wallace, M. (1994). Towards a contingency approach to development planning in schools. In D. Hargreaves, & D, Hopkins (Eds.), *Development planning for school improvement*. London: Cassell.

Globalization and Educational Change

AMY STUART WELLS
University of California Los Angeles

SIBYLL CARNOCHAN
University of California Los Angeles

JULIE SLAYTON
UCLA Graduate School of Education and Information Science

RICKY LEE ALLEN
UCLA Graduate School of Education and Information Science

ASH VASUDEVA
UCLA Graduate School of Education and Information Science

There is no greater context for educational change than that of globalization, nor no grander way of conceptualizing what educational change is about. Wells and her colleagues analyze how economic and political globalization are affecting the identity and independence of nation states, and the ways in which public education (like public health and welfare) are undergoing change within the states. They acknowledge that there is no agreement about how political and economic globalization have affected public education precisely, and they review and evaluate different theoretical claims about the globalization effect: from neo-liberals, liberal-progressives (or modernizers), realists and critical theorists. The paradoxical juxtaposition of educational markets, privatization and decentralization with standardization of assessment and growing emphases on nationhood in the agendas of school reform is analyzed through these different approaches to globalization theory.

This chapter also looks at the social and cultural effects of globalization on education again from different theoretical standpoints in terms of the growth of communism and the spread of visual and eletronic imagery. Wells and her colleagues examine the consequences of these influences for teaching and learning, the curriculum, and the ability to deal with difference. Globalization is reshaping students lives through market influences and symbolic concerns with identity and nationhood. Wells and her colleagues demonstrate how the immensely broad phenomenon of globalization is having very concrete effects on contemporary agendas of educational reform.

In the last two decades, a growing number of economists, political scientists and cultural theorists have turned their attention to the study of "globalization." Although globalization has been called "the central political phenomenon of our day," only recently have scholars in the field of education begun to explore the relationship between this global transformation and the conditions of schooling ("Incorporating . . .," 1996, p. 3; Green, in press). In fact, much of the literature

A. Hargreaves (ed.), Extending Educational Change, 42-68.
© 2005 *Springer. Printed in the Netherlands.*

on educational change focuses on the school as the unit of analysis and does not consider macro-level forces that shape the conditions for school change. We argue, however, that the global shifts discussed in this chapter could shape the very meaning of schooling in the 21st century.

In this chapter, we first briefly note the conditions that comprise the phenomenon of globalization. We then focus on two of the most powerful themes that are emerging from, and contested within, the globalization literature. The first of these overlapping and intertwined themes – the economic and political implications of globalization – is prevalent in the writing of economists and political scientists. It focuses on the effect of globalization on economic inequality and the role of nation-states in providing public services. Public educational systems, state-run institutions that reflect social conditions, stand to be strongly affected by the political and economic dimensions of globalization.

The second theme – the social and cultural implications of globalization – is primarily addressed by cultural theorists. This theme considers the effects of globalization on culture, arguing that globalization both homogenizes and fragments cultural identities across the world. The phenomenon of simultaneous cultural homogenization and fragmentation raises important questions regarding the culture of schools and the direction school change might take.

In the chapter's final section, we suggest avenues for future research into the relationship between globalization and educational change.

GLOBALIZATION AT A GLANCE

The term "globalization" is generally used to refer to a complicated set of economic, political, and cultural factors. At an economic and political level, the term signifies the diminishing of economic borders and the simultaneous increase in international exchange and transnational interaction (Dolon, 1993, p. 259). As a result of expanding world trade, nations and individuals experience greater economic and political interdependence. New technologies, particularly communications technology that facilitates expanded world trade as well as cultural interaction, are considered essential to the emergence of globalization. Economic exchange across borders leads, ultimately, to "global enmeshment", as "money, people, images, values, and ideas flow ever more swiftly and smoothly across national boundaries" (Hurrell & Woods, 1995, p. 447). As economic forces reach across borders and cultures are reshaped by new and expanded communications, the role of the nation-state as arbiter of exchange shifts. The magnitude and effects of each of these phenomenon – economic exchange, the role of the nation-state, and cultural shifts – are all contested within the globalization literature. But all theorists of globalization might agree with the statement of Kumar (1995): "Political, economic and cultural life is now strongly influenced by developments at the global level" (p. 121).

In the sections that follow, we consider the debates within the literature on globalization. Before we continue, we must make clarify one element: We do not mean to imply in our review of the literature that any one theorist or author fits neatly into one theoretical category or another. Rather we hope to help explain distinct, but often overlapping, theoretical lenses through which globalists view their subject. Furthermore, we suggest that disagreements over the extent and implications of globalization are significant and should be debated, not only because they point to a possible scholarly over-reaction to contemporary trends but also because the ideology of globalization affects the shape and scope of educational reform.

THE ECONOMIC AND POLITICAL IMPLICATIONS OF GLOBALIZATION: EDUCATIONAL POLICY DEVELOPMENT FROM DIFFERENT STANDPOINTS

Since the late 1960s, social theorists have written about the coming of a post-industrial era in which technology would lead to new and faster methods of acquiring, processing and distributing information across the globe and thus a revolutionary transformation of modern, industrial society. But the nature, magnitude, and outcomes of globalization are hotly contested by theorists. We present the theoretical positions of neo-liberals, liberal progressives, realists, and post-Marxists. The differences among these groups of theorists revolve around two issues that are central to educational policy and governance: the relationship between globalization and the distribution of material resources, and the relationship between globalization and the role of nation-states. In the following sections, we examine different authors' stances on these issues and consider the implications of each view for educational change.

1. Neo-liberalism and Globalization

Neo-liberalism represents the current manifestation of the classical political and economic laissez-faire liberalism of the 18th and 19th centuries. Classical liberalism describes society as "a collection of atomistic individuals whose rational self-interested choices lead to optimal social efficiency" (Jonathan, 1990, p. 117–8; also see Cookson, 1994; Wells, 1993). The 1990's version of "social efficiency," could be defined as the optimal arrangement for the production and distribution of goods, services, and wealth. In essence, neo-liberalism promotes free, unregulated markets coupled with aggressive individualism. Neo-liberals espouse the superiority of the market, as opposed to the state, as the allocator of resources, and they argue that capitalist markets – unfettered in this global age by national economies or regulations – maximize economic efficiency and serve as the main guarantor of individual freedom. For neo-liberals, then, unrestricted global markets are the ultimate symbol of social progress (Mander, 1996).

According to Korten (1995), neo-liberals, whom he refers to as free-market ideologues,[1] advocate the removal of barriers to the free flow of goods and money anywhere in the world based on the belief that free international markets will spur competition and economic growth, increase economic efficiency and consumer choice, create jobs, and lower prices. The idea of a "national economy" is no longer helpful, according to neo-liberals, because all countries are best off when goods and services move freely across national borders in mutually rewarding exchanges and when nation-states allow for and facilitate this flow (Frieden & Lake, 1995).

Furthermore, neo-liberals argue that Fordist economies based on the principles of protected national markets, organized labor unions, mass production of standardized products, bureaucratic and hierarchical management, and fragmented and standardized work tasks are no longer feasible in a global economy spurred by new technology and new relationships between management and labor (Harvey, 1990). Neo-liberals call for Fordism to be replaced by "neo-Fordism" in which global competition forces corporate downsizing, cost cutting and flexibility in labor organization, which reduces wages and shrinks the bargaining power of unions. This global competition reportedly facilitates an "enterprise culture" as entrepreneurs seek out niche markets and move toward flexible production of goods using a work force of part-time, temporary, and contractual employees. Neo-liberals argue that nations' and corporations' economic prosperity will depend on their ability to make use of the skills, knowledge, and insights of workers in these more adaptable neo-Fordist ways (Brown & Lauder, 1997; Harvey, 1990).

There appears to be little concern among neo-liberals that globalization will increase inequality between or within nation-states. Rather, they believe the invisible hand of the market will assure a more efficient world economy, thereby improving the material conditions of people across the globe. The role of the nation-state, which historically has played some role in mitigating unequal benefits of capitalist economies, shifts within the neo-liberal paradigm. The nation-state should, according to neo-liberals, step out of the way of the free-market only intervening to assure the freedom of corporations to trade, compete and invest. Under the neo-liberal paradigm, state-run services, including education, should be turned over to competitive market forces (see Callaghy, 1993). In fact, neo-liberalism seeks to increase corporate earnings and economic efficiency by privatizing public institutions, reducing state regulation and taxation, and rolling back the "costly" welfare state (Carl, 1994, p. 298). Such policies, the neo-liberals argue, will increase the efficiency of the state while decreasing the tax burden on corporations and wealthy individuals, who will in turn invest their earnings in enterprises that will create new jobs (Torres, 1995).

Economists such as Milton Friedman have long espoused the neo-liberal ideology, and the fall of communism in Eastern Europe has only strengthened the neo-liberal argument that highly deregulated, free-market capitalism is the only logical economic system – for individual countries and for the world economy at large. "The market, and the market alone, rules. No one doubts it" (Thurow, 1996, p. 1). Bryan and Farrell (1996) argue that the fall of communism has opened the door for unfettered global markets. They note that in the past, centralized political elites controlled the flow of capital within their nations, but that increasingly, millions of global investors, operating on their own economic self-interest, are determining interest rates, exchange rates, and the allocation of capital, irrespective of the wishes or objectives of political leaders.

In this way, neo-liberal ideology legitimizes globalization not just in Western countries, but also in Latin American and African countries that have been strongly influenced by the neo-liberal monetary policies of the International Monetary Fund (IMF) and the World Bank (Barber, 1995; Pannu, 1996). The influence of the IMF and the World Bank has become more pronounced since the debt crisis of the early 1980s, which left Third World countries increasingly dependent on First World countries and banks. In Latin America, for example, the goals of IMF policies have been to reduce public expenditures and eliminate the government's deficit; the objectives of the World Bank include removing trade barriers, deregulating markets, reducing the size of government, and privatizing public institutions in order to "bring development and prosperity to the Third and Second Worlds" (Dolon, 1993, p. 261; also see, Boron & Torres, 1996). According to Bryan and Farrell (1996), the economic policies in developing countries have often worked to repel the market, reduce productivity, and discourage efficient allocation of resources. The neo-liberal argument for First World intervention in the Third World via the IMF and World Bank is to make developing nations more responsive to global market forces, especially by encouraging them to privatize state-run services and industries.

To summarize, the neo-liberal paradigm calls for policies that promote capitalist expansion across the globe and decrease the role of nation-states in the regulation of private exchange and the delivery of public services.

The Neo-liberal View of Educational Change

From the First to the Third World countries, one of the most obvious targets of neo-liberals is state-run public education. Bureaucratic, regulated, "monopolistic," and socialistic public school systems are the antithesis of the neo-liberal ideology of free markets, competition, deregulation, and individualism. Public schools, from the neo-liberal perspective, operated by the state represent a form of "big government" that nations can no longer afford if they are to remain globally competitive. This leads to a push for privatization of educational systems through contract management agreements with non-public agencies and decentralization of educational services from national to provincial and municipal governments (see Torres, 1995). Part and parcel of these market-oriented reforms is the neo-liberals' call for greater parental and student choice of schools and thus greater competition between schools for "clients" (see Tooley, 1996).

One of the main proponents of this neo-liberal perspective as it applies to education reform is Milton Friedman, who argues that the government should give parents vouchers to spend on "approved" educational services from private, public, for-profit, or non-profit institutions (Friedman, 1962). More recently Chubb and Moe (1990) have built on Friedman's proposal, arguing that schools should be cut free from public sector bureaucracies and allowed to sink or swim in a deregulated educational marketplace. Much like the unfettered global market for which neo-liberals long, the educational marketplace, according to Chubb and Moe, should be unconstrained by a particular geographic area or bureaucratic jurisdiction. Parents would receive tuition vouchers or "scholarships" to spend in the educational marketplace, and schools would be forced to respond to parents' individual demands or go out of business. They note that the beauty of the marketplace is its freedom from democratic politics, which represents a "coercive" power of public authority. In a market-based educational system, individuals and groups achieve their ends through voluntary exchange with others (p. 30).

Within this paradigm, government-run educational programs targeted toward the poorest or most disadvantaged students – e.g. Title I compensatory education, special education, or bilingual education – are problematic because they are regulatory in nature, discourage school-level autonomy or responsibility, and contribute to the increased fiscal deficit of the state (see Boron & Torres, 1996).

On a global level, this neo-liberal ideology of educational change has become increasingly hegemonic in the last ten years, as more corporate leaders and policy makers argue that governments cannot support the public sector. The neo-liberal ideology of school reform is reflected in world-wide efforts to dismantle state-run public education systems and replace them with more market-responsive systems. From Britain's set of Education Reform Acts in the 1980s and early 90s that led to grant-maintained schools and city technical colleges, to the charter school movement sweeping across the United States and Canada, to the competitive and deregulatory choice programs in Australia and New Zealand, reforms that are at least partly grounded in neo-liberal ideology have caught on in many Western countries (Whitty, 1996). Furthermore, Third World countries are implementing similar policies of deregulation and privatization of educational systems, as leaders respond to pressure from the World Bank and IMF to reform their economic systems and shrink their government bureaucracies (Fiske, 1996; Pannu, 1996).

More specific and localized efforts to privatized public education in the U.S. include contracts between school districts and private, for-profit companies, including Education Alternatives Inc., the Edison Project, Alternative Public Schools Inc., and the Disney Corporation, to manage specific schools. More piecemeal efforts to privatize public education occur when school districts or individual schools opt to contract with fast food chains to provide lunch services instead of using unionized district employees to prepare meals. In addition, the growth of private fund-raising efforts by public schools, in lieu of bond measures or tax increases, which have traditionally been considered more "public" forms of school financing, signal yet another form of privatization that pushes schools to become more responsive to market forces (see Ascher, Fruchter, & Berne, 1996).

In sum, the neo-liberal paradigm of educational change calls for the dramatic restructuring of public education by minimizing government's involvement in the daily operation or oversight of schools and increasing the role of private interests and investments in deciding how schools are run and whom they serve.

2. Liberal Progressives and Globalization

Liberal progressives, or modernisers, are distinct from neo-liberals in their more cautious and conditioned embrace of globalization, still they tend to remain optimistic about the potential of a more technologically sophisticated and truly global economy to benefit those who are educated to take advantage of rapid developments. According to Giddens (1994), liberal progressivism is the "notion that there is a direction to history and that the appropriate sorts of political intervention can help us locate it as well as speed up the journey" (p. 51). Thus, unlike the neo-liberals who embrace "market capitalism" and its profit motive as the central criteria for enterprise, the liberal progressives maintain that nations must play a more active role in confronting the challenge of a global economy by making those at the bottom of the labor market more powerful against employers. "They recognize that the provision of a floor of protective rights, entitlements and conditions for workers in the context of the global auction is both socially desirable and economically essential" (Brown & Lauder, 1997, p. 12).

Robert B. Reich, a political economist and U.S. Secretary of Labor during the first Clinton Administration, is perhaps the best known spokesperson for many of the liberal progressive views. In The Work of Nations (1991), Reich describes a global economy in which corporations no longer hold allegiance to particular nations, there are no national products or technologies, no national industries, and no national economies. At the same time, corporations are shifting rapidly from high-volume to high-value production in which they cater to the needs of a more specific set of customers. Firms will scan the globe in search of needed high-value components for their products.

Thus, manufacturing, trade and service provision increasingly occurs at a global, transnational level, within a new web of enterprise. Each point on this web represents a unique combination of skills, as famous brand products and services are "cobbled together from many different courses outside the formal boundaries of the firm" (p. 97). Products are international composites; the concept of "foreign" or "domestic" products is an out-dated one. Reich notes that 11 percent of the industrial workforce in Northern Ireland is employed by American corporations. What is traded between nations is less often finished products than specialized symbolic and analytical services – problem-solving, problem-identifying, and brokerage – as well as more routine services.

In Reich's view of an international labor market encompassing Africa, the Americas, Asia, Western Europe and increasingly Eastern Europe, the competitiveness of any one nation will soon depend not on the fortunes of its corporations or industries per se, but rather on the functions its citizens can perform. Workers' ability to provide symbolic-analytic services is, according to Reich (1991), the only asset that grows more valuable as it is used; "Each nation's primary assets will be its citizens' skills and insights" (p. 3). Peter Drucker (1993) uses the term "knowledge workers" to describe the new value of educated and skilled workers in the global economy.

Another well-known economist, Lester Thurow (1996), makes similar liberal progressive arguments, although he tends to be more pessimistic about the ability of nation-states to make new investments in human capital in this globally competitive age. He argues, for instance, that the nation-state is in a bind because the rise of global capitalism and transnational "state-less" corporations diminishes the power of governments to make necessary investments in citizens' "brain power." Thurow argues that the increased mobility of capital and transnational firms signals the end of the era of government regulation and taxation of business. Firms will simply move elsewhere. "A substantial disconnect arises between global business firms with a world view and national governments that focus on the welfare of 'their' voters" (p. 9). This situation, he notes, makes it very difficult for governments to invest in the educational programs needed to prepare their citizens for the better-paying brainpower industries.

Despite these differences, each of these liberal progressives or "modernisers" recognize that while socialist "welfare state" policies must be rethought they also acknowledge that those on the Left need to develop a credible response to the global economy. At the top of this agenda is a commitment to invest in human capital and "strategic investment" to move toward a high skilled, high waged "magnet economy" capable of attracting industry within an increasingly global labor market (Brown and Lauder, 1997). Thus, modernisers advocate an sometimes called "producer capitalism," comprising two principals: (1) long-term investment in the development of knowledge and skills; and (2) a strong state enforcement of labor laws, including a minimum wage, to protect employees within a post-Fordist economy. According to progressives, this agenda is critical to mitigating the downsides of globalization, such as corporate downsizing in Western countries, and the potential for greater inequality as corporate profits grow while individual and family incomes decline (see Cassidy, 1995, 1996).

Liberal Progressives' or Modernisers' View of Educational Change

Central to the liberal progressives' educational agenda is the call for greater investment in educational systems to prepare the next generation for a high-skill, high-wage economy (Baron & Torres, 1996; Drucker, 1993). An updated educational system, progressives argue, will not only spur economic growth but also further the goal of social justice, as governments commit to providing all students – not just a privileged few – with a challenging curriculum to prepare them for a lifetime of "creative problem-solving, identifying and brokering" (Reich, 1991, p. 228).

Traditional school curricula, emphasizing rote learning and static skills, must be altered to accommodate the flexible specialization required by new production techniques (Ball, 1994). In Britain, for instance, the Technical and Vocational Initiative emphasizes process and experiential learning (some times referred to as post-Fordist vocationalism) rather than the transmission of non-transferable craft skills (Hickox & Moore, 1990), and thus embodies the ideas of the modernizers. In the U.S., liberal progressives advocate "systemic reform," calling for the adoption of high standards for all students across all types of curriculum coupled with greater school-site autonomy (O'Day & Smith, 1993). The notion of systemic reform is embodied in the Clinton Administration's Goals 2000 legislation and the school-to-work vocational programs.

Yet in recent years, Goals 2000 has come under increasing criticism from conservatives who fear its imposition of standards signals a loss of local control over what is taught in schools, which could subject students to a more "Leftist" form of humanistic and multi-cultural curriculum at the expense of a more traditional, Western European canon (Diegmueller, 1995). This backlash led the Republican-controlled Congress to cut the federally funded standards-setting agency out the federal budget, but other privately funded (generally corporate-sponsored) groups have emerged to fill the void. As the battle continues to rage at the federal level, some states and local school districts are setting standards and attempting to devise performance and portfolio assessments to measure how well students are learning the content of new standards.

Yet it is the other half of systemic reform, the effort to decentralize decision-making by allowing schools more autonomy, that seems to have spread more quickly across the U.S. and other countries. Schlechty (1990) notes, for instance, that if schools are to be structured as effective knowledge-work organizations, they will have to operate with considerable more flexibility than is now the case. In particular, schools need to attract highly competent people, who seek out environments in which they can exercise their own judgment and respond quickly to opportunities and problems: "[I]t is this need to increase the capacity of schools for quick and flexible response to the needs of students, as much as any other factor, that leads reformers to urge the decentralization of school administrators" (p. 79).

Yet, inherent in the proposals and initiatives set forth by the liberal progressives is the assumption that nation-states have a vital role to play in upgrading their state-run educational systems to prepare students for the 21st Century. According to Thurow (1996):

> The proper role of government in capitalistic societies in an era of man-made brain power industries, is to represent the interest of the future to the present, but today's governments are doing precisely the opposite. They are lowering investments in the future to raise consumption in the present. (p. 16)

Thus, the clearest distinction between the neo-liberals and the liberal progressive modernizers in education is the different roles they see the state playing in response to globalization. While the neo-liberals call for an end to the burdensome and out-dated "welfare state," which includes state-run educational systems, the liberal progressive modernizers call upon policy makers to invest more heavily in the state-run educational system and to create higher, more challenging goals and standards.

3. Realists and Globalization

Another cluster of theorists interested in the political and economic dimensions of globalization are the realists, who argue that the extent and novelty of globalization is frequently exaggerated by both the neo-liberals and the liberal progressives.

This less declamatory view is grounded in realists' reading of the history of capitalism and thus their argument that the current "global economy" is not really much more global than in the past. In this way, the realists align themselves with an anti-state view presented in the world-system's perspective of Wallerstein (1979), who argues that capitalism has never allowed its aspirations to be determined by national boundaries in a capitalist world economy. "Capitalism was from the beginning an affair of the world-economy and not the nation-states" (p. 19).

Like the many Marxist political economists, the realists see nation-states as playing a significant role in the expansion of capitalism, but they do not – unlike many Marxists today – necessarily see the new era as significantly more global than in the past. Hirst and Thompson (1996) write that globalization has become a "fashionable" concept among social scientists on both the Left and the Right. Yet the authors note that these claims are based solely on the increasing salience of foreign trade and the international flow of capital, which have been features of the international economy since 1914, and not on evidence of a new and distinct phenomenon or a new economic structure.

Frieden and Lake (1995) note that the "new international order" was born in the 1930s and took root at the end of World War II, when the Bretton Woods agreement established a new series of international economic organizations – namely the IMF, GATT, and the World Bank. And while globalists argue that the power of these institutions has been greatly enhanced with the development of a more global economic system and the debt crisis of the Third World, Frieden and Lake point out that First World countries, particularly the U.S.'s, control of the IMF and World Bank, is nothing new, nor is the trade liberalization that opened the huge American market to foreign producers or American overseas investment and economic aid. In fact, Hirst and Thompson (1996) argue that the power and influence of both the IMF and the World Bank has been somewhat undermined in recent years due to the spread of floating exchange rates and the growth of regional economic configurations such as the European Union and the North American Free Trade Agreement.

Furthermore, Hirst and Thompson (1996) contend that even the very powerful multinational corporations are not truly "global." For instance, they found that two-thirds of these corporations are based in just 14 countries and that both their operations and sales are fairly circumscribed to their home region, and often home country. For this reason, realists note that the mythology of globalization overstates the nation-states' degree of helplessness in governing global markets or in reacting to the demands of corporations (Cox, 1995; Hirst & Thompson, 1996; Harvey, 1990). While realists do not deny that the nation-states' exclusive control of territory has been reduced by international markets and new communication media, they maintain that these states still play an essential role (Hirst & Thompson, 1995, 1996). Frieden and Lake (1995) write: "Realists believe that nation-states pursue power and shape the economy to this end. They assume that nation-states are the dominant actors within the international political economy" (p. 12). They base this claim on their argument that people are less mobile than money, goods or ideas. Thus most people remain "nationalized" and dependent on such things as passports, visas and labor qualifications.

Some realists note that even as nation-states cut back social services, they are not necessarily becoming weaker. Rather, they have increased strategic control through new forms of contractual governance, periodic interventions, and performance-based funding (Green, in press; Haggard and Moon, 1995; Harvey, 1990). According to Green (in press), "the role of the nation-state today may be changing, but internationalization does not of itself necessarily reduce the scope or importance of its functions" (p. 37).

The Realists and Educational Change

Green (in press) is one of the very few educational theorists who writes about globalization, and he does so from what political economists would consider a realist's perspective. Green (in press) traces the historical relationship between the nation-building practices of states and their national educational systems. Echoing the work of Collins (1979) on the role of the public education system in developing a more common national culture and identity, Green (in press) maintains that throughout the modern era, national educational systems have been the pre-eminent author and guardian of national identity and culture, forging principles of common purpose and values. This "romantic nationalism" led to an educational emphasis on common language, tradition, and, oftentimes, race or ethnicity. While the "nation-building" project of schools has been contested in recent years, with racial and ethnic group's calling for recognition of identities beyond the dominant "national" identity, the project continues nonetheless (Green, in press).

In response to claims by globalists that the sovereignty and autonomy of nation-states, and thus their power to shape their educational systems, have been eroded in the new global world order, Green states that such arguments are far too extreme. Like Hirst and Thompson (1995; 1996), Green writes that globalization theory hinges on the notion that current developments represent not merely an extension of long-established trends, but a significant acceleration of such an order. "The problem with much of the writings by globalists is that there is insufficient historical depth and global reach, both in the evidence and arguments, to allow us to assess their claims properly" (p. 28).

Furthermore, Green (in press) notes that the trends of globalization are uneven and play out the differently in different states or different areas of state control. Thus, he argues that in certain cases, central governments of many nation-states have reduced their control over certain areas of public life, by cutting back or privatizing administrative aspects of education, health, and transportation. Yet he notes that for every area where governments have ceded some direct responsibility, there are others, such as the environment and surveillance and monitoring of information, where they have become increasingly active. Thus, he writes that, in many countries, the trend toward marketization and privatization may have led to the devolution of decision-making in education, but not necessarily to the end of state control over what is taught in school. National curricula and tests linked to performance-based funding and other accountability measures are examples of state "quality control" measures that tend to spring up where direct administrative controls are relaxed.

Ultimately, Green (in press) argues that national educational systems have become more porous in recent years, as they have engaged in "policy borrowing" and grown more like each other in certain ways. But he adds that rather than a full-scale globalization of education, the evidence suggests a partial internationalization of educational systems and not the end of national education per se.

4. The Post-Marxist[2] Critique of Post-Fordism

Like the realists, social theorists influenced by a Marxist perspective discuss the historical, complimentary relationship between nation-states and global capitalism. In this way, many aspects of the Marxist perspective is traceable to Wallerstein's (1979) World System Theory, which, as we mentioned above, states that the formation of nation-states is iterative with the imperialistic spread of global capitalism. The liberal state, in this paradigm, is complicitous with capitalism rather than powerless against it. Most Marxists also accept Wallerstein's argument that the dominant core-capitalist countries' reliance upon capitalism coupled with the economic interrelatedness of nation-states has had negative consequences for economically "weaker" or peripheral and semi-peripheral countries that are "underdeveloped." Thus, Marxists argue that capitalism is experienced differently across geographic contexts (Kearney, 1995; Wallerstein, 1979).

The resulting power imbalances across nation-states leave underdeveloped countries dependent and therefore exploitable by powerful capitalist nations. Capitalism's creation of these underdeveloped spaces, filled with cheap labor or raw materials, is a major source of its "growth" and longevity over the last 400 years. In this way, Marxists, like the realists, contend that capitalism has always been global, but they add that late capitalism has brought abrupt changes that transform its ways of shaping social relations (Best & Kellner, 1991; Harvey, 1990; Hobsbawm, 1987; Hobsbawm, 1994). One of the most profound ways in which capitalism is currently evolving into late capitalism, argue many Marxists, is by using technology to change the meaning and reality of "skilled" labor in such a way that allows for greater exploitation of workers regardless of country.

Post-Marxist are especially critical of the social inequities wrought by globalization and are quick to note that technology is often less a harbinger of progress than a capitalist tool to replaced salaried workers with fixed-price machinery. For instance, Aronowitz and DiFazio (1994) proclaim that all the contradictory tendencies involved in the restructuring of global capital lead to the same conclusion for workers of all collars: "unemployment, underemployment, decreasing skilled work, and relatively lower wages" (p. 3). According to Aronowitz and DiFazio (1994), high-quality and well-paid permanent jobs once available in core-capitalist countries are being destroyed by three closely related developments:

- The massive restructuring of patterns of ownership in the global economy means that fewer companies dominate larger portions of the world market in many sectors and that national boundaries are becoming less relevant to the way in which goods are produced and distributed.
- New technology has made human labor less necessary and enabled transnational corporations to "deterritorialize" their production, making them independent of geographic proximity to markets. Particularly in financial, retail and wholesale industries, production and services can be dispersed throughout the world, allowing corporations to seek out the cheapest and politically weakest labor markets.
- Not only is manual labor being displaced by machines and global competition, but even workers in the new "quality" jobs – those that Reich (1992) refers to as the strategic brokers within the brain-power industries described by Thurow (1996) – are being replaced by less expensive counterparts in other countries.

Similarly, Rifkin (1995) argues that the record high global unemployment rates of the early and mid-90s are due to the technological revolution that is fast replacing human beings with machines in virtually every industry. He notes that post-Fordist corporations are discovering countless new ways to use technology to "re-engineer" their organizations to compress time and reduce costs. Computers are replacing salespersons, account executives, truck drivers, warehouse handlers, and shipping department personnel. U.S. corporations are eliminating more than two million jobs annually; new jobs are generally at the bottom of the pay scale.

According to Rifkin (1995), the development of new labor-displacing technologies and the availability of inexpensive labor in Third World countries is unraveling the post-World War II "truce" between management and labor in the U.S. By the early 80s, corporations "began a concerted drive to weaken organized labor's influence and reduce the cost of the labor component in the economic process" (Rifkin, 1985, p. 170).

Rather than describing corporate policies and nation-states' accommodation of these policies as simply a reaction to the competitive demands of the global economy, Rifkin posits that corporations are making downsizing and cost-cutting decisions mainly so that the people at the top – the CEO's, executives, and large investors – can become wealthier at the expense of the rest of the workforce. Furthermore, Rifkin argues that good jobs – those in the "knowledge sector" of research, engineering, computer software, law and banking – are small in number and require a great deal of specialized training. He writes: "It is naive to believe that large numbers of unskilled and skilled blue and white collar workers will be retrained to be physicists, computer scientists, high-level technicians, molecular biologists, business consultants, lawyers, accountants, and the like" (Rifkin, 1985, p. 36).

In general, post-Marxist theorists see traditional nation-states as continually accommodating global trends. And while they acknowledge that the global economy does not respect national boundaries and that the impact of national fiscal and industrial policies are severely limited, they argue that we are witnessing the formation of what might be called the "metastate," in which "the intersection of the largest transnational corporations and the international political directorates of many nations constitute a new governing class" (Aronowitz & DiFazio, 1994, p. 22).

Thus, the post-Marxists argue, inter-dependent relationship between the state and the capitalist economy may not be lessening with globalization but may be becoming stronger. For instance, Barlow and Clarke (1996), writing about the roll back of the welfare state in Canada, note that both the political and economic elite bought the current ideology that in order for Canada to remain competitive in the new world order of a global economy they had to dismantle a social infrastructure of welfare, and collective bargaining agreements with government workers, along with environmental regulations. As a result, according to the authors, corporate profits are soaring, as is the rate of child poverty.

In Third World countries, where the growth of a liberal democratic state is more of an exception than a rule, both the state and the economy are extremely vulnerable to globalization and neo-liberalism. Here the IMF and World Bank have sought to restructure the state and privatize the public sector (including education) in countries which are greatly indebted to the First World countries driving these reforms (Pannu, 1996). The efforts of these supranational institutions are orchestrated by transnational corporations and powerful Western states and driven by a neo-liberal ideology of free market reform. Pannu (1996) argues that these supranational organizations adopt a very undemocratic approach, forcing neo-liberal policies onto the weaker debtor nations. With the help of the World Bank, IMF and Inter-American Development Banks, these multinational corporations, especially the banks, are able to force Third World governments to implement policies that are favorable to their efforts to produce, market and distribute their products globally for the least amount of cost and the greatest profit (Trazi, 1995).

In short, Marxists have historically viewed the state as complicitous with capitalist enterprises by providing full protection of private property and capital; rights to ownership and accumulation; social stability; and the physical, social and legal infrastructures, including educational systems, that allow it to maintain control (Torres, 1995; Pannu, 1996). In this way, Marxists have always been critical of the welfare state, emphasizing its reproductive tendencies (Pannu 1996; Torres 1995). The only solution, according to Marxists, would be an international labor movement to challenge global trends of transnational exploitation within and across nation-state borders and to ultimately "achieve redistributive justice" (Aronowitz & DiFazio, 1994, p. 9).

Post-Marxist Theories and Educational Change:

In the 1970s, Marxist theorists, most notably Bowles and Gintis (1976), provided detailed critiques of educational systems in capitalist societies. They argued that the schools played an important social reproduction function due to the correspondence between the capitalist system and the educational system. This correspondence theory has highlighted the parallels between the Fordist production line compliance of workers in a hierarchical and unequal industrial society and the traditional tracked structure and authoritarian pedagogy in the schools.

In a post-Fordist age, post-Marxists see the correspondence between a new, more decentralized, mobile, and flexible modes of production and the deregulated, market-driven educational reforms, such as school choice and privatization (Hickox & Moore, 1990). Thus, the focus of post-Marxists theorists is frequently not on the school change process per se but rather on the economic and political forces that shape the educational system into the likeness of capitalist systems.

Similarly, as educational theorists examine the relationship between the educational system and capitalist systems, many have developed a sophisticated critique of the neo-liberal market metaphor for educational change. Thus, they are critical of reform efforts, such as deregulated school choice policies, that force schools to compete with each other for students and resources. According to Ball (1994), the implementation of market reforms in education "is essentially a class strategy which has as one of its major effects the reproduction of relative social class (and ethnic) advantages and disadvantages" (p. 103).

Recent reform efforts to turn over educational governance to the private sphere, especially tuition voucher plans (now in Milwaukee and Cleveland in the U.S.) and the practice of hiring for-profit firms to manage public schools in various states, including Massachusetts and Michigan, have been shaped by the powerful rhetoric of devolution, deregulation and parent and community control (Troyna, 1994). According to its post-Marxist critics, this international educational reform movement is part and parcel of an ideological shift in which democracy is framed in terms of individualism and education is framed in terms of consumerism. As Aronowitz and Giroux (1993) note: "Ideologically, this meant abstracting schools from the language of democracy and equity while simultaneously organizing educational reform around the discourse of choice, reprivatization, and individual competition" (p. 1).

In the global economic transformation to the post-Fordist information age, the substitution of market forces for government-run services becomes a "natural" evolution and educational systems become increasingly commodified or reified, which means that social relationships between educators and families become material objects in the sphere of market exchange. The resulting shifts in the educational system lead to market-based solutions such as increased competition, choice, and individualism. Such shifts, write Kenway et al., (1993), "position education in a consumer/product discourse" (p. 112).

According to Troyna (1994), the impact of these shifts on the shape and provision of education "has been both fundamental and pervasive," creating a dynamic "where providers are encouraged to compete against one another and consumers are encouraged to express their preferences" (p. 1). Ball and other educational researchers argue that market-oriented reforms tend to ignore issues of social justice and fail to account for the existing asymmetric distributions of resources, as the market rewards those with material resources and provides less to the children from families with the fewest economic resources. As Pannu (1996) notes, the neo-liberal vision of globalization pushes for marketization of education worldwide, leading to differentiated access to quality education according to social class.

Thus, Aronowitz and DiFazio (1994) are critical of policy proposals by national leaders in the U.S. and other Western countries to invest "human capital" through various education and job training programs – most of which, they argue, will be highly stratified based on the wealth and status of the students' families – while providing tax incentives for corporations to invest in labor-saving technology. They argue that unless public and private investment is geared toward hiring labor rather than purchasing labor-saving machines, then investments in educational programs will not result in significant net gains in employment and will certainly not help those students from the poorest countries and the poorest families, regardless of country.

THE SOCIAL AND CULTURAL EFFECTS OF GLOBALIZATION

While the bulk of literature on globalization appears to be written by political economists concerned with economic and political aspects of recent change, cultural theorists are also writing about cultural and social effects of globalization. Despite some theoretical overlaps between political economists and cultural theorists, the cultural dimensions of education in a global economy are too often overlooked. According to Dehli (1996), some feminist and other Leftist authors, in their effort to critique neo-liberal ideology and the marketization of education, may have placed too exclusive an emphasis on the economic and structural processes involved in contemporary school reform, "while rendering marginal or invisible the cultural, ideological and moral(izing) dimensions of change" (pp. 9–10).

Filling this void, cultural neo-Marxists' focus on, among other things, the interrelatedness between capitalism and underdevelopment, global "consumer culture" and neo-liberal ideology, and the hegemony of national culture and identity politics (Lefebvre, 1974; Soja & Hooper, 1993; Soja, 1989; Wallerstein, 1991). In this section, we present some of the main arguments emerging from cultural studies literature – most of which are based on neo-Marxist interpretations of globalization – and discuss their implications for educational change.

5. Neo-Marxists and Globalization

While neo-liberals believe that deregulated markets will serve everyone equally and modernisers attempt to develop universal policies to "lift all boats," neo-Marxists accentuate the contextual nature of experience. They study "the cultural" in order to capture the unexpected social creations resulting from the global impact of neo-liberal ideology and local policies of nation-states (Kearney, 1995). Similar to the anti-state themes of the post-Marxists described in the prior section, neo-Marxists criticize social institutions, such as schools, for representing the global-local crystallization of cultural, linguistic, economic, and ideological hegemony (Fine, 1991; Giroux, 1992; Hargreaves, 1994; Lamphere, 1992; McLaren, 1994).

Cultural neo-Marxists also focus on the "homogenized" consumer culture that accommodates the free market by spreading demand for products across the globe. They critique arguments for global consumption utopias, such as that espoused by the president of Nabisco, who said the goal of economic globalization is the creation of "a world of homogeneous consumption," in which people everywhere eat the same food, wear the same clothing, and live in houses built from the same materials. The logical conclusion of such a view is a world in which every society employs the same technologies, depends on the same centralized economy, speaks the same language, consumes the same media images, and offers its children the same Western education (Norberg-Hodge, 1996, p. 20).

Cultural neo-Marxists argue that the globalization of culture is linked to the capitalist processes of standardization, routinization, and streamlining that Golding refers to as the "McDonaldisation of everywhere."

> This is a culture that is supremely 'wedded to the pastiche and superficial variation,' 'deals in slick symbol and diffuse connotation' and does not resonate well with the 'real experiences of non-mobile inhabitants across the variety of national, stratified, and local cultures. Indeed it often mistakes the surface appearance for the material reality of sharply differentiated experience of life chances' (cited in McLaren, 1995a, p. 6).

Central to the neo-Marxist critique of neo-liberal ideology and mass consumerism has been the argument that it engendered a form of "social amnesia" among the working class, eroding any class consciousness of domination and alienation in a capitalist system. This relates to Marx's concept of "commodity fetishism," or the way in which the exchange of commodities masks the conditions and struggles associated with the production of commodities (see Gill, 1995). Any broad-based critique of global capitalism or the multi-national corporations' never-ending search for new markets is subsumed beneath the visual images of Reeboks and Coke. "Buying and eating become the wages of the alienated labor, the means by which the hunger for recognition, satisfying work and play, and decent human relationships are spuriously satiated. . . the love of things rather than persons that fills the void created by the suppression of the memories of degraded labor" (Aronowitz, 1990, p. 247).

Many cultural neo-Marx examine the media's role in educating a global populous about this homogenized consumer culture. Green (in press) notes that from a cultural lens, globalizing trends are "unambiguous," as electronic information technology has increased the ease, economy, and rapidity of communications, providing unprecedented corporate access across to the global flow of ideas. No country is immune to the effects of international television, film, video, and computer networks, and governments cannot or will not constrain their impact.

What is especially significant about these "predatory times" in which the United States continues its dependency on capitalist expansion, write McLaren and Gutierrez (in press), is that "U.S. citizens have become trapped by the ecocidal desire to endlessly consume" (p. 4). In linking this desire to consume to global communication, McLaren (1995a; 1995b) examines the role of the mass media in creating the images, signs and symbols of a postmodern age that mask the spread of the capitalism, the growth of the "global assembly line," the international division of labor, and the uneven development causing the destruction of village life and the creation of more urban slums. McLaren argues that we are situated "in the twilight of modernity" and that it is becoming more obvious that "old forms of production and consumption have given way to a new universe of communication which celebrates the look, the surfaces, the textures, and the uniformation and commodification of the self" (1995b, p. 59). In this new universe of communication, the seductive symbolic power of goods – the surface textures and signs – rather than products become the primary foci of late capitalist consumption (Gill, 1995; McLaren, 1995b).

Many post-modern neo-Marxists argue that the media today do not so much communicate as they construct a new electronic reality. This hyperreality is a condition Baudrillard calls the "ecstasy of communication" in which the world becomes a world purely of simulation, of simulacra or images (Baudrillard, 1988; Kumar, 1995). But unlike conventional images, simulacra are copies that have no grounding in authentic originals. Truth is therefore not a question of accurately representing an unquestionable, original, objective truth. Instead, the "truth" of simulacra is more closely related to what is believed by the consumer or reader of the message (Baudrillard, 1983; Soja, 1993). Thus, in global marketing and consumption, the images themselves, not the products, become the objects of consumption; individuals receive their identity from the signs and meanings they consume – to drink Pepsi-Cola is not so much to consume a carbonated beverage as it is to become part of the multi-cultural community featured in the Pepsi ad (Poster, 1995).

Trend (1994) notes, however, that control of transnational media is not distributed across the globe, but rather dominated by the U.S. The mass media, particularly television, creates a shared virtual community that has spread transnationally, but originates mostly in Los Angeles. Thus, a global homogenization, driven by U.S. cultural representations, results in a subjugation of other cultures. The U.S. benefits as a nation by creating a global market of consumers desiring "American" culture.

This neo-Marxist critique of consumer culture and neo-liberalism highlights what is often referred to as the "postmodern paradox": increasing cultural homogeneity occurring simultaneously with increasing cultural heterogeneity. In other words, as consumer culture spreads globally across electronic media, bringing more people into direct contact with the symbolic messages of Western core-capitalist countries, those who are the target of these messages are constructing their own meaning of these images based on their local context, life experiences, and language. Therefore, the globalization of consumer culture structures social relations in a multitude of ways at the level of "local" context. Consumer culture may be able to transcend the physically demarcated borders of its nation of origin, or territory, but it still must contend with socio-cultural "borders" (Marcus, 1986).

Thus, some theorists argue that the world is increasingly comprised of a network of loosely connected communities, inventing their own forms of life and finding their own means to express them. There are no longer scientific laws of society, but local customs and usage (Kumar, 1995). The seeming contradictions of globalization is the focus of Benjamin Barber's book *Jihad vs. McWorld* (1995). One the one hand, Barber notes, the global distribution of products such as MTV, McDonalds, and Reebok presses nations into one homogenous global theme park, "one McWorld tied together by communications, information, entertainment, and commerce" (p. 4). On the other hand, the phenomena that Barber refers to as "Jihad," balkanizes nation-states as culture is pitted against culture, tribe against tribe, and localized social movements fight against interdependence and search for a local identity. Such searching often results in "peripheral nationalism" in which small nations incorporated into larger units such as the U.K. France, Spain, and now Italy struggle for greater freedom and independence (Kumar, 1995). Barber argues that these two seemingly disparate movements of Jihad and McWorld are interconnected, as both the centralization of global capital and the cultural decentering of political and social movements share some common themes: They both, he argues, "make war" on the nation-state, thereby undermining democratic institutions, belittling democratic citizenship, and eschewing civil society.

Still, most neo-Marxists are less critical than Barber of "Jihad." They point to the emancipatory potential of localized social movements and the struggles of marginalized people for greater freedom from oppressive nation-states. They see the so-called fragmentation of nations along cultural lines as one aspect of post-modernity's rejection of the totalizing meta-narratives of cultural identity related to national identity. "Post-modernism proclaims multi-cultural and multi-ethnic societies. It promotes the 'politics of difference.' Identity is not unitary or essential, it is fluid and shifting, fed by multiple sources and taking multiple forms" (Kumar, 1995, p. 122).

Thus, some neo-Marxists choose to examine the dialectic between national culture and counter-hegemonic cultural movements. Foster (1991), for instance, notes that national culture is itself a segmentation of humankind. One of the primary features of national culture is the delineation of boundaries and territories, to separate "insider" from "outsider." Because nation-states extend horizontally across local community contexts, national cultures can only survive by creating national identities that seem natural, logical, unquestionable, and primordial. Teaching people that it is natural and logical to be governed "from afar" by a majority-rules system is also a key cultural component to nationalism (Trend, 1994). The social institutions of a nation-state are both products and reifiers of national culture, playing a central role (Collins, 1979; Green, in press) in the national homogenization process (Blomley, 1994) that masks social, historical and geographical struggles for meaning and identity.

Thus, counter-national communities problematize nation-state hegemony and global capitalism and represent spaces and social networks that transcend territorial nation-state boundaries. Kearney (1991; 1995) notes that diasporan communities include members who are globally dispersed, yet share a common myth of a "homeland" and a reason for the separation from that homeland. The myth, or diaspora, combined with local experiences of alienation act to tie together the community beyond the initial dispersed generation (Hall, 1990). Kearney (1995) and Kumar (1995) argue that as localized counter-national groups recognize their connection to the global society through more sophisticated communication systems, they will be able to draw upon the power of non-governmental organizations to protect their own rights in the face of abusive state actions. Kumar notes that several social movements, including feminism, ecological movements, and religious revivals have united local groups to global causes. "Numerous indigenous groups have been able to reframe their disadvantageous relationships with the nation-states that encompass them by defining their projects in the global space of environmentalism and human rights" (Kearney, 1995, p. 560).

Thus, although some postmodern neo-Marxists critique the commercialism, consumerism, neo-liberal ideology and the increasing inequality that results from global capitalism, they also embrace certain aspects of globalization, especially its deleterious impact on traditional nation-states' ability to preserve a hegemonic national identity. As a result, these theorist, like the post-Marxists sometimes find themselves loosely aligned with neo-liberals, who would like to roll back the welfare state because of its intrusion into the market. This odd coalition of neo-liberals who espouse free markets and competition and post-modern theorists who support the splintering off of various suppressed cultural groups suggest the power of the pressures placed on nation-states and national social welfare programs, including education, from divergent political perspectives (see Rosenau, 1992).

Neo-Marxism and Educational Change

Cultural neo-Marxists argue that the ways of thinking about education and society need to be significantly and continually transformed. This rethinking of schooling considers the issues of consumer culture, national culture, and identity in a global flow of capitalism.

For instance, neo-Marxists are generally supportive of the critical media literacy programs designed to develop a citizenry of socially conscious viewers that are being founded in several countries faced with the constant influx of

U.S. consumer culture via electronic media. Trend (1994) describes how the Canadian Ministry of Education produced a workbook called *The Media Literacy Resource Guide* to assist educators and students in deconstructing the cultural imperialism of U.S. television by focusing on the various ways that television shows present problematic versions of race, sex, desires, pleasures, and needs through "'structured absences' that systematically exclude certain viewpoints" (p. 236). Paradoxically, however, the Canadian struggle against U.S. culture entails a simultaneous effort on behalf of the Canadian Ministry of Education to create a "distinctly Canadian identity."

The simulacra of consumer culture is concerned with the aesthetical, not the ethical, and education has its own version of simulacras that go undetected, thus perpetuating the more general trend of avoiding direct interrogation of social problems. Hargreaves (1994), for instance, positions cooperative learning as a "safe simulation" that purports to fill a cognitive and social void that the system itself ironically produces through its own technocratic procedures. When students are viewed by educators as lacking "appropriate" mental and social abilities, cooperative learning is then implemented to ameliorate their "civil" behavior and learning. However, students already have their own ways of learning and socializing that are contradicted by rules such as discipline and grading practices. Cooperative learning then becomes a means to avoid the real issue of institutional hegemony.

Cultural neo-Marxists argue that other popular pedagogical tools fall into the same category of safe simulations that side-step race, class, and gender production in a global capitalist society. For instance, standards-based assessment and portfolios are technical reforms that allow schools to merely reconfigure their own hegemonic culture into new modes of control. The learning that teachers do in obtaining these methods rarely includes critical social theories that deconstruct the ways that such methodologies mask the spread of domination. The same holds true for certain versions of "integrated curriculum," which merely intermingle traditional disciplines that have never centered their concerns on the theories and experiences of and about marginalized "others." The result is a simulated "worldliness" that one has considered issues from a broad perspective.

From the cultural neo-Marxist perspective, national culture also poses problems for curriculum. In the face of perceived globalization that renders nation-states more or less obsolete, national elites try to re-impose cultural control over schools by formulating what they consider to be "basic" knowledge and skills that all national citizens should know (National Educational Goals Panel, 1995). They also try to attach public funding to the implementation of the national standards and curriculum, money that the poorest urban school districts with large percentages of minority students cannot afford to ignore. Although, as we mentioned earlier in this chapter, in the U.S. the modernizers and more social conservative groups do not always agree on the specific content of educational standards, the drive to create a set of "high" or "world-class" standards and assessment – at least as an abstract goal – remains strong. And poor urban students are the very populations that many national culturalists feel need to be most "nationalized."

Also, cultural neo-Marxists tend to be less concerned about the "fragmentation" of state-run educational systems that may result from an increased emphasis on market-based organizing principles of deregulation, parental choice, competition and individualism (see Ball, 1994). Apple and Oliver (1996) argue that schools, as state-run institutions, have always been complicitous in the production of "fragmentation" or difference. Cultural neo-Marxists recognize that marginalized cultural groups who have had an historical, geographical, and social experience of oppression by educational institutions should be allowed to create their own type of learning from which they can draw strength.

In this way, neo-Marxists help to explain how educational institutions produce identity in global capitalism. McLaren and Gutierrez (in press) state that the micropolitics of urban classrooms have become the local instantiations of the sociopolitical and economic consequences of a rapidly expanding global market.

Various educational ethnographies have used this framework, asking how individuals or groups get into a particular mental, physical, or social "locale" in relation to global capitalism (Marcus, 1986). For example, Willis (1981) describes how boys at one school in England form separate identities – one groups was called the "ear'oles" and the other the "lads"- by contrasting their interactions in a variety of settings, including the school site. Ultimately, the differences partially produced in school developed into a division of labor that was observable in local factory settings as the ear'oles became management and the lads became labor in the global realm of production. Willis shows how seemingly unconnected interactions at a local level work to reinvent the hegemony of global capitalism (Marcus, 1986).

Finally, cultural neo-Marxists promote critical pedagogy as a way of allowing students to explore their own localized alienations and identities (McLaren, 1994). Since modernistic institutions and global capitalism mask the difference that they create with their homogenizing tendencies, critical pedagogy seeks to make central the everyday struggles of the marginalized (Hooks, 1993; Soja, 1993). Students are pushed to form a conscience and discourse of alienation that can then be used to resist global capitalism in everyday life in local, regional, and global spheres.

CONCLUSION

Given the array of theoretical and epistemological perspectives presented in the general social science literature on "globalization," it is difficult to assess not only the dimensions of globalization but also what it might mean to the field of education. Because few educational researchers or theorists have attempted to make connections between the economic, political and cultural dimensions of globalization and the policies and practices of education, the aim of this chapter has been to present a broad overview of the multiple meanings of globalization and work through the various implications of these meanings for schools and children.

Based on our review, we believe that the global trends and developments cited in much of this literature will continue to have a major impact on schools, communities, parents and students. As we head into the 21st Century, it appears as though the ability of nation-states to build a redistributive, universal and standardized educational system is greatly undermined by the neo-liberal agenda for globalization, the commodification of culture into a more centralized transnational media industry, and the pluralization of cultures that arise through fragmentation and diversification.

We do not intend to deny the emancipatory potential of schools that are more closely tied to local communities of marginalized ethnic, social class, or religious groups, as these very groups struggle for autonomy from potentially oppressive nation-states. But we are interested in investigating the untenable position in which educators across the world are placed as they try, simultaneously, to respond to local demands in a more decentralized educational system, give all students the knowledge and skills to participate in a global economy, and navigate the international flow of culture and commodities via mass media – all of this despite persistent (and exacerbating) conditions of inequality and uneven development.

Thus, it appears as though the phenomenon of globalization will mean many different things for education. Most certainly in the near future it will mean a more competitive and deregulated educational system modeled after the free market but with more pressure on it to assure that the next generation of workers are prepared for some amorphous "job market of 21st Century." It will also mean, we believe, that educational systems will increasingly provide the sites of struggle over the meaning and power of national identity and a national culture. And finally, schools will no doubt also be the sites of various counter-hegemonic movements and pedagogies.

As we noted at the beginning of this chapter, educators must simultaneously recognize the conditions created within globalization that allow counter-hegemonic and counter-national social movements to flourish while remaining aware of potential for growing inequality in terms of material conditions and, at the same time, a diminishing ability on the part of nation-states to respond to these unequal conditions. We encourage educators to further the journey we have started here by thinking more carefully and more frequently about "globalization," the different theoretical lenses through which various scholars and leaders view it, and the various ways in which it affects the educational change process taking place in local schools across the country. In particular, we suggest that a critique of the hegemonic neo-liberal perspective, presenting a one-sided vision of "globalization" as advantageous without noting the unequal distribution of its benefits across, race, class, and national borders – should be the focus of an emancipatory research agenda and liberatory practices in the next century. In this way, educators and researchers will themselves become part of the global discussion, shaping the debate and influencing its outcomes.

ENDNOTES

[1] Korten (1995) makes an important distinction regarding the different names used to describe neo-liberal or free-market ideology in different parts of the world. Neo-classical, neo-liberal, or libertarian economics; neo-liberalism, market capitalism, or market liberalism are some of the most popular terms. In Australia and New Zealand, the term economic rationalism is common; in Latin America, the term neo-liberalism is more popular. He notes, however, that in most counties, including the United States, this ideology goes without a generally recognized name. "Unnamed, it goes undebated – its underlying assumptions unexamined." (p. 72).

[2] We use the term "post-Marxist" to refer to those theorists who write in the area of political economy and who are critical of capitalist expansion while remaining anti-state and anit-hierarchy. We use the term "neo-Marxists" to define more cultural Marxists who maintain their essential identity and primary affiliation with a Hegelian form of Marxism (see Aronowitz, 1990 and Rosenau, 1992). We realize that such distinctions between these two groups are often arbitrary and artificial; they re overlapping categories that permit individuals to move between them over time (Rosenau, 1992).

REFERENCES

Apple, M. (1993). *Official knowledge: Democratic education in a conservative age.* New York, NY: Routledge.

Apple, M. W., & Oliver, A. (1996). Becoming right: Education and the formation of conservative movements. *Teachers College Record,* **97**(3), 417–45.

Aronowitz, S. (1990). *The crisis in historical materialism: Class, politics and culture in Marxist theory.* Minneapolis, MN: University of Minnesota Press. (2nd Edition).

Aronowitz, S., & DiFazio, W. (1994). *The jobless future: Sci-Tech and the dogma of work.* Minneapolis, MN: University of Minnesota.

Aronowitz, S., & Giroux, H. (1993). *Education still under siege.* Westport, CT: Bergin & Garvey.

Ascher, C., Fruchter, N., & Berne, R. (1996). *Hard lessons: Public schools and privatization.* New York, NY: Twentieth Century Fund.

Ball, S. (1994). *Education reform: A critical and post-structural approach.* Buckingham: Open University Press.

Barber, B. R. (1995). *Jihad vs. McWorld.* New York, NY: Times Books.

Barlow, M., & Clarke, T. (July 15/22, 1996). Canada – The broken promise. *The Nation.* 23–26.

Baudrillard, J. (1983). *Simulations* (Paul Foss, Paul Patton & Philip Beitchman, Trans New York: Semiotext[e].

Baudrillard, J. (1988). Simulacra and simulation. In M. Poster (Ed.), *Selected writings.* Cambridge, UK: Polity Press.

Best, S., & Kellner, D. (1991). In search of the postmodern. In S. Best & D. Kellner (Eds.), *Postmodern theory: Critical interrogations,* (pp. 1–33). New York: The Guilford Press.

Blomley, N. K. (1994). *Law, space and the geographies of power.* New York: The Guilford Press.

Boron, A. A., & Torres, C. A. (1996). The impact of neo-liberal restructuring on education and poverty in Latin America. *The Alberta Journal of Educational* Research, **32**(2), 102–114.

Bowles, S., & Gintis, H. (1976). *Schooling in capitalist America.* New York, NY: Basic Books.

Brown, P., & Lauder, H. (1997). Education, globalisation and economic development. In C. Hawley, H. Lauder, P. Brown, & A. S. Wells (Eds.), *Education: Culture, economy and society.* Oxford, UK: Oxford University Press.

Bryan, L., & Farrell, D. (1996). *Market unbound: Unleashing global capitalism.* New York, NY: John Wiley & Sons, Inc.

Callaghy, T. M. (1993). Vision and politics in the transformation of the global political economy: Lessons from the second and third worlds. In R. O. Slater, B. M. Schutz, & S. R. Dorr (Eds.), *Global transformation and the third world.* Boulder, CO: Lynne Rienner Publishers.

Carl, J. (1994). Parental choice as national policy in England and the United States. *Comparative Education Review,* **38**(3). 294–322.

Cassidy, J. (October 15, 1995). Who killed the middle class? *The New Yorker,* 113–122.

Cassidy, J. (April 22, 1996). All worked up. *The New Yorker,* 51–55.

Cherryholmes, C. H. (1988). *Power and criticism: Poststructural investigations in education.* (Vol. 2). New York: Teachers College Press.

Chubb, J. E., & Moe, T. M. (1990). *Politics, markets & America's schools.* Washington, D.C.: The Brookings Institution.

Clifford, J. (1994). Diasporas. *Cultural Anthropology, 9*(3), 302–338.

Collins, R. (1979). *The credential society.* Orlando, FL: Academic Press.

Cookson, P. W. Jr. (1994). *School choice: The struggle for the soul of American education.* New Haven, CT: Yale University Press.

Cox, K. R. (1995). Globalization, competition and the politics of local economic development. *Urban Studies, 32*(2). 213–224.

Dale, R. (1994). Applied education politics or political sociology of education?: Contrasting approaches to the study of recent education reform in England and Wales. In D. Halpin & B. Troyna (Eds.), *Researching education policy: Ethical and methodological issues.* Washington D.C.: The Falmer Press. 31–42.

Dehli, K. (1996). *Between market and state? Modalities of power and difference in the marketization of education.* Paper presented at the annual meeting of the American Educational Research Association. New York, NY.

Diegmueller, K. (1995a, January 11). Backlash puts standards' work in harm's way. *Education Week,* 1 and **12.**

Dolon, M. (1993). Global economic transformation and less developed countries. In R. O. Slater, B. M. Schutz, & S. R. Door (Eds.), *Global transformation and the third world* (pp. 259–282). Boulder, CO: Lynne Rienner.

Drucker, P. (1993). *Post-capitalist society.* New York, NY: Harper Business.

Fernandez-Kelly, P. (1988). The "maquila" women. In J. Cole (Ed.), *Anthropology for the nineties.* New York: Free Press.

Fine, M. (1991). *Framing dropouts: Notes on the politics of an urban public high school.* Albany, NY: State University of New York Press.

Fiske, E. (1996). The politics of decentralization. New York, NY: The World Bank.

Foster, R. J. (1991). Making national cultures in the global ecumene. *Annual Review of Anthropology,* **20,** 235–60.

Frankenstein, M. (1989). *Relearning mathematics: A different third r – radical math(s).* London: Free Association Books.

Frieden, J. A., & Lake, D. A. (1995). Introduction: International politics and international economics. In J. A. Frieden & D. A. Lake (Eds.), *International political economy: Perspectives on global power and wealth* (pp. 1–16). New York, NY: St. Martin's Press.

Friedman, M. (1962). *Capitalism and freedom.* Chicago, IL: University of Chicago Press.

Giddens, A. (1994). *Beyond left and right: The future of radical politics.* Stanford, CA: Stanford University Press.

Gill, S. (1995). Globalisation, market civilisation, and disciplinary neo-liberal. *Millennium: Journal of International Studies, 24*(3). 399–423.

Gilroy, P. (1987). *Diaspora, utopia, and the critique of capitalism, 'There ain't no black in the union jack':* The cultural politics of race and nation (pp. 153–222). Chicago: University of Chicago Press.

Giroux, H. A. (1992). *Border crossings.* New York: Routledge.

Giroux, H. A., & McLaren, P. (1992). Writing from the margins: Geographies of identity, pedagogy, and power. *Journal of Education,* **174**(1), 7–29.

Green, A. (in press). *Education, globalization and the nation-state.*

Gupta, A., & Ferguson, J. (1992). Beyond "culture": Space, identity, and the politics of difference. *Cultural Anthropology,* 7(1), 6–23.

Haggard, S., & Moon, C. (1995). The South Korean state in the international economy: Liberal, dependent, or mercantile? In J. A. Frieden & D. A. Lake (Eds.), *International political economy: Perspectives on global power and wealth* (pp. 47–60). New York, NY: St. Martin's Press.

Hall, S. (1990). Cultural identity and diaspora. In J. Rutherford (Ed.), *Identity, community, culture, difference.* London: Lawrence and Wishhart.

Hargreaves, A. (1994). *Changing teachers, changing times.* New York, NY: Teachers College Press.

Harvey, D. (1990). *The Condition of postmodernity.* Cambridge, MA: Blackwell.

Hirst, P., & Thompson, G. (1995). Globalization and the future of the nation-state. *Economy and Society,* **24**(3), 408–442.

Hirst, P., & Thompson, G. (1996). *Globalization in question.* Cambridge, UK: Polity Press.

Hobsbawm, E. (1987). *The age of empire 1870–1914.* New York: Pantheon Books.

Hobsbawm, E. (1994). *The age of extremes, 1914–1991.* New York: Vintage Books.

Hooks, B. (1993). Transformative pedagogy and multiculturalism. In T. Perry & J. Fraser (Eds.), *Freedom plow* (pp. 91–7). New York: Routledge.

Hurrell, A., & Woods, N. (1995). Globalization and inequality. *Millennium: Journal of International Studies*, **24**(3), 447–470.

"Incorporating the World." (July 15/22, 1996). *The Nation*, 3.

Jonathan, R. (May, 1990). State education service or prisoner's dilemma: The 'hidden hand' as source of education policy. *British Journal of Educational Studies*, **38**,(2), 116–132.

Kearney, M. (1995). The local and the global: The anthropology of globalization and transnationalism. In W. H. Durham (Ed.), *Annual Review of Anthropology*, (Vol. 24, pp. 547–65). Palo Alto, CA: Annual Reviews Inc.

Kenway, J. (with Chris Bigum and Lindsay Fitzclarence). (1993). Marketing education in the postmodern age. *Journal of Education Policy*, **8**(2). 105–125.

Korten, D. C. (1995). *When corporations rule the world*. West Hartford, CT: Kumarian Press.

Kumar, K. (1995). *From post-industrial to post-modern society: New theories of the contemporary world*. Cambridge, MA: Basil Blackwell.

Lamphere, L. (1992). *Introduction: The shaping of diversity*. In L. Lamphere (Ed.), Structuring diversity: Ethnographic perspectives on the new immigration (pp. 1–34). Chicago: University of Chicago Press.

Lefebvre, H. (1974). *The production of space*. Oxford: Basil Blackwell.

Lindbloom, C. E. (1977). *Politics and markets: The world's political-economic systems*. New York, NY: Basic Books.

Mander, J. (July 15/22, 1996). The dark side of globalization: What the media are missing. *The Nation*, 9–14.

Marcus, G. E. (1986). Contemporary problems of ethnography in the modern world system. In J. Clifford & G. E. Marcus (Eds.), *Writing culture: The poetics and politics of ethnography* (pp. 165–193). Berkeley: University of California Press.

McLaren, P. (1994). *Life in schools: An introduction to critical pedagogy in the foundations of education*. (second ed.). White Plains, NY: Longman Publishing Group.

McLaren, P. (1995a). Critical pedagogy in the age of global capitalism: Some challenges for the educational left. *Australian Journal of Education*, **39**(1), 5–21.

McLaren, P. (1995b). *Critical pedagogy and predatory culture*. New York, NY: Routledge.

McLaren, P., & Gutierrez, K. (in press). Global politics and local antagonisms: Research and practice as dissent and possibility. In D. Carlson & M. Apple (Eds.), *Critical pedagogy in unsettling times*. Boulder, CO: Westview Press.

National Education Goals Panel. (1995). *The national education goals report: Building a nation of learners* (ISBN 0–16–048364–6). Washington, D.C.: U.S. Government Printing Office.

Norberg-Hodge, H. (July 15/22, 1996). Break up the monoculture. *The Nation*, 20–23.

O'Day, J., & Smith, M. (1993). Systemic reform and educational opportunity. In S. H. Fuhrman (Ed.), *Designing coherent educational policy*. San Francisco: Jossey-Bass.

Ong, A. (1987). *Spirits of resistance and capitalist discipline: Factory women in Malaysia*. Albany, NY: State University of New York Press.

Pannu, R. S. (June, 1996). Neo-liberal Project of Globalization: Prospects for democratization of education. *The Alberta Journal of Educational Research*, **32**(2), 87–101.

Poster, M. (1995). *The second media age*. Cambridge, MA: Basil Blackwell

Pratt, M. L. (1986). Fieldwork in common places. In J. Clifford & G. Marcus (Eds.), *Writing culture: The poetics and politics of ethnography* (pp. 98–121). Berkeley: University of California Press.

Reich, R. (1991). *The work of nations: Preparing ourselves for 21st-Century capitalism*. New York: Alfred A. Knopf.

Rifkin, J. (1995). *The end of work: The decline of the global labor force and the dawn of the post-market era*. New York: G.P. Putnam's Sons.

Rodrigues, N. P. (1995). The real 'new world order': The globalization of racial and ethnic relations in the late twentieth century. In M. P. Smith and J. R. Feagin (Eds.), *The bubbling cauldron: Race, ethnicity and the urban underclass*. Minneapolis, MN: University of Minnesota Press.

Rosenau, P. M. (1992). *Post-modernism and the social sciences: Insights, inroads, and intrustions*. Princeton, N.J.: Princeton University Press.

Rouse, R. (1991). Mexican migration and the social space of postmodernism. *Diaspora*, **1**, 8–23.

Schlechty, P. C. (1990). *Schools for the twenty-first century: Leadership imperatives for educational reform*. Jossey-Bass Publishers: San Francisco.

Soja, E., & Hooper, B. (1993). The spaces that difference makes: Some notes on the geographical margins of the new cultural politics. In M. Keith & S. Pile (Eds.), *Place and the politics of identity* (pp. 183–205). London: Routledge.

Soja, E. W. (1989). *Postmodern geographies: The reassertion of space in critical social theory.* New York: Verso.

Soja, E. W. (1993). Postmodern geographies and the critique of historicism. In J. P. J. III, W. Natter, & T. R. Schatzki (Eds.), *Postmodern contentions: Epochs, politics, space* (pp. 113–36). New York: The Guilford Press.

Strike, K. (1996). *Centralized goal formation and systemic reform: Some liberty arguments.* Unpublished manuscript.

Tarzi, S. M. (1995). Third world governments and multinational corporation: Dynamics of host's bargaining power. In J. A. Frieden & D. A. Lake (Eds.), *International political economy: Perspectives on global power and wealth* (pp. 154–164). New York, NY: St. Martin's Press.

Thurow, L. C. (1996). *The future of capitalism: How today's economic forces shape tomorrow's world.* New York, NY: William Morrow and Company, Inc.

Tooley, J. (1996). *Education without the state.* London, UK: The Institute of Economic Affairs.

Torres, C. (1995). State and education revisited: Why educational researchers should think politically about education. In M. W. Apple (Ed.), *Review of research in education.* Washington D.C.: American Educational Research Association. 255–331.

Trend, D. (1994). Nationalities, pedagogies, and media In H. A. Giroux & P. McLaren (Eds.), *Between borders: pedagogy and the politics of cultural studies,* (pp. 225–241). New York: Routledge.

Troyna, B. (1994). Reforms, research and being reflexive about being reflexive. In D. Halpin & B. Troyna (Eds.), *Researching education policy: Ethical and methodological issues.* Washington D.C.: The Falmer Press. 1–15.

Wallerstein, I. (1979). *The capitalist world-economy.* New York, NY: Cambridge University Press.

Wallerstein, I. (1991). *Culture as the ideological battleground of the modern world-system, Geopolitics and geoculture: Essays on the changing world-system* (pp. 158–183). Cambridge: Cambridge University Press.

Wells, A. S. (1993). *Time to choose: America at the crossroads of school choice policy.* New York: Hill and Wang.

West, C. (1993). *Prophetic thought in postmodern times.* Monroe, ME: Common Courage Press.

Whitty, G. (1996). Creating quasi-markets in education: A review of recent research on parental choice and school autonomy in three countries. *Review of Research in Education, 22.*

Willis, P. (1981). *Learning to labour: How working class kids get working class jobs.* New York: Columbia University Press.

Markets, Choices and Educational Change

WILLIAM BOYD

College of Education, The Pennsylvania State University

Market forces have been widely proposed as a solution to the alleged inflexibilities and inefficiencies of school bureaucracies in a rapid changing postmodern world. Subjecting public education to the rules of the market arouses great passion among educational reformers, whether they are in favour or opposed. In this chapter, Boyd and Lugg review the arguments and, most importantly the evidence about the effects that market forces of school choice have had upon public education.

Seeking the "pragmatic, but precarious middle ground", Boyd & Lugg move beyond absolute opposition to market influences of any kind, and beyond the nostalgic distortions through which past public bureaucracies are lavished with fake praise, to evaluate the evidence on marketization, as it has been played out in different contexts. They examine the contexts and causes of market-oriented influences in education, and succinctly summarize the key arguments of proponents and opponents.

What is especially interesting about the chapter is the way its authors tread beyond conventional "left" and "right" positions on this issue, by sketching out what the moral and regulatory boundaries of market systems in education might reasonably be. The chapter contributes strongly to the debate on school choice and charter schools that are taking place in many jurisdictions.

Market forces, especially in the form of "school choice," have been proposed as a panacea capable of curing mediocre government school monopolies (Chubb & Moe, 1990). Proponents claim that with one "silver bullet" school choice not only can improve schools but resolve governance conflicts by allowing divergent groups to cluster in their own schools. Critics of choice and market forces reply with apocalyptic visions of the injustice and fragmentation such measures will visit upon schools and society. As a result, views on school choice are so polarized, and writing and research on the topic are often so partisan, that it is not easy to assess the merits of the competing claims. Neutral observers – if any exist – are likely to be confused, because advocates and opponent of school choice are inclined to draw conflicting conclusions from the *same* evidence.[1] This happens, time and again, because advocates value liberty or choice above all, whereas the overriding value for opponents is social equality. Each side heavily discounts the opponent's primary value, so rapprochement is unlikely.

As we shall elaborate, the evidence from school choice programs internationally provides less support for the claims of advocates than for the fears of critics, but much of the research and debate on both sides is characterized by inadequate evidence, exaggerated claims, and signs of partisanship.[2] Little doubt exists, however, that choice policies do transform the environment and governance of

A. Hargreaves (ed.), Extending Educational Change, 69-94.
© 2005 *Springer. Printed in the Netherlands.*

schools. Depending on how they are designed and regulated, choice policies can either promote desirable reforms or cause serious problems (OECD, 1994). As Glenn (1989, p. 220) concludes from his research:

> The experience of other nations yields no conclusive evidence that parent choice has a decisive effect, either positive or negative, on the *quality* of schooling. Evidence is extensive, however, that choice may have either a positive or negative effect upon *equity*, depending upon how the process is structured and what incentives are included for ethnic and class integration.

What parent choice of schools *does* affect powerfully is the satisfaction of parents, their sense of being empowered to make decisions about their own children, the accommodation of their deeply-held convictions about education.

For better or worse – depending on one's viewpoint – school choice increasingly seems to be an idea whose time has come. Parents tend to be attracted to it, and policy makers see it as a way to reform stagnant public school bureaucracies. Since a problem for all organizational change is finding the incentives to overcome the status quo, the dynamics unleashed by market forces appeal to many policy makers. At the same time, choice and market forces challenge core beliefs about the non-competitive structure and democratic purposes of public schools. Consequently, choice and market forces antagonize those deeply invested into the tradition and ideology of public education.

Elsewhere in this Handbook, Tom Sergiovanni argues persuasively that deep or fundamental improvement in the quality of teaching and learning in schools is more likely to be achieved through efforts to build a caring and professional community within schools than it is through bureaucratic or market-driven devices. The latter, he contends, can produce quicker and more efficient change in schools, but of a more superficial nature. We agree with much of his analysis, and with the growing consensus (see, e.g., Newman & Wehlage, 1995; Elmore, 1995) that simply changing the structure of schools (e.g., by introducing school-based management or intensive scheduling) does not, by itself, guarantee real improvement in their core functions, teaching and learning.

In addressing school choice, however, two things need to be recognized. First, the market-driven changes that Chubb and Moe (1990), Milton Friedman (1955, 1962), and others advocate alter the *institutional structure* of schools (their incentives, accountability mechanisms, and ultimately, their culture), not merely their organizational arrangements. That choice advocates are right about this is seen in the fears of critics that market-driven policies will distort the culture of schools and lead to the "commodification" of education. Second, and equally important, school choice is being advocated not only in the belief that it will lead to school improvement and efficiency, but often even more because it can enhance freedom, parental empowerment, and the ability to create schools as "communities" of shared values (Glenn, 1989, 1995). In our highly secularized western societies, the religious and cultural values of parents – especially those outside the mainstream values of the society – are too often discounted or dismissed as irrelevant or undesirable when it comes to the provision of schooling or the choice of schools

(Glenn, 1989; Hull, 1995). Thus, to focus only (or mainly) on the efficiency and school improvement side of the issue is to miss what many see as essential driving forces behind the school choice movement.

Indeed, the problem of "community" lies at the heart of the issues dividing partisans on the topic. This is so because, as Peshkin (1978, pp. 201–202) has observed, there are limits on the "goodness" of the boundaries of any community. Whether the "shared community" is at the neighborhood, local, regional, or national level, it inevitably excludes some people, often with serious social consequences. Rather than being limitless, therefore, freedom and choice must at some point be balanced against other values: "Freedom for the shark," as the saying goes, "is death for the minnows." Thus, some limits on choice and the exercise of individual and family freedom are necessary for the good of the larger community or society. Exactly where these limits should be, alas, is not easily determined: The limits on the "goodness of community boundaries" can also include attempts by governments to impose artificial or unwelcomed communities. Thus, although liberals or "progressives" applaud attempts to impose inclusive communities on those whose social class, racial, ethnic, and religious biases cause them to favor exclusion, they are likely to be upset if a conservative majority uses government to impose moral codes or religious practices on them.

At the risk of offending partisans on both sides of the school choice issue, we are drawn toward seeking the pragmatic, but precarious middle ground on this topic. Realistically, school choice already occurs and is difficult to prevent, short of using totalitarian measures.[3] Moreover, the "genie is out of the bottle;" school choice as a policy option is now increasingly accepted (Glenn, 1989; OECD, 1994).[4] Rather than try to eliminate choice or, at the other extreme, allow it to be completely unregulated, the challenge is to design and maintain policies that structure and control school choice in fair and socially desirable ways. Advocates of public schools, of course, can continue to try to renew ebbing public commitment to the old model of a "common" public school for everyone (Glenn, 1988) or, better, to a "reinvented" model that provides some choice among public schools. Further, they can document the social costs when school choice is inadequately regulated, and can lobby for the correction of these problems. But, they are unlikely to be able to turn back the clock on the choice issue.[5]

Unrealistic assumptions about markets are often matched, on the opposing side, by unrealistic beliefs about the beneficence and efficacy of central planning and public service bureaucracies (Kerchner & Boyd, 1987). If markets can fail, so can government policies and agencies, including public schools. Present-day policy makers and reformers need to steer a course between the opposing dangers of market failure and government failure (Weimer & Vining, 1989).[6] Such a course may invite the disdain of ideologues, but empirical evidence reveals that governments take pains, even with ostensibly "free-markets," to ensure that their national interests (however determined) are not undermined by undue competition (Zysman & Tyson, 1983; Tyson & Yoffie, 1991). Indeed, markets and government regulation can be highly complementary (Gintis, 1995). Given educational policy's concern with balancing competing values – e.g., equality, excellence, liberty, efficiency, and community – a better model than "free-markets" to follow, in assessing the merits of market-based choice proposals, would be "fair or managed markets."

APPROACH OF THIS CHAPTER

Advocates of school choice expect a wide range of benefits to flow from choice policies. They believe that competition will cause schools to improve, that a wider range of schooling choices will become available, that the poor will be freed from the shackles of public bureaucracies and empowered (like the affluent) to chose good schools to attend, and so forth. We shall argue here, however, that school choice is neither a panacea nor a single policy. Like public policies in general, its effects depend crucially on the specifics of how each choice policy is designed. Moreover, its effects depend on complex relationships between the policy, those affected by it, and the socio-cultural context within which these relationships take place (Whitty, 1997). Murnane and Levy (1996, pp. 211–213) put it this way:

> [S]chool choice, like more money, is no panacea. To begin with, the impact of any choice plan – including who wins and who loses – is determined by its details. Talking about "choice" in broad terms is not useful. But even a fair choice plan, by itself, has limited power to boost student achievement. A fair choice plan will stimulate school change. But as in all market systems, the nature of change will be driven in large part by schools' attempts to satisfy customers. Families that value [needed career and workplace] skills will seek out schools that have organized around teaching [such] skills . . . Families that are satisfied with their children's skills will seek out other kinds of schools, and achievement levels will not rise.

Although advocates expect school choice to open up both the *demand* and *supply* sides of market activity in education, research shows that choice policies usually fall far short of doing this, with very significant limitations on both sides of the demand-supply equation. In drawing conclusions about the merits of choice policies, and their possibilities when properly regulated, however, it is important to remember that their shortcomings should be compared realistically, not to some utopian ideal, but to the typical performance of bureaucratized government school systems. In this chapter, we begin with a discussion of the international context giving rise to demands for school choice. Next, drawing on international research evidence, we discuss the constraints on the *demand* and *supply* sides of education markets, and we consider how school choice policies should be designed and regulated. Finally, we conclude by highlighting the policy implications of our assessment of this subject.

THE CONTEXT OF MARKET-BASED EDUCATIONAL REFORM

In international school reform efforts, alternative models of governance are competing, based upon quite divergent logics: bureaucracy, professionalism, decentralization, and market forces. To make the situation even more confusing, these divergent logics sometimes are combined in a single, multifaceted policy "package" (e.g., in British reforms since 1988). In the English-speaking world, market forces (especially, school choice) is perhaps the leading trend. But, there and elsewhere it competes with older views that emphasize either bureaucracy, the professionalism of educators, or forms of decentralization that emphasize participatory management or participatory democracy. While "governance" may imply democracy to the western mind, ambivalence about democracy fuels continued interest in bureaucracy, professional expertise, or market forces as alternative approaches that may avoid the "dangers" of democracy (Chubb & Moe, 1990; Plank & Boyd, 1994). The policy significance of these various efforts flows from the consequences of the alternative logics for both school effectiveness and democracy.

Market forces and, especially, school choice have become increasingly popular as possible mechanisms to spur national educational reform. Much of this popularity can be linked to broader changes in the political and economic global order. Starting with the OPEC oil embargo in 1973, both Western countries and the Soviet bloc were forced into an era of economic retrenchment and political uncertainty, as neither bloc could adequately insulate themselves from the resulting economic turbulence (Tyson, 1986). This global economic reordering eventually triggered profound political changes in both blocs.

In the West, *stagflation* (low growth and high unemployment, coupled with high inflation) and increased international economic competition propelled nations into an era of economic restructuring and massive de-industrialization (Biven, 1989). Many industrial centers scaled back and/or closed down, throwing blue-collar employees out of work in numbers not seen since the Great Depression. By the late 1970s, the global economic decline had triggered a crisis in public confidence about the welfare state and the efficacy of public services. In particular, political conservatives in both Great Britain and the United States claimed that social service provision was far too costly.

Bolstered by the claims of neoclassical economists, conservative politicians argued that the taxes needed to maintain generous services impinged upon the economic health of their respective nations (Biven, 1989; Walford, 1994). While they usually failed to fully enact their broader social agendas, western political conservatives met with a good deal of electoral success, seen especially in Australia, the United Kingdom, New Zealand, the United States, and (more recently) in Canada. Additionally, they made enormous ideological progress in eroding popular support for the welfare state, and this included enthusiasm for public education (Henig, 1994). Their success is dramatically confirmed by the widespread adoption of neoconservative social and economic policies by the *opposition* parties, e.g., the Labor Party in Australia, "New Labour" in the U.K., and the "New Democrats" in the USA. Even in Sweden, long the exemplar of a successful welfare state, school choice policies have been adopted (Miron, 1993, 1996).

Conservative politicians and educational reformers were aided by a series of unanticipated events. In particular, the increased international economic competition, coupled with the recession in the early 1980s, accelerated the notion that public education was in crisis (Henig, 1994). This idea was particularly powerful in the United States, which has a history of equating national economic stability with the quality of public schooling (Callahan, 1962). In 1983, the *A Nation at Risk* report was released, again linking academic excellence with economic competitiveness. The public schools were deemed to be so inadequate as to be a menace to the national economic health (Tyack, 1993). Consequently, the rhetoric of educational reform quickly shifted from focusing upon educational equity to ensure social justice and stability, to academic excellence to ensure economic competitiveness (Best, 1993).

Further, the collapse of the Soviet empire added ammunition for the critique of the welfare state, lending credence to conservative warnings regarding the dangers of state-run monopolies. With the end of the cold-war, centralized governmental agencies were viewed with a high degree of suspicion by the public and many politicians. Moreover, the slow progress seen in educational reform efforts fueled frustration. Rightly or wrongly, government education systems were perceived as quasi-monopolistic bureaucracies with little incentive to perform or improve. As they seemed to have successfully resisted most efforts to improve them on their own terms, the idea that only radical reform (especially market forces and privatization) could save them has gained strength.

The growing support for radical reform in public schooling coincided with the broader global movement towards market-based national economies. If markets were good for economic development, why not "open up" the markets for social service provision, and in particular, educational services? Market forces, privatization, and choice were seen as the "answer" to poorly functioning state educational systems. Here was a potent cure for educational ills and its bolder proponents proclaimed that "choice is a panacea" (Chubb & Moe, 1990, p. 217).

Much of the early theoretical basis for market-based educational reform (or school choice) was developed by the Nobel laureate economist, Milton Friedman (1955, 1962). While his over-riding intellectual concern was to rebut the then long-standing Keynesian consensus, Friedman expanded his vision of the possibilities of the free-market (or freer-markets) to a myriad of public policy concerns (for example, the now the all-volunteer U.S. military). Friedman's (1955, 1962) early arguments for a market-based approach to public education centered upon moving the discussion from a government-provided service to a government-subsidized service. He acknowledged that government had both a responsibility for ensuring children received an education, and for setting minimum educational and fiscal standards. However, he disagreed that the state should be the sole provider of the actual service. Friedman's (1962) elegant premise was – and remains

– that competitive markets are far superior to state-run bureaucracies for allocating social services.

The development and propagation of the philosophy of the "New Right" in the 1970s in Britain has been ably chronicled by Stephen Ball (1990), who emphasizes the influence there, on the Thatcherites, of the writings of Friedrich von Hayek. Here, we shall sketch out parallel developments in the United States. Friedman's market-based educational ideas (which included a voucher scheme for both public and private schools) failed to attract much attention in America until the mid-1960s (Henig, 1994). There are compelling historical reasons for this lack of attention. Starting in the mid-1950s with the *Brown vs. Board of Education* decisions, and continuing through to the mid-1970s, the U.S. underwent a period of racial desegregation of its public schools, thanks to a series of Supreme Court decisions baring the racial segregation of public services. School desegregation was a rancorous process, filled with enormous political and social stakes and, at times, more than a measure of violence (Kraft, 1970).

During this turbulent period, school choice took on a meaning that was vastly different from Friedman's original conception, which was grounded in economics. Those who favored racial segregation, especially southern segregationists, invoked the "choice" rhetoric in the name of white supremacy (Griffith, 1969). Seven southern states enacted voucher plans which funded "segregation academies," in hopes of maintaining maintain a dual system of education, one white and private, another black and public (Henig, 1994; Hershkoff & Cohen, 1992; Hafter & Hoffman, 1973). Additionally, southern school districts facing desegregation implemented "freedom of choice" plans, ostensibly to desegregate their public schools. But such plans placed the burden of "choice" upon African-American parents and children, and the operating environment was openly hostile to desegregation. The effect was to maintain segregation. As U.S. Commissioner of Education Harold Howe II told the House judiciary committee in December of 1966, "the community atmosphere is such that Negro parents are fearful of choosing a white school for their children" (*Phi Delta Kappan*, 1967, p. 249). Both plans were eventually found to be in violation of the U.S. Constitution (Morris, 1989).

While the racist rubric of "choice" was being dismantled by the U.S. federal court system, Friedman's notion of market-based school-choice gained legitimacy in the mid-1960s from unlikely liberal supporters, such as Christopher Jencks and Theodore Sizer, then dean of Harvard University's graduate school of education. For some liberal school reformers, market-based school choice schemes were viewed as powerful tools for spurring otherwise intransigent and unresponsive (if not irresponsible) state educational bureaucracies towards better "behavior" in their treatment of poor and/or minority students (Ambler, 1994; Henig, 1994). Competition between schools for students was also seen as a way of fostering better teaching and reducing administrative bloat.

But for all of their intellectual support, market-based school choice plans faced enormous political opposition during the 1970s. The on-going problem of segregation remained, in both Southern and Northern public schools, and "choice" as an educational reform was viewed with more than just a degree of suspicion (*North*

Carolina Education, 1970). Additionally, some early market-based plans were incapable of passing either U.S. or state constitutional muster, for they would have provided state moneys directly to sectarian schools. Other plans, such as the Office of Economic Opportunity (OEO) voucher scheme, ran into blistering opposition from both teachers' unions and school administrators' associations (Henig, 1994).

In the U.S., widespread political support for market-based educational provision only came in the late 1980s, when the social climate had substantially shifted, from focusing upon educational equity and access to a concern for academic excellence to foster national economic competitiveness.[7] This shift was emblematic of the greater political change within the country with the election of an avowedly conservative president in 1980, Ronald Reagan. President Reagan consistently voiced his support for educational choice throughout both his terms. The call for choice was bolstered by the landmark 1983 report *A Nation at Risk*, which decried the poor condition of U.S. education. While Reagan's political motivations regarding "choice" were rather mixed, lending support to both radical reformers and outright racists (Lugg, 1996), he helped legitimate public school experimentation with market-based choice (Henig, 1994).

School choice gained further political and international visibility when the Education Reform Act (ERA) of 1988 was enacted in Britain, establishing the first widescale provision of market-based educational choice (Walford, 1994). The actual British reform (affecting England and Wales) rested upon five premises: (1) Parent's had the fundamental right to determine all matters regarding their children; (2) Parents were better judges of their children's needs than a bureaucracy; (3) Choice would increase parental involvement and in turn, the child's motivation; (4) Competition between schools would lead to better performing schools; and finally (5) Competition would lead to schools being more 'consumer responsive' (Walford, 1994, pp. 2–5; Bagley, Woods, & Glatter, 1996). Such notions dovetailed quite nicely with American proponents' assertions, and further popularized the British/American public policy connection. Prime Minister Margaret Thatcher and President Ronald Reagan had much in common in their conservative political philosophy, and their governments stressed the unique nature of the Anglo/American relationship in a number of policy areas (Boyd, 1995).

Further theoretical support for an American system of market-based school choice came with the publication of John Chubb and Terry Moe's (1990) *Politics, Markets and America's Schools*. Employing an institutional perspective, and presenting survey research evidence that they claimed supported their conclusions, Chubb and Moe (1990, p. 188) argued that America's institutions of democratic control in education bred "bureaucracy and undermine[d] autonomy," two key variables affecting whether schools were effective. Thus, they stunned the education community by calling for an end to the direct democratic control of public schools. In agreement with Milton Friedman, Chubb and Moe argued that while the state had a responsibility to subsidize and regulate educational services, it should not be the sole provider of education. Competition between public and private schools for students (and the dollars that followed the students) would lower costs, foster greater equality of opportunity, and spur academic excellence

(Chubb & Moe, 1990). Reaching beyond American borders, Chubb and Moe (1992) made a brief and superficial examination of British school reform and proclaimed that it was on the right track, but ought to go even further in applying market principles to the education system.

Chubb and Moe's efforts reinvigorated both the intellectual and political debate in America over school choice (Henig, 1994). They were also aided by local efforts. By the early 1990s several states and municipalities had enacted their own limited school choice plans, with multiple and varied social and educational objectives. Many of these programs (e.g., Milwaukee, Cambridge, East Harlem, and the state of Minnesota) were trumpeted as early success stories. However, studies of these ventures revealed a more mixed picture of actual academic achievement, and critics questioned the extent to which "choice" played a role in improving educational achievement (Henig, 1994).

Nevertheless, the growing number of choice programs, both in the U.S. and Great Britain, lent political support for a national plan. In 1991, President George Bush proposed his *America 2000* plan, which set forth national education goals that were to be achieved by the year 2000. Included in the plan was a small, market-based school choice program, which would have included government funds for private and sectarian schools. While the Bush administration pushed the plan as a major reform, the proposal for school choice fell upon deaf ears politically. With the election of President Clinton in 1992, *America 2000* was transformed into *Goals 2000*, minus the choice scheme. School choice has gained in popular support in American public opinion polls, especially when limited to choice among public schools or public "charter schoolschools" – about which we will say more later. While charter school laws are making headway at the state level, school choice schemes have yet to gain consistent support at the national level in the United States, due to our tradition of local control of education and resistance to the expansion of the federal government's role in education.

CONSTRAINTS ON THE EDUCATIONAL MARKETPLACE

As noted earlier, under ordinary policies and circumstances the education market is at best a constrained "quasi-market" (Levacic, 1995; OECD, 1994; Whitty, 1997). Neither the demand nor the supply side of the education market functions in an ideal way.[8] On the *supply* side, government schools rarely are allowed to go out of business. Popular schools rarely expand very much to accommodate the demand for their services. The supply of nontraditional or innovative schools is likely to be very limited. On the *demand* side, consumers face substantial information problems in choosing among schools. Better educated families are better informed and more likely to use choice actively and effectively than those less well-educated and advantaged (Ambler, 1994; Citizens' Commission on Civil Rights, 1997; Fuller & Elmore, 1996). Further, parents often appear to prefer more traditional schools, reducing the incentives for a more diverse supply of school types.[9] Finally, in choosing schools, parents often value the school's location and (especially) the social composition of the student body more than the reputed pedagogical quality of the school, which is, in any event, a more difficult attribute to determine (Adler, Petch, & Tweedie, 1989; Ball, Bowe, & Gewirtz, 1996; Whitty, 1997).

To their credit, Chubb and Moe (1990) recognized aspects of the constraints on the "supply side" of the education market. Consequently, they called for policies to encourage and increase the supply and variety of schools from which consumers could choose. More broadly, in the OECD (1994) report on school choice prepared by Donald Hirsch – based on country reports from Australia, England, the Netherlands, New Zealand, Sweden, and the United States – all four of Hirsch's recommendations emphasize supply side problems. He recommends that policies be adopted for "active diversification of educational supply," "measures to improve the supply of chosen options," "intervention to create choices for educationally underserved groups," and "clear criteria for schools' choice of pupils" (OECD, 1994, pp. 50–51).

With regard to diversification of educational supply, Hirsch notes that, "Demand-led choice does not on its own tend to create educational pluralism: schools subject to open enrolment are more likely to compete at the margin for extra pupils than to redefine their character to serve a 'niche' market" (p. 51). In regard to the supply of chosen options, he stresses that, "The biggest frustration to parents and pupils is to be promised free choice of school, only to find that the most attractive schools are full" (p. 51). Thus, he says popular schools should be helped to expand and less popular schools helped to copy the qualities of the more popular schools. Interventions to create choices for underserved groups are needed for a variety of reasons, including the fact that the disadvantaged rarely live near the more popular schools and need help in finding out about them, in securing transportation to attend them, and in obtaining admission to them. Finally, although students are supposed to choose their schools, the reality may be the other way around. Consequently, Hirsch says that, "In many cases where demand for a school exceeds supply, the fact that schools will need to select pupils must be openly accepted; and the criteria on which selection is made should be openly debated" (OECD, 1994, pp. 51–52; see also Hirsch, 1995).

On the demand side, one of the best documented findings internationally is that better educated and more affluent families are usually more active and effective choosers in the education marketplace than their less advantaged counterparts (Ambler, 1994; Adler, Petch, & Tweedie, 1989; Ball, Bowe, & Gewirtz, 1996; Citizens' Commission on Civil Rights, 1997; Fuller & Elmore, 1996; OECD, 1994; Willms & Echols, 1992). Most researchers, such as those just cited, fear that this pattern of behavior will exacerbate social class segregation and the disadvantages of the lower classes, a point that Ball, Bowe and Gewirtz (1996) elaborate with detailed empirical evidence. Hirsch puts the problem this way:

> There is strong evidence in a number of countries that choice can increase social segregation. Sometimes this is because more privileged groups are more active in choosing "desired" schools. Sometimes it is because such schools are in more prosperous neighborhoods, whose residents continue to get

privileged access to them once they are full. Crucially, a new "choice" of school does not work well in cases where a high proportion of choices cannot be met, because of a concentration of preferences on a few schools with limited capacity (OECD, p. 7).

In a study of magnet schools in Cincinnati, Ohio, Nashville, Tennessee, and St. Louis, Missouri, conducted by Ellen Goldring and Claire Smrekar for the Citizens' Commission on Civil Rights (1997), the Commission concluded that magnet schools were worthwhile devices to help equalize educational opportunity, but that they must operate with safeguards to insure that disadvantaged families were informed of their opportunities to choose these schools, and that every effort should be made to minimize the isolation and other inequalities these families face. With regard to the finding that higher socioeconomic status families were more likely to choose the magnet schools, the Commission concluded that:

> The lower participation rates of low-income families in magnet schools in the three communities studied is not a result of the failure of the school districts to provide information about magnet opportunities. The districts studied use many techniques of affirmative outreach . . . in an effort to make parents and students aware of the program. However, the research showed that higher income parents have available to them a wider variety of sources of information than low-income families. Access to people knowledgeable about schools either through their social networks or contacts at the workplace often gives middle class parents a basis for choice not available to those less well-off. Higher income families who have cars and flexible work hours are better able than others to visit schools before making a choice (Citizens' Commission on Civil Rights, 1997, p. 2).

A study of a largely unregulated interdistrict school choice plan in effect in Massachusetts found that "92 percent of the families participating . . . were white.[10] And they had higher incomes on average than both the families who remained in their home districts and the state as a whole. Moreover, they tended to choose to move their children to wealthier districts" (Viadero, 1997, p. 12). However, the study found that the choice plan had not hurt the racial balance of the districts affected, because of the small number of students using the plan. Moreover, it found that some of the districts losing students under the plan had responded with efforts to improve their services (consistent with the expectations of choice theorists), while other districts, "deciding that the loss of students had affected them only slightly or not at all, made no changes" (Viadero, 1997, p. 12).[11]

DESIGNING AND REGULATING CHOICE PLANS

As Hirsch emphasizes in his OECD (1994) report, policies can be developed to regulate and moderate many of the problems associated with school choice plans. Similarly, Herbert Gintis (1995) – famed for his collaboration with Samuel Bowles in producing *Schooling in Capitalist America* (Bowles & Gintis, 1976), and hence, hardly a member of the "New Right" – has presented an elegant case, in which he argues that a "regulated competitive delivery" of educational services can be more efficient and effective than the bureaucratic, non-competitive delivery of educational service by government-operated institutions. Under a competitive delivery system, he contends that social and educational goals can be protected and pursued through specific regulations and incentives aimed, for example, at such things as encouraging "appropriate social values" or a socially diverse student body. Further, he points out that:

> Appropriate regulation increases the effectiveness of consumer choice by lowering the cost of acquiring the information needed to make informed choices. Financial institutions, for instance, are regulated in virtually all economies, because individual investors cannot be expected to make exhaustive investigations of each insurance company, mutual fund, pension plan, or bank with which they do business. . . [V]irtually every successful universal health care system in the advanced economies allows client choice, but because of client inexpertise, the conditions for accreditation as a health care provider are quite stringent (Gintis, 1995, p. 499).

The best U.S. experiments in educational choice illustrate the positive potential of properly regulated plans. These arose out of our Constitutional crisis over racial segregation. During the 1970s and 1980s, "magnet schools" were developed as means of voluntary desegregating public school districts. Schools were encouraged to develop specialties (for example, a performing arts school) as a means of attracting a diverse student clientele while simultaneously meeting court-specified racial ratios (OECD, 1994; Henig, 1994). Given the political rancor, violence, and "white flight" associated with *mandatory* desegregation plans, magnet schools were viewed as a far more desirable alternative, as they contributed to desegregation through voluntary participation.

An example of a very successful magnet plan is found in Montclair, New Jersey. Established in 1977 as part of a desegregation agreement with the State Commission of Education, *every* school was reconceptualized as a magnet, offering a broad "ethos" rather than a heavily specialized curriculum. Parents can request any school, listing three possible choices. The school district places students in schools considering (1) siblings already in a given school, (2) race and gender ratios (3) and whether the school is oversubscribed. Placements for oversubscribed schools are then made at random (OECD, 1994).[12]

The results of such a tightly controlled and monitored school choice plan have been generally positive (Henig, 1994). First, over 90 percent of students are placed according to their parents' first or second choice. Parents tend to choose schools according to their general atmosphere, with more affluent parents searching more carefully and thoroughly. Second, after the plan was introduced, the schools became more racially balanced. Third, standardized tests scores improved. Subsequently, the departure of more well-to-do families to private schools was halted. Finally, pupil turnover has been low, indicating that parents are generally satisfied with student placement (OECD, 1994; Henig, 1994).

Whereas magnet school plans usually involve a mixture of magnet and regular schools, which can have adverse effects for the reputation and morale of the "unspecial," non-magnetized schools (Metz, 1986), the Montclair plan is an example of broader, "open enrolment" plans designed to provide what Alves and Willie (1987) called *controlled choice*, i.e., the use of quotas within voluntary, open enrolment plans to enhance racial and social class balance in schools or, at least, to see that segregation is not increased (see also Yanofsky & Young, 1992). In its application to foster equal educational opportunities in Massachusetts, Glenn (1991) described "controlled choice" as operating in this way: Automatic assignment of pupils on the basis of where they live is abolished, and the parents of children new to the school system or moving to the next level of schooling receive information and, if they wish, counseling about all options before indicating preferences. Then assignments are made, satisfying these preferences so far as is consistent with available capacities and local policies and requirements. According to Glenn (1991, pp. 91–92):

Controlled choice is intended to accomplish four objectives:

(1) to give all pupils in a community (or in a geographical section of a larger city) equal access to every public school, regardless of where their families can afford to live;
(2) to involve all parents (not just the most sophisticated) in making informed decisions about where their children will go to school;
(3) to create pressures for improvement, over time, of every school through eliminating guaranteed enrollment on the basis of residence; and
(4) where necessary, to achieve racial desegregation of every school with as few mandatory assignments as possible.

Regarding rationales for regulating school choice, Frances Fowler (1992) notes that while advocates of choice can draw on elegant economic theories in support of relatively unregulated plans, critics of school choice lack a well-defined – not to mention, compelling – theory showing why school choice, if granted, should be carefully regulated. In an effort to fill this gap, Fowler proposes a theory based on a "neopluralist" framework derived from the work of political scientist Robert Dahl (1982). This theory highlights four risks to democracy that unregulated choice plans might bring: 1) reinforcing social inequalities; 2) deforming "civic consciousness," by encouraging groups to lobby for their own educational needs while neglecting the needs of the whole country; 3) distorting the public agenda, as some groups might become so powerful they could push their preferences onto the agenda and deflect attention from other preferences; and 4) alienating final control over education policy, as some groups might become strong enough to exercise control over education policy that legitimately belongs to government (Fowler, 1992, pp. 456–457).[13]

Fowler (1992) applies her theory to an evaluation of the French experience with government funding for Catholic schools, from the Debré Act in 1959 enabling this to an act in 1985 amending this policy.[14] For the French to achieve a stable and non-divisive arrangement for public funding of Catholic schools was a remark-able accomplishment, because of the profound cultural division of the nation into "'two Frances:' Catholic France and her enemy, secularized France" (Fowler, 1992, p. 462). Based on documentary analysis and interviews in 1989 with 16 French policy actors, she concludes that the French experience shows:

> that regulated school choice plans can work. . . . [The framers of the Debré Act] were able clearly to conceptualize both their policy goals and most of the potential problems posed by any school choice plan. They were also able to structure their policy so as to accomplish those goals and to minimize the risks that they foresaw.
>
> The French experience also suggests that it is difficult to foresee some of the issues that choice plans raise. When they developed their policy in 1959, French leaders were concerned about solidarity and equality issues. They also understood that they risked the alienation of final control over educa-tion to the Catholic church and other private groups. They did not foresee the more abstract problems of financial control and conflict between governmental jurisdictions. Nor did they anticipate distortions of the public agenda (Fowler, 1992, pp. 467–468).

Surprisingly, Fowler found that equality was not a major issue in the French case, evidently because the French view their public schools as superior to private schools, and private education, as a consequence, is "not an important political resource in France" (p. 461). From this, Fowler concludes that in nations such as the United States, where private schools are thought to be superior to public ones, it would be desirable to make all school choices seem attractive:

> When all schools offer similar political resources to their students, choosing among them ceases to be a search for advantage and is reduced to a matter of taste. In such a situation, the inherent risks of choice plans in an unequal society are reduced. Paradoxically, the best way to develop an effective choice plan may be to so improve *all* schools that choice ceases to be a major issue (Fowler, 1992, p. 468).

Fowler's insightful analysis of the French experience brings us to the perplexing issue of how to achieve and maintain policies which promote "parity of esteem" between public and private schools. International comparative research suggests that such parity of esteem requires a delicate balance in policies for the funding and regulating of public and private schools, as well as a supportive socio-cultural context (James, 1987, 1988). The issues here can be illustrated by briefly discuss-ing the contrasting cases of the Netherlands – where there is a high degree of par-ity – and Australia, where private schools are much preferred to public schools.

The circumstances that contribute to parity in the Netherlands are unusual (Dronkers, 1995; James 1984; Louis & van Velzen, 1990/91). These social and politi-cal circumstances flow from the unique *verzuiling* or "pillarization" of Dutch society into three roughly equal social sectors: Catholic, Protestant, and secular.

This balance of forces has produced laws, policies, and social behavior that combine to make government and private schools equal in prestige, financing, and social support.

The current Dutch education system was established by the 1917 Constitution as part of a political compromise between the emergent Socialist party and an alliance of Catholics and Calvinists. It was designed to reduce tensions among the three "pillars" of Dutch society (Ambler, 1994). The result was a guarantee of full state funding for all schools, including religious schools (what the Calvinists and Catholics desired), and full manhood suffrage (what the Socialists desired) (Ambler, 1994; OECD, 1994). Consequently, the Dutch have had a subsidized system of private/public school-choice for well over 70 years. The government pays for teachers, building and related instructional costs, whether the school is public or private, secular or non-secular, and sets specific requirements regarding minimum enrollment, administration and curriculum (OECD, 1994; Ambler, 1994).

Generous government funding has produced a vast private-school sector. About seventy percent of all primary and secondary pupils are enrolled in privately governed schools, "the great majority of them either Protestant or Catholic and the rest mainly non-religious" (OECD, 1994, p. 67–68). It is important to note that the foundation for the Dutch choice scheme was in allowing parents to choose a school that fostered a desired philosophical and/or theological world-view for their children (OECD, 1994), not to stimulate competition between schools for students. In fact, the government has rather rigid strictures to inhibit such competition (Ambler, 1994). This has significant implications for efficiency, as costs run 10–20 percent higher "due to diseconomies of scale" (Ambler, 1994, p. 470; see also Dronkers, 1995; Louis & van Velzen, 1990/91). The fact that the system is highly decentralized and contains "massive duplication" is not particularly problematic for Dutch taxpayers (OECD, 1994, pp. 67–71).

The original educational agreement has endured even while churches in the Netherlands have suffered real declines in both membership and political influence. Overall pupil enrollment also has declined, forcing some schools to close and others to diversify. For example, some Catholic schools are now majority Muslim (OECD, 1994). Religion has become but one of several reasons for choosing a school (Dronkers, 1995). The others factors affecting choice include proximity to home, academic quality, and the social and racial composition of the school. While the degree of social and racial segregation is high, it is not a big worry to the Dutch:

> because it is not associated with profound *educational* difference. 'Black' schools here are not always seen as 'sink' schools. The idea of equal access to resources is matched by the concept of equal provision of a good standard of schooling. Underwritten by such guarantees, school choice is seen by most Dutch people as a positive influence in society (OECD, 1994, p. 71).[15]

The Australian experience in funding independent schools is much more problematic than that of the Netherlands (see Anderson, 1993; Boyd, 1987; Hogan, 1984). Even though equality has been an important value in Australia historically, government subsidized school choice has encouraged a growing exodus from Australian government schools (particularly at the secondary school level and especially by upper middle-class families) in favor of independent schools, which are perceived to be superior. Since the time this policy was initiated, government schools have declined in prestige and in their share of student enrollment (Anderson, 1993). The private share in Australia, which grew from about 20 percent to 27 percent during the 1980s (Anderson, 1993), now stands at 29.4 percent and the Government projects that it will reach 31.1 percent by the year 2000 (McCollow, 1996).

Like many countries, Australia initially relied on schools provided by church groups. In 1872, however, the Colonial parliaments passed legislation making education "free, compulsory, and secular" and, at the same time, ending the financing of denominational schools. This arrangement continued until 1952, when a law was passed allowing small tax deductions for school fees. Then, in 1964, when the Catholic schools were in severe fiscal straits, a program of more substantial state aid was introduced.

The expansion of state aid continued in the 1970s, under both Labor and Liberal governments. The Labor Party, which had opposed funding for nonpublic schools, felt that it had to compete for the large and important bloc of Catholic votes. It decided that nonpublic schools should be funded on the basis of need, with wealthy schools getting no aid. This idea ultimately failed politically, as the Catholic school lobby, fearing they might be the next target, supported the elite wealthy schools when 41 of them were threatened with a funding cutoff in 1983.

As Anderson (1993) documents with trend-line data, although the Catholic school sector enrolls the largest proportion of those not attending state schools, the elite private schools exert disproportionate and growing social and political influence within Australia. They not only cream-off the upper middle-class students, but have a lock on the power elite of the society. Even committed socialists, not to mention public school educators and government officials, prefer to send their children to the high status independent schools (Boyd, 1987).[16]

Since independent schools charge fees, this state of affairs disadvantages less affluent families, who must use either the state schools or the less expensive Catholic schools, neither of which enjoy the posh facilities found in many independent schools. The decline of public schools continues and critics complain that government schools are now on "reduced rations," as the Howard Government's federal budget included an additional $150 million for nonpublic schools over four years, while at the same time cutting funding for state schools:

> The balance sheet for government schools over the next four years will show a net reduction of well over $400 million – and it could be as high as $550 million. Taken as a package, the measures announced in the 20th August Budget represent an assault on the very notion of a strong, universally-provided, free and secular public schooling sector (McCollow, 1996, p. 2).

Needless to say, the politics surrounding efforts to achieve, maintain, or change policy and funding arrangements affecting the parity between public and private schools are highly sensitive and potentially explosive in most nations. Even in the countries that have achieved stable and successful approaches to the issue, such as the Netherlands and France, threats to the status quo can touch off intense controversy and, in the French case, bring millions of people into the streets in protest (Glenn, 1989).

In closing this discussion of the problem of parity of esteem, we turn to recent developments in the United States and, very briefly, in Britain. In Britain, elite private schools and state funding for denominational schools have been long established; in the former, U.S. schools are less important and funding has been prohibited for sectarian schools. Despite these differences, parity issues abound, as both nations have been experiencing campaigns to transform the character of their public schools through the introduction of market forces and privatization (Whitty, 1997). Of course, the British Conservative government was been able to go much further with this than the more decentralized and divided U.S. government and, for the Conservatives, the private, independent school was the ideal toward which they pushed the state system.

Provisions for parents in England and Wales to vote to have their state schools "opt out" of their Local Education Authority, to become autonomous "Grant Maintained" (GM) schools directly funded by the central government (Fitz, Halpin, & Power, 1993), are paralleled, in some ways, in the USA by our charter schoolschools movement.[17] Although the result in both nations is nominally a new kind of "public" school, critics in both countries fear these schools are but "stalking-horses" or "way stations" on the road to a full privatization characterized – unlike the Dutch model – by social class and racial segregation. With "New Labour" now in power in Britain, these fears should become less acute there.[18]

In the United States, however, the process of legislation for charter schoolschools, and for experiments with limited voucher plans, is proceeding mainly at the state, rather than federal level. One result is great variation in the legislation for charter schoolschools among the twenty-nine states that have passed such laws, as of this writing. Briefly, a charter school is "an autonomous, results-oriented, publicly funded school of choice that is designed and run by teachers or others under contract with a public sponsor" (Buechler, 1996, p. 4). This sense of choice is firmly rooted in market forces. Charter schools are intended to be exempted from many state regulations affecting other public schools, and are supposed to be given wide discretion in policies relating to personnel, curriculum and budget. Conceptually, charter schoolschools are a hybrid, fusing elements from both public and private schooling. Like a private school, a charter school must be able to attract students, since funding is tightly linked to consumer appeal. Yet, like public schools, a charter school must remain non-sectarian, accept all students who enroll free of charge, and also be held accountable by the charter to a public entity (Buechler, 1996).

The devil is very much in the details of the charter schoolschools laws passed to date. Thus, the twenty-nine states can be arrayed along a continuum from highly permissive to highly restrictive, in terms of their provisions affecting the startup and operation of charter schoolschools and the specific requirements of their public accountability (Buechler, 1996; Millot, undated). At the permissive extreme, for example, is Arizona, which has been called the "Wild West" of charter schools-chools and which even the laissez faire *Wall Street Journal* recognized as in need of more regulation (Stecklow, 1996). At the other extreme are states with laws so inhospitable to charter schoolschools that none have yet been formed.

For the most part, the initial results with charter schoolschools are inconclusive. Generally, charter schoolschools are small in size, and serve an elementary aged population. Parental involvement tends to be higher in charter schoolschools, but this might be due to a frequently required "involvement contract" that must be signed by parents (Buechler, 1996). A study of twenty charter school proposals in three school districts (Grutzik, Bernal, Hitschberg, & Wells, 1995) concluded that when charter schoolschools require parents to commit time to attend school events and to volunteer to support the schools' work more generally, this may lead them inadvertently to limit access to certain kinds of families – notably ones whose cultural and other capital is such that they are able to participate.

The data presently available, however, suggest that the student population in charter schoolschools tends to be comparable to the public school population in both racial composition and socioeconomic status. Perhaps most intriguing is the variety in instructional approaches. Some schools are using interdisciplinary instruction, while others concentrate on parental involvement. Other charter schoolschools favor performance assessments and portfolios, while others focus upon back-to-basics instruction (Buechler, 1996; see also Finn, Bierlein, & Manno, 1996).

Even states with laws friendly to charter schoolschools, may have significant barriers to establishing and maintaining a charter school. According to Buechler these include: (1) lack of capital funds, (2) lack of legal and business expertise, (3) the extra costs involved with special education, (4) problematic relationships with the local district, (5) lack of clear legislation, (6) hidden constraints such as transportation schedules and funding formulas, and (7) heavy teacher workloads (Buechler, 1996, pp. 29 – 33).

Despite ambiguity surrounding the topic, in the North American context the charter schoolschools concept has attracted an enthusiastic following from those dissatisfied, for a variety of reasons, with regular public schools. This is demonstrated by the interest the idea has drawn even in Canada, where most provinces already fund a variety of denominational as well as state schools. The nerve that seems to have been struck, in many cases, is weariness with the bureaucracy and lack of responsiveness to parents on the part of some state schools and school systems (Freedman, 1995, 1996; Lawton, 1995). In the USA, even communities that have prided themselves in the high quality of their public schools, such as Princeton, New Jersey, are not immune from the interest in, and threat – or opportunity – represented by, charter schoolschools (Ritter, 1997). On balance, however, it is still too soon to know how much impact charter schoolschools, and variation in how they are designed and regulated, will have on pupil achievement and on the reputation, competitive standing, and response of regular public schools.[19]

CONCLUSION

To reiterate our assessment of the evidence on school choice, we have argued that, rather than try to eliminate choice or, at the other extreme, allow it to be completely unregulated, the real challenge is to design and maintain policies that structure and control school choice in fair and socially desirable ways. School choice is neither a panacea nor a single policy. Its effects depend crucially on the specifics of how each choice policy is designed, and on complex relationships between the policy, those affected by it, and the socio-cultural context within which these relationships take place. Although advocates expect school choice to open up both the *demand* and *supply* sides of market activity in education, choice policies usually fall well short of doing this, with very significant limitations on both sides of the demand-supply equation. These limitations, interacting with the social inequalities found in most societies, create an imperative for very careful regulation and monitoring of school choice plans.

Fortunately, the lessons from international comparisons of school choice schemes indicate that policies and regulations can be crafted to control or ameliorate most of the problems found in these plans (Glenn, 1989, 1991; OECD, 1994). Although the policy design problems are clearly challenging, the issue ultimately is more political than technical: Will policy makers be able, politically, to enact and maintain well-regulated choice plans, and will they choose to do so? This, of course, begs the question of how to get agreement on what a "well-regulated" choice plan is. The propensity of opposing interest groups to see things very differently on this count makes agreement very difficult to achieve.

Reflecting ten years ago on the implications for the United States of Australia's experience with school choice, the senior author wrote as follows:

> In the final analysis, Americans are left with this question: Is it politically feasible and socially desirable to undertake public funding of private schools if it can work constructively only through changes in the system of regulations that are sure to provoke strong political opposition from *both* public and private school supporters? If policy were made solely on rational grounds, and if the advocates of public and private schools were willing to accept regulatory changes that would modify the character of *both* sectors, we might easily achieve and maintain the delicate balance necessary for parity in this arena. But in the rough and tumble world of American politics, with committed lobbies on both sides of the issue, it is far more likely that the balance will shift substantially one way or another (Boyd, 1987, p. 195).

Developments since the time of that writing make the possibility of achieving a new balance in the United States, though still quite difficult, greater now than in 1987. The charter schoolschools movement has led to discussions about reducing the regulations constraining public schools, to make for a more "level playing field" on which regular public schools and charter schoolschools might compete. Also, as noted earlier, many people, including even some American teachers union leaders, are coming to acknowledge the need for substantial change in the character of public schools (Hill,

Pierce, & Guthrie, 1997; Urbanski, 1996).[20] Involving private and, above all, sectarian schools would be far more difficult, because of our Constitutional separation of church and state. But even that could change if our Supreme Court should reinterpret our first amendment, as some legal scholars think is possible (and as the Australian High Court ruled in adjudicating a similar clause in their Constitution), to permit state aid to religious schools so long as no religion is favored over another.

Pressures for increasing school choice, in the United States and other western nations, arise from the intersection of several contemporary trends: better educated, more quality-conscious parents and consumers; discontent with bland, generic government schools; increasing social and cultural diversity, due to immigration, the reawakening of ethnic identities, and the rise of evangelical and fundamentalist religions; and mounting concerns about the deterioration of the family and moral order in today's highly secularized and hedonistic western societies. The result has been the rise of a "politics of excellence and choice" in education (Boyd & Kerchner, 1988) compounded by what has been called "culture wars" in the United States and "Jihad versus McWorld" or "tribalism versus globalism" internationally (Barber, 1995). The tensions and centrifugal forces generated by these developments rip at the fabric of society and overwhelm the capacities of secularized and monochromatic government school systems.

As a consequence, there are growing efforts to gain space and support for religious schools, moral education, and diversity within schools and society, even in situations where only minorities desire these things. Given that we now know a good deal about how to regulate school choice plans to minimize their inegalitarian social consequences – through such approaches as "controlled choice" – minorities' desires should receive more consideration in formulating policy. Thus, if Glenn (1989, p. 210) is correct in his conclusion, based on his research in six nations, that "public funding of nongovernmental [and sectarian] schooling is neither destructive of national loyalties nor a guarantee of religious loyalties," then his contention that the balance in policy making should "tip toward freedom and diversity" needs to be taken seriously in debates about school choice.

Here, we confront concerns about the tensions encountered in trying simultaneously to educate for diversity and educate for social cohesion. Discussing this problem, O'Keeffe (1988, p. 4) quotes from Craft (1984), who observed that the problem is one of "deciding on the *minimum* level of acculturation necessary for full participation in society and the *maximum* extent to which diversity might be encouraged." About this, O'Keeffe (1988, p. 4) notes that, "Disagreements at all levels of theory and practice are evident between those who stress social cohesion at the expense of social diversity."

Increasingly, thoughtful observers agree that the complex problems of modern societies – including the challenges of multiculturalism and the decline of civility, sense of community, and social responsibility – cannot be adequately solved either by the working of markets or of governments. Consequently, attention increasingly turns to efforts to reinvent "community" (Etzioni, 1993) and to renew the "civil society," that is to revitalize the crucial social sphere of "mediating structures" (Berger & Neuhaus, 1996) between atomized individuals responding to markets and, at the other extreme, governments trying to mount broad policies and programs to alleviate social problems. As Whitty (1997, p. 37) concludes his thoughtful discussion of "quasi-markets in education":

> Part of the challenge must be to move away from atomized decision making to the reassertion of collective responsibility without re-creating the very bureaucratic system whose shortcomings have helped to legitimate the current tendency to treat education as a private good rather than a social responsibility.

We agree with Whitty's (1997, p. 37) observation that those favoring "the idea of a common public school are still faced with the need to respond to increasing specialization and social diversity." Finding an acceptable response is made all the more difficult because many parents and citizens neither desire nor welcome diversity in schooling or society. The problem we are left with, then, is the challenge to create education systems that can honor and support individual and group cultural identities while at the same time maintaining broader societal unity. In this challenge, we believe that creative and properly regulated school choice systems can have an important role to play.

ENDNOTES

[1] As an example of this, at the same time that Australian critics (e.g., Hogan, 1984) were denouncing what they saw as the inegalitarian consequences of their nation's approach to school choice, through government funding for wealthy as well as needy private schools while state schools were frequently less than adequately funded, some American observers (including, somewhat later, a U.S. Secretary of Education, Lamar Alexander) were proclaiming that Australia provided a good example of how the United States ought to fund both private and public schools (Sherman, 1982). For the details of this episode, see Boyd (1987). For other examples of protagonists disagreeing about the merits of specific instances of school choice, see Glenn (1989, p. 47) concerning the Dutch approach, which is generally viewed as a success story, and the acrimonious dispute (Olson, 1996) between researchers John Witte and Paul Peterson over the merits of the Milwaukee, Wisconsin experiment with state-funded vouchers permitting poor inner-city children to exit public schools and attend non-sectarian private schools.

[2] In recent years, the literature on school choice has mushroomed and more thoughtful, data-based, and sophisticated studies have appeared. (See, for example, Cookson, 1994; Glatter, Woods, & Bagley, 1997; Glenn, 1989; Henig, 1994; OECD, 1994; and Whitty, 1997).

[3] While not insisting on the total abolition of school choice (e.g., by prohibiting the existence of non-public schools – which has been found unconstitutional in the United States), many public school educators would prefer that state schools not encourage choice. But use of "attendance areas" to zone students into their schools scarcely ensures equality, as the more affluent and mobile families can move to other attendance areas or "exit" to non-public schools.

[4] For American evidence of this, consider the fact that Adam Urbanski, one of our best-known teachers union leaders, has published a proposal (Urbanski, 1996) to "make public schools more like private schools" by introducing choice, market incentives, public accountability assessments, etc. in public school systems.

[5] In the United States, the school choice issue divides into two debates: The most heated debate involves proposals for government funding to subsidize choice between public and private schools, usually referred to as "voucher" proposals. This controversy is complicated by our Constitutional separation between church and state, which our Supreme Court has interpreted to prohibit government funding to religious schools. The second debate involves proposals for greater choice among public schools, an idea that has caught fire with the advent of the "charter school" concept. Charter

school laws have been passed in twenty-nine states, permitting the creation of new "charter schools-chools" that are public schools of choice *independent* of local school districts. Although intended to be *deregulated* schools, charter schoolschools may not discriminate, on the basis of race, religion, or gender, in admitting students. For more on the American debate on school choice, see especially Cookson (1994), Fuller and Elmore (1996), Henig (1994), and Wells (1993).

[6]   For an insightful and thought-provoking analysis that moves beyond the stereotypical thinking of conservative "marketeers" and "radical" socialists, see Giddens (1994).

[7]   Concern continues about equity issues, however, with fears about the racial implications of school choice plans. See Parker and Margolis (1996).

[8]   For a sophisticated economic analysis of demand and supply issues in the international provision of public and private schooling, see James (1987, 1988, 1989).

[9]   Note, however, that based on their important Parental and School Choice Interaction (PASCI) study, Woods, Bagley, and Glatter (1997) emphasize that parents value, *alongside* the schools's academic role, the personal, social and pastoral aspects of schooling. Thus, they conclude that this does not mean they necessarily favor "traditional schools;" it all depends on what is meant by "traditional schools."

[10] On the politics that led to the creation of "irresponsible" school choice plans in Massachusetts, see Glenn (1993).

[11] For a classic discussion of the complex dynamics triggered by the "exit" of customers, see Hirschman (1970).

[12] For an interesting proposal to use random assignment of students to oversubscribed schools as a device to promote the common good and ameliorate the inequitable effects of privatization, see Walford (1994). Under his scheme, the intent would be to motivate parents to insure that all state schools are good, and not just the ones they expect to use.

[13] For another framework for considering the *public* as well as *private* implications of school choice policies, and the consequent need for careful regulations, see Woods and Bagley's (1996) analysis and discussion of the differences between "public markets" and "free markets."

[14] On the French experience, see also Ambler (1994).

[15] This country report within the OECD (1994) study was prepared by Jaap Dronkers.

[16] Anderson (1993) emphasizes that Australian state schools have hurt themselves, in their competition with nonpublic schools, by refusing (except in a few instances), on philosophical grounds, to offer any academically selective stream to cater to the desires of parents who wish to have their children prepared for the top universities and professions.

[17] Although superficially similar, the "grant maintained" and "charter schoolschools" initiatives differ in important ways. GM schools are *existing* state schools, usually secondary schools, that vote to opt out of their LEA. Charter schools are usually *new* schools created under charter schools-chools legislation, and most of them are small, primary schools.

[18] For a helpful overview and discussion of the British school reforms, see Stearns (1996).

[19] According to Vanourek, Manno, and Finn (1997), there were about 500 charter schoolschools in the United States as of May, 1997 (as compared to some 83,000 regular public schools) and these charter schoolschools enrolled "barely two-tenths of 1 percent of American school children" (p. 46). Those interested in schools with 'charters,' should also examine developments in this vein in Australia and New Zealand. See Townsend (1996), Whitty (1997).

[20] Here, we need to acknowledge the uncertainty that surrounds the future of current reform efforts: The existence of charter schoolschools in the USA is still being very much contested by those who prefer the traditional public school system. Thus, charter schoolschools face many political campaigns, either to prevent their existence or to regulate them so heavily that they become no different from other public schools and, hence, no competition for them. See Vanourek, Manno, and Finn (1997).

REFERENCES

Adler, M., Petch, A., & Tweedie, J. (1989). *Parental choice and educational policy.* Edinburgh, Scotland: Edinburgh University Press.

Alves, M. J., & Willie, C. V. (1987). Controlled choice assignments: A new approach to desegregation, *Urban Review,* **19**, 67–86.

Ambler, J. S. (1994). Who benefits from educational choice? Some evidence from Europe. *Journal of Policy Analysis and Management*, **13**(3), 454–476.
Anderson, D. S. (1993). Public schools in decline: Implications of the privatization of schools in Australia. In H. Beare & W.L. Boyd (Eds.), *Restructuring schools: An international perspective on the movement to transform the control and performance of schools* (pp. 184–199). London: Falmer Press.
Bagley, C., Woods, P. A., & Glatter, R. (1996). Scanning the market: School strategies for discovering parental perspectives. *Educational Management and Administration*, **24**(2), 125–138.
Ball, S. J. (1990). *Politics and policy making in education: Explorations in policy sociology*. London: Routledge.
Ball, S. J., Bowe, R., & Gewirtz, S. (1996). School choice, social class and distinction: The realization of social advantage in education. *Journal of Education Policy*, **11**(1), 89–112.
Barber, B. R. (1995). *Jihad vs. McWorld*. New York: Times Books.
Berger, P. L., & Neuhaus, R. J. (1996). *To empower people: From state to civil society* (2nd ed.). Washington, D. C.: The AEI [American Enterprise Institute] Press.
Best, J. H. (1993, June). Perspectives on deregulation of schooling in America, *British Journal of Educational Studies*, **41**(2), 122–133.
Biven, W. C. (1989). *Who killed John Maynard Keynes? Conflicts in the evolution of economic theory*. Homewood: Dow Jones-Irwin.
Bowles, S., & Gintis, H. (1976). *Schooling in capitalist America*. London: Routledge and Kegan Paul.
Boyd, W. L. (1987, Fall). Balancing public and private schools: The Australian experience and American implications. *Educational Evaluation and Policy Analysis*, **9**(3), 183–197.
Boyd, W. L. (1995, September). *The "loyal opposition" and the future of British and American school reform*. Paper prepared for the European Conference on Educational Research. University of Bath, Bath, England.
Boyd, W. L., & Kerchner, C. T. (Eds.). (1988). *The politics of excellence and choice in education*. London: Falmer Press.
Buechler, M. (1996, January). *Charter schools: Legislation and results after four years*. Bloomington: Indiana Education Policy Center, Policy Report PR-B13.
Callahan, R. E. (1962). *Education and the cult of efficiency*. Chicago: University of Chicago Press.
Chubb, J. E., Moe, T. M. (1990). *Politics, markets, and America's schools*. Washington, D.C.: The Brookings Institution.
Chubb, J. E., Moe, T. M. (1992). *A lesson in school reform from Great Britain*. Washington, D.C.: The Brookings Institution.
Citizens' Commission on Civil Rights. (1997, Spring). *Difficult choices: Do magnet schools serve children in need?* Washington, D.C.: author.
Cookson, P. W. (1994). *School choice: The struggle for the soul of American education*. New Haven: Yale University Press.
Craft, M. (1984). Education and diversity. In M. Craft (Ed.), *Education and cultural pluralism*. Lewes: Falmer Press.
Dahl, R. (1982). *Dilemmas of pluralist democracy*. New Haven, CT: Yale University Press.
Dronkers, J. (1995, September). The existence of parental choice in the Netherlands. *Educational Policy*, **9**(3), 227–243.
Elmore, R. F. (1995, December). Structural reform in educational practice. *Educational Researcher*, **24**(9), 23–26.
Etzioni, A. (1993). *The spirit of community: Rights, responsibilities, and the communitarian agenda*. New York: Crown Publishers.
Finn, C. E., Bierlein, L. A., & Manno, B. V. (1996, Spring). What are we learning about charter schools? *Jobs & Capital*, (Vol. 5, 11–17). (Published by the Milken Institute for Job & Capital Formation, Santa Monica, CA.)
Fitz, J., Halpin, D., & Power, S. (1993). *Grant maintained schools: Education in the market place*. London: Kogan Page.
Fowler, F. C. (1992, November). American theory and French practice: A theoretical rationale for regulating school choice. *Educational Administration Quarterly*, **28**(4), 452–472.
Freedman, J. (1995). *The charter school idea: Breaking educational gridlock*. Red Deer, Alberta: Society for Advancing Educational Research.
Freedman, J. (1996). *Charter schools in Ontario: An idea whose time has come*. Unionville, Ontario: Ontario Coalition for Education Reform.
Friedman, M. (1955). The role of government in education. In R. A. Solo (Ed.), *Economics and the public interest*. New Brunswick: Rutgers University Press.

Friedman, M. (1962). *Capitalism and freedom*. Chicago: The University of Chicago Press.
Fuller, B., & Elmore, R. (Eds.). (1996). *Who chooses, who loses?: Culture, institutions, and the unequal effects of school choice*. New York: Teachers College Press.
Giddens, A. (1994). *Beyond left and right: The future of radical politics*. Cambridge, U.K.: Polity Press.
Gintis, H. (1995, Spring). The political economy of school choice. *Teachers College Record*, **96**(3), 492–511.
Glatter, R., Woods, P. A., & Bagley, C. (Eds.). (1997). *Choice & diversity in schooling: Perspectives and prospects*. London: Routledge.
Glenn, C. L. (1988). *The myth of the common school*. Amhurst, MA: University of Massachusetts Press.
Glenn, C. L. (1989, December). *Choice of schools in six nations*. Washington, D.C.: U.S. Government Printing Office.
Glenn, C. L. (1991, Spring). Controlled choice in Massachusetts public schools. *The Public Interest*, No. 103.
Glenn, C. L. (1993). Creating an irresponsible school choice program. In C. Marshall (Ed.), *The new politics of race and gender*. London: Falmer Press.
Glenn, C. L. (1995). *Educational freedom in eastern Europe*. Washington, D.C.: Cato Institute.
Griffith, K. (1969, October). "Segregation academies" flourish in south. *South Today*, **1**(4), 1, 6 – 7.
Grutzik, C., Bernal, D, Hitshberg, D., & Wells, A. S. (1995). *Resources and access in California charter schools*. Paper presented at the annual meeting of the American Educational Research Association, San Francisco, April.
Hafter, J. C., & Hoffman, P. M. (1973, June). Segregation academies and state action. *Yale Law Journal*, **82**(7), 1436–1461.
Henig, J. R. (1994). *Rethinking school choice: Limits of the market metaphor*. Princeton: Princeton University Press
Hershkoff, H., & Cohen, A. S. (1992, Winter/Spring). School choice and the lessons of Choctaw County. *Yale Law & Policy Review*, **10**(1), 1–29.
Hill, P., Pierce, L. C., & Guthrie, J. W. (1997). *Reinventing public education: How contracting can transform America's schools*. Chicago: University of Chicago Press.
Hirsch, D. (1995, May 31). *The other school choice: How should over-subscribed schools select their pupils?* Open lecture at the Institute of Education, University of London.
Hirschman, A. O. (1970). *Exit, voice, and loyalty: Responses to decline in firms, organizations, and states*. Cambridge, MA: Harvard University Press.
Hogan, M. (1984). *Public versus private schools: Funding and directions in Australia*. Ringwood, Victoria, Australia: Penguin Books.
Hull, J. M. (1995). The theology of the Department for Education. *Educational Review*, **47**(3), 243–253.
James, E. (1984, November). Benefits and costs of privatized public services: Lessons from the Dutch educational system. *Comparative Education Review*, **28**(4), 605–624.
James, E. (1987). *The political economy of private education in developed and developing countries*. Washington, D.C.: World Bank.
James, E. (1988). The public/private division of responsibility for education: An international comparison. In T. James & H. Levin (Eds.), *Comparing public and private schools* (Vol. 1, pp. 95–127). New York: Falmer.
James, E. (1989). Public and private education in international perspective. In W. L. Boyd & J. G. Cibulka (Eds.), *Private schools and public policy: International perspectives* (pp. 213–235). London: Falmer Press.
Keeping abreast in education. (1967, January). *Phi Delta Kappan*, **47**(5), 249.
Kerchner, C. T., Boyd, W. L. (1987). What doesn't work: An analysis of market and bureaucratic failure in schoolIn W. L. Boyd, & C. T. Kerchner (Eds.), *The politics of excellence and choice in education* (pp. 99–115). New York: Taylor & Francis.
Kraft, I. (1970, June). 1970: The year of the big sellout on integration. *Phi Delta Kappan*, **51**(10), 523–526.
Lawton, S. B. (1995). *Busting bureaucracy to reclaim our schools*. Montreal, Quebec: Institute for Research on Public Policy.
Levacic, R. (1995). *Local management of schools: Analysis and practice*. Buckingham, U.K.: Open University Press.
Louis, K. S., & van Velzen, B. A. M. (1990/91, December-January). A look at choice in the Netherlands. *Educational Leadership*, 66–72.

Lugg, C. A. (1996). *For God and country: Conservatism and American school policy.* New York: Peter Lang.

McCollow, J. (1996, September 13). Social justice: Government schools on reduced rations. *Directions in Education* (published by the Australian Council for Educational Administration), 5(15), 1–2.

Metz, M. H. (1986). *Different by design, the context and character of three magnet schools.* New York, Routledge & Kegan Paul.

Millot, M. D. (undated). *What are charter schools? An introduction to the concept and the statutes.* Seattle, WA: RAND/University of Washington Program for Reinventing Public Education.

Miron, G. (1993). *Choice and the use of market forces in schooling: Swedish education reforms for the 1990s.* Stockholm: Institute of International Education, Stockholm University.

Miron, G. (1996, October). Free choice and vouchers transform schools. *Educational Leadership*, 54(2), 77–80.

Morris, A. A. (1989). *The constitution and American public education.* Durham: Carolina Academic Press.

Murnane, R. J., & Levy, F. (1996). *Teaching the new basic skills: Principles for educating children to thrive in a changing economy.* New York: The Free Press.

Newman, F., & Wehlage, G. (1995). *Successful school restructuring.* Madison, WI: Center on Organization and Restructuring of Schools, Wisconsin Center for Educational Research, University of Wisconsin.

North Carolina Education. (1970, October). *Issues & Answers*, 1(2), 21.

O'Keeffe, B. (1988). *Schools for tomorrow: Building walls or building bridges.* London: Falmer Press.

Olson, L. (1996, September 4). New studies on private choice fan the flames. *Education Week*, 1 & 20–21.

Organization for Economic Co-operation and Development (OECD). (1994). *School: A matter of choice.* Paris: Centre for Educational Research and Innovation, OECD.

Parker, L., & Margolis, F. (1996). School choice in the U.S. urban context: Racism and policies of containment. *Journal of Education Policy*, 11(6), 717–728.

Peshkin, A. (1978). *Growing up American: Schooling and the survival of community.* Prospect Heights, IL: Waveland Press. (Reissued, 1994).

Plank, D. N., & Boyd, W. L. (1994, Summer). Antipolitics, education, and institutional choice: The flight from democracy. *American Educational Research Journal*, 31(2), 263–281.

Ritter, J. (1997, March 27). Princeton charter school adds up to division. *USA Today*, p. 6A.

Sherman, J. D. (1982, October). Government finance of private education in Australia: Implications for American policy. *Comparative Education Review*, 26(3), 391–405.

Stearns, K. (1996). *School reform: Lessons from England.* Princeton, NJ: Carnegie Foundation for the Advancement of Teaching.

Stecklow, S. (1996, December 24). Arizona takes the lead in charter schools – for better or worse. *Wall Street Journal*, pp. A1 & A4.

Townsend, T. (1996). *Schools of the future: Does the reality match the rhetoric?* Melbourne, Australia: South Pacific Centre for School and Community Development, Monash University.

Tyack, D. (1993). School governance in the United States: Historical puzzles and anomalies. In J. Hannaway & M. Carnoy (Eds.), *Decentralization and school improvement: Can we fulfill the promise?* (pp. 1–32). San Francisco: Jossey-Bass.

Tyson, L. D. (1986, July). *The U.S. and the world economy in transition.* The Berkeley Roundtable on the International Economy, University of California, Berkeley. BRIE Working Paper #22. Paper prepared for the meeting of the Western Economics Association, Berkeley, CA.

Tyson, L. D., Yoffie, D. B. (1991, August). *Semiconductors: From manipulated to managed trade.* The Berkeley Roundtable on the International Economy, University of California, Berkeley. BRIE Working Paper #47.

Urbanski, A. (1996, January 31). Make public schools more like private. *Education Week*, pp. 31 & 33.

Vanourek, G., Manno, B. V., & Finn, C. E., Jr. (1997, April 30). The false friends of charter schools. *Education Week*, pp. 60 & 46.

Viadero, D. (1997, April 16). Massachusetts study supplies ammunition to supporter and critics of choice. *Education Week*, p. 12.

Walford, G. (1994). *Choice and equity in education.* London: Cassell.

Weimer, D. L. & Vining, A. R. (1989). *Policy analysis: Concepts and practice.* Englewood Cliffs, NJ: Prentice-Hall.

Wells, A. S. (1993). *Time to choose: America at the crossroads of school choice policy.* New York: Hill and Wang.

Whitty, G. (1997). Creating quasi-markets in education: A review of recent research on parental choice and school autonomy in three countries. In Michael Apple (Ed.), *Review of Research in Education* (Vol. 22, pp. 3–47). Washington, D.C.: American Educational Research Association,

Willms, J. D., & Echols, F. (1992). Alert and inert clients: The Scottish experience of parental choice of schools. *Economics of Education Review*, 11(4), 339–350.

Woods, P. A., & Bagley, C. (1996). Market elements in a public service: An analytical model for studying educational policy. *Journal of Education Policy*, 11(6), 641–653.

Woods, P. A., Bagley, C., & Glatter, R. (1997, March). *Dynamics of choice: School responsiveness in a competitive climate*. Paper presented at the annual meeting of the American Educational Research Association, Chicago.

Yanofsky, S., & Young, L. (1992, February). A successful parents' choice program. *Phi Delta Kappan*.

Zysman, J., Tyson, L. (Eds.). (1983). *American industry in international competition: Government policies and corporate strategies*. Ithaca: Cornell University Press.

New Information Technologies and the Ambiguous Future of Schooling – Some Possible Scenarios

CHRIS BIGUM

Faculty of Education, Central Queensland University

JANE KENWAY

Faculty of Education, Deakin University

Few change issues are more compelling for schools today than the introduction of new technologies. Computers in particular are widely advocated as harbingers of an educational revolution where children will have independent access to rich sources of information, be able to integrate and apply knowledge in sophisticated ways and where their teachers will become coaches, guides and facilitators to assist young people in the new forms of learning that will engage them. At the same time, critics of the computer revolution argue that much of it replaces education with entertainment, that the quality of information that can be accessed is often very poor, that children will learn in more and more isolated ways from each other, and that critical elements will be drained out of the educational process by focussing on technical competence alone.

Bigum and Kenway take their readers through this highly contested and controversial field with a balanced and thoughtful review and evaluation of the main standpoints that educators take towards new technologies in education. They describe and critique the positions of groups they call the Boosters, the Doomsters, the Anti-Schoolers and the Critics – leading to their own exposition of a practically workable and educationally justifiable stance that schools might best take towards high technology and future schooling.

INTRODUCTION

Nowadays, computerisation is a term commonly associated with change in many fields of human endeavour. In education, computer technology has promised much over the past fifteen years and schools, together with other educational institutions, especially in the main Anglophone nations, have invested considerable sums of money over this period in coming to terms with this technology. As the ubiquity and power of computer technology have increased, so too has the pressure on schools to respond. More recently, the growth of the Internet and its public prominence have added it to the growing list of computer technologies with which schools believe they have to contend.

Two features of the uptake of computers by schools over the last fifteen years are noteworthy: the relatively short time it has taken for computers to become an "essential" component of most 'first world' classrooms and the broadly held views concerning their educational importance. Schools and school systems have been

A. Hargreaves (ed.), Extending Educational Change, 95-115.

sufficiently persuaded of the importance of computers in classrooms that they have made significant and ongoing expenditure on computer hardware, software and support, so much so that today, the major consideration is not whether to buy but what to buy[1]. The investment in computer technology by policy makers, administrators and teachers is consistent with a widely held discourse which associates computers in classrooms with technological progress, future employment opportunities of students as well as enhanced learning in the classroom (Iacono & Kling, 1996).

The relationship between computer use in schools and the educational value of computer technology is not as obvious as it might first appear. In the early 1980s, the educational merits of computers in classrooms were yet to be established. Schools acquired modest numbers of the first eight-bit microcomputers such as the Apple IIe and Commodore 64. Acquisition of more computers and the replacement or upgrading of out-of-date machines continued while teachers worked hard to establish useful things to do with them in classrooms (Bigum et al., 1987). In the 1990s, many schools boast networks of many computers and some schools have adopted policies which require all students to own a laptop computer. As schools continue to improve and add to their computing resources, Becker (1996) has estimated that to properly equip a school with computer technology and support teachers in their use will cost an additional $2,000 per pupil, per year. The investments schools have made and are likely to continue to make are clearly substantial. Apart from diverting resources from other areas of the curriculum, the growing use of computers in schools gives computer technology an educational legitimacy that otherwise it would not have. Regardless of what they are used for in classrooms, computers are now firmly linked to public perceptions of modern educational practice and their growing use in the home appears to be linked to a now general acceptance of their educational worth.

In terms of a growing social acceptance of computer technology, the educational worth of computer technology, aided by the ongoing purchase of computers by schools has meant that some school age students have better access to better hardware and software in their homes. The change in home ownership of computers is only one of a number of changes associated with the growing use of computers that have taken place outside schools since the early 1980s (Bigum, Fitzclarence, Green, & Kenway, 1994). The world in which schools first began to use computers is much changed, largely due to increasing computerisation and global computer networks (Sassen, 1991; Castells, 1991) but schools have continued to respond to computer technology in much the same way as they always have (Bigum, 1995), acting in accord with a rather narrow and limited view of the role of computer technology in education and in the world more generally (Kenway, in press-b).

In an era in which government expenditure on education is declining (Kenway, Bigum, Fitzclarence, Collier, & Tragenza, 1995) and the promotion of the new information and communication technologies continues apace (Kenway, 1995a), schools will find it increasingly difficult to finance the acquisition of contemporary computer technology. The commitment of most schools to a discourse of technological progress locates them in a broad social movement that supports computer-based education (Iacono & Kling, 1996). Schools would argue that they have little choice given the increasing competition for students between schools and the need to have at least a gloss of high technology to show parents. Although reluctant to admit it, schools are clearly caught in an increasingly expensive pattern of consumption of high technology products. We believe that schools can no longer continue to operate in this way and would be better able to adapt to the changed techno-social conditions if they engaged a more pluralistic and contextually sensitive view of computers and related technologies in classrooms. In this chapter we briefly indicate four broad discourses which portray and position teachers and schools with respect to the use of computer technology. We briefly develop elements of the scenarios (Schwartz, 1991) for schools that each of these positions implies and conclude with a set of principles that derive from a more balanced approach for using computers in schools.

FRAMING COMPUTERS IN SCHOOLS

Categories for describing computer use in schools have been in existence since the early eighties (Taylor, 1980) and generally are based around different pedagogies associated with computer use. The discursive categories we offer here reflect a broader set of educational and social beliefs and practices that come together around the use of the new information and communication technologies in education. We acknowledge that the boundaries of our categories are not sharp but that each category reflects a set of family resemblances in terms of the assumptions about and orientation towards computer technology. We use the terms *Booster, Anti-schooler, Critic* and *Doomster* to label each set of discourses. Each discourse frames what teachers and schools do with computers, the stories they tell about them and the imaginings they have of the future. In order to make the distinctions sharper, we have constructed a set of ideal types formed in each of the discourses. This allows us a shorthand to talk about particular set of ideas and the individuals who promote them and provides a set of types which teachers can use to identify and perhaps make better sense of particular positions on technology in the classroom. We use the plural form of our labels to refer to these types. So we speak of boosters, for example, both individually and as a camp or broad collection of people strongly positioned in the overall Booster discourse.

Our second purpose is to speculate on the shorter and longer term scenarios which are implied by these different ways of understanding information technology in education. In so doing we draw from the work of Schwartz (1991) who with others[2] has developed an approach to scenario writing that distinguishes three broad elements: *driving forces* (things that drive the plot of a scenario), *predetermined elements* (things that are more or less fixed) and *critical uncertainties* (elements of the scenario that are the least certain and also the most important to the scenario). A scenario is not a prediction but a way of developing alternative images that are not simply extrapolations of current conditions. Done well they expose 'blind spots' in our thinking and provide a rigorous basis for testing policy and plans.

We undertake this scenario work for the following reason. Each discourse either explicitly or implicitly points to a future. However, these futures are rarely taken to their longer term conclusion. Seldom do proponents or opponents adopt the 'the art of the long view'. Those involved in changing schools and those being changed by schools should understand the implied future of each discourse rather than uncritically accepting its promises and prognostications and automatically taking up its imperatives. In its proper form, scenario work is a rich theoretical and practical methodology for anticipating and planning for change. Its value is to open up debate rather than closing it down before it has properly begun.

On the basis of reviewing these different discourses and their future implications, we end our paper by suggesting some basic principles for working with new information technologies in schools in such a way that the associated processes of change are educationally, culturally and socially astute.

FOUR DISCOURSES

Like all categorisations, the four broad camps in the field of the new information and communication technologies in education that we will now outline are arbitrary. Of necessity, most of these ideas are speculative; at best, to be seen as useful 'intuition pumps' (Dennett, 1995). Each of the groups we describe, in effect both represents and constructs scenarios for the future relationships between new information and communication media and schools. We uncover the basic elements of their scenarios pointing to the assumptions they make in order to tell their stories about the future. In this way, we can identify the way their discourse limits and shapes their proposals for how schools should change, or not, in order to come to terms with the new information technologies.

1. Boosters

By far the dominant group, boosters are the unequivocal promoters of new information technologies in education. Their pronouncements are easily found in print and broadcast media. Most books, articles and policies concerning new technologies in education fit into this camp; so it is difficult to select one author as prototypical. Bill Gates is undoubtedly one of the group's prominent intellectual and moral leaders (Gates, 1995). Boosters tend to be characterised by an unswerving faith in the technology's capacity to improve education and most other things in society, often coupled with a sense of inevitability concerning the growth and use of computer technology. They have few if any doubts about the educational merits of their vision for change.

To Boosters, the duty of teachers is to make the best use of these technologies as they become available, as if they all have intrinsic educational value. Boosters are therefore preoccupied with *how* questions: how to engineer new technologies into classrooms, how to encourage teachers to use it, how to measure the learning gains, how to convince school districts to spend more money on technology – and so on. The educational claims made on behalf of the technology are almost never challenged seriously and tend to surface as narrow technical questions such as "What is the effect of word processing on children's writing?"

The lexicon typically found in Booster discourse includes terms like instructional design, multimedia, 'smart', 'intelligent', computer-based, computer-aided, and computer-managed. In short, boosters employ an educational technology lens with which to view the world. It matters less to them *what* computers are (or are not) used for in the classroom or *why* they are used at all.

The rationale that Boosters use to justify technology in the classroom typically derives from what Sproull and Kiesler (1991) call 'first level effects'. Such effects are claims made on behalf of a new technology in order to justify its acquisition. These claims are invariably in terms of improvements to existing processes. So computers are promoted as improving learning, improving access to jobs, and with the Internet, improving access to information. These claims are so entwined with the belief in the self-evident benefits of technological progress that the claims become more like slogans, tapping the genuine concern of all teachers to improve student learning and the anxiety of parents for their children's future.

Booster scenarios tend towards utopian visions of schooling in which most if not all educational problems will be solved by the application of new technologies. Commonly, there is a vision of computers doing most of the 'teaching' or at least occupying students most of the time, leaving the teacher 'free' to 'facilitate learning' (Tiffin & Rajasingham, 1995). The technology is seen in terms of replacing 'inefficient' human activity and such replacements are seen as unproblematic (Hiltz, 1994). To Boosters, there is little or no uncertainty associated with technological advance, only with the particular direction it takes. Social costs and disadvantage associated with the adoption of a particular technology are necessary obstacles to be overcome and are the price of progress.[3]

For some Boosters, the critical uncertainty in the stories they tell about the future concerns the unknown path the technology will take, the next new development that is often totally unanticipated. The decisions and choices that are made in research laboratories and high tech engineering sites become a source of wonder, awe and amazement. Excitement about the new provides the energy that drives their stories. Each new product in turn poses an educational engineering challenge: how to develop classroom applications.

Experienced Boosters see high technology industries as a driving force in their scenarios. Their continual capacity to produce successive waves of technology, each one an improvement on what went before, gives these boosters a faith in finding a technical solution to virtually any educational problem, including those produced by using technology!

The 'big picture' scenarios for Boosters tend to be scaled-up versions of what they are interested in at a classroom level. Equity issues such as the low level of access for disadvantaged groups in society to technology and understandings about it, are translated into problems of inadequate resources. They rarely ask questions about their own privileged positions with regard to access to hardware, software and the necessary expertise in using it. The massive social and economic dislocation that has accompanied the global development of computing and communication technologies (Kenway, Bigum & Fitzclarence, 1993) is to them, simply a phase that we need to pass through in order to reach technological and educational nirvana.

A Booster future scenario for high technology and education is a totally 'wired' world, in which classrooms, kids, teachers and the home are all permanently connected to a global computer network (Hiltz, 1994). They see such a world offering high quality access to information, remote and world-wide-expert teachers and other learners around the globe. Teachers who have not adapted to this massive shift in the way that schools operate will be discarded. There are no problems in terms of equity and access since the technology will become so affordable and available. A major focus becomes how to deal with the staggering volumes of information that are available. Technical solutions that are superior forms of the know-bots touted in the 1990s are planned. Education generally is enmeshed in a booming economy of 'bits' (Negroponte, 1995), in which schools are significant traders. The gift economy of the earlier Internet still survives alongside a commercial version. Public schools tend to rely upon publicly available information whereas private schools subscribe to private information sites and sources for their students.

Broadly, this scenario retains the school, but in a much modified form. The dream of a totally technologised school and curriculum is realised. The 'weak link' in the new schools proves to be students. They don't learn fast enough. So there is a renewed emphasis on cognition and learning science, as teaching is now described. Schools provide a mix of high technology resources that more or less replicate what is in the home but they also continue to help socialise the young into a high technology world in which national identity has been largely subsumed within a new global culture.

2. Anti-schoolers

An interesting sub-set of the Boosters is a group who use their analysis of the relationship between schools and the new information and communication technologies to propose the demise of schooling. Schools, from this perspective, are past their sell-by date. As products of the industrial revolution, it is argued, schools are unable to be reconstructed or reconfigured using computer technology. They should simply be scrapped. As Perelman (1992) has suggested, putting computers into schools is akin to putting an internal combustion engine into a horse.

Unlike the Boosters, this group provides a broad social analysis to argue that the origins of schools and their association with the rise of industrial work are incompatible with the social practices and structures that are emerging around the growth of the new information and communication technologies. The anti-schoolers imagine a utopian, high technology-based educational future in which there are no schools. These critics of schooling embrace the populist claims made about technology-driven epochal social and economic shifts as proposed by Toffler (1980) and Drucker (1993), and celebrate the digital dreams of Kelly (1994) and Negroponte (1995). Kelly described his own book thus[4]:

> A book about how machines are becoming biological, how distributed systems will take over, and the Net will become the reigning metaphor in the coming decade. It's a dose of techno-transcendentalism. As a bonus I enumerate the nine laws of God.

And from Negroponte's recent book:

> Today kids are getting the opportunity to be street smart on the Internet, where children are heard and not seen. Ironically, reading and writing will benefit. Children will read and write on the Internet to communicate, not just to complete some abstract and artificial exercise. What I am advocating should not be construed as anti-intellectual or as a disdain for abstract reasoning – it is quite the opposite. The Internet provides a new medium for reaching out to find knowledge and meaning. (Negroponte, 1995, p. 202)

Perelman (1992), Papert (1993) and the less prominent Davis and Botkin (1994), Lemke (1994) and Spender (1995) seem to be broadly representative of this camp. The driving force for their scenarios is general technological advance and, the spread of the Internet in particular. An underlying assumption in their scenarios is that schools as we know them will decline in the face of the onslaught of technology. Anti-schoolers also express some distaste for the operations and operators of schooling and seek to replace or diminish contemporary forms of schooling via technological means.

The Internet already hosts a number of experimental 'schools' and 'universities' in which classrooms and curriculum are reproduced digitally, linking students and teachers from around the world. These experiments in reproducing the real world with a virtual analogue are early attempts to explore the educational potential of this new medium. They represent the beginning of a much desired end as far as Lemke (1994), for example, is concerned. He sees schools as supporting a monolithic and restrictive curriculum model of education compared with what the Internet can offer –an information access model of learning in which he envisages learners to be like adult scholars, selecting areas of interest that can be pursued free of adult interference. Spender (1995) compares the possibilities and excitement of *Nattering on the Net* with the dreariness of 'boring old teachers'. She seems to speak on behalf on the Vidkid generation when she calls for more educational life on line. Perelman (1992) is in no doubt that schools should be replaced by more efficient and effective technologies.

Other writers in this group are more moderate. Papert (1993) is critical of the top-down command systems of school bureaucracies and large schools, and argues for a diverse network of what he calls 'small schools', with good access to networked information and the technical support to form rich and varied electronic communities in cyberspace. Davis and Botkin (1994) see a knowledge-for-profit revolution transforming business and education. They argue that as businesses become more concerned with the production and distribution of knowledge, they will become unwitting competitors with schools which have been unable to adapt to the demands of technology-based change, and over time business will win out. They point to the enormous size of educational activity in corporations at present and see the uptake of new technologies by the young as a crucial element in their scenario in which there is a slow shift from the public provision of education to one which is supported by business. They argue that,

> Public schools will stop trying to be all things educational to all citizens. Like steel and other basic industries, those who succeed in transforming themselves do so only by becoming smaller, more focused, and very agile in the limited markets they choose to serve. (Davis & Botkin, 1994, p. 133)

A key element in anti-schooler scenarios is the growing importance of the home as a key site for delivering entertainment and information. For many secondary schools around the world, home ownership of computers means that some students can have better access to better technology in the home than they do in their classroom. Indeed, all Anti-schooler scenarios have in common the Booster assumption that easy access to broadly based digital information will be sufficiently commonplace to allow, if not to trigger the decline of formal schooling. The critically uncertain element in these stories is how schools and school systems will respond. The difficulty is imagining how such an entrenched institution can be dismantled or fundamentally restructured. Papert imagines a Soviet-style collapse, sudden and sweeping, whereas Davis and Botkin imagine a gradual shift to business funding and influence which they identify as already under-way. They point to the 140,000 explicit school-business relationships in the United States and the increasing influence of market influences on schooling around the world.

In educational policy reports, new information technologies have fired a great deal of discussion about "Open Learning" (Department of Employment, 1994). The convergence of computing and telecommunication technologies has given the proponents of open learning a new means of promoting their ideals (Hiltz, 1994). They point to the possibilities that the new communication technologies offer for reducing the existing boundaries between classes, schools, and sectors. Even state and national boundaries do not limit the communications carried by computer, modem and telephone line. However, other possible convergences or disappearances are ignored, for example the weakening of the nation state's capacity to fund public education, or the emergence of new, global education services delivered via fibre optic cable into the home. Thus educational policy makers' wishful expectation that, despite techno/market forces, education will remain largely institutionalised and under state control appears to be based in a selective reading of the impact of the new technologies. Open Learning in

conjunction with the emerging parallel education industries in On-Line libraries, museums and art galleries, with the networking of homes and with the
privatisation and commercialisation of education, point to the probability that
education will look quite different in the years to come (Kenway et al., 1995).
You don't have to be an anti-schooler or indeed, a de-schooler to see these trends.

An anti-schooler future scenario for high technology and education is that
there are no longer any schools. Universities have been reduced to tiny, highly
specialised, privately subsidised research institutes. Learning is life-long and
delivered on-line. Just-in-time learning emerges as a huge industry, delivered to
students at any time and anywhere. Teachers have become private tutors who
work for individual or consortia of students. Education is totally negotiated or
in Drucker's (1993) terms becomes 'mass customised'. Business funds the basic
infrastructure through communication cartels that subsidise the sorts of
knowledge production which meet corporate interests. A lower quality, public
education facility for the poor operates alongside the business-funded
enterprises. The decline in the nation state's ability to raise revenue in a world
in which most commerce operates on the Net produces a residualised state-
based system and a dominant business-funded system.

3. Critics

In contrast to the numerically larger group of boosters and their sub-group the
anti-schoolers, other writers are critical of the rush to technologise schools and
education more generally. These critics are sceptical of many of the claims
advanced for using the new information and communication technologies in education. While not totally opposed to the use of new communications media in education, they urge caution and draw on socio-cultural analyses of technological change
to support their views. This rather diverse group tends to ask *why* and *what*. Its
members challenge the taken-for-granted assumptions about the use of computers in schools and elsewhere. Some point to social justice concerns in matters of
access to and use of technology (Kenway, 1995a). Others adopt the role of child-
protectors and point to problems associated with Net pornography and harassment, and argue for mechanisms to control children's access to such things – at
least at school. Others raise questions about the educational minimalism of some
technology-based approaches to teaching and learning (Bromley, 1992). Others
point to new technologies as technologies of control by the state over educational
institutions (Bigum & Green, 1993). As computer networking between schools
develops, the opportunities for increased electronic surveillance of schools by
central authorities grows. In some systems, schools are provided with and are
required to use administrative software which is networked to central computers,
allowing easy access via these computers to a school's electronic records.

Some of the key issues taken up by critics derive from computers being used to
do things that some regard as being the domain of humans (Weizenbaum, 1984).
The distinction Weizenbaum makes is between what a computer *can* do and what

it *ought* to be used to do. He argues that simply because a computer can carry out a function, it ought not necessarily be used to do so. In education, for instance, anti-schoolers have argued that computers can be used to replace teachers. This issue is complex and cannot be dealt with adequately here. The prospect of using computers to teach derives largely from the claim that much of teaching is 'rule-based' or follows the form, that "if this is that case, and that is the case, then do this". A description of this kind locates teaching in the realm of knowledge-based or expert systems software which employs propositional logic of the if-then kind to 'reason' (Bigum, 1987b) which it is claimed, is able to be converted into computer programs.[5] Such claims about computer reasoning and its application in fields like education have been strongly contested (Boal & Lakoff, 1995; Dreyfus, 1992) by the view that human reason is embodied in our feelings and purposes, much of it is metaphorical, and it is therefore not amenable to the precision of a computer program.

Critical literature on computer use outside education is reasonably common-place (Kling, 1996a; Brook & Boal, 1995). However, apart from an early collection by Sloan (1984), critical education collections concerned with computer use in the classroom are harder to find. Interestingly, what is remarkable about schools when compared to other social institutions is how successful they have been in resisting computers. As critical historians Tyack and Cuban (1995, p. 126) put it: ". . . computers meet classroom; classroom wins." Resistance or the lack of acceptance by the broad population of teachers has been commonplace in schools around the world and is documented generally by Cuban (1986) in the case of a range of classroom technologies in North America and by Hodas (1996) and Bigum et al. (1987) in Australia with respect to computer use in schools.

Critics turn boosters' givens into uncertainties or raise questions about the assumptions underlying boosters' proclaimed benefits. For example, in the case of the claim or assumption that computers in schools are essential for the future employability of students, critics point to the macro changes in the employment market world-wide, where the significant growth in jobs will be in poorly paid service occupations. The contribution of well paid high technology employment to the total job market, they argue, is minimal (Henwood, 1995).

In the case of claims about improved learning for students using computers critics point to the problems of attempting to compare learning outcomes that purportedly derive from the use of different media. Papert (1972) parodied the comparison of computer-based teaching to other teaching methods. He suggested that the failure to find significant differences in favour of computer-based approaches was like the failure of a 19th century engineer who failed to show that engines were better than horses.

> This he did by hitching a 1/8 HP motor in parallel with his four strong stallions. After a year of statistical research he announced a significant difference. However it was thought that there was a Hawthorne effect on the horses . . . the purring of the motor made them pull harder. (Papert, 1972, p. 2)

Critics also argue that the technology amplifies some ways of knowing and diminishes others. For example, in mathematics, the more widespread use of computers has meant that numerical approaches which require computers to do many iterative calculations to achieve a solution, have become more prevalent than analytical approaches, requiring formal reasoning and proof (even though computers can still be used even with this kind of mathematical reasoning). Interestingly, there is now virtually nothing of what is taught in mathematics from primary to tertiary levels of education that computers cannot do. From a critic's perspective, this poses important curriculum questions about what is worth knowing not only in mathematics, but in many disciplines (Bigum, 1987a).

Critics tend to focus on the human, social or cultural dimensions of technological change. They emphasise the human costs of widespread computerisation and argue for a more balanced assessment when computers are to be employed in any situation (Cooley, 1992). They raise questions associated with the implications of new communications media for the ways in which we live, work and play and observe that if such matters are ignored by schools, students will be ill equipped to be critical consumers of new technologies (Mackay, Young, & Beynon, 1991). They see technology as a resource for learning but also as a context for learning. They argue it is a context about which learning must itself occur (Bigum & Green 1993).

In common with boosters, critics see technological development as a driving economic, cultural and thus educational force. But they draw the critical uncertainties for their scenarios from a wider social context than do boosters (Kenway et al., 1993). For instance, the rise in the ownership of computers in the home (in some sections of the community at least) and the manner in which this is to be negotiated by schools is a key element for the scenarios of some critics. Other critics point to the difference in computing skills and familiarity between students and their teachers. Barlow argues that the students are the natives in this arena and the adults are the immigrants (in Tunbridge, 1995). Seen in this light, computer literacy programs for many students in schools are misguided. Other critics emphasise the largely equity-blinkered development of computer technologies in schools. They argue that all technology amplifies advantage and computers are no exception (Zakariya, 1984). They predict a future of information rich and information poor schools and students.

The critical discourse around computers in schools is not simply negative. Many critics see both benefits and dangers in the use of the new information media in schools. More specifically, they see severe limitations in many popular current approaches and in the ideas which inform them but at the same time they want to contribute positively to educational developments (Bigum & Green, 1993; Williams & Bigum, 1994). At the same time they are constantly alert to the difficulties, dilemmas and dangers. For example Kenway (in press-a) draws on work associated with liquid identity and electronic scholarship, to consider new ways of exploring gender issues in schools. Cummins and Sayers (1995) adapt the ideas associated with critical pedagogy to develop cross cultural literacies on-line. Green and Bigum (1993) point to the need for schools to attend more effectively to the needs of the Nintendo generation. Ultimately, this group identify the genuinely new educational issues and opportunities that such technologies generate.

A scenario for the future of schooling and computing, according to critics, is one where technologization of schooling and most other aspects of society has occurred, but where it is also dramatically uneven. The patterns of disadvantage that emerged in the 1980s and 1990s have become clearer and extend most markedly to the poor nations of the world and to the poor in all nations of the world. The 'digital economy' has meant even more massive job losses than in the 80s and 90s. Low paid service jobs are available as middle income earners and the wealthy 'out source' most of the work done in the networked home. But service jobs are drying up as the middle class and its overall purchasing power shrinks due to the extensive application of new information technologies to most forms of work.

Schools continue to exist because they still offer the best but not the least expensive solution for minding the young. Parents teleworking at home has meant that most children attend school part-time, when their parents are not at home to supervise them. Some schools have been able to continue to embrace each new wave of technology, but the majority, as they lost revenue due to diminishing attendance, keep only the barest repertoire of technology. The home has become the central site for the delivery of prepackaged and global educational materials. It is the place where most people maintain their own information systems and data stores. Schools continue to teach a more or less traditional curriculum but what is taught in schools is determined more than ever by business, a trend that was established in the late 1980s and early 1990s. The desire by business to have a highly flexible and adaptable worker has meant that the pursuit of 'generic skills' has intensified and teachers who are paid according to how many students they are able to have placed in well paid jobs, have lost the little say they had over curriculum.

Despite commonplace talk about preparing students for the 'knowledge economy', the number of well paid high technology related jobs in the knowledge economy remains very small in comaparison to the total employment market. Many students are encouraged through enterprise education to learn about establishing small businesses based upon service provision and entertainment but as the middle income sector of the economy continues to shrink this avenue for employment appears to be short-lived.

4. Doomsters

Doomsters are unqualified opponents of the new information and communication technologies. They see much damage to society and education arising from the uncritical acceptance of new media forms ranging from television to the Internet (Postman, 1993). Doomsters are nostalgic for the period when these technologies did not exist or for the practices and institutions that are being replaced by new technologies. While their concerns are about all of society, they have a particular concern for the young and what they see as being neglected in their schooling. This discourse is a broadly conservative one that emphasises the value of past educational practices and knowledge and is critical of contemporary, computer-based pedagogy and curriculum (Bowers, 1988).

Postman (1986; 1993) is a well-known doomster who presents a wide ranging critique of most electronic media from television to computers. He expresses a number of fears about the psychological fallout of the Internet – that it will breed a cop-out society by feeding fantasy, escapism and nostalgia. He writes about the loss of meaning and the trivialisation associated with the media age; the feelings of alienation, confusion and inertia that it produces. In Postman's view, as the home increasingly becomes the site for accessing shopping, entertainment and work, 'cocooned and isolated individuals will be produced who find it difficult to distinguish between reality and simulation'. For schools, to go 'on line' is to undermine their critical capacities and to subject them to the same problems. More recently, Stoll (1995) has also offered a controversial but detailed critique of the Internet attacking many of the claims made on its behalf and providing some down-to-earth appraisals for users and would-be users.

If boosters are the blinkered romantics of scenario writing for high technology in education then doomsters are the writers of tragedy. In many respects, members of this group are closest to the Luddites of industrialising England in that they have created well-developed arguments for rejecting the technology (Sale, 1995; Roszak, 1994). None have been known however, to go around smashing it – except metaphorically, of course. Key indicators for this group are a singular and nostalgic valuing of books, libraries, print literacy, face-to-face interaction etc. In their stories, schooling is represented as having a golden age before the arrival of electronic media and technology. Doomster scenarios portend social decline if tech-nologization is not reversed. They also ask *why* questions; in particular "why replace perfectly good practices and institutions with technology-based ones"?

In schools, doomsters are concerned at what they see as a deskilling of students who use calculators, spelling checkers and other computer-aids for work. The rise in popularity of the Internet poses important questions about how students are taught to select and judge information from a source in which the quality controls of print-based resources don't exist. Postman points to problems associated with information glut and information junkies in the use of the Internet (Roszak, 1994). He argues that the Internet is unnecessary because we already have an over-abundance of information. Lakoff (Boal & Lakoff, 1995) agrees and argues that what is confused is the amount of information that is available and the amount of information a person can actually use.

The scenarios that doomsters describe, tell of societies over-run with technol-ogy in which human interaction, sense of community and the ability to deal with issues at other than the superficial level offered by electronic media are much diminished (Slouka, 1995). Yet the doomster dream of a technology-free world ironically and in many respects exists now, in our far from perfect schools.

Relative to the world outside, most schools are technology impoverished places. Indeed, for many teachers, working without technology in the classroom is often not a matter of pedagogical choice. It reflects the practicalities of working in a poorly resourced school with little or no technical support. Under these circumstance, it makes little sense to base too much teaching on computers. To doomsters at least, this is a good thing. It means that schools may yet represent an important bastion for protecting what they see as important knowledge and skills.

A doomster scenario for education and the new information and communication technologies, is one which accepts but also greatly regrets the widespread technologization of most aspects of society. Society has split into three broad groups: a technological elite who produce, and distribute most forms of information, entertainment and educational services; a massive middle group who consume information products, and a displaced lower section of community who have largely rejected a high technology way of living and have returned to a more subsistence lifestyle, maintaining their own schools and keeping alive (but not through choice), the practices and traditions swept aside by the high technology revolution. At the top, the highly technologically literate group controls and determines the techno-social agenda, while at the bottom, people build a lifestyle around print literacy. The glitterati are the digerati – but they are hollow and shallow people psychologically tied to their machines.

Schools reflect these social divisions and though much diminished in social status they continue to fight a losing battle against global information and entertainment systems for the minds of their students. They have continued to adapt however and provide patchy but important opportunities for students to retain a basic level of print and critical literacy.

'THE ART OF THE LONG VIEW'[6]

The discourses, their associated ideal types and the scenarios that we have briefly described offer different views of the development of technologies in schools. Taken together they enable a more pluralistic perspective on the nature and implications of a more electronic educational world; one that is not tied to a single view of the world or of society's capacity to engage or reject the new information and communication technologies. The future of new communications media will likely remain uncertain for a long period to come. If we are witnessing something akin to the replacement of steam with electric power then it may be many decades before the impact of the digital revolution becomes clear. It is thus wise to remain open minded and indeed pluralistic about its long term implications for schooling. Indeed, as we implied at the outset, a useful way to develop a more balanced and reflective view of technology-based change in schools is to adopt 'the art of the long view'[7]. The identification of driving forces, predetermined elements and critical uncertainties on which this approach (Schwartz, 1991) is based, allows any proposed technological development to be analysed and critiqued thoroughly.

The scenarios we have painted for each of the four groups may appear exaggerated but they serve a number of purposes. They open up blind spots in the ways that schools think about these issues. They can prompt educators of all kinds into rethinking how schools should come to terms with computer technology and other new communication media. In this respect we offer a set of principles that we have developed over many years of working with teachers, schools and in our own practice as distance learning educators, with regard to using new technologies. These principles are designed to support teachers to develop ways of understanding and using the new information and communication technologies in the context of a broad commitment to social justice.

TOWARDS AN EDUCATIONALLY SOUND AND SOCIALLY JUST HIGH TECHNOLOGY FUTURE OF SCHOOLING

1. Communities of learners and knowers

Students and teachers can usefully think about what is worth knowing about education and new technologies along three dimensions -*operational, cultural and critical.*[8] The *operational* dimension attends to the skills that are necessary to use the new information media: computers, modems, networks and so on. However, how these skills are acquired is just as important as what is acquired. It is useful to model the learning of these skills on the way in which computer professionals learn and work. They employ an elaborate human network of support, and learn to rely upon a 'collective' approach to knowing and problem solving. This ethos, clearly evident in the early days of the Internet, is also a rich and powerful way to learn and to know. Instead of everyone trying to know everything, individuals have a basis for specialist and shared knowledge that enables them to participate in a collective knowing.

The *cultural* dimension involves stepping into the culture that supports the practices of using computers for educational purposes – no matter what one's level of expertise or orientation. It acknowledges the importance of multiple perspectives on new technologies and their uses, and on the human processes that are needed to build, sustain and maintain the effective use of particular technologies in classrooms and elsewhere. For novices, what is required is a kind of cultural apprenticeship in which they learn to mimic expert performance (Lave & Wenger, 1991). Knowing and being able to tell stories that both critically and supportively sustain the use of computers in schools is essential. This requires teachers to move beyond a purely instrumental role for the technology as an educational add-on, to regarding technology as something that poses interesting and important questions for administration, curriculum, pedagogy and for what is worth doing and knowing, educationally.

The *critical* dimension invites the teacher and student to step outside the culture, read "against the grain" and ask questions about the taken for granted assumptions that are embedded in the stories about computer technologies in and outside of schools. This is the most difficult of the three components because it calls for self-questioning, critical dialogue, analysis before action, time for talking and think-ing, willing colleagues to think with, and research resources to provoke and expand one's thinking. Our references provide some starting points here.

2. Teachers first

Counter-intuitively, it is important to attend properly to the personal and profes-sional needs of teachers vis-à-vis computer technologies *before* the needs of students. Teachers' needs are often neglected because of the widespread percep-tion that students needs are especially urgent; that if they are not properly prepared in the classroom for living in a world with computers then they will be seriously disadvantaged. Concern about students has been a powerful influence in shaping how schools have come to terms with computer technology. In the 1980s it led to a spate of computer literacy courses and programs in schools. Now, in the 1990s, the Internet has prompted a fresh wave of anxiety about students, with calls for 'Net literacy'. In retrospect, literacy courses about current computer technologies can be seen as educational panics, largely prompted and promoted by sections of the computer industry.

Computers have become more commonplace in the home and increasing numbers of children now grow up in environments in which they have access to an array of electronic media devices and computers of various types outside school. By the time some children reach school they have considerable skills in using computers and have little or no fear of them. Many teachers, on the other hand, grew up in an environment that had far fewer electronic technologies available and find the adaption to working with computers more difficult than their students.

Adopting a principle of teachers first means supporting teachers to make use of computer and communication technologies in connection with their personal work, before using the technology in their classrooms. It encourages teachers to attend to their own needs and interests before those of their students. It is based on the premise that if teachers are to make sound educational choices about using the technology in their classroom, they must use it for their own purposes first. The emphasis upon personal use and adoption comes from a broader view that locates technology use in schools as a part of a larger process of social acceptance of computer technology (Franklin, 1990) in which the period of the 1980s and 90s is the early phase of a thirty or forty year process (King, 1996).

3. Complementarity

The adoption of a particular technology must be understood in as broad a context as possible. For example, for each high technology 'tool' that is employed, the skills that complement its use should also be taught. Take the case of the hand-held calculator. In order to use this technology, a student requires at least two complementary skills: an ability to approximate or estimate an answer and a knowledge of significant figures. For a technology like the Internet, the complementary skills are less obvious. The Internet poses unique problems for students and teachers in learning how to find, select and appraise information that for the most part has none of the quality assurance methods normally associated with print publications. There are few useful precedents for working with information in a space like this and it will take time to identify the necessary complementary skills a student needs in order to use the resources of the Internet in an educationally sound manner.

This principle is useful at a number of levels. The steady and sometimes dramatic rise of home computer ownership to support the school education of children, makes new complementary relationships between school and home important. Here we do not mean simply enabling compatibility between the two sites. In an era of limited resources, it makes little sense for schools to duplicate what is in the home, particularly if the student has better access at home to better technology. Schools might do better to offer access to computer resources that are more specialised, such as computer-aided design facilities, music composition facilities or robotics. An important aspect of complementarity between home and school is is what to do for students who have little or no access to computers. Schools clearly have a critical role to play here in ensuring that the least advantaged of the school community receive support which may well mean giving privileged access in school time to the "have-nots".

4. Workability

A key test for implementing any new technology in schools is "does it improve the working conditions for student or teacher?" This is not a simple matter. The time-scale over which such issues are judged is important given the costs associated with learning to adapt a workplace to the requirements of computer technology (Kling, 1996b). The adoption of computers in schools has often been a matter of direct or implied compulsion. Yet it is the work of teachers and students that should be the priority in determining whether or not to adopt or implement a particular technology. All too often the technology and its educational claims are the major basis for making judgements about whether or not to purchase. At best the costs of hardware and software are a consideration, but expenditure on these items is always less than the cost of teachers' time in learning how to use the technology, and then designing and implementing classroom activities. The principle of workability draws attention to the complex and unpredictable nature of technological change and provides an additional basis for decision making in ways that will lead to practical benefits for teachers and students.

5. Equity

The use of computers in schools always involves choices about resource allocation. The "logic" behind much resource allocation in schools is driven by prior
access to information and resources. The technically able and well-equipped
are able to make more compelling cases for re-equipping ahead of those who
have poor or no resources. In classrooms, just as elsewhere, technology tends to
amplify advantage. The principle of equity draws people's attention to this and
provides an alternative basis for supplying access to information and allocating
resources.

As Negroponte (1995, p. 6) says "Computing is not about computers any more.
It is about living". Given this, technological competence has become a new basics
of education. Equal access and equal competence must therefore be a key concern
for educators. Such competence will eventually have an impact on students' quality of education; on their access to jobs (no matter how menial), to retraining, to
government information and to learning about critical issues which affect their
lives. Considering how all basic needs can be met is crucial. In addition, as Negroponte implies, as new technologies converge and develop, they will have an ever-
increasing impact on our work, leisure, health, lifestyles, national and cultural
identities and social relationships. At the moment, little educational attention is
being paid to how we produce and consume such technologies and to associated
issues of politics and justice. Be it in the workplace, the home or elsewhere, students
need to be in a position to assess the costs and benefits of the new communications media and to make wise choices which maximise the economic, social and
cultural benefits and minimise the risks and costs. Teaching students about technology is just as important as teaching them to use it. For, in the words of Mitch
Kapor from the Electronic Frontier Foundation,

> We are not just consumers, we are also citizens. With all this talk about
> markets and profits in the new digital world-order perhaps it's time to start
> thinking about what kind of world we want it to be. (quoted in Burstein &
> Klein, 1995, p. 17)

CONCLUSION

For fifteen years, schools have adopted a largely technically oriented, 'heads in'
approach to the use of the new information and communication technologies.
The transformation of computers into communication devices with a global
range and the implications of all these developments for the future of schools
requires a more 'heads up' approach instead, "one that examines the social
choices of whether and how to computerize an activity, and the relationships
between computerized activity and other parts of our social world" (Kling,
1996c, p. 2). It is only with such an approach that schools can move beyond

their current tendency to imagine that if they adopt computer use and networking they will have dealt with the issues associated with being in a global, wired world. This 'immunisation' stance is untenable because schools are deeply implicated in the economic and cultural changes associated with globalisation. Teachers must therefore pull their heads out of their schools to some extent and critically consider the educational issues associated with globalisation. Blind faith in technological progress has not served schools well. It has limited how teachers think about the complex and confusing issues associated with new information media. Schools must be informed, critical and creative in how they use these media if they are to create worthwhile and workable educational futures rather than pander to technological utopias.

ENDNOTES

[1] Becker (1996) reports that each year, schools in the United States purchase between 300,000 to 500,000 computers. In Victoria, $25,000,000 a year is spent on computer hardware and software in government schools.
[2] The Global Business Network has used scenario development in a wide range of fields. More detail about the process and examples are available at: http://www.gbn.org/Main/Scenarios.html
[3] The adoption of any new technology entails decision making that advantages some and disadvantages others. Analyses such as those of Franklin (1990) and Marvin (1988) illustrate the social costs associated with the social adoption of electricity and the telephone among others.
[4] Reported by Stewart Brand in his review of Kelly's book, http://www.gbn.org/BookClub/
[5] The *Journal of Artificial Intelligence in Education* represents the current debates about using computers to teach.
[6] From (Schwartz, 1991).
[7] Useful examples and references can be found at: http://www.gbn.org/
[8] This framework was initially developed by (Green, 1988) in the context of subject-specific literacies and was further developed by (Green & Lee, 1994). Most recently it has been generalised to computing in education.

REFERENCES

Becker, H. J. (1996). How much will a truly empowering technology-rich education cost? In R. Kling (Ed.), *Computerisation and controversy : value conflicts and social choices.* (2nd ed.). San Diego: Academic Press.
Bigum, C. (1987a). *The convivial spreadsheet.* Geelong: Deakin University.
Bigum, C. (1987b). *Natural intelligence meets artificial stupidity.* Geelong: Deakin University.
Bigum, C. (1995). *Learning about limits: Yesterday, today and tomorrow as knowledge resource.* Paper presented at the Australian Computers in Education Conference, Perth.
Bigum, C., Bonser, S., Evans, P., Groundwater-Smith, S., Grundy, S., Kemmis, S., McKenzie, D., McKinnon, D., O'Connor, M., Straton, R., & Willis, S. (1987). *Coming to terms with computers in schools. Report to the Commonwealth Schools Commission* : Deakin Institute for Studies in Education, Deakin University.
Bigum, C., Fitzclarence, L., Green, B., & Kenway, J. (1994). *Connecting schools to global networks one way or another.* Paper presented at the Apitite 94 Conference, Brisbane.
Bigum, C., & Green, B. (1993). Changing classrooms, computing and curriculum: critical perspectives and cautionary notes. *Australian Educational Computing, 8*(1), 6–16.
Boal, I. A., & Lakoff, G. (1995). Body, brain and communication. In J. Brook & I. A. Boal (Eds.), San Francisco: City Lights.

Bowers, C. A. (1988). *The cultural dimensions of educational computing: Understanding the non-neutrality of technology.* New York: Teachers College Press.

Bromley, H. (1992). Culture, power and educational computing. In C. Bigum & B. Green (Eds.), *Understanding the new information technologies in education: A resource for teachers.* Geelong: Centre for Studies in Information Technologies and Education, Deakin University.

Brook, J., & Boal, I. A. (Eds.). (1995). *Resisting the virtual life: The culture and politics of information.* San Francisco: City Lights.

Burstein, D., & Kline, D. (1995). *Road warriors: Dreams and nightmares along the information highway.* New York: Penguin Books.

Castells, M. (1991). *The informational city.* Oxford: Basil Blackwell.

Cooley, M. (1992). Human-centred education. In C. Bigum & B. Green (Eds.), *Understanding the new information technologies in education: A resource for teachers.* Geelong: Centre for Studies in Information Technology and Education, Deakin University.

Cuban, L. (1986). *Teachers and machines: The classroom use of technology since 1920.* New York: Teachers College Press.

Cummins, J., & Sayers, D. (1995). *Brave new schools: Challenging cultural illiteracy through global learning networks.* Ontario: OISE Press.

Davis, S., & Botkin, J. (1994). *The monster under the bed. how business is mastering the opportunity of knowledge for profit.* New York: Simon and Schuster.

Dennett, D. (1995). Intuition pumps. In J. Brockman (Ed.), *The third culture: Beyond the scientific revolution.* New York: Simon & Schuster.

Department of Employment, Education and Training. (1994). *Inquiry into the present and future role of open learning in education and training,.* Canberra: Submission to Senate Standing Committee on Employment, Education and Training.

Dreyfus, H. L. (1992). *What computers still can't do: A critique of artificial reason.* Cambridge, Mass: MIT Press.

Drucker, P. F. (1993). *Post-capitalist society.* Oxford: Butterworth-Heinemann.

Franklin, U. (1990). *The real world of technology.* Montreal: CBC Enterprises.

Gates, B. (1995). *The road ahead.* New York: Viking.

Green, B. (1988). Subject-specific literacy and school learning: A focus on writing. *Australian Journal of Education, 32*(2), 156–179.

Green, B., & Bigum, C. (1993). *Aliens in the classroom, 37*(2), 119–141.

Green, B., & Lee, A. (1994). Writing geography: Literacy, identity and schooling. In A. Freedman & P. Medway (Eds.), *Learning and teaching genre.* Portsmouth, NH: Heinemann/Boynton Cook.

Henwood, D. (1995). Info fetishism. In J. Brook & I. A. Boal (Eds.), *Resisting the virtual life: The culture and politics of information.* San Francisco: City Lights.

Hiltz, S. R. (1994). *The virtual classroom: Learning without limits via computer networks.* Norwood, NJ: Ablex.

Hodas, S. (1996). Technology refusal and the organizational culture of schools. In R. Kling (Ed.), *Computerisation and controversy: Value conflicts and social choices.* (2nd ed.). San Diego: Academic Press.

Iacono, S., & Kling, R. (1996). Computerisation movements and tales of technological utopianism. *Computerisation and controversy: Value conflicts and social choices.* (2nd ed.). San Diego: Academic Press.

Kelly, K. (1994). *Out of control: The rise of non-biological civilization.* New York: Addison-Wesley.

Kenway, J. (1995a). Reality bytes: education, markets and the information super-highway. *The Educational Researcher, 22*(1), 35.

Kenway, J. (1995b). Technological trends: Issues for schooling. In B. Lingard & F. Rizvi (Eds.), *External environmental scan.* Brisbane: Department of Education, Queensland, Australia.

Kenway, J. (in press-a). Backlash in cyberspace and "why girls need modems". In L. Roman & L. Eyre (Eds.), *Dangerous territories.* New York: Routledge.

Kenway, J. (in press-b). The information superhighway and postmodernity: The promise and the price. *Comparative education: Special issue on postmodernity*

Kenway, J., Bigum, C., & Fitzclarence, L. (1993). Marketing education in the postmodern age. *Journal of Education Policy, 8*(2), 105–123.

Kenway, J., Bigum, C., Fitzclarence, L., Collier, J., & Tragenza, K. (1995). New education in new times. *Journal of Education Policy, 9*(4), 317–333.

King, J. L. (1996). Where are the payoffs from computerisation? Technology, learning, and organizational change. In R. Kling (Ed.), *Computerisation and controversy Value conflicts and social choices* (2nd ed.). San Diego: Academic Press.

Kling, R. (Ed.). (1996a). *Computerisation and controversy: Value conflicts and social choices* (2nd ed.). San Diego: Academic Press.

Kling, R. (1996b). Computerisation at work. In R. Kling (Ed.), *Computerisation and controversy: Value conflicts and social choices.* (2nd ed.). San Diego: Academic Press.

Kling, R. (1996c). Heads-up versus heads-in views of computer systems. In R. Kling (Ed.), *Computerisation and controversy: Value conflicts and social choices.*(2nd ed.). San Diego: Academic Press.

Lave, J., & Wenger, E. (1991). *Situated learning: Legitimate peripheral participation.* Cambridge: Cambridge University Press.

Lemke, J. L. (1994,). *The coming paradigm wars in education: Curriculum vs information access.* Paper presented at the Computers, Freedom, and Privacy Conference, Chicago.

Mackay, H., Young, M., & Beynon, J. (Eds.). (1991). *Understanding technology in education.* London: The Falmer Press.

Marvin, C. (1988). *When old technologies were new: Thinking about communications in the late nineteenth century.* New York: Oxford University Press.

Negroponte, N. (1995). *Being digital.* New York: Knopf.

Papert, S. (1972). Teaching children thinking. *Mathematics Teaching* (Spring).

Papert, S. (1993). *The children's machine: Rethinking school in the age of the computer.* New York: Basic Books.

Perelman, L. J. (1992). *School's out: Hyperlearning, the new technology, and the end of education.* New York: William Morrow.

Postman, N. (1986). *Amusing ourselves to death: Public discourse in the age of show business.* London: Heinemann.

Postman, N. (1993). *Technopoly : The surrender of culture to technology.* New York: Vintage Books.

Roszak, T. (1994). *The cult of information: A neo-Luddite treatise on high tech, artificial intelligence, and the true art of* thinking (2nd ed.). Berkeley: University of California Press.

Sale, K. (1995). *Rebels against the future: The Luddites and their war on the Industrial Revolution: Lessons for the computer age.* Reading, Ma.: Addison-Wesley.

Sassen, S. (1991). *The global city.* Princeton: Princeton University Press.

Schwartz, P. (1991). *The art of the long view.* New York: Doubleday.

Sloan, D. (Ed.). (1984). *The computer in education: A critical perspective.* New York: Teacher's College Press.

Slouka, M. (1995). *War of the worlds: Cyberspace and the high-tech assault on reality.* New York: Basic Books.

Spender, D. (1995). *Nattering on the net.* North Melbourne, Australia: Spinifex Press.

Sproull, L., & Kiesler, S. (1991). *Connections: New ways of working in the networked organization.* Cambridge, Ma.: The MIT Press.

Stoll, C. (1995). *Silicon snake oil: Second thoughts on the information highway.* New York: Doubleday.

Taylor, R. (1980). *The computer in the school: Tutor, tool, tutee.* New York: Teacher's College Press.

Tiffin, J., & Rajasingham, L. (1995) . *In search of the virtual class: Education in an information society.* London: Routledge.

Tunbridge, N. (1995). The cyberspace cowboy. *Australian Personal Computer,* September.

Tyack, D., & Cuban, L. (1995). *Tinkering toward utopia: A century of public school reform.* Cambridge, Ma.: Harvard University Press.

Weizenbaum, J. (1984). *Computer power and human reason: From judgement to calculation.* Harmondsworth, Middlesex: Penguin.

Williams, M., & Bigum, C. (1994). *Networking Australian schools: preliminaries, problems and promise.* Paper presented at the Apitite 94, Brisbane.

Zakariya, S. B. (1984) . In school (as elsewhere), the rich get computers, the poor get poorer. *American School Board Journal,* (March), 29–32.

Public Education in a Corporate-Dominated Culture

HEATHER-JANE ROBERTSON

Professional Development Services, Canadian Teachers Federation

In this chapter, Heather-jane Robertson critiques the growth of corporate interest and involvement in public education. The chapter pulls no punches. It critiques the trend towards the corporalization of everything, including education.

With extensive exemplification, Robertson describes how the corporate community has dramatically redirected educational policy, reshaped the discourse and language in which policy is conducted, intruded into the curriclum, redirected resources, influenced the standardization and testing movement, developed partnerships seeking to influence the practices of many individual schools, engaged in sponsorships, and other things besides. There is nothing necessary or inevitable, Robertson concludes, about the influence of the corporate sphere on educational change and she urges us to choose, for democracy, how or whether that influence should persist.

In 1936, G.K. Chesterton denounced business education as a subject of study in schools, claiming:

> ... that it narrows the mind; whereas the whole object of education is to broaden the mind; and especially to broaden it so as to enable it to criticize and condemn such narrowness ... If he [the student] is immediately initiated into the mysteries of these institutions themselves, if he is sworn in infancy to take them as seriously as they take themselves, if he becomes a trader not only before he becomes a traveller, but even before he becomes a true citizen of his own town, he will never be able to denounce those institutions – or even to improve them. (p. 75)

Judged by modern standards, Chesterton was lamenting a very modest intrusion of commercialism into public education. Today's schools accommodate "traders" with little protest: corporate sponsors place their logos on new schools, boards of education sell advertising space on school buses and the media praise the inspired corporate leadership that forces schools to operate more like businesses. Yet, on the whole, the discourse surrounding school reform is dominated by technicist and strategic concerns, and silent on the increased power and visibility of corporations. Chesterton's comments would seem peculiar if they were published today; it is taken for granted that childhood preparation for a world overrun by traders is unavoidable in a corporate-dominated culture.

The shadow of the private sector is being cast over all aspects of school reform,

A. Hargreaves (ed.), Extending Educational Change, 116-137.

from how we think about learners and learning to how schools should be governed and financed; from who produces curriculum to who (or what) "delivers" it; from whether public education is viewed as a remarkable accomplishment or an anachronistic failure. One of the purposes of this paper is to call attention to the nature and consequences of corporate influence on public education. The other is to call attention to how little we seem to worry about it.

EDUCATION IN CORPORATE TIMES

It is not just education that has been invaded by the logic of "traders." Recently Canada's Justice Minister defended an impartial justice system by arguing "it was good for global competitiveness." Two weeks later, the Prime Minister announced that Canada would send peacekeepers to Haiti because that country "is an important trading partner." In Alberta, a politician proposed disbanding that province's human rights commission, asking "if the marketplace doesn't want it, then why should government fund it?" (Nikiforuk, 1995) Key elements of democracy, justice and human rights are thus reduced to levers of commercial interests.

This confusion between the public good and private interests is one of the dislocations of post-modernity, and perhaps its most perilous. While the marketplace has been an exceedingly effective mechanism to generate wealth, on the whole its success has been achieved because of, not despite, its lack of a moral core. This is not a character flaw but a characteristic. Markets are not moral; they are necessarily preoccupied with self-interest and advantage, and, as such, are unfit arbiters of what constitutes our collective well-being. The best of Canada's public policies have recognized that public interest cannot be measured – or determined – by private profit.

But Canada is changing. The ascendency of neoliberal ideologies to the status of conventional wisdom has transformed the accommodation between private interest and public good that has marked modern democracies (Brooks, 1995). The corporate sector is prescribing the exact dimensions of the level playing field of public policy it desires, marked by less government, rapid deregulation and low corporate taxes. In Canada, despite an allegedly oppressive level of public debt, corporate tax rates have fallen to well below both American and OECD averages (Jorgenson, 1996). The not-for-profit sector, including public education, is coming to understand that its role is no longer to negotiate its space inside a mixed economy, but to justify its existence in terms of how well it serves the for-profit sector. Under these rules, cherished educational goals, such as attempting to reduce the social and economic marginalization of certain groups of students, are allowed to proceed only if they can be shown to be good return-on-investment propositions. Goals formerly defended from a moral framework must be redefined as serving the priorities of the corporate sector or risk being discarded.

If necessary, much of what public education attempts to accomplish can be put in utilitarian terms – a task made less difficult by the vacuity of some of the language used to describe educational goals. But not all goals can be redescribed simply by using the "value-added" language of the day; if choices are to be consistent with an economically functionalist perspective, sooner or later some goals must be left behind. Other goals would be enhanced: the "sorting" function of schools would become much more rigid and transparent if economic efficiency were to become entrenched as the overriding priority guiding education reform. Given that factors associated with social class are already a strong predictor of student achievement (Levin, 1995), we would skew public resources towards the well-off right from the beginning and accept in deed as well as word a Darwinian model of student survival. Utilitarianism has no room for sentimentality: we would be obliged to discard not only less "productive" curriculum components, such as the Arts, but also less "productive" students.

While few would promote education reform by using such indelicate phrases, if the same premises are given the right spin, many citizens seem prepared to accept public policy that grants self-interest precedence over public interest, and to harbour a growing indifference towards those who cannot compete successfully (Kopvillem, 1995; 1996). Those with little ideological sympathy for reforming from the Right are silenced by claims of inevitability and assurances crafted from words like "responsibility" and "self-sufficiency." Schools designed to adapt to these new premises and to train students to fend for themselves are essential to perpetuating neo-liberalism into future generations. Yet schools are said to be notoriously out of touch with tough-minded realities; left to their own devices, there is some doubt that they would retool with sufficient dispatch (Lacey, 1994). There is growing agreement across many constituencies that education's "competitive alignment" requires hands-on corporate involvement (Bertrand, 1993).

EDUCATION AND CORPORATE INTERESTS: AN HISTORICAL PERSPECTIVE

The currents that shape Canadian public discourse about education often flow from Canada's American neighbour (Prentice, 1970), where historically, schools have been expected to deliver what corporate North America has demanded. This sector's contemporary preoccupation with public education reform thus marks a vigorous return to a familiar agenda. At the beginning of the industrial revolution, the movement in support of basic public education was very much driven by the captains of industry (Calvert & Kuehn, 1993). Since the need for greater numbers of reasonably literate workers was growing, powerful industrialists advanced the convenient idea that the public should be taxed to finance the basic education of more children. A moderately literate workforce was seen as a distinct competitive advantage; transferring this cost to the public purse markedly limited the expense incurred by employers in training their workforces. Of course, many early champions of public education had no particular sympathy for the interests of industrialists; public education was seen as capable of serving a wide range of desirable personal and social ends (Prentice, 1970). Surely public education was a concept sufficiently grand to accommodate multiple goals!

During the prosperous post-World War II period, the public good was assumed to be synonymous with corporate interests: "What's good for General Motors is good for America" included its schools. During this time, it was not so much that education fell from Corporate America's agenda, but that the private sector rested, satisfied with the role schools were playing in maintaining healthy levels of general and corporate prosperity (Berliner & Biddle, 1995). This complacency ended with the frenzy of soul-searching and school reform that characterized post-Sputnik America. America, the "leader of the free world," had been surpassed, and Corporate America blamed schools, demanding, in particular, a renewed emphasis on creative approaches to the teaching of mathematics and sciences as elements essential to winning the Cold War (Berliner & Biddle).

The persistence of the Cold War and the space race spurred economic investment and corporate expansion. Pleased with its profits, Corporate America was pleased with schools. But the shock caused to the American economy and psyche by the oil crisis of the early 1980's stimulated another round of education criticism, now led quite transparently by a new generation of the captains of industry. Appointed by President Reagan, the corporate-dominated task force responsible for A Nation at Risk left no metaphor unturned in condemning America's schools, describing them as having undermined America's competitiveness and virtue more perniciously than any invading army (National Commission on Excellence in Education [NCEE], 1983). This alarmist portrayal that Berliner and Biddle (1995) call the "mother of all critiques" frightened many Americans, and the criticisms it leveled arguably contaminated other nations' confidence in their own school systems.

The release of A Nation at Risk coincided with other significant political and economic shifts. Corporate America saw the advantage of consolidating its political power if it was to compete successfully in what was beginning to be called the global marketplace. American corporations found that they could promote their public policy goals – including their education agenda – through an assortment of roundtables, think tanks and lobbying organizations. With the Free Trade Agreement on the horizon, the harmonization of North America's power structures soon began in earnest, and corporations on both sides of the border (but very much rooted in American ownership and interests) became better organized (Calvert & Kuehn, 1993). In Canada, lobbying structures parallel to their American counterparts were created. These included the Business Council on National Issues (BCNI), a lobby group representing 160 of Canada's largest corporations with combined assets exceeding one trillion dollars, and the Conference Board of Canada, directed by CEOs representing one hundred corporations determined to pursue a very active role in education (Barlow & Campbell, 1995). The Corporate-Higher Education Forum was created. Influential think tanks such as the C.D. Howe Institute, comprised of corporate members and dedicated to neo-liberal economic policies, and the Fraser Institute, once considered an extreme-right think-tank, but now among the most-quoted sources of "expert opinion,"

(Campbell, 1995) began to advance the interests and opinions of Corporate Canada not only to receptive governments, but to the general public. Each signaled Corporate Canada's intention to enhance its influence on all aspects of public policy, from Free Trade to social investment. Education would be no exception; indeed public education was selected as key strategic territory to be captured (Economic Council of Canada [ECC], 1992).

CAPITALIZING ON SCHOOL FAILURE

Politicians on both sides of the Canada-U.S. border have been welcoming big business – their strongest political allies – to the determination of education policies, an alignment predicated on the need for urgent, cross-sector measures in the face of public education's "failure." Former Xerox CEO and American Deputy Secretary of Education David Kearns claims: "The business community has treated the schools with kid gloves. To be successful, the new agenda for school reform must be driven by competition and market discipline, unfamiliar ground for educators. Business will have to set the new agenda" (Shenk, 1995). The much-touted "Education Summit '96," attended by State Governors, CEOs of America's leading corporations (and exactly two teachers) excluded students and national education organizations. At this meeting, criticism of American schools allegedly reached new allegorical heights: Nevada Governor Bob Miller complained: "Too often we seem too willing to accept underachieving standards for a Beavis, a Butthead, or a Bart Simpson . . . The nation's CEOs are fed up with passive acceptance of mediocrity." ("You can forget Goals 2000," 1996, p. 6)

One of Canada's Education Ministers recently declared – unaware that he was being videotaped – that it was his intention as Minister to "create a crisis" in public education; he admitted that precipitating a crisis would require some "skill," and that to achieve his goal he would have to be "more negative" than the facts would warrant (B.C. Teachers' Federation [BCTF], 1996). Some of Corporate Canada's leaders have been more than prepared to assist the Minister in nourishing a manufactured crisis. Addressing a national consultation of education "partners" organized by the Council of Ministers of Education, Canada, the editor-in-chief of Canada's "national newspaper," The Globe and Mail, mused that the "lackadaisical" and "crude" characteristics of public education in Canada would be "scandalous and bankrupting if applied to the design and manufacture of auto parts" (Thorsell, 1996, p. 3). Like his American counterparts, Thorsell advised "looking to market forces" as the means of systemic restructuring. He subsequently printed the text of his speech in his own newspaper – it is not every critic who has such ready access to the press. Consultation participants formally demanded that, given the many errors of fact that appeared in the article, the Ministers respond in defense of the systems they govern. The Ministers of Education declined (Jonasson & Morris, 1996).

Mr. ThorsellThorsell's attack was not unique. Criticism of Canada's education system routinely focuses on comparisons of student achievement selectively presented and often egregiously distorted (Ireland, 1995). In a 1500-word condensation of education's problems and solutions, business-education activist Byron Price (1995) misrepresents Canada's spending on education, teachers' salaries, class size, the length of the school year and student results on international tests in just two paragraphs. He concludes that competition and customer choice would be maximized by making public each school's "records" on "specialization, scholastic achievement, comparative student progress, discipline, and ethos" (p. 12). How the latter would be measured is not explored, although "ethos indicators" have no doubt been generated. Whether they would be valid, however, is unclear. As Bracey (1994) observes, "there appears to be an inverse relationship between the importance of an educational outcome and its measurability: trivial outcomes are easy to measure, crucial ones defy instrumentation" (p. 7). He might have added that what is easy to measure is a delight to report.

Media oversimplifications of test results, featuring headlines such as "schools must smarten up" (Bell & le Riche, 1995, p. 4) have lent credence to high-profile corporate criticism of education. In part, the media's distortions of education's weaknesses and accomplishments explain growing public receptivity to the myth of school failure; the manufactured crisis becomes a crisis of confidence rather than one of school quality. Books such as Pandora's Box (Calvert & Kuehn, 1993) and Class Warfare (Barlow & Robertson, 1994) are among those that track the criticisms and deconstruct the myths used to prop up the claim of Canadian education's failure, but they also argue that discrediting schools is a key component of the reform agenda that would transform and privatize the institutions Canadians have built over many decades. The neo-liberal premises of deregulation, privatization and competition are in direct conflict with public education and the values that sustain it: "The assault on public schools is not an isolated movement. It is part of, and grows out of, the assault on universality, and the privatization of social security, and democracy itself. A public education system cannot survive as an island in a sea of privatized services." (Barlow, 1996, p. 5) If public education is to be sacrificed to advance a market-driven state, then first its quality must be discredited. The public will be more amenable to losing its institutions once convinced that they are worthless as well as unaffordable and uncompetitive.

As public opinion in support of schools has begun to falter, citizens have become more open to expert solutions – as long as the experts are not educators and the solutions are not complex. The private sector lives or dies by focusing exclusively on "results"; perhaps schools could be dragged into the competitive realities of the present by adopting the same focus. It is not surprising that the broadsides fired at public education by Mr. Thorsell occurred as part of an event convened to discuss "accountability." No strategy is more potent than determining how success will be described and measured, unless it is to control how that success will be reported and interpreted. Consistently used as a proxy for "measuring outcomes," the term accountability is a favourite of education's business-suited critics, some of whom have ingenuously professed disinterest in what is to be measured, so long as the measurements were standardized, frequent, inexpensive and easy-to-understand (ECC, 1992). Using the language of accountability and excellence, in the early 1990's Corporate Canada began a successful lobby that demanded a system of standardized, national testing. Without having to be explicit about the reform of educational content it had in mind, Corporate Canada was able to alter the curriculum simply by ensuring the high-stakes testing of certain kinds of outcomes. Conveniently, the content areas they wished schools to stress were those tested most cheaply and efficiently: mathematics and sciences. The well-documented associated effects of test-dominated education systems (Meaghan & Casas, 1995), including the placing of greater emphasis on the subject areas being tested (Herman & Golan, 1993), could serve to "rebalance" the curriculum while circumventing tedious debate. High-stakes testing ensured that those domains less easy to quantify would receive less attention, not only in planning documents, but in the day-to-day life of the classroom.

Results of high-stakes standardized tests have been used to leverage changes to curricular content and process across the country. Catch-22 applies: provinces faring less well on interprovincial tests, even by a margin not exceeding statistical error, were told that "reforms were on their way" to improve results. When Manitoba students performed particularly well on one set of exams, the Minister used the occasion to denounce the mediocrity the tests countenanced, and similarly promised that "reforms were on their way" (Robertson, G. 1995, p. 5). Among the most significant of these reforms has been a weakening of jurisdictional prerogatives that would have been unthinkable a decade earlier. The adoption of national standardized tests is one of the factors that has lead to growing support for the idea that Canada "needs" a national standardized curriculum on which to base these tests, despite decades of jealously-guarded provincial jurisdiction over curriculum (Bacon, 1994; Livingstone, Hart, & Davie, 1995). In 1993, two projects initiated by Ministry consortia of the Western and Eastern provinces to develop common mathematics and science curricula were begun, violating long-standing protocols for involving teachers and community members in curriculum design (Basarab, 1996). In her assessment of current curriculum reform in Canada, Basarab concludes that "curriculum change is not being driven by actual deficiencies in curriculum; instead, curriculum is being adjusted to meet predetermined outcomes in the name of accountability" (p. 11). Indeed, as part of this study, Education Ministry officials surveyed to describe curriculum reforms in their jurisdictions answered in the language of accountabilism. Asked to describe how curricula (rather than students) were being evaluated, Ontario's Ministry responded: "Although the curriculum is not yet fully developed, there are several ways in which accountability will exist. The regular testing [of students] by the Education Quality and Accountability Office [a new, arms-length government body with significant corporate representation] will provide a public means of ensuring accountability." (p. 25)

Increasingly, education's "accountability" extends to the health of the economy. Politicians at all levels have encouraged the public to see "skills" – that is to say, young people and their education – as the key economic problem facing Canada. Both Prime Ministerial candidates in Canada's last Federal election attempted to divert inconvenient questions about the performance of the economy and how it happened that a "jobless recovery" could simultaneously fuel record-breaking corporate profits and record-breaking unemployment. Prime Minister Jean Chrétien – a politician more indebted to Corporate Canada than any before him (Cléroux, 1996) – just weeks before his election, claimed in a campaign speech that "[t]here are 300,000 jobs vacant in Canada because our young people lack the relevant skills training" (Barlow & Robertson, 1994, p. 46). In the spirit of investigative reporting, the Canadian Broadcasting Corporation (CBC) pursued the basis of this claim and found no support for either his estimate or this alleged cause of job vacancies, and the comment was purged from subsequent campaign speeches. Nonetheless, the myth has been repeated before and since, and has taken on the status of fact, demonstrating Cameron's claim ". . . that for neo-liberals, repetition replaces logical demonstration; truth becomes what the media repeat over and over" (Cameron, 1996, p. 5).

The "skills deficiency" argument still fuels much debate about public education, and justifies re-tooling the curriculum to give greater prominence to "skill sets" related to employment. Turning the public towards their schools – while simultaneously blaming schools for having created the nation's economic woes – has its advantages, both for corporations and for politicians. Blaming workers, and those who prepare them, for high unemployment distracts the public from expecting governments to deliver on their promises to create jobs, and from scrutinizing the advantages which accrue to employers during times of high unemployment and employee insecurity (Menzies, 1996). To a citizenry reeling from rapid social change and the disappearance of jobs, the argument for prosperity through school reform, although feeble, is at least familiar. Certainly, it is easier to blame schools than to wade through analyses explaining the relationships among fiscal and economic policies, price stability, interest rates, unemployment and trade policies.

THE CORPORATE CURRICULUM

In 1992, The Conference Board of Canada, on behalf of its one hundred corporate members, began to promote its "Employability Skills Profile": "the generic skills, attitudes and behaviours that employers look for in new recruits" including the willingness to show "initiative, energy and persistence to get the job done," to "listen to understand and learn" and to "understand and work within the culture of the group" (Conference Board of Canada, undated).

The twenty-six employability skills have been treated reverentially by those designing curriculum reform; they are directly cited, for example, in documents such as Ontario's Common Curriculum (Basarab, 1996). In practical application, this employability skills focus has resulted in a greater emphasis on technology, the use and production of "business English," entrepreneurship as a subject of study, a growing emphasis on "work-study" placements, and, above all, a concentration on outcomes (Basarab, 1996). As part of Ontario's secondary school reform initiative (known as the "business plan" for education), Education Minister Snobelen has advocated a mandatory "jobs-for-credit" component, occupying up to one third of high school course hours, saying this would ensure young people could "learn job skills, learn the value of showing up, learn how to work in teams,[and] learn how to serve people" (Ibbitson, 1996, p. A1). He didn't mention that it would also ensure lower corporate taxes: the Government had just introduced a "cooperative education tax credit" that would allow cooperating private sector employers to write-off up to $1,000 per student placement (McCay, Duff & Company, 1996). The Ottawa Citizen newspaper pointed out that working for credits, especially when legitimate job-preparation and adult retraining programs had been cancelled, was little more than a push to "insert several new career-oriented courses into an already shrinking high school curriculum" in response to the myth that "young people don't know enough about the "real" world inhabited by computer programmers, insurance agents and journalists" ("Education: Idea lacks credit," 1996, p. A12).

Students, parents and editorial writers may be dubious, but representatives of the business community seem close to getting what they have asked for: an unending supply of cheap, flexible, pliable workers prepared to "think on their feet, learn on the job, and take on new challenges," in the words of the Conference Board of Canada (1993a). Put more colloquially, Gary Johncox, vice-president of McMillan Bloedel, a giant forestry products corporation, told an education-business conference that if he had his way, only six core subjects would be taught in high school: "(1) English, (2) Mathematics, (3) Physics, (4) Chemistry, (5) The importance of showing up for work, (6) How to get along with others. With only half my tongue in my cheek, I think we get all the geography, law, ethics, and probably more than enough biology from TV" (Barlow & Robertson, 1994 p. 123).

Ironically, Mr. Johncox's opinions about what is worth knowing seem closer to realization than the multiple (and often less tangible) goals most Canadians want their schools to pursue (Ontario Royal Commission on Learning, 1995). Argued on its merits, the narrowing of curriculum and its re-alignment with tenuous employability skills seems unlikely to have prevailed; in 1994 a public opinion survey of Ontarians concluded that "a plurality . . . think that people generally have more education than jobs require," and a majority thought "the failure of the economy to generate jobs is the main cause of youth unemployment" (Livingstone, Hart & Davie, 1995, pp. 27, 31).

While "skills" may be the issue that receives the most attention, the curriculum alignment that is sought by corporate Canada is not intended to serve only economic and political goals, but social and structural ones as well. When a public high school aligns itself with American Express, (CBO Radio, 1996) winning the right to pilot a "Travel and Tourism" curriculum by outbidding its competitors – using "existing resources" and "volunteer teacher time," as bargaining chips-more than skills is involved. When the price of receiving an American Express Travel and Tourism certificate requires that fully one third of a student's academic credits be related to the travel industry – and when neither students nor teachers are able to admit that there are tradeoffs involved – more has shifted than the curriculum.

To the extent that resistance to such corporate adventures has been raised, it has been voiced by those dismissed as representing special interests. Control is the key issue whenever terrain is contested, and it is clear that the neoliberal education reform agenda will proceed much more smoothly if those closest to the complexities of education are frozen out of public debate. This shunning is made palatable to the public by repeated accusations that some combination of teachers, bureaucracies, politicians or teacher unions are guilty of ruining schools (Lawton, Freedman, & Robertson, 1995). Most governments have skilfully ensured that the "education establishment" has been excluded, by staging consultations which ignore informed input, by encouraging the public to see educators' opinions as the bleatings of self-interest, or (as in the recent case of the province of New Brunswick), simply by dissolving elected school boards in favour of appointed parent advisors (Saunders, 1996).

Shifting power from educators and elected decision-makers to representatives of each schools' "clients" is not only consistent with a market-place ideology, it ensures local decision-makers will be isolated and more inclined to worry about school level issues than macro-level policies. Parental influence on schools, now facilitated in legislation in every Canadian province, (Alberta Teachers' Association [ATA], 1996) follows the pattern established in Great Britain and New Zealand. "Parent power" sells well in a climate of institutional distrust and populism; it poses no threat to corporate interests now convinced that ordinary citizens have absorbed their messages about competitiveness and the need to control and shrink the public sector. The devolution of increased responsibility to the level of the individual school constitutes exactly the kind of deregulation corporations seek; it maximizes the potential for competition; it brings a marketplace paradigm to decisions about what schools should attempt to accomplish. Parent governance of schools provides a starting-place for transferring the expense of public education to "clients" (i.e. parents) thus, in time, shrinking even further the expense to corporations posed by general taxation.

This characterization of parent governance hardly describes the motives of most parents who want to play a more active role in their schools; they willingly give of their scarce time to make the school a better place, not to serve an agenda of deregulation. Most would be astonished to learn that the World Bank is trying to leverage a greater role for parents in education decisions; the World Bank sees parents as key players in counterbalancing the "vested interests" who might object to introducing school-by-school competition and a more market-driven education system in developing countries (1994). Apparently, the World Bank believes that when the future of their children is alleged to be at stake, parents will be most prepared to make compromises.

THE PARTNERSHIP COMPROMISE

While corporations continue to seek to influence the macro-issues facing public education, many are attempting to increase their corporations' visibility within individual schools as well. This is where a corporate presence is most evident to teachers, students and parents, and often it is welcomed. Teachers rightly assume an implicit political imperative to be more responsive to the overtures of business; the school which has managed to snag a corporate partner is regarded by central administrators and trustees as being progressive and "on the right track."

Research conducted for Canada's influential newspaper, The Financial Post, on business-education partnerships claims to have documented that "the barriers between business and the educational establishment are breaking down" (1994, p. 8). Ninety-nine per cent of business respondents said business could play "a major role in improving the quality of education"; 98 per cent of school boards responding agreed. The Post praised this new spirit of harmony and its contrast with "what in the past has seemed an almost perpetual state of confrontation," a time when "schools [were] perceived as uncommonly anxious to resist the "taint" of any commercial influence." The Post's coverage neglected to mention that survey respondents on the education side were exclusively school boards, even though Boards indicated that school principals and teachers were most likely to be involved directly with partnerships. On the corporate side, 88 per cent of respondents said they were "active" in education; 96 per cent of school boards said they were involved or planned to be involved in a corporate partnership. Yet only 16 per cent of corporations had a public education policy, and among those, only one in three had consulted with educators in its development. Twenty-seven per cent of school boards had policies; 80 per cent had developed them in consultation with the business community or their "partners."

The lack of cogent policy regarding the ground rules of partnerships is either an expression of high trust or considerable naivete on the part of school districts. It is unlikely that the same Boards would approach negotiations with their employees in such a laissez-faire manner. In this policy vacuum, it is the individual school, often through the office of the principal, that is left to work out the ground rules and the details. Yet as Ekelund (1994) observes, "[a]ny business that considers entering into a partnership with a school will know what it wants to gain from the merger . . . [h]istory is strewn with lessons detailing the consequences of negotiations between a party that knows what it wants and a second party driven by need." (p. 121)

According to the Post's survey, motives for entering into partnerships vary, as do perceptions of who should benefit from the arrangement. Eighty-one per cent of corporations rated the public relations value of partnerships to be of greatest benefit; 43 per cent believed they were contributing to a better-educated and trained workforce. School boards chose "increased ties with the community" as their primary benefit (at 94 per cent); gaining access to "material and support" they could otherwise not afford was checked off by 75 per cent of respondents. Both groups rated technology, mathematics and science as desirable areas of concentration for partnerships; however, while Boards budgeted 33 per cent of their partnership dollars towards special needs programs, only 1 per cent of corporate dollars were directed to this area.

Other needs are apparently unmet: Boards would like to see corporations more active in developing "teacher resources, tools and materials" for use in the classroom. The survey analyst suggested that corporations' apparent lack of interest in the humanities, and school districts' needs in this area, suggest "a new area for partnership activities."

Teachers may not support the whole package of educational reforms proposed by business, but they understandably react to what is most immediate. Student need is more tangible than corporate greed, and it is this need which blurs the lines. It is one thing to reject an overture from a corporation which supplies "free" technology for an unsavoury price (and nets a tax writeoff); it is another to realize the choice is between tainted technology or none at all. Often it comes down to bartering ethics for resources.

In 1994, the large Toronto Board of Education entered into a one million dollar agreement with Pepsi-Cola Canada, giving Pepsi a three-year exclusive contract for drink and juice-vending machines within the District (Duffy, 1994). Pepsi negotiated the distribution of its own videos on substance abuse and the importance of staying in school, although it did not succeed in having Pepsi declared "the official drink of Toronto schools." Trustees defended their decision despite student, parent and even national media criticism by claiming financial hardship. An envious trustee from a neighbouring district thought the deal made sense, even if its ethics were a bit dubious; if the arrangement meant revenue, she admitted "her principles would have to go out the window a little bit" (Warburton, 1994). In response to a stinging column in a national newsmagazine, Pepsi-Cola's CEO defended the deal: "An initiative like this demonstrates the fruitfulness of enterprising, innovative partnerships between the public and private sectors. Regarding Canadian education, we are proud to be part of the solution" (McEachern, 1994, p. 4).

The arrangement between Pepsi-Co and the Toronto Board is perhaps most notable for its quite transparent quid-pro-quo of partnership in return for profit. Other partnerships – now more common than not at the high school level, and growing in numbers at the elementary school level – take different forms. (Dubé, 1995; Ontario Secondary School Teachers' Federation [OSSTF], 1995) In several schools, the fast-food retailer Subway "sponsors" the peer-counselling program, but the public relations value is purchased at the bargain price of a few year-end sandwiches. Other partnerships have resulted in banks setting up weekly banking days in elementary schools (complete with take-home brochures for Mom and Dad). Many partnerships involve work placements for students, guest speakers from the "partnering" corporation for school events, and some include the use of curricular "supplements" (Lewington, 1996).

Educators struggle – often unsuccessfully – to reconcile corporate goals with the goals of education. In a discussion paper prepared by the Nova Scotia Teachers' Union on partnerships, the authors recognize:

[that] (b)usiness is ultimately concerned with the maximizing of profits . . . business must see a return on investment through increased economic activity either by a growth in goodwill or through a more efficient utilization of

resources. Second, business is concerned with the employability of graduates as described, for example, in the Conference Board of Canada's Statement of Employability Skills (Association of Teachers of English of Nova
Scotia [ATENS], 1996, p. 9).

The paper goes on to state, "(s)chools are ultimately concerned with the development of students who are not only employable, but also autonomous, responsible,
moral individuals who are effective members of society." Rather than dwelling on
any inherent contradictions between these sets of goals, the paper simply concludes
that "ultimately, the concerns of schools and businesses are the same" as long as
one takes "an extremely long view" of their convergence. (p. 9)

A newsletter published by the Faculty of Education of Queens University puts
a blunter twist on what is at stake. One article testifies to the success of "Bird's
Hill School" in rural Manitoba, a school that has entered into dozens of partnerships, and as the result of national recognition (again, through the Conference
Board of Canada), it has been hailed as an exemplary model of an "entrepreneurial"
approach to school improvement (Lee, 1996). The school's "partnerships spokesperson," presumably a teacher, advises attention to values – "if educational values
are too different from business values it may be difficult to work together" – but where
differences exist, it is clear that education must do all the accommodating, even if
this means distancing itself from its own roots.

> In our dealings, we have never represented ourselves as part of the educational
> establishment. We have represented ourselves as being independent-minded
> and entrepreneurial. The terms we use are business terms. We describe
> ourselves as educational entrepreneurs staking our limited resources on find-
> ing solutions to the needs in the educational marketplace. (p. 4, [insert])

One can avoid disappointments by knowing one's place, he continues: "Even the
best of partners must sometimes make a choice between keeping a commitment
to you or to a customer. The customer wins hands down!" (p. 4, [insert])

Even schools prepared to look and sound more like their prospective business
partners still have to compete with each other to snag a particularly desirable
"mate". Huybreghts (1996) refers to such arrangements as "marriages," and says
Districts and schools "have to be prepared to give up some decision-making
autonomy and allow business to access students and teachers" (p. 27). For example,
"the few school boards with district policies on school-business partnerships usually deny companies on-site advertising, but companies expect the goodwill and
word-of-mouth exposure generated by their contributions to pay dividends in
increased sales" (p. 28). A software spokesperson explains, "Schools are basically
ignorant of business. I understand that boards and schools have to be careful in
their relationships with business, but they need to develop a culture that emphasizes
a certain amount of hard work on the part of a business should bring a reward"
(p. 29).

Corporate Canada rejects any suggestion that business-education partnerships
are usurious. David McCamus, formerly CEO of Xerox Canada, sees them as
providing reciprocal benefits:

A successful partnership is a two-way relationship. Business can give students experience on sophisticated, high-tech equipment, which is beyond the scope of the school. The schools can help business by enabling students to develop their entrepreneurial skills, and their sense of enterprise, as well as by developing skills and attitudes necessary for success in the world of work (Conference Board of Canada, 1993b).

To McCamus, everything from exposing students to technology to developing new skills and attitudes is framed as "helping business." If education is to be "helped," it is to be helped to serve business better. Curiously, students' interests, if they are thought of at all, are presumed to be synonymous with the interests of employers.

Recently, I was telephoned by a local senior high school student who wanted my opinions on school-business "partnerships." Motivated by duty and the lack of a convenient excuse, I began the conversation I had assumed, paternalistically, would be awkward and superficial. Instead, it served as a window into students' lived experience of the transformation of their schools, their culture, and even their furniture. Toward the end of the conversation, I asked the student why he had chosen this topic for his research paper. He told me that one day he had walked to his buddies' usual hangout in the foyer of the school. Where once there had been a student gathering place, furnished with imitation park benches, there was now nothing but empty space. He asked his principal about the disappearance of the benches. "They're gone," she said, "because it's not very business-like to have students sitting around on benches talking to each other. Our partner is [high tech transnational] Corel. Do you think Corel wants its employees to be just sitting around when they should be on the job?"

Stung by criticism that some kinds of corporate involvement in education were bald exploitation, the Conference Board of Canada, corporate mentor of partnerships, developed "Ethical Guidelines" to shape business-education arrangements (1995). Yet it seems unlikely that statements intended to leave partners "free to express their individuality" and to "agree on what the guidelines mean to them" have much clout. Indeed, the Conference Board recently declined to join a group that came together to fight an attempt to resurrect the Youth News Network (YNN) (Canadian Teachers' Federation [CTF], 1996).

Modelled on American Chris WhittleWhittle's Channel One, the promoters of YNN were allegedly offering "free" technology – a satellite dish and TV monitors-to schools which would sign on to YNN. The first stage of programming would feature nine and one-half minutes of YNN-produced news, interspersed with two and one-half minutes of youth-targeted commercial advertising (Krueger, 1996). Schools were to commit their students to daily, uninterrupted viewing; teachers were not to be allowed to excuse students nor to mute the commercials. A grass-roots coalition opposed to YNN, along with sustained national media interest, drew public attention to YNN and the questionable manoeuvres of its promoter. The Conference Board declined to denounce YNN, apparently seeing no contravention of its "ethical partnership" guidelines. This outcome casts some doubt on the potency of statements the Conference Board proudly describes as being grounded in "utility ethics."

MODELLING THE MENTORS

Funding cutbacks ensure that partnerships are thriving, but there may not be enough partners to go around. Schools wishing to be judged worthy are trying to look more like the partners they wish to court. Nowhere is this more evident than in the attempt to import Albert Deming's Total Quality Management approach to enterprise; money, energy and a great deal of teacher time are being invested in achieving certification for Canadian schools as Quality Assurance sites. Businesses using TQM describe their conversion as the process of building "a strong corporate culture which encourages the workforce to accept the company's goals as its own" (Barlow & Robertson, 1994 p. 89).

Bensimon (1995) summarizes the three precepts of TQM: Quality is defined by customer satisfaction; Quality is the reduction of variation; and Quality must be measurable. Her reading of the move to TQM by American post-secondary institutions, fostered as it is by corporate giants like IBM, is that the "customer" to be satisfied is not the student but the corporation as future employer, that reduction in variation is the last thing to which an inclusive system serving diverse needs should aspire, and that selecting goals on the basis of their ease of measurement is detrimental to the setting and valuing of other goals. Definitions of quality, she points out, "always reflect particular interests, values, and beliefs about goodness, and these do not always benefit all members of the community in the same ways." (p. 595)

The "Quality commitment" is far from superficial, indeed it comes with a built-in analysis of cause and effect. As promotional materials explain, it is assumed that "most quality problems derive from poor processes or poor delivery or both" ("Quality in Action," undated). This emphasis on the "downstream" factors, of course, hides the corporate-unfriendly reality that it is "upstream" factors, particularly the characteristics of the students served by the school, that most accurately predict student success.

According to a Total Quality supporter and one of Canada's leading school district directors, Veronica Lacey (1994), both just-in-time manufacturing and the concept of zero defects can be imported to education:

> In my view, education needs to approach its challenges by subjecting our policies and procedures to the same kind of fundamental scrutiny that business has employed in responding to the changing conditions within which the world now operates. The half-hearted attempts which have been made to date are not sufficient. (p. 6)

If it is only a matter of effort, school systems will prove their mettle. At least one Ontario school district is offering product guarantees (Cosgrove, 1995), first reported as an entrepreneurial leap by the Los Angeles Unified School District, and now being considered by a number of other Canadian districts. Should the student "product" turn out to be deficient, in the view of his or her employer, then retraining is guaranteed. It is worth noting that it is only the employer who has access to consumer protection; should the student, or the student's parent, be unhappy with the student's school experience, no retooling is available. This kind of arrangement perpetuates the schools-as-marketplace paradigm, and vests employers, rather than citizens, with the status of "customer." This matters a great deal when, as they say in business, it's the customer who should be in the driver's seat.

Bringing schools closer to the customer is becoming a physical as well as a philosophical matter. Following the lead of large American corporations, at least one Canadian employer has negotiated a work-place school, referred to by the media as a "brave new innovation" (Mitchell, 1995). Alberta Government Telephones, a private company, negotiated a school for the children of its managers and employees on site, thus creating what is probably a Canadian first – an entire student body with at least one parent employed. Despite promises that it will maintain a hands-off relationship, questions about the involvement of the employer in curriculum and staffing raise some obvious concerns. The district will have to be responsive to certain sensibilities. Is this school likely to be lead by a union activist? Is its curriculum likely to be technologically "advanced"? Will the employer ensure that these students, at least, enjoy reasonable class sizes? Who is the "customer" of this "brave new innovation" and what is the logical next step?

Still, it is not difficult to find corporations or schools willing to defend partnerships as having provided genuine benefit to both students and partners. Certainly, the neighbourhood enterprise that donates time and energy to its local school does not deserve to be condemned as the dupe of the interests of transnational capital. Good intentions, however, must not mask the consequences of engineering school reform around either deep pockets or charitable impulses. To allow private interests to dominate education policy and practice is to retreat from the hard-won progress of years of democracy. To allow private interests to demand public policies that increase the number of students at risk, and then to profit from the public relations value of "rescuing" them is not just cynical, it is unconscionable.

SHAPING THE CUSTOMER

The increasing North American interest in charter, voucher and other quasi-private schools has been fuelled, in large part, by a common goal shared by apparently disparate special interest groups. The religious Right and ideological ultraconservatives resist and suspect the role of the state in anything as important as the education of children, although it is fair to assume their preferred curricula would differ substantially. Neoliberals are attracted by the prospect of reshaping a public institution according to private sector and marketplace principles; the increasingly taxed – both emotionally and economically – middle class yearns for an end to what they have been told is a wasteful, bureaucratic swamp of indifference and self-interest (Robertson, 1995b). The "revolt of the elites" (Lasch, 1995) includes their abandonment of any sense of attachment to, or responsibility for those relegated to public schools. Overwhelmed teachers yearn to escape the edu-babble of conflicting and unworkable policy directives in the face of decreasing resources. Politicians see their electability contingent on reducing debt. Everyone seems to have something to gain if public education can be culled from the public space and edged, delivered or dragged into the private space.

The gains could be quite tangible. To some, the $5.5 billion spent annually in Canada on public education is not an expense, or even an investment, but a business opportunity. A few high profile corporate misfortunes-most notably the American company Education Alternatives, Inc. – suggest that the business of running for-profit "public" schools may not turn out to be easy or lucrative ("Privatization Experiment in Hartford," 1996). Yet even corporations not much interested in the messy work of running schools are attracted to the "business within a business" opportunities these ventures offer. Chris WhittleWhittle (best known for his Channel One venture) is said to be intending to set up mini-malls within selected schools, providing retailing opportunities for those selling books, videos, CDs, children's clothing and the like. Says Whittle, "the biggest contribution business can make to education is to make education a business" (Barlow & Robertson, 1994 p. 182). Taco Bell and other fast food outlets see this privatization of what was once public space as a windfall ("Taco Bell," 1995). McDonald's is negotiating with some British Columbia schools to compete with school cafeterias (and provide unidentified education services) for an undisclosed sum of cash (A school principal expressed surprise at the newsworthiness of this transaction: "I think they're just being good corporate citizens," he said.) (Helm, 1994).

Both quasi- and full-privatization of schools are so attractive that corporations are prepared to put their political clout behind any move that will allow them more access to schools and to the enormous market potential children represent. It is in this climate that increasingly resource-starved classroom teachers have turned to corporate-sponsored contests and curriculum resources to augment their students' diets. When you are hungry, even a Big Mac begins to look good.

Some corporate-written materials intended for student use are seeking quite blatantly to imprint brand names and to influence students' consumption patterns. Campbell's "Prego Thickness Experiment" promises to teach "scientific thinking" by having students compare brand-name spaghetti sauces (Karpatkin & Holmes, 1995). Other sponsors pursue slightly more subtle goals, such as shaping students' opinions regarding the forestry industry or the role of banks in the economy. Exxon distributes a videotape "Scientists and the Alaska Oil Spill" that claims the company's cleanup of the Valdez oil spill was flawless (Winans, 1996). Proctor and Gamble's curriculum on the environment claims that it uses clear-cutting "because it most clearly mimics nature's own processes" (Shenk, 1994). The Ontario Farm Animal Council (OFAC) –i.e. meat producers – has a unique take on vegetarianism to be shared with students, along with posters of pop culture heroes who advocate the use of animals in research (OFAC, 1992). School mail-boxes are full of corporate-written materials that are becoming more slick, more appealing and more "teacher-proof" than ever before. Like everyone else, teachers are becoming more inured to commercialization, and in their time-deprived situations, more prepared to trade a corporate logo for a turnkey lesson plan.

This fact is not lost on some promoters, who, at least among themselves, can be less restrained about their ambitions. A two-day conference in Toronto appealing to senior-level corporate executives (with a registration fee of $1171.65 US) taught "Creative Kid-Targeted Marketing Strategies" by exposing participants to "winning tactics, case studies and hard facts from top Canadian and American companies" (Robertson, 1995a). The promotional brochure boasted:

> Learn how and why you should use school-based programs to support your kid marketing activities! Leverage partnership programs to reach kids! Hear how to make sure your product positioning idea is strong enough to be targeted to kids, not gatekeepers for kids! (p. 10)

This is a tricky business, marketers were warned; there is money to be made, but first "you must win the hearts of your customers." In a workshop titled, "Using school-based programs to support your kids' marketing activities," participants were told not only "how school-based programs can be parleyed into product launches and kids clubs," but, "how new Canadian education developments will impact on marketing." It is this all-important public policy climate which will determine whether corporations can take full advantage of their 2 to 12-year-old customers (Robertson, 1995a).

HEARTS, MINDS, AND PUBLIC POLICY

If public education is to avoid capture by the special interests of corporations, those of us whose chief preoccupations are not stock exchange fluctuations must be more explicit about setting boundaries. We must restate that schools are intended to serve all citizens, and as such have no "privileged" clients. The continuous dialogue on renewing schools must engage Corporate voices – but just as it must engage the voices of all individuals and groups with an interest in the success of schools.

Corporations wishing to contribute to this success can begin by paying fair taxes. They can advocate for a vigorous public sector – the strength of which, in Canada, has been responsible for much corporate profit. Corporations can advance public policy that supports healthy children, stable families and literate homes. They can ensure that their employees, many of whom are parents, can fulfill that role with fewer penalties and less conflict. They can fund arms-length research on promising educational innovations and their implementation. They can create jobs from their prosperity and give students hope for the future. They can celebrate our national good fortune to have inherited an education system that is among the best in the world. They can use their power to strengthen public education – or cause its collapse.

The neoliberal reform of public education is advancing only in part because of corporate power and political advantage. It also benefits from the paradox of short-term private good co-existing with long-term public peril. In other words, at the level of individual experience, much of what has been described could be viewed positively: parents are unlikely to speculate on the end-product of educational reform when their child describes his classroom's exciting new "donated" computer; a teacher frustrated with an inflexible bureaucracy is attracted to the promises of "empowerment" offered by "partnered" schools. The child who is rewarded with a free pizza for reading the most books is not perplexed by the long-term consequences of reducing reading to a competitive activity; the student who enjoys her co-op placement in a high-tech setting thinks of résumé possibilities, not of the dubious link between training and employment.

The corporatization of education shares this paradox with some of the other great problems facing society. Many environmental problems, from disappearing rainforests to excessive energy consumption, are rooted in the same dilemma: short-term private advantage adds up to long-term collective devastation. To the extent that progress has been made on environmental issues, it has been achieved by exposing this paradox, and by calling on the public to recognize the links between individual choices and collective consequences. This strategy has been potent if not perfect. It rests on a conviction that there is fundamental goodness in ordinary citizens, and the belief that once we as citizens, rather than as consumers, come to understand the connections across issues, we will forgo convenience and short-term advantage in the interests of the common good. This may sound naive in a climate so disabused of its idealism, but what is left of public education if its champions become as cynical as its critics?

Those of us whose vocation is public education must find our voices. As John Ralston Saul so brilliantly writes in The Unconscious Civilization, the ideology of corporatism too often begets a debilitating passivity in the face of crisis (1995). The temptation to dismiss corporate-dominated education – or corporate-dominated society, for that matter – as merely paradoxical is to fall victim to the comforting seduction of denial. To see it as inevitable is to forget that no society has been asked to choose corporatism, nor the fascism of markets, as its deity or its government. It has "snuck up on us," so to speak, its way paved by leaders who either deny their intentions or who are themselves blind to their own ideologies, including the ideology of inevitability.

Two hundred years ago, William Pitt said "Necessity is the plea for every infringement of human freedom. It is the argument of tyrants; it is the creed of slaves" (Saul, 1995, p. 111). Democracy is threatened when we are told by the tyrants that we have no choice; democracy dies when we come to believe that this is true. If education seeks to illuminate, or (more modestly) to make the apparent more transparent, then unmasking the ideology of the markets and their grasp on us is a compelling matter, but alone these insights are of little value. We must reclaim the consciousness that requires us to own up to the presence of the choices before us. Pitt's creed of slaves is a sorry excuse for a millennial mantra for public education.

REFERENCES

Alberta Teachers' Association. (1996). *Agenda-driven governance.* Ottawa, ON: Canadian Teachers' Federation.

Association of Teachers of English of Nova Scotia [ATENS]. (1996, January). *A shared vision: A report on education-business partnerships.* Halifax, NS: Nova Scotia Teachers' Union.

Bacon, A. (1994, November 2). *Open letter to the Honourable Jean Garon, Chair, The Council of Ministers of Education, Canada.* Ottawa: Canadian Teachers' Federation.

Barlow, M. (1996, April 28). *The winds of change.* Presentation to the Women in Education Central Regional Symposium of the Canadian Teachers' Federation in Aylmer, Quebec.

Barlow, M., & Campbell, B. (1995). *Straight through the heart: How the liberals abandoned the just society.* Toronto, ON: Harper Collins Publishers Limited.

Barlow, M., & Robertson, H.-j. (1994). *Class warfare: The assault on Canada's schools.* Toronto: Key Porter Books.

Basarab, C. (1996). *Truncation of curriculum: In search of accountability.* Ottawa: Canadian Teachers' Federation.

Bell, R., & le Riche, T. (1995, September 28). Schools must smarten up: Dropout rate too high, Math grades too low. *The Edmonton Sun,* 4.

Bensimon, E. M. (1995, Winter). Total quality management in the academy: A rebellious reading. *Harvard Educational Review,* 593–611.

Berliner, D. C., & Biddle, B. J. (1995). *The manufactured crisis: Myths, fraud and the attack on america's public schools.* Don Mills, ON: Addison-Wesley Publishing Company.

Bertrand, L. (1993, May 5). Canada's schools failing the grade: Business leaders. *The Montreal Gazette.*

Bracey, G. W. (1994, January). A critical look at standards and assessments. *Principal,* 7.

Brooks, N. (1995). *Left vs. right.* Ottawa, ON: Canadian Centre for Policy Alternatives.

B.C. Teachers' Federation [BCTF]. (1996). *Inventing crisis: The erosion of confidence in canadian public education.* Ottawa, ON: Canadian Teachers' Federation

Calvert, J., & Kuehn, L. (1993). *Pandora's box. Corporate power, free trade and canadian education.* Toronto, ON: Our Schools Our Selves Education Foundation.

Cameron, D. (1996, May). Mad economist's disease. *Canadian Forum,* 5.

Campbell, M. (1995, December 2). Wonks. *The Globe and Mail,* p. D1-D2.

Canadian Principal. (1996, March). Privatization experiment in Hartford comes to an end. *Canadian Principal,* 7(6), 1–2.

Canadian Teachers' Federation [CTF]. (1996, February 14). *Teachers don't want youth news network.* Press release. Ottawa: Author.

CBO Radio (1996, May 21, 5:17 p.m.). Travel and tourism academy. *All in a day.* [Transcript of cassette]. Interview with Cairine Wilson High School in partnership with American Express. Cassette obtained from Bowden's Electronic Media.

Chesterton, G. K. (1936). *As I was saying: An anthology of G.K. Chesterton's varied works.* Grand Rapids, MI: William B. Eerdman's Publishing Company.

Cléroux, R. (1996, April). The party of corporate Canada. *Canadian Forum,* N847, 15–18.

Conference Board of Canada, (undated) *Employability skills profile.* [Brochure]. Ottawa, ON: Author.

Conference Board of Canada. (1993a, April). *Matching education to the needs of society. A vision statement working paper.* Ottawa: Author.

Conference Board of Canada. (1993b, June). *Reaching for success.* [Conference brochure]. Ottawa: Author.

Conference Board of Canada. (1995). *Ethical guidelines for business-education partnerships.* [Draft]. Ottawa: Author.

Cosgrove, G. (1995, May 31, 12:10 p.m.). *CBO-FM radio noon.* [Transcript of cassette.] Interview with G. Cosgrove, Director of Education of the Frontenac-Lennox and Addington County Roman Catholic Separate School Board. Cassette obtained from Bowden's Electronic Media.

Dubé, F. (1995, November 18). Corporate classrooms: Are we letting the moneylenders loose in our temples of learning? *The Ottawa Citizen*, B1-B2.

Duffy, A. (1994, January 19). Pepsi deal 'dangerous in schools' students say. *Toronto Star*.

Economic Council of Canada [ECC]. (1992). *A lot to learn: Education and training in canada.* Ottawa: Author.

Education: Idea Lacks Credit. (1996, April 25). *The Ottawa Citizen*. [Editorial].

Educational Partnership, An. (1994, November 10). *The Financial Post.* [Editorial to study conducted by Spencer Francey Peters Inc. and Cunningham Gregory and Company, (1994, November) *National Survey on Corporate Support of Education.*].

Ekelund, G. (1994, november). Ethics and the corporate classroom. *Our Schools, Our Selves*, 1(37), V6, 119–128.

Helm, D. (1994, October 12). McDonalds' in saanich school? May, but no arches. *The Times Colonist*.

Herman, J. L., & Golan, S. (1993, Winter). The effects of standardized testing on teaching and schools. *Educational Measurement: Issues and Practices*, 20.

Huybreghts, G. (1996). Business partnerships: Helping schools keep pace with technology. *Spectrum*, 28–30.

Ibbitson, J. (1996, April 26). Plan makes jobs compulsory part of high school. *The Ottawa Citizen*.

Ireland, D. S. (1995). Dispelling myths of student underachievement: The international status of Canadian education. *Orbit*, 26(4).

Jonasson, E., & Morris, M. (1996, May 14). Letter to the editor of the Globe and Mail. [Unpublished].

Jorgenson, B. (1996, March 2). Low taxes? Try Canada. *The Financial Post*.

Karpartkin, R. H., & Holmes, A. (1995, September). Making schools ad-free zones. *Educational Leadership.* p. 74.

Kopvillem, P. (1995/1996, December 25/January 1). Unemployed, without a safety net. Maclean's CBC News Poll. *Maclean's*, p. 21.

Krueger, L. (1996, February 9). Schools don't need 'partners' like YNN. *The Globe and Mail*, p. A24.

Lacey, V. S. (1994, April). *The role of information management in restructuring education.* Paper presented to the Invitational Conference on Restructuring Education, Haarlem, the Netherlands.

Lasch, C. (1995). *The revolt of the elites and the betrayal of democracy.* New York, NY: W.W. Norton.

Lawton, S. B., Freedman, J., & Robertson, H.-j. (1995). *Busting bureaucracy to reclaim our schools.* Montreal, QB: Institute for Research on Public Policy.

Lee, N. (1996, April). Schools as learning organizations. *MSTE News*, 5(2), [4-page insert], Faculty of Education, Queens University. Kingston, Ontario, Canada.

Levin, B. (1995, Summer). Poverty and education. *Education Canada*, 35(7), 28–35.

Lewington, J. (1996). A marriage made in heaven or hell? *The Globe and Mail*.

Livingstone, D. W., Hart, D., & Davie, L.E. (1995). *Public attitudes towards education in Ontario: 1994.* Toronto, ON: The Ontario Institute for Studies in Education.

McCay, Duff & Company. (1996, May). *1996 Ontario budget highlights.* [Prepared for the Council of Canadians, Ottawa.]

McEachern, R. (1994, February 21). [Letter to the Editor]. *Maclean's*, 4.

Meaghan, D., & Casas, F. (1995, January/February) Don't jump on the standardized testing bandwagon. *The ATA Magazine*, 75(2), 15–17.

Menzies, H. (1996). *Whose brave new world? The information highway and the new economy.* Toronto, ON: Between the Lines.

Mitchell, A. (1995, January 6). Calgary board plans to take school to work. *The Globe and Mail*.

National Commission on Excellence in Education. (1983, April). *A nation at risk: A report to the U.S. Department of Education.* Washington, DC: U.S. Department of Education.

Nikiforuk, A. (1995, April 9). A Loyal grunt in Klein's revolution. *The Toronto Star*.

Ontario Farm Animal Council [OFAC]. (1992). *Issues: teachers' guidelines for sensitive issues in agriculture and food production.* Mississauga, ON: Author.

Ontario Royal Commission on Learning, The. (1995). Making it happen. *For the love of learning, 4.* Toronto, ON: Author.

Ontario Secondary School Teachers' Federation [OSSTF]. (1995, September 15). *Commercialization in Ontario schools: A research report.* Toronto, ON: Author.

Prentice, A. (1970). The American example. *Canadian education: A history.* J. D. Wilson, R.M. Stamp and L-P. Audet. Scarborough, ON: Prentice-Hall of Canada, Ltd., 41–58.

Price, B. (1995, October). Independent public schools: Countering government and union monopolies. *The Canadian School Executive*, 12.

Quality in action. (undated). [Promotional brochure].

Robertson, G. (1995, October 20). *Benefits and pitfalls of standards and standards-based examinations in Manitoba.* Paper presented to the Manitoba Association of Teachers of English.

Robertson, H.-j. (1995a, December). Marketing to kids. *Canadian Forum*, 10–15.

Robertson, H.-j. (1995b). Restructuring from the right: School reform in Alberta. *The trojan horse, Alberta and the future of Canada.* Edmonton, AB: Black Rose Books.

Saul, J. R. (1995). *The Unconscious civilization.* Toronto, ON: Anansi Press.

Saunders, D. (1996, February 23). New Brunswick eliminates school boards. *The Globe and Mail.*

Shenk, D. (1995). Tomorrow's classroom today. Available from http://condor.depaul.edu/ethics/shenk.html.

Taco Bell. (1995, March 7). *The Globe and Mail.*

Thorsell, W. (1996, May 9). *Notes for keynote address* at Second National Consultation on Education in Edmonton, Alberta. Consultation by the Council of Ministers of Education, Canada.

Warburton, W. (1994, January 29). Corporate intrusion in the classroom. *The Ottawa Citizen.*

Winans, D. (1996, March). Trash or treasure? *NEA Today,* 14(7), 4–5.

World Bank, The. (1994, June 1). *Priorities and strategies for education.* [Draft]. Geneva: Education International.

You can forget Goals 2000, now it's Summit 1996. (1996, May). *The Executive Educator,* 8(5), [Editorial], 6.

Cultural Difference and Educational Change in a Sociopolitical Context

SONIA NIETO

School of Education, University of Massachusetts

Sonia Nieto's chapter points to the significant phenomenon of growing cultural diversity and the challenges it presents for educational change. Reviewing the evidence on ways of learning and what counts as learning in diverse cultures, and on the strong association between various levels of cultural diversity and poverty, Nieto argues that beyond the rhetoric, differences of race, culture, and language are rarely taken very seriously in educational reform efforts. Yet, she shows how taking cultural and linguistic diversity into account in educational reform initiatives, can make a real difference in student learning and achievement – and she outlines numerous, concrete and practical examples of how this can be and sometimes has been achieved.

In the second part of her chapter, Nieto spells out some educational change implications of her findings. She argues for better preservice teacher education that will prepare teachers effectively to work in contexts of diversity; for a more positive view of the strengths to be drawn from cultural difference; for whole-school policies that are sensitive to diversity issues; and for making social justice central rather than peripheral to an educational reform agenda that is currently too preoccupied with other interests and concerns.

Change and reform have become the educational buzzwords of the late twentieth century in many countries throughout the world, especially in highly developed industrialized societies with large immigrant populations. What is meant by reform has differed according to the society in which reform initiatives take place and the effect on various populations within particular societies. Given the dramatic demographic changes taking place in many Western societies at the close of the twentieth century, as well as the history of unequal educational opportunities available to culturally dominated and marginalized students within those societies, it is imperative to pay special attention to the meaning of educational change in a sociopolitical context.

In this chapter, I will first briefly define what I mean by cultural difference, educational change, and a sociopolitical context. I will also review some of the relevant research and related literature on cultural differences and educational achievement. Specifically, the chapter will address how a positive perception of student diversity can result in successful learning outcomes. The discussion will center on three general areas: culture and its potential influence on student learning; adaptations of curriculum and pedagogy that can foster academic success; and the impact of school policies and practices on achievement. I will conclude the chapter with a number of implications for understanding difference in relation to educational reform.

138

A. Hargreaves (ed.), Extending Educational Change, 138-159.

A note about the scope of this chapter is in order. Although the stated purpose of this volume is to review and highlight educational reform within an international perspective, the term *international* is misleading. If indeed we are concerned with educational change on a global scale, we would be dealing with scores of countries. Yet the literature included in most "international" reviews is limited to a few countries, notably Western, technologically advanced societies where those in power are European or of European descent and English is the dominant language. (A conspicuous exception is Japan, which is also often included under the "international" rubric). Given that the majority of accessible literature has been produced by scholars in this handful of countries, it is also the research from which I will draw most of my examples. I want to emphasize, however, that I do not consider this an international focus, but rather one steeped in Western, European traditions of scholarship. Needless to say, much that is important and enlightening concerning educational change will be missing. Nevertheless, even within this very limited framework, there is much that can be learned because most of the countries generally included in the "international" literature (for example, the United States, Britain, Australia, New Zealand, and Canada) are also highly diverse, multicultural, and multilingual societies, if not in policy at least in reality.

DEFINING KEY CONCEPTS

There are three key concepts that need further explanation in beginning a discussion of the impact of difference in the arena of educational reform. First, cultural difference and educational change will be defined as they are used in this chapter. Also included is a brief definition of sociopolitical context, since it is the lens through which I view and evaluate educational change efforts.

Cultural Difference

Many discussions of cultural difference are based on limited conceptions of culture that take into account only ethnicity, race, and language. This is understandable given the history of the deplorable educational conditions in which students of non-majority cultures are educated, especially in Western societies. Thus, for example, bilingual, multicultural, intercultural, and anti-racist education in the United States, Britain, and the rest of Europe have focused on addressing inequities in educational outcomes for those whose ethnicity, race, and/or language are different from the "mainstream" culture (Banks & Lynch, 1986; Skutnabb-Kangas & Toukomaa, 1976; Santos Rego, 1994; Banks, 1995; Allan & Hill, 1995; Figueroa, 1995; Moodley, 1995; Hoff, 1995; Pérez-Domínguez, 1995). For the purpose of this chapter, I define *culture* as *the ever-changing values, traditions, social and political relationships, and worldview created and shared by a group of people bound together by a combination of factors (which can include a common history, geographic location, language, social class, and/or religion), and how these are transformed by those who share them* (Nieto, 1996, p. 390). Culture includes not only language, ethnicity, and race, but other crucial dimensions such as social class and gender, because they may be key factors in explaining educational achievement. In fact, the problem is that cultural differences are often separated from one another as if this is how they existed in the real world. Yet differences such as race and social class often combine to place Black and other students of color at a disadvantage for learning; the same is true of ethnicity and gender, and of any number of other combinations.

It is important to mention how race and racial differences will be considered in the discussion of cultural differences. Although the concept of *race* as a biological trait that determines behavior and intelligence has been largely abandoned, the existence and persistence of *racism* as both institutional practices and personal bias, and its corollary, White privilege based on White supremacy, cannot be denied (McIntosh, 1988; Weinberg, 1990). Consequently, it is necessary to consider not racial differences *per se*, but rather *how racial differences are socially constructed*. Racial differences are primarily constructed by the larger society, which often perceives them in only negative ways. Therefore, what is important to remember is that race itself is not what makes a difference in people's attitudes, behaviors, and values, but rather how particular racial groups are valued or devalued by society.

In addition, many students classified as "linguistically and culturally diverse" are in fact also from poor or working class backgrounds; thus, the challenge is to understand the impact of poverty and its connection to how particular cultural differences are perceived in the larger society. That is, sometimes children from non-dominant backgrounds suffer academically not simply because their culture is at odds with the culture of power, but *because their schools and teachers are materially ill-equipped to give them an adequate education*. What often happens in such cases is that a singular focus on race, culture, language, or other differences overshadows the effect of the actual dismal conditions in which these children are educated, including dilapidated buildings and scarce resources (Kozol, 1991). These issues are crucial to understand because it is not *simply* the cultural differences of students, and the negative perception of these differences in the larger society, that places students at risk: they are also placed at risk of academic failure because they are simply not given the minimal resources with which to learn.

As a result, poor teaching methods and approaches are often institutionalized as what children "need," and the result is usually watered-down curriculum, a focus on "basic skills" that never progress to more rigorous standards, and low expectations of students. Knapp (1995), reporting on the first large-scale study in the United States of systematic attempts to enrich the educational experiences of students attending schools in high-poverty areas, has found that enrichment efforts yield results superior to those of the conventional practices associated with schools of children who live in poverty. The study, which described and analyzed instructional practices in about 140 classrooms located in 15 schools in low-income communities, discovered that meaning-centered strategies were similar to the goals of current reform movements. In terms of diversity, he also found that teachers who connected learning to students' backgrounds were much more likely to be successful in their efforts.

Finally, it is imperative that culture be understood as dynamic rather than fixed, as process instead of just content, and as historically and socially contextualized rather than insulated. Too often, quaint artifacts or isolated ethnic traditions and folklore are the elements by which culture is defined. When this is the case, educational decisions affecting curriculum, pedagogy, and other school practices are not likely to improve academic achievement. Erickson (1990) maintains that this conception of culture actually supports the status quo, leaving little room for transformative practice. In a cogent criticism of the kinds of superficial implementations of multicultural education that are based on an understanding of culture as frozen traditions and fascinating artifacts, he writes, "A serious danger lies in treating culture traits in isolation, fragmenting and trivializing our understanding of people's lifeways as we freeze them outside time, outside a world of struggle in concrete history" (p. 34). Instead, Erickson (1990) calls for a critical understanding of culture that leads to pedagogy that is genuinely transformative rather than "cosmetically relevant" (p. 23).

Educational Change

From the 1980s and continuing into the 1990s, educational change and reform took center stage in the social and political discourse in many countries. How educational change is defined, however, makes a difference in the kinds of initiatives promoted. For instance, based on educational reform policies in six countries, Beare and Boyd (1993) concluded that there is an almost universal trend towards such reforms as school-based management and other efforts that aim primarily at the control and governance of schools and school systems, that is, the *management* of schools. Yet educational change cannot simply be thought of as a "technical process of managerial efficiency" but must also be considered a political process (Hargreaves, Earl, & Ryan, 1996, p. 233). This means that political considerations as well as structures in schools and communities that either promote or inhibit reform need to be taken into account. Furthermore, given the growing influence of governments and businesses on the enterprise of education, an economic imperative has been at the heart of a majority of school reform initiatives (Beare & Boyd, 1993). The outcome of some of the practices that have emerged (such as increased "high-stakes" testing and the further institutionalization of ability grouping) is that schools, teachers, and students have been the primary targets of blame for poor achievement.

Another consequence of the focus on management in educational change is that issues of pedagogy and curriculum become marginalized. Darling-Hammond (1991), in a review of testing legislation in the United States in terms of equity and diversity, concluded that instead of improving learning outcomes, such legislation was having a negative impact on students who were already disproportionately represented among poor achievers in school, especially African American and

Latino youngsters. Similar findings were reported by Corbett and Wilson (1990) concerning the impact of state-wide testing initiatives in Maryland and Pennsylvania. One reason for negative results was that gross inequities in instructional quality, resources, and other support services are conveniently ignored when testing takes precedence over pedagogy; another is that teachers' creativity is diminished when they have to "teach to the test" and are discouraged from implementing more engaging pedagogical practices. Darling-Hammond (1991) found a decline in the use of teaching and learning methods such as student-centered discussions, essay writing, research projects, and laboratory work when standardized tests were required. Furthermore, Fullan and Stiegelbauer (1991) found that there is a tendency in relatively stable communities to promote innovations that do not favor those who are most disadvantaged (what they call the "bias of neglect," p. 58). Given this situation, students who are already facing substantial obstacles to learning are further jeopardized.

In this chapter, *student learning* will be the lens through which educational reform efforts are judged. In contrast to the focus on management and control, relatively little attention in educational policy has been paid directly to student learning. Yet student learning is at the very center of the purpose of schooling, regardless of country or educational system. Generally missing from reform efforts are questions that focus directly on how and to what extent students of diverse backgrounds best learn, and the implications of these questions for academic achievement (Nieto, 1997). Without this kind of inquiry, educational reform can become just an empty exercise in bureaucratic shuffling or can result in the imposition of national policies that have little impact on the actual learning that goes on in classrooms.

Questions about student learning are especially incisive for societies with heterogeneous populations and those with a history of rampant educational failure among those who are most disadvantaged and powerless. How cultural differences are taken into account in teaching and learning, what the sociopolitical implications of difference are, and what educational change means in such settings are crucial questions for consideration.

Sociopolitical Context

School reform with a focus on diversity needs to begin by addressing what is meant by a *sociopolitical context* (Nieto, 1996). A sociopolitical context takes into account the larger societal and political forces in a particular society and the impact they may have on student learning. A sociopolitical context considers issues of *power* and includes discussions of structural inequality based on stratification due to race, social class, gender, ethnicity, and other differences; it also includes the relative respect or disrespect accorded to particular languages and dialects.

School reform strategies that do not acknowledge macro-level disparities are sometimes little more than wishful thinking because they assume that all students begin their educational experiences on a level playing field. In spite of the rhetoric of meritocracy espoused in most democratic countries, social stratification is based on *groups,* not on individuals (Ogbu, 1994). Given this perspective, educational decisions about such policies as ability grouping, testing, curriculum, pedagogy, and which language to use for instruction are also *political* decisions (Freire, 1985). Embedded within all educational decisions are also assumptions about the nature of learning in general, the worthiness and capability of students from different social groups, and the inherent value of languages other than the dominant one. Thus, even seemingly innocent decisions carry an enormous amount of ideological and philosophical weight, and these are in turn communicated to students either directly or indirectly (Cummins, 1989). Furthermore, education remains a gatekeeper to future opportunities for most youth, and these opportunities are influenced by the quality of education to which students have had access. Consequently, educational changes tend to favor the interests of those who are most powerful in a given society (Hargreaves, Earl, & Ryan, 1996). Corson (1993, p. 11) describes the impact of such policies and practices on students who tend to be the most disadvantaged in societies: "The members of some social groups, as a result, come to believe that their educational failure, rather than coming from their lowly esteemed social or cultural status, results from their natural inability: their lack of giftedness."

CULTURAL DIFFERENCES AND EDUCATIONAL ACHIEVEMENT

How differences are taken into account when educational reform takes place is a central question for researchers and practitioners to consider because cultural diversity is often either ignored or assumptions about the appropriateness of particular policies or pedagogical strategies are primarily based on the dominant culture in a society. Stubbs (1995), writing about England and Wales, could just as well be speaking about numerous other societies when he describes the unstated premise in much of British educational language policy and planning: "the situation of a monolingual majority should be altered as little as possible" (p. 34). That is, the underlying assumption has generally been that assimilation is both desirable and necessary and most educational reform strategies echo this view. On the other hand, relatively little attention has been paid to how cultural differences, in combination with power differentials, affect student learning.

The foundational work of Cole and associates concerning culture and learning is instructive here (Cole, Gay, Glick, & Sharp, 1971). Although this research is over a quarter century old, it holds important lessons for understanding the learning experiences of children of dominated cultures in Western societies. Cole and his associates were particularly interested in discovering why the Kpelle children of north-central Liberia experienced a great deal of difficulty in Western-style mathematics. First, it is necessary to understand that the Kpelle children's Western-style education generally took place in schools that were physically and culturally separated from the towns in which the children lived. Because of the inherent tensions between tribal traditions and Western-style education, these schools were, in the words of the researchers, "a source of culture contact and culture conflict" (p. 51). It is no surprise, then, that Western-style education represented a tremendous challenge to the children in more ways than one.

When Cole and his associates explored the context of the children's educational and home experiences, they found that while the children did indeed have difficulty in some tasks such as measuring lengths, for example, they were more skilled than American children at other tasks, such as estimating various amounts of rice. Rice farming is, of course, central to their culture and involves a network of related activities. However, measuring lengths is a very specific and isolated activity that depends on what is being measured. Consequently, the metric for cloth is different from the metric for sticks. The axiom that people learn to do best those things that are important to them and which they do often was reinforced. Finally, the researchers suggested that culture and cognition cannot be separated: "To study cognition is to study cognitive behavior in a particular situation and the relation of this behavior to other aspects of the culture" (Cole et al., 1971, p. 18).

In another example of the necessity to understand learning within the context in which it takes place, an early analysis of reading failure among Black students in U.S. schools challenged deficit theories about learning. McDermott (1977) suggested that failing to read is "culturally induced" behavior. That is, because of the conflict between the child's culture and the culture of school, McDermott hypothesized that success in reading and success in social interaction with peers are often mutually exclusive. Thus, *learning not to read* was a necessary adaptation to the cultural conflict. This kind of behavior can be defined as *resistance* (Giroux, 1983; Skutnabb-Kangas, 1988), and it is related not only to ethnic cultural differences, but also to power differentials between students, their teachers, and the institution of school. In the words of McDermott (1977, p. 17),

> The bicultural child must acquire a sometimes mutually exclusive way of knowing how to act appropriately, one way for when Whites are present and another for when the interaction matrix is all Black. Where code shifting is most difficult is apparently in the bureaucratic setting in which the White code, in addition to being the only acceptable medium of information exchange, is also the medium for the expression of host group power and host group access to the essential and even luxurious utilities of contemporary America.

Recently this point has been made even more powerfully by Kohl (1994), who has termed resistance a kind of "creative maladjustment." How students, particularly those from culturally dominated groups, resist learning has serious implications for school policies and practices.

A related issue that has emerged in the past several years is that progressive educational strategies are sometimes used uncritically with students from culturally dominated groups. That is, if such strategies are successful with middle-class mainstream students, the assumption is that they will therefore be appropriate for all children. Although their use may be well-intentioned, uncritically adopting such strategies may result in marginalizing those students whose communities have the least power in society. By using the dominant culture as the standard, educational decisions that affect all children are made. This is the case, for instance, with wholesale applications of process approaches to literacy if they do not take into account the diversity of the student population (Delpit, 1995). In reviewing whole language approaches used with linguistically diverse students, Reyes (1992) has also critiqued what she calls "one-size-fits-all" approaches that do not consider students' specific cultural or linguistic characteristics. In another example, an early case study of a progressive primary school in Britain found that the assumptions of "open education" actually worked against children with working class backgrounds (Sharp & Green, 1975). When children failed to thrive in such settings, their home backgrounds were blamed, rather than the educational approach that was used with them. As Fullan and Stiegelbauer (1991) point out, innovations often fail because *means* become *ends* in themselves, and the fundamental reasons for change are forgotten. This is especially true where marginalized students are concerned.

It is clear from the above examples that race, culture, language, and other differences, although usually acknowledged to be important considerations in educational reform efforts, are in fact often not taken seriously. A growing number of studies, however, are documenting how taking into account cultural and linguistic diversity in educational reform initiatives, whether at macro or micro levels of implementation, can make a real difference in student learning and achievement.

Using Students' Linguistic, Cultural, and Experiential Backgrounds as Resources

The cultural knowledge and experiences of students from disempowered and culturally dominated communities are frequently dismissed or denied in schools. Perhaps an example from a field unrelated to schools can illustrate how this takes place. Based on several years of ethnographic research, Jordan (1989) described the participation of Mayan midwives in government-sponsored training courses in the Yucatán region of Mexico. She found that the courses, for all their good intentions, generally failed. That is, although the midwives received years of training, their day-to-day practice did not change as a result, partly because the teaching strategies to which they were exposed were based on the unstated premise that they had nothing to contribute to their own learning. Teachers thus tended to dismiss the local culture and its values and practices which would have made learning not only more relevant for the midwives, but also might have provided a challenge to the teachers' imperialistic worldview. Jordan concluded,

> The enterprise of teaching and learning, whether it involves midwives, school children, or an industrial work force, is always an enterprise in the service of multiple agendas. Although it is ostensibly about the transmission of knowledge and skills, in a hierarchically organized society it is also always

about the imposition, extension and reproduction of lines of power and authority (Jordan, 1989, p. 925).

It is not too farfetched to apply this description of cultural imperialism in the training of midwives in the Yucatán to the way children's cultures and life-styles are devalued every day in schools, especially in Western pluralist societies. Although the settings are very different, the process is an all-too-familiar one: the cultures and languages of culturally dominated children are often disregarded and replaced within the school setting.

Bourdieu (1977) is instructive in explaining how this process takes place in schools. Because schools primarily reflect the knowledge and values of economically and culturally dominant groups in any society, they validate and reinforce what Bourdieu calls the *cultural capital* that students from such groups bring from home. This validation takes place through the curriculum and environment both overtly and covertly in the school setting, and it represents a *symbolic violence* against devalued groups. The cultural model held up for all, however, is not within easy reach of all; that is, only token members of students from less valued groups can achieve it. If even a few members of disempowered groups learn and take on this cultural capital (usually losing their own culture, language, and values along the way), they may succeed in school. Consequently, the myth of the meritocracy in Western societies is maintained.

In spite of the overwhelming influence of dominant cultural capital, recent research on the education of students whose cultures differ from the mainstream has pointed out that using their cultures, languages, and experiences in their education can lead to academic success. This line of research implies that educational reformers need to learn about cultural and linguistic diversity and become aware of how these can influence learning as a first step in understanding the relevance of diversity in change efforts. Otherwise, their judgments about students' educational potential, if based on incomplete or biased assessments of culture, language, social class and other differences, can actually create or reinforce barriers to achievement. That is, reformers' judgments are often based on societal expectations and criteria where one race, language and culture are afforded higher status, and therefore more credibility, than others. Such judgments become, in effect, the guiding principle of some reform initiatives. Bilingual education is a good example. Although mired in contentious debate and controversy in many countries, research results on an international scale are almost unanimous in their conclusion: children from language minority backgrounds benefit from bilingual programs when their native language plays a major role in their instruction. This is the case in countries such as Mexico, Sweden, and Canada (Moorfield, 1987); the Netherlands (Vallen & Stijnen, 1987), the United States (Ramírez, 1991; Thomas & Collier, 1995), and other countries in Europe and Africa (Skutnabb-Kangas, 1988).

Using students' linguistic, cultural, and experiential backgrounds as resources has proven to be effective in their learning. An important study concerning Latino language-minority students in the United States (Lucas, Henze, & Donato, 1990) documented the positive effect of a shared belief among teachers, counselors, and administrators that all students are capable of high levels of learning. When such beliefs permeate the school climate, concomitant changes are made in policies and practices. In the case of the six high schools studied, researchers found eight features that were especially important in promoting the success of the Latino language-minority students in the schools. One of these, a high value placed on students' language and culture, was epitomized by treating their native language ability as an advantage, encouraging them to continue their study of Spanish and staff members to learn it, and promoting in-depth approaches to affirming cultural diversity rather than superficial "one-shot" professional development workshops or decontextualized diversity programs.

In Auckland, New Zealand, the Richmond Road School is another example of using the cultural and linguistic strengths of children to promote their learning. Rather than a focus on what May (1994) has called a "benevolent multicultural education," this school has been internationally recognized for implementing a critically conceived approach to diversity in which total school reform is the goal. The school, with a 48% language minority student and staff population, offers bilingual programs in three languages and supports the biliteracy of all its students. In addition, there is a communal and consensual approach to decision-making, an approach based on the recognition of the cultural appropriateness of this approach for the ethnic minority children who attend the school. More important, however, *both* cultural maintenance *and* access to power (through an emphasis on teaching skills needed to live in the wider society) are at the core of the program (May, 1994).

Although the preceding are noteworthy examples that may hold important lessons concerning school reform, there is an inherent problem with using model schools or programs as examples of transformational change because they represent what have been called an "extreme case of the limitations of school improvement" (Hargreaves, Earl, & Ryan, 1996, p. 238). Often, these schools are built on the reputation, charisma, and vision of individual leaders. When such leaders leave the particular school or program they inspired, the changes they started are usually short-lived. Thus, it is necessary to search for examples of educational transformation that do not rely on single individuals. In the words of Hargreaves, Earl, and Ryan, ". . . while we have learned a lot about how to create exceptional islands of improvement, we know less about how to construct archipelagos and still less about how to build whole continents of successful change" (1996, p. 237).

Nevertheless, the above examples may represent an important beginning to reflect on how to view cultural diversity in order to provide more effective learning opportunities for students. The assumption that students' cultural and linguistic backgrounds can be important resources in their learning can be understood within the framework of what have variously been called *culturally compatible, culturally congruent, culturally responsive, bicultural,* or *culturally relevant pedagogy* (Au & Kawakami, 1994; Darder, 1991; Ladson-Billings, 1994; Hollins, King, & Hayman, 1994). These approaches are based on using students' cultures as an important source of their education, particularly in the case of those whose communities have been omitted or denied in the educational setting. There is, of course, no simple panacea for remedying the wholesale academic failure of students from these communities; nevertheless, culturally responsive approaches offer important insights for understanding it. An exploration of how *cultural motifs* can be successfully incorporated in instruction follows.

Using Cultural Motifs

Family and cultural motifs, that is, the use of values, traditions, and themes central to the lives of non-dominant groups, have been found to be effective in a number of situations. In effect, bringing the family culture and practices into classroom instructional and curricular processes can benefit the educational experiences, and therefore the academic success, of students. A powerful example of the use of cultural knowledge can be found in the research in the Piedmont Carolinas by Heath (1983). In exploring the language of African American children at home and at school, she found that different family and cultural ways of using language resulted in certain tensions between the children and their mostly White teachers in the classroom. As a result of becoming aware of these differences, teachers began to experiment with different ways of asking questions, thus helping children bridge the gap between their home and school experiences. Consequently, the children's language use in the classroom and their academic success were enhanced.

Another example can be found in the Kamahameha Elementary Education Program (KEEP) in Hawaii (Vogt, Jordan, & Tharp, 1993). Here, the researchers found that certain cultural discontinuities in instruction were a major problem in the poor academic achievement of Native Hawaiian children. The KEEP Program was established to explore remedies for the children's chronic academic underachievement by changing certain educational practices. For example, teachers changed from a purely phonetic approach to one that emphasized comprehension. In addition, heterogeneous groups were substituted for individual work desks, and individual praise was de-emphasized in favor of more indirect and group praise. These changes more closely paralleled the children's cultural styles. For instance, the move from phonics to comprehension allowed the students to use a speech style called the "talk-story," a familiar linguistic event in the Hawaiian community (Vogt, Jordan, & Tharp, 1993). The KEEP Program has had great success, including significant gains in reading achievement.

Deyhle (1995) investigated the lives of Navajo youth in the United States in and out of school. She found that those youths who had little sense of their Navajo identity and who were not accepted by non-Navajos were most at risk for school failure. Thus, the reservation school was more successful than non-Navajo schools because it helped students to affirm and retain their cultural identity. She concluded:

For Navajo students, one of the most life-affirming strategies is to embrace reservation life and traditional Navajo culture. Indeed, the students in my study who were able to maintain Navajo/reservation connections gained a solid place in Navajo society and were also more successful in the Anglo world at school and workplace (Deyhle, 1995, p. 404).

In contrast, Hartle-Schutte (1993), highlighting the experiences of four academically successful Navajo students, found that the school system failed to capitalize on their culture and experiences. Their academic success happened *despite*, rather than *because of*, the instructional and assessment practices of the school. In effect, he found that the four students, who were characterized by what are often considered insurmountable "risk factors" such as poverty and language and cultural differences, had literacy experiences at home that helped them to become successful readers (Hartle-Schutte, 1993).

Another researcher who has explored Indigenous "ways of going to school" among a number of American Indian nations has concluded that Indigenous schools serve an important role as sites of negotiation between cultures in contact (Stairs, 1994). She also found that Indigenous classrooms are different from traditional U.S. classrooms in a number of ways. In Indigenous classrooms, there tends to be more interaction and collaborative learning and peer teaching, less direct questioning of individual students and little performance in front of the class, more personal narratives, closer physical proximity, and many references to community life and culture. Traditional U.S. classrooms can learn a great deal from these examples of the use of cultural motifs, but Stairs warns of the pitfalls of what she calls the "two-column schemes" characterizing Indigenous learners as compared to others. That is, although these descriptions of Native students' learning styles can be helpful, they can also backfire by characterizing these students with fixed traits within rigid boundaries.

Another example of using cultural motifs in education is provided by Abi-Nader (1993) in a description of a classroom of Latino youths in a large, urban high school in the Northeast United States. She found that interactions between the teacher and his students were largely based on Latino cultural values of *familia* (family): that is, the classroom was characterized by a deep sense of support and affection, students developed collective responsibility for one another through such practices as peer tutoring and mentoring, the teacher acted as a family member and friend to the students, and students were encouraged to do well in order to make their families proud of them. The result: unlike the dramatic dropout rates of Latinos in general, which tend to be the highest in the nation (ASPIRA, 1993), up to 65% of the students in this program went on to college.

Why the use of cultural motifs is effective in promoting educational success may be explained by the fact that students from culturally dominated groups receive, if anything, only negative support for their cultures and languages in the school setting. Consequently, because they are under constant attack, their cultural identities become extremely important to these young people (Corson, 1993). An interesting example of this is found in research on Romani youths ("gypsies") in

Hungary (Forray & Hegedüs, 1989). Gender expectations of Romani boys and girls tend to be fairly fixed. Yet because the family is often the only place where most culturally dominated students can positively strengthen their self-image, girls may perceive, quite correctly, that breaking free of even limited expectations of their future life options also results in giving up their ethnic identity. Through questionnaires collected from elementary school teachers of Romani children, the researchers concluded that teachers' negative attitudes and behaviors concerning the differential expectations for boys and girls were at least partly responsible for strengthening the expected gender-based behavior among girls in school. It is conceivable that, had teachers been able to develop a more culturally sensitive approach to their behaviors, the children might have felt safe to explore other options without feeling that they were cultural traitors.

The significance of an emphasis on family motifs is that this framework can be used to weave all instructional strategies together in a way that is easily understood by the students because it is part of their ethnic behavior (Bernal, Knight, Ocampo, Garza, & Cota, 1993). It is true that the actual family lives of some students may be quite different from the ideals expressed in the motifs, especially because of the difficult social and political contexts in which they live. Nevertheless, the students' cultures are important to embody in educational programs and approaches because they allow students to see less of a cultural discontinuity between their homes and schools than is normally the case. Tharp (1989) in a review of the school achievement of learners from culturally dominated groups found that schools consistently supported two major practices in all cases of academic achievement: language development, and contextualized instruction, that is, instruction based on students' previous knowledge and experience.

Delgado-Gaitán and Trueba (1991) have commented on the impressive resilience of youths from culturally dominated backgrounds, and their insights hold lessons for the schools these students attend. Reflecting on their ethnographic research on immigrant students in the United States, they state, "The children's talent for integrating values, priorities, and demands from home and school reveals their significant potential for accomplishing their goals in schools and in life in general" (p. 14). The fact that newcomers, in spite of being young, feeling isolated, and facing what can be a terrifying situation in an unfamiliar environment, can nonetheless incorporate the cultural motifs of disparate values and behaviors speaks well for them. Schools also can learn to incorporate students' cultural motifs into their policies and practices.

IMPLICATIONS OF CULTURAL DIFFERENCES FOR EDUCATIONAL REFORM

In numerous societies, cultural differences have been generally placed within a framework of cultural deficit. As is evident from the above discussion, a growing body of research is suggesting that the very view of *diversity as deficit* needs to be reframed if educational reformers are serious about affording all students an equal opportunity to learn. A number of implications emerge from the reframing of educational reform that includes a reconceptualization of the salience of diversity. Three implications will be briefly addressed.

1. Reform Needs to Take Place in Multiple Contexts

It is becoming increasingly clear that substantive changes in education will occur only through reformation of the *entire learning environment*. This includes not only curriculum and materials, but also institutional norms, attitudes and behaviors of staff, counseling services, and the extent to which families are welcomed in schools.

Positive changes in the learning of individual students or the restructuring of particular classrooms and schools are often used as examples of what might be possible if individual teachers, principals, or other administrators take the leadership in promoting educational success (Abi-Nader, 1993; May, 1994; Lucas, Henze, & Donato, 1990). These are meaningful examples because they point out the salutary effects of pedagogical, attitudinal, and structural changes in specific contexts. In addition, they provide classroom- and school-based models that may contain important lessons for other educators. Nonetheless, in spite of the positive changes that may occur as a result of reform at the individual classroom or school level, a sociopolitical framing of education is needed alongside these examples because it underscores the institutional nature of schools. A good example of how particular classrooms are profoundly influenced by the sociopolitical context can be found in research by Gutierrez, Rymes, and Larson (1995). Analyzing a narrative concerning current events in a 9th grade classroom, the researchers pointed out how students were able to insert their "local knowledge" into a teacher's virtually incontestable script. Students' actions helped create the possibility of a "third space," that is, a context in which various cultures, discourses, and knowledge are made available to all classroom participants, and therefore become resources for mediating learning. In effect, the "third space" is an opening in which the classroom can become a site for social change. Without it, classrooms can remain isolated from their sociopolitical context.

To divorce schools from the societies in which they operate is impossible: although schools may with all good intentions attempt to provide learning environments free from oppressive conditions, once students leave the classroom and building, they are again confronted with inequities in their communities and societies. The implication is that educational reform must take place in multiple contexts: classroom, school, district, nationally, and ideologically. Until this happens, isolated stories of individual hope and inspiration may be the best concrete results of reform we can achieve. Although these stories may be impressive catalysts for further educational reform, they leave most students unaffected.

Educational reform must also take place in the context of professional development, where much remains to be done to prepare teachers to work with students of diverse backgrounds (Banks & Lynch, 1986). Because teachers are drawn primarily from the majority culture in most Western societies, and because schools and colleges of education are slow to analyze their own practices critically, both pre-service and in-service education have been slow to change. Even when multicultural and anti-racist education principles and strategies are addressed, there is often fierce resistance on the part of teachers. For example, a study reported by Solomon (1995) on the perspectives of over 1,000 teachers from five school jurisdictions across Canada found that, although teachers expressed the need for content in diversity, many of them nevertheless resented the implication that they were not adequately prepared to teach students of diverse backgrounds. In addition, White teachers resisted inservice programs that focused on race and ethnicity because of the guilt they experienced as a result. Teachers also resisted addressing issues of race and culture because they felt that such discussions were antithetical to harmonious racial relations.

The result of educators' lack of preparation for teaching students of backgrounds different from their own often results in a serious mismatch between teachers' perceptions of their students' abilities and the actual abilities these students may have. Delgado-Gaitán and Trueba (1991), in discussing the education of immigrant students in the United States, describe the situation in this way:

> The best of intentions on the part of teachers cannot compensate for the way that the teachers' education system fails them. Teachers are not prepared for the challenges of teaching children who, from their perspective seem to be failures, when in fact these children possess a wealth of knowledge and skills which can be harnessed and transformed into creative ideas. . . (p. 136).

At the national level, pronouncements of reform are frequently couched in the discourse of control rather than in the discourse of equality or social justice (Beare & Boyd, 1993). As a consequence, suggested policies are based on a compensatory framework, that is, on compensating for the supposed shortcomings of students. This is certainly the case with transitional bilingual education approaches that, although encouraging the use of native language in instruction, do so only as a bridge to the second language. A more positive view of cultural differences has yet to be articulated in most educational reform national policy statements.

Troyna (1992), a passionate advocate of anti-racist education, argues nevertheless that anti-racist professional development pays insufficient attention to successful change strategies. Reflecting on how one particular school responded to the recommendation that it should prepare policies that declare a commitment to cultural pluralist ideals, he found that such policies are likely to have a limited impact on the practices of schools unless those involved in their implementation also participate in their formulation. He concluded that it is overly deterministic to suppose that not institutionalizing multicultural education derives completely from the unwitting racist attitudes of teachers. For one, this policy implies ignorance and failure on the part of teachers, and teachers in his study found this to be insulting. The result in the school he studied was the articulation of a watered-down principle that basically absolved staff from a commitment to anti-racist pedagogy. Thus, although teachers may indeed collude with a racist system, blaming teachers alone was an unproductive basis on which to develop effective change in school. Consequently, Troyna concluded that the struggle to achieve racial equality in education is much more complex than is generally assumed.

Given the relatively recent development of anti-racist professional development, little attention has been given to its possible impact. One of the few documented studies concerns the effect of an anti-racist professional development course for White teachers (Lawrence & Tatum, forthcoming). The course, which was taken by a group of forty teachers and administrators, took place in 3-hour sessions over a period of seven months. Taught by a bi-racial team of instructors, the content included topics such as racism, White privilege, and racial identity development, with specific attention given to the role of Whites as "allies" rather than simply as bearing the entire guilt for racism. The researchers were especially interested in whether White teachers' understanding of their own racial identity influenced their thinking and daily classroom practice. Results indicate that in their essays and reflective papers as well as through interviews with the researchers, the course had a profound impact on most of the participants. Especially important was the influence on the participants' behaviors in their classrooms and schools. For example, teachers began discussing race and race-related topics more frequently with their students, they made a conscious effort to include the experiences and histories of people of color in their curriculum, they changed their teaching practices, and they reconceptualized their relations with parents. Although this study is limited by the fact that it was primarily based on self-reported data, it provides some direction for the positive impact that professional development can have on teachers' attitudes and behaviors.

Finally, a profound shift at the ideological level is needed if educational reform is to work. School policies and practices are the living embodiment of a society's underlying values, educational philosophy, and hopes and dreams for its young people. That is to say, policies and practices in schools – whether curriculum, pedagogical strategies, assessment procedures, disciplinary policies, or grouping practices – do not emerge from thin air, but instead are tangible reminders of a society's beliefs, attitudes, and expectations of students. Thus, for example, retention, ability grouping, and testing are policies laden with value judgments about students' capabilities. It is clear to see, then, that a society's ideology can either promote or retard the kind of learning that prepares students for productive and satisfying lives in a multicultural and democratic society. In practice, this implies that schools can serve as models of pluralism and democracy, or conversely, that they can distort the messages of democracy and pluralism that are conveyed in exalted mission statements and idealized treatments of history in school textbooks.

Similarly, issues of institutional power and privilege in society are played out in daily interactions in a school through its policies and practices. Unfortunately, these issues are rarely made part of the public discourse (Freire, 1985; Fine, 1991). Instead, in modern Western industrialized societies, individual merit, ambition, talent, and intelligence are touted as the sole basis of academic success, with little consideration given to the impact of structural inequality based on race, ethnicity, gender, social class, and other differences. Meritocracy, while a worthy ideal, is far from a reality in most cases. As a consequence, students whose difference may relegate them to a subordinated status in society are often blamed for their lack of achievement (Nieto, 1997). Although it is true that individual differences are also important in explaining relative academic success or failure, they must be understood in tandem with the power and privilege of particular groups in society (McIntosh, 1988). What this means at the ideological level is that until societies believe and act according to the belief that all children are worthy and capable of learning, most students of non-dominant groups will be doomed to academic failure.

2. Both Assimilation and Structural Separation as the Goal of Education Need to Be Contested

Western societies have generally responded in one of two ways to the cultural, racial, and linguistic diversity of students in their schools: either they have emphasized the goal of assimilating these students into the dominant cultural group; or they have supported the goal of structural separation of students who are different from the "mainstream." In general, the first strategy has operated in societies where the students are part of an indigenous or enslaved group, or an immigrant group with intentions to remain in the country (as is usually the case in Canada and the United States). The second strategy has usually operated in Western Europe when immigrants are "guest workers" and expected to leave the country after a specific length of stay. In either case, students from culturally dominated communities learn to feel inferior to the mainstream because their differences are perceived in negative ways. In the words of a young Finn educated in Sweden, "When the idea had eaten itself deeply into my soul that it was despicable to be a Finn, I began to feel ashamed of my origins" (Jalava, 1988, p. 164). If cultural and other differences are to be taken into account in substantive reform efforts, both of these goals need to be challenged.

Assimilation of newcomers into the so-called "mainstream" has been a fundamental goal of education in the United States and, to a lesser extent Canada, for the past century. In the United States, the "melting pot" metaphor has been heralded as proof that assimilation works. Assimilation has operated on the assumption that one must lose something in order to gain something else. Thus, linguistic assimilation has meant not only learning the national language, but also forgetting one's native language; cultural assimilation has meant not only learning the new culture, but also learning to eat, dress, talk, think, and behave like those in the dominant group. To go through this process almost certainly means the inevitable loss of a great part of one's identity. Thus, the process itself poses a wrenching dilemma for culturally dominated youths: either assimilate to a homogeneous model, or resist assimilation and in the long run lose out on the educational and other resources that might provide more enriching life options (Skutnabb-Kangas, 1988).

Studies concerned with the importance of cultural maintenance are beginning to challenge the equation *education=assimilation*. For instance, in a study of successful Punjabi students in the United States (Gibson, 1987), the researcher found that parents consistently admonished their children to maintain their culture, making it clear to them that adopting the values and behaviors of the majority group would dishonor their families and communities. Also in the United States, a study of Southeast Asian students found that higher grade point averages correlated with the maintenance of traditional values, ethnic pride, and close social and cultural ties with members of the same group (Rumbaut & Ima, 1987). Elsewhere, similar results have been reached with reference to bilingual education (Baker, 1993).

The inevitable conclusion that maintaining native languages and cultures will help students in their academic achievement turns on its head not only conventional educational philosophy, but also the policies and practices of schools that have done everything possible to eradicate students' culture and language. Rather than attempt to erase culture and language, recent research is suggesting that schools need to do everything in their power to use, affirm, and encourage them as a foundation for academic success. In order to do this, a constructivist model of teaching and learning needs to be in place whereby students and their teachers begin with what students know, rather than with a transmission model which assumes that students know nothing and need to be "filled up" with knowledge (Freire, 1970; Cummins, 1994).

3. Social Justice Needs to be Placed at the Center of Educational Reform

A final implication when considering cultural diversity as a central concern in educational reform is that social justice must be at the heart of such efforts. As elegantly expressed by Corson, "Working with minority children is often more than a skill; it is an act of cultural fairness" (Corson, 1993, p. 179). Yet it is too often the case that students from culturally disempowered groups are considered objects of pity or scorn. The result is that the kinds of interventions provided are patronizing and partial because they are located within a model of *diversity as deficit*.

By having a social justice perspective at the center of reform approaches, structural and social inequities that stand in the way of student achievement can be squarely confronted. For example, a social justice perspective forces reformers to consider how youngsters are *disempowered* by schools and society, rather than simply blaming students, their families, communities, and cultural differences for their supposed deficits. During the 1960s, this was the operating assumption, but it was squarely challenged by Ryan (1972) when he coined the phrase "blaming the victim." Ryan turned the argument of cultural deprivation on its head by suggesting:

> We are dealing, it would seem, not so much with culturally deprived children as with culturally depriving schools. And the task to be accomplished is not to revise, amend, and repair deficient children, but to alter and transform the atmosphere and operations of the schools to which we commit these children (Ryan, 1972, p. 61).

One way in which social justice is placed at the center of reform, whether in individual classrooms or through more broad-based efforts, is by engaging in what Cummins has called *collaborative relations of power* rather than traditional *coercive relations of power* (Cummins, 1994). This approach operates on the assumption that interpersonal and intergroup relations can serve to empower rather than disempower students. Such a process involves challenging the hegemony of the dominant cultural capital as well as redefining the relationships among students, their families, and the schools. In this way, teachers are encouraged to consider the worthwhile contributions and insights that students and their families can bring to the educational experience. This means that everybody can contribute on an equal basis, but all have to undergo some change, not only students and their families (Skutnabb-Kangas, 1990).

Finally, in order for a social justice agenda to have any meaning in educational reform, students themselves need to be involved. In the words of Fullan and Stiegelbauer: "Students, even little ones, are people too. Unless they have some meaningful (to them) role in the enterprise, most educational change, indeed most education, will fail" (1991, p. 170). Numerous examples of student engagement in their own education, and in the design of school policies and policies that affect their learning on a daily basis, confirm that their views are important and necessary ingredients for educational reform (Nieto, 1994).

CONCLUSION

Educational change strategies are often developed with the best of intentions but with little thought given to the enormous diversity of backgrounds and experiences that students bring to their schooling. When this is the case, educational reform tends to be a prescription for the "remedy of diversity" and those students who have been most severely marginalized and alienated from schools tend to be the ones who once again suffer the most. The perception of diversity as an ailment that needs to be cured is based on the view that in order to be successful in school students need to assimilate and accommodate to the dominant culture. While a certain amount of accommodation and adaptation are indeed necessary, a wholesale assimilation may result in promoting even more academic failure among those who differ from the mainstream. Many reform strategies consequently fail to capitalize on student diversity as a strength to be used in the service of learning. Yet all students have talents, skills, insights, and experiences that can be used to promote learning. Educational reform and change strategies need to take these differences into account in a serious way.

REFERENCES

Abi-Nader, J. (1993). Meeting the needs of multicultural classrooms: Family values and the motivation of minority students. In M. J. O'Hair & S. Odell (Eds.), *Diversity and teaching: Teacher education yearbook* (pp. 212–236). Ft. Worth, TX: Harcourt Brace Jovanovich.

Allan, R., & Hill, B. (1995). Multicultural education in Australia: Historical development and current status. In J. A. Banks & C. A. M. Banks (Eds.), *Handbook of research on multicultural education*, pp. 763–777. New York: Macmillan.

ASPIRA Institute for Policy Research. (1993). *Facing the facts: The state of Hispanic education, 1993.* Washington, DC: Author.

Au, K. A., & Kawakami, A. J. (1994). Cultural congruence in instruction. In E. R. Hollins, J. E. King, & W. C. Hayman (Eds.), *Teaching diverse populations: Formulating a knowledge base*, pp. 5–24. Albany: State University of New York Press.

Baker, C. (1993). *Foundations of bilingual education and bilingualism.* Clevedon, U.K.: Multilingual Matters, Inc.

Banks, J. A. (1995). Multicultural education: Historical development, dimensions, and practice. In J. A. Banks & C. A. M. Banks (Eds.), *Handbook of research on multicultural education.* New York: Macmillan.

Banks, J. A. & Lynch, J. (Eds.). (1986). *Multicultural education in Western societies.* London: Holt, Rinehart and Winston.

Beare, H., & Boyd, W. L. (Eds.). (1993). *Restructuring schools: An international perspective on the movement to transform the control and performance of schools.* Washington, DC: The Falmer Press.

Bernal, M., Knight, G., Ocampo, K., Garza, C., & Cota, M. (1993). Development of Mexican American identity. In M. Bernal & G. Knight (Eds.), *Ethnic identity formation and transmission among Hispanics and other minorities*, pp. 31–46. Albany: State University of New York Press.

Bourdieu, P. (1977). *Outline of theory and practice.* Cambridge, Eng.: Cambridge University Press.

Cole, M., Gay, J., Glick, J. A., & Sharp, D. W. (1971). *The cultural context of learning and thinking: An exploration in experimental anthropology.* New York: Basic Books.

Corbett, H. D., & Wilson, B. (1990). *Testing, reform, and rebellion* Norwood, NY: Ablex.

Corson, D. (1993). *Language, minority education and gender: Linking social justice and power.* Clevedon, England: Multilingual Matters, Ltd.

Cummins, J. (1989). *Empowering minority students.* Sacramento, CA: California Association for Bilingual Education.

Cummins, J. (1994). From coercive to collaborative relations of power in the teaching of literacy. In B. M. Ferdman, R-M. Weber, & A. Ramírez, (Eds.), *Literacy across languages and cultures.* Albany: State University of New York Press.

Darder, A. (1991). *Culture and power in the classroom: A critical foundation for bicultural education.* New York: Bergin & Garvey.

Darling-Hammond, L. (1991). The implications of testing policy for quality and equality. *Phi Delta Kappan,* 73(3), 220–225.

Delgado-Gaitán, C., & Trueba, H. (1991). *Crossing cultural borders: Education for immigrant families in America.* London: The Falmer Press.

Delpit, L. (1995). *Other people's children: Cultural conflict in the classroom.* New York: The New Press.

Deyhle, D. (1995). Navajo youth and Anglo racism: Cultural integrity and resistance. *Harvard Educational Review,* 65(3), 403–444.

Erickson, F. (1990). Culture, politics, and educational practice. *Educational Foundations,* 4(2), 21–45.

Figueroa, P. (1995). Multicultural education in the United Kingdom: Historical development and current status. In J. A. Banks & C. A. M. Banks (Eds.), *Handbook of research on multicultural education,* pp. 778–800. New York: Macmillan.

Fine, M. (1991). *Framing dropouts: Notes on the politics of an urban high school.* Albany: State University of New York.

Forray, K. R., & Hegedüs, A. T. (1989). Differences in the upbringing and behavior of Romani boys and girls, as seen by teachers. *Journal of Multilingual and Multicultural Development,* **10**(6), 515–528.

Freire, P. (1970). *Pedagogy of the oppressed.* New York: Seabury Press.

Freire, P. (1985). *The politics of education: Culture, power, and liberation.* New York: Bergin & Garvey.

Fullan, M. G., & Stiegelbauer, S. (1991). *The new meaning of educational change* (2nd ed.). New York: Teachers College Press.

Gibson, M. A. (1987). The school performance of immigrant minorities: A comparative view. *Anthropology and Education Quarterly,* **18**(4), 262–275.

Giroux, H. A. (1983). *Theory and resistance in education: A pedagogy for the opposition.* New York: Bergin & Garvey.

Gutierrez, K., Rymes, B., & Larson, J. (1995). Script, counterscript, and underlife in the classroom: James Brown versus Brown v. Board of Education. *Harvard Educational Review,* **65**(3), 445–471.

Hargreaves, A., Earl, L., & Ryan, J. (1996). *Schooling for change: Educating young adolescents for tomorrow's world.* London and Philadelphia: Falmer Press.

Hartle-Schutte, D. (1993). Literacy development in Navajo homes: Does it lead to success in school? *Language Arts,* **70**(8), 643–654.

Heath, S. B. (1983). *Ways with words.* New York: Cambridge University Press.

Hoff, G. R. (1995). Multicultural education in Germany: Historical development and current status. In J. A. Banks & C. A. M. Banks (Eds.), pp. 821–838. *Handbook of research on multicultural education.* New York: Macmillan.

Hollins, E. R., King, J. E., & Hayman, W. C. (Eds.). (1994). *Teaching diverse populations: Formulating a knowledge base.* Albany: State University of New York Press.

Jalava, A. (1988). Mother tongue and identity: Nobody could see that I was a Finn. In T. Skutnabb-Kangas & J. Cummins (Eds.), *Minority education: From shame to struggle,* pp. 161–166.

Jordan, B. (1989). Cosmopolitan obstetrics: Some insights from the training of traditional midwives. *Social Science and Medicine,* **28**(9), 925–944.

Knapp, M. S., Shields, P. M., & Turnbull, B. J. (1995). Academic challenge in high-poverty classrooms. *Phi Delta Kappan,* **76**(10), 770–776.

Kohl, H. (1994). *'I won't learn from you' and other thoughts on creative maladjustment.* New York: New Press.

Kozol, J. (1991) *Savage inequalities: Children in America's schools.* New York: Crown.

Ladson-Billings, G. (1994). *The dreamkeepers: Successful teachers of African American children.* San Francisco: Jossey-Bass Publishers.

Lawrence, S. M., & Tatum, B. D. (forthcoming). White educators as allies: Moving from awareness to action. In M. Fine, L. Weis, L. Powell, & M. Wong (Eds.), *Off-White: Critical perspectives on race.* New York: Routledge.

Lucas, T., Henze, R., & Donato, R. (1990). Promoting the success of Latino language-minority students: An exploratory study of six high schools. *Harvard Educational Review,* **60**(3), 315–340.

May, S. (1994). *Making multicultural education work.* Clevedon, Eng.: Multilingual Matters.

McDermott, R. P. (1977). The cultural context of learning to read. In S. F. Wanat (Ed.), *Papers in applied linguistics,* 10–18. Linguistics and Reading Series: 1. Arlington, VA: Center for Applied Linguistics.

McIntosh, P. (1988). *White privilege and male privilege: A personal account of coming to see correspondences through work in women's studies.* Working paper n. 189. Wellesley, MA: Wellesley College Center for Research on Women.

Moodley, K. A. (1995). Multicultural education in Canada: Historical development and current status. In J. A. Banks & C. A. M. Banks (Eds.), pp. 801–820. *Handbook of research on multicultural education.* New York: Macmillan.

Moorfield, J. (1987). Implications for schools of research findings in bilingual education. In W. Hirsch (Ed.), *Living languages,* pp. 31–43. Auckland: Heinemann.

Nieto, S. (1994). Lessons from students on creating a chance to dream. *Harvard Educational Review,* **64**(4), 392–426.

Nieto, S. (1996). *Affirming diversity: The sociopolitical context of multicultural education* (2nd ed.). White Plains, NY: Longman Publishers.

Nieto, S. (1997). School reform and student academic achievement: A multicultural perspective. In J. A. Banks & C. A. M. Banks (Eds.), *Multicultural education: Issues and perspectives,* 3rd ed., pp. 387–407. Boston: Allyn & Bacon.

Ogbu, J. U. (1994). Racial stratification and education in the United States: Why inequality persists. *Teachers College Record,* **96**(2), 264–298.

L Cultural Difference and Educational Change in a Sociopolitical Context 159

Pérez-Domínguez, S. (1995). The European dimension in education within cultural and ethnic diversity: The challenge of multi-intercultural education. Paper presented at the conference *1996: A Plan for Europe? Politics, Economics, and Culture,* sponsored by the AIESEC International and the Fountainbleau Youth Foundation, Brussels, September, 1995.

Ramírez, J. D. (1991). *Final report: Longitudinal study of structured English immersion strategy, early-exit and late-exit transitional bilingual education programs for language minority children.* Washington, DC: Office of Bilingual Education.

Reyes, M. de la Luz (1992). Challenging venerable assumptions: Literacy instruction for linguistically different students. *Harvard Educational Review,* 62, 427–446.

Rumbaut, R. G., & Ima, K. (1987). *The adaptation of Southeast Asian refugee youth: A comparative study.* Final Report. San Diego, CA: Office of Refugee Resettlement.

Ryan, W. (1972). *Blaming the victim.* New York: Vintage Books.

Santos Rego, M. A. (Ed.). (1994). *Teoría y práctica de la educación intercultural.* Universidade de Santiago de Compostela, España: Promociones y publicaciones universitarias.

Sharp, R., & Green, A. (1975). *Education and social control: A study in progressive primary education.* London: Routledge & Kegan Paul.

Skutnabb-Kangas, T. (1988). Multilingualism and the education of minority children. In T. Skutnabb-Kangas & J. Cummins (Eds.), *Minority education: From shame to struggle,* pp. 9–44. Clevedon, Eng.: Multilingual Matters.

Skutnabb-Kangas, T. (1990). Legitimating or delegitimating new forms of racism: The role of the researcher. *Journal of Multilingual and Multicultural Development,* 11(1 & 2), 77–100.

Skutnabb-Kangas, T., & Toukomaa, P. (1976). *Teaching migrant children's mother tongue and learning the language of the host country in the context of the socio-cultural situation of the migrant family.* Helsinki: Finnish National Commission for UNESCO.

Solomon, R. P. (1995). Beyond prescriptive pedagogy: Teacher inservice education for cultural diversity. *Journal of Teacher Education,* 46(4), 251–258.

Stairs, A. (1994). Indigenous ways to go to school: Exploring many visions. *Journal of Multilingual and Multicultural Development,* 15(1), 63–76.

Stubbs, M. (1995). Educational language planning in England and Wales: Multicultural rhetoric and assimilationist assumptions. In O. García & C. Baker (Eds.), *Policy and practice in bilingual education: Extending the foundations,* pp. 25–39. Clevedon, Eng.: Multilingual Matters.

Tharp, R. G. (1989). Psychocultural variables and constants: Effects on teaching and learning in schools. *American Psychologist,* 44(2), 349–359.

Thomas, W. P. and Collier, V. P. (1995). Language-minority student achievement and program effectiveness studies support native language development. *NABE News,* 18(8), 5, 12.

Troyna, B. (1992). *Racism and education.* Buckingham: Open University Press.

Vallen, T., & Stijnen, S. (1987). Language and educational success of indigenous and non-indigenous minority students in the Netherlands. *Language and Education,* 1(2), 109–124.

Vogt, L. A., Jordan, C., & Tharp, R. G. (1993). Explaining school failure, producing school success: Two cases. In E. Jacob & C. Jordan (Eds.), *Minority education: Anthropological Perspectives.* Norwood, NJ: Ablex.

Weinberg, M. (1990). *Racism in the United States: A comprehensive classified bibliography.* Westport, CT: Greenwood Press.

Language Issues and Educational Change

JIM CUMMINS

Ontario Institute for Studies in Education, University of Toronto

With cultural diversity comes linguistic diversity. This diversity has been created by growing rates of migration since the 1960s and by greater inter-cultural contact among nations as they try to resolve ecological and diplomatic problems together. In this chapter, Jim Cummins looks at the implications of linguistic diversity for educational change

    Cummins asks what it means to provide education in a growing number of contexts which are not merely bilingual, but which serve students from many different linguistic backgrounds in classrooms and their schools. Bilingualism, linguistic immersion, heritage languages, second language learning, and transformations in the entire organization of teaching and learning to accommodate classroom populations of great diversity are among the issues that Cummins addresses.

    The importance of these issues is pressed home with reference to research findings which indicate that when students lag behind in first language proficiency, they also lag behind in academic achievement and intelligence test scores despite their abilities in their own language. Failing to address the issue of linguistic diversity effectively leads to failure to capitalize on children's academic potential. Cummins concludes with policy recommendations to address language issues as a focus for educational change, including changes in curriculum, teaching and learning, and the climate of the school.

Linguistic diversity has always been characteristic of human societies. However, at no time in human history has linguistic diversity been associated with such volatile conflicts and power struggles in countries around the globe. These power struggles are evident in a variety of societal institutions and particularly so in public education systems. During much of this century, education systems in Western countries were expected to assimilate immigrants and "melt" cultural and linguistic differences into obscurity. These assimilationist policies, however, have been challenged since the 1960s as a result of the increased prominence of human rights and equity provisions in national and international policies and covenants and the dramatic growth in ethnic and linguistic diversity in Western countries.

    Cross-cultural contact has never been greater in both domestic and international arenas. This increase in diversity has resulted primarily from economic migration to Northern Europe, Australia, and North America whose economies expanded rapidly during the 1960s and from efforts to resettle refugees from countries devastated by war and famine. At the same time as diversity is increasing within societies, cross-cultural and linguistic contact between countries is increasing as a result of globalization of economic activity together with international attempts to resolve ecological and diplomatic problems.

    This paper considers the educational implications of this changing cultural and

A. Hargreaves (ed.), Extending Educational Change, 160-179.
© 2005 *Springer. Printed in the Netherlands.*

linguistic landscape. In many countries, educators and policy-makers are grappling with issues such as: What programs and methods will be most effective in teaching bilingual students the primary language of schooling and of the wider society? What role, if any, should students' mother tongues have within the public education system? What initiatives are required to teach additional languages to dominant or majority language group students so that they can operate effectively in a broader European Union or global context? How can persistent patterns of educational failure among certain linguistic and cultural minority groups be overcome?

In analyzing these issues, I shall first sketch the context of linguistic diversity in two broad geographic regions: the European Union and North America. These regions have been selected not because issues of linguistic diversity are in any sense more pressing than in other regions (e.g. Africa, Asia, Australia, Central and South America) but because a considerable amount of research has been carried out in these contexts and this research potentially lays the groundwork for theoretical analysis.

LINGUISTIC DIVERSITY IN EDUCATION WITHIN THE EUROPEAN UNION

By the early 1990s, about ten percent of the European Union (formerly European Community) school-age population came from families that had a language and/or cultural background different from that of the majority of the country in which they lived (Reid & Reich, 1992). In major metropolitan areas such as London, Amsterdam, Berlin, and Stockholm, concentrations of culturally and linguistically diverse students are much greater. For example, by the turn of the millenium, about 40 percent of school-age children in Amsterdam will have been born outside the Netherlands. In the Stockholm area, Runfors and Sjögren (1994) report that municipalities with high rates of immigrant settlement experience yearly increases in the proportion of children with parents of non-Swedish origin; for example, schools in Botkyrka have between 40 and 95 percent non-Swedish origin students (usually still referred to as "immigrant" even though most are at least second generation and born in Sweden). Sixty home languages are taught at school (usually for about 3 hours per week). At the preschool level, 75 percent of students have a foreign background.

Within Europe, the policy context for educational initiatives related to linguistic diversity issues is still defined in relation to the European Community's (EC) 1977 Directive to Member States on the education of children of migrant workers. The Directive emphasized the right of children to receive adequate teaching of the language of the receiving country and the obligation of the receiving countries to promote the teaching of the mother tongue and culture of the countries of origin, although this latter "obligation" was very much diluted by restrictive clauses (Reid & Reich, 1992).

A variety of pilot projects were initiated in member countries in response to the

EC Directive but, with some exceptions, the long-term impact of these projects appears to have been slight. An assessment of 15 projects implemented between 1986 and 1991 (Reid & Reich, 1992) suggested that for a large majority of the pilot projects mother tongue teaching remained a marginal activity, minority communities were not systematically involved in the development and planning of school subject content, teaching of the majority language tended to be "naively assimilatory" or was seen as "culturally neutral" (p. 241), and structural changes in educational provision were not a concern. Furthermore most of the pilot projects collapsed after EC financing came to an end and were not taken any further by the national or local authorities. Altogether, in the authors' view, "the tangible effects are slight" (p. 237). Teunissen (1992), in discussing the same projects, points out that many educators saw an opposition between teaching for diversity (linked to mother tongue instruction) and teaching for equity (linked to instruction in the majority language).

A similar opposition was noted in the Swedish context by Runfors and Sjögren (1994). Since 1974, Swedish policy in relation to the education of immigrant students was based on the principles of "equality, freedom of choice, and partnership." The principle of "freedom of choice" referred to the right of families to choose to maintain their language and culture of origin and was implemented by means of the teaching of students' home languages in the school for several hours per week. While some groups of immigrant students appear to perform well in Swedish schools (e.g. those with parents from East European countries), there is considerable concern about the underachievement of students who grow up in predominantly immigrant areas where there may be little contact with Swedish outside the school. Teachers in these areas are highly committed to help children succeed in Swedish society but perceive cultural and linguistic diversity as a disadvantage to students, a barrier to be overcome, and thus they tend to devalue the teaching of the home language. According to Runfors and Sjögren:

> For nearly twenty years the main issue was how to support immigrant children in maintaining and developing their mother tongue and to make them bilingual. The acquisition of Swedish was more or less taken for granted. Today, with a growing number of children of the second and third generation with an immigrant background, coupled with the recession of recent years as well as with an increase in the number of refugees, the central authorities question the principle of home-language teaching. The structures established during the last twenty years to provide this teaching are being revised and funds are diminishing. Emphasis is now being put on the necessity of mastering "proper" Swedish, rather than maintaining the home language. The principle of equality is given priority over the principle of freedom of choice. (1994, pp. 302–303)

Runfors and Sjögren report studies conducted with pupils of Assyrian/Syrian, Turkish, and Kurdish origin in North Botkyrka which showed that these children had few opportunities to speak Swedish outside the classroom and most had no Swedish-speaking friends. One survey conducted in 1991 in North Botkyrka reported that 86 percent of pupils required supplementary teaching in Swedish. Another reported that the majority of immigrant pupils made little progress in catching up to Swedish academic language norms during the first six years of schooling.

The apparent devaluation of home language instruction in the Swedish context echoes the recommendations of the Swann Report in Britain (Department of Education and Science, 1985). The report strongly endorsed initiatives to promote racial equality and the teaching of English as a second language but saw mother tongue teaching as an activity best left to the family and community without formal support from the school. The report did concede a role for bilingual support teaching in the primary school as a bridge to the acquisition of English. A considerable number of school systems in Britain do employ bilingual support teachers and assistants at both primary and secondary levels. According to Edwards and Redfern (1992) the aim of this movement towards "multilingual education" is "to encourage children to make use of the full range of their linguistic repertoire in communication and in learning, with the support of multilingual teachers, assistants, parents and resources" (p. 65).

To illustrate, the need to acknowledge bilingual learners' first language is articulated as follows in the language policy of Tower Hamlets, an inner city borough in London, with more than half its student population coming from home backgrounds other than English and many schools whose student population is over 90 percent bilingual:

> Encouraging the use of the first language in the classroom helps pupils' language and learning development particularly in the early stages of learning English. For example, concepts and their ideas can be explained in the first language and consolidated through English appropriate to the bilingual learner's stage of English development; experience of narrative can be given to beginner bilinguals through stories in their first language when their English has not developed beyond a few simple sentence structures. As pupils' acquisition of English develops, their first language remains a resource which supports their learning. Teachers need to be sensitive to this, at the same time as aiming to provide maximum opportunities for pupils to discuss and articulate their ideas and understanding in English. (Tower Hamlets Education, no date, p. 13)

This sketch of some initiatives within the EU is illustrative of the provision and debates during the past 20 years. However, it barely hints at the range of programs that exist in different countries. For example, in the area of provision for immigrant students, Finnish students in Sweden have the option of attending programs that use Finnish as the primary language of instruction throughout elementary school with Swedish occupying a secondary role (Skutnabb-Kangas, in press). One of the most impressive programs for culturally diverse students anywhere in the world is the trilingual Foyer program in Brussels that operates in six schools serving students from Italian, Spanish, Turkish and Morroccan backgrounds with the goal of developing proficiency in students' first language (L1), Dutch, and French (Byram & Leman, 1990; Reid & Reich, 1992).

In addition, a wide variety of bilingual and immersion programs exist for established national minorities such as Frisians in The Netherlands, Swedes in Finland, Gaelic speakers in Ireland and Scotland, Welsh speakers in Wales, and Basque and Catalan speakers in Spain. Many of these programs also serve speakers of the major language of the society who wish to develop full bilingual skills through immersion in the minority language (Beardsmore, 1993; Skutnabb-Kangas, 1995). In some cases, immersion programs are designed to serve speakers of the majority language only (e.g. Swedish immersion programs for Finns [Buss & Laurén, 1995]) while in other situations majority and minority language speakers are mixed in the same classes.

One model of multilingual education which is unique to the European context is the European Schools model that involves instruction through at least three languages at different stages of students' school careers. These schools serve students from a variety of language backgrounds in major European cities and they aim to maintain students' home language while also teaching the language(s) of the country in which the school is located and other major European languages. Beardsmore (1993) cautions that this model is expensive to operate, is not destined for expansion, and might be perceived as somewhat elitist. Nevertheless, the model illustrates how it is possible to organize schooling for mixed populations on an equal footing and to implement a program that is multilingual both in its operation and outcomes.

In summary, the European situation illustrates the range of educational provision in multilingual contexts (see also Centre for Educational Research and Innovation, 1991; Cummins & Skutnabb-Kangas, 1988; Extra & Verhoeven, 1993; Jaspaert & Kroon, 1991; Skutnabb-Kangas & Phillipson, 1994). In general, second language teaching innovations designed for dominant or majority groups in particular societies have been non-controversial and strongly supported by the EU; programs designed for well-established national minorities have also received strong support (e.g. from the EU's Bureau for Lesser Used Languages). More controversial, however, have been programs that aim to address the educational needs of migrant students (whether newly-arrived or second or third generation). Central EU agencies have provided both financial and moral support for programs that promote intercultural education and mother tongue teaching but many member states have tended to be ambivalent in relation to mother tongue provision. This has resulted in isolated and often short-lived initiatives that exert relatively little impact on the educational system as a whole. An exception to this has been Sweden which has had a stable policy infrastructure for more than 20 years supporting home language teaching; however, commitment to this policy appears to be weakening at the present time.

LINGUISTIC DIVERSITY IN EDUCATION WITHIN NORTH AMERICA

Canada and the United States differ from European nations insofar as both can be characterized as *settler societies* (Ogbu, 1992) that have long histories of immigration and which continue to admit large numbers of immigrants. By contrast, European countries have tended to be much more homogenous, often denying the diversity that has existed within their boundaries, and admitting migrants largely for narrowly-defined economic functions. Even countries such as Sweden that have granted migrant workers and their families full citizenship rights after several years residence, still erect psychological and institutional barriers to full societal participation (e.g. through segregated housing and schooling) (Runfors & Sjögren, 1994).

In spite of the different orientations to immigration and diversity in Europe and North America, many of the educational issues are similar in the two contexts. Among policy-makers and the general public in both Canada and the United States, there is considerable ambivalence in relation to immigration in general and strong opposition to publically-funded educational support for cultures and languages other than English. This opposition tends to be expressed more vehemently in the United States than in Canada and organizations such as the 700,000 strong *U.S. English* have run vigorous campaigns to restrict the use of languages other than English in schools, the workplace, and government-funded institutions.

In Canada, four classes of second language program can be distinguished based on the target population. Best known are the French immersion programs intended to develop bilingual French-English proficiency among mainly English-speaking students. Approximately 300,000 students participate in programs across the country that start in kindergarten or grade 1 (early immersion), grades 4 or 5 (middle immersion) or grades 7 or 8 (late immersion). All three variants are characterized by an initial intense exposure to French (50–100%) followed by instruction through both French and English in subsequent grades (Swain & Lapkin, 1982). These programs have been evaluated extensively and found to develop reasonable fluency in French at no apparent cost to English academic skills.

A second form of bilingual program serves official language minority students (anglophones in Quebec and francophones in other parts of Canada). These programs usually provide most of the instruction through the minority language (students' mother tongues) throughout the grades.

A third program variant involves the teaching of aboriginal languages to First Nations students. Extensive programs of bilingual instruction involving Inuktitut operate for Inuit students in Quebec and the Eastern Arctic and there are also bilingual programs involving Cree and Mohawk. In the case of Mohawk, programs in Quebec and Ontario are usually termed "immersion" programs insofar as English is the predominant home language of students. This reflects the pattern of rapid language loss in First Nations communities across the country with only three languages (Inuktitut, Cree, Ojibway) expected to survive long into the next century.

Finally, heritage or international language programs operating in most provinces teach languages other than the official and aboriginal languages. Enrolment in particular programs is open to any interested student and is not restricted to students from particular linguistic or cultural heritages. In the prairie provinces of Manitoba, Saskatchewan, and Alberta, as well as to some extent in British Columbia, some of these programs are fully bilingual usually involving about 50 percent of instructional time through both the heritage language and English. In Ontario and Quebec the languages are taught as subjects either outside the regular school day or within an extended school day. Ontario has the largest program with more than 120,000 students, reflecting the fact that Ontario is the most frequent destination of immigrants and close to half the student population in metropolitian Toronto school systems come from non-English-speaking home backgrounds. Heritage language programs (recently renamed "international languages" in Ontario) were implemented in the wake of the 1971 federal policy of multicultur-alism but were hotly contested in many contexts (e.g. metropolitan Toronto) on the grounds that teaching languages other than the official languages was potentially divisive and discouraged assimilation into the Canadian mainstream (see Cummins & Danesi, 1990).

All of these four program types would fall into what Ruiz (1988) terms the language planning categories of "language-as-resource" or "language-as-right". Official language minorities and First Nations students are seen to have either constitutional or treaty rights to protection of their language while French immer-sion programs and heritage language teaching are both regarded as enrichment initiatives that promote the linguistic resources of both the individual and the broader community.

In the United States context, these two orientations to language planning have been overshadowed by the "language-as-problem" orientation. This orientation focuses on the resolution of societal problems associated with language learning or linguistic diversity (Ruiz, 1988). Widespread implementation of bilingual educa-tion for bilingual students began in response to the judgement of the U.S. Supreme Court in the *Lau v. Nichols* case in 1974. The Court ruled that the civil rights of non-English-speaking students were violated when the school took no steps to help them acquire the language of instruction

> . . . there is no equality of treatment merely by providing students with the same facilities, textbooks, teachers, and curriculum; for students who do not understand English are effectively foreclosed from any meaningful educa-tion. Basic English skills are at the very core of what these public schools teach. Imposition of a requirement that, before a child can effectively participate in the educational program, he must already have acquired those basic skills is to make a mockery of public education. We know that those who do not understand English are certain to find their classroom experi-ences wholly incomprehensible and in no way meaningful. (Crawford, 1992, p. 253)

The Court did not mandate bilingual education but did require that schools take effective measures to overcome the educational disadvantages resulting from a home-school language mismatch. The Office of Civil Rights, however, interpreted the Supreme Court's decision as effectively mandating transitional bilingual education unless a school district could prove that another approach would be equally or more effective. This interpretation of the Supreme Court decision by the Office of Civil Rights sparked outrage among media commentators and educators in school districts which, for the most part, were totally unprepared to offer any form of bilingual instruction.

The ensuing debate was (and continues to be) volatile. Bilingual education is seen as just one manifestation of the legitimation and institutionalization of cultural diversity that threatens to fragment the nation. The prevailing neo-conservative attitude towards bilingual education is clearly expressed by Arthur Schlesinger Jr. in his best-selling book *The Disuniting of America*:

> In recent years the combination of the ethnicity cult with a flood of immigration from Spanish-speaking countries has given bilingualism new impetus. . . Testimony is mixed, but indications are that bilingual education retards rather than expedites the movement of Hispanic children into the English-speaking world and that it promotes segregation rather than it does integration. Bilingualism shuts doors. It nourishes self-ghettoization, and ghettoization nourishes racial antagonism. . . Using some language other than English dooms people to second-class citizenship in American society. . . Monolingual education opens doors to the larger world. . . institutionalized bilingualism remains another source of the fragmentation of America, another threat to the dream of 'one people.' (1991, pp. 108–109)

Schlesinger's claims that "bilingualism shuts doors" and "monolingual education opens doors to the wider world" are laughable if viewed in isolation, particularly in light of considerable research to the contrary (see Cummins, 1996) and the obvious reality of global interdependence. These views become interpretable only in the context of the extreme paranoia in relation to cultural and linguistic diversity that grips a significant segment of the U.S. population at the present time.

In spite of the sustained opposition to bilingual programs, these programs have become established in many states during the past 20 years and considerable evidence has accumulated regarding their effectiveness in reversing patterns of school failure among bilingual students (see Collier, 1995 and Cummins, 1996 for reviews). The two program types that have the most clear-cut research support are "developmental" or "late-exit" programs that maintain L1-medium instruction for part of the day throughout elementary school (Ramirez, 1992) and "two-way bilingual immersion" programs that serve both majority and minority students in the same classes with 50–90 percent of instruction in the early grades taught through the minority language and continuing for about half the instructional time in the later grades of elementary school. Collier summarizes the conclusion of her large-scale research (involving 42,000 students) on different program models as follows:

In our current research (Thomas & Collier, 1995), we found that two-way bilingual education provided for students at the elementary level is the most promising program model for the long-term academic achievement of language minority students. It is the only program where language minority students consistently maintain their academic success throughout high school, even though they may not have the opportunity to continue to develop their first language academically once they reach secondary school. The confidence that language minority students gain in classes where they are challenged with meaningful academic instruction through two languages is unparalled. By adding to that the stimulus of working academically with English-speaking peers, learning appears to accelerate, as the two groups serve as peer tutors for each other. (1995, pp. 35–36)

Developmental programs also emerged as very successful in Thomas and Collier's (1995) research. The least successful program model for students' long-term academic success was ESL pull-out in the early grades with no L1 support.

The outcomes of bilingual education in different parts of the world are consistent with the findings of basic research on second language learning and bilingualism. These findings and their policy implications are reviewed in the next section.

RESEARCH ON SECOND LANGUAGE LEARNING AND BILINGUALISM

Length of Time Required for Second Language Learners to Catch up Academically

Several large-scale studies conducted in Canada and the United States have reported that, on the average, at least five years is required for second language learners to attain grade norms in academic aspects of English proficiency (Collier, 1987; Cummins, 1981; Klesmer, 1994). Other research suggests that a much shorter period of time (about two years) is usually required for students to attain peer-appropriate levels of proficiency in conversational aspects of their second language (e.g. Gonzalez, 1986; Snow & Hoefnagel-Höhle, 1978).

The general pattern of findings can be illustrated with reference to Klesmer's findings. Klesmer's sample of almost 300 12-year-old English-as-a-second-language (ESL) students (most of whom were in grade 7) was representative of the ESL student population in the North York Board of Education in metropolitan Toronto. Students' length of residence in Canada varied from six months to more than six years. Detailed assessments of English proficiency and background data, as well as teacher ratings, were obtained. Klesmer reported that teachers considered most ESL students as average for their age in speaking, listening and reading after 24 to 35 months in Canada. In the area of writing, teachers considered ESL students to have almost reached the mean for Canadian born students after 5 or 6 years. However, the test data showed significant gaps between the ESL students and a control group of English first language students (N=43) in all areas, except non-verbal ability, even after six years length of residence. The control group of English L1 students performed at the level of test norms whereas the ESL students were considerably below test norms on verbal academic measures even after 6 years length of residence. These data are consistent with the findings of Collier (1987) and Cummins (1981) and also with the fact that both majority and minority students in two-way bilingual immersion programs in the United States require most of the elementatry school years to attain grade norms in their second language (Dolson & Lindholm, 1995; Thomas & Collier, 1995).

There are two reasons why such major differences are found in the length of time required to attain peer-appropriate levels of conversational and academic skills. First, considerably less knowledge of language itself is usually required to function appropriately in interpersonal communicative situations than is required in academic situations. Contextual cues provided by the concrete situation as well as by intonation, gestures, facial expressions, etc. greatly facilitate communication of meaning in face-to-face contacts. These cues are largely absent in academic situations such as reading a text or writing an essay.

The second reason is that native speakers of the school language are not standing still waiting for ESL students to catch up. Every year their literacy skills are expanding and thus second language learners must catch up with a moving target. It is not surprising that this formidable task is seldom complete in one or two years. However, as Klesmer's data suggest, ESL students' facility in English conversational skills may give a misleading impression of their overall competence in the language.

Some policy implications of these data are very clear. First, it is clearly not feasible for second language learners to receive special withdrawal teaching of the language for the five to ten years it may take to reach native-like proficiency in academic language skills. Thus, mainstream classroom teachers must define their roles to include the teaching of academic language, in addition to particular content, to second language learners. Until recently, few mainstream teachers were prepared (in either sense of the term) to undertake this task despite considerable policy rhetoric in countries such as Britain and Canada about teaching language across the curriculum. In most European and North American contexts pre-service education of teachers still pays scant attention to the implications of linguistic diversity for mainstream teachers even in contexts when second language learners constitute the mainstream school population.

A second policy implication of the length of residence data concerns the administration of standardized tests either for general monitoring of school progress or for diagnostic purposes when students encounter learning difficulties. The data suggest that administration of verbal ability or achievement tests will underestimate second language learners' academic potential until they have been learning the school language for at least 5 years. In the Cummins (1981) study, such tests underestimated the academic potential of students with three years length of residence by the equivalent of 15 IQ points (one standard deviation). Clearly, the entire structure of special education assessment and identification in several North American and European countries needs to be critically examined particularly in light of other data suggesting significant overrepresentation of bilingual students in special education programs (Centre for Educational Research and Innovation, 1987; Ortiz & Yates, 1983).

Bilingual Development among Second Language Learners

Considerable research has focused on the effects of various types of bilingual education and on predictors of L2 and L1 proficiency among second language learners (e.g. Harley et al., 1990; Verhoeven, 1994). A consistent conclusion to emerge from these studies is the fragility of students' L1 in situations where it is not strongly supported by the school. There is also considerable evidence of a moderate positive relationship or interdependence between the development of academic skills in the bilingual child's two languages. Concepts and knowledge developed in one language can transfer to the other (either L1 to L2, or L2 to L1) when sociolinguistic and educational conditions support the development of both languages (see Cummins, 1996 for a detailed review of this literature).

This "interdependence principle" accounts for the fact that for both majority and minority language students, bilingual education does not result in adverse effects on their academic development in the majority language, despite considerably less instructional time spent through that language.

An implication of the data on bilingual education is that, at both elementary and secondary levels, using bilingual students' L1 for instructional purposes is a valuable strategy to assist them in gaining access to mainstream curriculum content while they are acquiring proficiency in the major school language. Developing students' conceptual knowledge and literacy skills in this way helps make academic input through the L2 more comprehensible.

The basic research findings on time required for language learning and students' bilingual development reviewed above assist in interpreting some of the observed outcomes of different programs. For example, it is clear why "quick-fix" solutions such as providing a short period of time in an ESL or bilingual program are often unsuccessful if no modifications are made within the mainstream classroom or in the culture of the school generally. These findings also illustrate the need for the development of explicit language policies at the level of the school in order to ensure that all teachers are providing an appropriate learning environment for bilingual learners (Corson, 1990).

However, the psychoeducational data do not explain the variability in academic performance among culturally diverse students exposed to apparently similar educational experiences. Nor do they fully explain the significant enhancement of student performance in certain kinds of bilingual programs (Thomas & Collier, 1995). These issues are addressed in the next section.

EXPLAINING PATTERNS OF BILINGUAL STUDENT ACHIEVEMENT

In both European and North American contexts there is considerable variation among minority groups in patterns of educational success and failure. It is clearly not the case that a home-school language switch inevitably results in academic difficulties (as implied by the U.S. Supreme Court in the Lau v. Nichols case). The success of majority language students in immersion and two-way bilingual immersion programs illustrates this reality as does the strong academic performance of certain groups of minority students in both European and North American contexts despite a home-school language switch.

A variety of factors are likely at play in different contexts. Runfors and Sjögren (1994), for example, highlight the gap between the orientation to literacy required for success in Swedish schools and the multilingual but predominantly oral traditions of Turkish, Kurdish, and Assyrian/Syrian communities. Factors related to socioeconomic status are also relevant but cannot fully explain the data (Cummins, 1984; Krashen, 1996).

Factors related to power and status relations between groups in the wider society appear to play a significant role in determining patterns of minority student academic performance. In this regard, Ogbu (1978, 1992) has emphasized the differences between voluntary and involuntary minorities. The former come to host countries as immigrants to better their lives and to escape difficult economic or political circumstances. They are positively oriented to the dominant group in their new society and want to integrate rapidly. At the same time they are usually positively oriented to their home culture and have little ambivalence in regard to their sense of identity.

Involuntary minorities, on the other hand, were originally brought into the society against their will through slavery, conquest, colonization or forced labor and henceforth have been relegated to menial positions and denied true assimilation into the mainstream economic and political life of the society. Within the American context, Ogbu cites African Americans, Latinos (with the exception of Cubans), Native Americans, and Hawaiian Americans as examples of involuntary minorities. Involuntary minorities tend to experience long-term persistent underachievement whereas voluntary minorities are often highly successful academically (Gibson & Ogbu, 1991; Ogbu, 1978).

Although both types of minority may experience discrimination and hardship, voluntary minorities have a comparative frame of reference such that their present circumstances may appear preferable to those in their homeland. Their response to hardship is often to work harder to succeed. Involuntary minorities, on the other hand, do not have access to a comparative frame of reference and are very much aware of the "job ceiling" that limits how far they are likely to succeed in the society. In response to persistent devaluation of their identities and barriers to full participation in the society, they often develop either an ambivalent or oppositional collective identity in relation to the dominant group. They either partially internalize the devaluation of their identity or resist this process by taking on certain cultural behaviors that are opposed to dominant group norms in order to maintain their sense of security and self-worth. Adoption of an oppositional identity is one way of resisting the devaluation of their culture and language by the dominant group. Within schools, for example, African American adolescents are reported to regard academic success as "acting White" (Fordham, 1990).

The examples Ogbu cites from around the world suggest convincingly that inter-group power and status relations play a major role in determining minority students' academic success or failure. However, the voluntary/involuntary distinction must be seen in terms of dynamic rather than static categories. Immigrants such as Turks in Europe and Latinos in the U.S. may initially arrive in the host country with the positive orientation characteristic of voluntary minorities but over time adopt the oppositional identity of longer-term residents from their group as a result of strong prejudice and various forms of institutional discrimination which prevent genuine access to the mainstream society.

Power and status relations in the broader society are reflected in various societal institutions including schools. For example, the lower status of bilingual students in school has often been reinforced by punishing students for speaking their L1 and making them ashamed of their cultural background. The ways in which educators define their roles together with the structures of schooling (e.g. curriculum, assessment, language of instruction, teacher preparation, etc.) result in patterns of educator-student interaction that mirror the patterns of intergroup interaction in the broader society. In a societal context of coercive relations of power to which involuntary subordinated minorities have been subjected for generations, student identities have typically been devalued in these classroom interactions (Cummins, 1996).

This perspective suggests that program interventions aimed at reversing the underachievement of culturally diverse students will be successful to the extent that these interventions result in educator-student interactions that challenge patterns of coercive relations of power in the broader society. Thus, communicating to students that their bilingualism is a valuable asset both for them and their society challenges the societal discourse that proclaims "bilingualism shuts doors." Involving parents and minority communities as partners in a shared educational enterprise challenges the societal discourse that attributes students' academic difficulties to their cultural, linguistic, or genetic backgrounds (e.g. the popular and academic literature is littered with assumptions regarding minority students' "cultural deprivation," "linguistic deficits," "bilingual confusion," and "genetic inferiority"). Similarly, instruction that acknowledges and builds on students' prior experience and addresses issues that students see as relevant to their lives is much more likely to engage students academically than transmission-oriented instruction that effectively suppresses students' experience – what Paulo Freire (1983) termed a "banking" education where teachers define their roles in terms of depositing information and skills in students' memory banks.

To what extent is the research on educational effectiveness for culturally diverse students consistent with this theoretical framework?

EDUCATIONAL EFFECTIVENESS FOR CULTURALLY DIVERSE STUDENTS

The findings of two syntheses of the research and two major research studies will be summarized here. Both Garcia's (1991) and Stedman's (1987) syntheses include elementary and secondary school data. Stedman's also includes all "minority" students (i.e. African-American as well as language minority students). Lucas, Henze, and Donato's (1990) study, by contrast, focused on Latino students at the secondary level. The international case study project conducted by the Centre for Research and Innovation (1991) of the OECD analyzed 23 detailed case studies conducted in three continents. Despite this variation in student populations and contexts, there is considerable consistency in the factors these investigations point to as significant for students' school success.

Garcia groups effective instructional practices under five categories:

(a) *High Levels of Communication*: Effective classrooms were characterized by a high level of communication emphasizing student collaboration on small group projects organized around learning centers. Worksheet exercises were minimized in favor of an informal family-like social setting in which the teacher assisted individuals or small groups as they worked on their projects.

(b) *Integrated Thematic Curriculum*: Instruction of basic skills and academic content was organized around thematic units. In the majority of classrooms studied, students had considerable input into the choice of themes.

(c) *Collaborative Learning*: Collaborative learning has proved particularly effective in studies involving Latino students. According to Garcia, student-student interactions evoked higher order cognitive and linguistic discourse than did typical educator-student interactions.

(d) *Support for L1 Language and Literacy Development*: In early grades Spanish-English bilingual instruction was common and in later grades students were allowed to use either language. Students progressed systematically from writing in L1 to writing in English and their English writing emerged at or above their grade level of writing in Spanish.

(e) *Educator Perceptions and Role Definitions*: According to Garcia, educators in effective schools demonstrated a coherent pattern of high academic expectations for their students and perceived themselves as advocates for students. They also saw themselves as instructional innovators and had a strong commitment to school-home communication. They felt they had the autonomy to innovate and support from their principals to do so.

On the basis of this pattern of findings in effective schools, Garcia concludes that all students need to be intellectually challenged and academic content must be closely related to students' own environment and experience. Students should have ample opportunities to study topics in depth and to engage in active learning in a collaborative context through group projects that investigate issues relevant to their own lives.

Stedman's (1987) conclusions are similar. First on his list of factors contributing to low-income students' academic success is *cultural pluralism*. He argues that effective schools acknowledge the ethnic and racial identity of their students through having role models in high status positions and offering opportunities for students to develop their linguistic and cultural talents through programs such as bilingual education.

Among the other factors stressed by Stedman are *parental participation* and *academically rich programs*. Parents are encouraged to become involved in their children's education and students are actively engaged in their own learning through projects and tasks that capitalize on their prior experiences. The other factors identified by Stedman related to allocation of resources and permitting students a genuine role in school decision-making.

Lucas et al.'s (1990) study of six successful high schools serving primarily Latino students in Arizona and California documented eight factors that appeared to distinguish these schools. These factors are as follows:

1. Value is placed on students' languages and cultures;
2. High academic expecations are communicated to language minority students;
3. School leaders make the education of language minority students a priority;
4. Staff development is explicitly designed to help teachers and other school staff to serve language minority students more effectively;
5. A variety of advanced and basic courses and programs for language minority students is offered;
6. School counselors are committed to and capable of providing appropriate guidance to language minority students as a result of speaking students' language and coming from similar cultural backgrounds;
7. Parents of language minority students are encouraged to become involved in their children's education;
8. School staff members share a strong commitment to create contexts both inside the school and in the community wherein a sense of empowerment can be generated among language minority students.

The picture that emerges from these studies of school effectiveness for language minority students has three specific and one general component that contribute to student academic success. The three specific components are: (a) affirmation of students' cultural identity and encouragement of L1 literacy and language development; (b) encouragement of active parental participation; and (c) cognitively-challenging instruction that provides opportunities for students to draw on their background experiences while working collaboratively to explore issues and topics that are relevant to their lives.

These specific interventions are implemented in a school context where issues related to the education of language minority students have moved from the periphery to the center of concern for the entire school. Educators, both individually and collectively, have defined their roles in such a way that their interactions with language minority students affirm rather than devalue students' identities.

The educational structures established in the school reflect these role definitions. In the Lucas et al. research, this whole school shift in role definitions and structures is indicated in features 3, 4, 5, 6, and 8.

The affective dimension of these interactions between educators and students is clear in student comments reported by Lucas et al.:

> At all of the schools, students mentioned teachers who had given them special help and attention, often crediting them with providing personal counseling as well as academic support. Typical student comments included the following: 'The teachers here don't just teach; they care about you' and 'Teachers stay after school to explain what we didn't understand.' (p. 336)

Consistent findings emerged from the analysis of 23 case studies of schools addressing issues of cultural diversity in Europe, North America, and Australia conducted by the Centre for Educational Research and Innovation (1991). Innovations were analyzed according to the extent to which they fostered greater respect for students' language and culture, greater parent and community involvement, and instruction that provided meaningful cognitive challenges while building on students' background experience. Successful schools appeared to

> depend on the use and recognition of each student's cultural and linguistic background; on forms of participation of parents and communities which take into account cultural perspectives and linguistic abilities in meaningful ways; and on curriculum content which relates, in part, to each student's experiences and perspectives and permits each student to critically interpret curriculum content in relation to these experiences and perspectives as well as alternative perspectives. (1991, p. 121)

In addition, the culture of the school was found to be a key to successful change. The extent to which the whole school culture was affected by a particular approach or innovation was crucial to its eventual success (see Hopkins, 1987).

IMPLICATIONS FOR POLICY AND PRACTICE

There is a considerable gap between the "best practices" identified in the research reviewed in the previous section and the reality of educational practice in many European and North American schools. North American findings (e.g. Goodlad, 1984; Olsen & Minicucci, 1992; Ramirez, 1992; Sirotnik, 1983) suggest that teacher-centered transmission approaches predominate across the grade levels and particularly so at the high school. In addition, language minority students are frequently segregated and do not get access to mainstream curriculum content. Olsen and Minicucci (1992), for example, report data relating to the degree of integration/segregation of second language learners in 27 California secondary schools. They found that these students were tracked into separate classes and rarely had opportunities to interact with mainstream English-speaking students.

The fact that only English was generally used in these classes channelled students away from their first language and culture but yet they were not getting the kind of academic input in English to permit them to succeed academically in that language.

In the Dutch context, a similar problematic picture of secondary level instruction has been presented by Hajer (1994) in an analysis of 56 lessons given to a class of students from a variety of linguistic backgrounds in Amsterdam. The students were in their third year of secondary school (average age 15.2) and had an average length of residence in the Netherlands of 13.1 years.

Preliminary analysis indicated that neither students nor teachers considered learning through Dutch to be a problematic issue despite the fact that students' written Dutch evidenced considerable semantic and morpho-syntactic difficulties. In all subject areas observed, students had very limitied opportunities to produce Dutch, oral or written. In fact, "when pupils had to write in tests, it was often their first opportunity to use the subject language, and they were immediately judged on this, without getting any feedback" (p. 8). Also, according to Hajer, "many opportunities were missed to relate the course content to the pupils' background, thus diminishing the possibilities of providing the pupils with a context for the themes involved. Activating prior knowledge seldom took place" (p. 8). The case studies analyzed by Reid and Reich (1992) and the Centre for Educational Research and Innovation (1991) also reveal the preponderance of transmission approaches to teaching culturally diverse students in many contexts.

In summary, although the available data are limited in scope, there is evidence of a considerable gap between actual patterns of classroom interaction in both North America and Europe and the types of patterns that research and theory suggest might be optimal for academic development in the second language. The fact that in most contexts issues related to cultural and linguistic diversity remain marginal in the pre-service preparation of teachers clearly contributes to the absence of effective language policies in most schools serving culturally diverse student populations. Similarly, only a very small proportion of bilingual students receive any form of L1 support in either Europe or North America, despite the research suggesting the potential significance of this type of intervention.

CONCLUSION

The increasing linguistic diversity in education presents major challenges to educators and school systems that have traditionally operated according to monolingual and monocultural assumptions. Innovations that serve the interests of dominant groups in society (e.g. French immersion programs in Canada or the European Schools in Europe) are generally non-controversial and supported by government policy and funding. By contrast, innovations that are perceived as serving the interests of minority groups (e.g. bilingual education in the United States or heritage language programs in Canada) tend to be the subject of volatile debate in which sociopolitical and psychoeducational arguments become intertwined.

Despite the controversies, there is in fact considerable consistency in the research findings emerging from different contexts relating both to the general outcomes of program interventions and more specific issues related to language learning and bilingual education.

All of the interventions that research highlights as potentially successful entail an entire school commitment to make instruction accessible to second language learners. In other words, rather than expecting culturally diverse students to adapt to the school as it is, the school commits itself to change in order to meet the students half-way. Issues related to linguistic and cultural diversity become a central focus of school policy rather than just a footnote to business as usual.

Within the classroom, this change in overall school policy will manifest itself in interactions between educators and students that value students' prior experience, language and culture. Failure to activate students' prior experience in the instructional process is akin to teaching in a vacuum. All cognitive theorists agree that we learn new information by integrating it with our existing cognitive schemata – in other words, with our prior experience. Yet too often culturally diverse students are viewed as blank slates and no attempt is made to mobilize their prior knowledge.

There is considerable agreement among applied linguists about the kinds of teaching strategies that will integrate language and content, which is essential if students are to catch up academically. In addition to activating students' prior experience, students' L1 development should be reinforced to the extent possible. Instruction will emphasize two-way communication and cognitively challenging content. Specific approaches will include strategies such as cooperative learning, use of "key visuals" or "graphic organizers," verbal presentation that builds in considerable redundancy, and a focus on encouraging students to become self-regulated learners through helping them acquire efficient learning strategies (see Chamot & O'Malley, 1994).

However, the extent to which individual educators and entire schools adopt these strategies will depend on the extent to which they perceive culturally diverse students as having important contributions to make to the process of intellectual exploration within the classroom and, by extension, within the society itself. If educators reflect the prejudices towards subordinated groups that are prevalent in the broader society, then they are unlikely to value students' prior experiences nor use them as the foundation for future learning. They are also likely to rely on transmission approaches to teaching that communicate to students that their role is to internalize dominant group wisdom rather than engage in a collaborative process of generating knowledge.

In short, pedagogical practices in relation to culturally diverse students are intertwined with patterns of power relations in the broader society. Effective instructional practices will inevitably entail a process of identity negotiation between educators and students that challenges patterns of prejudice and discrimination in the broader society. Educational planning that fails to acknowedge this fundamentally political dimension of the change process is unlikely to be successful.

REFERENCES

Beardsmore, H. B. (1993). *European models of bilingual education.* Clevedon, England: Multilingual Matters.

Buss, M. & Laurén, C. (1995). *Language immersion: Teaching and second language acquisition> From Canada to Europe.* Proceedings of the University of Vaasa Research Papers. Tutkimuksia No. 192. Vaasa: The University of Vaasa.

Byram, M., & Leman. J. (1990). (Eds.). *Bicultural and trilingual education.* Clevedon, England: Multilingual Matters.

Centre for Educational Research and Innovation (CERI), Organization for Economic Co-operation and Development (OECD). (1991). *Education and cultural and linguistic pluralism: Synthesis of case studies.* Effective strategies and approaches in schools. Paris: OECD/CERI.

Chamot, A.U., & O'Malley, J. M. (1994). *The CALLA handbook: Implementing the cognitive academic language learning approach.* Reading, MA: Addison-Wesley.

Collier, V. P. (1995). *Promoting academic success for ESL students: Understanding second language acquisition for school.* Elizabeth, NJ: New Jersey Teachers of English to Speakers of Other Languages.

Collier, V. P. (1996). Age and rate of acquisition of second language for academic purposes. *TESOL Quarterly, 21,* 617–641.

Corson, D. (1990). *Language policy across the curriculum.* Clevedon, England: Multilingual Matters.

Crawford, J. (Ed.). (1992a). *Language loyalties: A source book on the Offical English controversy.* Chicago: University of Chicago Press.

Cummins, J. (1981). Age on arrival and immigrant second language learning in Canada: A reassessment. *Applied Linguistics, 2,* 132–149.

Cummins J. (1984). *Bilingualism and special education: Issues in assessment and pedagogy.* Clevedon, England: Multilingual Matters.

Cummins, J. (1996). *Negotiating identities: Education for empowerment in a diverse society.* Ontario, CA: California Association for Bilingual Education.

Cummins, J., & Danesi, M. (1990). *Heritage languages: The development and denial of Canada's linguistic resources].* Toronto: Our Schools Ourselves/Garamond.

Department of Education and Science. (1985). *Education for all.* London: HMSO.

Dolson, D., & Lindholm, K. (1995). World class education for children in California: A comparison of the two-way bilingual immersion and European Schools model. In T. Skutnabb-Kangas (Ed.), *Multilingualism for all.* (pp. 69–102). Lisse: Swets & Zeitlinger.

Edwards, V., & Redfern, A. (1992). *The world in a classroom: Language in education in Britain and Canada.* Clevedon, England: Multilingual Matters.

Extra, G., & Verhoeven, L. (1993). *Immigrant languages in Europe.* Clevedon, England: Multilingual Matters.

Fordham, S. (1990). Racelessness as a factor in Black students' school success: Pragmatic strategy or pyrrhic victory? In N. M. Hidalgo, C. L. McDowell, & E. V. Siddle (Eds.), *Facing racism in education.* (pp. 232–262). Reprint series No. 21, Harvard Educational Review.

Freire, P. (1983). Banking education. In H. Giroux & D. Purpel (Eds.), *The hidden curriculum and moral education: Deception or discovery?* Berkeley, CA: McCutcheon Publishing Corporation.

Garcia, E. (1991). *Education of linguistically and culturally diverse students: Effective instructional practices.* Educational Practice report 1. Santa Cruz: The National Center for research on Cultural Diversity and Second Language Learning.

Gibson, M. A., & Ogbu, J. U. (Ed.). (1991). *Minority status and schooling: A comparative study of immigrant and involuntary minorities.* New York: Garland Publishing.

Gonzalez, L. A. (1986). *The effects of first language education on the second language and academic achievement of Mexican immigrant elementary school children in the United States.* Doctoral dissertation submitted to the University of Illinois at Urbana-Champaign.

Goodlad, J. I. (1984). *A place called school: Prospects for the future.* New York: McGraw Hill.

Hajer, M. (1994). *Learning through a second language: Insights from classroom research.* Unpublished manuscript.

Harley, B., Allen, P., Cummins, J., & Swain, M. (Eds.). (1990). *The development of second language proficiency.* Cambridge, England: Cambridge University Press.

Hopkins, D. S. (1987). Improving the quality of schooling. Lewes, England: The Falmer Press.

Jaspaert, K., & Kroon, S. (Eds.) (1991). *Ethnic minority languages and education.* Amsterdam/Lisse: Swets & Zeitlinger.

Klesmer, H. (1994). Assessment and teacher perceptions of ESL student achievement. *English Quarterly*, **26**(3), 8–11.

Krashen, S. (1996). *Under attack: The case against bilingual education*. Los Angeles: Language Education Associates.

Lucas, T., Henze, R., & Donato, R. (1990). Promoting the success of Latino lanuage-minority students: An exploratory study of six high schools. *Harvard Educational Review*, **60**, 315–340.

Ogbu, J. U. (1978). *Minority education and caste*. New York: Academic Press.

Ogbu, J. U. (1992). Understanding cultural diversity and learning. *Educational Researcher*, **21**(8), 5–14 & 24.

Olsen, L., & Minnicucci, C. (1992, April). *Educating limited English proficient students in secondary schools: Critical issues emerging from research in California schools*. Paper presented at the American Education Research Association annual conference, San Francisco.

Ortiz, A. A. & Yates, J. R. (1983). Incidence of exceptionality among Hispanics: Implications for manpower planning. *NABE Journal*, **7**, 41–54.

Ramirez, J. D. (1992). Executive summary. *Bilingual Research Journal*, **16**, 1–62.

Reid, E., & Reich, H. (Eds.) (1992). *Breaking the boundaries: Migrant workers' children in the EC*. Clevedon, England: Multilingual Matters.

Ruiz, R. (1988). Orientations in language planning. In S. L. McKay & S. C. Wong (Eds.), *Language diversity: Problem or resource?* (pp. 3–25). New York: Newbury House.

Runfors, A., & Sjögren, A. (1994). Language, dominance, and resistance: An ethnological perspective on teaching and learning Swedish in an immigrant environment in Sweden. *Migration*, **23/24**, 293–314.

Schlesinger, A. Jr. (1991). *The disuniting of America*. New York: W.W. Norton.

Sirotnik, K. A. (1983). What you see is what you get – consistency, persistency, and mediocrity in classrooms. *Harvard Educational Review*, **53**, 16–31.

Skutnabb-Kangas, T. (Ed.) (1995). *Multilingualism for all*. Lisse: Swets & Zeitlinger.

Skutnabb-Kangas, T. (in press). Bilingual education for Finnish minority students in Sweden. In J. Cummins & D. Corson (Eds.), *Bilingual education*. New York: Kluwer.

Skutnabb-Kangas, T., & Cummins, J. (Eds.). (1988). *Minority education: From shame to struggle*. Clevedon, England: Multilingual Matters.

Skutnabb-Kangas, T. & Phillipson, R. (Eds.) (1994). *Linguistic human rights*. Berlin: Mouton de Gruyter.

Snow, D. E. & Hoefnagel-Höhle, M. (1978). The critical period for language acquisition: Evidence from second language learning. *Child Development*, **49**, 1114–1128.

Stedman, L. C. (1987). It's time we changed the effective schools formula. *Phi Delta Kappan*, **69**, 215–224.

Swain, M., & Lapkin, S. (1982). *Evaluating bilingual education*. Clevedon, England: Multilingual Matters.

Teunissen, F. (1992). Equality of educational opportunity for children from ethnic minority communities. In E. Reid & H. Reich (Eds.), *Breaking the boundaries: Migrant workers' children in the EC*. Clevedon, England: Multilingual Matters.

Thomas, W. P., & Collier, V. P. (1995). *Language minority student achievement and program effectiveness*. Washington, DC: National Clearinghouse for Bilingual Education.

Tower Hamlets Education. (no date). *Tower Hamlets language policy*. London: Borough of Tower Hamlets.

Verhoeven, L. (1994). Transfer in bilingual development: The linguistic interdependence hypothesis revisited. *Language Learning*, **44**, 381–415.

The Politics of Gender and Educational Change: Managing Gender or Changing Gender Relations?

JILL BLACKMORE

Faculty of Education, Deakin University

One of the strongest social forces driving educational change – in classrooms, curriculum, teaching and leadership – is the changing role and position of women in society. But the effects of changing configurations of gender relations in education are not straightforward. In this chapter, Jill Blackmore discusses how stronger orientations to gender equity in children's learning and educators' careers frequently run against the grain of deep-seated cultural assumptions about gender, long-standing institutional practices that don't easily accommodate changed gender relations, and parallel patterns of reform that seem to contradict or undermine many of the new directions otherwise being pursued in the name of gender equity.

In particular, Blackmore scrutinizes how gender-based reforms fare in the context of an increased market orientation to educational change, where many gender-sensitive practices in classrooms, curriculum and even the hiring of school principals are often construed as bad for the school's image in the marketplace of parental choice. Gender based reforms are also analyzed in the context of a new managerialism in education, where emphases on financial constraint and centralized accountability in rational systems of measurement and management, paradoxically mean that the growing numbers of women entering the school principalship turn into emotional 'middle-managers' of educational change – motivating their staff to work reasonably and committedly in an increasingly unreasonable world.

Blackmore concludes by saying that gender-based reform in educational change is about much more than recruiting women into educational leadership, or embracing their caring styles of emotional managment, but also engineering much more fundamental shifts in the wider policy context of educational reform so that schools can be more responsive to gender based issues.

Change has become a prime focus of attention in education. It is widely argued that postmodern workplaces and social organizations need new kinds of workers and citizens: and these in turn call for new forms of schooling, new types of leadership and new ways of teaching. At the same time, issues of gender that had long been ignored in educational policy research has moved increasingly into the mainstream. What is it that has changed so that gender can no longer be ignored so readily? Also, what can research in gender equity tells us about the nature and effects of educational change?

The changing demographics and workforce patterns of post-industrial society have meant that women's role and position in society have changed. Women are now viewed as important producers and consumers in the post-industrial economy. In a period of political and economic volatility women also act as powerful political constituencies (Yeatman, 1992). Clearly, therefore, gender can no longer be

A. Hargreaves (ed.), Extending Educational Change, 180-201.

ignored in projects of social and educational change. But just how fundamental are effects of social change and educational restructuring on gender relations? And how has gender reform informed social change? Are they first level or second level effects? First level effects operate at the level of discourse. They are typically claims about the efficiency and effectiveness of a particular reform, and are often called upon to justify change after the event, and if change occurs it is fleeting and superficial. Second level effects are those that actually occur when a reform is implemented and that produces fundamental changes in social practice in terms of new contact patterns between individuals and the changes in what individuals believe to be important (Cuban, 1990).

Policies of educational reform have, while largely drawing upon more optimistic accounts of postmodernism about multi-skilling, team work and the democratising tendencies of new information technologies, often produced unpredictable and inequitable effects. Such effects are made more obvious when the question is asked: What impact will this policy have on Aboriginal girls or that program on working class boys? Seemingly progressive initiatives can reproduce social inequities if difference (of gender, race, ethnicity and class) is not addressed as a central and integral aspect of educational change. Furthermore, new policy initiatives seeking to promote changes such as gender equity, for example, are situated in contexts which may inhibit the capacity for those expected to produce reform to do so. Thus in many schools in Australia, while there is a popular rhetoric about gender equity reform for girls and women, it is in a time of reduced resources in schools, scarce university and training places, and a more competitive and market oriented environment. These factors reduce many schools' capacities to deal with social justice issues. Finally, many policymakers assume that policies are adopted as they intend. Thus the adaptation and interpretation of gender reform policies, as well the significant resistances, at the level of school are rarely addressed.

In this chapter, I consider why we should be 'uneasy' about the effects of educational restructuring and recent policy initiatives on gender equity. I draw from a number of research studies[1] which have focused upon gender reform, leadership and educational change over a period of radical restructuring of education in Victoria, Australia, since 1989. One project draws upon the experiences of female educational bureaucrats in seeking to produce educational policy; another was a three year project considering the reception by teachers and students of Equal Opportunity (EO) policies for girls; a third and ongoing project focuses upon women and leadership in schools; another considered the impact of the restructuring of educational work on women educators. A fifth project examined the claims of Schools of the Future, the policy which introduced self-managing schools in Victoria, from the perspective of how principals, schools and parents 'manage change'. The data were collected through unstructured interviews, documentation, observation, survey, and focus groups. This chapter highlights patterns, critical incidents, life stories and case studies which arose out of these projects. I use these to explicate the complexities of gender equity reform in the context of rapid and radical educational restructuring. By looking through the lens of gender, I consider how particular reforms have affected women and girls, and what studies on gender equity can suggest are strategies we may follow to produce greater gender equity in new hard times. I first deal with the wider contextual issues of restructuring and gender, and then focus upon the dilemmas these produce for principals in schools and conclude with some suggestions about gender reform practice which are conducive to a more socially just education.

RESTRUCTURING AND THE RE-GENDERING OF EDUCATIONAL WORK

Workplace restructurings in most post industrial states have called upon discourses which connect the globalisation of the marketmarket to local workplace flexibility (Lash & Urry, 1994). The global nature of the problems confronting Western nation-states has led to significant 'policy borrowing' across the world as different governments seek to find solutions to similar problems (Ball, 1995). By restructuring, I refer to major changes in school organization, curriculum, pedagogy and assessment practices as well as to teachers' and principals' work. Educational restructuring in Victoria and elsewhere has the following characteristics: devolution of responsibility to schools and principals to prioritise within global budgets; increased principal power; an intensification of teachers' and principals' work; new career structures based upon performance management; and a shift away from collective bargaining to individual contracts in teacher employment (Ball, 1995). This constitutes a radical restructuring of education – in school governance, teaching and learning – in order to provide greater flexibility to principals and to enable schools to maximise resources and increase effectiveness and efficiency. While equity has not been central to this restructuring, it is assumed that in addressing market diversity and providing students opportunities to exercise individual choice, that equity concerns will be met.

But while there have been radical changes in the relationship between schools and their communities, and within schools between teachers, parents and the principal, such changes have not necessarily been progressive when gender is considered. The restructuring of schools has, while changing certain fundamental social relationships, exacerbated not ameliorated, the historical division of labour in education in which men manage and women teach although along different lines (Blackmore, 1996a). Three aspects of school restructuring have been particularly important to the processes re-gendering educational work: devolution of decison-making and responsibility to schools; the reorganization of education along quasi-market lines; and the internal processes of restructuring by which jobs are re-defined and re-allocated in schools and bureaucracies.

Devolution in education systems has usually been accompanied by declining public expenditure and a rhetoric of small government (Moller, 1993; Whitty, 1996; Blackmore, 1995a). Women's equity gains during the twentieth century have largely relied upon a strong interventionist state in the areas of welfare, equity policies and guaranteeing basic wages[2]. Women employees have been concentrated in the public sector; women and children tend to be the majority of the recipients of welfare; women also benefit from Equal Opportunity legislation (Wernerson, 1989; Middleton, 1988; Eisenstein, 1991). These are the areas in which the state is withdrawing. We are now in a period of transition away from the modern welfare state to a smaller contractualist state which intervenes selectively only to modify the excesses of the market (Yeatman, 1992). Whereas the state assumed responsibility for health, education and welfare as basic citizenship rights for the public good, now education is increasingly perceived as a private good to be paid for by the user (Peters & Marshall, 1996). Together with the shift from centralised wage systems of collective bargaining towards decentralised systems of enterprise based and individual work contracts, women's dependence upon the paternalistic state to provide a 'safety net' in employment and welfare is in jeopardy (Hyman, 1994). As a feminised public sector profession, teaching sits in a precarious position with this shift in the role of the state, the rise of the market and competitive individualism in education, and the decline of unionism in the workplace. The trend is for teachers' work to become casualised and feminised, trends which reflect changes in the wider labour market (Pillinger, 1993). Under enterprise and individual wage bargaining agreements, women in feminised industries tend to tradeoff higher wages and status to gain the 'flexibility' to undertake family responsibilities[3] (Blackmore, 1996a; Hyman, 1994). Furthermore, a core-periphery model is emerging in the deregulated teacher labour market in the consumer / service oriented economies of USA, UK, Canada, Australia, New Zealand, Sweden and Israel. On the one hand there is the casualisation and feminisation of teachers' work forming a peripheral labour market amongst teachers and on the other hand a 're-masculinisation' of the central administration at executive management level as women exit due to the 'chilly climate' and as curriculum and professional development is devolved down to schools (Lash & Urry, 1994; Ozga, 1993; Möller, 1993; Goldring & Chan, 1993). These factors have long term consequences for teaching as a profession in terms of salary decline and status (Acker, 1996).

Second, devolution has usually been accompanied by the development of quasi-market systems in education in most nation states (Kenway, 1996; Gewirtz, Bowe, & Ball, 1995). Global budgets dependent upon per capita funding means that in a declining school population, schools compete for students with other public schools and, in some instances, a private school sector[4]. Gender then becomes a significant factor in the market – in terms of images of good leadership and the marketability of gender equity programs (Blackmore, 1996b). The dominant value systems of the market-oriented school tend to focus upon individual choice and competition. They often lead to educational practices which are selective and exclusionary practices, success being judged upon narrow academic outcomes, and the ranking and streaming of students. These values can work against those central to gender equity reform with its focus upon integration, welfare, community, student needs, curriculum issues, disadvantage, inclusion and caring social relationships. While the claim is often made that the market will be the mechanism by which individual choice is exercised and diversity is thereby addressed, market advantage is normally maintained by conforming to, and being ranked against, particularly narrow images of what constitutes an effective school (Gewirtz et al., 1995; Blackmore, 1996b).

Such images are more often than not premised around strong and entrepreneurial models of leadership more closely associated with masculinity than femininity. In such a context, equity and social justice are not 'marketable' commodities, with few exceptions such as single sex girls schools which attract a particular 'niche market' of expert consumers – middle class parents with daughters.

Finally, restructuring also provided possibilities for the male bias of institutional structures and cultures to be 'mobilised' as organizations are internally restructured along managerialist lines (Burton, 1990). Discourses of efficiency and effectiveness tend to be privileged in the 'rational processes' of organizational restructuring over those of equity and social justice. The maintenance rather than dismantling of the gendered division of labour has often occurred in organizations although the rationale is for flexibility. This maintenance work occurs when decisions are made about what is open to be changed and what is left unchanged. Do we change the way we organize schools to be more representative or do we focus upon inclusive curriculum and ignore the organisational context? The mobilisation of bias occurs in the ways in which merit and skill are defined in job descriptions and what forms of knowledge are valued. It occurs in the overt and covert rules governing organisational restructuring. In Victoria, many women 'separated' voluntarily from the central educational bureaucracy in part due to the 'chilly climate' which excluded women from the decision-making processes (Still, 1995); in part due to reduced opportunities as rules for re-deployment re-located the many senior male staff into the new jobs for which experienced women had been 'waiting in the aisles'; and in part as middle management was 'hollowed out' as curriculum and professional development (areas where women were largely located) were devolved to schools. Finally, a conscious political strategy of the conservative government was to dismantle the Gender Equity units within the central administration and to change the language by replacing equal opportunity and gender with the more 'value neutral terms' of merit and equity. The effect was the loss of many women with histories in gender equity reform as they moved out into areas not concerned with gender equity or left the system altogether. They were replaced by 'multi-skilled' managers without experience in neither education or social justice policy development. The consequence was a significant loss of institutional memory in gender equity reform at the centre where many initiatives had begun.

Thus, seemingly 'rational' and 'neutral' processes of restructuring produced outcomes which were antithetical to equity because gender equity was not a central organising principle embedded in the policies and processes of restructuring or integral to all phases of planning and implementation. Equity was more an afterthought, and any individuals who criticised the new policies were positioned as 'tired old feminists', 'out of date' or 'resisters to change'. Such managerialist rationalities, particularly when imbued with notions of the market, which is not gender neutral, as the mechanism by which educational resources will be distributed, have implications for school based management.

DEALING WITH DIFFERENCE AND THE MARKET

At the level of the school, the dissonance between the rhetoric of professional autonomy and discretionary judgement and the reality of the self managing school meant principals and teachers in Victoria, as elsewhere, are now confronted with difficult dilemmas (Ball, 1995). Specifically, the tension was between the principal's role as educational leaders in the community and school and as line managers with responsibility to the central administration in terms of more efficiently managing finance, staffing and public relations in accordance with government policy. In Victoria, as elsewhere, the centralising tendencies of 'the self managing school' have become stronger than the decentralising tendencies because of the accountability mechanisms which provide feedback to the centre. Principals and teachers are increasingly monitored and managed through such measures as curriculum standards frameworks, standardised testing, career structures based upon performance management, and school charters with three year priorities. In 1994, a national report on Australian principals in all state systems referred to the "pressure of unrelenting change which is not seen as being necessarily to education's advantage; the increasing, multiple and sometimes conflicting expectations which result in an excessive workload for the principal filled with a growing tension, stress and, increasingly, burnout; and the perception that education has become an economic / political football in which the principalship is not valued" (Grady, McPherson, Mulford, & Williamson, 1994, p. 36).

Principals perceive their energies are being deflected away from the core work of education, teaching and learning; are experiencing a depersonalisation of the system; and are having to cope with burgeoning administrative paperwork due to the increased reporting and accountability demands back to the centre. Furthermore, each school's global budget is reliant upon enrolments in a more competitive and deregulated educational market in which reputation and image are all important. A school's (and principal's) survival is dependant upon 'market performance' which is judged against a range of externally imposed indicators, e.g. standardised tests and parent questionnaires. Such outcomes based evaluations, merely due to their emphasis on quantitative not qualitative measures, tend to use narrow definitions of success. Leadership was seen by many principals in our research studies to be more about image management to gain and maintain their market advantage than about educational issues of teaching and learning (Blackmore, Kenway, Willis, & Rennie, 1996a; Grady et al., 1994). Yet principals are positioned in the principal-centred policies of Schools of the Future as key change agents. The 'faxing of the crisis down the line' to schools has meant that principals in self-managing schools are therefore positioned as instruments of radical change over which they have little control and in which they have reduced discretionary decision-making due to limited and fluctuating budgets (Watkins, 1993).

Paradoxically, alongside all these managerial shifts in Victoria, a 'radically conservative' Liberal-national Coalition government has invested in Women and Leadership Programs (e.g., Victorian *Ministerial Review of Employment Equity for Women Teachers,* 1996). Building upon the gains of the previous decade of equal opportunity policies which had created a pool of eligible, experienced and enthusiastic women teachers. These Victorian 'initiatives' included strategies of women-only programs on mentoring, learning about leadership from shadowing of principals, as well as how-to-do-it training in financial management, application writing and presentation at interview. From 1992–5 there was an increase from 20% to 30% of women in the principal class (Ministerial Review, 1996). These policy initiatives drew heavily upon the new management discourses about 'women's special contribution to leadership' (Shakeshaft, 1987; Adler, Laney, & Packer, 1993; Ozga, 1993). Women, as good communicators, facilitators, collaborative managers and change agents, are the new sources of leadership talent for the self managing school.

While most principals experience the ambiguities and tensions of centralised-decentralisation of self-managing schools, gender is still an issue. First, many female principals have been appointed for their 'caring and sharing' attributes and democratic styles of leadership. Once in positions of leadership, these principals in particular found they lacked the power or resources to implement change in the consultative and collaborative way they desired. Not only did the intensification of their work and shrinking budgets reduce their discretionary capacities, but the values and managerialist practices which emanated from the centre were antithetical to their preferred way of working with staff, parents and students (see also Ozga & Walker, 1995; Whitty, 1996; Gewirtz, Ball, & Bowe, 1995 for comparable English studies). Instead, these newly appointed principals have overseen the downsizing of the teaching workforce in Victoria, the casualisation and feminisation of the profession, and the reduction of resources being allocated to public education.

Second, the pattern has been for women principals to be located in schools with high ethnic, socioeconomic and racial diversity. This was often a consequence of their profile as active change agents and their stated commitment to social justice. Such schools were often less attractive to many experienced (usually male) principals, and had experienced a high turnover of leadership. Women principals were also more likely than men to be located in smaller rural primary schools where the workload doubled because they have to be both teachers and principals (Grady et al., 1994). Schools with either the above demographic profiles tend to be more resource stretched due to the wider range of the demands made upon them because of diversity, size or lower socioeconomic background. In such schools specialist programs for girls and other disadvantaged groups compete for resources with mainstream programs of drama, art and music, gifted student programs compete with students with disabilities. Thus the deregulated educational market and the climate of rampant competitive individualism between students, schools and teachers produced personal and professional dilemmas for those women principals, many active feminists, with a deep concern for social justice. They spoke of the policy and resource vacuum about issues of multiculturalism, socio-economic disadvantage, pastoral care, welfare and community, and the difficulty of maintaining awareness of these in schools where success was based upon a narrow range of academic outcomes. This was captured in one female secondary school principal's lament:

> How does one measure on a scale from 1 to 10 the feeling of pleasure and belonging gained from a day in which students from over 20 different national backgrounds perform items at a festival celebrating multiculturalism? If we can't measure it and put it into our reports and charters, such experiential social learning is ignored and ultimately devalued. Yet this is what makes this school good although judged against academic student results with more homogenous school populations it could be perceived as not so good. But we do high quality educational work here. And it is much harder and fraught with risk and disaster than in other schools. Diversity and difference cannot be ignored here!

Many of these women came to see themselves as failures. Quite a few signalled that they were ready to leave the system, not just because of the emotional, physical and intellectual demands of the job[5], but more because of their growing unease and sense of loss of integrity arising from the widening gap between their values and professional principles, the actions required of them as principals, and their sense of powerlessness to change direction (Blackmore, 1996b).

Furthermore, the widening gap between rich and poor schools has increased as educational costs are increasingly privatised and school communities are expected to raise funds or gain business sponsorship (Gordon, 1994a; Gewirtz et al., 1995). It is not good business to sponsor losers no matter how creative and entreprenurial a school principal may be. And the image of the principal is paramount in the market. A female principal in a suburban secondary college with a high level of cultural diversity, single parent families, aboriginal students and socio-economically disadvantaged students commented:

> We have gone from a huge school to one with 365. Now we have declining enrolments, declining resources in a declining value system which all interact in a self-fulfilling spiral. I am increasingly aware that the school is vulnerable to the strengths and weaknesses of the principal. The market driven model of devolution is driven to doom innocent kids and staff because it only has a crude range of adjustment mechanisms based upon image and outcomes.

And the market is not gender neutral. The market, often through the media, constructs images about good education and good leadership. The market also plays upon commonsense and traditional views about women and leadership which associates authority, rationality and entrepreneurship with particular models of male leadership, as indicated in the following case study.

In a Victorian rural secondary college, Hillcrest, there was particular concern expressed by parents and teachers that the school now had female principal and deputy principal. One female teacher on the local principal selection committee who had actively supported the appointment of the woman principal, commented that having a female deputy principal imposed by the region as well was 'too much' for the school and the community. This school had built its reputation and student base around strong discipline. A totally female leadership team was seen to be a considerable disadvantage in this rural community where gender equity reform was perceived to have 'gone too far' and 'against nature' and where authority was closely associated with masculinity. Despite the fact that the new female principal was seen by all staff as exemplary in her leadership, and by those parents interviewed as excellent, the myths about weak discipline perpetuated. Yet most teachers and students at Hillcrest secondary college believed that discipline had improved since the discipline policy now shifted responsibility onto the students and teachers in a pastoral care program. Discipline was no longer dependent upon the authority of the single male deputy principal. Although the principal did considerable public relations work in her community, she was conscious that she did not have access to many of the traditional male networks. This rural school lost students in the following years to a male led local Catholic school which marketed itself as being highly disciplined (Blackmore, 1995b).

Principals are expected to 'work the market'. On the one hand, principals construct parental desire by promoting particular images of successful schools. Yet the market encourages conformity not diversity, the dominant image of successful schools being those with academic and sporting achievers, well dressed and well disciplined students in a pleasant and safe environment. On the other hand, principals are also expected to uncritically respond to the market by meeting parental demand. In so doing, the professional integrity and knowledge of educators is increasingly devalued and the parent consumer, in making choices about schooling, is positioned as knowing what is best educationally *for their child*. The collective and accumulated professional knowledge of teachers and principals, and a sense of public education for the common good, is thus subverted. One principal commented:

> There is increasingly less loyalty to a public system of education by parents and teachers under current policies. A lot are still committed to public education, as I am, and I am reluctant to adopt the robber baron mentality about our kids and the schools at the expense of other schools.

In such contexts, issues of social justice and equity as principles basic to a democratic society are rendered irrelevant except to the extent that individual parents can make claims upon the system to redress their child(ren)s disadvantage. Community is equated to the aggregate of individual consumer choices, and not about social relationships arising out of interdependence and shared values.

In turn, the individualising tendencies of the market also redefine disadvantage. Any individual can make claim upon resources on the basis of individual difference in which there is no ranking of difference (Blackmore, 1995a). The claims for additional resources for the gifted male student of a dual income middle class, and all the cultural capital that brings with it, are seen to be equal to the claims of a black girl whose mother is on welfare. In one inner city primary school, a parent whose child had just been identified as 'gifted' requested that the after school child care progam establish a special gifted program. There were no similar programs for girls, or children from lower socio-economic backgrounds, of whom there were many. The principal of this school spoke of how it was necessary to have clear policies in order to respond to what were, she felt, increased pressures by middle class parents for special programs for their children. The implicit threat was that the child would be withdrawn and sent elsewhere.

> What we did was to produce our gifted student policy which emphasised the need for mainstreaming gifted children, not creating special programs. It had a clear educational position which satisfied this particular parent. It was not a knee jerk response to an individual case which would have been a disaster. We had already thought this through carefully as we could see giftedness becoming an issue as it was being promoted by the Ministry as a big promotional initiative with the election. We guessed this would mean pressure to do something more overtly although we did address giftedness in clasroom pedagogies and curriculum.

The market treats all differences equally. As the above example indicates, as the market infiltrated into schools, principals and teachers increasingly found the need to establish clear hierarchies between differences in ways which did not undermine such important educational categories as race, gender, socio-economic status and non English speaking background (Blackmore, Kenway, Willis, & Rennie, 1996b).

And finally, principals were also being positioned as the 'emotional managers' at the level of the school in this quasi- market education system. They operated in the context of increased financial constraint but with greater demands for accountability to the centre and to the community. They experienced increased external pressure to produce easy solutions to such complex social problems as unemployment, violence, drug abuse and youth alienation as judged annually by parent questionnaires. Principals also had to do the emotional management work arising out of declining teacher morale. While teacher morale is seen as an issue by the Ministry of Education, it was dealt with in technicist ways premised upon behaviourist psychology. These individualised the problem by focusing upon conflict management, stress management, and a range of therapeutic or 'internal solutions' such as reflective practice, personal narrative and school-based action research (Hargreaves, 1996, p. 10). Such processes sheet blame home onto individual principals and ignore the context in which teachers' work is being deskilled and devalued. Thus at one level the people management skills, the so called feminine skills of leadership, for the emotional management work, are deemed necessary. At the same time, while teachers in our studies viewed educational vision, people skills, compassion, trust, genuine love of the job, humility, respect and pride of others achievements, reciprocity, life long learning, collegiality and professionality as central to good educational leadership, the system through its job descriptions and reward systems prioritised management skills in getting more for less, measurable outcomes, good public relations, financial skills and 'strong' entrepreneurial leadership (Grady et al., 1994; Blackmore, 1995b). Principal-led leadership in turn effected how teachers viewed change.

THE CULTURES OF CARE, COMPLIANCE AND CHANGE

Educational change as shaped by restructuring in Victoria has been principal not teacher centred. Central to most educational reform policy texts and professional development in Australia is the notion of principals as culture builders (Caldwell, 1994; Ball, 1995). As Hargreaves (1996) points out, the means to produce such cultures may be inclusive, involving, built around team work, caring, and collaboration. But they are usually from a management perspective. They often result in the colonisation of the most valued aspects of teachers' cultures which are most conducive to good practice. In practice the shared visions and consensus encapsulated in various policy texts such as school charters were not necessarily the product of consultative or collaborative processes out of which teachers gained a sense of ownership. This became obvious when educational issues such as the introduction of standardised testing in primary school divided the community and positioned teachers as against change. So while much of the management literature on strong corporate culture assumes that the 'social glue' of strong cultures results from shared visions, equally often such visions are imposed by the principal and not contested and negotiated by equal partners.

Fineman (1993) suggests fear, in a period of rapid change and uncertainty, was an equally 'binding' factor in building consensus – but that it often produces superficial short term change; lip service but not commitment. Many women principals spoke of the detrimental impact of recent reforms to principal/teachers staff relations which were now premised upon fear as much as upon collegiality. 'They have put a wedge between principals and teachers' commented one female primary school teacher. These reforms included new principal and teacher career structures based upon performance management, legislation which undermined tenure and collective bargaining, and gave increased power to principals over staffing, promotion and job allocation in schools. The new social relationships shaped by principal-centred views of leadership have significant implications for innovative change and how teachers and schools solved problems. One principal felt that

> the staff feel less committed to collectively working together because they feel disempowered and come running to me for solutions, of which I have few, given the constraints. So I am caught in that you almost have to create an environment of fear about our very survival in order for people to be re-committed to what is important in education again.

These hierarchies were premised upon monetary incentives and bonuses and did not tap into the satisfaction teachers get from teaching and collaborative work. What most teachers and principals asked for and saw as critical to quality planning and reflective practice was time and recognition of what they did with kids.

Now management prerogative now rested with the principal and 'lead' teacher group in most schools and no longer with the representative elected committee systems which had previously been negotiated under collective bargaining legislation. This shift in the location of decision making power further distanced principals from the possibility of more collegial relationships with their staff (cf. Ozga & Walker, 1995; Court, 1995). Although some principals, and nearly all women principals in these studies indicated that their preferred way of working was to maintain democratic practices based upon consultation and collaboration, the demands for instant decisions from the centre led to the exercise of increased executive discretionary power.

Many principals also described themselves as a 'buffer' against the deluge of policies and change initiatives so that the teachers could get on with the real work of teaching and learning (Blackmore et al., 1996a). They were a buffer against the top-down policies of the Ministry, against the demands of the community, but they were equally a buffer in deflecting teacher resistance away from the centre by 'coping' at the level of the school (Tickell, 1994). Being able to control one's teachers and school council is the sign of a good principal,' said one primary school principal. 'This means not too much debate about government policy'. Acting as a buffer was at significant emotional, physical if not moral cost to principals. One spoke of the pain in her right arm when she was confronted with a difficult moral issue. Most referred to the isolation and how they missed being able to socialise or 'just being friendly' with their staff at a close personal level, as now, they could not be seen to 'favour' individuals. Many women referred to how they distanced themselves from decisions they 'morally could not uphold if it was up to me. I just say – I am instructed to do this' (Blackmore, 1996b). Being a buffer also meant principals took on the responsibility to sift through the proliferation of curriculum, assessment, school organization and careers initiatives (as well as a burgeoning marketing literature from business which sees schools as new market opportunities) in order to select what issues to 'run with' and what to reject. This last response was more typical of primary than secondary schools where the pressures with regard to post compulsory education were greater and principals had to run faster to keep up with other schools (Blackmore et al., 1996a).

Another aspect of being a buffer was that principals adopted a caring position towards their staffs. This culture of care, often associated to female styles of leadership, was a positive response to rapid change and uncertainty by providing certainty and direction. And many of the women in the studies had been appointed as principals because of their caring and sharing leadership skills (Limerick & Lingard, 1995). Ironically, the new hierarchies between principal and teachers led to the reassertion of maternalism or paternalism. One female principal spoke of how the current relationships in the new model of decision-making, with reversion of authority to the principal, 'was infantilising not only the kids but the bloody staff as well'. It was, she felt, constructing a dependency upon the principal to take all the initiative, define directions and push people along. It did not encourage informal leadership. It was not conducive to maintaining professional relationships premised upon equality and mutual engagement, or which encouraged problem solving approaches. As one principal commented: 'We overprotected teachers to some extent and when the crunch came they were ill-prepared'.

The downside of fear of uncertainty and this urge to protect was what one female principal of a small primary school in a working class suburb described as a 'culture of compliance' amongst teachers. There was, she argued, no longer any debate about educational issues when new policies were introduced. Instead, when teachers were informed of a new initiative, 'all they wanted to know was how to do it as painlessly as possible because they were exhausted and defeated'. Since 'all policies emanated from the centre outside the school', or had to fit with the array of departmental policies, school charters and principal performance plans, local teacher-based initiatives were discouraged. There was little financial flexibility or spontaneity in responding to problems which arose in the daily work of classroom teaching. Another female principal of a secondary school commented that provided little scope for action for teachers when there was quite legitimate conflict or a problem to be resolved within the school.

It means that the staff reaction is to strike or give in. There is little or no scope for the types of creative solutions where you work together and learn ways of talking to each other. While we learnt in the old system of participatory school based democracy where such a dialogue was possible that there were limitations to democratic processes, because these problems were not resolved it was possible for the new government to highlight them to justify this new system of devolution which is non participatory and managerialist. While we incorrectly assumed that if we got the structures right then everything was OK. . . at least then there was some ownership of decisions and collectivity. Now there is neither the dialogue nor the ownership as we are in a moral vacuum as well.

This distancing of principals from teachers, while not necessarily atypical, did not resolve the internal and highly personal dilemmas many principals felt with regard to their long term commitment to progressive educational reform and social justice. A strong unionist and now secondary school principal reflected:

I consciously decided not to be a unionist member because then the staff would get ambiguous messages about what my position was personally and officially. They were disappointed in me because they hoped my support of the union would strengthen its negotiating position.

Teachers viewed the failure of another secondary female principal to renew her union membership as signalling that she had 'given up the fight' on matters of social justice. This widening gap between administrators' and teachers' work and values (and their wages) has been a key aspect of educational restructuring worldwide (Whitty, 1996; Ozga & Walker, 1995), as seen with the demise of the 'teacher leader', in places like Sweden (Wernersson, 1989) and in the assertion of more managerialist and entrepreneurial models of leadership in the UK and elsewhere (Whitty, 1996; Pringle & Timperley, 1995; Evetts, 1994).[6] Ultimately, many principals felt that the culture of fear and dependency promoted by reforms which were principal and not teacher-centred actively worked against innovation.

And whereas a usual response by teachers to uncertainty and change is often to focus upon teaching and learning as their 'escape', one principal commented:

> Teachers can't even withdraw into the classroom and enjoy that any more, because class sizes have risen. You have things like the new standardised assessment which are in direct antithesis to what they believe, increased administrative tasks due to accountability demands, depleted resources and higher community expectations. In our school the problems of the students are greater – family unemployment, violence etc. The pleasure previously gained out of teaching (and out of leading) is gone.

The culture of care also has the potential for entrapment, particularly for women. The culture of care taps into dominant professional discourses, particularly in primary schools, where women are concentrated. Sandra Acker (1995) in her case study of two primary schools in England argues, the ways in which teachers cared for and supported one another 'can be understood at least in part as a response to the difficulties and paradoxes that caring for children contained' (Acker, 1995, p. 21). But she also argued that in a female dominated profession, women, more often subordinates in organizations, tended to have to be more sensitive to the needs of those in power as well as to others for their collective survival. Caring for each other was one response to the struggle by teachers to protect their material conditions and social practices in the context of frustration, stress, and reduced resources. 'Their close knit culture stemmed in part from the need to find collective strategies to compensate for the frustration of their work; the culture gave them the impetus to keep doing what often seemed an impossible job' (Acker, 1995, p. 21). But it did not, she suggested, necessarily provide them with collective agency, and indeed gave the appearance that all was well.

Teacher professional identity and self is also closely tied up with caring about children and 'liking children'. So when national curriculum assessments were introduced into primary schools, 'many primary teachers spent vast amounts of personal time in extra preparation and marking, so much so that their health and personal lives and even the quality of relationships with pupils was suffering' (Acker, 1995, p. 24). Hargreaves maps out a similar terrain in Canada where teachers felt guilty if they changed their pedagogy to more 'lean and mean' pedagogies due to the intensification of labour (Hargreaves, 1994). Likewise in Victoria, with the introduction of a range of reforms in curriculum, standardised tests, reporting and increased class sizes, primary teachers spent considerably greater amount of time working at home to *protect* what they valued about teaching and learning, rather than change their child centred and idealised professional practices according to the new reforms (Blackmore et al., 1996a). Caring for their colleagues and students had detrimental effects on their health. As one school office manager commented: 'Teachers rarely take sick leave now even when they are sick. They are aware that in so doing, because there is limited funding for substitutes, that their class is distributed across other classes. That was bad for students and intensifies the load for their colleagues. When they get sick, they really get sick, and often take more time'.

The culture of caring raises the expectation that women principals, for example, are more caring as it is closely associated with 'female' styles of leadership. The downside is that women are judged as bad leaders if they display negative emotions – anger is equated to not being caring. Particular images of woman leaders as caring and sharing therefore add to the constraints upon women principals. Common in all the interviews with women principals was a sense of emotional intensity they felt about their work but their incapacity to show the depth of their emotions publicly. While they regretted the loss of pleasure in the job in recent times, there were frequent references to how they had learnt to silence their anger. Anger was inappropriate for women – and if displayed they were depicted as being bitchy, unpleasant and destructive (Court, 1995; Fineman, 1993). Jenny Ozga (1993) refers to the anger that women feel, and usually contain, when confronted with their sense of powerlessness in leadership or socially unjust practices. For those women in leadership who did have a strong sense of responsibility to gender reform, but lacked the power and resources to practice what they valued as desirable forms of leadership, the effect was despair and disillusionment. They were isolated from their earlier source of emotional support and strength – other women teachers – who now often judged them for their apparent failure to effect change. Their responses varied at different moments: to distance themselves from their work, to focus upon minute detail in a desire to control their lives, to become alienated or to exit the profession (Blackmore, 1996b). The dilemma for women arises out of an unproblematic notion of caring. Acker (1995) is critical of the popular essentialist stance which regards caring as 'naturally female' rather than viewing caring, as Noddings (1992) argues, as something which is learnt. It is an educative process to learn through caring for someone, as well as by being cared, and the benefits arising out of both providing and not just receiving care. Reciprocity and interdependence are fundamental elements.

Another effect was that in this kind of context, many eligible women, often leaders to their colleagues in curriculum and pedagogy, indicated that they were now choosing not to become principals. Formal leadership meant rejecting what they were passionate about – their teaching and their professional and personal values: 'I entered teaching to teach because I love children. To become a principal or administrator requires me to change my job!' 'I don't want to become and behave like that'. A principal teacher in a small rural school commented:

> My own position of myself as an educator was challenged by my desire to take on a school leadership role. The inclination brought about by my socialization to maintain the gender order by nurturing and teaching young children was jeopardised or compromised by my pursuit of leadership. I was positioned in really contradictory ways'. She wrote in her journal: "I have invariably felt that the encouragement of women to aspire to leadership roles causes a dilemma. Being a teacher who thrives on classroom teaching, enjoys being with children, takes up challenges of changing educational theory and practice, I have often questioned whether a principal leadership role is in

fact what I want or whether I would be happier with curriculum leadership. Certainly, when women are successful in obtaining leadership roles they are viewed as reaching the ultimate and 'having made it'. But the concept of exemplary classroom practice also requires a high measure of success which has been increasingly devalued with current changes. My dilemma has been which direction to follow (Gunn, 1995, p. 31).

Nor were the 'superwomen' in the principal positions the role models to which many women aspired, as they saw those women in leadership positions struggle to uphold their long held values and beliefs about education and social justice, working long hours, and 'putting their family and social life on hold' in the face of an increasingly unsympathetic, if not antagonistic, system. Women teachers watched their female colleagues struggle with these moral dilemmas between educational leadership and management, and often 'chose' not to undertake the considerable physical, emotional and ethical burden that leadership involves. So at the same time that individual women were being positioned as the new leaders, even the more positive images of leadership as superwomen and carers were disempowering for leadership aspirants. So for women, the discourses of caring or 'female styles of leadership' which tap into the more positive aspects of the emotional investment of teachers and principals in their work, are both seductive and dangerous. They are seductive in that the rhetoric of self management promises the possibility to produce change in schools. And they are dangerous for those who profess to value social justice and a preference for more democratic and collaborative models of leadership when the system works against their capacity to meet such expectations.

INFORMED GENDER REFORM: LEARNING FROM RESEARCH AND THINKING STRATEGICALLY

Any limited successes for gender equity reform under a predominantly liberal feminist legislative framework have been implemented in a rapidly changing context. First, the context of the backlash against feminism and a more radically conservative politics; second, the market and commodification of education; and finally the radical restructuring of educational work. Briefly, the combination of strong state interventions in moral agendas and weak state intervention in the market has dangerous potential for gender equity. At the same time, gender can no longer be ignored by schools, given the conditions I have outlined above. But downstreaming and mainstreaming gender through new structures and policies does not necessarily mean that change will be effected. We need to consider more closely what happens to such policies, how they are received, resisted and transformed. We also have to pay close attention to those aspects about change which have largely been ignored – the emotional (as well as material) investment of individuals in the status quo; the material and cultural constraints which work against change (lack of resources, policy constraints, resistance); as well as the presence or the absence of social conditions conducive to change (collegial environments, policy guidelines, resources and professional development).

What our studies indicated was that there has to be an overt commitment of educational leaders in schools to gender equity, followed by well informed and exemplary practice. In the complex information feedback and accountability systems of devolved school systems, there is some opportunity to integrate gender equity as a clear indicator of good leadership and school practice. Gender equity outcomes can be embedded into all aspects of school charters; in performance management contracts of managers and principals at all levels of educational governance; and as an indicator of success in all school programs and evaluations. But we need to go beyond the statistical mapping of how many teacher days have been spent on gender equity professional development or how many girls participate in science or boys in conflict management skills, to explore how teachers and students read these gender reform messages or whether practices have actually changed in classrooms or school administration.

Gender equity reform often works against the grain of our taken for granted assumptions about administration, teaching and learning. Gender equity discourses and reform are marginal to more dominant professional knowledge bases (eg. child centred learning). When asked whether they addressed gender in their classrooms, many teachers in our studies responded that they dealt with each child individually according to their needs and capacities. Likewise, school objectives often refer to 'treating everyone according to their individual needs'. This often translates into practice as not seeing gender as a systemic issue but as an individual problem. In so doing, a range of organizational and cultural valuing and practices are not addressed. Gender must be an organising principle and remain central through planning. Gender reform requires a whole school and not piecemeal approach so that gender is consciously and continuously addressed in all aspects of school life – curriculum, classroom and play ground behavior, school governance and pedagogy. Students receive quite contradictory messages when male principals advocate gender equity for girls and then position their female colleagues as weaker, lesser, or unimportant through their language, body movements or style of leadership; or when a male teacher introduces group work or the life history of a female scientist into his lessons, but talks mainly to the boys, often about sport; or when time allocations and timetables favor maths and science (into which girls are encouraged) over the humanities and creative arts (into which boys are not encouraged). At the same time, there is no predicability in how gender equity texts are read in schools, in that many girls and women read gender equity discourses quite selectively due to their personal life histories around a range of differential experiences according to their race, class, ethnicity as well as gender, and sometimes even subversively. But the existence of such policy texts has important symbolic power and provides a language for change. Gender reform studies indicate the need for a range of changes – institutional, cultural and personal – and a range of strategies – top-down and bottom-up. As Lingard and Limerick (1995, p. 3) suggest, equal opportunity legislation 'is a necessary, but not sufficient, condition for improvement'.

Gender reform also requires us to think about change more closely – as an emotional experience and not just an intellectual exercise. The assumption in much gender equity reform is that knowledge will lead individuals to change. The raising of gender awareness is just the first step. Knowledge is a necessary but not a sufficient condition, to promote real change. There are a range of factors such as the material and social conditions of any school which make some institutions and cultures more open to change. But there is also the issue of personal receptivity at the level of the emotional as well as the intellectual. Mainstream organizational change theory has emphasised the intellectual to the detriment of the emotional dimensions of personal change, the organizational to the detriment of the personal. This is because organizations have been constructed upon a split between rationality and emotionality, the public and the private, which is itself gendered (Fineman, 1993). While there is a significant body of literature in educational administration arising out of cultural feminism about how an ethics of care would reconstruct school organization and educational leadership which focuses upon emotional attachment and engagement (Beck, 1994; Noddings, 1992), these still portray the positive dimensions of emotion – caring, sharing, attachment, pleasure and not the more negative aspects of emotion which often accompany radical and rapid change – alienation, detachment, disengagement, isolation, fear, guilt and anger.

Gender equity reform is not just about positive emotions eg. sense of wellbeing or care, or desire, but also negative emotions – desire, fear, pleasure, distrust, anger (Hargreaves, 1995). Much gender equity reform, for example, has relied upon guilt to motivate individuals to change – making girls feel guilty that they make the wrong subject choices, boys feel guilty that they do not fit more sensitive models of masculinity, women feel guilty that they are not caring, and men feel guilty for oppressing women. Guilt can often paralyse individuals and thus inhibit rather than promote change in that it does not provide alternative ways of seeing and doing things. For those seeking to produce gender change in schools, it is necessary to tap into people's desires and ambitions, to give them a sense of ownership and involvement at all stages and levels of change, and to develop a high level of trust, mutual engagement and reciprocity (Fullan, 1993; Hargreaves, 1994).

Gender equity reform requires a capacity for self reflection and sense of collective action. It is particularly difficult because it requires self reflection on one's own gender subjectivity and of long held institutional, cultural *and* personal practices and beliefs. It is about personal change which is both informed by and informs cultural change. It is closely tied to power relationships at home, school and work and connected to emotion. Many men who actively went out of their way to encourage and promote gender equity reform, when questioned about whether their initiatives reflected any change in their attitudes, spoke of their close-hand experiences as 'partners of feminists' and 'fathers of daughters' to what gender inequity and discrimination in schools and at work meant on a daily basis for women and girls (Blackmore, 1996a; Sinclair, 1994). It was their emotional connectedness to those who experienced the impact of overt and covert sexism, structural and cultural discrimination, and often ongoing harassment, which allowed them to empathise and better understand the ways in which women and girls were positioned unequally.

Finally, I would suggest that the gap between hope and happening in gender equity reform has been in part because educational change, particularly with regard to gender, has been inadequately theorised. Change tends to be seen as something which is stimulated by outside forces upon us in education (e.g., Naisbett & Aburdene, 1990). Many educational reforms have called upon management rather than educational theories and research on change (e.g., Senge, 1990; Drucker 1992) which treat change as a generic process without regard to substance: what it is we seek to change and why. The same processes of change necessary to improve profits in business are assumed to be equally applicable to improving student outcomes or producing active citizens. The processes of change are decontextualised and the substance of change is ignored. By focusing upon change, the historical intransigence of class, gender and race power relations and the considerable evidence with regard to the exacerbation, not amelioration, of social inequality in many Western nations is played down. Failing to deal adequately with the social and differentiating dimensions of change, Anna Yeatman suggests, means that management gurus promote a 'new individualism' premised upon the abandonment of the post-war 'rhetoric of social citizenship' (Yeatman, 1992, p. 4). While feminist educational researchers would agree with the recent change literature in education that change is about process, uncertainty, conflict; that change is about cultural 'sea changes' at the level of organizations; that it is about deeply personal changes in attitude and values, feminist research also indicates that gender reform is also about a political commitment to social justice built upon an energy and passion to initiate change to gain social justice. While still emphasising the importance of procedural justice and due process, feminists tend to argue that change must focus upon more equitable outcomes and substantive moral and ethical value positions. What we seek to change and for what, not just to change for its own sake. We need to ask: whose 'vision' is followed, whose 'interests' are achieved, who is effected by change and how.

ENDNOTES

[1]   I wish to acknowledge the support of the Australian Research Council in all these projects as well as the work of Jane Kenway, Jenny Angwin, Chris Bigum, Louise Laskey and John Hodgens at the Deakin Centre for Education and Change as well as Sue Willis at Murdoch University and Leonie Rennie of Curtin University.

[2]   While there are similarities cross nationally in both the content of gender reform policies and also the reliance upon the state to initiate and resource gender equity programs, there are also considerable differences which lead to variations in effects. Australia and particularly Victoria are seen to produce relatively more successful programs on a range of indicators eg. level of institutionalisation of gender equity reform and range and types of activities in schools (Stromquist, 1992, Weiner, 1995, Arnot, 1993). Differences between USA, Canada, UK, New Zealand, Sweden and Australia can be explained by a range of factors: strength of state intervention, level of resourcing, and compliance requirements, the level of decentralisation of industrial bargaining and of educational governance more generally. There are cross national comparisons which indicate, for example, that nation

states(eg Sweden and Australia) with more centralised and collective systems of wage bargaining have a smaller gender gap between average male and female wages than those with decentralised systems such as England, USA and Canada) (Whitehouse, 1990).

3   In Israel, for example, Goldring and Chan (1993) view the feminisation of the principalship as the result of a long term lowering of the professional status of the occupation due to devolution and new collective bargaining conditions in which feminised industries 'trade off' salary gains to achieve flexibility to maintain domestic and paid labour, a pattern being replicated in enterprise bargaining agreements in Australia (Blackmore 1996c) and individual contracts in New Zealand (Hyman, 1994).

4   In Victoria, over 30% of students attend either the Catholic system or elite private schools.

5   The annual survey of the Schools of the Future undertaken by the Cooperative found a significant gender difference between hours worked by and expectations of women principals in Schools of the Future (Caldwell, 1994).

6   This gap is heightened by principal salary claims being based in collective bargaining on the differences between principals' and teachers' work. Principals receive up to 15% of salary in bonuses if there are improved outcomes as outlined on their performance plan although there is little empirical research which *directly* links principal leadership to student outcomes. Instead, recent Victorian research indicates that students outcomes are effected by teacher/student relationships in specific classrooms (Hill, 1993)

REFERENCES

Adler, S., Laney, J., & Packer, M. (1993). *Managing women: Feminism and power in educational management*. Milton Keynes: Open University Press.

Acker, S. (1995). Carry on caring: The work of women teachers. *British Journal of Sociology of Education*, **16**(1), 21–36

Acker, S. (1996). Gender and teachers' work. In M. Apple (Ed.), *Review of educational research*. Washington DC: AERA

Arnot, M. (1993). A crisis in patriarchy? British feminist educational politics and state regulation of gender. In M. Arnot & K. Weiler (Eds.), *Feminism and social justice: International perspectives*. Sussex: Falmer Press.

Beck, L. (1994). *Reclaiming educational administration as a caring profession*. New York : Teachers College Press.

Ball, S. (1995). *Education reform*. Buckingham: Open University Press.

Blackmore, J. (1995a). Policy as dialogue: Feminist administrators working for educational change. *Gender and Education*, (7)3, 293–313

Blackmore, J. (1995b). Towards a post-masculinist politics in education. In B. Limerick, & B. Lingard (Eds.), *Gender and changing educational management*. Sydney: Hodder.

Blackmore, J. (1996a). *The re-structuring and re-gendering of educational work*. Keynote Address to the 9th Congress of Comparative Education, University of Sydney.

Blackmore, J. (1996b). Doing emotional labor in the educational market place: Stories from the field of women in management. *Discourse*, **17**(3), 301–314.

Blackmore, J., Kenway. J., Willis, S., & Rennie, L. (1996a). Putting up with the put down: Sexual harassment, power and policy. In L. Laskey & C. Beavis (Eds.), *Sexuality and schooling* (pp. 201–220). Geelong: Deakin University Press.

Blackmore, J., Kenway, J., Willis, S., & Rennie, L. (1996b). Feminist dilemmas: An Australian case study of a whole school approach to gender equity reform. *Journal of Curriculum Studies*, **28**(3), 253–79

Burton, C. (1990). *The promise and the price: The struggle for equal opportunity in women's employment*. Sydney: Allen and Unwin.

Caldwell, B. (1994). Australian perspectives on leadership: The principal's role in radical decentralization in victoria's schools of the future. *Australian Educational Researcher*, **21**(2), 45–62.

Court, M. (1995). Good girls and naughty girls. Rewriting the scripts of women's anger. In B. Limerick & B. Lingard (Eds.), *Gender and changing educational management* (pp. 150–161). Sydney: Hodder.

Cuban, L. (1990). A fundamental puzzle of school reform. In A. Lieberman Ed.), *Schools as collaborative cultures: Creating the future now* (pp. 71–77). Lewes: Falmer.

Drucker, P. (1992). *Managing the future*. New York: Dutton

Eisenstein, H. (1991) . *Gender shock: practising feminism in two continents.* Sydney: Allen and Unwin.

Evetts, J. (1994). *Becoming a secondary headteacher.* London: Cassell.

Fineman, S. (1993). Organizations as emotional arenas. In S. Fineman (Ed.), *Emotion in organizations* (pp. 9–35). Newbury Park: Sage

Fullan, M. (1993). *Change forces.* London: The Falmer Press.

Gewirtz, S., Ball, S., & Bowe, R. (1995). *Markets, choice and equity in education.* Buckingham: Open University Press.

Goldring, E., & Chan, M. (1993). The feminisation of the principalship in Israel. In C. Marshall (Ed.), *The new politics of race and gender* (pp. 175–182). Sussex: Falmer Press.

Gordon, L. (1994a). Rich and poor schools in Aotearoa. *New Zealand Journal of Education,* **29**(2), 35–47.

Grady, N., MacPherson, M., Mulford, W. R., & Williamson, J. (1994). *Australian school principals: A profile.* South Australia: Glenelg Press.

Gunn, E. (1995). *A taste of school leadership: A feminist perspective.* Masters of Educational Administration Research Paper, Faculty of Education, Deakin University.

Hargreaves, A. (1994). *Changing teachers, changing times: Teachers' work and culture in postmodern times.* New York: Teachers College Press.

Hargreaves, A. (1995). Development and desire. In M. Huberman & P. Guskey (Eds.), *Professional development: New paradigms and practices* (pp. 9–34). New York: Teachers College Press.

Hargreaves, A. (1996). Cultures of teaching and educational change. In B. Biddle, T. Good, & I. Goodson (Eds.), *International handbook of teachers and teaching.* The Netherlands: Kluwer Press.

Hill, P. (1993). *Report on 150 effective schools in victoria.* University of Melbourne, Unpublished paper.

Hyman, P. (1994). *Women and economics: A New Zealand feminist perspective.* Wellington: Bridget Williams Books.

Kenway, J. (1996). A feminist perspective on marketing. *Discourse* (in press).

Lash. S., & Urry, J. (1994). *The economies of signs and space.* Oxford: Polity Press.

Limerick, B., & Lingard, B. (Eds.). (1995). *Gender and changing educational management.* Sydney: Hodder.

Middleton, S. (1988). Women, equality and equity in liberal educational policies 1945–88: A feminist critique. In S. Middleton (Ed.), *Women in Aotearoa 1.* Wellington: Allen and Unwin.

Ministerial Review. (1996). *Ministerial review of employment equity for women teachers.* Melbourne: Department of Education.

Möller, J. (1993). *Restructuring in the Norwegian context: A combination of efforts towards decentralisation and centralisation.* Paper presented to OISE.

Naisbitt, J., & Aburdene, P. (1990). *Megatrends II.* New York: Warner Books.

Noddings, N. (1992). *The challenge to care in schools: An alternative approach to education.* New York: Teachers College Press.

Ozga, J. (1993). *The deprofessionalisation of teaching in the UK.* Paper presented to Australian Association of Research in Education Conference, Perth.

Ozga, J., & Walker, L. (1995). Women in educational management: Theory and practice. In B. Limerick & B. Lingard (Eds.), *Gender and changing educational management* (pp.34–43). Sydney: Hodder.

Peters, M., & Marshall, J. (1996). *Individualism and community: Education and social policy in the postmodern condition.* London: The Falmer Press.

Pillinger, J. (1993). *Feminising the market.* Basingstoke: MacMillan

Pringle, J., & Timperley, H. (1995). Gender and educational management in New Zealand: Cooption, subversion or withdrawal. In B. Limerick & B. Lingard (Eds.), *Gender and changing educational management* (pp. 162–173). Sydney: Hodder.

Senge, P. (1990). *The fifth discipline.* New York: Doubleday.

Shakeshaft, C. (1987). *Women in educational administration.* Newbury Park: Sage.

Sinclair, A. (1994). *Trials at the top: Chief executives talk about men, women, and the Australian executive culture.* Melbourne: Melbourne Business School.

Still, L. (1995). Women in management: Glass ceilings or slippery poles? In B. Limerick & B. Lingard (Eds.), *Gender and changing educational management* (pp. 106–120). Sydney: Hodder

Stromquist, N. (1992). Sex equity legislation in education: The state as the promoter of women's rights. *Review of Educational Research,* **63**(4), 379–408.

Tickell, G. (1994). Principal as line manager or educational leader. In *Deakin Centre for Education and Change Schooling: What Future?* Geeling, Australia: Deakin University.

Watkins, P. (1993). Faxing the crisis down the line. In J. Smyth (Ed.), *A Socially critical view of the self-managing school* (pp. 153–172). Sussex: Falmer Press.

Weiner, G. (1995). A question of style or value? In B. Limerick & B. Lingard (Eds.), *Gender and changing educational management* (pp. 22–23). Sydney: Hodder.

Wernersson, I. (1989). Gender equality – ideology and reality. In S. Ball & S. Larsson (Eds.), *The struggle for democratic education* (pp. 137–159). Sussex: Falmer Press.

Whitehouse, G. (1990). Unequal pay: A comparative study of Australia, Canada, Sweden and the UK. *Labour and Industry*, 3(2/3), 354–71.

Whitty, G. (1996). Creating quasi-markets in education: A review of recent research on parental choice and school autonomy in three countries. *Review of Research in Education*, 22.

Yeatman, A. (1992). Women's citizenship claims, labour market policy and globalisation. *Australian Journal of Political Science*, 27, 449–61

School–Family–Community Partnerships and Educational Change: International Perspectives[1]

MAVIS G. SANDERS

Center for Research on the Education of Students Placed at Risk, Johns Hopkins University

JOYCE L. EPSTEIN

Center on School, Family, and Community Partnerships, Johns Hopkins University

The last decade has seen a rise in research on and practices of school, family and community involvement in the education of youth. This trend can be attributed to a number of factors. Low achievement and high dropout rates, especially for poor and marginalized youth, have led educators and social scientists to become more aware of the importance of family and community involvement for school effectiveness and positive student outcomes. Moreover, communitarians and others have pointed to the loss of community and collective life that many people feel in their neighbourhoods, workplaces and schools as well. In this chapter, Sanders and Epstein make the case that in order for schools to educate all youth effectively, families and communities must become full partners in the process.

Not all schools and not all nations, they point out, are at the same point in their work on partnerships. Some focus on parent participation on school councils; others concentrate more on choice of schools than on what happens to involve families after the choice is made; some are looking deeply into helping families understand their children's school subjects and curricula; and others are working on improving general communications. Drawing on Epstein's model of different forms of school-community relationship, this chapter summarizes and discusses research studies collected from social scientists in twenty nations to increase our understanding of how partnership approaches are linked to the processes and outcomes of educational change and school improvement.

INTRODUCTION

The last decade has seen a rise in research on and practices of school, family and community involvement in the education of youth in the United States and abroad. This trend can be attributed to a number of factors, both social and political. From a social perspective, low achievement and high dropout rates, especially for poor and marginalized youth, have led educators and social scientists to become more aware of the importance of family and community involvement for school effectiveness and student outcomes. From a political perspective, the fall of communism in the former Soviet Union and the spread of democratic systems of government in countries in Eastern Europe and Latin America have sparked dialogue about and policies to promote equal educational opportunity, and parental and community participation in the educational process (Prucha & Walterova 1992; Glenn 1989).

A. Hargreaves (ed.), Extending Educational Change, 202-224.
© 2005 *Springer. Printed in the Netherlands.*

Whatever the reasons for this trend, there is a strong, common desire to make schools more effective institutions of learning. Concurrent with this goal is the realization that schools neither exist nor function in a vacuum. In order for schools in any nation to effectively educate *all* youth, families and communities must become partners in the process.

Epstein's theory (1987) of overlapping spheres of influence provides a framework for research and practice that reflects this viewpoint. This theory integrates and extends educational, sociological and psychological perspectives on social organizations, as well as research on the effects of family, school and community environments on educational outcomes (for details, see Epstein, 1987, 1992). Acknowledging the interlocking histories of the major institutions that socialize and educate children, the theory posits that certain goals, such as student development and academic success, are of interest to all of these institutions and are best achieved through their cooperative action and support. Pictorially, this perspective is represented by three spheres symbolizing school, family and community, whose connections are determined by the attitudes, practices and interactions of individuals within each context.

Based on years of research, Epstein (1995) has identified six types of school-family-community involvement that are important for student learning and development, and more effective schools and families. These are: 1) parenting – helping all families establish home environments that support children as students and helping schools understand families; 2) communicating – designing and conducting effective forms of two-way communication about school programs and children's progress; 3) volunteering – recruiting and organizing help and support for classrooms, school functions and student activities; 4) learning at home – providing information, ideas and opportunities to families about how to help students at home with academic decisions, homework, and curriculum-related activities; 5) decision-making – including parents in school governance, and 6) collaborating with community – identifying and integrating resources and services from the community to strengthen and support schools, students and their families, and from schools, families and students to support the community.

Although most schools are not yet implementing practices that effectively foster all six types of involvement, many elementary, middle and high schools are conducting practices that foster one or more of them. Some schools in this and other nations are focussing on parent representation on school councils, or on choice of schools as a form of family and student academic decision-making. Others are looking deeply into helping families understand their children's subjects and curricula. Still others are working at more general communications. It is clear that investments and actions are increasing in many nations to understand and implement productive school-family-community partnerships. This chapter summarizes and discusses research studies collected from social scientists in twenty nations[2] to better understand how partnership approaches are linked to the processes and outcomes of educational change and school improvement. The studies referenced here were selected from those sent by members of the International Network of Scholars of the Center on Families, Communities, Schools and

Children's Learning. Although selective, these studies illustrate the significant progress in research and development in school, family, and community partnerships that has occurred in many nations over the past decade. The chapter has six sections that link the international studies with others conducted in the United States and that enrich our understanding of the six major types of family/community involvement in schools: 1) Variation in levels of family involvement; 2) Governmental policies to promote greater family involvement; 3) Programs to enhance family practices that support children's learning; 4) Community involvement with schools and families; 5) Identifying and dismantling barriers to school-family-community partnerships, and 6) Crosscutting themes about partnerships and their meaning for educational change, school improvement and future research.

VARIATION IN LEVELS OF FAMILY INVOLVEMENT

Studies in all nations show that some parents are highly involved in their children's education and others are not. In a qualitative study of parent involvement in primary schools in Cyprus, Phtiaka (1994) found that families could generally be characterized into three types. The first type was the highly involved family. Phtiaka described these families as university-educated professionals with "privileged access to the school." They participated in and were leaders of parent groups, and were satisfied with their children's school, the information they received from the school and their children's school performance. The second group, or "middle group" comprised skilled laborers. Although they contacted the schools when they had specific concerns, these families desired more information and feedback from the school and the opportunity to be more involved in school activities. Phtiaka described the third category of families as "marginalized." Fathers, if present, were often unskilled laborers and mothers were generally housewives. This group had difficulty communicating with the school and often felt a sense of powerlessness before the school's position and authority. These families experienced more anxiety than the other two groups about their children's school work and homework. While acknowledging that it was their responsibility to assist in their children's learning, these families reported a lack of knowledge, time and energy to do so.

From her data, Phtiaka concluded that although wealthier, more educated families are more involved in the educational process, all families, even the most disadvantaged, care about their children and are interested in their education. They are willing to help and are receptive to teacher advice. However, their present perceptions of the school make them hesitant to initiate contact with teachers, and this is often perceived by schools as a lack of interest. According to Phtiaka, to bridge this gap, schools must learn to communicate with *all* families, especially those that are marginalized, and respond to these families with the understanding that they too want the best for their children.

Distinctions among groups of highly involved to uninvolved families have also been made in studies in other nations. For example, Toomey (1989) contrasts "enthusiasts" with a "silent majority" in Australia.[3] The former become involved on their own, whereas the latter need guidance from their children's schools. He concludes that schools need to take innovative approaches (such as programs to assist families in becoming more involved with their children's reading at home) in order to involve those who would not become involved on their own, and to improve the skills of students who often have difficulty succeeding in school.

For such approaches to be successful, however, schools have to tailor them to meet the specific needs of their students' families. For example, Sanagavarupu and Elliott (1996) found that Indian and Australian parents take different approaches in guiding their children's preschool education. Mothers in India regulated and monitored their children more, and expected preschoolers to complete extensive homework assigned daily by the school. They are influenced by a highly competitive and selective higher education system for which preparation starts in the earliest grades. By comparison, Australian mothers were more flexible, encouraging greater independence and expecting preschoolers to learn through developmentally appropriate play. The authors suggest that these and other differences in parenting need to be understood by schools in order to work effectively with students and their families who immigrate and enter new school systems. These and other studies underscore the importance of school programs that encourage greater communication, cooperation and interaction between families and their children's schools to enhance children's learning and development.

GOVERNMENTAL POLICY CHANGES TO PROMOTE GREATER FAMILY INVOLVEMENT

Recognizing the need for *all* families to have opportunities to become more involved in their children's learning, many nations have developed policies to promote family-school connections, including – parent choice of their children's schools and parent representation on school councils or decision-making boards.

School Choice. One of the first policy changes for increasing family involvement in many nations is to offer families a choice of the school their children attend. This is often a first step for nations moving toward democracy because it is a focussed, mechanical process that can be designed and regulated by educational officials. Systems of choice are explained in terms of marketing and competitive forces; policy and business leaders are comfortable viewing parents as "consumers" (Woods, 1993). As the following research suggests, however, in order for choice systems to be effective, communication between families, schools and children is necessary.

In their study of school choice, Shapira and Haymann (1991) found that, in Israel, choosing primary schools is an option primarily exercised by upper-middle class families who have greater access to school information. The authors contend that this disparity in information may undermine the goal of integrating students with diverse socioeconomic status and academic abilities. According to Shapira and Haymann, for school choice to be equitable and non-segregated in Israel, information about schools must be extended to lower income parents.

Similarly, researchers studying school choice in Amsterdam and the United States concluded that within the currently operating educational system, most parents choose schools without having adequate information (Salganik & Carver, 1992; Van Der Wolf, 1995). They recommend providing all parents with objective information to make sound choices of schools, thereby making schools more accountable to educational consumers and more responsive to competitive market forces.

Edge, West and David (1996) also stress the importance of information in school choice decisions in Britain, and point out the importance of parent-child communication when choosing secondary schools. These authors found that school test scores are secondary to parents' and children's main concerns for programs that are responsive to students' interests, talents and needs. In addition, Edge and her colleagues report that there is room for improvement in the information that is provided to families on British secondary schools. Good choice systems, therefore, should provide all important school information in understandable terms and allow families to weigh the data as they see fit.

School Decision Making

There are natural connections between a nation's goal of democratization and the establishment of school boards and councils that include parent representatives (Prucha & Walterova 1992; Vantuch, 1996). The hope is that such representation will make dramatic improvements in school programs and lead to all kinds of social and economic advances. Most councils, however, are ineffective (Mac Beath, 1994, 1995; Beattie, 1985; Marques, 1996). Parent representatives and school personnel are not usually prepared to serve and communicate with the rest of the parent population (Wilkomirska & Marek, 1996).

As in many nations, parents in Hong Kong were found to have minimal participation in school governance or substantive decision-making (Shen, Pang, Tsoi, Yip, & Yung, 1994). The most popular vehicles for initiating parent involvement in school decision-making are parent associations (PAs) and parent-teachers organizations (PTOs) (Beattie, 1985). The majority of kindergarten, elementary, and high schools in Hong Kong have neither, although membership in PTAs is growing (I-wah, 1996). When surveyed, school supervisors, principals, and teachers stated that PTO's should primarily help to improve communications and relationships between families and schools. These school personnel did not think that parent organizations should help in formulating school policies or in monitoring the work or quality of the school. Their attitudes reflect a concern that parent organizations might interfere with the professional responsibilities and autonomy of administrators and teachers.

Other studies also show that concerns about professional autonomy inhibit many administrators and teachers from encouraging parental involvement at school, especially in the area of school governance and/or decision-making (Krumm, Moosbrugger, & Zwicker, 1992: Phtiaka, 1994; Zagoumennov, 1996). In a series of interviews with twelve primary school teachers in Australia, Newport (1994) found that although teachers believed that parents should be informed about changes in school policies and curriculum developments, most did not believe that parents should be involved in the decision-making process. Newport argues that central to teachers' resistance to parental participation in school governance are their beliefs and definitions of teacher professionalism. She found that teachers' belief in "teacher-as-expert" created a perceived hierarchy of knowledge, value, and status that affected some teachers' collaboration with parents as equals in the process of educating children. The author contends that this belief reflects insufficient teacher training in the knowledge, skills and attitudes needed to facilitate the development of effective partnerships between schools, families and communities.

By contrast, in an evaluation of New Zealand's Project CRRISP, designed to promote parental participation in decisions about curriculum development and design, Ramsay (1992) found that with appropriate training and support for families and school staff, parents and teachers can become partners in school governance with substantial educational and social gains for all stakeholders. Observation, interview and questionnaire data gathered from four schools found that schools that allocated the necessary resources, and allowed time for parents and teachers to discuss issues and decisions were most successful in promoting collaborative decision-making about curriculum. In addition, the authors found that ethnic minority and low-income parents were most involved in the process when they felt that their opinions were valued. No one strategy for promoting collaboration was found to be the best. Rather, a repertoire of strategies was necessary to ensure that parents from all ethnic and income groups believed their input and participation were welcomed. Lastly, the authors found that as schools and parents collaborated on curriculum decision-making, parents became more involved in their children's learning at home, parents and teachers communicated more easily and frequently, and teachers had the opportunity to know their students better.

It is evident that educators must work to give families the information and support they need to feel competent and comfortable enough to make decisions about where their children will attend school, and to become more active in school decision-making and other school activities. This work may not be easy given the concerns of many teachers and administrators about their professional status and autonomy, and the concerns of families about the special needs of their children. However, such attitudes can be modified. In a report about the changing role of parent involvement in Dutch schools, Smit and Van Esch (1995) concluded that experiences with parent participation in school governance have, generally, increased teachers' and students' sense of well-being. Similarly, Townsend (1996) reports increased parent satisfaction in a "self managed" school in Australia. Studies and field tests in the United States and other nations also indicate that negative attitudes that teachers and families hold about each other become more positive after partnership practices are implemented (Bastiani, 1988; Epstein 1996).

PROGRAMS TO ENHANCE FAMILY PRACTICES THAT SUPPORT CHILDREN'S LEARNING

In contrast to the initial governmental approaches that emphasize mechanical changes, in school choice and decision-making, most families' concerns about involvement focus on fulfilling their parenting roles, and helping their children reach their fullest potential. To families, partnerships with schools require respect, relationships, and responsiveness to children and families' needs and goals. School-family-community connections involve interpersonal relations among teachers, principals and parents, and long term commitments to communication about children and their schools.

Of all the types of involvement, the one that most families in most nations want to know most about is how to enhance their children's learning at home. This includes how to be an effective parent at each age level, and how to interact with children at home about classwork, homework and academic plans and decisions across the grades. Recognizing the need to reach out to families in order to improve the academic success and educational experiences of students, more schools are conducting programs and practices to strengthen parenting skills and to help parents provide home environments to support their children's learning. Research suggests that activities, such as workshops and home visits, have positive influences on families' practices at home, parent and student attitudes about schools, and students' academic achievement.

Villas-Boas (1996) conducted a study to measure the effects of workshops and home visits that were designed to inform parents about literacy development on the literacy skills of low-income, first-grade Indian children in Portugal. The study compared a control group to an experimental group who attended parent workshops and received regular home visits during which story books were delivered and parents were assisted in reading these stories to their children. Children's reading gains were measured using pre- and post- standardized reading exams. Changes in parental and teacher attitudes were measured using pre- and post- questionnaires.

Villas-Boas (1996) found that the intervention program had significant, positive effects on the literacy performance of students in the experimental group. In addition, more parents in the program reported that they could talk freely with teachers about their children's learning problems, that they had higher expectations for their children's school performance, and that they better monitored their children's completion of homework. Teachers' attitudes toward parents also became more positive. Before the intervention, teachers described Indian parents as difficult to reach. After the intervention, more teachers reported that these parents were cooperative and willing to help their children at home. The Villas-Boas (1996) study confirms findings from Epstein's (1990) study that teachers who involve families at home rate poor families with less formal education more positively than do other teachers. The study in Portugal also shows that positive subject-specific practices of school-family partnerships can positively affect students' learning in the targeted subject, as well as teacher and parent attitudes.

Similar results showing the positive effects of subject-specific school-family collaborations on students' skills and related family and teacher outcomes have been found in numerous studies in the United States (Balli 1995; Epstein, Salinas, & Simon, 1996) and in other countries. Several studies in Chile indicate that when Chilean parents were provided parenting education and subject-specific training in mathematics by educators, they became more effective "teachers" or "tutors" at home as evidenced by students' statistically significant gains in mathematics achievement (Pizarro, 1992; Sanchez, 1994). Sanchez and Baguedano (1993) caution that such gains are not guaranteed for all home-school links, however. They argue that in order for desirable educational and instructional outcomes to occur, several elements are required including: 1) well-designed and well-implemented training for parents; 2) sufficient funds to implement the practice effectively; 3) sufficient time to ensure parental competence and understanding; 4) committed and knowledgeable education specialists, teachers and counselors, and 5) clear, specific subject content. If these elements are in place, the authors are optimistic about the positive influence of family-school collaborations on students' learning.

Others conducting evaluations of school-family connections and student academic outcomes have also reported favorable results. Topping (1995) found that Scottish student's spelling skills and their self-concept of ability in spelling were enhanced when their parents tutored them using a cued spelling strategy.

Results of a comprehensive study on the effects of homework on students' learning English as a foreign language (Villas-Boas, 1993) also support the belief that parental involvement in well-designed homework can enhance achievement. The study's participants were seventy-seven 6th graders from an urban, preparatory school located in the metropolitan area of Lisbon, Portugal. The boys and girls were eleven to twelve years of age and from lower and middle-income families. Students were randomly assigned to two experimental groups and one control group. A criterion-referenced language pre-test was administered to each child at the start of the study.

The experimental groups were assigned homework especially designed to develop vocabulary, listening, reading and writing skills, while members of the control group received regular homework assignments. In addition, randomly selected parents of students in one of the experimental groups attended an hour-long training session on how home environmental factors affect children's learning, and what parents can do to encourage and support their children's work at home. Two weeks after the training session, parents were contacted by phone or mail to check for and encourage their involvement in their children's learning.

At the end of the four-week treatment, a post-test was administered to all students. The experimental groups' test scores were significantly higher than the test scores of the control group. Furthermore, students in the experimental group whose parents were involved in their homework, performed significantly better than students in the experimental group whose parents were not.

Additional studies emphasize other important school-related outcomes that result from effective subject-specific school-family collaborations. In his evaluation of Effective Partners in Secondary Literacy Learning (EPISLL), an Australian program designed to support and raise parent participation in literacy learning and the study skills of students in grades 7–10, Cairney (1995) found that the program had several positive effects. The program's participants were a diverse group of 17 families drawn from a socioeconomically disadvantaged suburb in Sydney, Australia. EPISLL consisted of 11 two-hour sessions over six weeks that introduced parents to learning strategies to use with their children at home. The content of the program included the importance of developing positive parent-child relationships, helping students to set realistic personal goals, understanding the nature of reading and writing processes, and locating and using community resources.

Written evaluations of EPISLL and structured interviews with parents and teachers revealed that parents reported improved communications and better personal relationships with their children. Parents also reported gaining new knowledge about literacy and learning, and greater confidence in themselves and their ability to help their children succeed in school. Teachers reported that the program helped open channels of communication and interaction between themselves and parents, and teachers and parents reported that students had acquired new competencies, including better study skills, and more positive academic self-concepts.

Similar outcomes were found in evaluations of IMPACT, a project that originated in England to involve parents in their children's mathematics learning. In a two-year qualitative evaluation of the program, Border and Merttens (1993) found that parents reported that IMPACT made mathematics more enjoyable and less frightening for their children, helped them to understand how their children learned mathematics, and provided opportunities to share and discuss their children's curriculum with other parents and teachers. However, parents also voiced concerns over the program, including complaints about activity instructions, unclear connections between homework activities and mathematics learning, and lack of teacher follow-up in the classroom. The authors concluded that although IMPACT successfully involves many parents in their children's school work, it may also lead to "disruptions" due to differing expectations and attitudes between teachers and parents.

Another program that reports positive results for schools, parents and their children is the Home-School-Community Liaison Scheme (HSCL) in Ireland. Ryan (1995) found that students' attitudes and skills improved as a result of increased communication and interaction between their families and schools. The HSCL program was introduced in Dublin in 1990 to increase the academic success and school persistence of economically disadvantaged students through greater cooperation between families and schools. Through parent courses and activities and home visits, the program encourages the involvement of parents of primary school aged children at home and at school.

Outcomes for students, teachers and parents participating in HSCL have been positive. Teachers have observed improvements in students' classroom behavior, attendance, attitudes towards teachers, parents, the school and themselves, and care in completing school work. Teachers have also noted that, at the primary level, the presence of parent volunteers has had positive effects on students' sense of well-being. In addition, teachers have reported greater comfort with parental involvement and improved parent-teacher relations.

Over two-thirds of the families involved in HSCL reported that as a consequence of their involvement, they have learned how to help their children with school learning. Parents who volunteered in classrooms reported learning more about the teacher's job and problems, and about the classroom life of a child. As a result, they found it easier to talk to teachers and ask questions. Parents have also reported that they have more positive attitudes about the school, greater trust of school personnel, greater confidence in approaching the school and teachers, and increased attendance at parent-teacher meetings.

Some parents in HSCL, however, did not get involved. Compared to more involved parents, less-involved parents were more likely to be single-parents, have more children, be unemployed, and/or perceive their children as low-achievers. According to Ryan, increased efforts are needed to advance the level of involvement of families who, for economic and social reasons, are most in need of assistance.

Similarly, Toomey (1989) followed 79 working class families of preschool students in a study of home reading activities. He found that subject-specific information and training for families in reading helped many become involved who would not otherwise have done so. Controlling on students' earlier reading competencies, those whose families participated in the program significantly increased their reading skills. He concluded that in economically disadvantaged communities, special efforts need to be made to reach parents who are less confident about assisting their children's reading and/or contacting schools. If that effort is made, parents respond and children benefit.

COMMUNITY PRACTICES OF PARTNERSHIP WITH FAMILIES AND SCHOOLS

Schools are not the only institutions committed to educational change. Internationally, community-based institutions and programs are becoming involved in improving educational outcomes for today's youth. Community agencies are increasingly working with families and schools to increase the support that all children need to be successful citizens in the 21st century. The following studies show how community programs can benefit children and their families.

A community-based program in Colombia, South America that has been successful in helping children and families is PROMESA (Garcia, 1995). One of PROMESA's goals is to promote greater school attendance in rural areas in Colombia through grassroots, participatory action. The project began in 1978 with 100 families and continues today, serving about 2,000 families. Community leaders, many of whom are mothers, primary education agents, and other parents are involved in different aspects of program planning and implementation. Evaluation results show that PROMESA has led to more children going to primary school and staying longer. For example, the average grade level for a twelve year-old in one region served by the program increased from 2.5 to 4.2 between 1980 and 1989.

Another successful community-school collaboration is taking place in Poland (Kawecki 1993) through the Civic Educational Association (CEA), an independent organization in Poland led by teachers and parents. The CEA provides psychological and pedagogical guidance to schools serving children from economically disadvantaged families. Drawing from the knowledge and expertise of psychologists and other medical and social service specialists, the CEA provides on-site family therapy, and consultations for parents and teachers.

Research is beginning to show that the most effective community connections are well-implemented and responsive to the needs of families, students and schools. For example, Cairney and his colleagues (1995) reviewed literacy programs in Australia. Of the many literacy programs being implemented, most had not been evaluated, were often initiated by schools without family or community input, and varied greatly in content, process, purpose, and participant control. The authors argue that research and evaluation of the processes and results of literacy programs are needed to help us better understand the ways in which community groups and schools can share responsibility for program development and control. They suggest that shared community, school and family responsibilities will increase feelings of ownership among all participants and avoid the tendency of many programs to simply impose one group's cultural literacy practices on another.

Garreau (1996) extends our understanding of the need for school-family-community connections that are responsive to the needs of families and students in her study of children's return to school after cancer treatments. Doctors, nurses, treatment center administrators, families and schools must learn new ways to work together with student-patients and their peers when the students re-enter regular school. Her work suggests that in addition to working with children and families, health service providers need to connect with schools in order to improve the quality of life and education of children returning to school after severe illnesses.

Acknowledging the importance of shared responsibility and the essential role that communities can play in educational change and progress, Mawhinney (1994) conducted a study to better understand the process of school-community collaboration in Canada. Her study examined the theoretical and practical issues related to school-community collaborative efforts, and the changes needed in both practice and approach to accommodate collaborative action. Mawhinney found that the primary difficulties in establishing and maintaining school-community collaborations related to defining roles, clarifying goals for schools and community agencies, and finding and organizing funding to support programs. Her study and a study conducted by Nettles (1992) in the United States indicate that with the commitment and persistent action of key actors, successful collaborations such as tutoring, mentoring, counseling and "coaching" (Nettles, 1992) for youth and their families are possible, and increasingly necessary.

BARRIERS TO SCHOOL-FAMILY-COMMUNITY PARTNERSHIPS

The preceding studies provide information and corroborate previous findings in the United States and other countries on the potential success of school-family partnership activities at home. There are, however, potential barriers to the successful implementation of practices to involve all families (Epstein & Becker, 1982). Based on their work in Australia, Crump and Eltis (1995) remind us that although more teachers are attempting to collaborate with families, there are deeply ingrained individual and institutional histories that need to be addressed for good partnerships to develop. These include some teachers' perceptions of a lack of support or interest from the home, and some parents' negative experiences with education, either their own or their children's.

Most families have questions about how to best support their children's schooling, how to promote students' social, emotional and intellectual development at different ages, and how to help prepare them for post-secondary education and/or future employment. For answers to these and similar questions, the school is often the most convenient and accessible institution to which parents can turn. The school, therefore, can be an important source of information and support for parents in the care, socialization and education of their children. However, research (Calabrese, 1990) shows that some parents are reluctant to turn to the school for the help and information that they need. This reluctance may stem from social status or educational differences between parents and school personnel, or from the school's lack of pro-active and equitable practices of family and community involvement.

Research in Israel led Goldring (1991) to contend that a number of barriers must be removed if greater school-family interaction is to be achieved. These are: 1) lack of flexible, frameworks for interactions between parents and teachers; 2) disagreement among parents and teachers over definitions of teacher professionalism, and 3) vast differences in the ways that children relate to their teachers and parents.

Studies in the United States (Dauber & Epstein, 1993; Epstein & Dauber, 1991) show that schools and teachers who conduct positive, comprehensive partnerships with families can break down the barriers to effective communication, and help families overcome their reluctance to use the school as a resource. Studies in Canada also indicate that such practices help more families feel more comfortable with their children's schools, and improve the schooling experiences of children. Coleman, Collinge and Tabin (1993), for example, interviewed students in grades 6 and 7, their parents and their teachers in British Columbia, Canada. As in studies conducted in the United States, the interview data indicated that parent and student attitudes about schools and their ratings of teachers are strongly affected by teacher practices of parent involvement. Coleman, Tabin and Collinge (1994) also found that student responsibility for learning was enhanced when parents, teachers and students engaged in mutually supportive activities.

Other studies also point to the importance of understanding students' views

(McGilp, 1996; Ryan & Sykes, 1993; Yue & Ho, 1996) and students' roles (Montandon & Perrenoud, 1987) in education and in school-family-community partnerships. In country after country, research, development and evaluation reports indicate that barriers are beginning to be dismantled and that schools are developing successful partnerships with families and communities. Broad based commitment and support on national, state and local levels appear vital to the success of programs of school-family-community partnerships. For example, changes in Spain and Portugal's educational policies that encourage greater parental participation in school decision-making, and better in-service teacher education stressing family-school partnerships have resulted in more communication and interaction between families and schools (Martinez, Marques, & Souta 1994). The Talk to a Literacy Learner program (TTALL), designed to promote home-school connections to help children develop literacy skills, was developed in response to an initiative of the New South Wales state government of Australia, as part of the International Literacy Year in 1990. As another example, the Ministry of Education in Chile (Icaza 1995), established policies and sponsored a number of programs to integrate families into the educational process. Progress during the past decade in the United States and elsewhere in school-family-community collaborations to improve students' learning has been noteworthy and promises to continue because of national, state and local policies, and the hard work and commitment of schools, families and communities.

SUMMARY AND DISCUSSION

"A school door must open from both sides."
(From a statement by Jana Matousova, school principal,
Czech Republic interviewed by Walterova, 1996).

Crosscutting Themes about Partnerships. Research on school-family-community partnerships is international in scope and central for understanding children's learning and development. Most children learn academic subjects in school, but how well they learn, what else they learn, and why they learn are influenced by schools, families, communities, and their connections. Research on school, family, and community partnerships is also central for understanding the social organization of schools. Most schools are directed by educators and education policy, but how effectively schools are run and how successfully teachers teach all students are influenced by school, family, and community connections. These conclusions are true across countries. International studies of the connections of families, schools, students and communities contribute to an understanding of requirements for school change and school improvement.

Research on school-family-community partnerships differs from country to country due, in part, to each nation's history of education, social research, and partnership approaches. For example, Australia has a long history of literacy programs, and so research on family, school, and community connections to literacy learning is prominent. By contrast, Poland and the Czech Republic are developing educational structures and processes that reflect their new democracies, and so studies of families-choice of schools and participation in school decision making are prominent. Despite important differences, common themes are emerging from studies across countries that extend findings from any one nation and strengthen the knowledge base about the importance of partnerships for successful schools and successful students. Our review of selected studies by researchers in twenty nations reveals these common findings:

Parents vary in their level of involvement with schools. In just about all nations, some parents are closely connected to their children's schools and interact easily with teachers. Others, particularly parents with less formal education, are reluctant to contact their schools if they view them as hostile places. Family structure, family life, and parents' work patterns are changing in many countries. More mothers are educated and more are employed outside the home during the school day. Family forms are diversifying as parents divorce and remarry. Close ties with relatives are stretched as families immigrate to new communities or new countries. These factors affect families, children, and schools in all nations, and require schools to consider many different ways to communicate with the families of their students. There is more involvement by more families in the elementary than in the secondary grades, in part because, internationally, more parents feel comfortable and familiar in the early grades, and in part because educators in the early grades do more to involve families. Most parents in most countries are eager to become more involved in their children's education in all grade levels at home or at school, but need to know that they are welcomed and respected by the schools, and need useful information from the schools about how to assist their children.

Parents are most concerned about their children's success in school. Parents want their children to be happy and successful in school. In different cultures, these concerns are expressed in different ways. Interestingly, even when they are free to choose the schools their children attend, parents and students select schools based on a number of factors (not just academic test scores) to maximize children's chances of success and happiness. Parents want their schools to understand and respond to their children's talents and needs.

Students need multiple sources of support to succeed in school and in their communities. Students in all nations report that their families love and care for them, and that they learn things at school and at home. Surveys in many locations indicate that children and parents are often more in tune with each other than with teachers when asked about family goals, students' aspirations or about the kinds of assistance that students and families need to reach their goals. Research, however, shows that students who receive support from home, family and community are triply benefitted, and are more likely to be academically successful than those who do not (Sanders 1996a).

Teachers and administrators are initially resistant to increasing family involvement. Some educators in most locations fear that involving families and others will decrease their professional status. There is more resistance to involving families in school decision-making and curriculum design, and less opposition to involving families in fund-raising, volunteering, and communicating in traditional ways from school to home. Other types of involvement (i.e., two-way communications and involving families with their own children on schoolwork at home) meet mild, initial resistance, but are growing areas for action and improvement.

Teachers and administrators need pre-service, in-service, and advanced education. Education and training is necessary in order for teachers and administrators to understand diverse families and to obtain the knowledge and skills needed to establish and maintain good programs of partnerships with all families and communities. Most educators in all nations are unprepared by their education and training to understand and work with families. In some countries, educators are required to accrue credits or other evidence of continuing education every five years, but these improvements do not have to include school-family-and community partnerships.

Schools need the input of families and communities. Schools need assistance from their students' families and their communities to provide rich and varied educational experiences to help all students succeed in school and in life. In most nations, funding for education is too low to meet all needs. School systems need to be able to identify, mobilize, and organize all available resources and talents to support and extend programs and opportunities for all students. Most parents need assistance to understand their children, the schools and ways to help both. Schools are in a unique position to address the fears and concerns of uninvolved parents by establishing programs and practices that encourage all parents to participate in their children's education.

Taken together, these conditions – parents' readiness, students' needs, teachers' resistance, schools' insufficiencies – set the stage for action to improve school-family-community partnerships. The studies reviewed in this chapter show that researchers and educators have identified some common approaches to increase partnerships. Researchers in more than one country conclude:

Policies are important precursors to program development. Progress in family participation in education has been made, in large part, by national, state, and local policies. There is, presently, a mismatch between the official policies to increase family involvement and the actions that most parents want to take to support their children's education. Most governmental policies begin with tightly controlled mechanical systems for parents to choose their children's schools or to include a few parent representatives on existing decision-making bodies. If well designed, these mechanical systems may become part of full programs of partnership, but they cannot take the place of more responsive systems that involve all families in school activities, children's progress, decisions about courses, and other aspects of their own children's learning and development. The information and activities that families seek are based on relationships and regular communications with educators. The studies summarized in this chapter suggest that, across countries, programs and practices tend to evolve from mechanical systems to also include interpersonal practices of partnership. Researchers may help to hasten the development of more responsive partnerships by collecting and interpreting data from parents and students on their educational interests and needs.

Programs and practices of partnership make a difference in whether, how, and which families are involved in their children's education. Well-designed and well-implemented programs and practices enable families to become involved at school and at home, including families who are unlikely to become involved on their own. Good programs provide the climate, tools, skills, and confidence that parents need to assist their children and the schools. Positive effects of programs that reach out to involve families have been reported by researchers in such diverse locations as Australia, Chile, the Czech Republic, Cyprus, Ireland, Portugal, New Zealand, Spain, the United Kingdom and the United States. In particular, teachers' attitudes about parents' interests and skills change after they begin to work with families; parents learn how to help at home and conduct many more activities with their children and schools; and students benefit in various ways when they see that their parents and teachers know and respect one another and communicate regularly.

Subject-specific practices involve families in ways that directly assist students' learning and success. Studies across nations indicate that students benefit when they interact with family members about topics they are learning in class. Examples tested across countries include parent-child reading, cued spelling, or interactive math or writing homework that children conduct with family members at home. Benefits are reported in studies in more than one country in mathematics and language arts. Across cultures, however, researchers caution that in order for all families to become involved, subject specific interventions must be clear, appropriate for the skills and needs of students and families, monitored and rewarded by teachers, and continually improved with input from all participants.

Programs will be most useful to schools and to families if they are customized, comprehensive, and continually improved to help meet goals set for students by students, families and schools. Epstein (1995) identifies a set of challenges and redefinitions for each of six major types of involvement that are essential for effective programs. The redefinitions and challenges help schools establish a varied menu of practices to involve present-day families at home, at school, and in the community. Researchers in several countries (e.g. Czech Republic, Chile, Ireland, Portugal and Spain) have taken an action team approach for organizing programs of partnership (Davies & Johnson, 1996; Epstein, Coates, Sanders, Salinas, & Simon, 1996; Sanders, 1996b) and have addressed the challenges of the six major types of involvement to improve their programs over time (Gonzalez, 1996; Icaza, 1995; Marques, 1996, Ryan, 1995, Villas-Boas, 1996; Walterova, 1996). For example, Walterova's school team in the Czech Republic initiated and expanded their partnership program with school-parent meetings, newsletters/bulletins, visiting times for parents, homework assistance, volunteers, and other activities. She reports that teachers' attitudes about parents, and parents' attitudes about the school and about their involvement improved over one year. Many studies show that *when* schools implement appropriate practices, many more parents communicate with their school and their children, and have more positive attitudes toward the school.

The Contributions of International Research on Partnerships. This chapter summarizes research collected from members of the International Network of Scholars of the Center on Families, Communities, Schools and Children's Learning[3] which includes researchers from more than forty countries. The Center sponsors and supports international round tables and symposia to encourage communication and exchanges among researchers studying various aspects of school-family-community partnerships, from birth through high school.

The collection of studies demonstrate that small and large studies contribute to a stronger knowledge base with common, replicated results. Although many of the studies reported in this chapter are case studies or local surveys of small samples of parents, teachers or students, the common or linked results of several studies from different nations using varied methods make any one study's findings more credible. The studies summarized here also point to new directions for future research:

Research is needed that collects data from multiple reporters. Several studies confirm that families, students, and others in the community have important messages for schools about their programs and their connections with each other. It is not enough to know what educators think or what policy leaders proclaim about school successes or needed improvements. Indeed, researchers should strive to examine and analyze the perspectives of all key stakeholders in the educational process, including students' views.

Research is needed on community connections with schools, families, and students. Policies, practices, and research have focused more on family-school connections than on how community members and groups can assist schools, families, and students. A broad agenda across countries is emerging on the organization and effects of integrated community services, including the links of schools and families with community health, civic, religious, cultural, recreational, and other community groups and agencies.

Research using different methods is needed on the results of specific practices to involve families and communities. Case studies, surveys, interviews, histories, and evaluations of particular practices are needed to understand the results of school-family-commmunity connections for students at all age and grade levels. Studies in many nations are needed on short- and long-term results of specific practices of all six major types of involvement, separately, in combination, and in full programs of partnership.

Research is needed to understand differences in family involvement across countries. In addition to common themes, approaches, and results across nations, we need to better understand the unique influences of history, geography, politics, and legal frameworks on policies, programs, practices, and expectations for family involvement in different countries. For example, research in Hong Kong has focused on the implications of family-school partnerships when old schools close in urban centers with declining populations and new schools open in expanding suburban areas (Ho, 1995). Various topics linked to patterns of mobility and school transitions are pertinent in all nations.

New topics are emerging that are linked to other social, educational, and economic changes in third world nations. For example, patterns of family-school-community connections change when mothers gain more education. Many countries are increasing the number of years of compulsory education and equal educational and occupational opportunities for males and females. Educational expansion will, over time, produce new patterns of family involvement in children's education by encouraging more mothers and fathers to feel comfortable in school and by alerting schools to the need for new ways to communicate with parents who have one or more jobs during the school day and evening.

International studies have helped researchers in many nations broaden their views and deepen their understanding of processes of school-family-community partnerships that may help all students succeed in school. New investments in education and emerging global economies ensure that school-family-community partnerships will remain an exciting and important field of study.

ENDNOTES

[1]   This work is supported by grants from the Office of Educational Research and Improvement (OERI) to the Center on Families, Communities, Schools and Children's Learning and the Center for Research on the Education of Students Placed At-Risk (CRESPAR) at Johns Hopkins University. The opinions are the authors' and do not necessarily reflect the policies of OERI. Either author may be contacted for more information.

[2]   These nations in alphabetical order are: Australia, Belarus, Canada, Chile, Colombia, Cyprus, Czech Republic, Hong Kong, India, Ireland, Israel, Netherlands, New Zealand, Poland, Portugal, Scotland, Slovakia, Spain, Switzerland, and the United Kingdom.

[3]   (now the Center on School, Family and Community Partnerships at John Hopkins University).

REFERENCES

Balli, S. (1995). *Family involvement with middle-grades homework.* Ph.D. Dissertation, University of Missouri-Columbia.

Bastiani, J. (1988). *Parents and teachers: From policy to practice.* NFER. Nelson: Windsor.

Beattie, N. (1985). *Professional parents: Parent participation in four western european countries.* London: Falmer.

Border, R., & Merttens, R. (1993). Parental Partnership: Comfort or Conflict? In R. Merttens & J. Vass (Eds.), *Partnerships in maths: Parents and schools project,* London: The Falmer Press.

Cairney, T., & Munsie, L. (1995). Parent Participation in Literacy Learning. *The Reading Teacher,* 48(5).

Cairney, T., Ruge, J., Buchanan, J., Lowe, K., & Munsie, L. (1995). *Developing partnerships: The home, family and commununity interface, summary of findings and recommendations.* Department of Employment, Education and Training under the Australian Language and Literacy Policy, Commonwealth of Australia.

— (1995). Developing Parent Partnerships in Secondary Literacy Learning. *Journal of Reading,* 38(7) 520–26.

Calabrese, R. (1990). The Public School: A source of alienation for minority parents. *Journal of Negro Education* 51(1).

Coleman, P., Collinge, J., & Tabin, Y. (1993). *Learning together: The student/parent/teacher triad.* British Columbia, Canada: Simon Fraser University.

Coleman, P., Tabin, Y., & Collinge, J. (1994). *Taking control: developing student acceptance of responsibility for learning.* Presented at the Annual Meeting of the American Educational Research Association. New Orleans.

Crump, S., & Eltis, K. (1995). *School-home connections: Political relations in policy implementation.* Presented at the Annual Meeting of the American Educational Research Association. San Francisco, CA.

Dauber S. L., & Epstein, J. L. (1993). Parents' attitudes and practices of involvement in inner-city elementary and middle schools. In N. Chavkin (Ed.), *Families and schools in a pluralistic society,* pp. 53–71. Albany NY: SUNY Press.

Davies, D., & Johnson, V. (Eds). (1996). *Crossing boundaries: multi-national action research on family-school collaboration.* Report 33. Baltimore MD: Center on Families, Communities, Schools and Children's Learning.

Edge, A., West, A., & David, M. (1996). *Secondary school choice and involvement in education: a family process* (London: Center for Educational Research, London School of Economics). Paper presented at the annual meeting of the AERA, New York.

Epstein, J. L. (1987). Toward a theory of family-school connections: Teacher practices and parent involvement. In K. Hurrelmann, F. Kaufmann, & F. Losel (Eds.), *Social interventions: Potential and constraints,,* pp. 121–136. New York: DeGruyter.

Epstein, J. L. (1990). Single parents and the schools: Effects of marital status on parent and teacher interactions. In M. Hallinan (Ed.), *Change in societal institutions,* pp. 91–121. New York: Plenum.

Epstein, J. L. (1992). School and family partnership. In M. Alkin (Ed.), *Encyclopedia of educational research,* pp. 1139–1151. New York: MacMillan, 6th ed.

Epstein, J. L. (1995). School-family-community partnerships: Caring for the children we share. *Phi Delta Kappan,* **76**. pp. 701–712.

Epstein, J. L. (1996). Perspectives and previews on research and policy for school, family and community partnerships. In A. Booth & J. Dunn (Eds.), *Family-school links: How do they affect educational outcomes?* (pp. 204–246). Hillsdale NJ: Lawrence Erlbaum.

Epstein, J. L., Becker, H. J. (1982). Teacher practices of parent involvement: Problems and possibilities. *Elementary School Journal,* **83,** 103–113.

Epstein, J. L., Salinas, K. C., & Simon, B. (1996). *Effects of the teachers involvement parents in schoolwork (tips) language arts interactive homework process in the middle grades.* Paper Presented at the Annual Meeting of the AERA, New York.

Epstein, J. L., Coates, L., Salinas, K.C., Sanders, M. G., & Simon, B. (1996). *Partnership-2000 schools-manual: Improving school-family-commmunity connections.* Baltimore: Center for Research on the Education of Students Placed at Risk, Johns Hopkins.

Epstein, J. L., & Dauber, S. L. (1991). School programs and teacher practices of parent involvement in inner-city elementary and middle schools. *Elementary School Journal.,* **91**: 289–303.

Garcia, M. C. (1995). *Promesa: A community development model for healthier environments for young children.* CINDE, Bogota, Colombia. (mimeo).

Garreau, M. C. (1996). *Conquering heroes: parents' perspectives of the child's schoolingexperiences after the child's diagnosis of cancer.* Ph.D. Dissertation, University of Alberta, Edmonton.

Glenn, C. L. (1989). *Choice of schools in six nations.* Washington: U.S. Department of Education.

Goldring, E. D. (1991). Parents, participants in an organizational framework. *International Journal of Educational Research,* **15**(2) 215–228.

Gonzalez, R. M. (1996). *Parent involvement in schools in spain: A case study.* In D. Davies & V. Johnson (Eds.), *Crossing boundaries: multi-national action research on family-school collaboration.* Report 33, pp. 103–143. Baltimore, MD: Center on Families, Communities, Schools and Children's Learning.

Ho, K. (1995). Relocation of secondary schools from the urban area: The hong kong experience. *The educational research journal of the Hong Kong educational research association* , **10**(1), 60–66.

Icaza, B. (1995). *Project "educando juntos."* Santiago, Chile: Centro de Investigacion y Desarrollo de la Educacion, CIDE.

I-wah, P. (1996). *Functions of the parent teacher association (PTA) and PTA networking* Paper Presented at the Annual Meeting of the AERA, New York.

Kawecki, M. (1993). Polish initiatives to enhance cooperation between schools and educational organizations. *Unidad.* Winter. Baltimore, Center on Families, Communities, Schools and Children's Learning. Johns Hopkins University.

Krumm, V., Moosbrugger, M., & Zwicker, T. (1992). *Parent involvement in Austria and Taiwan: Results of a comparative study.* Paper Presented at the Annual Meeting of the AERA, San Francisco.

Mac Beath, J. (1994) *Taking account: A role for parents in school development planning.* Paper presented at the annual meeting of the AERA, New Orleans.

Marques, R. (1996). Family-school partnerships in three portuguese schools. In D. Davies & V. Johnson (Eds.), *Crossing boundaries: Multi-national action research on family-school collaboration,* Report 33, pp. 25–46. Baltimore, MD: Center on Families, Communities, Schools and Children's Learning.

Martinez, R., Marques, R., & Souta, L. (1994). Expectations about parents in education in Portugal and Spain. In A. Macbeth and B. Ravn (Eds.), *Expectations about parents in education: European perspectives*, pp.44–58. Glasgow, Computing Services Limited.

Mawhinney, H. B. (1994). Institutional effects of strategic efforts at community collaboration. *Educational Administration Quarterly*.

McGilp, E. J. (1996). *Students' perceptions of how they learn at home, in school, and in the community –and partnerships with parents*. Paper presented at the Eighth Annual International Roundtable of the Center on Families, Communities, Schools and Children's Learning, New York.

Montandon, C., & Perrenoud. (1987). *Entre parents et ensignants un dialogue imposible*. Berne: Lang.

Nettles, S. M. (1992). *Coaching in community settings*. Report 9. Baltimore, Center on Families, Communities and Children's Learning. Johns Hopkins University.

Newport, P. (1994). *Construction of teacher beliefs and practice: Parent participation in the primary school and classroom*. Dissertation. The University of Sydney.

Phtiaka, H. (1994). *Each to his own? Home-school relations in Cyprus*. Presented at the Twentieth Annual BERA Conference. St. Anne's College, University of Oxford.

Pizzarro, R. (1992). *Quality of instruction, Home environment, and cognitive achievement* (Chile). Paper Presented at the Annual Meeting of the AERA. San Francisco.

Prucha, J., & Walterova, E. (1992). *Education in a changing society: Czechoslovakia*. Instituteof Educational and Psychological Research. Faculty of Education, Charles University: Prague.

Ramsay, P. (1992). Sharing curriculum decisions with parents: An overview of the findings of project CRRISP. *New Zealand Journal of Educational Studies*, 27(2).

Ryan, M., & Sykes, H. (1993). *Support requirements for senior secondary students*. Victoria University of Technology, Australia. (mimeo).

Ryan, S. (1995). *Home-school-community liaison scheme: Final evaluation report*. Dublin, Educational Research Center.

Salganik, L. H., & Carver, R. (1992). *Strategies for informing families about school choice*. Report 5. Baltimore MD: Center on Families, Communities, Schools and Children's Learning.

Sanagavarupu, P. & Elliot, A. (1996). *Cultural specificity in parents' guidance of young children's learning*. (University of Western Sydney Nepean). Paper presented at the annual meeting of the AERA, New York.

Sanchez, R. P. (1994). *Educational quality, curriculum of the home and math achievement*. Paper presented at the Sixth Annual International Roundtable on Families, Communities, Schools and Children's Learning, New Orleans.

Sanchez, R. P., & Baguedano, M. M. (1993). *Curriculum of the home and mathematics achievement*. Presented at the Fifth Annual International Roundtable on Families, Communities, Schools and Children's Learning, Atlanta.

Sanders, M. G. (1996a). *School-family-community partnerships and the academic achievement of African-American urban adolescents*. Baltimore: Center for Research on the Education of Students Placed at Risk. Johns Hopkins University.

Sanders, M. G. (1996b). Action teams in action in the Baltimore School-Family-Community Partnership Program. *Journal of Education for Students Placed At Risk*, 1(3).

Shapira, R., & Haymann, F. (1991). Solving educational dilemmas by parental choice: The case of Israel. *International Journal of Educational Research*, 15(3/4) 277–291.

Shen, S., Pang, I., Tsoi, S., Yip, P., & Yung, K. (1994). *Home-school cooperation research report*. Hong Kong: Education Department.

Smit, F., & Van Esch, W. (1995). *Evaluation of the New Educational Partnership Act in the Netherlands*. Paper Presented at the Annual Meeting of the AERA. San Francisco.

Toomey, D. (1989). *Bridging the home-school gap: A link between research and practice* , la Trobe University. Paper presented at the First Annual International Roundtable of the Center on Families, Communities, Schools and Children's Learning, San Francisco.

Topping, K. (1995). Cued spelling: A powerful technique for parent and peer tutoring. *The Reading Teacher*, 48(5), 374–383.

Townsend, T. (1996). *Community perceptions of the self managing school*. (MonashUniversity, Australia). Paper presented at the Eighth Annual International Roundtable of the Center on Families, Communities, Schools and Children's Learning, New York.

Van Der Wolf, K. (1995). *School choice and school improvement: the role of bureaucracy, professional autonomy and parental satisfaction*. Pedagogische Wetenshappen, Amsterdam, Netherlands.

Vantuch, J. (1996). *Changes in education after the velvet revolution: A slovakian elementary school case study*. (Comenius University, Bratislava, Slovakia)). Paper presented at the Eighth Annual

International Roundtable of the Center on Families, Communities, Schools and Children's Learning, New York.

Villas-Boas, A. (1993). The effect of parental involvement in homework on student achievement. *Unidad*, Winter, Issue 2. Baltimore Center on Families Communities and Children's Learning. Johns Hopkins University.

Villas-Boas, A. (1996). The role of Indian immigrant families in their children's literacy acquisition. In D. Davies & V. Johnson (Eds.), *Crossing boundaries: multi-national action research on family-school collaboration.* Report 33, pp. 69–97. Baltimore, MD: Center on Families, Communities, Schools and Children's Learning.

Walterova, E. (1996). Building school-family-community partnerships in the process of social transition in the Czech republic. In D. Davies & V. Johnson (Eds.), *Crossing boundaries: multi-national action research on family-school collaboration.* Report 33, pp. 145–180. Baltimore MD: Center on Families, Communities, Schools and Children's Learning.

Wilkomirska, A., & Marek, J. (1996). *The teachers assessments of changes in the educational system in Poland since 1989.* (University of Warsaw, Poland). Paper presented at the Eighth Annual International Roundtable of the Center on Families, Communities, Schools and Children's Learning, New York.

Woods, P. (1993) *Parental perspectives on school choice in the United Kingdom.* Paper Presented at the Annual Meeting of the AERA. Atlanta.

Yue, X., & Ho, K. (1996). *Causes and management of students behavioral problems in junior high schools in Hong Kong: Views from students, parents, and teachers* (Chinese University of Hong Kong). (CHECK -Paper Presented at the Annual Meeting of the AERA, New York.

Zagoumennov, I. (1996). *Identifying a "good school" – Views of educators, students, families and communities* (Belarus Educational Center for Leadership Development). Paper Presented at the Annual Meeting of the AERA, New York.

II: Challenges

Restructuring and Renewal: Capturing the Power of Democracy

LEW ALLEN
League of Professional Schools, University of Georgia

CARL D. GLICKMAN
Program of School Development, University of Georgia

Allen and Glickman begin Part 2 of this section of the Handbook by examining restructuring and renewal as strategies of educational change. They draw on their own experience of establishing and working with The League of Professional Schools in order to do so. Schools belonging to this league commit to "a belief in the powers of democracy to guide school restructuring in order to bring about on-going school renewal that focussed on students." Changing the governance of the school to more shared, democratic forms is regarded as one fundamental way of enacting this belief.

Allen and Glickman describe The League of Professional Schools and provide research evidence on its processes and effects as a form of school restructuring. Developing trust, creating understanding through action-research, and building a vision together characterize some of the core aspects of League school activities. Allen and Glickman flush out what these things mean in practice, and analyze the obstacles and difficulties that schools encountered and sometimes overcome when they tried to convert them into reality.

Successful school change efforts recognize that simply changing the organization or structure of schools isn't sufficient to bring about meaningful change. The hearts and minds of the people in schools ultimately dictate what happens in classrooms, not changes in policies or procedures.

Sarason (1995) places teachers at the center of school change when he points out that if teachers are not provided stimulating conditions that nurture their growth and learning, they will not be able to create rich learning environments for their students. Peterson, McCarthey, & Elmore (1996) in studying efforts that go beyond tinkering and result in changes in classrooms, conclude that before instruction is affected, teachers' must become a part of a community of learners that shares a common vision of what could be for students and is continuously seeking to develop new skills and understandings to bring that vision to life. Gitlin, Bringhurst, Burns, Cooley, Myers, Price, Russell, & Tiess (1992), relate the experiences of one of the authors, a 6th grade teacher, "The empowerment for which I so longed in my profession and my life was within me. That is not to say there

A. Hargreaves (ed.), Extending Educational Change, 225-248.
© 2005 *Springer. Printed in the Netherlands.*

were and are no structural barriers, but as I addressed the self-imposed restrictions, the other barriers were more clearly defined and understood" (p. 93). Finally, Fullan (1992) simply states "[that] teacher development and school development are very intimately related" (p. 24).

If building the capacity of the people in schools is central to schoolwide change, then the question becomes, How does a school go about such a task? Simply put, the answer is to govern according to the foundational aspects of public education and democracy. As Jefferson wrote:

> I know of no safe depository of the ultimate power of the society but the people themselves, and if we think them not enlightened enough to exercise their control with a wholesome discretion, the remedy is not to take it from them, but to inform their decision.
>
> (Wagoner, 1989, p. 1)

Democracy is predicated on philosophical and psychological assumptions about humans; specifically, that every individual as an active, curious learner who – given information, materials, and directions – will be able to utilize learning in meaningful ways: to see connections, to discover applications, and to participate with others (Dewey, 1916; Glickman, in press; Snauwaert, 1993).

High performance on the part of both students and teachers is found in schools that use their organizational structures of shared governance, site-based decision making, and action research to infuse democracy throughout their normal, routine activities – including staffing, scheduling, curriculum, student placement, assessment, discipline, staff development, and involvement with parents and community (Newman & Wehlage, 1995; Aiken, 1942).

THE LEAGUE OF PROFESSIONAL SCHOOLS

The mission statement of the League of Professional Schools reflects a belief in the power of democracy to guide school restructuring in order to bring about on-going school renewal that is focused on students: "To Promote the school as a learning community that is democratic, professional, and student-oriented." Bringing this mission statement to life has profound implications for how schools deliver instruction; how schools are governed; how leadership is defined; what roles students and teachers assume in classrooms, the school, and the larger community; and what role district personnel, parents, and community members play in the life of the school.

What have we learned about what happens when schools move from following hierarchical decision-making procedures to following democratic procedures where the governance concerning teaching and learning is shared and informed by each school's own research efforts? What are the characteristics of this type of schoolwide change that can be identified, studied, and understood in such a way as to be helpful to other schools wanting to make similar changes?

Since the mid 1980's, staff of the University of Georgia's Program for School

Improvement have been collaborating with practitioners from Georgia public schools to learn more about using democratic principles to guide school renewal. The League of Professional Schools, founded in 1989, has been the chief vehicle for this collaboration. Schools joining the League (membership is voluntary) make a commitment to implement a three-part framework for renewal that guides the school's restructuring efforts (Glickman, 1993):

1.   The governance of the school is democratized (charter).
2.   The focus of the governance is driven by the school's own shared vision of exemplary teaching and learning (the covenant).
3.   Action research is conducted to inform the governance process (the critical study process).

Implementing this framework leads schools to create inclusive procedures for gathering and reflecting on information for problem identification, problem solving, and acting collectively. The League's view of the focus of school improvement is exemplified by the words of Hopkins, Ainscrow, and West (1994):

> We regard school improvement as a distinct approach to educational change that enhances student outcomes as well as strengthening the school's capacity for managing change. In this sense school improvement is about raising student achievement through focusing on the teaching-learning process and the conditions which support it. (p. 3)

League schools are not just a collection of schools that have a common focus, nor are they passive subjects of the research of others. League schools actively network together to provide mutual support and to study the process of implementing the League's three premises. Studies conducted in League schools since its inception include five doctoral dissertations, 19 collaborative research projects spearheaded by League staff and university associates, 25 case studies by League practitioners, and a number of collaborative books, chapters, and research presentations. To understand the research on these schools' journeys to become democratic, self-reflective, educative places, it is important to know the commitments made by and services available to member schools.

League Services

Before schools join the League, they first send a team that includes the principal and that has a majority of teachers to a two-day Orientation and Planning Workshop. Teams may include various staff members, parents, and district personnel. At this workshop, the framework of shared governance and action research, focused on curricular and instructional issues, is presented. Teams are given opportunities to hear from veteran League schools, and a significant amount of time is provided for teams to reflect on how the information and examples given might be relevant to their school. The teams then return to their schools, share what they learned with others, and, if they receive 80% approval by faculty (on a secret ballot), they commit themselves to the premises and to participation in the League.

When schools become members of the League a number of services are offered to facilitate their work (Lunsford, 1995). The following services and all major activities of the League are determined and governed by the League Congress. The Congress consists of a representative from each League school and a representative from the League staff.

1. Four days of central and regional meetings are provided annually for teams of six. All activities at these meetings (key note addresses, breakout sessions featuring school practitioners, structured and informal dialogues) are related to the League's framework. Each meeting includes a significant amount of time for team planning.

2. A newsletter and school directory are distributed. A bi-annual newsletter features articles by League practitioners about their work, reflections on the League's premises, and items noting outstanding achievement of the schools and their staffs. Schools wanting more information on any of the information and work described in the newsletter are encouraged to contact the contributing school. Also, the school directory lists each school's initiatives so schools pursuing similar goals can keep in touch.

3. Schools have access to an information retrieval system which honors school requests for information about issues, concerns, and practices dealing with the League framework. This system also helps connect League schools with those who have similar instructional interests or common concerns in implementing the framework.

4. Schools receive an annual site visit by a League staff member, university associate, or League practitioner. The purpose of the visit is to provide each school an opportunity to reflect with a knowledgeable colleague about the school's progress, concerns, successes, and future plans. Following the visit, the school receives a written summary of what the visitor heard and observed during the course of the day. Schools can request additional on-site assistance for a nominal fee.

5. Special summer institutes provide schools teams with extended time to address issues that are of concern. Examples of past summer institutes are team building, analyzing qualitative data, conflict resolution, and grant writing.

6. League staff provide schools with assistance in identifying resources and with consultation regarding the implementation of the League premises via telephone, fax, and electronic mail communication.

Huberman and Miles (1984) point out the importance of ongoing facilitation in bringing about complex schoolwide change. League practitioners find networking with other member schools provides needed facilitation through stimulating and informing their thinking, enabling them to put their work into perspective with other schools, and providing teachers and principals with on-going opportunities to share their expertise with other professionals (Allen & Lunsford, 1995). A case study from a League middle school states:

We are actively involved in whole language, interdisciplinary instruction, care teams for at-risk students, and cooperative learning. The League of Professional Schools was the catalyst for our immersion in these programs. . . . Gradually, from the teachers outward, we are changing the structure of our school to reflect a more democratic, common sense approach to education. (Loe, Rogers, Shams, & Williams, 1992, p. 23)

The responses to a recent survey of veteran League schools revealed that League services overwhelmingly made a significant contribution to the schools' efforts in implementing the League's framework for renewal. For example, when asked about the value of exchanges with other schools at League meetings, 99% indicated they were of value to their schoolwide efforts.

METHODOLOGY

The following findings are drawn from the information found in the on-site reports and studies described earlier. When the yearly on-site reports are written, each school receives a copy as does the League office. Each year these reports are analyzed by League staff members first, individually, and then collectively. Through extensive dialogues and multi-year comparisons, patterns of school behaviours, common concerns and successes, and degrees of implementation of each of the League premises are culled from these reports (Glickman, Allen, & Lunsford, 1994). The data gained from this on-going process provides the foundation for the findings that follow.

INTRODUCTION TO FINDINGS

The efforts of League schools to move from traditional, bureaucratic decision-making to democratic decision-making informed by each school's action research are an on-going process as people define, modify, then refine and clarify new roles and areas of influence for groups and individuals. In doing this work there is a constant need to increase the school's depth of understanding of shared governance and action research, to build the level of trust among the people in the school, and to clarify the school's vision of what can be accomplished.

Sometimes schools move forward, sometimes they reach a plateau, and sometimes they lose ground. In making a presentation about her school's efforts, one principal showed an overhead transparency of a train going down perfectly straight tracks. This is how she hoped the journey to a more democratic, self-reflective school would look. She then showed the same train teetering precariously on tracks that twist and circle off into the distance. This, she reported, is a more accurate depiction of the journey. What follows are the lessons we have learned to date, knowing full well that there are many more waiting around the next bend in the tracks.

As this principal learned, schools' progress in becoming democratic places is not linear. While the following findings are grouped into two basic categories, Building a Foundation for Change and Deepening the Work, it should be understood that schools continue to build and shore up the foundation for implementing the premises while they deepen the work. Under "Building a Foundation for Change" we have included sections on readiness for change that a school brings to the process, issues that need to be dealt with in getting started, the role that trust plays in the early stages, and how a schools' collective understanding of the work and the vision of what is to be accomplished is built. The "Deepening the Work" section includes using information, schoolwide actions that move the schools' work forward, how schools learn to use time, and the role of the principal.

BUILDING A FOUNDATION FOR CHANGE

Readiness for Change

Reasoning that schools joining the League already have some manner of decision-making in place, a League associate sought to learn how, if at all, a school's previous way of doing business affected its decision to join the League and whether it was related to later success in implementing the League's framework (Roberts, 1992). Participants in an Orientation and Planning Workshop were asked to write on a blank note card their reasons for attending the workshop. They were also asked on an open-ended survey to describe recent instructional changes that had been made in their school, to clarify how these decisions had been made, to identify the school's instructional priorities, and to list the enhancing and impeding factors at work in their school regarding the implementation of the League's framework. The data from these answers were subdivided between schools which subsequently chose to join the League and schools which chose not to join the League. It was found that schools exhibiting the following characteristics were more likely to join the League:

- a collegial atmosphere where formal and informal discussions about instruction take place,
- a principal who encourages risk taking, buffets the school from outside mandates, and encourages teacher input in decisions, and
- faculty members who are informed about and understand the basic purpose for attending the Orientation and Planning meeting.

In other words, a predictor of a school's willingness to embrace shared decision-making and action research was tied to whether its current decision-making process already valued professional reflection, was open to change, recognized teachers as having expertise, and reflected some basic knowledge of the role that democratic values should play in school renewal. This study made League staff members sensitive to how past experiences not only influenced whether a school joined the League but also to how the school approached implementation of the League's framework. Subsequently our experiences have confirmed the key role that a school's history plays in its efforts to change. The significance of this factor will be explained further throughout this chapter.

Getting Started

By the end of the second day of an Orientation and Planning Workshop, team members are typically excited about the possibilities of the League's framework for their school and for the opportunity to network with other schools as they take on this ambitious task. Their job then, is to return to school and share this information and excitement with their colleagues. It is at this stage that key events take place which lay the foundation for schoolwide change in their school's renewal process.

Faced with the dilemma of how to propose a major schoolwide change to their colleagues and involve them in it, these teams enter unfamiliar territory. Most teachers have spent a majority of their professional lives in classrooms isolated from the other adults in the school. One of the lessons learned by teachers and principals from the League's charter schools, as they struggled to initiate a change in governance, has been that simply inviting colleagues to voice their opinions at full faculty meetings is often not enough to gain a true understanding of how people feel about the proposed change. Nor does such a process help a school collectively reflect upon and develop the needed commitment to making the change. Schools that held faculty meetings where information from the Orientation and Planning Workshop was shared and a vote was then taken found that, even if this resulted in the 80% favorable vote needed to join the League, people did not have a clear understanding of what was being proposed. In these circumstances, where faculty members had not been given formal opportunities to share their thoughts and concerns about joining the League, it was also not unusual to find that informal communications often took place without any input from those trying to lead the change effort. As a result, discrepant theories arose as to why this change was being proposed, what it would accomplish, and who it would benefit. These theories then circulated throughout various parts of the school. Consequently, when leadership teams moved forward, even through they had the formal consent of their colleagues, they found there was little real ongoing support or understanding for what they were trying to accomplish. A team of teachers documented what happened in their school when adequate opportunities for reflection on a proposed change in governance was not provided:

> At first there seemed to be a general lack of understanding about the process and what was involved, a "fear of the unknown." Many felt they would not be taken seriously because their ideas would need additional funding. Some indicated that they believed a select few would make all the decisions. Many worried about power struggles within groups, more paper work, and

too many meetings which might take up valuable time without accomplishing anything. (Aiken, Burdeshaw, Cook, DiVito, Handley, Robinson, Spurlock, & Westlund, 1993, p. 10.)

Another case study reported that, "Problems arose from the fact that many faculty members did not realize when we initially joined. . .what a tremendous impact this involvement in the League would have on our school." (Loe, Rogers, Shams, Williams, 1993, p.16.)

Fullan's (1992) findings support the need for ongoing, schoolwide reflection.

Vision is not something that someone happens to have; it is a much more fluid process and does not have to be – indeed it must not be – confined to a privileged few. In a real sense, implementation of any policy will be superficial unless all implementers come to have a deeply held version of the meaning and the importance of the change for them. (p. 92)

Schools that provided multiple opportunities for people to discuss their thoughts about the school's possible commitment to implementing the League's premises found it paid dividends. When people were given opportunities to take part in a dialogue where they were encouraged to ask questions, express their skepticism or support, seek clarification, and hear what others were thinking, they were much more likely to have a deeper understanding of what the change was about. They were also more likely to be active participants once the decision to embrace the premises had been made because they understood the commitment the school had made and because they felt their voice had been a part of the decision-making process (Allen, 1994).

Once schools moved past the initial stages of committing to the change process, they did not suddenly become democratic centers of inquiry where the governance of teaching and learning was fully shared and where action research was an integral part of the school's decision-making process. Rather, schools began acting in more democratic, inclusive, and reflective ways only as the people in them earned one another's trust, developed a deep understanding of what shared governance and action research can accomplish, and created a shared, schoolwide vision of what the school ultimately wanted to accomplish. As these concepts began to take shape in the minds of the people in the school, these people then began in act in new ways. If these concepts were not developed, expanded, and grasped by a sizeable majority of the faculty, the school could only make simple changes that did not affect the nature of teaching and learning.

Trust

The initial reaction many teachers have to the idea of shared governance is skepticism. They wonder if they will really be allowed to make decisions or if the principal will exercise a veto if things do not go his or her way, reducing their participation to what Nias (1989) calls "mock democracy." Or, they worry that they are going to be victims of what Hargreaves (1994) calls "contrived collegiality" where the shared governance process is used as a front to further the goals of the principal rather than the collective will of the teachers. Principals worry that teachers do not see the "big picture" and might make decisions that are not in the best interests of the school. Everyone worries that the wrong people will get in power for the wrong reasons and make decisions that will be detrimental to their work.

Many veteran teachers have seen many different "great ideas" come and go and suspect that this might be just one more. Teachers' concerns in League schools are hauntingly similar to concerns Huberman (1993) found in his study of secondary teachers in Switzerland. He quotes a veteran teacher: "Now I believe less that we can change the world by changing teaching. I realized that most of the reforms ran up against the weight of the institution and the system" (p. 170).

Teachers worry that action research will be used to force them to make changes that are unwarranted, that it will require large amounts of resources to discover what everybody already knows, or it will result in other people prying into their teaching methods which they consider their own private domain (Calhoun, Allen, Halliburton, & Jones, 1995). Cochran-Smith and Lytle (1993) note school based educators have become leery of educational research because it generally involves people from outside of schools studying, not always respectfully or helpfully, those based inside schools.

Until these types of concerns are addressed and people begin to trust each other and the process, a school is severely limited in its ability to move forward. Trust is the grease that keeps the machinery of shared governance and action research running. Blase & Blase (1994) concluded from their work in League schools that:

> Without trust, people are likely to close up, to keep to themselves, to even close ranks in cliques or special interest groups. Without trust, issues are seldom discussed and never resolved. Without trust, a school cannot improve and grow into the rich, nurturing microsociety needed by children and adults alike. The reward of a trusting environment is immeasurable, yet the price of a lack of trust is dear. (p. 20)

Building trust takes time and hard work, the amount of which depends on the history of the school and the larger contexts in which the school is situated. Some schools begin the change process with certain elements that foster trust already in place: i.e., past and present administrators of the school have not acted and do not act in autocratic ways, the district is perceived as being respectful of teachers' professionalism, a majority of the people in the school feel they have always had at least some input in school decisions, and there is no external pressure to join the League. At the other end of the spectrum are schools with histories of top-down decision-making policies; that are situated in districts which provide schools with very little room for curricular and instructional decisions, where the decision to join the League was made with a minimum of discussion and reflection among the staff; and where there has been subtle pressure on faculty to support what the hierarchy wanted.

Ultimately, trust is built by actions, not words. Teachers learn to trust a principal's commitment to shared decision-making as they observe her supporting a school's decision even when she personally spoke against it, or when teachers observe that no reprisals are forthcoming when they voice opinions different from the principal's. Principals learn to trust teachers when they observe that, given adequate information and opportunities to interact with each other, teachers are capable of making decisions that reflect a schoolwide perspective and concern for all children. People begin to trust the process when their opinions and thoughts are listened to and respected, when they see that action research can produce information that has practical value to the decision-making process and is not used as an evaluative tool on individual teachers, and when schools reach decisions through open democratic means that lead to purposeful action.

Building Understandings

When a school begins to implement the League's framework, its understanding of shared governance is generally limited in breadth and depth. Initially, there are only a small number of people in the school who have an understanding of shared governance and their understanding is somewhat rudimentary. The school's commitment to shared governance is interpreted by some as simply freeing them from any restraints. Therefore, it is perceived as a lack of authority where no one can tell anyone else what to do; everyone is free to do as they please. Others believe that shared governance means replacing the principal's sole authority with a committee or council which assumes that role as the school's decision maker. Experience and collective reflection, both within and across schools, however, eventually leads schools to a more complex understanding of shared governance. Schools come to define shared governance as a way for all people to work together, to learn from each other, to grow in their understanding of what others in the school are thinking and doing, and to take collective action. People begin to see that it is not about personal autonomy, but about schoolwide autonomy. People begin to value working in groups, having collegial dialogues, thinking in terms of "we" rather than "I" (Little, 1982), and knowing how to reach consensus instead of worrying about political clout and who gets to make what decisions (Hays, Glickman, & Allen, 1994). A case study in an elementary school revealed that:

> The decision-making process was perceived as being painful and slow. Group members had to learn to communicate their opinions without fear of reprisal from their peers. Several teachers identified a need for training in conflict resolution. This need became most apparent when the discussion involved emotional issues. Sometimes when difficulties arose, group members wanted an administrator to take over the group. In these cases, the administrator showed the group a way to resolve the problem themselves by gathering data or redirecting the group's focus. As a result, the teachers learned to work

together more democratically. The teachers developed a better understanding of their peers and developed faith in the process. The decisions made by the committees have received better acceptance than past decisions made exclusively by administrators. (Hix, 1992, p. 30)

As schools grow in their understanding of shared governance, they also face similar challenges in dealing with action research. Action research is initially thought of as something to avoid. The word "research" conjures up memories of complicated statistical manipulations focused on theoretical questions far removed from the real world of schooling (Anderson, Herr, & Nihlen, 1994). Yet, as people are given more information and exposure to action research and how other practitioners in schools use it, they begin to understand that it can serve a vital purpose in the school's decision-making process. A comprehensive study of schools' efforts with action research over the past five years concluded:

Schoolwide action research is not something that a school can simply add to what it is already doing. Changes in the normative behaviours in the school must be made; substantial time must be set aside for collecting and analyzing data; the school's governance process must be able to respond to action research findings; new roles must be assumed by teachers and administrators; and external support must be secured. A school faculty that just starts "doing" action research without addressing these changes will find action research has little effect on the life of the school. (Calhoun, Allen, Halliburton, & Jones, 1995, p. 7).

Schools' experiences with action research help them discover that it is within their capabilities to conduct action research, and, having done so, that they can then directly apply the findings to their work.

Teachers saw themselves growing as researchers. Lisa said that she and Mary Jane had initially felt at a loss about what to do with all the data they had collected. . . but together, her group designed meaningful ways of analyzing the data. . . . Teachers learned about research from the inside out. . . . The group was thinking like researchers. . . . Everything was becoming a research question. . . .Teachers recognize the role research played in their lives. 'We seem to have become a more professional group by looking at issues from a research standpoint and not just what we think. . . .' (Allen, 1994, pp. 208–209)

As teachers and principals networked with educators from other League schools, they further broadened their perspectives of various methodological approaches to and benefits of action research. An elementary principal wrote:

I am most pleased that we are beginning to take a more active role in evaluating curriculum initiatives within our school. . . . We are certainly not experts at action research and evaluation techniques but we are not attempting to qualify and quantify what we do instructionally. I believe teachers have always had the innate ability to say what works and what doesn't in their classrooms. Now, I think we can begin to evaluate school programs in terms of what students have accomplished, how we need to modify existing programs, and what we need to try next. (Deweese, Duke, Inglett, Reabold, Robertson, Thomas, & White, 1992, p. 43)

Building a Schoolwide Vision

Over time, schools learn the importance of being able to provide clear answers to the question, "What are we working towards?" Until there is a common vision of education, shared governance and action research are ends unto themselves and not means for making appreciable schoolwide progress in teaching and learning. It is important to note that schools don't simply work on and then arrive at their collective vision. Sometimes the initial vision that guides the work is, in reality, that of the principal or a handful of people in the school (Hargreaves, 1994). Consequently, building a schoolwide vision is an ongoing process. In writing about schools developing a vision, Michael Fullan (1991) cautions, "its formation, implementation, shaping, and reshaping. . .is a constant process" (p. 82).

The initial excitement of trying something new and connecting with other schools can give people the impetus to start and can sustain them in the early stages of schoolwide change, but as that excitement begins to wane, people need a larger vision to keep them moving and excited. It is hard for a staff to pull together until there is agreement as to which direction everyone wants to go. The following quote from a League school case study reflects the school's understanding of the importance of having an educational vision to guide its change efforts. It is instructive to note that the following case study was written in the school's third year of League membership.

> Communication, involvement, reflection, focus, and vision are the goals of our future. We must continue to improve the way we communicate to each other. Lack of time, combined with a large number of issues to be discussed, often results in cursory treatment of important issues. What we are doing has not been made clear to everyone. We must create an understanding of our decisions so that we are able to support and defend them. . . . We need to articulate the focus of the work in our school so that those teachers, who are feeling fragmented by the size of the school and the complexity of so many issues, can have a direction to climb toward. (Hix & Nall, 1993, pp. 57–58)

A common vision is built as people have on-going dialogues focused on school-wide issues of teaching and learning. These are not simply conversations in which people share accounts of failures or successes that happened in their classrooms, but collegial conversations about what instruction, curriculum, schedules, placements, and relations should look like across the school.

These increased understandings of school direction are manifested in the methods schools use to form leadership teams, the parameters or guidelines followed by leadership teams, the inclusive nature of a school's governance process, and the focus of task forces and study groups. It is important to note that because schools do not start at the same levels of readiness and work in differing circumstances, all schools do not move at the same pace or in the same way.

DEEPENING THE WORK

Use of Information

Information distribution is a key factor in developing trust, understanding, and vision. If a school seeks widespread involvement in its renewal efforts, it must create a system for getting information to those it wants to involve and it must provide time and opportunities for people to study and reflect upon the information (Fullan, 1991). "Learning- enriched" schools value information and go out of their way to gather it and make it available to teachers (Rosenholtz, 1989).

Todd's (1994) study of how four League schools use information to facilitate their implementation of the League's framework provides insight into understanding schoolwide change.

1. Information can lead or entice teachers to become active participants in the change process. A teacher reported that information provided "the foundation, and the courage, that they needed to stand up and state their beliefs to their colleagues" (pp. 78–79).

2. Information helps teachers begin to work together by providing a stimulus for collective reflection. A teacher observed that information "helped draw us a little bit closer and took away some of that isolation that we had experienced in the past" (p. 83).

3. Learning that others are having similar experiences with an innovation can rekindle teachers' commitment to continue. "In schools where. . . teachers were becoming actively involved in the instructional decision-making process apparently for the first time, the use of information that affirmed their actions was very comforting and encouraging" (p. 82).

4. Information provides teachers with new ideas and perspectives that can motivate them to see the need for change. It opens up new worlds and in some instances provides a blueprint for change.

Information generated from a school's action research can also help get a school moving and draw people into the decision-making process. After studying the efforts of League schools in conducting action research, Calhoun (1992) concluded:

> The public sharing of data has a confrontational connotation to some of our teachers and administrators. Some sites have reported that problem-identification linked to specific personnel is very uncomfortable and difficult for them to handle productively. . . . Some types of confrontation can be beneficial, however, as I observed occasionally. One faculty was shocked when

they counted the number of children who were failing the ninth grade and the number who had traditionally dropped out. Recovering from the shock, they responded by taking action. I observed other faculties where the same type of pattern occurred – data collection, shock at the evidence, and (not without struggle) redirection of their initiatives. I think that it may be necessary for schools to experience this kind of confrontation if school improvement is to become serious. (p. 127).

Actions Reflect Collective Understandings

As schools develop their collecting thinking and understanding of key issues and concepts, their actions begin to change. What follows is a composite picture of the successive actions that League schools have taken over the past five years.

Selecting Leadership Teams

As charter League schools began creating schoolwide leadership teams, they used a variety of approaches which reflected different levels of democracy. Initially, in some schools, the principal appointed teachers to serve on the team. As schools began to understand the democratic implications of shared governance, they also began to move to electing members and/or using volunteers. En route to eliminating the principal's appointments, a few schools used a combination of appointments by the principal and elected members. In one school, the team was created by the principal selecting the members from a pool of volunteers. Electing members to leadership teams has eventually become the mostly widely accepted method of forming a leadership team. The complexity, however, does not end there.

As schools discover the importance of providing everyone with formal access to the decision-making process, they create increasingly democratic ways of selecting their leaders. Some schools move from selecting leaders through schoolwide elections to electing representatives from departments or grade level, to breaking faculty into small heterogeneous groups and having each group select its representative. These schools concluded that as the group electing a leader/ representative becomes smaller, the stronger each person's voice in the decision-making process becomes and consequently the more democratic the process (Allen, 1994). Schools have further refined the selection process, and made it more democratic, by creating a rotation system that calls for members of the leadership team to rotate off so that others may serve.

Schools have also learned that distributing the opportunity to serve on leadership teams equally has another positive effect. It builds the capacity of the faculty. A principal in a League school concluded:

Ignoring all other advantages, the self governance process provides a significant opportunity for growth in the area of leadership. . . . Sometimes it is a quiet staff member or one who has very little interaction with co-workers who suddenly demonstrates an uncommon insight or ability to express an idea or solve a problem. . . . Always, the role of constituency representative lifts the rank and file staff member to new insight, new confidence and frequently to a new self-awareness. These skills continue to benefit the staff member, constituency group and the staff as a whole, even after the representative rotates off the Leadership Team. Examples of this phenomenon now abound at Windsor Forest where as many as 30% of the staff have cycled on and off the Leadership Team over 4 years. These individuals have a more balanced view of the decision making role in the school. They tend to be more cooperative, more open to alternatives and more willing to negotiate. (Reese, 1994, p. 15)

As schools deepened their understanding of the role and the effect of serving on a leadership team, they also realized that diverse perspectives enhanced the work of the team and ultimately the school. Consequently, they began to be more inclusive in their thinking about who should sit on the teams. Support staff, parents, and students were added to many teams. This inclusive behaviour was also influenced by teams gaining confidence in the process and seeing the value of open and honest dialogue. They lost their fear of airing their dirty laundry in front of those outside the teaching profession and felt comfortable with inviting them to serve on the team.

Becoming More Inclusive

Initially, leadership teams discussed issues, gathered information, fleshed out concerns, and then made decisions or took recommendations to the whole faculty for a vote. As those serving on leadership teams noted that colleagues not serving on the teams were either indifferent or somewhat hostile to the process, they began to modify the teams' actions. School leaders came to realize that the heart of the decision-making process was not the leadership team, but the quality of involvement of everyone in the decision-making process (Weeks & King, 1994). Schools learned that while it is relatively simple to create a leadership team, it takes hard work to keep everyone involved in the process after leaders have been identified (Hensley, Calhoun, & Glickman, 1993).

Given this realization, teams began to open up the process to the whole school (Glickman, Allen, & Lunsford, 1994). They began to make meeting times and locations public and to stress that the meetings were open to everyone in the school. They started meeting in rooms large enough to accommodate extra people. Methods were devised to give everyone opportunities for placing items on the agenda. Information about issues being discussed (Shedd & Bacharach, 1991) and copies of the minutes from leadership team meetings were widely distributed. Task forces made up of those not on the leadership team were utilized for fact finding and for drafting recommended actions. Operating procedures were clarified, put in writing, and communicated to everyone (Allen & Glickman, 1992). Leadership team members stopped defining themselves as decision makers and became coordinators of the involvement of all. Decisions were no longer made within the closed confines of leadership team meetings. Small groups, formal and ad hoc, gave anyone who wanted the opportunity to participate in defining the issues, structuring courses of actions, and monitoring the effects of the actions.

Becoming More Focused on Teaching and Learning

In spite of their commitment to focus on improving teaching and learning, many of the initial issues focused on by schools dealt with adult concerns such as sign-in procedures, smoking in the teacher's lounge, and improving building maintenance. Over time, in most schools, the issues became more outwardly focused, more concerned with the bigger picture of renewing the school's efforts with students and parents (Allen & Glickman, 1992).

Schools walk a fine line between addressing non-instructional issues to build confidence and understanding in their new system of governance and not getting struck dealing with the myriad of "administrivia" issues that arise.

Kirby (1992) examined the focus of leadership teams' efforts in four League schools and concluded that school improvement teams will be more likely to address issues of greater significance under the following circumstances:

- when minor faculty concerns are resolved first, thereby fostering trust in the process and facilitating a more professional culture. . .
- when schools are able to focus their own work through formal structures for goal setting, determining agendas, and reaching decisions. . .
- when more people are involved in prioritizing concerns and when those people declare a stake in the outcomes . . . and
- when the data base for generating concerns, alternatives, and solutions is both comprehensive and objective (e.g., a discrepancy analysis of optimum and existing school effectiveness criteria to generate concerns or a literature review to generate alternative). . . (pp. 148–150).

While Kirby found that it is important for schools to work out some of the kinks in the governance process before moving on to more substantive issues dealing with students, Darling-Hammond (1995), warns that "some of the initial difficulty in making progress on a serious restructuring agenda may have been due to the [school's] initial focus. . .on procedures rather than purpose. . . . [This] focused attention on the divisive questions of who would be allowed to make which decisions, rather than on what people in the school wanted to do that could be facilitated by a governance group or team." (p. 162)

This is an on-going concern with which schools constantly grapple. Like many issues involved with schoolwide change, staying focused on students is a constant battle.

Learning How to Network

As the people in schools develop confidence in their collective work and realize the value of collegial behaviours, they begin to recognize opportunities to learn from others so as to improve learning for students. For example, they welcome visitors into their school not only because they enjoy sharing what they have learned but because they seek to learn what others are doing and to hear visitors' candid observations about the work of their school. People also begin to take better advantage of the networking possibilities at League meetings. They aggressively seek to learn what other schools are doing. They return from League meetings with notes, names, and phone numbers of people who might serve as resources to their school (Glickman, Allen, & Lunsford, 1994).

Managing Time

We found that teachers apparently go through developmental stages as they approach sharing with each other on a collegial level. It was difficult at times to communicate, articulate, and evaluate personal needs and philosophies as well as to see the whole picture. Working through this required a major time commitment. (Deweese, Parks, Inglett, & Reed, 1993, p. 24)

Time is a critical issue when schools seek to implement the League's framework. As schools learned from their own experiences and the experiences of other League schools, they developed ways to deal with the lack of time in the school day for collective activities (Glickman, Allen, & Lunsford, 1994). Lack of time is not an obstacle that schools have completely mastered. It continues to be an issue.

Initially, people simply did this work before or after school. Then schools began to realize that people were being overworked and that alternatives needed to be explored. Also, as schools began to understand the positive effects of bringing people together, collegial activities became a priority that schools didn't want to short change.

Some schools began to include time for groups to work together into their yearly calendars. For example, in planning for the upcoming school year, an elementary school set aside five days during the school year for its action research team to get together and analyze data. The cost of substitutes for team members was built into the school's annual budget. Some schools provided leaders with extra planning times. The principal of a high school taught a course, in part, to help provide teachers with more time to work together. Schools sought grants either to pay for substitutes or to pay people for putting in extra hours. Schools learned to make optimum use of meeting time by carefully constructing agendas that limited the number of items to be covered and limited the amount of time spent on each item.

Hargreaves (1990) suggests that schools would benefit by providing "more responsibility and flexibility to teachers in the management and allocation of their time and to offer them more control over what is to be developed with that time" (p. 319). He makes this point in the context that it is difficult for people working outside of classrooms to understand what time feels like to those working inside classrooms. Similarly, League schools have found that communication and understanding can help various members come to an understanding about how time is spent.

For example, a high school leadership team arranged for a teacher to be given an extra planning period so she could provide leadership for the school's action research efforts. This was met with enough skepticism from other teachers that she resumed teaching a full load. Later, when her colleagues came to value the contribution that action research could make to the life of the school, she was able to take back the extra planning period with the approval of most of her colleagues. Teachers in an elementary school who were provided substitutes to analyze data generated by the school's action research initially were questioned about what they were doing and why did they needed extra time to do it. As the fruits of their labor became evident, the skepticism abated.

Principal's Actions

The principal's leadership is critical to this work. When teachers in League schools are asked what advice they have for schools wanting to become more democratic and reflective, the response most often given is "make sure the principal believes in and understands what this is all about." So, what do League principals do to help move schools through this change process? A study (Glickman, Allen, & Lunsford, 1994) that involved interviewing all veteran League principals produced the following insights:

- Principals stop trying to be the fixer and start enabling others' efforts to reach solutions to problems. "Three years ago it was the kind of thing in which people would bring problems to me and then wait for an answer. . . . Now if its a big problem, schoolwide. . . we organize a task force." (p. 208)
- They model what's important by getting more involved in curriculum, instruction, staff development, and student learning. "The things I'm taking care of now are a lot more curriculum oriented and student oriented." (p. 209)
- They exhibit trust and respect for teachers. "My style is to listen to them and relate. . . as if they were the smartest people that I ever knew, which I believe." (p. 209)
- They encourage involvement from a wide range of people in the life of the school. "I have seen that groups expand almost like a concentric circle when you dropped a pebble into the pond." (p. 211)

It is important to note that principals stressed that they did not start acting in radically different ways immediately. As one principal said, "I guess learning to share my responsibilities in that area [curriculum and instruction]. . .has been sort of a developmental process. I've learned from my mistakes. (p. 212) Another pointed out the developmental nature of this work when he said,

Its just like when we founded this country. We established a constitution. We called it the Articles of Confederation. It didn't work. We sat down and wrote another constitution. And then it still didn't work as it ought to. So we amended it a few times. And we're basically in that stage right now. (p. 213)

Blase and Blase (1994) asked teachers in League schools, via an open-ended survey, what principals did that encouraged and facilitated their involvement in the life of the school. Their investigation supported the findings of the Glickman, Allen, and Lunsford (1994) study and added the following actions which principals take that teachers found empowering:

- Systematically structuring the school to encourage authentic collaboration by establishing readiness and common goals and by responding to the school's unique characteristics.
- Supporting teacher experimentation and innovation, granting professional autonomy, and viewing failure as an opportunity to learn.
- Modeling professional behaviour, especially by exhibiting caring, optimism, honesty, friendliness, and enthusiasm.
- Supporting shared governance efforts by providing professional development and basic resources.
- Encouraging risk taking and minimizing threat (or constraints on teacher's freedom and growth). (p. 127)

Another study of League principals emphasized the situational, contextual nature of the roles that principals assume in democratic schools. Principals in this study stressed that they alternately acted as facilitators, bosses, members of groups, and sometimes, one of the faculty depending on the circumstances and conditions surrounding issues. Principals must understand where people are in this developmental change process and act accordingly. What was appropriate last year may not be appropriate this year (Dougherty, 1995).

Principals play a major role in this change process by encouraging teachers to come out of their classrooms and become active participants in schoolwide action research and the governance of schoolwide curricular and instructional initiatives. Principals boost people's willingness to do this work by showing confidence in their abilities, ensuring that everyone's voice is nurtured and respected, marshalling the necessary resources so that those participating in the process experience success and feel supported, and modeling the type of collegial behaviours that are expected and needed.

Sergiovanni (1996) adds to our understanding of the role of the principal in a democratic school when he points out that the co-directors of Central Park East Secondary School in New York City, Deborah Meier and Paul Swartz, successfully lead their school's efforts because their leadership is idea based.

The sources of authority they appeal to are the values that are central to the school, and the commitments that everyone has made to them. And because of this, their supervisory responsibilities do not compromise democratic principles, dampen teacher empowerment, or get in the way of community building. (pp. 91–92)

CONCLUSION

On a recent survey (Tashlein, 1995) given to 159 teachers and principals in 46 League schools, the respondents reported almost unanimously that their school's efforts in implementing the League's framework had resulted in improvement for students in learning, participation in classroom decision-making processes, participation in schoolwide decision-making processes, ownership of the implementation of decisions, and attitudes toward learning. They also reported marked improvement in faculty learning, participation in schoolwide decision-making processes, ownership of the implementation of decisions, and improved attitudes toward improving teaching and learning. Further, they reported improvement in parent's learning about the education of their child, their participation in schoolwide decision-making processes, and their attitudes toward the educational programs of the school.

Some of the instructional accomplishments of League schools include transition programs for ninth graders that lowered drop out rates and improved academic achievement, programs that have lowered retention rates, academic initiatives that have made the curriculum more student-centered, and programs to reduce the number of students removed from the classroom for discipline purposes and to increase students' ability to control their own behaviour.

Students are also increasingly involved in the governance of some League schools. Many of the secondary schools now have students who are either members of their leadership teams or who are involved in some direct way with the governance process and with the action research activities. Some elementary schools have created students councils that address meaningful issues regarding teaching and learning (Allen, 1995).

Before schools joined the League, they were places where teachers taught in isolation and many of the major decisions that affected the school's teaching and learning were made by one individual or a small inner group. Renewal efforts were aimed largely at what individuals or small groups proposed to do apart from, rather than with, the school as a whole. Continuous conversations about teaching and learning were not considered to be a part of what educators discussed or acted upon.

Trying to change schools into democratic, professional communities where action research and shared governance are focused on schoolwide teaching and learning is not a simple, quick, or one-time task. In fact, people in League schools find this type of schoolwide change, between moments of great exhilaration, to be mainly difficult, slow, and inevitably frustrating work. The following quotes from school cases studies illustrate some of the problems schools encounter when trying to implement the League's framework.

- The volume of information brought to the Executive Council was overwhelming and we have had to find a way to deal with these issues and keep our meetings to a reasonable length. (Loe et al., 1992, p. 21)
- Our March Executive Council meeting featured petty grievances, unkind statements that were not thought out, and an atmosphere that appeared to be self-centered rather than school-centered." (Loe et al., 1992, p. 21)
- The building is undergoing renovation. It is too small and currently the school uses 14 trailers to provide for the overflow of students. Additional trailers will be needed for the next school year. There is a shortage of bathrooms, storage space, parking places, and telephones." (Hix, 1992, p. 27)
- I think that I can be perceived as weak, or not wanting to take the responsibility and/or blame for some matters. Perhaps, I can even be thought of as too busy or too lazy! For whatever reason, some teachers prefer an autocratic style. (Deweese, Duke, Inglett, Reabold, Robertson, Thomas, & White, 1992, p. 45)
- As the principal walked out of the door, they all looked at each other. The first thought was to bolt out the door and not return. Many put their heads in their hands and waited. Surely, the principal would come back and give more direction. (Harwood, 1994, p. 31)
- The team made regular attempts to communicate to the faculty what it was learning about self governance, instructional initiatives and action research. . . One team member offered, 'We spent the year taking in information and talking within the Leadership Team.' The team began to experience a feeling of frustration, compounded by lack of a formula for establishing a self governance process." (Weeks & King, 1994, p. 40)
- Then, to our despair, the principal announced she was leaving. Panic, anxiety, excitement, frustration, fear, and confusion were some of the faculty's emotions." (Hutchins, J, 1994, p. 69)
- Because of the emotional impact of confronting this issue, there was a feeling that a wedge had been placed between the special area teachers and other faculty members. Some members commented that they would never serve on that committee again. Some felt that the structure of the scheduling committee should be re-evaluated. Some felt that the scheduling task should be given back to the administration, and others felt satisfied that the conclusion was a consensus and the best solution had been reached. (Hix & Nall, 1993, p. 45)

Despite the many obstacles awaiting schools trying to make this type of change, League schools are living testimony that it can be done. Not that League schools have met all their goals and are finished products, but they are acting in new democratic ways that are benefiting teachers, administrators, parents, and most importantly, students.

Schools have been able to sustain this on-going change process by continuing to define for themselves, above all else, their collective mission – their single most important reason for existing. Then, revisiting and modifying structures and guidelines that help them work toward attaining their ultimate purpose. In essence, they have learned to talk to each other in honest and forthright ways about their common work of education. To do so, they had to earn each other's trust. They had to change the culture of the school to support the different ways people learn and assume new roles. They have benefitted from the on-going facilitation provided by networking with other like-minded schools.

All of the research from League schools has left us without a clear, step-by-step prescription for other schools to follow because each school is uniquely individualistic. However, we have learned how schools can get better and how such information can fuel the efforts of others involved in schoolwide change.

Emily Calhoun (1992) concluded one of her longitudinal studies of League schools with an open letter to the schools that reads, in part, as follows.

> Each time I have visited your school, I have wanted to cheer about your school improvement efforts. I do not know if you can feel the difference between the sense of staff unity focused on students' social and academic achievement and the degree of staff efficacy as a professional community that have developed at your school in contrast to the norms of isolation that operate in so many schools. For an outsider, the contrast is sharp. Your School has become a learning community. . . .There are some rough spots: everything is not moving as rapidly as it could, and everyone is not one hundred percent happy about the collection and use of schoolwide data or about the [shared governance] operation. . . . I wish the League of Professional Schools had a magic wand to give you a reward for all you have accomplished; instead, all we can do is acknowledge your accomplishments and encourage you to continue to move gently but firmly forward in school improvement. (p. 140)

REFERENCES

Aiken, K., Burdeshaw, P., Cook, C., DiVito, M., Handley, M., Robinson, J., Spurlock, R., & Westlun. (1993). In *Lessons from the league: Improving schools through shared governance and action research*. (pp. 5–16) (Monograph No. 2). Athens: University of Georgia, Program for School Improvement.

Aiken, W.F. (1942). *The story of the eight-year study*. New York: Harper and Brothers.

Allen, J. (1995). Friends, fairness, fun, and the freedom to choose: Hearing student voices. *Journal of Curriculum and Supervision*,10(4), 286–301.

Allen, J. (1994). Where's the action? In L. Hansen & L. Allen (Eds.), *Lessons from the league: Improving schools through shared governance and action research*. (pp. 150–164) (Monograph No. 3). Athens: University of Georgia, Program for School Improvement.

Allen, L., & Lunsford, B. (1995). *How to form networks for school renewal*. Alexandria, VA: Association for Supervision and Curriculum Development.

Allen, L., & Glickman, C. D. (1992). School improvement: The elusive faces of shared governance. *Nassp Bulletin*, **76**(542), 80–87.

Allen, L. R. (1994). The role of voice in shared governance: A case study of a primary school. In L. Hansen & L. Allen (Eds.), *Lessons from the league: Improving schools through shared governance and action research*. (pp. 150–164) (Monograph No. 3). Athens: University of Georgia, Program for School Improvement.

Anderson, G. L., Herr, K., & Nihlen, A .S. (1994). *Studying your own school: An educator's guide to qualitative practitioner research*. Thousand Oaks, CA: Corwin Press.

Blase, J., Blase, J., Anderson, G. L., & Dungan, S. (1995). *Democratic principals in action: eight pioneers*. Thousand Oaks, CA: Corwin Press.

Blase, J,, & Blase, J. R. (1994). *Empowering teachers: What successful principals do.* Thousand Oaks, CA: Corwin Press.

Calhoun, E. F. (1992). *Lessons from the league: Improving schools through shared governance and action research.* (pp. 25–42) (Monograph No.1). Athens: University of Georgia, Program for School Improvement.

Calhoun, E. F., Allen, L., Halliburton, C., & Jones, S. (1995). *Action research on action research: A quest for understanding.* Paper presented at the annual meeting of the American Educational Research Association, San Francisco.

Cochran-Smith, M., & Lytle, S. (1993). *Inside outside: Teacher research and knowledge.* New York: Teachers College Press.

Darling-Hammond, L. (1995). Policy for restructuring. In A. Lieberman (Ed.), *The work of restructuring schools.* New York: Teachers College Press.

Deweese, P., Duke, S., Inglett, B., Reabold, T., Robertson, J., Thomas, E., & White, S. (1992). In C. D. Glickman & L. Allen (Eds.), *Lessons from the league: Improving schools through shared governance and action research.* (pp. 9–24) (Monograph No.1). Athens: University of Georgia, Program for School Improvement.

Deweese, P., Parks, J., Inglett, B., & Reed, L. (1993). In *Lessons from the league: Improving schools through shared governance and action research.* (pp. 5–16) (Monograph No.2). Athens: University of Georgia, Program for School Improvement

Dewey, J. (1916). *Democracy and education: An introduction to the philosophy of education.* New York: Macmillan.

Dougherty, G. W. (1995). *Principals' perspectives of their role when implementing shared governance.* Unpublished doctoral dissertation, University of Georgia.

Fullan, M. G. (1991). *The new meaning of educational change.* New York: Teachers College Press.

Fullan, M. G. (1992). *Successful school improvement: The implementation perspective and beyond.* Bristol, PA: Open University Press.

Gitlin, A., Bringhurst, K., Burns, M., Cooley, V., Myers, B., Price, K., Russell, R., & Tiess, P. (1992). *Teachers' voices for school change.* New York: Teachers College Press.

Glickman, C.D. (1993). *Renewing America's schools: A guide for school-based action.* San Francisco: Jossey-Bass.

Glickman, C. D. (in press). *Sustaining school renewal in frenzied times: Personal essays on democracy, pedagogy, and change.* San Francisco: Jossey-Bass.

Glickman, C. D., Allen, L. R., & Lunsford, B. F. (1994). Voices of principals from democratically transformed schools. In J. Murphey & K. S. Louis (Eds.), *Reshaping the principalship: Insights from transformational reform efforts* (pp. 203–218). Thousand Oaks, CA: Corwin Press.

Glickman, C. D., Allen, L., & Lunsford, B. F. (1994). Factors affecting school change. *Journal of Staff Development,*15(3), pp. 38–41.

Hargreaves, A. (1990). Teachers work and the politics of time and space. *Qualitative Studies in Education,* 3(4), 303–320.

Hargreaves, A. (1994). *Changing teachers, changing times: Teachers' work and culture in the postmodern age.* New York: Teachers College Press.

Harwood, N. L. (1994). In L. Hansen & L. Allen (Eds.), *Lessons from the league: Improving schools through shared governance and action research.* (pp. 30–36) (Monograph No. 3). Athens: University of Georgia, Program for School Improvement.

Hays, R., Glickman, C. D., & Allen, L (1994). In L. Hansen & L. Allen (Eds.), *Lessons from the league: Improving schools through shared governance and action research.* (pp. 129–139) (Monograph No. 3). Athens: University of Georgia, Program for School Improvement.

Hensley, F, Calhoun, E., & Glickman, C. (1993). In *Lessons from the league: Improving schools through shared governance and action research.* (pp.118–141) (Monograph No. 2). Athens: University of Georgia, Program for School Improvement

Hix, B. (1992). In C. D. Glickman & L. Allen (Eds.), *Lessons from the league: Improving schools through shared governance and action research.* (pp.25–42) (Monograph No. 1). Athens: University of Georgia, Program for School Improvement.

Hix, B., & Nall, J. (1993). School improvement at Lilburn elementary 1991–1992. In *Lessons from the league: Improving schools through shared governance and action research.* (pp. 32–58) (Monograph No.2). Athens: University of Georgia, Program for School Improvement.

Hopkins, D., Ainscrow, M., & West, M. (1994). *School improvement in an ear of change.* New York: Teachers College Press.

Huberman, M. (1993). *The lives of teachers.* New York: Teachers College Press.

Huberman, M., & Miles, M. (1984). *Innovation up close.* New York: Plenum.

Hutchins, J. (1994). In L. Hansen & L. Allen (Eds.), *Lessons from the league: Improving schools through shared governance and action research.* (pp. 129–139) (Monograph No. 3). Athens: University of Georgia, Program for School Improvement.

Kirby, P. C. (1992). In *Lessons from the league: Improving schools through shared governance and action research.* (pp.5–16) (Monograph No. 2). Athens: University of Georgia, Program for School Improvement.

Little, J. W. (1982). Norms of collegiality and experimentation: Workplace conditions of school success. *American Educational Research Journal,* **19**(3), 325–340.

Loe, C., Rogers, J., Shams, M., & Williams, L. (1992). Pinckneyville middle school: Developing shared governance in a middle school. In C. D. Glickman & L. Allen (Eds.), *Lessons from the league: Improving schools through shared governance and action research.* (pp. 9–24) (Monograph No.1). Athens: University of Georgia, Program for School Improvement.

Lunsford, B. (1995). A league of our own. *Educational Leadership,* **52**(7), 59–61.

Newman, F. M., & Wehlage, G. G. (1995). *Successful school restructuring: A report to the public and educators by the Center on Organization and Restructuring of Schools.* Madison, WI: Wisconsin Center for Education Research.

Nias, J. (1989). *Primary teachers talking: A study of teaching as work.* New York: Routledge.

Peterson, P. L, McCarthey, S. J., & Elmore, R. F. (1996). Learning from school restructuring. *American Educational Research Journal.* **33**(1), 119–153.

Reese, G. (1994). In L. Hansen & L. Allen (Eds.), *Lessons from the league: Improving schools through shared governance and action research.* (pp. 129–139) (Monograph No. 3). Athens: University of Georgia, Program 'for School Improvement.

Rosenholtz, S. J. (1989). *Teachers Workplace: The social organization of schools.* New York: Teachers College Press.

Sarason, S. B. (1995). *School change: The personal development of a point of view.* New York: Teachers College Press.

Sergiovanni, T. J. (1996). *Leadership to the schoolhouse: How is it different? Why is it important?* San Francisco: Jossey-Bass.

Shedd, J. B., & Bacharach, S.B . (1991). *Tangled hierarchies: Teachers as professionals and the management of schools.* San Francisco: Jossey-Bass.

Snauwaert, D. T. (1993). *Democracy, education, and governance.* Albany, NY: State University of New York Press.

Tashlein, K. (1995). [*League of professional schools 1994 impact survey: Summary of significant findings*]. Unpublished raw data.

Todd, M. L .B. (1994). *Information dissemination and school reform: A case study of an information retrieval system.* Unpublished doctoral dissertation, University of Georgia.

Wagoner, Jr., J. L. (1989). Letter from Thomas Jefferson to William C. Jarvis. In *Public education and enlightened society: Selected quotations.* Unpublished manuscript: University of Virginia.

Weeks, K., & King, J. (1994). In L. Hansen & L. Allen (Eds.), *Lessons from the league: Improving schools through shared governance and action research.* (pp. 37–45) (Monograph No. 3). Athens: University of Georgia, Program for School Improvement.

Redefining Teachers, Reculturing Schools: Connections, Commitments and Challenges

LYNNE MILLER

College of Education, University of Southern Maine

While strategies of school restructuring often attend to the governance and descision-making, timetabling and programming aspects of school life as a lever for change, school reculturing buries deep into the heart of human attitudes and relationships that hold the school together and move it forward (or fail to do so). Drawing on four school case studies, Lynne Miller describes how successful school reculturing involves schools and their staff moving towards building professional community, putting learning before teaching, engaging in inquiry as a guide to improvement, developing their own systems of accountability and standards of learning, taking a whole-school focus, and widening the responsibilities for leadership.

Reculturing, Miller shows, is no easy matter. It depends on committing to long time frames, on the support of excellent principals, on teachers who are prepared to become leaders of their colleagues as well as teachers of their classes, on access to supportive networks outside the school, and so on. This chapter describes not only the theory and principles of reculturing, but conveys a vivid sense of what it means to try and reculture one's school in particular cases.

School reform has as many meanings as it has forms and strategies. To limit the scope of this chapter, I use the terms *reforming schools* and *restructuring schools* interchangeably to refer to those schools that are striving for changes in how learning is conceptualized and how it occurs. These changes are not a matter of rearranging the furniture; they require a major re-design of the environment. Too often, schools with new bell schedules, multi-age classes, grade level teams, and integrated curriculum units continue to construct learning from taken-for-granted and unexamined assumptions. Linda Darling-Hammond (1990) terms these "superficial reforms" and sees them as short-lived and ineffective. On the other hand, what Darling-Hammond calls "structural reforms" occur in schools where learning proceeds from a new set of premises.

To be more specific, in reforming schools, learning engages children and young adults in rigorous academic work that encourages them to "use their minds well" (Sizer, 1984) and to make connections between ideas and their applications in the world beyond the school. Ultimately, such a conception of learning depends on teachers – not on schedules, grouping procedures, or policy manuals. It is teachers who provide the support and challenge that promote learning; it is teachers who encourage improvement through the feedback they provide; it is teachers who present materials and ideas that engage student interest; and it is teachers who safeguard the academic integrity of the work that gets done in school. Teachers in

A. Hargreaves (ed.), Extending Educational Change, 249-263.

reforming schools do not view themselves as "delivering" instruction or "transmitting" knowledge. Rather, they "teach for understanding" (Cohen, McLaughlin, & Talbert, 1993) and assume roles beyond that of the didact. They are child developers, coaches, guides, advocates, and critics; they create environments where students can achieve their best work.

The teachers I am talking about are creating a new culture of learning for their students. But that is not all that they are doing: they are also creating a culture of teaching for themselves. If culture is defined as "the way we do business around here" and if the way schools do business is changing for students and teachers, then what we are witnessing is a fundamental *reculturing* of school. By that, I mean a shift from one set of assumptions, beliefs, norms, behaviors, and practices to another. In the section that follows, I explore what reculturing means for teachers.

RECULTURING TEACHING

Teachers in reforming schools are re-constructing learning and teaching at the same time. They are discarding the assumptions and practices of their own teaching past. Since so many of them were trained, inducted, and tenured within factory-model schools, where the norms of "uncertainty, isolation, and individualism" (Fullan & Hargreaves, 1991) dominated, they are re-inventing themselves as well as schooling. In the old order, they worked in highly individualized and personal ways and learned to depend almost exclusively on their students for feedback, rewards, and indications of success. They lacked the collegial interaction and peer supervision that other professionals take for granted in their work. They developed teaching strategies that were highly idiosyncratic, based on trial and error, and guarded as professional secrets. If they participated in professional development at all, it usually took the form of workshops and clinics where discrete skills and behaviors were introduced and transmitted. Their work was viewed as technical, concrete, and formulaic. While their teaching was invisible outside the classroom, the behavior of their students was not. As a result, teachers spent a disproportionate amount of time establishing control norms, and they expended enormous time and energy on enforcing rules and keeping discipline. The factory-model school sent a very powerful message to teachers about their position in the hierarchy of the organization. If students were products, then teachers were workers, and principals were foremen or bosses. As an assembly-line worker, the teacher was only responsible for her piece of the final product.

When teachers move to reculture their schools, they begin to change the conditions of their work. They make some fundamental shifts in the way they do business. Among these shifts are:

From individualism to professional community: Teachers are replacing the individualism, isolation, and privacy of traditional schools in favor of new norms of collegiality, openness, and trust (Little, 1981; McLaughlin & Talbert,

1993; Rosenholtz, 1989). Working together on projects helps teachers make this transition. Teachers come together in small groups or as whole school staffs to decide on common goals, develop integrated programs. of study, craft shared assessments, and examine student work. They set time aside for planning together, teaching together, and talking together. Peer observation and consultation contribute to a shared professional culture where risks are encouraged, mistakes acknowledged, learning scrutinized, and secrets shared.

From teaching at the center to learning at the center: The shift from "What do *I* do as a teacher and transmitter of knowledge? to "How can I plan with others for what *students* do as learners?" means that student work determines the agenda for teacher work. Teachers do not plan their curriculum from abstract goals or from objectives divorced from the reality of the classroom. Rather they "plan backwards" (MacDonald, 1991), beginning with an examination of student work. Samples of writing, problem solving, logical thinking, and creative arts are collected and analyzed as a first step in building designs for learning. Rather than focusing exclusively on how they should teach (collaborative learning, direct instruction, questioning strategies, etc.), teachers focus on how students learn, and adjust their teaching accordingly.

From technical work to inquiry: Teachers in reforming schools reject the notion that teaching is the accumulation of discrete and unrelated behaviors, a tool box of techniques and methods that is more befitting a technician than a professional. Rather, reforming teachers view their craft as intellectual work that engages them in posing problems and in seeking solutions, in raising questions and seeking explanations, in creating knowledge and using it. Systematic inquiry, research, and reflection are at the core of teacher's work. Like their students, teachers are involved in a process of continuous learning and improvement.

From control to accountability: In traditional practice, teachers spent a good deal of time and energy in maintaining order and discipline to "keep the lid on." Being in control was a much admired attribute because it was the only part of teaching that was visible. In reforming schools, it is student performance – not behavior – that is made public. This makes accountability for student learning more important than accountability for control. Instead of working as individuals to establish standards of behavior, teachers work together as colleagues to develop standards of learning to which they hold themselves and their students accountable.

From managed work to leadership: When public student performances become the products that schools develop, the role of the teacher changes dramatically from being assembly-line workers to being designers, conductors, and leaders. As leaders in their classrooms, teachers relinquish "power over" their students in exchange for "power to" (Sergiovanni, 1987) affect improved student performance. Outside of their classrooms, teachers assume leadership roles as well. They gain responsibility in areas traditionally reserved for administrators – instruction, assessment, rules, procedures, and governance. Teacher leadership and administrative leadership work in collaboration to create more democratic and participatory school organizations.

From classroom to whole school focus: As teachers expand the traditional boundaries of their work, they move from individual concerns about *my* classroom and *my* students to concerns about *our* school and *our* students. They think about the culture of the whole school and how to develop and support it. They engage in conversations about what the school stands for, how learning should occur there, how well the school is fulfilling its missions, and how well they – as community members – are contributing to the big picture.

SCHOOL SNAPSHOTS

How do teachers make the transitions that their work in reforming schools require? How do they get from individualism to professional community? From technical work to inquiry? From managed work to leadership? Current research in school reform shows that the transitions are slow and steady; they occur over time. Change in teaching, like all change, is "a process, not an event." (Loucks-Horsley & Stiegelbauer, 1991). To find the answers to these questions, let us look at the experiences of four schools that are well along in the process of transformation. Taken together, these schools exemplify the transitions discussed above. In this section, each school is described in a brief snapshot that captures what a reforming schools looks like from the outside. The descriptions that appear below are of actual schools; their names have been changed to preserve anonymity.

New Orchard School: A rural elementary school serving student in grades K-6, New Orchard has been involved in a process of change for over ten years. The school has become a culture where learning for children and adults is placed squarely at the center of its work. The school is a fully inclusive program, combining special needs and other students in both multi-age and traditional grade level classrooms. Systematic and continuous teacher research has guided instructional practices for over a decade. In the last two years, it has led teachers to develop school-wide benchmarks and assessments for students. The results of these assessments are made public annually, making New Orchard a leader in developing a local accountability system for student learning. The goal of the school is to provide students with "a continuous journey, rather than a series of disconnected trips" ("fieldnotes", 1995). To that end, the New Orchard staff have taken on the ambitious agenda of involving the entire school district (six schools encompassing seven towns) in a comprehensive assessment and accountability system.

Wright Middle School: An urban middle school serving 520 students in grades 6, 7, and 8, King is a multi-cultural enclave in a city dominated by white, ethnic groups. Sixty-five percent (65%) of its students are on free or reduced lunch, and 20% are from homes where languages other than English are spoken. The school is divided into houses where teams of teachers spend an entire day with students. The program of study is built around a series of teacher-developed "Expeditions". These are interdisciplinary curriculum units that culminate in a major project intended for an audience beyond the teacher. Student work is displayed throughout the building and descriptors of good writing and criteria of good work are posted in every classroom. Every year, the school hosts a Demonstration Fair and invites parents and community members to view student work and to engage students in conversations about their work. The Fair lasts a full day; it begins at 8:00 a.m. and ends at 8:00 p.m. One team has successfully initiated "looping," moving the entire 7th grade class into 8th grade with the same team of teachers. Other teams are now moving in that direction. The culture of the school is best captured by the large sculpture of a book that first greets a visitor to the school. In bold print that cannot escape notice, the title of the book announces "Great Expectations."

Aronomink School: An early elementary building serving 450 rural and suburban students in grades 1–3, Aronomink School has evolved into a culture where personalization, reflection, metacognition, and attention to quality work are at the core of the enterprise. Teachers have resisted the pressure to merely adopt innovations. Instead, they have adapted new approaches to teaching and assessment while maintaining traditions that continue to serve them and their students well. Like New Orchard, the school combines multi-age and traditional classes. Appropriateness and utility, informed by investigation and reflection, guide the work at Aronomink. The school has been a leader in the district in using student exhibitions and portfolios to demonstrate achievement. It has also been a pioneer in designing units that integrate curriculum, instruction, and assessment, and in establishing conferences (at entry, progress, and exit points) involving parents and led by children. Aronomink is best characterized by the sign in front of the building, "Aronomink School, A Center of Inquiry," and the greeting that visitors encounter:

Welcome to Aronomink School – a Center of Inquiry. We recognize and respect the individual's talents and strengths. We value the opportunity to create and nurture a climate that promotes human potential.

Stratton High School: is a rural high school serving 900 students whose families range from the working poor to the lower echelons of the middle class. It is a school where state assessment scores rival those of wealthier suburban districts. Such achievement has not always been the norm at Stratton. The school has moved from a traditional high school structure to one where all classes (with the exception of seven A.P. courses) are heterogeneously grouped, where differentiated assessments provide students with the choice of whether to pursue honors grades in a course. Departments have been replaced by learning areas and department heads have been eliminated. Students participate in Socratic seminars as well as regular classes in blocks of 90 minutes each and are required to complete a Service Project in order to graduate. All students take four years of mathematics and science. Teachers have eliminated "basic" math courses. As a result, all ninth graders take algebra and all seniors take mathematics beyond algebra and geometry, usually calculus. In science, most seniors are enrolled in physics. In fact, the school has the highest percentage (almost 100%) of seniors in physics and advanced math in the state. Overcrowded and underfunded, Stratton High School has nineteen mobile units. Yet the school maintains a unified culture, best characterized by the words "a place where students learn to use their minds well."

MAKING THE TRANSITION: KEY ELEMENTS

These snapshots present a quick view of schools that are making transitions from one teaching culture to another. The snapshots describe what these schools are like, but not how they got that way. Close scrutiny of these four schools and their histories points to eight key elements in their reformulation. These are: (1) a long-term perspective, (2) principal leadership, (3) teacher leadership, (4) inquiry and reflection, (5) outside support and reference groups, (6) focus on student learning, and (7) attention to teacher learning.. Below, each element is explained in some detail, drawing on the four schools for examples.

1. Long-term perspective: Each of these schools has been engaged in a continuous process of improvement for some time, from seven to ten years. New Orchard began its process with a teacher research initiative in 1987. Aronomink, that same year, developed a vision to guide its work for the next decade. Wright Middle School adopted the principles of middle level education in the late 1980's, and Stratton High School began its steady change effort in 1990.

In all four schools, the process of change has been "steady work" (Elmore & McLaughlin, 1988), marked by persistence, diligence, and perseverance. None of these schools experienced smooth paths toward change. Oftentimes they were targeted for criticism in their own districts. Identified as "the jewels in the crown," within a district, the schools received attention they didn't seek and approbation they felt they didn't deserve. This often led to resentment from colleagues in neighboring schools who felt that their own good work was being ignored. There were also criticisms from within; teachers, parents, and students often voiced disagreement with the new direction the schools were taking.

Having a long-range perspective helped these schools deal with dissension and skepticism. Sometimes the schools slowed down; other times they backed off; and at other times they pushed forward. Aronomink consistently maintained a low-key approach, providing continual opportunities for people to come on board. Teachers were invited to investigate new practices and to talk about them. Multi-age classes and inclusion practices were implemented slowly and only after teachers expressed readiness. On the other hand, Stratton took a more assertive approach. Here the long-term perspective led to the implementation of changes that were considered good for learning in the long run, even if most current students and some staff didn't quite agree. Despite initial opposition to de-tracking classes from the majority of students and a vocal minority of teachers, the school forged ahead and implemented the changes quickly and efficiently. A recent study of seniors, who were freshmen when the de-tracking policy was initiated, reports that the students now like heterogeneous classes and prefer them to the grouping practices they experienced in junior high school. At Stratton, a long term institutional perspective took precedence over short term individual preferences.

2. Principal leadership: The element of persistence over time relates to the leadership of the principal as well. In each of the four schools, principals have been leading for seven to fourteen years. In fact, each principal was in office when the first steps toward change were undertaken. These principals are all place-bound. All live within thirty minutes of their schools and have strong local allegiances. They all brought long, regional teaching histories to their leadership positions.

The four principals represent very different leadership styles. If they were to be compared to colors, the two elementary principals would be pastels, while the high school and middle school principals would be bold primary colors. This may be due to personality, to the different natures of elementary and secondary schools, or to the needs of the schools at the time. The middle and high school principals were explicitly hired to "shake things up" by their superintendents, while the two elementary principals were viewed as helmspeople who would steer good schools steadily toward improvement. In fact, all four have assumed the mantle of agents of change and are recognized as such by their staff and their communities.

What grounds these four principals is what the New Orchard principal ("fieldnotes", 1995) calls the "leadership diamond": That is to say; they all evidence vision, courage, ethics, and reality. In terms of vision, each principal is clear and articulate. The New Orchard principal envisions a school where the quality of student work is collaboratively determined, rigorously evaluated, and publicly announced. At Aronomink, the principal's vision places the teacher as reflective practitioner at the center of innovation and as the model of metacognitive learning for students. At both Wright Middle School and Stratton High School, the principals' belief in equity and high standards for *all students* is impressed throughout the school.

Regardless of personality or style, all four principals demonstrate courage for innovation and action, responsibility to admit what needs to be changed, energy and commitment to complete the work, and confidence that changes are in the best interest of their students and the teachers who guide them. Finally, each principal is grounded in reality — the reality of his/her particular context, the reality of what it is to teach diverse and increasingly needy populations, the reality of what the world will require of students, and the reality of what resources are available and can be made available to support teachers in making change.

3. Teacher leadership: Strong principals can only do part of the work. To complete the work, principals need to work side by side with strong teachers. By "strong teachers," I mean educators with highly developed and effective teaching practices and with the ability to assume leadership among their colleagues. Teachers lead from different strengths (Miller & O'Shea, 1992) and they lead in different ways. (Wasley, 1991).

At the four schools, teacher leadership is deeply embedded and has become a taken-for-granted part of the culture. At New Orchard, three teachers have together led the way in moving toward full inclusion, multi-age classrooms, and collaborative assessment of student work. The entire staff has been involved in benchmarking student achievement, in identifying exemplars of student work, and in reporting publicly about the school. Aronomink teachers rotate in positions as team leaders and teacher-scholars. The teacher-scholar is released from teaching for a year to pursue research in the school about issues affecting student learning. At Wright Middle School, teacher leaders oversee teams to promote efforts to develop "Expeditions" that cross disciplines and lead to work products that can be displayed to and evaluated by audiences beyond the school. And at Stratton High School, teachers led in the de-tracking of courses and the development of an exit exhibition for all seniors. In all four schools, teacher leaders continue to collaborate to refine practice and to create new solutions for old problems. Working with their principals, they are in large measure responsible for the transformation of their schools.

4. Inquiry and Reflection: Teachers at the four schools are consistently involved in either formal research or informal inquiry and reflection about instructional practice, student learning, and assessment. New Orchard and Aronomink have made teacher-led inquiry central to their work. At New Orchard, teachers have had grant support for two action research projects, one which involved parents as researchers as well. Today, New Orchard teachers are involved in a project that gathers extensive data on student achievement and uses these data to inform decision-making. Aronomink has also used external funding to support teacher research. It began its restructuring efforts with a grant from the state to apply the notion of "school as a center of inquiry" to its work Its teacher-scholar position is clearly identifies and supports research as a critical element in the life of the school. Wednesday morning sharing sessions at Aronomink provide another way for teachers to reflect on their practice and on student work. At Wright Middle School, teachers spend considerable time collecting and analyzing data on student writing samples. They use these data to inform practice and to make recommendations for curriculum change. Stratton High School staff often refer to their school as "one grand seminar." Teachers are in the habit of holding their practice up to analysis. They use such reflective tools as the Tuning Protocol and Collaborative Assessment Conference to systematically look at and improve their practice. Finally, all four schools have developed structures that support and promote teacher inquiry and reflection. Regular release time days, restructured faculty and team meetings, and summer institutes all provide time and opportunity for this work .

5. Outside Supports and Reference Groups: The four schools extend themselves beyond their boundaries. They are all members of a regional school/university partnership, which has been in operation for twelve years. Through the partnership, they network with other educators, read and discuss articles and books over dinner, and engage in assessment and review activities. Aronomink and New Orchard were original members of the partnership and have been actively engaged in its activities since 1985. They were active participants in an Early Childhood Education Group that met monthly for four years. In this group, principals and teachers read and discussed articles and books about the education of young children. The aim of the group was not to go back to schools and immediately implement new ideas. Rather, the group promoted the norm of critical of inquiry, the power of conversation and reflection were acknowledged, and the teachers involved in the group developed a common language and a solid knowledge base as a springboard for action.

Wright and Stratton joined the partnership sometime later. Wright had already established itself as a middle school and was grappling with issues of appropriate curriculum when it became a member. It became one of three "demonstration" schools in the partnership to pilot a "planning backwards" model of assessment and learning over the course of three years. During that time, the Wright staff forged a close working relationship with a university faculty member. The result of this collaboration is the now annual Demonstration Fair. Stratton is a more recent member of the partnership, its district having four years ago. In a short time, the school became actively involved in partnership work and is now one of six high schools collaborating on ways to use the arts in student exhibitions of learning.

In addition to their partnership involvement, the four schools have developed independent affiliations with organizations beyond the region. Aronomink has long been associated with Project Zero at Harvard University and was one of four schools involved in the ATLAS Communities Project funded by the New Schools Development Corporation. New Orchard is an active member of John Goodlad's Network of Educational Reform and partners with a research and development group in developing its data-driven system of change. Wright Middle School is a member of the Expeditionary Learning Project, another New Schools Development Corporation project, and regularly connects with that organization in unit design and implementation. Stratton High School is a member of the Coalition of Essential Schools and is now involved with other Maine schools in an Annenberg Rural Challenge Grant project.

6. Focus on student learning: Unlike other schools where *what teachers do* is the focus of improvement efforts, these schools direct most of their attention to *how students learn.* They use student learning as the starting point and endpoint of their work. Here conversations are structured around students: what they know, what they don't know, what they need to know, and how they can demonstrate what they know. Student work is displayed prominently in hallways and classrooms. Archival data are maintained that track student progress over time. Instructional and structural decisions are based on knowledge of students and their particular needs.

The schools do not have exhaustive manuals about retention and promotion guidelines, grading policies, and disciplinary plans. Rather, decisions are made individually and are based on analysis of particular students and their needs. As in other schools, children may repeat grades at Aronomink and New Orchard and they may fail courses at Wright and Stratton, but unlike other schools, these decisions are made based on knowledge about individual students, not on general policies.

Teachers at these four schools use assessment of student work as their principal way of focusing on learning. By collecting student work samples and judging them against criteria of achievement, teachers develop a lens into student learning that is quite powerful. This process also helps refocus attention from what teachers do to what *students* do. For instance, New Orchard's benchmarking involves teachers in looking at student work on particular tasks in language arts and reading in second and fifth grade. Each work sample is scored by teachers who do not have the student in class, reinforcing the notion that it is what the student *does* that is important. Such close scrutiny gives the classroom teacher reliable information she can use in constructing learning for the student. Aronomink's exhibition project at grade 3 serves the same purpose. Here, outside juries evaluate student performance. Also, at Aronomink, a thorough reading inventory is conducted annually on each student. The results are used by teachers to plan instruction.

At Wright and Stratton, the emphasis on student learning is just as pervasive, despite the claim of some that large middle and high schools can't provide the individual attention that an elementary school does. Wright's Demonstration Fair is a culminating assessment. It is the work that goes on the in the day-to-day examination of student learning that is a basis for the Fair. The "house plan" at Wright is one way teachers have restructured their interactions with students and how they look at learning. In addition, almost all student assignments have accompanying rubrics or scoring guides. In this way, teachers and students are clear about criteria and expectations, and teachers can intervene more deliberately when they see precisely where students are experiencing success or difficulty. At Stratton, a team system also supports personalization. Student-developed rubrics are used extensively in classrooms. Ongoing discussions of student work and what the work tells about learning is an essential part of what happens at team meetings.

The schools use a variety of ways to look at student work. There are two tools that have proved particularly useful: the Collaborative Assessment Conference, and the "Slice". The Collaborative Assessment Conference, developed by the Coalition of Essential Schools, is a highly structured process that engages a group of teachers in conversation about and analysis of student work samples. The conference begins with teachers reading or observing the work, which can be pictures, videos, writing, etc. The teachers then respond to a set of questions: What do you see in the work? What questions do you have about the work? What do you think this child was working on most ardently in making this product? Silent to this point, the teacher presenting the work is now invited to provide additional observations, to address the questions raised, and to describe the child at work on the piece. The conference then becomes a general discussion of what strategies the presenting teacher should pursue with the child and the rest of the class. The conversation might consider future assignments, responses to the child, content issues, and questions to explore. The conference ends with a de-briefing of the process and its impact on the participants.

The "Slice" is a way to obtain a cross sampling of student work across a whole school. A representative group of students is identified and everything they create – homework, assessments, projects, worksheets, notes, drafts, videotapes – over one or two days is collected. Later, groups of teachers investigate the work, looking for trends and patterns. Stratton's Socratic Seminar lends itself to this exploration, but other schools use different approaches just as effectively.

Both the Collaborative Assessment Conference and the Slice enable teachers to know their students well so they can develop classrooms that are learner-centered. Teachers have developed the capacity to plan instruction from information that is collectively shared rather than from intuitions and impressions that are individually constructed. By focusing on assessment of student work, teachers at the four schools have learned to use data to develop strategies for instruction and to design particular interventions. More importantly, they have placed student learning at the center of the educational enterprise and made this "business as usual" in their schools.

7. Attention to teacher development and learning: Teacher learning goes hand-in-hand with student learning and is highly valued in the four schools. Professional development extends well beyond the traditional "make and take" workshops and direct instructional models that dominate elsewhere. As noted earlier, the four schools are all connected to local and national networks. These affiliations provide opportunities for teachers to expand their horizons beyond their localities and to connect with like-minded educators on a large scale.

On a smaller scale, staff development within the schools is more intimate, immediate, and continuous. No longer viewed as a commodity that is delivered in disconnected segments during "in-service days" that are scattered across the academic year, teacher development has become an integral part of teacher work. Teachers at the four schools have developed many tools for their own development. Among the most common and most promising are: teacher research, collegial reviews of practice, curriculum work, and standards/assessment development.

Teacher research is a well established tool in the four schools. Individually, or in small groups, teachers define a discussion-based problem, gather data that will help them learn more about the issue, analyze findings, and use the results to deepen understanding and improve practice. The "teacher scholar" position of Aronomink School is an example of one form of teacher research. Topics there have ranged from how students approach reading to how they use reflection to help them in their own learning. At New Orchard School, research has been conducted collectively on problems related to math and reading instruction, and on how students process emotional issues and the effects this has on learning. At Stratton High School, teachers researched student perceptions of de-tracking, and at Wright, there has been emergent research on the effects of keeping students with the same team of teachers over two years of middle school.

Collegial review of practice may take many forms. At root, these reviews are about the engagement of teachers in a critical and friendly analysis of their own practice. In fact, one of the strategies employed by Stratton High School is the "critical friend group", in which a trusted educator from outside of the school leads groups of teachers in a reflection on their work inside the school. At Aronomink, the teachers take part in a series of "rounds" where, as in medical rounds, a small group of practitioners visits another in her classroom and afterwards engages in a seminar aimed at identifying what went well and how things may have been done differently. A powerful tool that several of the schools have used is the "tuning protocol." The "tuning protocol " provides a process for reflection on teacher work.. It asks a teacher or team of teachers to present actual work (an assessment, a project, a unit, an idea) before a group of colleagues. The protocol has seven clearly defined and closely timed segments that move from presentation to critique to reflection. Central to the process is the idea of "warm" and "cool" feedback. Warm, supportive responses identify what is positive in the work, while more objective, cool responses address issues that are problematic or could be improved. Participants leave the "tuning protocol" with new insights about their own work and about that of the presenter.

Curriculum work is not a separate activity at the four schools. It is considered a valuable way for teachers to learn and grow together. Each of the four schools has been involved in significant joint curriculum work. Stratton High School's entire program has been revamped; courses have been eliminated; new requirements have been implemented; ability grouping has been abolished. This has led teachers to develop new ways of giving "honors" credit to students. They have developed a system of differentiated assessments in *all* classes that allow students to choose whether they want to work toward "honors" status. This required hours of intense conversation about course outcomes within and across disciplinary lines. The conversations provided an opportunity for people to examine expectations, assess their beliefs and practices, and make changes in their approaches to teaching and learning. The school's Socratic Seminar Program has had the same impact on teacher learning and practice.

At Wright Middle School, the whole staff has moved toward an Expeditionary model of curriculum development. Within their teams, teachers develop interdisciplinary "expeditions" with a core set of outcomes, subject-specific activities, and an integrated project. For example, one of the houses developed a culinary expedition where the students designed and constructed a restaurant on site, developed print and non-print materials, developed a menu and pricing procedures, designed management and service systems, and opened for business on two consecutive evenings. The teachers on the team, like those at Stratton, spent considerable time in conversation and planning activities. And as at Stratton, these conversations led to deeper understanding and changes in practice.

At the two elementary schools, curriculum work has been just as powerful a staff development approach. Both have moved toward multi-age, inclusive classrooms that required significant time and investment and learning for teachers. In addition, Aronomink School has collectively developed a template for designing interdisciplinary projects and New Orchard has involved teachers in a long-range program of curriculum review and improvement. As at the high school and middle school, these curriculum activities not only led to improved experiences for children, they also led to increased learning for adults.

Standards and assessment development is closely aligned with curriculum work. Earlier, Stratton's exit requirements for graduation, Wright's rubrics for writing, Aronomink's exhibitions, and New Orchard's benchmarks were mentioned. All these projects involved teachers working collaboratively in defining "What should students know and be able to do?" (the development of standards) and "How do students demonstrate what they know and can do?" (the development of assessments).

To take one example, New Orchard's benchmarking of student achievement has involved all the teachers in the school in close examination of student work. By analyzing what students were capable of doing in reading, writing, and mathematics, the teachers developed standards for what *all* students should achieve at grades 2 and 5. The standards that were developed reflected a school-wide consensus about what its desired ends are for all students. The complementary assessments represented the same kind of consensus about means. Teachers identified "anchor" papers of the standards and published a scoring guide for school-wide use. Every spring, they use the scoring guide in a blind review of student achievement at grades 2 and 5. They make results of the assessment available to parents and the community. Currently, teachers are meeting to develop individual interventions for each student who failed to achieve the benchmark standard. Having dismissed the stock response of retaining all students who don't meet the standard, the staff came up with an alternative. During the summer, teachers plan to meet in small groups to review the case of each child who achieved below the benchmark. These individual case review will focus on accumulating information and insights about specific children and their learning strengths and problem areas. Each case conference will result in an intervention plan for the student, to be implemented in the fall by the receiving teacher.

The New Orchard example epitomizes the power of collaborative assessment work for teachers. As was the case in joint curriculum work, standards and assessment development provides an arena for authentic teacher conversation about student learning. By focusing on the academic performance of their students, teachers are able to confront together the knotty issues about the nature of teaching and learning that were resolved individually in the past. These individual resolutions were, by their very nature, partial solutions forged in secret. Collaborative standards and assessment work promotes more comprehensive solutions that call on the collective experience and wisdom of teachers. By collecting wisdom from each other, teachers reflect on their own practices and acquire the insights and tools they need to get better.

These are but a few of the teacher development strategies employed at the four schools. Though these and other approaches are varied, they share similar features. That is, teacher learning is collaborative in nature. It strives for shared understanding about practice. It provides avenues for authentic conversation about teaching and learning. It recognizes the complex, layered, and conflicted nature of the work teachers do.

TEACHER MOBILITY: ANOTHER KEY ELEMENT?

As the four schools changed, an interesting phenomenon occurred in three of them. Though there is not sufficient evidence to place this issue among the seven key elements of cultural transition, it does seem worthy of note here. As three of the schools became more comfortable for some teachers, they seemed decidedly less so to others. Some dramatic shifts in personnel occurred. A number of teachers left for other positions, often in other schools in the same district. Those who remained were in a position to reinforce the emerging school culture through the hiring process. As a result, the school staff became more cohesive and more consensual in their values. As like-minded people joined the school faculty, the restructuring enterprise accelerated.

Such a shuffling of personnel, based on compatibility of belief and practice, leads to a strong and coherent school culture. It may well be an important piece of the reculturing process. In may ways, of course, it is a double-edged sword. The loss of resistant or recalcitrant teachers and their replacement with reform-minded educators enables some schools to enact their mission more effectively. At the same time, it may hinder the efforts of other schools – often in the same district – to move forward and improve. Some troubling questions emerge: What happens to the teachers who reject the need to revise their practices and choose to leave a reforming school? What happens to the schools that receive them? And what are the implications for the students whom they teach?

WHAT IT MEANS TO RECULTURE TEACHING

The key elements that are described above, – long term perspective, principal and teacher leadership, inquiry and reflection, outside supports and reference groups, focus on student learning, and attention to teacher development – all contribute to the development of a new way of doing business in schools. Separately, any one or two of these elements may exist in a school, and the school remains unchanged. Occurring together in a building, they are a powerful force that promotes the re-design of school, learning and teaching.

As evidenced by the four schools described in this chapter, school re-design depends on the establishment and sustainment of a professional teaching culture that is grounded in processes of collaborative learning and disciplined inquiry. Such a culture encourages and rewards teachers for accepting roles that transcend the boundaries of their individual classrooms. It provides the necessary conditions to support experimentation and risk-taking on behalf of student learning. It makes continuous improvement the goal for both teachers and students, and makes explicit the links between teacher learning and student achievement.

Changing roles and cultures is no easy task. It is the result of long and continuous "redesign conversations" (Wilson & Davis, 1994) that lead to the examination of practice, the articulation of beliefs, and the enactment of firmly held and consensual values. These "conversations" took place over ten years in the four schools. The cases demonstrate that change is possible and that teaching culture can be transformed. They also teach us that there are no shortcuts, no "magic bullets", no substitutes for hard and continuous work.

REFERENCES

Cohen, D., McLaughlin, M., & Talbert, J. (Eds.). (1993). *Teaching for understanding: Challenges for policy and practice.* San Francisco, CA: Jossey-Bass.

Darling-Hammond, L. (1990). Achieving our goals: Superficial or structural reforms? *Phi Delta Kappan,* **78**(4).

Elmore, R., & McLaughlin, M. (1988). *Steady work: Policy, practice, and the reform of American education.* Santa Monica, CA: RAND Corporation.

Fieldnotes, 1995, 1996

Fullan, M., & Hargreaves, A. (1991). *What's worth fighting for? Working together for your school.* Andover, MA: Regional Laboratory for Educational Improvement of the Northeast and Islands in association with the Ontario Public School Teacher Association.

Little, J. (1981). *School Success in Staff development: The role of staff development in urban desegregated schools.* Boulder, CO: Center for Action Research.

Loucks-Horsley, S., & Stiegelbauer, S. (1991). Using knowledge of change to guide staff development. In A. Lieberman & L. Miller (Eds.), *Staff development for education in the 90s: New demands, new realities, new perspectives.* New York, NY: Teachers College Press.

MacDonald, J. (1991). *Dilemmas of planning backwards.* Providence, RI: Coalition of Essential Schools.

McLaughlin, M., & Talbert, J. (1993). *Contexts that matter for teaching and learning.* Stanford, CA: Context Center on Secondary School Teaching.

Miller, L., & O'Shea, C. (1992). Learning to lead: Portraits of practice. In A. Lieberman (Ed.), *The changing contexts of teaching.* Ninety-first Yearbook of the National Society for the Study of Education. Chicago, IL: University of Chicago Press.

Rosenholtz, J. (1989). *Teachers' workplace.* New York: Longman.

Sergiovanni, T. (1987). The theoretical basis for cultural leadership. In L. T. Sheine & M. B. Schoenheit (Eds.), *Leadership: Examining the elusive.* Alexandria, VA: Association for Supervision and Curriculum Development.

Sizer, T. (1984). *Horace's compromise: The dilemma of the American high school.* Boston, MA: Houghton-Mifflin.

Wasley, P. (1991). *Teachers who lead: The rhetoric of reform and the realities of practice.* New York, NY: Teachers College Press.

Wilson, K., & Davis, B. (1974). *Redesigning education.* New York, NY: Henry Holt and Company, Inc.

The Micropolitics of Educational Change

JOSEPH BLASE

Department of Educational Leadership, University of Georgia

This chapter by Joe Blase, focuses on the micropolitics of educational change, an emerging area of educational inquiry. After a brief review of the relevant theoretical literature, the micropolitics of stability and change is discussed. Selected general studies are described to illustrate the pervasiveness of micropolitics to life in schools. Micropolitical studies of 1980s and 1990s reform and general studies of 1990s school reform/restructuring are then reviewed. This review is used to demonstrate the central thesis of the chapter: Micropolitics is a fundamental dimension of school change in general and, as such, a chief target of most approaches to school restructuring. A framework of ideas for further research on the micropolitics of change in schools is described. Such research is needed because few direct studies of this important phenomenon actually exist.

Schools and school systems are political organizations in which power is an organizing feature. Ignore [power] relationships, leave unexamined their rationale, and the existing system will defeat efforts at reform. This will happen not because there is a grand conspiracy or because of mulish stubbornness in resisting change or because educators are uniquely unimaginative or uncreative (which they are not) but rather because recognizing and trying to change power relationships, especially in complicated, traditional institutions, is among the most complex tasks human beings can undertake.

Seymour Sarason, *The Predictable Failure of Educational Reform*
(1990, p. 7)

The micropolitical perspective on organizations directly challenges traditional-rational (consensus) models of organization developed by such theorists as Weber (1947) and Taylor (1947). Burns (1961) was among the early theorists to discuss organizations as political systems consisting of both cooperative and conflictive elements; he argued that political alliances and political obligations were the "exchange currency" of organizational behavior.

Although Iannaccone (1975) first introduced the notion of micropolitics to education in the mid 1970s, it was not until the late 1980s that scholars produced significant theoretical and empirical work. Ball (1987), Bacharach and Mitchell (1987), Blase (1987a), and Hoyle (1986) were early pioneers in this new area of educational inquiry. Bacharach and Lawler (1980) constructed a political perspective on school organization that emphasized group-level analysis, bargaining relationships and tactics, and conflict in the context of formal decision making.

264

A. Hargreaves (ed.), Extending Educational Change, 264-277.

Ball's (1987) political perspective on schools, drawn from studies of British schools, also stressed group-level interactions: the interests of stakeholders, the maintenance of control by school heads (principals), and conflicts over decision making and school policy. Ball also discussed the politics of gender, race, age, and change.

Parallel theoretical work on schools as organizations, indirectly underscored the salience of micropolitics to everyday life in schools. Representative examples in this area include loose coupling theory (Weick, 1976), negotiated order theory (Hall & Spencer-Hall, 1982), and the interacting spheres model (Hanson, 1976) as well as intensive case studies of educational settings by Waller (1932), Beale (1936), Becker (1980), Lortie (1975), and Cusick (1983), among others. Such work pointed to the centrality of power and influence, value and goal diversity, and cooperative and conflictive processes in school organization. Indeed, like emerging micropolitical work in the area of education, such related work also suggested a view of organization that stressed the interactive, dialectical, strategic, ideological, interpretive, and conflictive/cooperative aspects of school life.

Researchers such as Ball (1987), Bacharach and Mitchell (1987), Blase (1987a, 1987b, and 1991), and Hoyle (1986) made important contributions to understanding the micropolitics of schools. However, most work has emphasized (a) conflictive "dark side" politics, (b) group-level behavior, and (c) formal decision-making processes. To address these limitations, Blase (1991) constructed an inclusive definition of micropolitics from the extant literature:

> Micropolitics refers to the use of formal and informal power by individuals and groups to achieve their goals in organizations. In large part political actions result from perceived differences between individuals and groups, coupled with the motivation to use power to influence and/or protect. Although such actions are consciously motivated, any action, consciously or unconsciously motivated, may have political "significance" in a given situation. Both cooperative and conflictive actions and processes are part of the realm of micropolitics. (p. 11)

Among other things, this definition of micropolitics addresses all types of decision-making structures and processes in school settings: conflictive and cooperative-consensual, group-level and individual, and formal and informal. It treats overt behavior as well as subtle and submerged processes (e.g., socialization) and structures (e.g., policies and procedures) as political phenomena. Blase's (1991) perspective on micropolitics is especially relevant to understanding school restructuring designed to create participatory governance structures (e.g., shared governance, site-based management, team leadership, teacher empowerment). School restructuring is driven by both conflictive-adversarial ("power over") and cooperative-consensual ("power with") political processes despite the participatory/democratic rhetoric stressing the latter (Fullan, 1991; Kreisberg, 1992; Malen & Ogawa, 1988). Kreisberg (1992) has observed that "the history of consensual decision-making in organizations is littered with power struggles [and] dissensus" (p. 124). Power-with political interaction focuses on mutual empowerment through a process characterized by reciprocity, co-agency, negotiation, and sharing to achieve goals. Because power-with political processes usually function within a larger power-over milieu of competition and domination, they are quite vulnerable to subversion (Kreisberg, 1992).

Blase's (1991) comprehensive perspective on micropolitics acknowledges the significance of all matters related to influence processes and the distribution of symbolic and tangible resources in school settings. Decision-making is considered only one micropolitical arena. For example, those with positional authority structure organizations to preclude issues from coming to a decision (e.g., via policies, rules, control of agendas). They also attempt to socialize others to accept the status quo. Such actions and processes, as well as actions by individuals and groups who lack formal decision-making status, are part of the micropolitics of a given school setting (Bachrach & Baratz, 1962; Blase, 1991; Galbraith, 1983; Hickson, Astley, Butler, & Wilson, 1981; Lukes, 1974).

MICROPOLITICS AND EDUCATIONAL CHANGE

Micropolitical structures and processes are fundamental to change and innovation as well as stability and maintenance of school settings. In fact, both divergent and convergent processes and structures constitute the political "state" of a school organization, although the salience of each in a given setting varies over time (Ball, 1987; Blase, 1991; Burlingame, 1988; Burns, 1961; Duke, 1976; Malen, 1994; Townsend, 1990).

During periods of stability, micropolitical processes and structures benefit some individuals and groups rather than others. In addition, the political power of individuals and groups is often taken for granted because it is imbedded in organizational and cultural structures that work to preserve the status quo (Blase, 1991; Cusick, 1992; Duke, 1976; Gronn, 1986; Lukes, 1974; Rollow & Bryk, 1995; Sarason, 1990). Mangham (1979) wrote, "so formidable is the collection of forces which underpin behavior in organizations that it is surprising that any changes ever manage to be promulgated let alone implemented" (p. 122). Sarason (1990) has argued:

> Schools will accommodate [change] in ways that require little or no change. . . . the strength of the status quo – its underlying axioms, its pattern of power relationships, its sense of tradition and, therefore, what seems right, natural, and proper – almost automatically rules out options for change in that status quo. (p. 35)

Relatedly, Marris (1975) contends that "dynamic conservatism" is a powerful force in all organizations: "social systems provide

> . . . a framework of theory, values, and related technology which enables individuals to make sense of their lives. Threats to the social system threaten this framework" (p. 51).

During periods of change, however, micropolitical interaction tends to intensify and become more visible in both formal and informal arenas of school life. Change dynamics – ambiguity, uncertainty, and goal complexity – provoke and exacerbate such intensified interaction.

Interestingly, most current restructuring approaches have been specifically designed to increase political activity in schools through, for example, the development of democratic decision-making structures. Such structures include new stakeholders with different ideologies and interests, who use different strategies to pursue a wide range of new issues (Ball, 1987; Baldridge, 1970; Blase & Blase, 1994; Cusick, 1992; Ferris, Russ, & Fandt, 1989; Hall & Spencer-Hall, 1982; Hardy, 1987; Mangham, 1979). These structures provide organizational stakeholders (with both similar and dissimilar interests and goals) new forums for political interaction, both adversarial and collaborative (Bolman & Deal, 1984; Mangham, 1979; Malen & McLeese, 1992).

In essence, power and politics dramatically affect and even drive all key dimensions of change and innovation in organizations. They typically reflect "the strong advocacy of some and the strong opposition of others. The self-interest of both groups is at stake and every trick and resource will be called into service to bring about or successfully oppose the innovation under consideration (Mangham, 1979, p. 133). In traditional organizations, change is often a top-down (hierarchical) imposition, a political strategy itself. "Setting a new image for the organization is essentially a political process by which 'dominant coalitions' (Thompson, 1967) impose their values on the organization and plans are articulated in light of the compromises that emerge from the political debate" (Baldridge, 1970, p. 26).

MICROPOLITICS AND EVERYDAY LIFE IN SCHOOLS

Political and nonpolitical studies demonstrate the centrality of micropolitics to everyday life in schools. Several studies have examined relationships between school administrators and teachers. To illustrate, Roberts and Blase (1995) found critical differences in the micropolitical interactions of supervisors and teachers participating in successful and less successful post-observation instructional conferences. Blase (1987b) described the political vulnerability of teachers in their relationships with parents and how this shaped instructional, social, and extracurricular dimensions of classroom life. Anderson (1991) investigated how school principals manipulated teachers through "cognitive politics"– the manipulation of language-and its profoundly oppressive effects on teachers' political participation and influence. From a large sample study of teachers, Blase and Blase (1994) studied effective traditional principals' use of powerful normative political strategies (e.g., giving praise) to gain teachers compliance with principals' goals. Greenfield (1991) examined how a common set of values among administrators and faculty in one elementary school provided the basis for developing a cooperative political culture devoted to serving the interests of children.

Studies of other relationships further demonstrate the importance of micropolitics in school life. Corbett (1991) researched the political influence of parents on one high school's discipline policy and how a principal's attempts to preempt such influence undermined the foundations of teachers' political influence with students. Osborne (1989) studied "power struggles" between Anglo and Zuni teachers in a public elementary school in Zuni, New Mexico. Schempp, Sparkes and Templin (1993) investigated the micropolitics of induction of three teachers in three schools. Spaulding (1994) described the complex web of micropolitical interactions that occurred in one elementary classroom and, in particular, the range of strategies used by a teacher and her students.

A host of nonpolitical studies in education also demonstrate the importance of politics to everyday life in schools. To illustrate, Hanson (1976) found that although formal structures of authority explain some of the political dynamics between teachers and school administrators, each group also controlled informal "spheres of influence." Brieschke (1983) described three strategic orientations – reinforcement, elite, fringe – teachers enacted in resisting and influencing school principals.

Other studies have reported that teachers exchange loyalty (and other intangible and tangible valued goods) for principal support in conflicts with students and parents. Specifically, teachers withhold valued goods in interactions with principals who fail to provide them with adequate political support (Becker, 1980; Cusick, 1983; McPherson, 1972). The subtle strategies teachers use to resist administrative control have also been discussed in the literature (e.g., Apple, 1986; Becker, 1980; McNeil, 1983).

A stream of studies have produced vivid descriptions of the "negotiated" nature of classroom life associated with teacher-student interactions about instructional and social issues (Cohen & Kottkamp, 1993; Connell, 1985; Lightfoot, 1983; McNeil, 1983; Nias, 1989; Pauly, 1992; Pollard, 1985; Powell, Farrar, & Cohen, 1985; Sedlak, Wheeler, Pullin, & Cusick, 1986; Waller, 1932; Woods, 1990). From their research, Powell et al. (1985) and Sedlak et al. (1986) found that classroom interaction is fundamentally political: Interaction is based primarily on power dynamics and negotiation between teachers and students and results in "understandings," "bargains," and "treaties," that define and control all aspects of classroom life. Pauly (1992), has concluded from his studies of schools that "education is the result of working agreements that are hammered out by the people in each classroom, who determine the rules, the power relationships, and the kinds of teaching and learning that will take place there" (pp. 13–14).

THE MICROPOLITICS OF EDUCATIONAL REFORM

Only a few studies conducted in Britain and the United States during the reforms of the 1980s have directly investigated the micropolitics of change in schools. These studies indicate that school administrators typically employ control-oriented power-over approaches to change. Ball (1987), for example, described how attempts to introduce mixed-ability grouping in several British schools led to conflict among groups of teachers with contrasting ideologies and interests. He demonstrated how micropolitical considerations (e.g., the use of strategies such as public debate, behind-the-scenes maneuvering, and lobbying by school factions) shaped efforts at innovation at the school level.

Ball and Bowe (1991) found that changes initiated by the 1988 Education Reform Act in Britain precipitated political struggles at the school site between those with a managerial orientation and those with an educational orientation. In another study of Reform Act effects, Radnor (1990) reported how school governance structures were bureaucratized, how school curriculum decisions were centralized, and how curriculum leaders (heads of departments) were transformed to curriculum managers (rather than initiators). Ball and Bowe (1991) and Radnor (1990) concluded that the responses of British school heads to externally initiated change were designed to create the appearance of schoolwide participation and consensus.

Sparkes's (1990) study of department head-initiated change in the physical education department of a British school described how the head dominated the direction, content, and outcome of meetings by using "contractive rhetoric" (i.e., the use of pejorative language by powerful stakeholders to trivialize the introduction of ideas and practices outside normative practice) and other political strategies to undermine faculty with opposing viewpoints. Noblit, Berry, and Dempsey (1991) investigated how teachers, in response to district initiatives to centralize personnel management and to professionalize teaching, used reform to increase their own political power, to discover their collective interests, and to define professionalism in their own terms.

The second wave of educational reform in the United States has been identified strongly with the goal of restructuring schools along democratic lines. Terms such as *site-based management, shared governance, participatory decision-making, decentralization,* and *empowerment* have been used to denote a move away from top-down control to the devolution of political power and authority to the school-building level (Glickman, 1993; Lightfoot, 1986; Maeroff, 1988). Restructuring has produced new formal governance structures and informal coalitions in schools; new interest groups with different ideologies and interests; and more public conflict, negotiating, mediating, bargaining, and persuading than ever before. Clearly, the form and substance of political interaction have changed significantly in successfully restructured schools (Peterson & Warren, 1994; Rollow & Bryk, 1995). (In other schools, of course, despite district-level initiatives, few substantive political changes have resulted, and "maintenance" politics has continued [Rollow & Bryk, 1995]).

The balance of this section examines the few extant micropolitical studies that have addressed innovative relationships and newly initiated governance structures and processes in schools. Some general studies of school restructuring are also interpreted from a micropolitical standpoint. *Taken together, these studies demonstrate the critical role of micropolitics in educational change, a role that appears to be quite significant as a positive, facilitative force and as a negative, impeding force in school restructuring efforts.*

The importance of the principal's role in *facilitating* change in schools is widely discussed in the restructuring literature (Blase & Blase, 1994; Blase, Blase, Anderson, & Dungan, 1995; Bredeson, 1989; Clift, Johnson, Holland, & Veal, 1992; Etheridge & Hall, 1995; Freeman, Brimhall, & Neufeld, 1994; Murphy & Louis, 1994; Reitzug, 1994; Rollow & Bryk, 1995). These studies emphasize the principal's political role in facilitating new governance processes and structures in school settings.

Blase and Blase (1994) found that the use of a facilitative leadership approach by shared governance principals (e.g., building trust, developing democratic decision-making structures, encouraging autonomy, encouraging innovation/risk taking) contributed significantly to teachers' sense of political efficacy. Facilitative principal leadership was linked to substantial increases in teachers' involvement in decision-making, voice, and commitment to democratically derived decisions.

In a study of the effects of the Chicago Reform on school-site restructuring, Rollow and Bryk (1995) found that the type of "political practice" that developed in the schools depended largely on principals' leadership. Facilitative leadership, based on trust in teachers, support for collective faculty action, and encouragement of parental participation in school decision-making was strongly correlated with the development of "strong democracy" in schools.

Facilitative successful school restructuring has also been strongly associated with various facets of the principal's political role, specifically managing internal conflict (Beck, 1993; Peterson & Warren, 1994), developing teachers' capacity for critique (Reitzug, 1994), maintaining balance between district- level initiates and school-based initiatives (Conley & Goldman, 1994), challenging teachers to transform schools (Prestine, 1994), maintaining accountability of organizational stakeholders (Bondy, Ross, & Webb, 1994), and developing collaborative relationships with parents (Flinspach, Easton, Ryan, O'Connor, & Storey, 1994).

Other studies have directly linked teachers' political participation in school-wide decision-making, classroom autonomy, and reflective critique of curriculum and instruction to successful school restructuring (Allen, 1993; Bredeson, 1989; Brimhall, 1993; Blase & Blase, 1994; Corbett & Rossman, 1988; Melenyzer, 1990). Smylie and Brownlee-Conyers (1990) described teachers' use of specific political strategies to develop innovative collaborative relationships with principals. In a micropolitical study of a school implementing site-based management, Reed (1992) discovered that teachers' perspectives of political efficacy significantly varied: Teachers who defined efficacy as greater formal authority in school-wide, as opposed to classroom, decision-making were seen as an important force in facilitating the implementation of site-based initiates.

Also found to be important factors in successful implementation of school restructuring have been a central office's efforts to protect a school involved in restructuring from interference (Slavin, Madden, Shaw, Mainzer, & Donnelly, 1993) and a superintendent's political support for newly developed school-based programs (McCarthy & Still, 1993). Smylie and Crowson (1993) found that central office support for training principals and teachers in collaborative processes facilitated implementation of school restructuring. A study of collaboration within an external coalition of partners (university, district, and computer manufacturer) highlighted the importance of both strategy and resource control to influence on school-level innovation (Baker, 1994).

Other political and nonpolitical studies point to the centrality of micropolitical factors to educational change by demonstrating how such factors significantly *impede* school restructuring and frequently contribute to the failure of restructuring efforts. School principals' unwillingness and inability to enact approaches to leadership consistent with democratic processes and principles have been a major impediment to successful school restructuring (Blase & Blase, 1994; Robertson & Briggs, 1994; Rollow & Bryk, 1995; Smith, 1995). Malen and Ogawa (1988) were among the first to report that even properly conceived approaches to restructuring (e.g., wherein school-based councils had broad jurisdiction and decision-making authority) were easily sabotaged by principals with "control" orientations to teachers and parents. Rollow and Bryk (1995) found that controlling and mediational forms of principal leadership impeded Chicago school reform and actually worked to maintain status quo politics or further consolidate principals' power.

Studies have found that principals' attempts to control decision-making, for example, through intimidation, misinformation, favoritism, and exclusion, have drastically interfered with restructuring initiatives (Etheridge & Hall, 1995; Gitlin et al., 1992; Reitzug & Cross, 1994; Smylie & Crowson, 1993. Lonnquist and King (1993) reported that principals undermined efforts to develop teacher-led schools by dismissing agendas and postponing meetings with teachers. Reitzug and Cross (1994) found that control and domination based on principals' traditional expectations for self, teachers' traditional expectations for principals, and access to knowledge not available to teachers "inadvertently" impeded school restructuring. Brown (1994) found that a principal's appointment of teachers to a leadership team without faculty consultation was sufficient to undermine the trust required for restructuring. Generally, the failure of principals to let go of power and to facilitate vigorously the development of political power in others has also been reported as a serious impeding factor in school restructuring initiatives (Blase & Blase, 1994; Bredeson, 1993; Murphy & Louis, 1994).

Teacher-related micropolitical factors have been found to impede school restructuring. These include classroom territoriality norms and protectionist orientations to outside intrusions, relationships of power and politics within classrooms (Cusick, 1992; Pauly, 1992; Powell et al., 1985; Sedlak et al., 1986), confusion about roles and authority in school-level decision making, and structural and socialization factors that prevent collegial dialogue (Gitlin et al., 1992). Other teacher-related micropolitical factors that interfere with restructuring are adversarial factions with competing interests who fail to share resources (Robertson & Briggs, 1994), domination of governance processes by particular groups and the types of strategies used to pursue their interests (Peterson & Solsrud, 1993), and compliant orientations toward principals (Allen, 1993; Blase & Roberts, 1994).

Several political factors at the school district level tend to impede restructuring initiatives. These include the failure to support school-site policy decisions, provide adequate time for decision making (Blase & Blase, 1994; Brown & Hawkins, 1988; Murphy & Louis, 1994), clarify the role of principals, and develop assessment criteria relevant to principals' new roles in restructured schools. Also found to hinder restructuring have been the failure to clarify procedural governance ambiguities (Bondy et al., 1994), trust the professional judgments of teachers, provide adequate funding/resources (Murphy & Louis, 1994), and support principals in conflicts with others (Crowson & Boyd, 1991). The use of top-down mandates to create school-based collegiality among teachers (Hargreaves, 1991) and extending inordinate power to school principals involved in site-based management have also been found to have an adverse effect on school restructuring (Smylie & Crowson, 1993). In one case, Louis and King (1993) discovered that restructuring efforts were impeded because a school board's need for accountability information required teachers to share negative data about restructuring that potentially threatened the school board's willingness to continue its support.

DIRECTIONS FOR FUTURE RESEARCH

Research on the politics of life in schools has advanced considerably during recent years. Indeed, several writers (e.g., Ball, 1987; Nyberg, 1981; Sarason, 1990) have argued that a failure to deal directly with the political dynamics of change will most likely prevent understanding and successful implementation of reform: Indeed, change stemming from the macropolitical environment of schools as well as its micropolitical environment will continue to thwart reform. However, despite the fact that 1990s reform in the United States and elsewhere, in large part, has focused on changing political structures and processes in schools, few micropolitical studies of school change have been undertaken. The following general framework of topics for research on the micropolitics of educational change and innovation applies particularly to the micropolitics of school restructuring.

Studies designed to investigate political *relationships* among parents, administrators, teachers, students, staff, central office, school board, community, state, and reform affiliates would be valuable. Likewise, studies of organizational *roles* associated with school restructuring would field important data. Pertinent roles might include facilitator, participant, decision-maker, partner, teacher as leader, leader as teacher, and parent/student as participants.

Another potentially rich area of research would be micropolitical studies of restructuring *processes* such as decision-making, teaming, influence, collaboration, problem solving, communication, consensus development, conflict resolution, planning, vision development, goal setting, empowerment, resistance, readiness, risk-taking, support, failure, action research, and confrontation. In addition, studies of particular formal and informal *structures*, for example, leadership, time, reward, and support, would contribute to our understanding of school restructuring.

Finally, studies specifically based in *theories* of conflict, change, communication, power, problem solving, leadership, dramaturgy, interpersonal and group dynamics, and socio-linguistics could generate valuable information about the micropolitics of school restructuring.

CONCLUSIONS AND IMPLICATIONS

Not only is politics a fundamental aspect of life in schools; it is also a fundamental aspect of change there. Micropolitical processes and structures tend to intensify during periods of change in schools. Current reform efforts to democratize schools are unique in that they aim to change (sometimes dramatically) the formal political governance structure of schools. However, different approaches to school restructuring are identified with different political processes and goals. Some approaches are conservative (e.g., Maeroff, 1988), others are liberal (e.g., Glickman, 1993), and still others are considered radical-emancipatory (e.g., Giroux, 1992).

Yet, the research literature tells us that those who initiate and implement school restructuring often fail to exhibit the essential knowledge and skill. Restructuring efforts often demonstrate a lack of micropolitically relevant knowledge and skill in facilitative leadership, interpersonal influence, team development/group dynamics, and collaborative-consensual vs. conflictive-adversarial processes, among other things (e.g., Bondy et al., 1994; Crowson & Boyd, 1991; Cusick, 1992; Hargreaves, 1991; Malen & Ogawa, 1988; Rollow & Bryk, 1995; Sarason, 1990). Preservice and inservice training of educators in these and other relevant knowledge and skill areas would be extremely valuable.

Historically, schools have not provided educators, students, or parents with opportunities for viable democratic participation in school life. Clearly, democratic values and principles have not governed everyday life in schools. Current approaches to school reform emphasize the development of democratic processes for school improvement: for these approaches school democracy is typically viewed as a vehicle for school improvement rather than an end in itself. Should the goal of school restructuring expand to encompass a vision of schools as models of democratic values and principles, then training in democratic theory and sophisticated micropolitical knowledge and skill would be required of all participants.

REFERENCES

Allen, L. R. (1993). *The role of voice in shared governance: A case study of a primary school.* Unpublished doctoral dissertation, University of Georgia.

Anderson, G. (1991). Cognitive politics of principals and teachers: Ideological control in an elementary school. In J. Blase (Ed.), *The politics of life in schools: Power, conflict, and cooperation* (pp. 120–130). Newbury Park, CA: Sage.

Apple, M. W. (1986). *Teachers and texts.* New York: Routledge & Kegan Paul.

Bacharach, S. B., & Lawler, E. J. (1980). *Power and politics in organizations: The social psychology of conflict, coalitions, and bargaining.* San Francisco: Jossey-Bass.

Bacharach, S. B., & Mitchell, S. M. (1987). The generation of practical theory: Schools as political organizations. In J. W. Lorsch (Ed.), *Handbook of organizational behavior* (pp. 405–418). Englewood Cliffs, NJ: Prentice Hall.

Bachrach, P., & Baratz, M. S. (1962). Two faces of power. *American Political Science Review,* **56**(4), 947–952.

Baker, L. M. (1994, April). *The politics of collaboration: How an educational partnership works.* Paper presented at the annual meeting of the American Educational Research Association, New Orleans.

Baldridge, J. V. (1970). *Images of the future and organizational change: The case of New York University.* (Report No. RDM58). Stanford, CA: Stanford Center for Research and Development in Teaching. (ERIC Document Reproduction Service No. ED 037 184).

Ball, S. J. (1987). *The micro-politics of the school: Towards a theory of school organization.* London: Methuen.

Ball, S. J., & Bowe, R. (1991). Micropolitics of radical change: Budgets, management, and control in British schools. In J. Blase (Ed.), *The politics of life in schools: Power, conflict, and cooperation* (pp. 19–45). Newbury Park, CA: Sage.

Beale, H. K. (1936). *Are American teachers free? An analysis of restraints upon the freedom of teaching in American schools.* New York: Scribner.

Beck, L. G. (1993). Cultivating a caring school community: One principal's story. In J. Murphy & K. S. Louis (Eds.), *Reshaping the principalship: Insights from transformational reform efforts* (pp. 177–202) Thousand Oaks, CA: Corwin Press.

Becker, H. (1980). *Role of the Chicago public school teacher.* New York: ARNO Press.

Blase, J. (1987a). Political interaction among teachers: Sociocultural contexts in the schools. *Urban Education*, **22**(3), 286–309.

Blase, J. (1987b). The politics of teaching: The teacher-parent relationship and the dynamics of diplomacy. *Journal of Teacher Education*, **38**(2), 53–60.

Blase, J. (1991). (Ed.). *The politics of life in schools: Power, conflict, and cooperation.* Newbury Park, CA: Sage.

Blase, J., & Blase, J. (1994). *Empowering teachers: What successful principals do.* Newbury Park, CA: Corwin.

Blase, J., & Roberts, J. R. (1994). The micropolitics of teacher work involvement: Effective principals' impacts on teachers. *The Alberta Journal of Educational Research*, **40**(1), 67–94.

Blase, J., Blase, J. R., Anderson, G., & Dungan, S. (1995). *Democratic principals in action: Eight pioneers.* Thousand Oaks, CA: Corwin Press.

Bolman, L. G., & Deal, T. E. (1984). *Modern approaches to understanding and managing organizations.* San Francisco: Jossey Bass Publishers.

Bondy, E., Ross, D., & Webb, R. (1994, April). *The dilemmas of school restructuring and improvement.* Paper presented at the annual meeting of the American Educational Research Association, New Orleans.

Bredeson, P. V. (1989). Redefining leadership and the roles of school principals: Responses to changes in the professional work-life of teachers. *The High School Journal*, **23**(1), 9–20.

Bredeson, P. V. (1993). Letting go of outlived professional identities: A study of role transition and role strain for principals in restructured schools. *Educational Administration Quarterly*, **29**(1), 34–68.

Brieschke, P. A. (1983). A case study of teacher role enactment in an urban elementary school. *Educational Administration Quarterly*, **19**(4), 59–83.

Brimhall, P. A. (1993, April). *Restructuring and teacher empowerment.* Paper presented at the annual meeting of the American Educational Research Association, Atlanta.

Brown, D. F. (1994, April). *Experiencing shared leadership: Teachers' reflections.* Paper presented at the annual meeting of the American Educational Research Association, New Orleans.

Brown, G. J., & Hawkins, J. (1988). Positive confirmation: Empowering others. *Contemporary Education*, **59**(4), 195–196.

Burlingame, M. (1988). [Review of *The micro-politics of the school: Towards a theory of school organization*]. *Journal of Curriculum Studies*, **20**(3), 281–283.

Burns, T. (1961). Micropolitics: Mechanisms of institutional change. *Administration Science Quarterly*, **6**, 257–281.

Clift, R., Johnson, M., Holland, P., & Veal, M. L. (1992). Developing the potential for collaborative school leadership. *American Educational Research Journal*, **29**(4), 877–908.

Cohen, M. M., & Kottkamp, R. B. (1993). *Teachers: The missing voice in education.* Albany: State University of New York Press.

Conley, D. T., & Goldman, P. (1994). Ten propositions for facilitative leadership. In J. Murphy & K. S. Louis (Eds.), *Reshaping the principalship: Insights from transformational reform efforts* (pp. 237–262). Thousand Oaks, CA: Corwin Press.

Connell, R. W. (1985). *Teachers' work.* Sydney: George Allen & Unwin.

Corbett, H. D. (1991). Community influence on school micropolitics: A case example. In J. Blase (Ed.), *The politics of life in schools: Power, conflict, and cooperation* (pp. 73–95). Newbury Park, CA: Sage.

Corbett, H. D., & Rossman, G. B. (1988, April). *How teachers empower subordinates: Running good schools*. Paper presented at the annual meeting of the American Educational Research Association, New Orleans.

Crowson, R. L., & Boyd, W. L. (1991). Urban schools as organizations: Political perspectives. In J. G. Cibulka, R. J. Reed, & K. K. Wong (Eds.), *Politics of education yearbook* (pp. 87–103). London: Taylor & Francis.

Cusick, P. A. (1983). *The egalitarian ideal and the American high school: Studies of three schools*. New York: Longman.

Cusick, P. A. (1992). *The educational system: Its nature and logic*. New York: McGraw-Hill.

Duke, J. T. (1976). *Conflict and power in social life*. Provo, UT: Brigham Young University Press.

Etheridge, C. P., & Hall, M. L. (1995, April). *Challenge to change: The Memphis experience with school-based decision making revisited*. Paper presented at the annual meeting of the American Educational Research Association, San Francisco.

Ferris, G. R., Russ, G. S., & Fandt, P. M. (1989). Politics in organizations. In R. A. Giacalone & P. Rosenfeld (Eds.), *Impression management in the organization* (pp. 143–170). Hillsdale, NJ: Lawrence Erlbaum Associates.

Flinspach, S. L., Easton, J. Q., Ryan, S. P., O'Conner, C., & Storey, S. L. (1994, April). *Local school councils during four years of school reform*. Paper presented at the annual meeting of the American Educational Research Association, New Orleans.

Freeman, D. J., Brimhall, P. A., & Neufeld, J. (1994, April). *Who's in charge now?: A principal's endeavors to empower teachers*. Paper presented at the annual meeting of the American Educational Research Association, New Orleans.

Fullan, M. G. (1991). *The new meaning of educational change*. New York: Teachers College Press.

Galbraith, J. K. (1983). *The anatomy of power*. Boston: Houghton Mifflin.

Giroux, H. (1982). *Ideology, culture, and the process of schooling*. Philadelphia: Temple University Press.

Gitlin, A., Bringhurst, K., Burns, M., Cooley, V., Myers, B., Price, K., Russell, R., & Tiess, P. (1992). *Teachers voices for school change: An introduction to educative research*. New York: Teachers College Press.

Glickman, C. D. (1993). *Renewing America's schools: A guide for school-based action*. San Francisco: Jossey-Bass.

Greenfield, W. D. (1991). The micropolitics of leadership in an urban elementary school. In J. Blase (Ed.), *The politics of life in schools: Power, conflict, and cooperation* (pp. 161–184). Newbury Park, CA: Sage.

Gronn, P. (1986). Politics, power and the management of schools. In E. Hoyle (Ed.), *The world yearbook of education 1986: The management of schools* (pp. 45–54). London: Kogan Page.

Hall, P., & Spencer-Hall, D. A. (1982). The social conditions of negotiated order. *Urban Life, 11*(3), 328–349.

Hanson, M. (1976). Beyond the bureaucratic model: A study of power and autonomy in educational decision making. *Interchange, 7*(1), 27–38.

Hardy, C. (1987). The contribution of political science to organizational behavior. In J. W. Lorsch (Ed.), *Handbook of organizational behavior* (pp. 96–108). Englewood Cliffs, NJ: Prentice Hall.

Hargreaves, A. (1991). Contrived collegiality: The micropolitics of teacher collaboration. In J. Blase (Ed.), *The politics of life in schools: Power, conflict, and cooperation* (pp. 46–72). Newbury Park, CA: Sage.

Hickson, D., Astley, W., Butler, R., & Wilson, D. (1981). Organization as power. *Research in Organizational Behavior, 3*, 151–196.

Hoyle, E. (1986). *The politics of school management*. London: Hodder and Stoughton.

Iannaccone, L. (1975). *Education policy systems: A study guide for educational administrators*. Fort Lauderdale, FL: Nova University.

Kreisberg, S. (1992). *Transforming power: Domination, empowerment and education*. Albany: State University of New York Press.

Lightfoot, S. L. (1983). *The good high school: Portraits of character and culture*. New York: Basic Books.

Lightfoot, S. L. (1986). On goodness in schools: Themes of empowerment. *Peabody Journal of Education, 63*(3), 9–28.

Lortie, D. C. (1975). *Schoolteacher: A sociological study*. Chicago: University of Chicago Press.

Louis, K. S., & King, J. A. (1993). Professional cultures and reforming schools: Does the myth of Sisyphus apply? In J. Murphy & P. Hallinger (Eds.), *Restructuring schooling: Learning from ongoing efforts* (pp. 216–250). Newbury Park, CA: Corwin Press.

Lukes, S. (1974). *Power: A radical view*. London: MacMillan Press.

Maeroff, G. I. (1988). A blueprint for empowering teachers. *Phi Delta Kappan, 69*(7), 473–477.

Malen, B. (1994). The micropolitics of education: Mapping the multiple dimensions of power relations in school politics. *Journal of Education Policy*, 9(5&6), 147–167.

Malen, B., & McLeese, P. (1992). *The policy and political influence domain: A definition of knowledge and skill requirements for principals.* Unpublished manuscript.

Malen, B., & Ogawa, R. (1988). Professional-patron influence on site-based governance councils: A confounding case study. *Educational Evaluation and Policy Analysis*, 10(4), 251–270.

Mangham, I. (1979). *The politics of organizational change.* Westport, CT: Greenwood Press.

Marris, P. (1975). *Loss and change.* New York: Anchor Press/Doubleday.

McCarthy, J., & Still, S. (1993). Hollibrook Accelerated Elementary School. In J. Murphy & P. Hallinger (Eds.), *Restructuring schooling: Learning from ongoing efforts* (pp. 63–83) Newbury Park, CA: Corwin.

McNeil, L. (1983). Defensive teaching and classroom control. In M. Apple & Luis Weis (Eds.), *Ideology and practice in schooling* (pp. 114–142). Philadelphia: Temple University Press.

McPherson, G. H. (1972). *Small town teachers.* Cambridge, MA: Harvard Univ. Press.

Melenyzer, B. J. (1990, November). *Teacher empowerment: The discourse, meanings, and social actions of teachers.* Paper presented at the National Council of States on Inservice Education, Orlando, Florida.

Murphy, J., & Louis, K. S. (1994). (Eds.). *Reshaping the principalship: Insights from transformational reform efforts.* Thousand Oaks, CA: Corwin Press.

Nias, J. (1989). *Primary teachers talking: A study of teaching as work.* London: Routledge.

Noblit, G., Berry, B., & Dempsey, V. (1991). Political responses to reform: A comparative case study. *Education and Urban Society*, 23(4), 379–395.

Nyberg, D. (1981). *Power over power.* Ithaca, NY: Cornell University Press.

Osborne, A. B. (1989). Insiders and outsiders: Cultural membership and the micropolitics of education among the Zuni. *Anthropology and Education Quarterly*, 20, 196–215.

Pauly, E. (1992). *The classroom crucible: What really works, what doesn't, and why.* New York: Basic Books.

Peterson, K., & Solsrud, C. (1993, April). *Leadership in restructuring schools: Six themes on the worklives of principals and teachers.* Paper presented at the annual meeting of the American Educational Research Association, Atlanta.

Peterson, K. D., & Warren, V. D. (1994). Changes in school governance and principals' roles: Changing jurisdictions, new power dynamics, and conflict in restructured schools. In J. Murphy & K. S. Louis (Eds.), *Reshaping the principalship: Insights from transformational reform efforts* (pp 219–236). Thousand Oaks, CA: Corwin Press.

Pollard, A. (1985). *The social world of the primary school.* London: Holt, Rinehart & Winston.

Powell, G., Farrar, E., & Cohen, D. K. (1985). *The shopping mall high school: Winners and losers in the educational marketplace.* Boston: Houghton Mifflin.

Prestine, N. A. (1994). Ninety degrees from everywhere: New understandings of a principal's role in a restructuring essential school. In J. Murphy & K. S. Louis (Eds.), *Reshaping the principalship: Insights from transformational reform efforts* (pp. 123–143). Thousand Oaks, CA: Corwin Press.

Radnor, H. A. (1990, April). *Complexities and compromises: The new era at Parkview School.* Paper presented at the annual meeting of the American Educational Research Association, Boston.

Reed, C. J. (1992, April). *Political basis of teacher response to opportunities for involvement in school site policy curriculum decisions.* Paper presented at the annual meeting of the American Educational Research Association, San Francisco.

Reitzug, U. C. (1994). A case study of empowering principal behavior. *American Educational Research Journal*, 31(2), 283–307.

Reitzug, U. C., & Cross, B. E. (1994, April). *A multi-site case study of site-based management in urban schools.* Paper presented at the annual meeting of the American Educational Research Association, New Orleans.

Roberts, J. R., & Blase, J. (1995). The micropolitics of successful supervisor-teacher interaction in instructional conferences. In D. Corson (Ed.), *Discourse and power in educational organizations* (pp. 55–70). Cresskill, NJ: Hampton Press.

Robertson, P. J., & Briggs, K. L. (1994, April). *Managing change through school-based management.* Paper presented at the annual meeting of the American Educational Research Association, New Orleans.

Rollow, S. G., & Bryk, A. S. (1995). *Politics as a lever for organizational change.* Manuscript submitted for publication.

Sarason, S. (1990). *The predictable failure of educational reform.* San Francisco: Jossey-Bass.

Schempp, R. A., Sparkes, A. C., & Templin, T. J. (1993). The micropolitics of teacher induction. *American Educational Research Journal,* 30(3), 447–472.

Sedlak, M. W., Wheeler, C. W., Pullin, D. C., & Cusick, P. A. (1986). *Selling students short: Classroom bargains and academic reform in the American high school.* New York: Teachers College Press.

Slavin, R. E., Madden, N. A., Shaw, A. H., Mainzer, K. L., & Donnelly, M. C. (1993). In J. Murphy & P. Hallinger (Eds.), *Restructuring schooling: Learning from on-going efforts* (pp. 84–113). Newbury Park, CA: Corwin.

Smith, W. E. (1995, April). *A case study of principal leadership: Dilemmas in implementing shared decision making.* Paper presented at the annual meeting of the American Educational Research Association, San Francisco.

Smylie, M. A., & Brownlee-Conyers, J. (1990, April). *Teacher leaders and their principals: Exploring new working relationships from a micropolitical perspective.* Paper presented at the annual meeting of the American Educational Research Association, Boston.

Smylie, M. A., & Crowson, R. L. (1993, April). *Principal assessment under restructured governance.* Paper presented at the annual meeting of the American Educational Research Association, New Orleans.

Sparkes, A. C. (1990). Power, domination and resistance in the process of teacher-initiated innovation. *Research Papers in Education,* 5(2), 153–178.

Spaulding, A. M. (1994). *The micropolitics of the elementary classroom.* Unpublished doctoral dissertation, Texas Tech University, Lubbock.

Taylor, F. W. (1947). *Scientific management.* New York: Harper.

Thompson, J. (1967). *Organizations in action.* New York: McGraw-Hill.

Townsend, R. G. (1990). Toward a broader micropolitics of schools. *Curriculum Inquiry,* 20(2), 205–224.

Waller, W. (1932). *The sociology of teaching.* New York: John Wiley.

Weber, M. (1947). *The theory of social and economic organization.* New York: Free Press.

Weick, K. E. (1976). Educational organizations as loosely coupled systems. *Administrative Science Quarterly,* 21(1), 1–18.

Woods, P. (1990). *Teacher skills and strategies.* London: Falmer Press.

The Emotions of Teaching and Educational Change

ANDY HARGREAVES

Ontario Institute for Studies in Education, University of Toronto

One of the most neglected dimensions of educational change is the emotional one. Educational and organizational change are often treated as rational, cognitive processes in pursuit of rational, cognitive ends. If emotions are acknowledged at all, this is usually in a minimalist way in terms of human relations or climate setting, where the task of leadership is to manipulate the mood and motivation of their staffs, in order to manage them more effectively. The more unpredictable passionate aspects of learning, teaching and leading, however, are usually left out of the change picture.

In this chapter, Andy Hargreaves makes a case for studying and energizing the emotions within the educational change process. Then, drawing on an empirical study of a group of change-oriented Grade 7 & 8 teachers in Canada, he describes how teachers' emotional goals for and bonds with their students permeate teachers' orientations and responses to all other aspects of educational change – such as curriculum planning, teaching and learning, and school structure. When the emotional aspects of teaching and educational change are considered seriously, Hargreaves argues, what is at stake in educational change and how best to manage it, will never look the same again.

INTRODUCTION

At the dawn of a new millennium, change is on most people's minds, not just the President's. Education prepares the generations of the future, and educational change is therefore front and center of all the talk about change in general. Educational reform is indeed pervasive right now. Learning standards are being defined for children, professional standards are being drawn up for teachers, assessment reform is extensive, new technologies are being widely advocated and implemented, schools in serious trouble are being reconstituted so they can make a fresh start, and school partnerships are being promoted everywhere with businesses, communities and universities. A growing change literature is also helping people understand how teachers and schools cope with educational change, and what sense they make of it (e.g., Fullan, 1991, 1993; McLaughlin, 1990; Miles & Huberman, 1984; Louis & Miles, 1990; Sarason, 1990; Newmann & Wehlage, 1995).

Important as all this reform work is, I believe that many of those who initiate and manage educational reform, or who write about educational change in general, ignore or underplay one of the most fundamental aspects of teaching and of how teachers change: the emotional dimension.

Emotions are at the heart of teaching. They comprise its most dynamic qualities – literally – for emotions are fundamentally about movement. Emotions are

A. Hargreaves (ed.), Extending Educational Change, 278-295.
© 2005 *Springer. Printed in the Netherlands.*

basically "mental states accompanied by intense feeling and (which involve) bodily changes of a widespread character" (Koestler, 1967, p. 226). The Latin origin of emotion is *emovere*: to move out, to stir up. When people are emotional, they are moved by their feelings. They can be moved to tears, overcome by joy, or fall into despair, for example (Höpfl & Linstead, 1993). Emotions are dynamic parts of ourselves, and whether they are positive or negative, all organizations, including schools, are full of them.

Good teaching is charged with positive emotion. It isn't just a matter of knowing your subject, being efficient, having the correct competences, or learning all the right techniques. Good teachers aren't just well-oiled machines. Computers can never replace them. They are emotional, passionate beings who fill their work and their classes with pleasure, creativity, challenge and joy. In Fried's (1995) terms, teaching is a passionate vocation. Good teachers are passionate about ideas, learning and their relationships with students. Woods and Jeffrey (1996) studied what made "exceptional" English primary school teachers especially creative. These teachers did more than teach to set standards or use approved techniques. Their classroom relationships featured "interest, enthusiasm, inquiry, excitement, discovery, risk-taking and fun". Their cognitive scaffolding of concepts and teaching strategies was "held together with emotional bonds" (p. 71).

Emotions are virtually absent from the literature and advocacy of educational change. Strategic planning, cognitive leadership, problem-solving, teacher reflection, higher-order thinking, and standards-based reform have virtually nothing to say about them. Even the idea of organizational learning which is on the very cutting edge of change theory, is almost exclusively cerebral in its emphasis. In so much writing about teaching and leading, it is as if educators only ever think, manage and plan in coldly calculative (and stereotypically masculine) ways. It is as if teachers think and act; but never really feel.

Even where feelings are acknowledged in discussions of how schools and other kinds of organization work

> the people presented are emotionally anorexic. They have 'dissatisfactions' and 'satisfactions', they may be 'alienated' or 'stressed', they will have 'preferences', 'attitudes' and 'interests'. Often these are noted as variables for managerial control. . . . We find little or no mention of how feeling individuals worry, envy, brood, become bored, play, despair, plot, hate, hurt and so forth.
>
> (Fineman, 1993, pp. 9–10)

Emotions are usually acknowledged and talked about only insofar as they help administrators and reformers "manage" and offset teachers' resistance to change, or help them set the climate or mood in which the "really important" business of cognitive learning or strategic planning can take place. The more volatile, passionate emotions (which are also the less easily managed ones) are kept off the educational agenda in favor of ones that encourage trust, support, openness, involvement, commitment to teamwork and willingness to experiment. This is so whether the emotions are positive ones like joy and excitement, or negative, like frustration and anger. Reformers and many change-managers tend to acknowledge the importance of teachers' emotions only when they can be treated as a gentle sedative (through collaboration, team-building, stress-management, wellness, etc.), and not as an unpredictable (yet potentially empowering) stimulant.

Another common misconception about the emotions is that they are somehow separate from reasoning. They might have their place, it's conceded, but only in a "handmaiden" role. Caring may matter, for instance, but only because it sets the climate for proper problem-solving at a higher level. In reality, though, feelings can't be parceled off in this way. Damasio (1994) and Sacks (1995) present compelling evidence that emotions are indispensable to rational decision-making. People who are emotionally flat might be able to perform abstract intellectual tasks, but they can't make practical judgments of human value. This is because they have lost the feelings, the in-built biases that narrow down the scope of potential judgment into a manageable range. You can't judge if you can't feel! Consistently dispassionate educators are therefore highly dysfunctional ones. They deny their feelings as teachers and leaders.

When educators and those who affect their lives act as if emotions aren't important, the consequences can be disastrous, because they still enter into things anyway – but this time by the back door! Festering resentment will undermine and overwhelm rationally made decisions; committee work will be poisoned by members with unresolved grudges and grievances, and curriculum planning will become stilted and boring when teachers have to plan things they don't care about and with people with whom they don't already have a relationship. Totally logical, step-by-step planning may be a satisfactory refuge for obsessive-compulsives, but planning doesn't *have* to be this way, as we shall see shortly.

Educational change initiatives do not just affect teachers' knowledge, skill and problem-solving capacity. They affect a whole web of significant and meaningful relationships that make up the work of schools. Educational change efforts affect teachers' relationships with their students, the parents of those students, and each other. Teachers make heavy emotional investments in these relationships. Their sense of success and satisfaction depends on them. This chapter focuses on one of the most significant emotional aspects of teaching; the emotional relationships that teachers have with their students. What is the nature and importance of these relationships? How do teachers feel about educational changes and change processes in terms of their impact on these relationships?

Caring occupations like teaching call not only for emotional sensitivity; they also require active *emotional labor*. In her classic text on the subject, Hochschild (1983, p. 7) writes:

> This labor requires one to induce or suppress feelings in order to sustain the outward countenance that produces the proper state of mind in others. . . . This kind of labor calls for a coordination of mind and feeling, and it sometimes draws on a source of self that we honor as deep and integral to our personality.

Teaching involves immense amounts of emotional labor. Not just "acting out" feelings superficially like pretending to be disappointed or surprised, but also consciously working oneself up into a state of actually experiencing the necessary feelings that are required to perform one's job well – be these feelings of anger or enthusiasm, coolness or concern. For Hochschild, emotional labor is a largely negative phenomenon. In Hochschild's (1983) view, emotional labor is a largely negative phenomenon – it involves trading in part of the self for the security and reward that people get from their employers, or for the profitable rewards that accrue from commercial encounters. Critics, however, argue that this underplays the pleasures of acting, interplay and playfulness that emotional labor involves (Fineman, 1993). There are also authentic elements of sincere emotional giving that are embedded in the idea of emotional labor, that Hochschild's partner concept of emotion work doesn't seem to capture.

Emotional labor is an important part of teaching, and in many ways, a positive one. It is a labor of love. Classrooms would be (and sometimes are) barren and boring places without it. With Hochschild, though, it is also important to recognize that emotional labor also exposes teachers, making them vulnerable when the conditions of and demands on their work make it hard for them to do their "emotion work" properly (Ben-Peretz, 1996).

METHODS

This chapter examines some aspects of the emotions of teaching and educational change among 32 Grade 7 and 8 teachers in four school boards (districts) close to the City of Toronto in Ontario, Canada. The teachers had all been identified by administrators in their school systems as having a serious and sustained commitment to implementing common learning outcomes, (or standards) integrated curriculum and alternative forms of assessment and reporting in their classes. These reforms were province (state) level priorities at the Grade 7, 8 and 9 level, and indeed a broad framework of common learning outcomes had been set by the province as a basis for school-level curriculum planning.

All teachers and their principals were interviewed individually in 1995 for between one and two hours about their perceptions of and responses to the changes in curriculum and assessment, about the relationship these changes had to their previous experiences in teaching, about their orientations to change in general, and about how these changes and the ways each teacher dealt with them, articulated with the demands and priorities of their lives outside school.

All interviews have been fully transcribed, generating over 1000 pages of text. Our overall analysis included searching for any references teachers made to the emotional aspects of their work. We picked out any references to how teachers felt about their work (though sometimes 'I feel' seemed to be used as a synonym for 'I think' or 'I know'). Excerpts that involved the use of emotion-words like angry, frustrated, guilty, happy, comfortable or excited, were also extracted. This created a large emotion-file that itself ran to hundreds of transcribed pages in length.

This file was then subcategorized into themes like emotional relationships with students, parents, administrators and other colleagues, or emotional responses to changes in curriculum, assessment, reporting etc. Where individual data extracts were relevant to several themes at once they were assigned simultaneously to several files. Every quote was then numbered in its subfile (e.g. emotional relationships to students). Many subfiles contained well over 100 quotations. Summary words or phrases were then assigned to each quotation to elicit further sub-themes within which all relevant quotations were clustered. For example, detailed sub-themes under emotional relationships to students, included references to caring relationships and caring climates; to changing contexts that generated a need for caring; and to structures that supported or inhibited caring. These detailed sub-themes provided the foundation for a narrative interpretation in each case.

We cannot claim that the emotional responses of the teachers in this study are typical of all teachers. Because our sample teachers had serious and sustained commitments to particular changes in curriculum and assessment, our findings cannot be generalized to teachers who are more suspicious of change or indeed resistant to it (Riseborough, 1984; Datnow, forthcoming; Bailey, 1995). Nor can they be generalized to circumstances where changes are unwanted or seen as peripheral to teachers' own purposes (Gitlin & Margonis, 1995). But we believe that our findings do offer significant insights into the emotional experiences of teachers on the leading-edge of particular kinds of change, and for the ways that educational change impacts on these relationships.

STUDENTS AS AN EMOTIONAL FILTER

It was soon obvious in our analysis that educational change affected teachers' emotional responses to the structures, practices, traditions and routines of their working lives by the way that the change was filtered through teachers' feelings about their students. Students were at the heart of their teaching, and at the heart of why many of these teachers diverged from the conventional teaching norm. The emotional goals that teachers had for students and the emotional bonds or relationships that teachers established with them, underpinned virtually everything else the teachers in our study did. Here, I will look closely at how teachers' emotional goals for and connections with their students impact on three more aspects of teaching and teachers' approaches to educational change in particular: planning, pedagogy and structure.

Many teachers' relations with their students are significantly emotional in nature. Indeed, like many elementary teachers, a number of the teachers we interviewed spoke of these relationships in terms of love (Nias, 1989). One teacher described her basic teaching technique as "I love you to death and work you to death and we can still have fun doing it".[2] Another proclaimed:

I love children. I love all ages. I have great deal of trouble with teachers who say "Oh I only like grade 1's. I won't teach anybody else. All other kids are awful." That makes my back just raise right up. I think to myself, "if you don't like kids, you shouldn't be teaching." You have to like kids. You have to like what you are doing a lot, and I do.

Not that these teachers were unrestrained romantics. The teacher quoted above was often tired and frustrated and had felt sick on the morning she was interviewed. Another candidly confessed he felt like strangling his students sometimes. But liking kids remained important; it was integral to the job. Just as Lortie's (1975) classic study of schoolteachers revealed, many of the rewards of teaching among the teachers in our sample were "psychic" in nature. They came from relationships with students, from seeing people change as a result of teachers' own commitments and efforts. "Working with young people and watching them grow" was "a real turn on," said one teacher. That was where her real strength was, "with individual kids". Indeed, as in Lortie's study, many teachers' psychic rewards were to be found in successes with individuals. "The kids; that's what keeps you going – I mean, if you can only help one in your year. . ." Individual students who come back later and have succeeded, who remember and are grateful, are particularly valued. One teacher said, "I'd much rather meet them in five years and say, 'I really remember when we did'. . .; to me that's more valuable". Another commented:

I feel very proud when they come back and say 'We're doing very well. We've got good marks. . . so I feel very good about that, so give us some strokes for that. . .' At the end of it all, they come back and thank you. . . So that makes us feel good that we are doing a lot of the right things.

As teachers talked about their work, they liked to celebrate stories of their efforts with individuals, and of what they had learned from them. One spoke of a "wonderful boy" just arrived at her school from the United States, for whom she had had to make a wide range of curriculum adjustments. Another told of a girl who had "started off completely lost at the beginning of the year" yet who, after involvement in self-evaluation, reflected that "I'm doing so much better and I feel really good, but I don't want to feel conceited". Another teacher described a previously "struggling" child who had responded exceptionally well to an integrated unit on flight, had constructed the most effective airplane, had revealed that he'd been making airplanes since Grade 1, and had thereby proved that in a supportive classroom environment "even an outcast" (as the teacher put it) could have a place to achieve.

The psychic/emotional rewards of teaching fundamentally affected what teachers did as they adjusted their teaching to what they learned about individual students, through conferencing, peer evaluation and other kinds of personal interaction. Teacher after teacher commented on why their emotional relationships with students mattered for the social outcomes they were trying to achieve and for establishing an appropriate emotional climate in which other kinds of learning could take place.

One teacher's "underlying truths" in the classroom included students having respect for themselves and each other. Another also felt that mutual respect was essential and was proud that none of her children were mean-spirited. Many teachers talked about the value of developing and displaying tolerance, especially in contexts of increasing cultural diversity so that "there's not a lot of this 'Oh, you're so stupid; you mean you can't do that?' It's like, 'no, it's not right but look what you've done here. It's just a small mistake." Cooperative groupwork was seen as especially valuable for fostering this kind of tolerance. Running through all these qualities of tolerance and respect, and through the ways teachers tried to develop them was an underlying ethic of care about which feminist writers like Gilligan (1982) and Noddings (1992) have written so eloquently. One of the younger teachers in our sample felt that the whole provincial reform philosophy was very much centered on providing better care for intermediate level students:

> I got a copy [of the Transition Years Reform document] and I looked through it. . . what I think it means is working with students, mentoring them, showing them the connections between school and the real world, showing them the connections between subjects that they are learning in the real world, helping them to develop at a very difficult time in their lives and just being caring and at the same time giving them an academic base for the future.

This teacher wanted students to know that teachers cared about their lives, was proud that she had built a reputation for being fair and caring and felt it important to know the students well if she was going to teach them well. She was aware she could be criticized for caring too much but, she retorted:

> People would say to me in the first few years, "Ah, you've got to toughen up, you're too soft, you're too sensitive, you take everything so seriously". And I'd say to them, even in my first year, I'd say "when I get tough and when I stop caring about what I'm doing then I won't be a teacher anymore and I will stop teaching, so I refuse now. . . and my philosophy of teaching has not changed and that is to be a caring and effective teacher".

Teachers we interviewed wanted to provide a safe, secure environment, a caring environment, a place of comfort that was "not like high school". Indeed, some teachers worried about students "getting lost" in high school when they transferred there in Grade 9.

Educational policies over the previous decade have brought a wider range of special education students into ordinary classes, and teachers' caring orientations were especially visible where this group was concerned. This care did not take the form of pity for or protectiveness towards children who were seen as fundamentally deficient, however. Rather, teachers were particularly pleased when special needs children were successfully integrated with all the others. "I love the fact that they are sitting in groups right now working with everybody else", said one.

Catering for a wide range of differences was technically and emotionally challenging work, however, especially when teachers were inexperienced or felt insufficiently skilled. One teacher "wasn't comfortable" at first because she didn't feel (she) was meeting the needs of both ends", although now, two years later, she felt she could. Committed as she was to caring for students who were exceptional and demanding, one teacher also worried about "the average child", "the gray kids" who were "getting lost", not "getting an equal shake" in all the reform effort.

High achievement did not insulate students from teachers' interventions. Teachers were also concerned about *their* attitudes, effort and emotional responses.

> I had two grade seven students whose parents were upset with me because, according to them, I was picking on them. They went home and told their parents I was picking on them and I was. Because they are two extremely bright children, and they were content to sit there and let everyone else do the work, and not lead, not volunteer, not risk in any discussions, so I picked on them to get them to do more and now both are. And suddenly their marks have gone up and they are both happier and now they are leading and now they are closer to what they could be.

One teacher whose school was in a mainly all-white community felt that it was these sorts of students in particular who needed their cultural horizons broadening, who needed to gain a better sense of being part of a wider global community. Sample teachers in this district increased students' awareness of cultural diversity by introducing "global education" in their integrated curriculum or by bringing visiting speakers of color into the school. In the three other and more culturally diverse districts in our study, teachers were confronted more directly by the changing multicultural context of their communities and society. Here, cultural diversity was a living, breathing feature of the student body itself. Teachers who commented on the issue, welcomed the opportunities that working in culturally diverse settings provided. One teacher said of her school that she "would be so bored if it wasn't multicultural". Although her example of being able to "talk about what you had for lunch or dinner last night" may be somewhat superficial, other teachers pointed to more dramatic and moving instances of multicultural engagement, such as linking the Holocaust to the lives of children whose relatives had died in other wars in Saudi Arabia, Vietnam or Japan. One recalled how "the little Japanese boy had tears coming down his face as he told how his grandfather had been killed". Another described one way in which he had connected the curriculum cognitively and emotionally, to his students' diverse lives:

> Yes, I really enjoy it (the multicultural dimension of his work). For example, we have a student who has just arrived from Turkey. He speaks very little English. He stays with us for math and then he has ESL. They divide differently. He didn't recognize this symbol when I was doing division. They do it like this, some other way. It is nice to share that. They don't do order of operation at all. The concept just floored him. Some other kids backed that up and said: "Yeah, my parents don't do that, they don't understand order of operation. They've never seen it before." So it is kind of neat for us to go, "yeah, just because we are doing this, doesn't mean that it is the be all and end all or it doesn't mean that everybody else is doing it." It allows me to do

things like that and to celebrate differences. We bring in different opinions about things, like women and how they are treated in other cultures. One of the girls did a report on a book about a Muslim girl who had to fight for independence in her family because of the role of women in that culture. . . It teaches them to be more tolerant. It makes an anti-racism unit a lot more meaningful than when you are doing it with an all-white, affluent group of kids going. "Yeah, we shouldn't be racist and feeling all pompous about it."

By focusing on the emotional responses of the project teachers, we were able to rethink what's important about educational change, indeed to revisit what educational change should be for. Our data clearly show that this classroom focus extends beyond issues of instruction. Teachers' classroom commitments also encompass their emotional relationships with and connections to students; their desire to care for students; to develop them as tolerant and respectful citizens and not merely high performing learners and future workers; to develop their students' social skills as well as their academic knowledge and to create an inclusive atmosphere where students with special needs from diverse backgrounds and/or from non-conventional home circumstances can feel equally comfortable and accepted.

Teachers' emotional connections to students, and the social and emotional goals they wanted to achieve as they taught those students, shaped and influenced almost everything they did, along with how they responded to changes that affected what they did. Teachers wanted to become better so they could help their students. The emotional bond teachers had with their students was central to how they taught them, how they evaluated them, what kinds of curriculum they planned and selected for them, and what kinds of organizational structures they adopted as a context for teaching them.

FEELINGS ABOUT STRUCTURE

How our sample teachers felt about something as seemingly abstract as the structures in which they work, was very much influenced by whether they felt these structures would benefit their students or not. The majority of teachers' remarks about structures and structural change came from the district where the most systematic attempts had been made to build curriculum integration, to establish a core-block of time for integrated studies within the timetable, and in some cases, to encourage teachers to follow their classes from one grade to the next. Teachers were consistently positive about the benefits of the new core structures for students, and for their relationships with students. They did not like the way conventional rotary timetables with separate teachers, subjects and short, lesson periods, fragmented their relationships with students. "The kids really need that one person they can relate to in school", said one teacher. A core-blocked timetable, where teachers were with the same class of students for at least half the day, made such relationships possible. It was now easier for "children through their adolescence to bond with one teacher". In one school, this had been very important for being able to care for one particularly difficult group of students, the "hell kids" who created immense problems for teachers with whom they did not have this kind of bond. Following students through from one year to the next meant that "because you know them so well, you know their moods and you can start right in with them". "You can see the change in growth". Because of following students year to year, "I know my kids, and I call them my kids, and I know what they're about. I know what they're doing inside and outside of school. I know their families, especially if you have them for more than a year", and as teachers see students grow and mature, it's wonderful to see that process.

A number of teachers commented on the advantages of the more open time structures that core blocking allowed. They "felt comfortable" with the open time-lines, didn't "feel constricted" by them and would "love having them (students) the whole day", if they could. Open timelines enabled teachers to keep "rolling" with the projects, to go with the flow.

> Where you have the children for a morning and there are no time lines, for example if you find you are rolling with a project or they start asking, "Can we go into the library to look up this" or "we want to find out more about this", there are a lot of teachers feeling comfortable saying, "Go for it! and maybe we don't get to math this morning, but yeah we'll do more math later on during the week".

> I can help any kid learn anything as long as he is motivated and I feel that I can motivate a kid through reality, natural situations, so that allows me to set-up, but in order to do that I have to be able to have block periods of time to set-up situations where I can show them the reality of this and to me that's a great thing. I get rolling on something and if the kids get rolling on something I don't want to be stopped by a bell telling me to move on, so I welcome it.

> . . .we had some kids involved in smoking in my class and I was really upset with them, and it was a perfect time. They were all upset, how could they have done that and be stupid enough and the kid had smoked so much. . . that she literally was drunk on it, she could not walk a straight line. They were so concerned. Whereas if it's a rotary class, pack up way you go. . . It was a good learning experience for the other kids to see. She sat there and she had her head on her desk and we talked about it. . . It was a wonderful learning experience that you won't get out of a textbook and that I'm not dictated to by a clock. I mean they don't come up everyday but when they do, you really appreciate that time that you can. . . bond with the kids.

While alternative structures made these change-oriented teachers feel they could care for their students and teach them more effectively, the persistence of more conventional structural arrangements could make it harder for them to do so, fracturing their relationships, undermining their planning, and overloading them with other obligations. A guidance teacher whose specialist teaching load was spread across many classes wanted time to do team-building, to "connect more" with the students. Another teacher mentioned how before the core blocking arrangements, the previous timetable was "horrible", "just brutal" in the way it fragmented contacts with students into 40 minute slots.

When teachers supported structures that supported their students, they did not do so in a self-sacrificing way, however. Teachers who worked in more open time structures felt more comfortable with them when many of their colleagues did not. When one school printed out its new timetable with a large allocation to core, some teachers were "more comfortable getting out their rulers and blocking the periods off and putting specific subjects back in". But teachers in our sample who worked in a larger core, liked to adjust the time to the learning rather than vice versa, and welcomed the flexibility to do that (see also Lieberman, 1995; Adelman & Walking-Eagle, 1997). In this respect, their desires for structures that would support students, and their own sense of what kinds of structures were comfortable for themselves as teachers, were closely aligned with each other. Their students' emotional needs and their own emotional rewards were attuned to each other.

FEELINGS ABOUT PEDAGOGY

Pedagogy is one of the great rhetorical battlegrounds of educational reform. Many studies portray classroom teachers as still being predominantly wedded to traditional patterns of instruction, such as lecturing, seatwork and question-and-answer methods (Hargreaves, Earl, & Ryan, 1996; Goodlad, 1984; Tye, 1985). Conversely, there has been an international assault on the supposed pervasiveness of and excessive adherence to groupwork and project work in elementary and intermediate teachers' classes, at the expense of whole class teaching (Nikoforuk, 1993; Woodhead, 1995). Meanwhile, new pedagogical approaches like reading recovery, cooperative learning, or manipulative mathematics, surface regularly, each with its own bold claims about achieving significant gains in student learning. Ideologically, teaching has become a pedagogical quagmire.

Interestingly, very few of our interviewees seemed to believe in one best approach to teaching. Most of them valued and said they actually used a wide variety of teaching strategies. Between them, the teachers we interviewed listed a formidable array of methods that they used in their teaching. These included concept attainment, mind-mapping, individual conferencing, "traditional" teaching, cooperative learning, individualization, "real time" assignments, visiting speakers, twinning with high school classes, special events like inventors' festivals, video, television, visual things in general, humor, enthusing students by doing "crazy things", creating "hands-on" experiences, setting puzzles or problems, organizing student oral presentations, using natural situations, having a "talking bucket" which children could use to speak about items of concern to them, computer data analysis, portfolios, out-of-school visits, kinesthetic learning such as walking around the circumference of circles, peer coaching, peer teaching, reading and writing workshops, roundtable discussions, working in pairs, role play, brainstorming and dramatic presentation.

Not all teachers claimed to use all these methods, of course. But the overall range is extensive; and indeed having and using a broad repertoire of teaching strategies mattered greatly to almost every teacher in this group. Teachers used "a lot of variety", "a combination of methods"; they saw themselves as "a multi-strategy person" and "liked to mix things". "I can't say that I have one strategy that I use", said one. Another teacher said that ideally, he would "love to see every teacher using a variety of strategies". Even a teacher who referred to being "indoctrinated with cooperative learning" said:

> I don't do one thing all the time. I do direct teacher teaching at the front of the room; I do pair work with the kids; I do cooperative learning; I do social skills teaching; I like an eclectic mix so that I can make things as interesting and effective as I can.

In opting for variety, what mattered most was making things interesting and effective for students. Having a wide repertoire could enable the teacher to "help any kid learn anything as long as he is motivated". As one teacher put it, "all I know is that I like to use as many different things as I can in my classroom to reach as many kids as I can in different ways and make things interesting". "Just anything that will work" would be a good pedagogical motto for most of the teachers in our sample.

Most of the study teachers included "traditional" teaching in what they felt would work with students. Few, if any of them were shrinking violets, happy to be quiet facilitators, mere "guides-by-the-side". While they favored cooperative learning, hands-on learning and learning that was like real life, these teachers also saw a strong place for traditional teaching, or "old teaching" as one called it, within their wider repertoire. One interviewee said about her teaching:

> You'd see a lot of variety and you'd see some pretty aggressive teaching. I like to be seen. I like to be heard. I like to move. I like to make sure that people are still with me. I like to be excited about what I'm teaching, even if its bland (material).

Many of the teachers portrayed themselves as vivid and vital presences in their own classrooms. They were not only facilitators; they were definitely teachers as well. One teacher was "not ashamed" that she "loved to present". She took pride in the fact. A teacher of French immersion said, "I think in second language teaching, you have to be prepared to dance and stand on your head and do just about anything to get kids to understand and respond and participate". As an example, she described how in one class, she had jumped from one table to the next as she role-played a naval battle in the middle of the Atlantic.

Teachers drew on a broad repertoire of strategies to try and reach their students, get them motivated, help them understand. The methods they used were determined, in many ways, by what they felt their students needed emotionally as well as intellectually. Teachers talked about changing their teaching so it meshed with what their students wanted, using support strategies that raised the comfort level of students with learning difficulties, trying "to involve the kids as much as possible – find out their interests", using portfolios to discover what children found "fun" so this could be incorporated into teaching them, not "acting as if I am the boss and as if I know everything" so that the classroom could "be a safe place where people can be free to express their ideas", creating an atmosphere where students could feel comfortable interrupting or asking questions, playing with students, encouraging them to share their feelings, finding ways to get students to support each other, and even playing soft background music if it helped children perform better in tests .

Through all this, some teachers felt that one of the most important strategies was humor. "I love to use humor as an effective tool", said one, "because it's a great equalizer. It breaks the tension and the stress". More than this, it was important to be yourself as a teacher, and to let your own emotions and feelings show through from time to time. As Farson (1996) says, it is indeed in moments when we *lose* control rather than exert it, that our humanity as leaders shines through. One teacher recalled how, "the more I imposed superstructures that were not me – and the kids knew it – it didn't function as well". Another described how he and his teaching partner would sometimes "do silly things together, in front of the kids", like throwing pies at each other. Humor was what made them human to each other and to their students – it was important that their emotional selves shone through, that they could "let go" occasionally, even to the point where students could sometimes scarcely believe what their teachers did (see also Woods, 1983).

The teaching strategies that teachers used were shaped by their own emotional needs, as well as those of their students. Excitement and enjoyment figured strongly among those needs. Teachers would talk about how they would "really enjoy getting them (their students) involved" or about the excitement of special events or performances like an innovation festival, where students could present their work authentically, to real audiences outside school. One teacher described her concept attainment lesson on relationships in ways that connected her own excitement to that of the students:

> I was so excited about it, and really when I started, I didn't know how it was going to work, but it took a long time, but oh, it was ever so powerful, because these kids, I'm sure if I went out in the schoolyard now, they'd tell me what "relationship" means because they developed it.

Another teacher recalled how he'd caused laughter in an inservice workshop by saying that cooperative learning had now passed sex on his list of priorities. A third teacher talked more generally about her ongoing emotional needs as a teacher:

> I also, myself as a person, I have to change every year. I have to get excited about what I'm doing and if I see myself going forward, I'm fine. Like probably the most exciting things are the fact that we are bringing in more 'real

time' people with the junior program and we're doing some more twinning with the high school, and so on. And I think for instance, if you're looking at global customs or man-made hazards globally, those are "real time" things and the kids get excited about those too.

As with many of her colleagues, this teacher's remarks pointed to the positive aspects of her work as emotional labor (Hochschild, 1983; Hargreaves, 1997). She cared for her clients and worked hard to get herself excited so she could meet their needs, while staving off the ever-present threat of boredom, routine and stagnation. Going forward, developing and changing pedagogical was important for many teachers in our sample (who by definition had been identified as having a serious and sustained commitment to educational change):

I'm a much better teacher than I ever was. I am much more aware of the kids' needs. I don't think I would say I was afraid of dealing with special ed. kids or gifted kids, but I don't think I was really confident in what I was doing and what was best for them. But now I know it is. I know what works for them.

For some, this sense of growing confidence and competence was especially accented in their early years of becoming a teacher. This time is typically one of early classroom survival, establishing your authority as a teacher, and moving beyond preoccupations with yourself and your own insecurities, to addressing the needs of your students, through a bank of knowledge and strategies that you have begun to accumulate over time (Sikes, Measor, & Woods, 1985; Huberman, 1993) as one of the teachers put it:

My first year, I never even looked at the kids. Looking back, I kind of go, "OK, that's OK – it was my first year and they all warned me that I would do that". You are so concerned with yourself and where you are at and whether your attendance is done and all of that stuff, that you have forgotten to look out to them and see where they are at and what their needs are. I am doing that a lot more now because I am feeling more comfortable about what I am doing. And I am realizing that the more interesting I make things and the more that what I do here is different from other classrooms, the more interested they are going to be. I feel freer to try new things and not worry if it goes overtime. If I don't finish one unit, I don't mind about it.

Part of the challenge of change and development for teachers was struggling with letting go of old conceptions, familiar practices, and comforting routines.

Well, I taught Math the first two years I was on staff and I was in a portable, the desk were in rows. This is what I left in '74. And that was a big change, getting the groupwork going in the core area. It was already set up in desks. And I thought the first couple of weeks, I was going to go nuts with the noise. But then I realized this is very productive.

Integrating new ideas and techniques recently acquired on professional development courses was equally challenging in both technical and emotional terms:

What I've been doing over my last two years of teaching is learn as much as I can and do things over and over again until I feel comfortable with them. So things that I learned in the cooperative learning institute the first time, I may only have used once or twice. But I have them in my teaching repertoire now, and when I know that it's going to be effective, I will use it again.

To sum up: most teachers were committed to having or developing a broad repertoire of teaching strategies. How they drew on this repertoire at any time was shaped by their relationships with students, their feelings about what would excite and engage students emotionally, and their feelings about what would excite and engage themselves as teachers. Building and maintaining such excitement and enjoyment was at the heart of the emotional labor of teaching, of what made teachers want to change and develop pedagogically, and of what made them take pride in that development over time.

FEELINGS ABOUT CURRICULUM PLANNING

Few areas of teachers' work seem as ostensibly unemotional as planning. Yet, for the teachers in our study curriculum planning was not constrained by stilted formats, excessively packed with overly detailed targets, or mapped backwards from abstract ends. Rather, teachers started with knowledge and feelings about their students, with *intuitive understandings* about what would be likely to excite and engage those students, and with their own passions and enthusiasms about ideas, topics, materials and methods that they could picture working with their classes. Teachers described how they loved writing curriculum, making things "richer for kids", in ways that were "practical" and "exciting".

Emotions as we saw earlier, are about psychological movement. In this sense, it is interesting that the teachers in our study described their excitement of developing ideas with colleagues in vivid, kinesthetic metaphors that portrayed planning as being full of creativity, movement and emotional intensity. Planning for outcomes began with teachers' own passions and their feelings about the students. Ideas for new integrated units were "brainstormed" by teachers together and sometimes with students who were made part of the planning process too. They were "piggy-backed" on one another, "bounced off" people, or generally "bashed around". Teachers would work together in teams to "capture those learners", be "springboards" for each other, "spin off" one another's ideas, "take risks", "go nuts" and engage in a "free-for-all", so that the planning process became "like a pinball machine" for them.

The feeling of freedom in planning was exceptionally important, for our sample teachers. It offered the opportunity to let the ideas and the brainstorming with colleagues flow. Indeed two of the teachers specifically talked about their experiences of planning in terms of recognizing the *flow* and making the meetings really *flow*. Csikzentmihalyi (1990) describes *flow* as a state of concentration so focused that it amounts to absolute absorption in an activity. Flow, he says, is the necessary ingredient for optimal experience and quality of life. For Goleman (1995:90)

> flow represents the ultimate in harnessing the emotions in the service of performance and learning. In flow, the emotions are not just contained and channeled, but positive, energized, and aligned with the task in hand.

"To be caught in the ennui of depression or the agitation of anxiety", Goleman continues, "is to be barred from flow". This is exactly what happened when planning processes and formats were imposed, when planning partners were not chosen, when planning purposes were unclear or not owned by those engaged in the planning, and when the "connections for the kids" were not evident. Teachers used very different metaphors to describe these kinds of planning – "stifled", coming across "stumbling blocks" or being "bogged down in cement". Rational planning has come in for criticism in recent years because of its failure to deal with the highly complex, uncertain and rapidly changing environments of today (Mintzberg, 1994). Our data suggest that rational planning models are also flawed because they take no account of the emotions.

Freer, flow-like approaches to planning among our leading-edge teachers did not exclude attention to goals or outcomes. But it was only later, as the course of study started to take shape, that many teachers would return to the list of prescribed outcomes, as a checklist, to see if they missed anything and to ensure their curriculum was balanced. Overall, while outcomes were still included in these more open-ended and flexible forms of planning, the emotionally charged way that our sample teachers appeared to plan in practice seemed sharply at odds with the more purely rational process of backward mapping implied by outcomes-based education. For them, curriculum planning engaged their emotions. It flowed. It was attentive to general goals and ends but not dominated by them. Such planning began with the teachers' emotional connections to students and was sustained by their emotional engagement in and excitement about the creative, interactive aspects of the process itself. Once more, students' emotional needs and teachers' emotional engagements in a creative, flexible labor process of teaching, were reciprocally attuned to each other.

CONCLUSION

Teaching cannot be reduced to technical competence or clinical standards. It involves significant emotional labor as well. The teachers in our study valued the emotional bonds they established with students, and valued educating their students as emotional and social beings as well as intellectual ones. Teachers' emotional commitments and connections to students energized and articulated everything these teachers did: including how they taught, how they planned, and the structures in which they preferred to teach. One important way in which teachers interpreted the educational changes that were imposed on them as well as the ones they developed themselves, was in terms of the impact these changes had on their own emotional goals and relationships. It is time for educational change strategies and reform efforts and definitions of teaching and learning standards to come to terms with and embrace these emotional dimensions of teaching and learning. For without attention to the emotions, educational reform efforts may ignore and even damage some of the most fundamental aspects of what teachers do.

REFERENCES

Adelman, N. E., & Walking-Eagle, K. P. (1997). Teachers, time and school reform. In A. Hargreaves (Ed.), ASCD Yearbook, *Rethinking educational change with heart and mind.* Alexandria, Virginia: Association for Supervision and Curriculum Development, 92–110.

Bailey, B. (1995). *Teachers marginalized by mandated change.* Unpublished doctoral thesis, Toronto, Ontario Institute for Studies in Education.

Ben-Peretz, M. (1996). Women as teachers: Teachers as women. In I. F. Goodson & A. Hargreaves (Eds.), *Teachers' Professional Lives.* London: Falmer Press.

Csikzentmihalyi, M. (1990). *Flow: The Problem of Optimal Experience.* New York: Harper Collins.

Damasio, A. (1994). *Descartes' error: Emotion, reason and the human brain.* New York: Grosset/ Putman

Datnow, A. (forthcoming). *The gender politics of educational change.* London & New York: Falmer Press.

Farson, R. (1996). *Management of the absurd: Paradoxes in leadership.* New York: Simon & Schuster.

Fineman, S. (1993). Organizations as emotional arenas. In S. Fineman (Ed.), *Emotion in organizations,* London: Sage.

Fried, R. L. (1995). *The passionate teacher.* Boston: Beacon Press.

Fullan, M. (1991). *The new meaning of educational change* (with S. Stiegelbauer). New York: Teachers' College Press

Fullan, M. (1993). *Change forces: Probing the depths of educational reform.* Philadephia, PA: Falmer Press

Gilligan, C. (1982). *In a different voice: Psychological theory and women's development.* Cambridge, Mass: Harvard University Press.

Gitlin, A., & Margonis, F. (1995). The political aspect of reform: Teacher resistance as good sense. *American Journal of Education, 103,* 377–405.

Goleman, D. (1995). *Emotional intelligence.* New York: Bantam Books.

Goodlad, J. I. (1984). *A place called school: Prospects for the future.* New York: McGrawHill.

Hargreaves, A, Earl, L. & Ryan J. (1996). *Schooling for change: Reinventing education for early adolescents,* London: Falmer Press.

Hargreaves, A. (1997). Rethinking Educational change: Going deeper and wider in the quest for success. In A. Hargreaves (Ed.), ASCD Yearbook, *Rethinking educational change with heart and mind.* Alexandria, Virginia: Association for Supervision and Curriculum Development, 1–26.

Hochschild, A. R. (1983). *The managed heart: Commercialization of human feeling.* Berkeley: University of California Press

Hopfl, & Linstead, (1993). Passion and performance: Suffering and the carrying of organizational roles. In S. Fineman (Ed.), *Emotion in organizations,* London: Sage

Huberman, M. (1993). *The lives of teachers.* London: Cassell and New York: Teachers' College Press.

Koestler, A. (1967). *The ghost in the machine.* London: Hutchinson.

Lieberman, A. (1995). *The Work of restructuring schools.* New York: Teachers' College Press.

Lortie, D. (1975). *Schoolteacher: A sociological study.* Chicago: University of Chicago Press.

Louis, K. S., & Miles, M. (1990). *Improving the urban high school: The what and how.* New York: Teachers' College Press.

McLaughlin, M. W. (1990). The Rand change agent study: Macro perspective and micro-realities. *Educational Researcher,* (December), 11–16.

Miles, M. B. & Huberman, A. M. (1984). *Innovation up close: How school improvement works.* New York: Plenum Press

Mintzberg, H. (1994). *The rise and fall of strategic planning.* New York, NY: Free Press

Newmann, F., & Wehlage, G. (1995). *Successful school restructuring.* Madison, Wis: Centre on Organization and Restructuring of Schools

Nias, J. (1989). *Primary teachers talking*. London: Routledge & Kegan Paul.

Nikiforuk, A. (1993). *School's out*: *The catastrophe in public education and what we can do about it*. Toronto: Macfarlane Walter and Ross

Noddings, N. (1992). *The challenge to care in schools*. New York: Teachers' College Press.

Riseborough, G. F. (1981). Teacher careers and comprehensive schooling: An empirical study. *Sociology*, **15**(3), 352–381.

Sacks, O. (1995). *An anthropologist on Mars*. Toronto: Alfred A. Knopf

Sarason, S. (1990). *The predictable failure of educational reform*. San Francisco, CA: Jossey-Bass

Sikes, P., Measor, L., & Woods, P. (1985). *Teacher careers: Crises and continuities*. Lewes: Falmer Press.

Tye, B. (1985). *Multiple realities: A study of 13 American high schools*. Lanham: University Press of America.

Woodhead, C. (1995). *Education – the elusive engagement and the continuing frustration*. TES p. 3: First Annual Lecture to HM Chief Inspectors.

Woods, P. (1983). *Sociology and the school*. London: Routledge and Kegan Paul.

Woods, P., & Jeffrey, B. (1996). *Teachable moments*. Buckingham: Open University Press

Organization, Market and Community as Strategies for Change: What Works Best for Deep Changes in Schools

THOMAS J. SERGIOVANNI

Department of Education, Trinity University

How one approaches changing a school or an educational system depends, fundamentally, on one's views about what kinds of places schools really are or should be. In this chapter, Tom Sergiovanni describes three dominant perspectives on schooling and the change strategies that spring from them – schools as bureaucratic organizations, schools as market systems, and schools as communities.

In each of these models, Sergiovanni describes how different forces of change can be used to leverage change in schools – bureaucratic forces of rules, requirements, procedures and outcomes; personal forces of leadership and personality; market forces of choice and competition; professional forces of self-set standards, codes of conduct and norms of service; cultural forces of values and relationships; and democratic forces of contracts and commitments to the common good.

Sergiovanni then charts how these forms and forces of schooling play themselves out in different patterns of reform – evaluating the strengths and weaknesses of each. In the end, he argues, "deep changes in schools, may well require that the basic metaphor for the school itself be changed from formal organization or market to community".

Organization, market and community are three strategies now being advocated by different reformers to leverage change in schools. The strategy preferred is a function of the reformer's theory for the school and the reformer's view of human nature. Different theories and views have different strengths. Organization and market are effective for bringing about efficient change in school structures over the short term. Community is effective for bringing about deep change in the operational core of the schools. Deep change involves changes in fundamental relationships, in understandings of subject matter, pedagogy and how students learn, in teachers' skills, in teaching behavior, and in student performance. Though many changes have taken place in school structures and arrangements, few can be considered as deep changes (see for example Newmann, Marks and Gamoran, 1995; Marks, Seashore, & Louis, 1995; Elmore, Peterson & McCarthey, 1995; and Elmore, 1995).

In accounting for the intractable nature of existing patterns of teaching and learning, Quartz (1995) proposes that schools are characterized by a "dominant culture of stabilizing reform" that aims to refine existing teaching practice but not to allow radical changes to occur (p. 240). Stability and change, it appears, co-exist because of the tendency of stability to absorb changes without altering underlying forms and assumptions. This tendency is reminiscent of Mannheim's (1940) observation that human beings and their institutions have a tendency to understand

A. Hargreaves (ed.), Extending Educational Change, 296-315.
© 2005 *Springer. Printed in the Netherlands.*

new things in terms of existing categories; and, of March and Simon's (1958) principle of uncertainty absorption which explains the predisposition of organizations to understand new things in old ways.

The tendency for schools to remain stable is attributed to a network of assumptions, beliefs, regularities and traditions that comprise norms which define, and then provide, meaning for teachers. These collective meanings help teachers make sense of their existing practices, affirm their sense of purpose, and help them to rationally accept the social situations they experience in schools. At root, then, changes in relationships, teaching practice and student learning involve changes in school culture. But before school culture can change, meanings that are both collectively and individually held must change. Perhaps things would be different if it were possible to move instantly from one set of meanings to another. The period in between causes the difficulty. Changing a culture requires that people, both individually and collectively, move from something familiar and important into an empty space. And then once they are in this empty space, to build a new set of meanings – a new set of norms, a new cultural order to fill it up. Deep change, in other words, requires the reconstructing of existing individual and collective mindscapes of practice. Mindscapes are implicit mental frames through which the reality of schooling and our place in it are envisioned.

SCHOOLS AS ORGANIZATIONS, MARKETS OR COMMUNITIES?

Perspectives on how to bring about change in schools are a function of the way change agents understand the nature of schools as organized entities and a function of the way change agents understand human nature itself. This section examines the first of these understandings noting that differences between these understandings lead to different kinds of policies, strategies and practices in educational change. Some of these policies, strategies and practices are more effective in bringing about deep change than others. Successful change it is argued, will result from approaches to change that match the unique cultural requirements of schools and match the unique operational requirements for new teaching and learning.

What are the images of schools that shape the way different change agents think about change? Most change agents view schools as formal organizations that share characteristics and features with other formal organizations. This view of organizations qua organizations allows for easy transfer to the school of assumptions and practices from the generic world of formal organizations. Thus, strategies for change (along with strategies for leadership, motivation, organization and accountability) that work well in formal organizations found in the corporate world and in other sectors of our society are generally assumed to apply to the school (Sergiovanni, 1996). This assumption accounts for why corporate restructuring images of downsizing, standards setting and accountability play such a large role in school reform efforts and why images from other sectors of our society (the worlds of civic, social and familial enterprises for example) are often overlooked.

Many respected voices in organizational theory, however, take a more differentiated view believing that formal organizations represent only one of several conceptions of human association. Ouchi (1980), for example, defines organizations as "any stable pattern of transactions between individuals or aggregations of individuals" (p. 140). He differentiates between three organizational types by the different ways organizations mediate transactions among people, and between people and their work. This mediation of transactions is necessary, he argues, to get cooperative effort towards organizational goals. Cooperation is a key issue because left alone, people are likely to pursue incongruent goals. Cooperative action requires that people become interdependent. Interdependence, in turn, calls for transactions among people and between them and organizational expectations. These transactions involve social relationships. "Social relationships denote the behavior of a plurality of actors in so far as, in its meaningful content, the action of each takes account of that of others and is oriented in these terms" (Weber, 1947 as cited in Eisenstadt, 1968: p. xxxv).

The three organizational types identified by Ouchi are bureaucracies, markets and clans. Bureaucracies mediate transactions by developing rational systems of expectations, by placing value on member contributions directed to achieving expectations, by providing supervision, rules and other means to guide and enable the process, and by compensating fairly. Markets mediate transactions by relying on the "natural" interdependence that emerges from interactions among people that take the form of trading compliance for desired incentives. Within markets, transactions between people and their different interests are viewed as commodities that, when traded, are capable of yielding mutual advantage in an efficient way. Clans, by contrast, mediate transactions and build interdependence by relying on connecting people to shared values and beliefs and relying on emergent norms that discourage opportunistic behavior and that promote commitment to the common good.

Ouchi's differentiation of organizational types raises important questions. If different organizational types exist, then a more effective approach to reforming schools would be to first identify the organizational type that best fits the school and then to adopt a particularistic approach to understanding change that leads to the development of unique change strategies for the school. Treating all organized entities the same and indiscriminately transferring practices from one to the other can result in a category error that raises questions of validity. If schools should not be viewed as formal organizations but as something else (perhaps markets or communities as discussed in this chapter) then a borrowed motivational, leadership or change strategy that may have been valid in its original context may not be valid in schools.[1]

CHANGE FORCES

Given this tradition of differentiating among organizational types, schools can be viewed in different ways. Different ways are embodied in different assumptions and beliefs that create different change realities. These realities become the basis for how we think and for the change policies and practices we create and use to reform schools. Three broad strategies for change now compete for attention. Each strategy stems from a particular view of the school: formal organization, market or community. Each view relies on different change forces for leveraging change in schools.[2] Six change forces are examined in this chapter: bureaucratic, personal, market, professional, cultural and democratic. Each of the forces rely on different change practices to leverage change:

- bureaucratic forces rely on rules, mandates and requirements to provide direct supervision, standardized work processes and or standardized outcomes to prescribe change.
- personal forces rely on personality, leadership style and interpersonal skills of change agents to motivate change.
- market forces rely on competition, incentives and individual choice to motivate change.
- professional forces rely on standards of expertise, codes of conduct, collegiality, felt obligations and other professional norms to build professional community.
- cultural forces rely on shared values, goals and ideas about pedagogy, relationships and politics to build covenantal community.
- democratic forces rely on democratic social contracts and shared commitments to the common good to build democratic community.

Table 1, summarizes each of the six forces for leveraging change in schools by comparing practices associated with each as well as their legacies, underlying theories of human behavior, how teachers are involved in change, and consequences for change in schools.

Bureaucratic and personal change forces are commonly chosen by those who view schools as bureaucratic or organic formal organizations. Bureaucratic forces rely on rules, mandates and requirements that provide direct supervision, standardized work processes, and standardized outcomes to prescribe changes. Personal forces rely on the personality, leadership styles and interpersonal skills of change agents to motivate people to change. Market forces, by contrast, are not organizationally oriented. Instead they rely on competition, incentives and individual choice to motivate change.

Reformers who view schools as communities advocate the use of professional, cultural and democratic forces to leverage change. Professional forces rely on standards of expertise, codes of conduct, collegiality, felt obligations and other professional norms to build professional community. Cultural forces rely on cultivating shared values, goals and ideas about pedagogy, relationships, and politics that provide norms of obligations and commitments to build covenantal community. Democratic forces rely on the development of social contracts and shared commitments to the common good to build democratic community. While bureaucratic personal and market forces strive to motivate or otherwise induce

Table 1: Change Forces, Theories and Consequencies in Organizations, Markets and Communities

Mindscapes for the School	Change Forces	Change Practices	Legacy	Theories of Human Nature	Teacher Involvement in Change	Change Consequences	Observed Changes
Bureaucratic formal organizations	Bureaucratic	1. Rely on rule, mandates and requirements to provide direct supervision, standardized work process and or standardized outcomes to presribe change.	*Bureaucractic Values* rationality efficiency uniformity	*constrained*: the visible hand of rational choice theory linked to penalties is necessary to motivate change	calculated	Teacher change just enough to avoid sanction. Change stops when sanctions are removed.	changes in structure, timetables and arrangements.
Organimic formal organizations	Personal	2. Rely on personality, leadrship style and interpersonal skills of change agents to motivate change.	*Human Relations Values* needs based motivational theories interpersonal leadership	*constrained*: the visible hand of rational choice theory linked to psychological rewards is necessary to motivate change.	calculated	Teachers change just enough to receive gratification of needs. Change stops when rewards are not available.	change in structures, timetables and arranagements.
Market Place	Market	3. Rely on competition, incentives and individual choice to motivate change.	*Market Values* Behavioural theory evolutionary biology economics	*constrained*: the indivisible hand of rational choice theory linked to individual self-interest is necessary to motivate change.	calculated	Teachers change just enough to win in the market place. Winning becomes less important after repeated losses.	mixed but not enduring

Table 1: Continued

Mindscapes for the School	Change Forces	Change Practices	Legacy	Theories of Human Nature	Teacher Involvement in Change	Change Consequences	Observed Changes
Professional Community	Professional	4. Rely on standards of expertise, coded of conduct, collegiality, felt obligations and other professional norms to build professional community.	*Professional Values* competence continuous learning altruism personal responsibility	*unconstrained*: the visible hand of professional socialization provides standards of practice and norms that compel change.	ethical	Teachers internalise norms of competence and virtue that compel change.	deep changes that endure
Conventional Learning Community	Cultural	5. Rely on shared values, goals and ideaqs about pedagogy, relationships and politics to build convenantal community.	*Community Values* convenantal relationships caring community personal responsibility	*unconstrained*: the invisible hand of community norms, values, and ideas that speak in a moral voice to compel change.	normal	Teachers internalize community norms that compel change.	deep changes that endure
Democractic Community	Democratic	6. Rely on democratic social contracts and shared commitments to the common goal to build democratic community.	*Democratic Values* constitution bill of rights civic virtue citizenship	*unconstrained*: the invisible hand of democratic traditions and internalized norms that compel change.	moral	Teachers internalize democratic norms that compel change.	deep changes that endure

change directly, professional, cultural and democratic forces seek to provide the conditions that result in the emergence of standards and norms that compel changes.

KEY MEDIATING VARIABLES

The deciding factor in determining whether change strategies based on a particular force are likely to be successful in bringing about deep changes in schools is their ability to influence key mediating variables in the change equation. These variables include the extent to which teachers are connected to shared norms that support proposed changes; the extent to which teachers understand differently the subjects they teach; the extent to which teachers have an expanded understanding of how students learn; and the extent to which teachers have the necessary skills to teach differently. If these key mediating variables are influenced positively by the change forces used, then enduring changes in relationships, teaching practice, and student learning are likely to occur. Patterns of influence among forces, mediating variables and change results are summarized in Figure 1 and discussed below.

Bureaucratic, personal and market forces generally result in changes in school structure. But because these three forces are only loosely connected to the mediating variables, they are less likely to result in deep changes in schools. Professional, cultural and democratic change forces, on the other hand, may or may not result in changes in structure. But because these forces are tightly connected to the mediating variables, they are more likely to be powerful enough to result in deep changes in relationships, teaching practices and student learning.

Prime among the key mediating variables is the capacity of shared norms to influence change. Deep changes require that new pedagogical, relational and political norms be cultivated (see for example Oakes, 1995; Quartz, 1995). Cultivating new beliefs points to the importance of strategies for change that invest heavily in teacher development. New norms, for example, must not only be learned and believed in, but be embodied in teaching practices as well. Embodiment in practice, in turn, presumes that teachers learn the new understandings and skill to practice differently.

Teacher development is advanced as professional community builds and as the school becomes a center of inquiry. Lieberman, Falk and Alexander (1995), for example, point out that teachers need to be "continually engaged in talk about work, values, processes, ideas and concerns" (p. 122). This kind of engagement is enabled by the development of a strong sense of collegiality, collaboration, and professional community in schools. A *situated* model of teacher development, linked to the changes being proposed and anchored in teachers' constructing knowledge for themselves, is an important strategy for influencing the key mediating variables.

Change strategies based on bureaucratic, personal and market forces overlook the importance of helping teachers to develop new understandings of the subjects

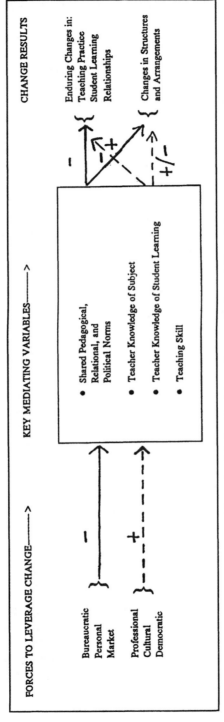

Figure 1:   Relationships between forces, mediating variables and change

they teach and new understandings of how students learn. Regardless of the presence of new norms that encourage change, unless teachers know how to change and are able to change, such change is not likely to occur. David Cohen (1995), for example, points out that systemic change "implies deep changes in at least three areas of instruction: knowledge of academic subjects, and teaching and learning; professional values and commitment; and the social resources of practice" (p. 14). He argues that deep changes require teachers to have a much greater grasp of the disciplines they teach and much more understanding and skill in using this knowledge about the discipline in their teaching. For Cohen it isn't an either/or question. He points out that "Without technical capacity, all the professional values in the world would be useless, but without those norms all the professional knowledge and skill would be impotent" (p. 15).

New relational norms are also key (Quartz, 1995). For the school to become a center of inquiry and for professional community to develop, a collaborative culture that supports deep change needs to be created. Finally new political norms that evolve democratically need to be constructed. These norms can provide the shared ideas that can become the source of authority for what goes on in the school.

THEORIES OF HUMAN NATURE

Different change forces are based on different theories of human nature. The change forces we rely upon are, in effect, statements about how we view people, their capacities, their moral propensities, and their motivational nature. Theories of human nature are at the center of prescriptions, legal systems, constitutions, contracts, socialization patterns, norm systems and other attempts to define human action and to codify human behavior. They determine how we treat others and others treat us. They determine what is just and good and what is unjust and evil. Theories of human nature define our existence.

Thomas Hobbes (1950) believed that human nature has both a reasonable side rooted in moral conceptions of goodness and a passionate side rooted in psychological egoism. The reasonable side includes our *capacity* to embody such virtues as altruism, moral bearing, self-sacrifice and cooperation aimed at the enhancement at what we believe to be the common good. The passionate side recognizes our *propensity* to satisfy our physical and psychological needs, to compete to win, and to accumulate wealth aimed at enhancing our own pleasure.

Hobbes (1950), reminiscent of Aristotle, believed that humankind's passionate side was a natural condition. The rational side by contrast, was artificial having been achieved by committing to covenants that are culturally determined. Development of the rational side depends upon our becoming morally responsive. As Frankena (1973) notes, "to have morality one must accept, believe in, or subscribe to, and judge by, some moral value system or other, though it need not actually be very systematic" (p. 28). And Kant (1959) believed that, for any action to have moral worth it must be done from duty (p. 16). Duty, in turn, is covenantal in nature because it is connected to conceptions of the common good and commitments to ideals (Sergiovanni, 1992).

The two sides of human nature exist in reasonable balance. Pursing self-interests helps us to navigate through the *Gesselschaft* world where "lets make a deal" is the norm. Moral bearing helps us to navigate through the *Gemeinschaft* world where connections to others are based on duties and commitments. Allocating resources among employees based on merit is an example of the first. Allocating resources among one's children based on need is an example of the second.

Despite this complexity of two dimensions in balance, most change agents operate from more simple, albeit implicit, theories of human nature. They tend to believe that people are either largely inclined toward good, or that people are largely inclined toward evil. The first inclination represents the unconstrained view of human nature and the second inclination represents the constrained view (Sowell, 1987). Constrained and unconstrained views of human nature are not discrete categories, but are ends of the same continuum. Few people are likely to be positioned in the same place on this continuum. Nonetheless, it is useful to think about two clusters comprised of people with similar enough views to be considered as holding either constrained or unconstrained theories.

Change agents who hold the unconstrained view believe that teachers can be trusted to act morally, and therefore must be provided with the freedom to optimize their moral propensity to do what is right. They have both the capacity and the need to sacrifice their self-interest for valued causes and for conceptions of the common good that they value. As professionals, they willingly accept responsibility for their own practice, and they commit themselves to the learning needs of their students above other concerns. When teachers do not respond to this ideal, it is thought not to be because of their human nature, but because of factors that they do not control. School arrangements and practices based on *Gesselschaft* values that now dominate the educational scene are the reasons frequently given for such lapses in human behavior.

Within the constrained view, by contrast, it is believed that teachers will act selfishly if given the chance. Their primary concern is to maximize their self-interest. Thus constraints in the form of incentives and penalties must be provided to force them to do the right thing. Advocates of this view believe that the moral limitations of human nature must be accepted, but can be manipulated in favor of the common good by the proper use of checks and balances such as rewards and punishments (Smith, 1937). Teachers may have the capacity to do the right thing, they reason, but this capacity will only be motivated if constraints are provided.

CONSTRAINED CHANGE FORCES

Bureaucratic and personal change forces both embody the constrained view. Bureaucratic forces rely on the application of rational choice theory linked to penalties for noncompliance to motivate teachers to implement changes. Personal forces rely on the application of rational choice theory linked to psychological rewards for compliance to motivate teachers to implement changes. In both cases, change agents propose to trade something thought to be of value to teachers and schools for their compliance with proposed changes. Bureaucratic forces require that formal systems be promulgated to propose, manage and monitor this trading on a day to day basis. Personal forces rely on formal and intensive leadership interventions to propose, manage and monitor this trading. Bureaucratic forces are inclined to emphasize material rewards and penalties. Personal forces are inclined to emphasize psychic rewards.

Market forces too rely on trades. But these trades do not require intensive administration by formal organizational arrangements. Nor do they require formal and intensive leadership intervention. Instead an unadulterated form of rational choice theory, linked to the propensity of people to function as individuals who seek to "maximize their gains and cut their loses" in an open market place, is depended upon to motivate change.

Since teachers play in this market as individuals, how can systemic change be leveraged by using market forces? Wouldn't self-interest work against the common good and provide instead a pattern of willy-nilly changes? Market advocates respond to questions of this kind by noting that the common good defies defining by bureaucratic means or by visionary leadership (or for that matter by shared covenants as assumed by community advocates). Instead the common good is defined by an aggregation of individual preferences. When the market game is played some individuals win and other individuals lose. But on the whole, and over time, benefits accrue for everyone and it is these benefits that define the common good.

RATIONAL CHOICE THEORY

Bureaucratic, personal and market change forces all rely on versions of rational choice theory to motivate change. The origins of rational choice theory are found in the fields of economics, evolutionary biology and behavioral psychology. From economics comes the image of the person as "economic man" who is always in pursuit of self-interest and who is never satisfied with what has been accumulated. Economic man operates alone, meaning that the drive to maximize gains and cut losses is pursued without regard for the welfare of others. In the extreme this kind of thinking is applied to all aspects of human life including those that are sacred. Marriage, for example, is assumed to result from a cost benefit analysis conducted by two individuals who reason that each has more to gain and less to lose by a union. Divorce is the inverse. A soldier gives her or his life not for country, but to make a personal point among friends and family or to win fame post-humously. Neither love nor patriotism are considered to be important in rational choice theory.

Adam Smith's *Wealth of Nations* (1937) is considered to be the formative text for rational choice theory. Smith's speculations emphasized that the individual pursuit of self-interest could be and needed to be harvested to serve moral interests and purposes. The means to this harvest, he proposed, is a system of incentives and penalties designed to constrain human kind's passionate nature. Charles Darwin's (1936) theories of natural selection expanded the emphasis on competition that plays a major role in market change force strategies. Competition, he argued, weeds out the weak players thus making the pool of survivors and new replacements for the weak stronger over time. Self-interest motivates competitive play. Darwin's theory provides the script for many school choice proposals that are based solely on free market principles.

Behavioral psychology contributed the "law of effect" (Skinner, 1953) to the market change forces equation. According to the law of effect human behavior is controlled by past consequences. Thus having received a reward or punishment in the past we are conditioned to repeat the behavior again and again to get the reward and to avoid the punishment in the future.

The modern expression of rational choice theory as the explanation for all of the social world can be found in Paul Samuelson's (1947) *Foundations of Economic Analysis*. Samuelson proposed a micro theory of human behavior based on the view that individuals and groups of individuals in the aggregate, motivated by self-interest, represented self contained rational systems that defined value. One particular variation of rational choice theory is "agency theory" (Moe, 1984). Agency theory assumes that the interests of managers and workers are not the same. Workers are interested in the best deal for the least effort. Managers are interested in the best performance at the least cost. Managers are dependent upon workers who have more information about how to do the job. Given the choice, workers will take advantage of this situation. Thus managers must use checks and balances and rewards and punishments to control and motivate workers (Bimber, 1993). Agency theory fits school change by substituting change agent for manager and teacher for worker; or, the state for manager and the school site for worker.

UNCONSTRAINED CHANGE FORCES

Professional, cultural and democratic change forces embody the unconstrained view of human nature. Professional forces, for example, rely on professional training, standards of practice and norms for behavior that, once internalized, are thought to compel change. Change behavior is motivated by professional virtues which function as substitutes for bureaucratic, personal and market change forces (Sergiovanni, 1994). One professional virtue is a commitment to practice teaching in an exemplary way by staying abreast of new developments, researching one's own practice, trying out new approaches and otherwise accepting responsibility for one's own development. Another professional virtue is to accept responsibility not only for one's own individual practice, but for the practice of teaching itself that exist in the school. Embodiment of this virtue transforms teaching from a collection of individual teaching practices to a single and shared practice of teaching. As teachers come to share the same practice a third virtue comes to play; colleagueship defined not merely as congenial relationships or even as patterns of working together, but as being connected together by morally held webs of obligations and commitments. Taken together the professional virtues enable the development of professional community.

Change agents who rely on cultural change forces believe that schools are not limited to being places where professional community is created. Schools can also become communities in their own right. They can become covenantal learning communities with cultures that compel changes among teachers and students that result in better teaching and learning. Cultural change forces rely on community norms, values and ideas that, when internalized, speak to everyone in a moral voice. Teachers, students and other members of this community, it is argued, are motivated by felt obligations that emerge from the shared values and norms that define the school as a covenantal community (see for example Etzioni, 1988; Sergiovanni, 1994).

Size is an important factor in creating a covenantal community. Everyone in a school might be connected together at one level by a commitment to certain shared democratic principles. But not everyone is likely to share the same views about the details of pedagogy, curriculum or assessment. Thus the creation of smaller covenantal communities within the same school building that allows like minded teachers, parents and students to function as independent schools is usually advocated by reformers who operate within the cultural change force frame (Sergiovanni, 1995).

Democratic change forces rely on commitment to democratic social contracts that function as the source for values to guide school decision making and as the source for patterns of obligations and duties that compel change. This strategy seeks to transform teachers and students into "citizens" committed to civic virtue. Civic virtue, defined as the willingness to sacrifice one's self-interest for the common good, is a key pillar undergirding American and Canadian democracy as well as other democracies with similar political and moral traditions.

Not only do professional, cultural, and democratic change forces all embody the unconstrained view to a greater extent than the constrained view, they all share the purpose of building community in schools as a means to leverage deep changes. When used together the three change forces seek to transform schools from organizations or markets to professional, learning and democratic communities.

The transformation to community depends upon the cultivation of a community of mind that becomes the source of authority for making decisions, establishing norms and otherwise directing human behavior (Sergiovanni, 1994). When professional, cultural and democratic change forces are combined, this community of mind takes on three major themes-ideas that define professional relationships and responsibilities; ideas that define broader questions of purpose, relationships, and behavior; and ideas that define the democratic ideal as the standard for making decisions. All three contribute to the school's moral voice that calls upon teachers, parents and students alike to respond on behalf of the common good.

CHANGE CONSEQUENCES

This section examines types of teacher involvement and consequences for change associated with each of the six change forces. Bureaucratic, personal and market forces all assume that change involves trading something presumed to be desirable for compliance with change goals. Bureaucratic change forces emphasize extrinsic rewards. Personal change forces add intrinsic rewards to this mix. Market change forces, by contrast, provide opportunities for teachers to pursue intrinsic and extrinsic rewards. In the first instance the state or the local school administration might mandate a change and announce formal rewards and penalties for compliance and noncompliance. In the second instance school administrators might emphasize providing for the higher order needs of teachers by offering interesting work and more satisfying work relationships in exchange for accepting and implementing desired changes. But in the third instance teachers decide for themselves what they want from a variety of offerings. To get anything, however, they must play the change game as prescribed by change agents.

In all three instances involvement of teachers is calculated (Etzioni, 1961, 1988). Teachers play the game of change as long as they get what they want, whether it be interesting work, cash bonuses, or the avoidance of penalties. But once they calculate that compliance is not worth the incentives or once they lose interest in the incentives, they are no longer willing to play the game by the change agent's rules.

When bureaucratic change forces are successfully used, teachers change just enough to avoid sanctions or to get rewards. But change stops when sanctions or rewards are removed. When personal change forces are successfully used teachers change just enough to get the incentives. But change stops when the incentives are no longer available or no longer valued. When market change forces are successfully used teachers change just enough to win in the market place. But change stops when they no longer like what they are winning or when they are no longer winning.

When professional, cultural and democratic change forces are successfully used, teachers become involved in change for internal reasons. They respond to standards and norms that compel them to behave in new ways. They willingly engage in the implementation phase of change. Successful adoption of a change presumes that teachers will have the necessary knowledge to implement desired changes and the opportunity to do so. Knowledge is provided as professional community and covenantal community builds and opportunity is provided as democratic community builds.

WHAT WORKS FOR SCHOOLS?

If the questions are "what works in bringing about quick changes in schools" and "what works in bringing about changes in schools structures and arrangements" then the answer is change forces that are based on various versions of rational choice theory as embodied in views of schools as either formal bureaucratic organizations, formal organic organizations, or as markets. But when questions such as "what works in schools over the long term" and "what works for leveraging deep changes in schools" are asked, then the answer is change forces that are based on views of schools as communities.

Not all reform efforts, however, that are intended to build community as a means to leverage change are the same. Some efforts are based on the High-Performance theory of organizations even though change agents may speak community language. High-Performance theory is an improved version of traditional Pyramid and Railroad theories of formal organizations. Pyramid, Railroad, and High-Performance theories share a pessimistic view of human nature and prescribe constraints aimed at controlling what teachers and schools do. Pyramid theory relies on direct supervision, rules and other top down arrangements. Railroad theory seeks control more impersonally by standardizing the work processes of teachers. This is done by scripting and tightly aligning goals, curriculum, teaching protocols, and assessment strategies. Both theories are institutionalized in present school structures and account for many of todays regularities in teaching.

The more "progressive" High-Performance theory, by contrast, allows for change agents to set and measure standard outcomes for the school. It then allows for "empowering" teachers, and "empowering" schools through site-based management and other means. Empowered groups are then responsible for figuring out how they will work to ensure that the change agent's standardized outcomes are achieved. Incentives and disincentives are then provided to be sure empowered groups make effective decisions that will accomplish the provided outcomes.

Instead of trying to control teachers by connecting them to hierarchies or scripts, High-Performance theory recommends seeking control by connecting teachers to outcomes, a strategy popularized by corporate theorists Peters and Waterman (1982) and widely imitated in schools. High-Performance theory assumes that effectiveness is achieved by loosely connecting teachers to means, but tightly connecting them to ends. In Pyramid and Railroad theories, planning *how* teaching will be done is separated from doing it. The reformers are responsible for the how and the teachers the doing. In High-Performance theory teachers get to decide how to do things. The planning of *what* to do, however, is separated from planning how to do it. Reformers are responsible for planning the former. All three organizational theories, it appears, share the same basic assumptions. While external controls may differ, they must always be provided. If you don't provide external controls, teachers will take advantage. If you trust teachers in schools too much, they will do the wrong things, if you don't provide incentives and disincentives, nothing constructive will happen.

Images of the school as covenantal learning community, professional community, and democratic community are based on more optimistic assumptions. Community advocates believe that given the opportunity and the right conditions (the right leadership, training, discretion, and support) teachers will make the right decisions. They will be morally responsive. Control need not be externally provided, but will come from within. And provided the opportunity, the needed training and support, the needed connections to colleagues in a shared practice, teachers will make the kinds of decisions about teaching and learning that will improve schools. Bring students, parents and administrators in as fellow citizens bound together by social contracts that define the school as a democratic community, and a revolution in change theory and practice will occur. Change in organizations is rules driven. And change in markets is incentives driven. But change in communities is norms driven.

Community views seem morally superior and more effective for levering change in schools than organizational and market views but reality is never as simple as portrayed above. Community views too have their problems. Prime among them is orientations towards change at different stages in the community's development. This chapter assumes that the stage in question is *emergent*. The issue under consideration is that of transforming schools from organizations or markets to communities. Emergent communities must strive to become communities of relationships, place and mind (Tönnies, 1957). A community of relationships emerges from the special kinds of connections among people that create a unity of being similar to that found in families and other close knit connections of people. Community of place emerges from the sharing of a common habitat or location. This sharing of place with others for sustained periods of time fosters a special identity and a shared sense of belonging. Community of mind emerges from the binding of people to common goals, shared values, and shared conceptions of being and doing. Together the three represent webs of meaning that tie people closely together by creating a sense of belonging and a common identity.

For schools to become communities it is necessary to address questions such as the following: "What can be done to increase the sense of kinship, neighborliness and collegiality among the faculty of the school? How can the faculty become more of a professional community where everyone cares about each other, helps each other to learn together, and leads together? What kinds of relationships need to be cultivated with parents that will enable them to be included in this emerging community? How can we redefine the web of relationships that exists among teachers and between teachers and students? How can teaching and learning settings be arranged so that they are more family-like? How can the school itself, as a collection of families, be more like a neighborhood? What are the shared values and commitments that enable the school to become a community of mind? How will these values and commitments become practical standards that can guide the lives community members want to lead, what community members learn and how, and how community members treat each other? What patterns of obligations and duties emerge as community is achieved? What are the patterns of mutual obligation and duties that emerge in the school as community is achieved?" (Sergiovanni, 1994, pp. 219–220).

During this formative stage of community building schools are ripe for change. Change agendas become important rallying points that provide the substance for creating the community of mind which becomes the schools source of authority for what will go on. As this process begins to accelerate, change becomes the means by which community norms are institutionalized as much as community norms become the means by which change is institutionalized. But as new ways of thinking and behaving become established and institutionalized, communities are no longer predisposed to change. Instead they use the powerful norms that they have constructed to reproduce themselves. Stability is no longer the means to achieve an end but becomes the end itself. For stability to endure, disciplined behavior from community members with respect to core values must be maintained. Community norms become expressed as social and cognitive controls designed to reduce discretion (Hannaway, 1993). Once this happens bucking the existing culture from the inside or changing the existing school culture from the outside becomes a formidable task.

WHY COMMUNITY THEORIES INSTEAD OF MARKET THEORIES?

Most reformers seem to agree that change forces based on conceptions of the school as a formal bureaucratic organization are not very effective. Some reformers are also unhappy with the use of personal change forces that emerge from conceptions of the school as a formal organic organization. The way to break out of this organizational thinking, they believe, is to look more and more to market forces that view schools and teachers as commodities within a free market place (Chubb & Moe, 1990).

Many advocates of market change forces seem comfortable with community ideas. They argue that while promoting community oriented schools cannot be guaranteed as the outcome of using rational choice theory in a free market setting, it is a possible and perhaps even a likely outcome. Teachers, students and their parents, they argue, would have free choice in an open market to build community oriented schools. All they need is to be successful enough to win as they compete with other conceptions of schooling. While such reasoning has appeal, the prospects for the success of market forces over the long run are dim.

Market forces for example, are more efficient than democratic forces but they may not be appropriate given the school's special importance and broader responsibility to promote societal interests. Choice is an important feature in both market and democratic images of schools. In markets individuals, motivated by self-interest, act alone in making preferred choices. Democratic choice, by contrast, is complex, cumbersome, time consuming and sometimes combative. Further, and unlike markets where theoretically the will of the majority is not imposed on everyone, once a democratic decision is made it applies to everyone.

Despite inefficiencies, democratic decision-making should be preferred for the things that society values – things like defense, legal codes, transportation and health care. "When, however, the things we are talking about are trivial – designer jeans, compact discs, deodorant soaps, different types of breakfast cereals – then democratic decision-making is a waste of effort. . . democratic politics should be the system we use for the distribution of everything important, and economic markets should be the system we use for the distribution of everything trivial" (Schwartz, 1994: p. 21). Given this reasoning, schools belong in the first category. Over time there is a danger that market values will drive out virtue. This tendency is particularly worrisome among the professions and for societal institutions that hold a special place in our culture. The commercialization of both sports and medicine are examples (Schwartz, 1994). Baseball and American style football, for example, have long been considered North American pastimes were loyalty, self-sacrifice, devotion to the game, duty and other virtues were enshrined. Today's baseball and football, however, are characterized by a canceled world series, team hopping as a result of free agent bidding, and the switching of franchises from city to city at the drop of a dollar. Similar stories can be told about tennis, football and other high profile sports played across the globe. Medicine has become so costly to practice that even physicians are soured by having to be part of the business of medicine where business too often comes first.

Imagine a group of educational marketeers switching school franchises from a declining social capital neighborhood to a rich social capital neighborhood as a way to attract more customers or more desirable customers. Imagine our best teachers, operating as free agents, switching from school to school to get "better" students to teach. While business may be business, this sort of thinking is unacceptable for schools and other social organizations. But the danger is there none the less. The very same market values that work so well for some sectors of our society can erode other sectors.

Similarly, the same strategies for change that might make sense for some sectors of our society seem not to work well for other sectors. Schools are a case in point. Deep changes in schools are difficult to achieve when using change forces that emerge from views of schools as formal bureaucratic organizations, formal organic organizations or markets. This difficulty is exacerbated by the negative effects that constrained theories and practices can have on teachers. Instead of nurturing professional community, constrained views breed cynicism, erode civic virtue and encourage the development of human nature's passionate side at the expense of human nature's rational side. Yet the voluminous literature on change in schools gives scant attention to this mindscapes problem.

In sum, mindscapes are expressed as idea systems. Idea systems become language systems. Language systems, in turn, become thought system (Greenfield, 1984). And finally thought systems become action systems. Thus changing the way we engage in the process of change in schools may have less to do with the particulars of a given strategy than it does with the fundamental idea systems that frame our views of schools as entities and our views of the nature of human nature. Deep changes in schools, for example, may well require that the basic metaphor for the school itself be changed from formal organization or market to community.

ENDNOTES

[1] Ouchi is not alone in differentiating among organizational types. In their seminal work *Formal*

Organizations: A Comparative Approach (1962) Blau and Scott, for example, make an important distinction between social organizations and formal organizations. They point out that "we would not call a family an organization, nor would we so designate a friendship clique, or a community, or an economic market, or the political institutions of our society" (p. 2). To them what differentiates formal organizations from more social enterprises is how human conduct becomes socially organized. By this Blau and Scott mean the regularities and behavior of people in the enterprise that are due to the social condition in which they find themselves rather than to their physiological or psychological characteristics as individuals.

Another classic work on organizational theory that differentiates among organizational types in Phillip Selznick's *Leadership in Administration: A Sociological Interpretation* originally published in 1957. Selznick proposes an "institutional" theory of leadership and organization as a more viable explanation for some societal entities than "organizational" theory. Institutions evolve naturally as a result of social needs. They become infused with values which enable them to become more responsive and adaptive than organizations. To Selznick "organizations are technical instruments, designed as means to definite goals. They are judged on engineering premises; they are expendable. Institutions, whether conceived as groups or practices, may be partly engineered, but they also have a natural dimension. They are products of interaction and adaption; they become the receptacles of group idealism; they are less readily expendable."

As a further example, Oakeshott (1975) distinguishes between two kinds of associations in our society: enterprise and civil. Enterprise associations are instrumental in the sense that they have formal goals and they require a layer of management whose job it is to decide the choice of means and to establish the structures needed to achieve the goals. Civil associations, by contrast, are substantive in the sense that they do not have goals in a formal sense. They are, instead, places within which members go about their self – determined pursuits guided by norms, standards, social contracts, and other artifacts of culture that informs the decisions that they make (see for example Elkin, 1993).

In enterprise associations people are connected to their work by organizational hierarchies, rules, systems of supervision and incentives. In civic associations member "citizens" are connected to their work by social contracts and norms.

2   Using "forces" as the change leveraging metaphor communicates both intent and inclusiveness. Force, for example, implies strength or energy brought to bear to move something or to resist movement. Force can also take many forms. Force can be power understood in physical terms, organizational conventions understood in bureaucratic terms, mental strength or attraction understood in psychological terms, felt obligations understood in moral term's and so on. Leadership, for example, can be thought of as comprising a set of forces that include technical competence, human relations skills, educational know how, symbolic messages, and cultural matters that school principals can use to influence people and events (Sergiovanni, 1984). Fullan (1993) coined the term "change forces" to communicate similar meaning aimed specifically at change issues.

REFERENCES

Bimber, B. (1993). School decentralization lessons from the study of bureaucracy. *Institute of Education and Training*. Santa Monica, CA.: Rand Corporation.

Blau, P. M., &Scott, W. R. (1962). *Formal organization: A comparative approach*. San Francisco: Chandler.

Chubb, J. E., & Moe, T. M. (1990). *Politics, markets, and America's schools*. Washington D.C.: Brookings Institutions.

Cohen, D. K. What is the System in Systemic Reform? *Educational Researcher*, **24**(9), 11–17, & 31.

Darwin, C. (1936). *The origin of species by means of natural selection*. N.Y.: The Modern Library.

Eisenstadt, S. N. (1968) Charisma and institution building; Max Weber and modern society." S.N. Eisenstadt (editor). *On charisma and institution building*. Chicago: The University of Chicago Press.

Elkin, S.L. (1993). Constitutionalism: Old and new. In S. L. Elkin & K. E. Soltan (Eds.), *A new constitutionalism*. Chicago: University of Chicago Press.

Elmore, R., Peterson P., & McCarthey, S. (1995). *Restructuring in the classroom: Teaching, learning, and school organization*. San Francisco: Jossey-Bass.

Elmore, R. (1995). Structural reform and educational practice. *Educational* Researcher, **24**(9), 23–26.

Etzioni, A. (1961). *A comparative analysis of complex organizations.* N.Y.: The Free Press.

Etzioni, A. (1988). *The moral dimension a new economics.* N.Y.: The Free Press.

Frankena, W. K. (1973). *Ethics.* Englewood Cliffs, N.J.: Prentice Hall.

Fullan, M. (1993). *Change forces.* New York: Falmer Press.

Greenfield, T. B. (1984). Leaders and schools: Willfulness and nonnatural order in organizations. In T. J. Sergiovanni & J. E. Corbally (Eds.), *Leadership and organizational culture.* Urbana: University of Illinois Press.

Hannaway, J. (1993). Challenging the standard paradigm. In J. Hannaway & M. Carney (Eds.), *Decentralization and school improvement: Can we fulfill the promise?* San Francisco: Jossey-Bass.

Hobbes, T. (1950). *Leviation* N.Y.: E.P. Duttons Company.

Kant, I. (1959). *Foundations of the metaphysics of morals.* Trans. L. W. Beck. N.Y.: Bobbs-Merrill.

Lieberman, A., Falk, B., & Alexander, L. (1995). A culture in the making: leadership in learner-centered schools. In J. Oakes & K.H. Quartz (Eds.), *Creating new educational communities.* Ninety-fourth Yearbook of the National Society for the Study of Education, Part I. Chicago: University of Chicago Press, pp. 108–129.

Mannheim, K. (1940). *Man and society in an age of reconstruction.* N.Y.: Harcourt, Bruce and World.

March, J. G., & Simon, H. A. (1958). *Organizations.* N.Y.: John Wiley.

Marks, H. & Seashore-Louis, K. (1995). *Does teacher empowerment affect the classroom? The implications of teacher empowerment for teachers' instructional practice & student academic performance.* Madison: Center on Organization and Restructuring of Schools, University of Wisconsin.

Moe, T. (1984). The new economic of organizations. *American Journal of Political Science, 28*(4), 739–777.

Newman, F., Marks, H., & Gamoran, A. (1995). Authentic pedagogy: Standards that boost student performance. *Issues in restructuring school*, Report No. 8, Spring. Madison: Center on Organization and Restructuring of Schools, University of Wisconsin.

Oakes, J. (1995). Normative, technical, and political dimensions of creating new educational communities. In J. Oakes & K. H. Quartz (Eds.), *Creating new educational communities.* Ninety-fourth Yearbook of the National Society for the Study of Education, Part I. Chicago: University of Chicago Press, pp. 1–15.

Oakeshott, M. (1975). *On human conduct.* Oxford: Clarendon Press.

Ouchi, W .G. (1980). Markets, bureaucracies and clans. *Administrative Science Quarterly.* **25**(1), 129–141.

Peters, T. J., & Waterman Jr., R .H. (1982). *In search of excellence: Lessons from American's best-run companies.* N.Y.: Harper Collins.

Quartz, K. H. (1995). Sustaining new educational communities toward a new culture of school reform. In J. Oakes & K. H. Quartz (Eds.), *Creating new educational communities.* Ninety-fourth Yearbook of the National Society for the Study of Education, Part I. Chicago: University of Chicago Press, pp.1–15 and pp. 240–252.

Samuelson, P. (1947). *Foundations of economic analysis.* Cambridge, Mass.: Harvard University Press.

Schwartz, B. (1994). *The costs of living how market freedom erodes the basic things in life.* N.Y.: W.W. Norton Company.

Selznick, P. (1957). *Leadership in administration.* Berkeley: University of California Press.

Sergiovanni, T. J. (1984). Leadership and excellence in schooling. *Educational Leadership.* 41(5), 4–14.

Sergiovanni, T. J. (1994). *Building community in schools.* San Francisco: Jossey-Bass.

Sergiovanni, T. J. (1995). Small schools, great expectations. *Educational Leadership*, 53(3), 48–52.

Sergiovanni, T. J. (1996). *Leadership for the school house: How is it different? Why is it important?* San Francisco: Jossey-Bass.

Skinner, B. F. (1953). *Science and human behavior.* N.Y.: Macmillan.

Smith, A. (1937). *An inquiry into the nature and causes of the wealth of nations.* N.Y.: Modern Library.

Sowell, T. (1987). *A conflict of visions.* N.Y.: William Morrowand Co.

Tönnies, F. (1957). Gemeinschaft und gesellschaft. In C. P. Loomis (Ed.), *Community and society.* New York: Harper Collins.

Weber, M. (1947). *The theory of social and economic organization.* (Tr. AM. Henderson and Talcott Parsons). Glencoe, IL.: Free Press.

Authenticity and Educational Change

DEBBIE MEIER

Coalition Campus Project New York, New York

One of the greatest clichés of educational change, indeed of our time, is that of authenticity. There is no shortage of advocates for authentic leadership, authentic learning and authentic assessment. In this chapter, Debbie Meier cuts through the hackneyed phrases to ask what, if anything there is to this idea of authenticity, and to the idea of authentic learning that motivates many change efforts.

What is authentic and what is artificial, Meier asks? How can anything in schools be truly authentic, when schools by their nature, are so artificial? Are authentic things necessarily good and inauthentic ones bad? How do we decide on these things? Meier teases her readers with examples that provoke creative discomfort around the idea of authenticity, which she uses to push the discussion much further than other writers in the area have done.

In the end, she finds some of the answers to these demanding conceptual questions in practice and draws upon her own experience of transforming Central Park East school in New York to do so. It is here, she shows, in attempts to build powerful, meaningful learning for students in disadvantaged neighbourhoods that the possibilities of authenticity are ultimately to be found.

Schools were invented as a replacement for the most authentic forms of education – those that stemmed naturally out of families, neighborhoods and work places. They were from the start, by their very nature, artificial. Schools have been in the business of imposing upon us, *out of context*, the stuff that "context", does not, it's assumed, naturally supply. It reminds me of modern nutrition: having taken all the natural nutrients out of food we spend a lot of money and energy devising systems for getting it back artificially.

The dilemma is that artificiality is both the raison d'être for schools and the stumbling block to their success. There are limits to how many nutrients we can absorb artificially, and how useful they are out of context; but there aren't alternatives unless we reorganize the entire society that surrounds us so that the raising of the young is once again woven into all aspects of modern life. We can probably only go so far in this direction, and the best solutions probably aren't accessible to vast numbers of our children – at least in the near future.

But artificiality doesn't have to be a bad word, and authenticity isn't a guarantee of good education. Playing scales on the piano over and over is surely "artificial" – but so is the piano and what we do on it. Whether it's justified depends both on how much we value its end purpose and whether we conclude it's a good route toward reaching such an end. The proof of the pudding doesn't even depend on how boring the task may seem, or how easy or hard it is to accomplish. We can

A. Hargreaves (ed.), Extending Educational Change, 316-335.
© 2005 *Springer. Printed in the Netherlands.*

only defend or attack the repetitiveness of the exercise if we examine it in relationship to its ostensible purpose. Any task can, in a way, be viewed as authentic if in our interpretation it's in keeping with its purpose. Practicing scales was, it so happens, an exercise I did with my mind and heart turned off, and the scales not surprisingly never helped me develop musicianship. But that's not to condemn scales, nor evidence against their potential authenticity under different circumstances. Let's look at some examples that might help us burrow more deeply into the meanings that authenticity might carry.

- A 9 year old student tells his teacher that he wants to make his story longer. "I want more words" he insists in Spanish – "mas palabras." He and his companion spend hours over a period of several days seeking words that will "add to" the story. It's not clear why he wants it longer, or what he thinks the new words add, or why his friend so eagerly joins him in this arbitrary self-assigned task. But his persistence, and his friend's eagerness to help him, stand out in a class that generally requires continuous external motivation. In some way that his teacher cannot discern, he is driven by a problem of interest to him.
- Teachers in a South Bronx school, seeking "authenticity", decided to study AIDS as a science topic: to think of ways to help their community tackle the crisis better. They read the most relevant daily accounts, and listened to local spokespeople on science and health-related issues. The students were bored, passive and unengaged. Could there have been a topic more "authentic"? Less than a mile away a similar group of students studied flatworms, about which they perceived no relevant purpose, except that it was the next chapter in their textbook. (No doubt the teacher could explain the purpose.) But they came into their lab eagerly, and were filled with enthusiasm at what appeared to me entirely trivial information about the anatomy of worms! Were they being scientists in a lab, much as a 4 year old is mommy in her play house? Had they created a make-believe but for them still authentic experience?
- My cousin learned to cook authentically – at her mother's side – and found it trivial and boring even though her mother was famous for her cooking skills. My neighbor learned to cook by loving food and poring over cook books to get it just right.
- A math teacher, in an effort to be authentic, has given students worksheets consisting solely of real-life examples in the use of ratios to solve real problems. The examples are both lively and amusing and require mental effort to solve. In fact, however, the students are no more intrigued by these "real life" examples, than by fantasized problems or pages of routine algorithmic tasks. Their value might lie in the fact that they more nearly represented what ratios are all about, not alas in their capacity to engage the minds of the students. Yet in talking with the teacher afterwards she explained her purpose as being to make math "more interesting and entertaining" by presenting students with real-life-like examples. She had been attracted to this particular program not because it was mathematically more authentic but because it might prove more

entertaining to the students. Her assumption was that its authenticity – these were real examples taken from real life – would lead to more engagement.

- A teacher in search of authenticity decides to group students in co-operative teams, and tells them their job is to publish a newsletter explaining what they have learned. It fizzles for lack of interest in producing anything of serious quality, even though the teacher tells them it will be used in a nearby elementary school. Meanwhile another teacher creates permanent year-long threesomes whose task, after every teacher-directed lesson of the most standard sort, is to be sure they all understand what's going on. The threesomes, over time, build enormous cohesion and solidarity and take on the task as an authentic collective enterprise.

- In the northern Italian city of Reggio Emilio, an ordinary group of working class children of ages one to six work over and over to get their models and drawings of the real world absolutely right. They persevere long after most of us might imagine giving up, for a purpose that seems far beyond their years. Their work is characterized by a perseverance that best characterized little babies as they obsessively practice getting new skills "just right" – for no apparent purpose: new sounds and words, new ways to formulate sentences, new physical capacities, new and seemingly trivial tasks like getting certain pegs in certain holes or seeing what happens if you keep dropping objects onto the floor – over and over like practicing one's scales.. And of course, these schools start with babies! The children aren't easily satisfied, but rarely downcast. Their curiosity is rarely idle, and appears joyous. The actual products of their work are rather startlingly sophisticated, as well as pleasing to the eye and ear. We'd be impressed if they were produced by far older students in a talented and gifted program.

Something in each of these vignettes speaks to the issue of authenticity in ways that also confuse it. Much of what passes for authentic curriculum and authentic assessment in the jargon of contemporary pedagogy, seems to miss the point; albeit, in a most well-intended fashion. There is an elusiveness to what we're seeking as educators, and authenticity is only a sliver of it. Until we are clearer about our purposes, the search for authenticity may be beside the point – a search to entertain better, to avoid the dreaded epithet of "boring"; instead of searching for what those Reggio Emilio students represent as a possibility for all our children.

We're right, of course, that no one can learn if they aren't paying attention, and boredom drives away attentiveness. To be alert, to notice, to take into account – these are dispositions that must be turned on high if we are to be in the mode to learn. So anything that helps elicit such qualities is worth exploring. But what it is that elicits such qualities is harder to put our finger on.

It may be that we can improve the odds that young people's minds and hearts will be engaged in their work if we can figure out how it can "appear" authentic *to them*. But this will take a lot more unpacking, because the word *authenticity* is layered with deceptive meanings that distract more than they reveal. If we are to use the concept of authenticity for more revolutionary purposes – creating schools that turn all our children into powerful, thoughtful and useful citizens – we can't use it as just a synonym for relevance or being true-to-life.

Insofar as schools serve ceremonial purposes – the anointing of particular elites – the authenticity of the tasks required is particularly irrelevant. Rites of passage often thrive on their lack of authenticity. It is part of their virtue. We do something absurd to prove our worthiness, and the mere arduousness and irrelevance of the tasks makes the victors all the more pure and celebrated. I remember years ago listening to a radio preacher explain why the most important of the ten commandments is precisely its most "absurd" – the keeping of the Sabbath on a particular day of the week. Efforts to explain the choice of Saturday rationally precisely miss the point, he explained. Its value lay, precisely in its arbitrariness, he argued. Anyone can be convinced to do what is sensible, but not everyone can be convinced to Believe. That takes Faith. Both winners and losers must have such faith for most Americans. The Academy is, such an accepted ritual exercise. It too requires our common Faith. We are not meant to make common sense of it.

To question the standard academic divisions of knowledge as presented in our schools (English, History, Math and Science) is already to acknowledge that one hasn't quite "got it", one isn't a proper "believer." For beyond the 3 R's, which serve ordinary daily purposes and whose rationale few have had trouble defending, the rest of the rite of passage is designed to be arbitrary. That it seems so to most youngsters – both those who accept it with relish and those most turned off by it – is to be expected. The staunchest defenders of pre-collegiate academics seem most often, in fact, to be using "academic" as a synonym for the 3 R's, or "the basics": weekly spelling tests, memorizing the times tables, and knowing the capitals of the states. Some insist that *any* act of interpreting text or weighing alternate views is an invasion of parental rights, and improper in an institution labeled "public." A steady dose of "facts, facts, facts" may seem boring, but for many defenders of tradition, that is what schooling is all about. It is not meant to be interesting!

And such traditionalists, in their ignorance, may be on to something. Because in its true and best sense, academics are in fact potentially dangerous stuff. And potentially interesting too. But because they have remained out of the reach of most Americans, who either learned them in their most watered-down and de-toxified forms or had a passing exposure to them as intimidating and over-their head, most Americans are truly unprepared to debate their merits. The long-standing American suspicion about what "they" are up to in our schools is not wholly illegitimate. The Academy, with its specialized jargon, has always been subject to popular suspicion. Unlike the proponents of "the basics", these other school folks are not speaking in plain language about plain matters. Ordinary things are dressed up in extraordinary language; those who break their peculiar code, the winners, are in danger of become alienated from their home and hearth. (If they go off to elite colleges they begin to slough off family values, religion, patriotism, etc.)

The Academy never tried, nor considered it part of its duty, to convince the populus of the merits of its traditions. Since few were to be chosen, it seemed unnecessary to convince the others. Popular tastes were presumed to be alright for most, as long as high culture was secure for the few. The task of the Academy was to preserve and protect. The masses might need to know what was Good and what was Bad taste, even if it didn't affect their daily habits. We all grew up knowing that popular music which we truly loved was less important than classical music which we did not understand. Most Americans lived comfortably side by side with such cultural elitism, grumbling on occasion, but only occasionally coming to blows. The school world was the meeting ground between the two worlds; but for most it was a short-lived interlude in a long life devoted to more practical concerns.

THE ACADEMY AS AN ANTIDOTE TO PRACTICALITY

The Academy was thus traditionally designed for those who could successfully bunker down and persevere without asking the reason why. Later on, presumably, if you made it through – and not all were intended to do so – the secret would be revealed. It was a strictly voluntary institution, after all. Few were exposed to any form of schooling for more than a half-dozen years or so. Those attracted to it had, perhaps, a natural bent for it, a true gift, or else came from a culture that had prepared them well to succeed at its arcane rules. The ordinary students who made it into such elite ranks – the upwardly mobile success stories – may have treasured this arbitrariness even more than the natural elites. It was an opportunity to soar out of mundane daily existence with all its compromises and disappointments.

In fact, as we all recognize, the very phrase "it's academic" has a double-meaning: that it's important and that it's unimportant, that it's the "real stuff" and that it's "moot". To write "academically" is both a sign of high status and a claim to dullness. But we all agree, it's a style, with little natural appeal. It has to be learned artificially and at some considerable effort. The personal and anecdotal is carefully weaned out of the best of academic styles. This goes not just for writing, but all aspects of academic demeanor. To be thought "popular" is to invite suspicion. To ask, "is this subject of practical use?" is taboo, or marks one as belonging to a lower status academic discipline. Practical math is instantly recognized as having less status than "impractical" math. The more relevant or catchy the course title, the less likely it is to carry status. Having denigrated the terms practical, popular and useful as for "the dummies only", have we merely invented the concept of authenticity as their replacement? Is it merely the latest euphemism, bound to pass into infamy over time? Probably so, unless we can use it to reexamine the heart of what it might mean to train ourselves in using our minds well without worrying overmuch about whether it's certified as Academic.

School is not and never has been the only place of learning. There is a whole genre of humor that reminds us that schooling can often interfere with learning. Schooling carries with it a whole panoply of historically rooted and not necessarily complimentary associations. The American nation was built, for example, upon a mythology of disdain for academia, and only the briefest of interest in schooling of any sort. Our popular culture is replete with examples of the effête eastern gentleman, with his fancy airs and school-based know-how going down to defeat to the real he-man – the Westerner with his street smarts, his quick and steady gun. There are urban versions of the same. One didn't need a white hat to know whose side we were expected to be on in any of these versions. A "real man" uses words sparingly; his actions speak louder than words. The reading of novels, the retrospective pose, the holding of doubt and uncertainty are marks of the feminine style at its more sickly and worrisome. Even the "real woman" is all action. I used to worry about the proliferating "hands-on" teacher workshops that so appealed to American teachers with their implicit message of "hands-on, minds-off." No more theory, teachers cried out, to the nods of their peers. My fellow teachers were being American to the core.

Yet, as we have celebrated our disdain for matters merely mental on the one hand, we also have traditionally allowed those who make it through "the academy" to hold positions of power and influence. On occasion they have found it necessary to disguise their well-educated roots – particularly if running for public office! The learned man has had power, although not as much as the true aristocracy of our times, the aristocracy of wealth. We secretly chuckled over the fact that the rich might not always have attended the best colleges or passed through them with high honors. The wealthy man and the well-educated man were not synonymous terms, in our or perhaps any other culture. It is only in modern times that the two are beginning to merge.

It is harder and harder to imagine that one could be powerful and not also rich, or rich and not also well schooled. Without quite acknowledging what has been happening, or digesting the implications, we have only very recently made doing Academia the preferred route to riches for *all* Americans. In the past decade we have insisted that *all* children should match the educational achievements of former elites. We have placed the floor where the ceiling once lay. Rhetorically anyway. Not surprisingly, in doing so, we have run into a conundrum. If we can't all be rewarded for being well-educated, getting rich, or moving up the ladder; why must we all be "well-educated"? Whatever would be its value if all succeeded at reaching it? If we truly want all citizens to be well-educated, regardless of immediate economic payoffs, can we afford the historic put-down of academic values.

The dual message of both disdain and respect is beginning to cause us trouble. It worked as well as it did only because we didn't demand that everyone succeed within the Academy, and didn't use its standards as a measure of *all* things worthwhile. In fact in my childhood less than half our citizens entered high school, far fewer received a high school diploma. Drop outs weren't on our mind; drop-ins were too new. And many an ambitious lad left school early precisely because he wanted to get on with those other worthwhile endeavors. Only a minority of those who earned diplomas took the "academic", college bound track. We honored something we called "smartness", and distinguished it from being school-educated. Those who weren't good at the school form of being smart took the business curriculum or vocational education, or dropped out, and dismissed academia as "not my style". They then went on with their life work without too many regrets, with their dignity largely intact. Everyone "knew" that academic success wasn't designed to be everyone's cup of tea.

Yet today we act surprised at the problems that arise when we insist that the Academy's rarefied definition of "well educated" become the universally accepted minimum competency for all citizens and all future employees. We expect this form of decontextualized, impractical knowledge to be second nature of all our children. We decry the schools for "watering the real stuff down", "popularizing" what was not meant to be popular in an effort to put it within the reach of everyone. The academy naturally see attempts to redefine academia as fooling with standards. They scold schools, teachers, parents and kids for failing to stick with the traditional fare of academic schooling, offered in the traditional way. What's wrong with today's youth? And even the non-schooled join in the chorus – after all "we had to do it" – why shouldn't they? We attack the young – and their teachers – for being lazy or just ignorant, and propose various carrots and sticks . On the carrot side we propose beefing the academic fare up with dollops of "authenticity"; maybe that way they'll swallow their medicine better. On the stick side we tie failure to reduced opportunities for further schooling and for decently paying jobs. What we haven't done is answered the question: "so, why is it all that important? What authentic claims does it have for our allegiance?"

"WHATEVER DO THEY WANT OF US?"

We're as loathe as ever to step back and ask those harder and more radical questions, which so often start off with "why?" We need to ask why youngsters are so easily alienated from schooling so that even our best efforts to create authentic tasks appear to them as tricky diversions or as still another pointless hoop. They are bored either way. They expect nothing more. "Just tell us what to do," they cry out, "don't pretend to give us reasons."

Behind the baffled cries lie serious questions that they do not know how to formulate. Convince me! Why these particular disciplines? What makes an "academic" discipline more valuable than a "nonacademic" one? How come success at extra-curricular activities is a better life predictor than success at the formal curriculum if "academia" is so important? What important talents does the former tap that the latter misses? Why is math four times more valuable than music or art? Why don't we honor academics except in school? What is the connection between being "academically learned" and the adult occupations that follow? Who ever uses their academic skills – show me! Do employers care whether I know my history or whether I'm reliable, hardworking and take initiative? Why must we all be trained for the one calling – "academia" – when we're hardly all slated to end up there?

Do the answers to these baffled cries appear more plausible if we try, for a moment, to distinguish between the school's role in preparing the young for gainful employment and its role in preparing them for the many other vocations they will occupy as adults? John Dewey suggested something of this sort when he argued that elite private schools have traditionally served to create a self-conscious and cohesive ruling class; and that democratic societies need public schools to do the same job for the rest of us. In this context the nature of academia required redefinition – and Dewey sought to do so. His claim required a new kind of institution to undertake this new kind of job. The questions he raised are perhaps just now being recycled. Will the outcome be any different? Does schooling serve the latter purpose any better than the former? And, even if it did, does our society suggest to the young that being a good citizen is of any great importance?

If schools were designed to serve as training sites for a democratic ruling class, as Dewey hoped, what are the dispositions, skills and knowledge that such a new kind of ruling class must have? Could the old Academy's definitions of being well-educated still serve such a new purpose? Probably not. Wasn't part of the value of the traditional academy's fare precisely that it separated the wheat from the chaff. If that were no longer its function then do we not have to reconsider the criteria we use for deciding what is the meat and potatoes and what the desert? What do the traditional disciplines have to offer us all in becoming such well-informed and well-disposed public actors? If every citizen must possess such dispositions, would that change the nature of how and who decides such matters?

We have relied for too long on defending the traditional school fare by noting the statistical correlation between years of schooling and lifetime earnings. Or, we argued on egalitarian grounds that if it worked for "us", how dare we deprive "them"? Or we fell back on the capacity – not likelihood – of this or that course of study to arouse reasoning powers in those who master it – like Latin and Greek. However, statistical predictions of success in life have, it turns out, precious little to do with school smarts, or with appreciating the beauty of calculus or the reasoning powers of Latin, and a lot to do with the number of years our parents went to school, how much money they have, our race and gender, and who is in our network of friends. We may be confusing correlation with causation.

The very success of our efforts to educate more students may oddly enough have only worked in the long run to disadvantage them further. As we educate a larger portion of our population, it takes more years of their unpaid labor to predict the same consequences. The rank order remains amazingly static. When incomes were generally rising, this fact was hidden behind a generally benign and expanding economy that created some space for upward mobility. Under current economic circumstances, its hollowness is more apparent. Which wouldn't be unfair, if the additional schooling could and would be defended on its own merits, or for its general social value, not its future private income producing effects.

Whereas in my childhood we heralded the revolutionary idea that everyone should have access to high school, by the time of my children's birth we had upped the ante to college, for the same reward. The GI Bill of Rights was an important marker in American history. Going to college became an American birthright, without which decently paying jobs were more and more out of reach. While we may have thus lowered the "standards" for what 12th graders could do, we raised the standard for what 18 year olds must know and know how to do. We have decried the former, and barely acknowledged the latter. Americans are better educated, even if 12th graders aren't.

Jobs remain scarcer than ever, and the "good life" is just as elusive, even as we all spend more years and more money on school! We have simultaneously elevated the status of the Academy and its demands by making them "the basics" for everyone, while also lowering their value by making them universal! (If everyone were to speak the King's English, it could no longer be used to divide and rank us. It is rank order that matters wherever scarcity exists.)

A high school diploma no longer brings delight, much less a job, and even a college education carries little classiness. Courses that were once symbols of status, are now requirements for all. New forms of status have to be invented. We can only brag about our kids if they attend "hard to get into" schools, where the number of winners is sufficiently small to mark their success as special. Going to the right college has become more and more important. We know a "high standard" only by setting the cut-off point high enough to ensure that few meet it. But that in turn creates a proclaimed crisis since we have declared the new high standard to be the minimum. We lurch from one self-induced crisis to another.

In short, we haven't found a way to establish educational legitimacy without reverting to the Academy to set it for us, and then to rank ourselves accordingly. How precisely the standard relates to the conduct of the "real" world is left unsaid and undefended. In such a climate, authenticity loses its original meaning, and too often becomes merely a way to induce the young to stick it out longer, to make it more entertaining, to bore them less. It becomes a pedagogical fad, not the purpose of schooling.

In disgust, some educators, tired of trying to entertain the young, are more and inclined to suggest a get-tough approach. In an economy of job scarcity such an "or else" approach is probably inevitable, as schooling reverts more openly to its older sorting function. The forms in which this get-toughness takes place vary: let's take away the right to a driver's license if they don't do well in school; make every employer insist that students show a satisfactory school transcript before they are allowed employment, punish parents (especially if they're on welfare) for their children's school transgressions, restore corporal punishment. The list is endless, dreary and perhaps inevitable. In such a climate, the call for authenticity is bound to appear as just another gimmick to avoid asking tougher questions about the purpose of the enterprise itself.

HOW MIGHT WE THEN DEFINE THE AUTHENTIC? AN EXAMPLE.

The trouble is that if we want to truly educate all of our citizens well, we need a more compelling explanation and a more compelling way to establish the meaning of high standards. Authentic practices will follow our announcement of authentic purposes, not the other way around. The millions of at-risk children who now drop out of school as failures know the risks. They have few illusions about their life's chances. It is hard to threaten them. They are without much hope and their anti-social behaviour is the consequence of that loss. While a direr set of threats may straighten out an occasional waverer, it is a short-term solution at the mere fringes of the problem For the problem is that our schools are not engaged in an authentic enterprise, the successes know that as well as the failures, and we are afraid to call attention to that fact. The emperor wears no clothes.

We need, in short, to create schools whose authenticity is self-evident. The task of schooling and the task of the school must be one and the same. When we do that we will more easily see that practicing scales is not demeaning, but related to the task of making good music, and that cooperative groups may or may not be more or less authentic depending on what has to get done. Good science work is generally collaborative; writing a poem perhaps not – although poetry too usually needs an audience. Authenticity cannot be a measuring rod until we know what we are measuring and, above all, why.

These were the questions with which we began when we created both Central Park East elementary schools and later Central Park East Secondary School. The elementary school, which had been created in 1974, had an easier task than the secondary school which started a dozen years later. Academic disciplines have always rested less heavily on the very young. Schools for pre-teens have always allowed for more playfulness, more experimentation, and a looser definition of what must be. Assuming we "took care of" the 3 R's, – which were once defined rather more narrowly – we are left a great deal to each family's and school's devices, even if only covertly. This is what made being a kindergarten teacher such a joy for me.

Thus Central Park East elementary school, like most progressive private schools, felt no compunction acknowledging that we followed no standard curriculum sequence. We would have said – had the words been fashionable in the early 70s – that we had standards for how we studied, but that virtually any and all subject matter seemed reasonable as a way to meet those standards. The criteria for selecting subjects to study was that they appealed to both teacher and student interest, offered lots of possibilities for activity, were rich in material resources and flexible enough to move in a variety of directions depending on the particulars of each group of children. Parents bought it; kids did too. Few were afraid that in doing so, we were shutting important doors in their faces.

We saw to it that in the course of the year children were confronted with topics that required them to tackle the world from a scientific viewpoint as well as a social scientific one. We were careful that our time with children included a wide range of human creative expression – poetry, dance, theater and fiction for example, as well as wonderful stories and narratives that constitute our shared and diverse histories. We didn't worry overmuch about these matters, but there was a kind of implicit backdrop that we accepted, although for any individual child the balance might vary quite substantially. Above all we believed that if the school could capture children's interest, stimulate their expanding curiosity, provide them with some sound craftsmanship and open them up to the viewpoint of often distant "others" we were well on the way. We also assumed that to be surrounded by a setting that valued ideas, enjoyed discourse, prized good communication and intellectual challenge, the kids would be "picking up" what it meant to be well-educated. We called it "natural". We believed that much of what we meant by being well-educated would be passed on effortlessly, much as children learned to talk, or as teens learned to drive. Not without effort on the part of the learner, of course; but without much effort on the part of the teacher, the modeler – other than designing sufficient models, examples, experiences.

We were encouraged to discover in interviews with graduates many years later that they had concluded that their later success had much to do with precisely such qualities as these during their unusual elementary school education. They were impassioned about the impact the school had on developing their lifetime interests, on their learning how to negotiate and converse with a wide range of people in persuasive and effective ways, and their considerable confidence in their capacity to tackle difficult and sustained work. They attributed part of it to good models, and to the continued faith their families had in them when the going got rough. Interviews with parents raised the possibility that the school's approach to their children had buttressed and influenced their own faith in them. While in earlier interviews, some had raised questions about "academic" preparedness, in these later reflections it virtually never came up at all.

This emboldened us to start our high school as a continuation of the work of the three Central Park East Kindergarten through 6th grade schools we had launched in East Harlem. We half-jokingly thought of ourselves as carrying the tradition of kindergarten all the way through high school. We knew, however, that it wouldn't be quite so easy. Even with our reputation and the support of Ted Sizer's new Coalition of Essential Schools, it would be harder to gloss over the ways in which we were different from traditional schools. We suspected that even our own students who selected to remain with us would want something that looked more like "real" school, and that parents would want reassurances that colleges would take us seriously. That meant that parents and kids, and we ourselves, would have to confront again the usual rationales for what and how we study, and this time with a set of different dilemmas. We would have to make a quite different set of compromises than had been possible in the work of our elementary schools. Looking back, it's hard to know if we made the right ones, or if we made too many of them, or not enough.

Seat time would not be our measuring rod, nor would Carnegie credit hours, nor would traditional exams. And kids would continue, as they had at CPE, to be known well by a small number of adults, and thus spend at least two years with the same teacher(s). Teachers would still be generalists, although maybe we would introduce slightly more specialization by traditional academic categories. And while we would continue providing detailed narrative reports to families, we would also introduce some form of grading. All kids would study the same basic "subjects" for the first four years, but would leave lots of room for personalization so that both the style, pace and focus of each student's work would vary depending on the student.

HABITS OF MIND? JUST ANOTHER WRINKLE?

The original core group tried to construct another vision of secondary school that was not in conflict with the elementary school but quite different from any that the original participants of the school had themselves seen, observed or experienced. We arrived, painstakingly but flippantly, at a different set of questions. Ted Sizer argued that the central function of high school was to educate the minds of its youngsters well. Big but vague words; how might we break high school down other than by listing subjects, facts, exams, years? We tried to tease out the ways in which we ourselves recognized others as being well-educated. We tried to distinguish between recognizing that they had attended a good school and what we ourselves meant by well-educated. Were these synonymous? Suppose we didn't know a friend's school history, what would we be looking for? How might we like to see our fellow citizens minds work? We introduced each other to our favorite authors, and emerged with bits and pieces from all of them.

These discussions led us to try and formulate a list of what uncomfortable, unnatural, not always easy habits of mind a democratic society might seek for it citizens. If they were "natural" then perhaps schools needn't worry overmuch about instilling them. But maybe some were hard to come by and needed lots of drill and practice. If schools didn't undertake this task, who else would? We found it hard to settle on any list of facts or domains whose value lasted a lifetime. We tried, but one of us always insisted that it would rule him or her out. In the end, we came up with a different kind of list, a list of habits of the mind that we thought were important to use even when no one was looking, whether one was in school or home, on the street or at one's job placement – and that were decidedly important to a democratic culture and decidedly difficult to sustain! (And not incompatible with work that paid decently, either).

We came up with many, but found a way to group them into a mere five. We were happy to note that they easily overlapped each of the traditional disciplines, as well as the everyday life of a citizen of our school. They weren't obscure or arcane, and yet they weren't easy to "master". To become habitual they'd need to be practiced in every realm of the school's organization – by adults as well as kids, in history classes as well as math classes, in discussions of classroom behavior as well as the behavior of famous men and women.

The first one we agreed on arose naturally out of our discussions of how we each envisioned "the good school". Our ideas were influenced by our own past histories, both our individual histories and the group identifications we brought with us. We coined this the habit of asking about "Viewpoint". This habit of mind was worded variously over the years. From whose viewpoint are we hearing this, to who's speaking? Would this look different if she or he were in another place or time? Most kids saw it at first as a justification for sticking with whatever idea they had "it's my viewpoint", they asserted dogmatically. By itself it seemed to be simply a way to denigrate any other ways of seeing the world! "She says that because she's ——." (fill in white, adult, Chinese, etc.). It took time to think of ways in which a good curriculum could help young people step into the shoes of others, to make deeper sense of the possible web of meanings that comes from standing elsewhere. It provided lots of tie-ins between science and history, history and literature, geometry and art. But it required deepening the question itself.

Closely connected, and useful in avoiding its pitfalls, was the issue of evidence. "How do we know what we know" became our second habit of mind. The school itself was simultaneously wrestling with precisely that question. How will we know what the kids do and don't really know? What evidence will we accept? How credible will such evidence appear to others? What rules of evidence are appropriate to different tasks? To provide kids with opportunities to develop such habits they needed, of course, curriculum that offered a lot of evidence that they could check out for validity without being entirely dependent on the word of a single authority. What mixture of authority and irreverence was appropriate? This was a habit central to "skepticism", but it needed to be carefully handled so that it didn't fit into a far easier habit, cynicism. All evidence is not equally compelling, after all, and learning how to weigh it for credibility is one hallmark of being well-educated, we declared.

In the process we added a third habit of mind: "connections, patterns." How is this over here connected to that over there? Have we ever encountered this before? Is there a discernible pattern here? What came first? Is there a clear cause and effect? What are the probable consequences that might follow from taking course x rather than course y? How probable? Is this a "law" of causality, a probability, or a mere correlation?

Closely following on issues of causality came conjecture. "What if" things had been different? Suppose King George had been a very different personality? Suppose the American colonies had followed the Canadian model? Suppose Napoleon or Martin Luther King Jr. or Hitler had not been born? Suppose King's assassin had missed? Suppose there hadn't been a storm, a heavy rain, a flood, or a particular brainstorm? Our fourth habit encompassed our belief that a well-educated person saw alternatives, other possibilities, and assumed that choices mattered. They could make a difference. The future wasn't, perhaps, inevitable.

And finally – who, after all, cares? Does it matter? And to whom? Is it of mere "academic" interest, or might it lead to significant changes in the way we see the world and the world sees us? Will it make us richer? More famous? More powerful? Can we know?

Over the years different people have worded these five differently; they never quite get said the same way. Sometimes the order itself is reversed, and in changing the order the meaning of each shifts slightly. In fact, the variety of ways in which it gets interpreted has become itself part of the intellectual life of the school. We also entertain, on occasion, the possibility of adding a sixth, or replacing one with another. We played once with: "compared to what?"

But each subject taught – and we tended to stick to traditional disciplinary categories – was supposed to be measured against its capacity to serve these five habits well. Some subjects, however they might appeal to us, seem ill-suited to the task. And a shallow skating-over of topics would be hopeless to serve such purposes. We could not expect kids to sift evidence if there weren't enough sources of evidence and the pace of the work prevented checking anything out carefully. "Less is more" can sometimes be a cover for doing little of anything. But given our concern for these five habits, less turned into a necessity.

SOME SPECIFIC POSSIBILITIES

But why would kids care any more for our habits than for any other rationale? We hoped that they would make more sense to them; that their clear relevance to everyday life would help. They became the basis for the kinds of questions we posed to kids who were sent to my office for misbehaving. So tell me what the teacher's viewpoint would be if she were here? And yours? And what evidence can you bring to bear on the credibility of your account? Is this part of a pattern of behavior or a once-in-a-lifetime mistake? Could you have acted otherwise? And anyway, why does any of this matter? Who cares?

But we also knew that we would have to design our course of study with more than these habits in mind. We'd also need to keep in mind what topics best provoked the students and staff to dig deeply, how to tease out of them their capacity to become engaged with ideas. We were a little leery of the 60's focus on "relevance" – since we knew that 8 year olds had a passion for dinosaurs. But what were the equivalent passions of 14 year olds? Sometimes just finding a way to ask a good question worked, sometimes it was selecting a topic that kids were naturally inclined to be curious about, or that seemed to appear in headlines and TV shows and thus offered lots of hooks and resources. The staff's own passions were, we knew, often contagious. Sometimes the hands-on pleasure of the work, and sometimes the drama of a topic would be enough. Sometimes a good topic had lots of unexpected connections to other strictly personal inclinations – from Latin to astrology! We wanted some of all the above.

We decided to ask kids to spend a whole year studying a host of topics that might help them answer one question: "who's an American, anyhow?" For some kids figuring out what is meant by an "American" vs a "foreign" name, how the continent got peopled over time, or how different people have chosen among their multiple possible identities, has become the center of their investigation, the heart of their interpretation of the question. It has led different kids down different paths, and did not always mean we were all even studying the same era of history, – or that we all read the same books. The possibilities the topic offered in literature were enormous, including similar struggles that took place at other times and places over this complex concept of "we-ness" vs "otherness." Was that O.K.?

We were comfortable with it because it could be justified as covering American history and much of what is considered the best of literature. For sanity's sake, teachers sometimes controlled the topic more tightly, choosing particular historic events and documents for everyone to focus on. Some decided to start in the present and work their way back. Others began with the vast, open, unpopulated continent and move forward. Still others were more free wheeling and left much to their student's choice. The adults themselves disagreed about how best to approach it.

But the topic itself was so engaging that most of the time it didn't matter. Almost any approach sometimes failed and sometimes worked – for different kids! The debates that ensued seemed at times to touch upon matters kids were really trying to figure out and that affected the way they were going to live their lives. We ourselves held different "answers" to the question, which was one criterion we had in mind in selecting good essential questions. There wasn't a Right Answer, although in pulling together one's point of view, some facts and some lines of reasoning could be objectively refuted, or at least made more difficult to sustain. Another thing we liked about it was that it would have later echoes as students studied other cultures: Who's a Jew? Who is really Chinese? What does it mean to be a Frenchman? An African American? A woman? A Central Park East Secondary School student?

Similarly we spent nearly two years of work in both math and science classes on a unified curriculum that is generally "covered" in less than one year in a traditional high school. It included both algebra and geometry, some elemental calculus, and lots of models, representations and real life problem solving involving force, motion, waves and energy. Issues of statistics, randomness and patterns arose naturally from this work. The kids enjoyed building roller coasters; but did that make it authentic? They studied musical sound waves and mapped appropriate equations? Was that more "real"? Did we convince kids they'd use it in their normal life? Probably not. Did it make kids more conscious of their physical world and of other natural and unnatural events that science sought to make sense of? Probably – but of course more so for some than others. Do they really know more physics, even in the areas studied, than their equivalent more traditionally educated friends?

It is hard to say. But we believe we can demonstrate that they have a much keener ability to explain how a scientist might go about using his or her observations to arrive at conclusions, what distinguishes a scientific theory from an opinion, how mathematics can be used in the service of science, and what scientists are engaged in. The conversations overheard between kids and between adults and students had the earmarks of real science talk, of puzzlement, of trial and error, of bemusement and playfulness as well as serious effort and diligence. They are aware that the nature of acceptable evidence in biology can sometimes be different than in physics, and they're aware that scientists argue about such matters because to them it truly "matters".

We constructed such curricula – painfully. We started out designing a science program that would be focused on the physics and biology of vision and seeing, and included lots of astronomy. It might have worked, but we gave it up. We spent many years trying to see whether everything could be taught in an integrated fashion, and whether everyone in the Humanities or Math/Science team could teach exactly the same material with the same questions at the same time. We found out they could, but felt the advantages were soon overwhelmed by the disadvantages. We began to use our student's community services experiences, which occupied several hours of their time each week while the faculty met, as sources of evidence for their regular course work, rather than as just an excuse to get them out of our hair.

But, if we went in the direction of having teachers and students range more widely and select more personally, we had to devise better and better ways to be sure we held commonly high standards and that not only the staff but the kids knew what the standards were. We worked out common "essential questions" and graded each other's student performances collectively. We tried to see that students presented their "habits" in a range of ways, but also insisted from the start, sometimes successfully, that the habits displayed should be judged by team standards, not only by individual teacher standards. It seemed easier when Grant Wiggins described it to us than when we tried to do it ourselves.

We also discovered we had to spend more time on habits of work – insisting on getting into the habit of attending class, being on time, meeting deadlines, handing in accurate and neat papers, conforming to certain standard formats for work (bibliographies, citations, etc.) than we had originally thought necessary. Sometimes these less lofty habits overwhelmed the others.

But perhaps our grandest leap forward came in the development of a schoolwide set of graduation expectations. To insure that these were valued we insisted, in fact, that they alone determined who would or would not receive a high school diploma. The diploma would be awarded by the vote of the faculty, upon recommendation of each student's Graduation Committee, whenever the student met the full requirements. The requirements consisted of presenting fourteen different portfolios covering the full range of a student's work with us. Each portfolio contained a body of work – some of which could not fit into a two-dimensional format. It might include attestations about musical performances, art shows, speeches given, service performed, as well as essays, videos, and visual representations. Seven of these portfolios would have to be presented orally and defended before a Graduation Committee consisting of two adults of the faculty's choice, one of the student's choice, a younger student, and any other persons who might be valuable for a particular portfolio or to a particular student. Since we began with just 7th graders and moved up year by year we had time to hone these a bit before trying them out for real.

We tried out various formats for "scoring" the portfolios – for developing both a common standard and ways to express our different values. While the assessment we devised was high stakes – everything depended on it – students could retake such portfolio demonstrations as often as they wished. They would retake the "exam" not just if they failed it, but also if they passed but wanted a higher grade. Over time these portfolios and presentations were more explicitly interwoven with the work of the earlier grades, not just confined to the final two years of high school.

The assessments were always public and open and the judgments made were discussable. The work remained with the school for review by others, although only the Graduation Committee members could alter a student's grade. The outsiders who evaluated the work of graduating students were judging us – the faculty and the school, not the individual student. We invited comments and criticism from outsiders in each of the major fields; holding one or two such reviews of our work each year. These reviews served as a check on our own judgments, biases, affections and loyalties. Without denying the existence and value of such "subjective" factors we balanced them thus with cooler ones.

The kids felt the authenticity of the process – it was tangible, it reminded them of real-life interviews and conversations, it was both intense and provocative. There were no secrets about it, and yet it was always a surprise. Unexpected things happened each time. And the cumulative impact was enormous. As kids saw their portfolios thicken, and the number of portfolios they completed accumulate, they had a visual sense of their own growth over time. And the work required not only the hard evidence within each portfolio, but the competence displayed in its broad defense. Finally all the work entailed in putting the work together, gathering the Graduation committee, arranging for its meetings and insuring that each member was properly prepared was hard evidence of good work habits. (One portfolio defense was video taped as well as form of evidence for future review).

Just as the elementary schools students' portfolios – which while less rigorously examined by others – served at the end of 6th grade as a form of confirmation of their growth, the high school seniors were impressed by how much they had produced and how many other people had taken it seriously. These were rites of passage, but the rites seemed "right", connected to both what had actually preceded them, as well as to the tasks that lay head.

Besides, by their concreteness, they held out hope for even those students who were late bloomers, who had for some reason taken far longer to prepare themselves. Once they reached the level of concentration and ambition required, it was possible to focus their attention on what was a "manageable" if arduous task. More arduous perhaps than completing three years worth of credit hours, but less frustrating and seemingly endless. Some kids dropped out before completing the work and came back later to finish it. A few transferred to "easier" schools or programs. And a few – our failures – left discouraged at the demands of the school. While nearly 90% of our students graduated high school (in a city where 50% was the norm), and 90% went on to college; the 10% who did not make it were a significant group.

These latter, while few in numbers at Central Park East, worried us. We knew that our colleagues starting schools like ours in even more homogeneously troubled areas of the city had student bodies composed of vastly more children of the kind with whom we had failed. So our concern for them loomed larger in our minds as we celebrated twenty-one years of success. What kept us from finding that common ground, a place of engagement for these youngsters?

We were also concerned with finding ways to improve the standards to which we held our graduates successes. We told the kids early on that not only would we keep fiddling with the graduation requirements, but we would hopefully over time be able to raise the standards for graduation. If we did, would we lose more? As we got to be better teachers, we said, what our students would be able to do would improve as well. But, it couldn't be just "upping"; we were concerned with getting it more "right." Were these the standards that held up over time?

OUR FAILURES: WHERE CENTRAL PARK EAST SECONDARY SCHOOL MISSED BEING AUTHENTIC.

We were especially troubled by what we came to understand about our failures: the marginal graduates and the drop-outs. Some of them, we noticed as we reviewed their stories, had done well in the various community service jobs they had held, as well as part-time internships that they had located for themselves. They were not always unreliable; and even their *school* unreliability may well have been a habit they developed to protect themselves from taking their failure too seriously. They weren't always the most anti-social, nor the kid we would least like to have as an ally in time of need. Some were quite terrific. Others had a kind of passivity in school that was either pathological or school-induced. We looked more closely. Had we failed to find the way to light a spark in them, to find the connections between their natural drive to make sense of life and the world of school? The kind of work demanded – a major portion of which was work aimed at pleasing the academic faculties of sister schools and colleges – had not been, we feared, well suited to catch their attention. If they had been my kindergarten students I would have started elsewhere. Had we been too fearful of straying from academia? They might turn in three, four or more drafts of an assignment and each might be worse, no different than the others or only minimally improved. And they would be crushed, bewildered by our failure to be pleased. Pleasing us remained, in fact, too important. But they didn't "get" what we were about, and we were unable to move ourselves into their shoes to catch them where they were.

Despite tutors and coaches and hands-on-experience, these students might find fractions mysterious unless they were in the midst of using them for a real and immediate purpose. No amount of practice in real-life prepared them for doing better in test formats. For others, reading a novel proved truly baffling – who cared what this make believe person thinks and feels, they moaned? Stepping into the shoes of others, particular others that they could not or chose not to identify with, was a habit they found so distasteful or boring that they read only assigned pages, and answered only assigned questions.

For many of these students college was not, at least at this period of their lives, a sensible path; and maybe most kinds of decontextualized intellectual work would remain puzzling. But they weren't bad citizens when confronted with a task that came in real-life forms. They weren't easily conned and were open to other people's arguments. They were potential employees who would never let you down, and they were certainly neighbors worth having. Why couldn't we give them a diploma that would allow them to leave us with their self-respect intact? Why did they feel obliged in the end to slink away, or drive us batty, or get pregnant as a respectable way out?

We felt trapped by our compromise with academia, our decision to demand that the five habits of mind be exhibited above all in the major traditional academic disciplines. It was our strength – it gave us immense credibility – but it stood as a cruel barrier to youngsters whose habits of mind and habits of work should have required no apology, except when it came to exhibiting them in the particular domains honored by The Academy. Who gave The Academy license to pass judgment on such youngsters?

And, in fact, had we done right for our more successful students whose growth was stunted by such demands, diverted from other more natural passions? I thought about what had been garnered in interviews with our elementary school graduates many years earlier, ten years after they graduated from 6th grade and long before we had a secondary school as follow-up. They too had done remarkably well. Far fewer had gone on to college, but they were holding up. They attributed their success to three things: Central Park East's support and encouragement of their own strengths and interests, their capacity to create useful and important relationships with a wide range of people, and the support they received from families who had themselves been influenced by the school. They looked back with the most detailed and pleasurable recall to the joyful times they had in school, at plays produced, trips taken, long term projects undertaken, concerts they sang at, instruments they learned to play, foods they cooked, games they invented. They acknowledged some drawbacks academically – in this or that domain. In some cases they overcame these easily, in others with considerable difficulty and some never did at all. But they compensated, got around, found alternate paths. They were resourceful. They thought that we had sent them on with respect and appreciation for who they were, and had helped their families sustain their belief in them as well.

That's the kindergarten way: and it's hardly surprising given the school's origins: a bunch of kindergarten teachers. But why had so much of the play disappeared as they got older? Didn't we ourselves, as adults, still view our work as a form of play? Wasn't play at the heart of intellectual life? We joked at how teaching had become our vocation, our calling; as much a hobby as a job. Was it also so for our students in high school' or had we allowed the particulars of Academia to narrow how we saw our youngsters, to literally clog our vision of their other strengths and passions, placing further barriers in lives already hemmed in by suffering and hopelessness.

We can keep at it working along the edges. And it helps. Far more of our students graduate and go on to better lives. What we have mostly given them is an authentic place where people treat each other with mutual respect, talk together in ordinary voices, and engage in things that interest them. It works wonders for many; and until we allow ourselves to ask bigger and braver questions, we may have to be satisfied with the results. More kids will graduate with somewhat more sophisticated and rigorous abilities to use their minds well, to make judgments and to ask and answer tough questions in credible ways. But we will lose far too many of the most vulnerable who cannot or will not jump our hoops. They deserve better answers to their question: why?

WHY SCHOOLING AFTER ALL: THE ESSENTIAL AUTHENTIC QUESTION.

Schools will explore authenticity more usefully when the enterprise of schooling itself is willing to be more honest about its role. What is it for? The Coalition of Essential Schools has a technique – called planning backward – that needs to be practiced more broadly. If we began by imagining a blank slate and asked ourselves: why fill it up at all? What is it we want that requires so much time and so many resources? What do we value so dearly that children must all learn it? And if all must learn it, why not learn it well? And – could we, their teachers – pass the test ourselves?

It might lead us to redesign the schooling that follows high school, as well as that which precedes it. We might wonder if far more young people shouldn't joy-fully leave high school for something other than academia, some other forms of vocational education; and if possibly the real academic work shouldn't be reserved for those who truly love it – at any time in their lives when it appears high on their agenda, except for those intending to become academics. And those aspiring to be professional academics might better apprentice themselves to one, as part of their own vocational training. We would meanwhile examine all the other possible media for imparting broader general education – in a voluntary nonjudgmental way. Television and interactive computers might offer us avenues for investing in our citizen's self-improvement.

But between the ages of 5 and 18 we had either better give up formal schooling or we must invent institutions more nearly resembling soccer camp; built on the most basic principles of cognition: that you can't learn to do something that you've never seen done, that you can't do it well if you can't imagine yourself belonging to the club of people who do it well; and that even then you need ample opportunities to do it yourself in a setting in which feedback is available. In contrast, the only thing kids see "done" in most schools, and to a considerable degree even at Central Park East Secondary School, is "teaching". For those who intend to become teachers they've had twelve years of exposure to the real thing – although not always played well, and with not much opportunity to try it out themselves. But for everyone else, we are far from having let the genie out of the bottle – and schools are not yet authentic enough so that the average 18 year old accomplishes what the least 5 year old does in the hills of Northern Italy in those remarkable little preschool classrooms and fields.

But it could be done. And in the meantime, kids are so hungry for the real stuff – starting with personal ties between young and old – that even if we just meet them part of the way we can produce what appears to be a miracle. They will mostly attend to even the most inauthentic school tasks if the school itself is an authentic experience, a place of mutual respect, grounded in our knowledge and concern for each other as human beings. That's the good news.

Organizational Learning and Educational Change

BILL MULFORD

Faculty of Education, University of Tasmania

The avant-garde of educational change theory is the idea that schools be treated and developed as learning organizations which do not pursue fixed plans in pursuit of set goals, but structure and develop themselves so that they and their members can continually learn from experience, from each other and from the world around them, so that they can solve problems and improve on a continuous basis.

In this chapter, Mulford takes this field of organizational learning, describes its key principles, discusses some of the research evidence that is beginning to emerge in relation to it; and engages critically with some of the field's claims and their limitations. Mulford's chapter is neither blindly euphoric nor sweepingly dismissive of organizational learning theory. Instead of uncritically applying the general theory to education as many other writers and advocates of educational change have done, he presents one of the few critical appraisals of the field and its relevance that have yet been written.

INTRODUCTION

In a time of massive change countries worry about themselves. This concern inevitably results in special attention being given to public institutions, including schools. We certainly seem fascinated, if not entranced, by the change that surrounds us in education (Berliner & Biddle, 1995; Hargreaves, 1995; Tyack & Cuban, 1995). Whether those in schools are thriving on the change is another matter. Some argue that "the decades of change, improvement and reform have left many educators – consciously or otherwise – confused, exhausted and disillusioned" (Deal, 1990, p. 131). Such a situation should be of concern not only for schools but also for the society they serve.

Peters is right when he says that the core paradox in a world of massive change "is fostering (creating) internal stability in order to encourage the pursuit of constant change" (1987, p. 395). Stability for change, moving ahead without losing our roots, becomes the challenge. This challenge may be able to be met in education and elsewhere by focussing on a change strategy where learning comes to be seen as "the single most import resource for organizational renewal in the postmodern age" (Hargreaves, 1995, p. 11). In this strategy the school is viewed and treated as a learning organisation.

In contrast to business where there has been a veritable explosion of books and journal articles on organisational learning (DiBella, 1994), a small but increasing number of educational writers have taken up the organisational learning 'baton'

A. Hargreaves (ed.), Extending Educational Change, 336-361.
© 2005 *Springer. Printed in the Netherlands.*

(Argyris, 1993; Argyris & Schön, 1978; Cousins, 1994; Fullan, 1993, 1994; Keating, 1995; Leithwood, Jantzi, & Steinbach, 1995; Louis, 1994; Miles, 1993; Mitchell, 1995; Senge, 1990; Watkins & Marsick, 1993) and an even smaller number of educational researchers have studied the area (Leithwood et al., 1995; Louis, Kruse, & associates, 1995; Mitchell, 1995; Russ, 1995; Sackney, Walker, & Hajnal, 1995). This literature and research, although small in quantity, raises a number of important issues that need to be taken into consideration if we are to see organisational learning as a change strategy likely to fulfil its early promise. But before turning to these issues which group around the two areas of developmental pathways and limitations of the current literature, we first need to examine the concept of organisational learning itself.

DEFINITION

Almost 20 years ago Argyris and Schön (1978) argued that those intervening in organisations "have had to recognize that their main challenge is not to help an organization become more effective at the performance of a stable task in the light of stable purposes, but rather to help an organization restructure its purposes and redefine its task in the face of a changing environment" (p. 320). Similarly, Peter Senge (1990) believes that the basic meaning of a learning organisation is one that is "continually expanding its capacity to create its future" (p. 14).

Argyris and Schon (1978) go on to say that we should give primary importance to organisational inquiry (or learning), that is, "an organization's capacity for conscious transformation of its own theory of action, and to individuals' ability to appreciate and transform the learning systems in which they live." (p. 331) The better organisations are at learning, the more likely it is they "will be able to detect and correct errors, and to see when they are unable to detect and correct errors" and the more likely they "will be at being innovative or knowing the limits of their innovation" (Argyris, 1993, p. 1).

Louis (1994) argues that existing models of change management in education are now inadequate but that the organisational learning model may be more promising because the "image of change that emerges in the organizational learning paradigm has elements of both managed change (organizational learning is affected by structure and leadership) and anarchy (the emergence of alternative paradigms and the selection of a new paradigm is a chaotic, largely unpredictable process)" (p. 20). Although, as she notes, "the frame is poorly developed in educational studies (see Dalin & Rust, 1983 for an exception), it has potential for helping to think about the problem of how schools change basic assumptions about 'what it is we do here' when demands for significant reforms are made" (p. 9).

Results of previous phases of a five year longitudinal study of policy implementation in the Canadian province of British Colombia (Leithwood et al., 1995) "increasingly have directed attention towards individual and collective learning processes [organisational learning] as explanations for variation in the productivity of school responses" (pp. 3–4). The authors (Leithwood & Aitken, in press) define organisational learning as ". . . a group of people pursuing common purposes (individual purposes as well) with a collective commitment to regularly weighing the value of those purposes, modifying them when that makes sense, and continuously developing more effective and efficient ways of accomplishing those purposes" (p. 63).

Fullan (1994) believes that in schools that are learning organisations "two things are key; learning is considered both 'essential' (important) and 'integral' (linked) to goals and activities" (p. 5). In contrast, Leithwood and his associates (1995) argue that it is a risky business trying to predict "the future social and economic consequences of present trends" and that therefore it is improbable that we can "accurately and precisely specify the characteristics of schools adapting to such consequences" (p. 2). Because of this position, they believe that, "Envisioning future schools as learning organizations does not require exceptional accuracy in predicting consequences for the future of current trends" (p. 2).

Given the relative youth of the literature on organisational learning, we should expect some of the confusion illustrated by the differences in emphasis in the above definitions. However, if the area is to be a change strategy that fulfils its early promise to address current educational agendas successfully, those involved must learn the lessons from those who have gone before and produce clear and agreed definitions. For example, one of the reasons that another promising change strategy for schools, Organisational Development (OD), eventually found itself out of favour, was largely one of semantics. OD came to mean many things to many people (Mulford, Conabere, & Keller, 1977; Mulford, 1978, 1982). All OD came to be judged by were the failures, even though there were some versions that were highly successful. Catch-alls that mean anything to anyone and that continue to rely on advocacy without research are doomed to repeat this sorry tale.

Keating (1995) points out that the area of organisational learning has many descriptions and case studies, but little comparative or systematic research. Yet he believes that "key elements noted by thoughtful observers can be summarized" (p. 20). For Keating, these elements include coordinated group effort towards commonly shared goals, active commitment to continuous improvement and to the diffusion of best practices throughout the organisation, horizontal networks of information flow to help bring together expertise as well as links with the external world, and the ability to understand, analyse, and use the dynamic system within which they are functioning.

Mitchell (1995), too, believes that much of the work on organisational learning "is theoretical in nature, based on literature reviews and anecdotal reports than on empirical evidence" (p. 47). She notes that in her reading of the organisational learning literature, she was reminded of the story of the three blind men trying to describe an elephant but each from a different vantage point. Nevertheless Mitchell (1995) concludes that there are points of convergence in the literature. These include the following set of indicators of organisational learning in a school:

Developing a spirit of trust

Developing common understandings

Developing shared vision

Sharing information openly and honestly

Engaging in collaborative practices

Engaging in professional learning and growth

Using reflective self-analysis to raise awareness of assumptions and beliefs

Examining current practices critically

Understanding the inevitability of conflict

Engaging in dialogue in order to understand the frames of reference of others

Raising sensitive issues for discussion

Experimenting with new practices

Changing personal frames of reference if warranted

Managing differences of opinion through inquiry and problem-solving

Understanding systemic influences and relationships

Correcting disruptive power imbalances

Despite the paucity of educational research on organisational learning, some consistency of definition and similar lists of identifying characteristics do seem to be emerging. In addition, some of the interrelationships among these characteristics are becoming clearer. For example, the identifying characteristics tend to describe organisational learning as a journey rather than a destination, and to group themselves sequentially and developmentally. The first stage of organisational learning largely focuses on developing common understandings, honesty, and trust through dialogue, sharing, and managing the inevitable conflict involved. These learning processes are then employed to make links to the outside, to examine current practice critically, to develop shared values as well as a vision for the school. The processes, the content (or identified changes), and shared values are employed to actually make the changes that have been identified, including a commitment and ability to repeat the stages, that is, to continuously learn and improve. These organisational characteristics are set within more or less powerful external parameters such as district policies, especially toward professional development, the student population, and the community.

As we improve our ability to monitor and understand these developmental pathways, we should be able to learn how to respond better to present problems and pressures and to optimise improvement in our schools. In other words, we should be able to establish effective organisational learning.

DEVELOPMENTAL PATHWAYS

There are at least three developmental pathways of organisational learning. These involve learning by individuals, learning by groups, and learning by the organisation itself. Because I believe that organisational learning is most effective when it takes the form of a social process that occurs in a community of practice, I will place particular emphasis on team or group development processes. However, it should be stressed that individual, group and organisation development are not distinct and mutually exclusive pathways of organisational learning but highly interconnected and interactive.

1. Individual Pathways

How, in individual terms, do teachers and principals learn? What pathways do their learning and development follow? There are a number of useful ways to examine this issue. Approaches include andragogy (Aubrey & Cohen, 1995; Brundage & McKerarcher, 1980; Loevinger, 1976; Mulford, 1979; Sheehy, 1976, 1995), study of career stages (Fessler, 1995; Huberman, 1995; Weiss & Cambone, 1994), and research on the steps through which educators proceed when they try something new (Beer, Eisenstat, & Spector, 1990; Carnall, 1986; Fuller, 1969; Hall & Loucks, 1976; Hall, Halland, & Hord, 1987; Redding & Catalandallo, 1994).

Understanding andragogy, or an individual's developmental stages, can help clarify the larger motives behind the investments of time, money and energy by many educational personnel. It can show us the more fundamental purposes that underlie undertaking further education, the pursuit of promotion or a career change, the desire to meet new persons, read more widely, explore new ideas and interests. It can remind us that the existential questions of meaning, purpose, vocation, social responsibility, dependence, and human relationships which many adolescents face with difficulty, are reconfronted by many thirty, forty, and sixty year olds.

Analysis of career stages is also useful because, unlike the recent past, change in schools increasingly depends on mid- and late-career teachers. These teachers, as Weiss and Cambone (1994) found, may sometimes be "more interested in planning for retirement than in planning for educational improvement" (p. 299). Huberman (1995) discusses the modal sequence of the teacher career cycle as entry and socialisation, followed by diversification and change, stocktaking and interrogations at mid-career, serenity and/or conservatism, and disengagement. This disengagement can be either serene or bitter. Some of the implications of career stages become clear when Huberman (1995) relates them to teacher satisfaction in times of change:

> Teachers who steered clear of reforms or other multiple-classroom innovations, but who invested consistently in classroom-level experiments – what they called "productive tinkering" with new materials, different pupil grouping, small changes in grading systems – were more likely to be "satisfied"

later on in their careers than most others, and far more likely to be satisfied than their peers who had been heavily involved in schoolwide or districtwide projects throughout their careers. This latter group felt that the time and effort expended on ambitious attempts to change on-going practices had essentially exhausted and embittered them, given the few concrete results they observed in their classrooms. . . . Yet – and this is noteworthy – these same teachers usually describe the first experiences of "experimentation" or "renewal" in which they were engaged with colleagues in these building-level changes as the most exciting and formative years of their career.

Three other factors were predictive of professional satisfaction later in the career cycle. . . teachers who spontaneously sought some sort of role shift when they began to feel stale . . . [having] specific cohorts or classes with whom they had enjoyed privileged relationships . . . [and] the experience of achieving significant results in the classroom. . .(p. 205)

Built on the earlier work of Fuller (1969), the most extensive research on the steps through which educators proceed when they try something new has been carried out by Hall and his associates (Hall & Loucks, 1976; Hall et al., 1987) under the title of the Concerns Based Adoption Model (CBAM). Two facets of CBAM are Levels of Use (LoU) and Stages of Concern (SoC). LoU focuses on the individual's behaviour and performance when facing something new. The teacher or principal begins by orienting him or herself to the change, actively engaged in looking over and reviewing materials, attending orientation workshops, examining the change and considering its use. The initial use of the change begins at the mechanical level where performance is somewhat disjointed and the user hangs on tightly to the 'user's guide'. A great deal of time is spent on logistical management matters. Focus is on the short-term, day-to-day use of the change with little time for reflection. Later there is a move to a routine use where systems are worked out and there is a way to work with the change. Little thought is given to improving the use of the change or its consequences. Finally refinement of the change may take place with the intention of increasing impact on students.

SoC focuses on the individual's perceptions, feelings and motivations about the change. During implementation, personal concerns such as those regarding one's adequacy to meet the demands of the change, one's role in relation to the reward structure of the organisation, and personal commitment will be most intense. As implementation progresses, management concerns regarding efficiency, organisation, timetabling, and time demands become more intense with personal concerns decreasing. With time, the impact or consequences of the change become the focus. Impact on students, then collaboration with other staff regarding the use of the change, and then refocussing to consider the possibility of major changes or replacement with more powerful alternatives become, respectively, most relevant.

One implication of LoU and SoC is that teachers involved in change are not able to work collaboratively until they have their 'own house in order'. Each staff member needs to master use of the change personally, in his or her context, before becoming active in effectively collaborating with other staff. The development implicit in concepts such as LoU and SoC also give us hope that, given time and support, those involved in change in schools will eventually move beyond the managerial to the educational standpoint.

These implications are consistent with other studies which have shown that, when it comes to spreading change throughout an organisation, it is often faster to 'reinvent the wheel' (e.g., Beer et al., 1990). It is also consistent with other developmental models such as that developed by Carnall (1986) which suggest that regardless of how well a change has proven itself elsewhere, each individual and group must go through a coping cycle. This cycle has five stages: denial where there is a lack of acceptance of the need for change that results from an implied criticism of past performance, defence usually to protect territories and maintain the status quo, discarding of the old, adaptation of the new, and, finally, internalisation. Redding and Catalandello (1994) stress that, "The coping cycle is inevitable, and each organizational unit must go through it. Leaders need to provide time and space for people to come to grips with the change" (p. 83).

What is consistent across each of these approaches to individual development is that few adults, including teachers or principals, progress as a matter of course through the various developmental stages (Mulford, 1979). Past experience enters into all adult learning. The learning process involves transformations rather than formations. Transformations require greater input of our energy and time because we invest considerable effort in maintaining established patterns, we need to bring meaning, values and skills to a conscious level and examine them thoroughly, and new behaviours need to be tested out in safe situations before being put into use in daily life (Brundage & MacKerarcher, 1980).

Ashton and Webb point out that work is likely to be satisfying "when we value what we do, when it challenges and extends us, when we do it well, and when we have ample evidence confirming our success" (emphasis added, 1986, p. 162). Movement from one stage of individual development to the next occurs through cycles of challenge and response, cognitive dissonance, cultural discontinuity, differentiation, and integration. It occurs when a person confronts situations for which old ways are not adequate, which require new ways of thinking and acting. This experience may be uncomfortable and does not always proceed simply and smoothly. The difficulty is achieving that optimal distance between where the teacher or principal currently is in terms of their thinking and behaviour, and what the new situations require so that he or she is challenged but not 'bowled over'; so that change is possible without provoking trauma, entrenchment, or flight.

Aubrey and Cohen's (1995) "working wisdom" model of organisational learning is consistent with these principles. The model was stimulated by the answers the authors received from asking managers "Where did you learn what is most useful to you in working life?" Answers did not include training courses, as had been expected, but took place, courtesy of episodes involving a non dogmatic mentor, a high pressure project, a major 'screwup', or a career change. Building on this insight, Aubrey and Cohen identified five key and evolutionary learning-management skills or tactics inherent in adult learning. Their model begins with a journey and an accompanist-learner manager (accompanying). Then it proceeds through planting the message, probably before the learner is ready to understand it (sowing), seeking the stressful, catalytic moment at which the learner is most likely to have a breakthrough – and nudging him or her to do exactly that (catalysing), providing numerous opportunities for dialogue among equals, as opposed to 'telling' (showing), and, finally, taking advantage of the prior learning, and moving on to the next stage (harvesting).

2. Group Pathways

Two sets of literature which help us in understanding group development in schools are those centred around the stages of staff and group development. In what follows, particular attention is given to the stages of group development and the importance of focussing on the stages involving conflict and then task accomplishment.

In discussing practices that support staff development, Lieberman points out that in contrast to the common strategy of a "transferable package of knowledge to be distributed to teachers in bite-sized pieces", people learn best "through active involvement and through thinking about and becoming articulate about what they have learned" (1995, p. 592). The change, as Lieberman succinctly summarises is "from 'teaching' to 'learning' " (1995, p. 592). Hamilton and Richardson's (1995) research confirms this conclusion. They examined the staff development program in two elementary schools which were implementationing a new reading program. They found that as group staff development processes proceeded, they "appeared to follow certain stages, each stage taking different lengths of time in the two schools" (p. 375). The introductory stage saw teachers familiarising themselves with each other and listening politely. The following 'breakthrough' stage resulted from a new way of thinking and "do you?" questions being asked of each other. The third and final stage involved empowerment where teachers "claimed ownership of the staff development itself and dominated the conversation" (p. 375). Staff were more likely to proceed through these three stages when there were "social norms within a school that encourage teachers to discuss their beliefs and practices" (p. 382).

Mitchell (1995) researched an urban Canadian elementary school that was involved in effective organisational learning. The research identified four processes, three basic assumptions, as well as three distinct phases in the school's organisational learning. To quote Mitchell:

> [Organizational learning] entailed four processes, two cognitive and two affective. The cognitive processes of reflection and conversation enabled the teachers to become aware of their practices and of those of their colleagues, to assess the desirability of those practices, and to discover new possibilities. The affective processes of affirmation [of each other as professionals] and invitation [into school deliberations] served to create positive working relationships by affirming the professional capabilities of individuals and by valuing the contributions of all staff members. (1995, p. 223)

These four processes were founded upon three basic assumptions: "that each individual was responsible for the welfare of the group and the success of the school; that diversity among individuals was recognized, honoured, and valued; and that psychological safety would be maintained in group deliberations" (Mitchell, 1995, p. 226).

The four processes also moved through three phases: naming and framing to clarify positions and opinions; analysing and integrating especially when new ideas are opened up for possible experimentation; and applying and experimenting" (Mitchell, 1995, p. 226). Indicators of organisational learning synthesised from the literature by Mitchell emerged at different points, over the three phases, implying that "these behaviours and processes do not develop overnight, but rather build on one another over time" (1995, p. 231).

This developmental nature of organisational learning highlighted for Mitchell

the importance of the 'naming and framing' and 'analyzing and integrating' phases. The comfort level with organizational learning grew as teachers developed their own understandings about the concept, analyzed their own practices in the light of those understandings, and applied appropriate aspects of what they had learned. . . Framing is an active process, and teachers need adequate time to talk about and to reflect upon initiatives . . . (1995, p. 243)

The message that emerges from these studies is that those in schools must learn how to lose time in order to gain time. Awareness of, and skill development in group and organisational processes is the first step in any effective change. Instead of others trying to insert something into a school's culture, the school, and especially its leadership, should first be trying to help that culture develop an awareness of and a responsiveness to itself (Mulford, Fisher, & Grady, 1991). This is similar to what Fullan and Hargreaves (1991) call "interactive professionalism" and Louis, Kruse and associates (1995) label a "professional community."

There is further evidence to support this position. Senge (1990) stresses the importance of team building and Watkins and Marsick (1993) focus on team relationships for effectice change. Russ' (1995) investigation of the features of school improvement that helped raise levels of pupil achievement in a small sample of secondary schools in the UK, highlighted the primacy of teams and collaborative staff development in a school's organisational learning. Sackney et al. (1995) research on the Saskatchewan School Improvement Program (SSIP), a provincially initiated school staff development program in 140 of the Province's 825 schools, based on effective schools research, found one of the three factors explaining the underlying structure of organisational learning to be collaboration. The other two factors were individual learning and alignment of the school's and the division's goals.

Fullan (1994) argues for promoting norms of collaboration, as do Leithwood and Aitkin (in press) who term it 'collective commitment'. Keating (1995) stresses coordinating group effort and Mitchell (1995) common understandings. Berliner and Biddle promote the concept of a community of learners stating that "once in place [they] . . . allow for meaningful discussion of change" (1995, p. 338). Darling-Hammond and McLaughlin (1995), Louis, Kruse and associates (1995), and McLaughlin (1994) argue persuasively for developing professional communities of teachers. As Murphy and Louis conclude, "[m]anaging reform turns out to be less an administrative task than a motivational one . . . defending and keeping the school vision alive is critical. . . [but] it is the richness of relationships that forms the taproot" (1994, p. 268).

One way to approach these processes is to base staff development, the increased cooperative effort, the increased sharing of power and responsibility, on predictable stages of group development. Borrowing from Mulford et al. (1980) and Wheelan (1994), a review of the accumulated research on group development suggests that groups move through sequential stages or phases. The initial stage of development focuses on issues of forming, of inclusion and dependency in which members attempt to identify behaviour acceptable to the leader and other group members. These early group meetings are also characterised as a time of member anxiety. This stage equates with Mitchell's (1995) naming and framing phase.

The next phase, storming, is described as a period of counter dependency, fight or conflict, and flight. Issues of power, authority, and competition are debated. Early struggles regarding authority and status, if resolved adequately, become prerequisites for subsequent increases in cohesion, cooperation, and trust. This phase also provides the opportunity to clarify areas of common value which can help to increase group stability. It equates with Mitchell's (1995) analysing and integrating phase. The third phase, norming, is devoted to the development of trust and more mature and open negotiations regarding goals, roles, group structure, and division of labour. This is followed by a performing or work phase characterised by an increase in task orientation and open exchange of feedback. This third stage equates with Mitchell's (1995) applying and experimenting phase.

There is also a mourning phase which can occur after any of the stages the group has reached. It is triggered by the impending dissolution of the group. At this phase members reassert their independence from the group and start to disengage. I also believe, although I have no research evidence to support the assertion, that there is a dorming phase that interacts at and with the performing phase. It is the time for 'pulling back on the oars' for resting and recuperating, for letting the momentum of success allow the group to 'coast' for a while.

Not only are there a number of clearly identifiable and sequential stages of development, but also much can be done to assist the group/staff through to a more effective later stage of 'performing'. If left to their own devices, groups may not progress beyond or may quickly revert to the earlier, less productive stages of 'forming', 'storming', and 'norming'.

Of all stages, the transition from storming to norming and then norming to performing are perhaps the most crucial. As Murphy and Louis have pointed out, principals need to be able to support teachers, especially through a "key stage" where together they change "from being managers of conflict to leaders who surface conflicts that must be addressed for reform to move forward" (1994, p. 274). This surfacing and productive use of conflict requires "'hard listening' that is alert to conflict, . . . active encouragement to voice frustration, [and] . . . respect and honesty, including permitting others to criticise the principal's decisions" (p. 277).

The educational literature and research on organisational learning seems divided on the importance and place of conflict. Mitchell's (1995) results reflect this division. On the one hand she found that there needs to be an "understanding of the inevitability of conflict" and the "raising [of] sensitive issues for discussion" (p. 232). On the other, she discovered that two of the three basic assumptions held by staff are that "diversity among individuals was recognized, honoured, and valued" and that "psychological safety would be maintained in group deliberations" (p. 226).

Valuable research by Jehn (1995) examined the structure of 105 work groups and management teams to address the question of whether conflict can be beneficial or not. Results show that whether conflict was beneficial depended on the type of task (routine or non-routine) and the norms of the group (in terms of openness versus conflict-avoidance).

> In groups performing very routine tasks, disagreements about the task were detrimental to group functioning. In contrast, in groups performing non-routine tasks, disagreements about tasks did not have a detrimental effect, and in some cases, such disagreements were actually beneficial. (p. 256)
>
> While openness norms did increase the beneficial aspects of task-related conflict on performance, they also increased the negative impact of relationship conflict rather than diminishing its negative effects. Groups with conflict-avoidance norms about relationship conflicts had more satisfied members than groups with openness norms. This finding contradicts much of the past group research . . . that suggests that open, honest communications and confrontation promotes effective group interaction. It is consistent, however, with more recent research. (Jehn, 1995, p. 277)

This more recent research includes a study by Murnighan and Conlon (1991) who found that successful British string quartets did not openly discuss heated interpersonal conflicts, recognising that these conflicts could be counterproductive. As Jehn reports, the "successful quartets resolved their conflicts by compromises (i.e., taking turns), staying focussed on the task, and leaving interpersonal or external conflicts (i.e., personality problems, trouble at home) aside" (1995, p. 277). A similar direction is hinted at in Mitchell's research when she discusses the importance of "managing differences of opinion through inquiry and problem-solving" (1995, p. 232) and in Louis, Kruse and associates' finding on the foundational nature of "a shared normative and value base paired with reflective dialogue" (1995, p. 206). In other words, trust and respect develops as a result of providing psychological safety in conflictual situations. This is achieved, in the main, by keeping focussed on the task, which in schools is teaching and student learning.

Achieving effective collaboration, especially through the inevitable conflict stage, may be difficult for many people in schools. Those who have been rewarded, by promotion and other means, on different criteria may be particularly disadvantaged. However, achieving this collaboration is a prerequisite for effective organisational learning.

The other prerequisite involves a second crucial transition, from norming to performing. This transition aims to ensure that the cooperative effort – the delegating, collaborating, and shared authority resulting from a successful negotiation of the storming stage, as well as the high morale that usually accompanies the norming stage – is focused on the task of schooling, that is, teaching and student learning. It aims to avoid the 'paralysis by analysis' suggested in studies of organisational learning in schools by both Dalin and Rust (1983) and Sackney et al. (1995). This transition is bound up with what Louis, Kruse and associates (1995) found to be the essential foundation for a mature professional community in a school – "a shared normative and value base paired with reflective dialogue" (p. 206). It involves Keating's (1995) "coordinated group effort towards commonly shared goals" (p. 20), Fullan's (1994) focus on multiple learning agendas and engagement in continuous learning, Leithwood et al's. (1995) coherent sense of direction, and Senge's (1990) and Mitchell's (1995) notions of shared vision. And it is consistent with Stoll and Mortimore's conclusion that for school effectiveness and improvement to be successful "people within the school [must] . . . take charge of the change process" (1995, p. 7).

A convenient bridge between the stages of group and organisational development is the importance of vision for establishing organisational learning in schools. There are different opinions on this issue in the literature, though Leithwood et al. (1995) found that a school's vision did not stimulate significant organisational learning and Sackney et al. (1995) reported that the willingness of teachers to align their activities with a school's or district's mission had no effect on school effectiveness. Reporting on research in 200 business organisations, Redding and Catalanello also state: "the quality of strategic plans did not seem to have much to do with companies' ability (or lack of ability) to change. Nor did the degree of effort devoted to the implementation of strategic plans . . . what seemed to matter most was the orgnization's readiness for change" (1994, p. xiii). These authors go on to conclude, as had Beer et al. (1990) and Kanter (1991) earlier, that "fundamental organisational change most often results from journeys of learning – of setting out in a direction, of gaining new insights and making discoveries en route, of going back, adjusting old maps, developing revised plans, and taking new actions" (Redding & Catalanello, 1994, p. 7).

Yet others, such as Hallinger and Heck (1995) and Weiss and Cambone (1994), have stressed the central importance of vision and/or goals in establishing effective organisational learning. If we substitute the word 'vision' for 'strategies' in the following quotation, Mintzberg may offer a resolution to this seeming confusion:

> . . . few, if any, strategies can be purely deliberate, and few can be purely emergent. One suggests no learning, the other, no control. All real-world

strategies need to mix these in some way – to attempt control without stopping the learning process. Organizations, for example, often pursue what may be called umbrella strategies: the broad outlines are deliberate while the details are allowed to emerge within them. Thus emergent strategies are not necessarily bad and deliberate ones good; effective strategies mix these characteristics in ways that reflect the conditions at hand, notably the ability to predict as well as the need to react to unexpected events. (1994, p. 25)

Redding and Catalanello put it as follows: "The major value of a strategic vision is that it compels the firm to act and to learn" (1994, p. 57) and that the "original vision is less important than perpetual 'revision.' The most effective vision is continually evolving, transformed by the insights derived from the actions of discovery that the vision itself inspires" (1994, p. 66).

In other words, a school involved in effective organisational learning has a vision that is constantly emerging and developing. "A vision that is kept purposely broad and open to allow for both the alteration of course over time and the involvement of the organization in the creation of the vision" (Redding & Catalanello, 1994, p. 179). Or as Russ concluded, a school that is successful at raising levels of pupil achievement "learns its way forward" (1995, p. 6). Similarly, Huberman found that the most satisfied teachers were those involved in "productive tinkering" throughout their careers (1995, p. 205). Tyack and Cuban put it as follows in their book *Tinkering Toward Utopia*, "We favor attempts to bring about . . . improvement by working from the inside out, especially by enlisting the support and skills of teachers as key actors in reform. This might be seen as a positive kind of tinkering, adapting knowledgeably to local needs and circumstances, preserving what is valuable and correcting what is not" (1995, p. 10).

3. Organisational Pathways

Griener (1972) was among the earliest to speculate about the changes that occur in organisations as they get older, bigger, and find themselves in higher growth rates. Just over ten years later, Quinn and Cameron (1983) reviewed nine models of organisational life cycles from the literature, including Greiner's. They constructed a summary model of life cycle stages that integrates each of these nine models. Each model is seen to contain "an entrepreneurial stage (early innovation, niche formation, creativity), a collectivity stage (high cohesion, commitment), a formalization and control stage (stability and institutionalization), and a structure elaboration and adaptation stage (domain expansion and decentralization)" (Quinn & Cameron, 1983, p. 40).

Hurst (1995) has recently renewed interest in the topic of organisational growth by refining and extending the above work. He has developed a model of the process of organisational change consisting of two loops that intersect to form the shape of an infinity symbol. One loop is the conventional S-shaped life cycle (or performance, technical systems loop) of the Greiner (1972) and Quinn and Cameron (1983) school of thought. In its most succinct form this involves a progression from emergent to rational to constrained action, i.e., from entrepreneurial action to strategic management to conservation (doing what we know and do best, sticking to the knitting). The new, reverse loop represents the process of renewal (or a learning, social systems loop of 'death' and 'reconception'). This returns through constrained to 'rational' to emergent action, i.e., from crisis and confusion (seeds of failure contained in fruits of success) to values-based charismatic leadership (walking the talk, envisioning) to a creative network (creating and nurturing contexts), choice and then entrepreneurial action once again. The model, which is summarised in what follows, is compatible with Louis' (1994) call to link both the managed change and anarchy paradigms for an effective model of how schools improve.

A number of features of Hurst's (1995) model are worthy of elaboration. First, change is seen as continuous, although the pace and nature of it vary greatly. Second, renewal also requires destruction and is an ongoing process. Third, there are two forms of rational action each taking the organisation in quite different directions. Strategic management in the performance loop is characterised by an instrumental, means-end rationality "which leads eventually toward organizations that become tightly connected and constrained" (p. 104). Charismatic leadership in the learning loop, on the other hand, is values-based rationality – "action taken for its intrinsic worth in demonstrating deeply held beliefs about human relationships . . . [and] develops loosely connected, creative networks from which new activities can emerge" (p. 104).

Fourth, managers "have to come to grips with both [the structural and process] loops in real time [especially at] the nexus of conflict . . . where the two forms of rationality cross – where the demand to live our values clashes with the requirement for instrumental behavior" (p. 167). It is where the "social vision

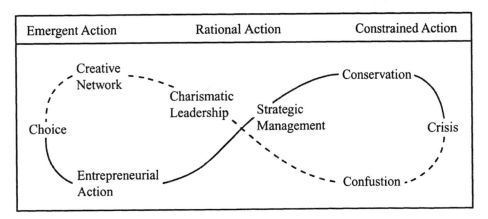

Figure 1

of an egalitarian, participative community clashes with the need to run a technically rational, hierarchical organization. Where the community may clash with individuality, as ambition vies with obligation; where cooperation meets competition; where the long run often trips over the short term" (p. 167).

And finally, healthy organisations "should . . . consist of 'patches' at different stages of development. One can use the . . . [model] both to locate all the patches at a moment in time and to track the evolution of particular patches over time" (p. 105).

Consistent with the directions suggested in the sections on individual and group pathways of development for those in leadership positions and the value of vision for organisational learning, Hurst (1995) sees that a manager's position in the renewal, or learning loop as analogous to that of a gardener:

> . . . the gardener cannot make the plants grow; he or she can only create the optimum conditions under which the plants' natural self-organizing tendencies can function. The gardener has to allow them to grow.
>
> This is why managers of the renewal process do not have to have any technical answers; they only have to understand the social contexts in which learning is possible. Thus, in the organizational renewal cycle, the emphasis is on action that creates contexts for action. On the learning loop, we have to act our way into a better mode of thinking. Logic is an output – an induction from successful action. (emphasis in original, pp. 136–137)

The above models of organisational development help us understand better the intricacies involved in moving any organisation such as a school, or part of a school, from where it is to becoming effective at organisational learning. They should help target appropriate interventions to ensure more effective progression through the stages as well as achieving the ultimate goal of being effective at organisational learning. In targeting interventions recognition needs to be given to the fact that actions at one stage may be inappropriate, or even counterproductive, at another stage.

Being effective at organisational learning may, in fact, mean that a school recognises and understands such stages and can take the appropriate action without being 'bowled over' by the change that surrounds it. It may mean understanding that you will be evaluated differently depending on the stage the school has reached. It may mean understanding the importance of both the 'dorming' stage in dealing with the psychological saturation arising from the amount of change and the intensity of teamwork, as well as the need to understand, if not balance, the rationality of the technical systems loop with the renewal involved in the social systems loop of organisational development. And it may mean understanding the crucial need to link the school closely with its wider environment, especially once it has developed to the more 'mature' stages.

LIMITATIONS

The theme I have been developing is that organisational learning has benefits for schools involved with educational change. This is especially so if this learning is based on an understanding of and an ability to act on individual, group and organisational development. However, organisational learning has somewhat uncritically become something of a cargo cult in the business community and shows signs of developing similar status in the educational community as well. Therefore, it is especially important to be aware of possible limitations of the approach. I therefore conclude this chapter by identifying six areas of concern – cultural and micropolitical limitations, the ideas of continuous improvement, self-determination and procedural illusions of effectiveness, and finally the deep seated limitations imposed by the grammars of schooling.

1. Cultural Limitations

Much of the literature in this chapter, is from North America – a part of the world with its own unique set of problems. Berliner and Biddle, for example, detail at some length the manufactured crisis in education in USA, the myths and fraud in recent bitter attacks on public schools that has diverted attention away from what they believe are the real problems faced by American education such as "income and wealth inequality; recent stagnation of the economy; racial, ethnic, religious, and linguistic diversity . . . ; prejudice towards . . . [those] of color; the ghettoization of . . . cities; violence and drugs; the aging of the population; the restructuring of work" (1995, p. 7).

But our world is also 'shrinking'. Access to international information, institutions, and expertise increasingly sees "policies and solutions to problems employed in one national context stand a far greater likelihood of being known and considered for use in other nations" (Hallinger, 1995, p. 4). Hallinger (1995) is one of a growing number who question this development. He wonders why, for example, "Western treatises on the nature of leadership . . . are often transferred across cultures with relatively little concern for cultural validity" (Hallinger, 1995, p. 4) To take but one example, it may be that Chinese cultures with their greater appreciation of the interconnectedness of life, processes, community, interdependencies, and long time-frame as compared with the Western emphasis on separateness, things, individuality, 'the answer', and short time-frame, are actually more amenable to the concept of organisational learning (Senge, Roberts, Ross, Smith, & Kleiner, 1994, p. 565).

2. Micropolitical Limitations: Genuine Involvement of All?

The skills promoted by change strategies such as organisational learning heavily favour the most literate and articulate members of the organisation. As "verbal facility is also probably related to the authority of the school . . . those lower in the hierarchy may find themselves at a disadvantage in pursuing their own interests . . . " (Morgan & associates, 1976, pp. 45–46). It may also be that the skills required for success, whether this be verbal ability or expertise in areas such as collaboration, favour other groups in schools, such as the principal and/or females (Caldwell, Lawrence, Peck, & Thomas, 1994; Shakeshaft, 1989; Thomas & Caldwell, 1994). Perhaps such 'favouritism' is not before time, but it is also to miss the point. The literature and research on schools involved in organisational learning suggests that all members of an organisation, articulate and inarticulate, females and males, old and young, superordinates and subordinates, and even those demonstrating expertise in different 'intelligences' (Gardiner, 1983) need to participate skilfully and with purpose in social interaction.

Schein (1996) believes that organisations will not learn effectively until we recognise and confront the implications of three different occupational cultures. He believes that until the executives, engineers (designers and technocrats who drive the core technology) and operators discover that they use different languages, make different assumptions about what is important, and until they learn to treat the other cultures as valid and normal, we will continue to see failures in organisational learning efforts. He provides an educational example:

> In the educational world we see the same conflict between teachers who value the human interaction with students and the proponents of sophisticated computerized educational systems on the one hand and the cost constraints imposed by school administrators on the other hand. If the engineers win, money is spent on computers and technologically sophisticated classrooms. If the administrators win, classes become larger and undermine the classroom climate. In either case, the operators, the teachers lose out and human innovations in learning are lost. (1996, p. 8)

3. Continuous Improvement?

As we have seen in other chapters of this book, the pressure on schools is for major and continuous improvement. Some call for nothing less than a paradigm shift (Louis, 1994). But as Hargreaves points out, "the commitment to continuous improvement can easily degenerate into interminable improvement where no value is given to heritage, continuity, consolidation and tradition (which are all vital ingredients of schooling); where only incurable change addicts prosper and survive" (1995, pp. 11–12).

It is important to heed Dalin and Rust's warning that it "is fatal to assume that the school is learning only if it is undergoing change. More crucial is its ability to monitor its own system constantly, and accept as well as reject new practices and new products as they are found to be appropriate and inappropriate (that is, to be a learning organisation)" (1983, p. 91). How to achieve the right balance between continuous improvement and the maintenance of a safe base from which to venture forth continues to be little discussed issue in the literature on organisational learning. How to achieve stability for change, how to move ahead without losing our roots, is the challenge.

4. Self-determination?

Effective organisational learning involves those in an organisation taking responsibility for outcomes. Yet how do we share responsibility for all problems, or to be more positive, learnings, when many matters are not within a school's control? Levin is one who points out that "arguably, the most powerful educative (and mis-educative) forces in our society lie outside the school system" and that "educational reformers might direct their efforts with greater effect to the mass media, popular culture, and the emerging Information Superhighway" (1994, p. 48). Hargreaves goes further in suggesting that, "the dynamics of blame. . . . the claim that we share responsibility for all our problems seems . . . pernicious. Schools and teachers have to deal with many mandates they do not control. Public schools are not bounded systems" (1995, p. 12). And Berliner and Biddle's (1995) book on the manufactured crisis in education, the recent myths, fraud and attacks on America's public schools, is ample testimony to just how permeable that boundary can be.

Leithwood et al's. (1995, p. 28) research employing interview data from 72 teachers and 6 principals in 6 schools in British Colombia, Canada, regarded as promising sites of organisational learning, concluded that district contributions to organisational learning in schools are underestimated. What seemed to be critical in order for districts to have such influence were their professional development policies and resources, especially policies that helped ensure the social processing of new ideas.

There are increasing calls by those in education for closer, more authentic links between the centre of a school system and its schools (Fullan, 1994; Miles, 1993; Mitchell, 1995). However, the evidence of the continuing influence of the centre for either good (Leithwood et al., 1995) or ill (Bishop & Mulford, 1996; Cohen & Barnes, 1993) and the emphasis in the organisational learning literature on the fundamental importance of the organisation being connected with the wider environment and remaining in control along with increasing evidence of the centre's reluctance to 'let go' (Stoll & Fink, 1994), point to continued difficulties in the relationship between the centre and the school over who is in control and over what.

This situation raises the question of how we could better handle the transition in this important and fundamental relationship. How to overcome the potential incompatibility between accountability and empowerment that lies at the heart of the relationship (Glickman, 1990) clearly needs to be understood better than it is at present. Teacher empowerment without accountability can lead to anarchy, whereas accountability without empowerment can lead to subservience.

An example of the difficulties involved when teachers have only partial control or none at all, can be found in the growing school based-management (SBM) literature. Evidence continues to mount that mandated moves to decentralisation of functions to the school level have occured only partially if at all, and that this has resulted in little substantive change in schools. A recent historical examination of how SBM evolved through earlier eras of decentralisation, as well as a review of the research literature on SBM over the last ten years, led Murphy and Beck, for example, to conclude that SBM "tends to wash over classrooms, leaving the instructional program largely unaffected" (1995, p. 154). Further, they state that there is "almost no evidence . . . that the current round of SBM measures is any more effective in enhancing student achievement than were previous decentralization initiatives" (p. 157). "In short," point out Murphy and Beck, "SBM – at least in its most recent incarnation – generally reinforces rather than helps overcome widespread inattention to the central issues of learning and teaching in schools" (1995, p. 177). (See also: Berliner & Biddle, 1995; Bishop & Mulford, 1996; Kirst, 1994; Louis, Kruse, & associates; 1995; Murphy & Louis, 1994; Mulford, 1994; Russ, 1995.)

5. Procedural Illusions of Effectiveness

One of the risks with accepting movement, or change for change's sake as proof of organisational learning, is that a school may be involved in what Sizer (1984) called "Horace's Compromise". That is, it may work toward a facade of orderly purposefulness, exchanging minimums in pursuit of the least hassle for everyone. Sometimes this compromise can be likened to 'doing things right' rather than 'doing the right things'. As Sergiovanni (1990) has pointed out, it has the same purpose as the latest military technology of building in canvas – that is, folding canvas tanks, canvas missile launchers, and so on, designed to serve as decoys and to create an illusion of strength. The purpose for schools becomes one of providing the 'right' public face (although such action could conceivably gain freedom within schools to interpret, decide, and function in ways that make sense).

In particular, procedural illusions can be employed to maintain the myth of education and function to legitimise it to the outside world (Meyer & Rowan, 1978). In the absence of clear-cut output measures we can turn to processes such as charters, strategic plans, and so on, as outputs. All these administrative processes give confidence to the outside (and to many of those inside) that schools are learning, that they know what they are doing. The structure of the school is the functioning myth of the organisation that operates not necessarily to regulate intra-organisational activity, but to explain it, account for it, and to legitimate it to the members outside the organisation and to the wider society.

Hargreaves (Hargreaves & Dawe, 1990) used the term "contrived collegiality" to describe one of the processes involved in such symbolic rather than substantive action. Here, of course, we are talking about a situation where, by being co-opted, schools and the staff in them may be involved in actions of high visibility and the impression of decisiveness – a situation which raises important moral questions. Deception should have little place in effective organisational learning in schools.

It is also worth pointing out that the research on organisational learning has hinted at a relationship between effective organisational learning in schools and better teaching and student learning. However the link between organisational learning and outcome variables such as these is, to date, very weak and in need of much greater attention by the educational research community.

THE GRAMMAR OF SCHOOLS

Other literature, also undergoing something of a revival, suggests that schools already have many structures and/or learning habits that will counteract any moves toward organisational learning. Some of the early literature in this vein pointed to the poor interpersonal relationships that can characterise schools (Campbell, 1976; Ogilvie, 1977), anti-collaborative norms (Mulford, 1982), the isolation or low interdependence among teachers (Bredo, 1977; Gregersen, 1978; Mulford, 1976, 1982), and isolation between strata (Hampstead, Ford, & Hird, 1980; Pusey, 1976). Other literature (Mulford, 1982) talks about the multiple, vague and/or disagreement on goals and processes in schools which can lead to action that is motivated merely by survival and to satisfy constraints. More recent examples of literature in this vein include that by Cohen (1994) and Hamilton and Richardson (1995).

Other more recent literature has shown a growing interest in what has been termed either the 'Grammars of Organisations' (Pentland & Rueter, 1994; Tyack & Tobin, 1994; Tyack & Cuban, 1995) or 'The New Institutionalism' (Boyd, Crowson, & Mawhinney, in press). Crowson and Boyd's (1993) article on coordinating services for children provides an example of literature in this mould. It argues that the 'deep structures' of schooling, that is, the fundamental ways schools work, make it difficult for cooperative, collegial, collaborative effort to occur. The public school is pictured as a "complex and intricate web of competition and collaboration" (p. 172), with its internal organisation "in many ways more a coalition of interests than it is a collegium" (p. 158).

Gitlin and Margonis (1995) also use evidence from a study of school site-based decision-making in USA to argue that the emphasis within the school change literature on promoting teacher engagement in reform endeavours obscures the political insights and potential good sense of those teachers who resist reform. They conclude, "our interpretation of the insights of resistant teachers indicates that reformers might be better focusing on the preconditions for reform: giving teachers the authority and the time they need to teach in ways they find educationally defensible" (p. 403).

Gitlin and Margonis (1995) suggest that if schools are to become effective at organisational learning then at least one of the 'grammars' of schooling, how they use time, will need to be profoundly reviewed. Louis, Kruse and associates (1995) and Lieberman (1995) make this same point, as does Mitchell when she points out that the behaviours and processes required for effective organisational learning "do not develop overnight, but rather build on one another over time" (1995, p. 231). Specifically, Mitchell found that her first phase of building effective organisational learning, naming and framing, "is an active process, and teachers need time to talk about and to reflect on initiatives" (1995, p. 243).

Based on a range of research findings, Berliner and Biddle's conclusion reinforces the importance of schools finding this time: " . . . communities of learners . . . takes time to establish, but once in place, such communities allow for meaningful discussion of proposed changes, provide appropriate environments to initiate and support change, and generate procedures to study the effects of change" (1995, p. 338). In brief, we could describe the need to find time as being about losing time to gain time. In other words, it is about schools first finding time to develop awareness of and skills in collaborative processes.

Yet how many of our schools are willing or able to find this time? As Mitchell's in-depth study of organisational learning in a Saskatchewan elementary school found:

> From time to time, endogenous influences distracted the teachers from thinking about and participating in organizational learning. . . . [e.g.,] Stalled contract negotiations resulted in a lock-out of all teachers in the system [and the] . . . illness [and subsequent death] of a fourth-grade student . . . .(1995, p. 221)
>
> . . . benefits can be gained when teachers talk with their colleagues about professional concerns, but the structure of the teacher's work-day does not expedite such an activity. Furthermore, teachers tend to be event driven. . . . [and thus] run the risk of losing sight of larger philosophical and pedagogical issues. (1995, p. 239)

CONCLUSION

We could sometimes be forgiven for wondering whether the essence of education – teaching and learning – has been displaced in the eyes of many of those both inside and outside schools. Has it been displaced because improvement of interpersonal relationships, curriculum and instruction calls for delayed gratification with the signs of progress being not easily detected? Have the tangible and immediate aspects (procedural illusions of effectiveness, restructuring, facts, knowledge, technical proficiency, and so on) replaced more nebulous, long-term considerations which, in my mind, are obviously more essential? I hope not.

The Ontario Royal Commission on Learning had the following to say about those in schools in today's turbulent times:

> Teachers are our heroes. We believe they should be everyone's heroes. Anyone who has watched a teacher begin a day facing a group of kids who'd rather be anywhere in the world than sitting in that classroom learning about something called geometry that they couldn't care less about understands

only too well what a frustrating, thankless, enervating task these mortal women and men face so much of their working lives. In return, they feel unappreciated, disrespected, the focus of twisted media attacks, caught in an almost war-like situation not of their making. It's hardly an accident that so many teachers love talking about themselves as the front-line troops of the education system, the ones that are in the trenches each and every day. Is this a happy metaphor for schooling?

... given the constant pressure they operate under, the seriousness of their responsibilities, the never-ending new obligations society foists on them and the never-ending new changes that boards or the Ministry impose on them, the anxiety about keeping up with their subject and with good practices that result from the explosion of knowledge both in their disciplines and in teaching methods – given all this, even the ordinary teacher seems heroic to us. (1994, pp. 13–14)

Yet despite this deep respect for those in schools, the Royal Commission went on to conclude that, "It's only when teachers are continually learning and thinking about how to improve their practice that collectively they can create the optimal conditions for students' learning" (1994, p. 16). In other words, in times of unprecedented change, paradox, and deep societal concerns over schooling, one of the Commission's major recommendations was for organisational learning.

The small but growing evidence available in the literature and research in the area supports such a recommendation. Organisational learning would appear to offer a way for a school to make sense of paradox, to ride the 'see saws' of change (Handy, 1994), and to establish and maintain a sense of connectedness, direction, and continuity. Organisational learning offers the potential of stability for change, an opportunity for schools to move ahead without losing their roots. In other words, it is a change strategy with the potential to address current change agendas. As such it is a change strategy worthy of further development and analysis.

REFERENCES

Argyris, C. (1993). *Knowledge for action: A guide to overcoming barriers to organizational change*. San Francisco, CA: Jossey-Bass.

Argyris, C., & Schon, D. (1978). *Organizational learning. A theory of action perspective*. Reading, MASS.: Addison-Wesley.

Ashton, P., & Webb, R. (1986). *Making a difference: Teachers' sense of efficacy and student achievement*. NY: Longman.

Aubrey, R., & Cohen, P. (1995). *Working wisdom: Timeless skills and vanguard strategies for learning organizations*. San Francisco: Jossey-Bass

Beer, M., Eisenstat, R., & Spector, B. (1990). *The critical path to corporate renewal*. Boston: Harvard Business School Press.

Berliner, D., & Biddle, B. (1995). *The manufactured crisis: Myths, fraud, and the attack on America's public schools*. NY: Addison-Wesley.

Bishop, P., & Mulford, W. (1996). Empowerment in four primary schools: They don't really care. *International Journal of Educational Reform*, 5(2), 193–204.

Boyd, W., Crowson, R., & Mawhinney, H. (Eds). (in press). *The politics of education and the new institutionalism: Reinventing the American school*. Washington, DC: Falmer Press (The 1995 Yearbook of the Politics of Education Association).

Bredo, E. (1977). Collaborative relations among elementary school teachers. *Sociology of Education*, 50(4), 300–309.

Brundage, D, & MacKeracher, D. (1980). *Adult learning principles and their application to program planning*. Toronto: Ontario Ministry of Education.

Caldwell, B., Lawrence, A., Peck, F., & Thomas, F. (1994). *Leading Victoria's schools of the future: Base-line survey of principals in 1993*. Paper presented at the Seventh International Congress for School Effectiveness and Improvement, Melbourne, Victoria, January.

Campbell, W. (1976). *Some consequences of the Radford Scheme for schools, teachers and students in Queensland*. Canberra: Australian Government Printer, AACRDE Report Number 7.

Carnall, C. (1986). Managing strategic change: An integrated approach. *Long-Range Planning*, 19(6), 105–115.

Cohen, D., & Barnes, C. (1993). Conclusion: A new pedagogy for policy? In D. Cohen, M. McLaughlin, & J. Talbert. (Eds.). *Teaching for understanding: Challenges for policy and practice*. San Francisco: Jossey-Bass, pp. 240–275.

Cohen, R. (1994). The ordeal of change: A true story of high school reform, *Teachers College Record*, 96(2), 148–166.

Cousins, B. (June 1994). *Understanding organizational learning for educational leadership and school reform*. Paper presented at the annual meeting of the Canadian Association for the Study of Educational Administration, Calgary. (To appear in Leithwood, K. (Ed) International handbook of educational leadership and administration. Norwell, MA: Kluwer Academic Publishers.)

Crowson, R., & Boyd, W. (Feb.,1993). Coordinated services for children: Designing arks for storms and seas unknown. *American Journal of Education*, 101, 141–179.

Dalin, P., & Rust, V. (1983). *Can schools learn*? Windsor, Berks: NFER-Nelson.

Darling-Hammond, L., & McLaughlin, M. (1995). Policies that support professional development in an era of reform. *Phi Delta Kappan.*, 76(8), 597–604.

Deal, T. (1990). Healing our schools: Restoring the heart. Chapter 7. In A. Lieberman (Ed.), *Schools as collaborative cultures: Creating the future now*. (Chapter 7). New York: The Falmer Press.

DiBella, A. (1994). *The Learning organization: A concept of being or becoming*? Paper presented at Eastern Academy of Management, Albany, New York, May.

Fessler, R. (1995). Dynamics of teacher career stages. In T. Guskey & M. Huberman (Eds.), *Professional development in education: New paradigms and practices* (pp. 171–192). NY: Teachers College Press.

Fullan, M. (1993). *Change forces*. London: The Falmer Press.

Fullan, M. (December 1994). *Teachers as leaders*. Report to the Joint Legislative Education Oversight Committee and the North Carolina State Board of Education.

Fullan, M., & Hargreaves, A. (1991). *What's worth fighting for? Working together for your school*. Toronto: Ontario Teachers' Federation.

Fuller, F. (1969). Concerns of teachers: A developmental conceptualization. *American Educational Research Journal*, 6(2), 207–226.

Gardiner, H. (1983). *Frames of mind: The theory of multiple intelligences*. New York: Basic Books.

Gitlin, A., & Margonis, F. (1995). The political aspects of reform: Teacher resistance as good sense. *American Journal of Education*, 103(4), 377–405.

Glickman, C. (1990). Open accountability for the 90's: Between the pillars. *Educational Leadership*, 47(7), 38–42.

Greene, M. (1995). Recapturing the political dimension. In M. Ginsburg (Ed.), *The politics of educators' work and lives*. New York: Garland Publishing.

Gregersen, J. (Ed). (1978). *Danish case study on evaluation of INSET programmes for teachers*. Paris: OECD.

Greiner, L. (1972). Evolution and revolution as organizations grow. *Harvard Business Review*, July-August, 37–46.

Hall, G., & Loucks, S. (1976). A developmental model for determining whether the treatment is actually implemented. *American Educational Research Journal*, 27(1).

Hall, G., Halland, G., & Hord, S. (1987). *Change in schools: Facilitating the process*. A lbany, NY: State University of New York Press.

Hallinger, P. (1995). Culture and leadership: Developing an international perspective on educational administration. *UCEA Review.*, 36(2), 1, 4–5, & 10–13.

Hallinger, P., & Heck, R. (1995). The principal's role in school effectiveness: An assessment of methodological progress, 1980 – 1995. In K. Leithwood (Ed), *The international handbook of research on educational leadership and administration*. New York: Kluwer Press.

Hamilton, M., & Richardson, V. (1995). Effects of the culture in two schools on the process and outcomes of staff development. *The Elementary School Journal* **95**(4), 367–385.

Hamstead, T., Ford, J., & Hird, W. (May, 1980). An administrative team development program. *Studies in Educational Administration*, 1–4.

Handy, C. (1994). *The age of paradox*. Boston: Havard Business School Press.

Hargreaves, A. (1995). Paradoxes of change: School renewal in the postmodern age. *Educational Leadership*, April.

Hargreaves, A., & Dawe, R. (1990). Paths of professional development: Contrived collegiality, collaborative culture, and the case of peer coaching. *Teaching and Teacher Education* , **6**, 227–241.

Huberman, M. (1995). Professional careers and professional development: Some intersections. In T. Guskey, & M. Huberman (Eds.), *Professional development in education: New paradigms and practices* (pp. 193–224). NY: Teachers College Press.

Hurst, D. (1995). *Crises and renewal: Meeting the challenge of organizational change*. Boston, MA: Havard Business School Press.

Jehn, K. (1995). A multimethod examination of the benefits and detriments of intragroup conflict. *Administrative Science Quarterly*, 40(2), 256–282.

Kanter, R. (1991). Change: Where to begin. *Harvard Business Review*, 69(4), 8–9.

Keating, D. (1995). *The learning society in the information age*. Toronto: The Canadian Institute for Advanced Research Program in Human Development, Working Paper No. 2.

Kirst, M. (1994). A changing context means school board reform. *Phi Delta Kappan*, **75**(5), 378–381.

Lave, J., & Wenger, E. (1991). *Situated learning: Legitimate peripheral participation* . Cambridge: Cambridge University Press.

Leithwood, K., & Aitken, R. (in press). *Making schools smarter: A system for monitoring school and district progress*. Newbury Park, CA: Corwin.

Leithwood, K., Jantzi, D., & Steinbach, R. (1995). *An organizational learning perspective on school responses to central policy initiatives*. Toronto: OISE.

Levin, M. (1994). New wine in old bottles: The limits of school reformation. *Orbit* , **25**(4), 45–48.

Lieberman, A. (1995). Practices that support teacher development. *Phi Delta Kappan*, **76**(8), 591–596.

Loevinger, J. (1976). *Ego development*. San Francisco: Jossey-Bass.

Louis, K. (1994). Beyond managed change: Rethinking how schools improve. *School Effectiveness and Improvement*, **5**(1), 2–24.

Louis, K., Kruse, S., & Associates. (1995). *Professionalism and community*. Thousand Oaks, CA: Corwin.

McLaughlin, M. (1993). What matters most in teachers' workplace context? In J. Little & M. McLaughlin (Eds.), *Teachers' work: Individuals, colleagues, and contexts*. NY: Teachers College Press.

McLaughlin, M. (1994). Strategic sites for teachers' professional development. In P. Grimmett & J. Neufeld (Eds.), *Teacher development in the struggle for authenticity: Professional growth and restructuring in the context of change*. (pp. 31–51). NY: Teachers College Press.

Meyer, J., & Rowan, B. (1978). Notes on the structure of educational organizations: Revised version. Paper prepared for the annual meeting of the American Sociological Association. Reported in Hannaway, J., Administrative structures why do they grow? *Teachers College Record*, 79(3), 416–417.

Miles, M. (1993). 40 years of change in schools: Some personal reflections. *Educational Administration Quarterly*, **29** (2), 213–248.

Mintzberg, H. (1994). *The rise and fall of strategic planning*. NY: The Free Press.

Mitchell, C. (1995). *Teachers learning together: Organizational learning in an elementary school*. Unpublished PhD thesis, University of Saskatchewan, Saskatoon.

Morgan, C., & associates. (1976). *Organization development (OD): The case of Sheldon High School*. London: The Open University Press.

Mulford, B. (1976). Open education and administrative styles. *The Educational Administrator*, **7**, 7–13.

Mulford, B. (1978). Organisational development in schools: An octet of dilemmas, *ACEA Bulletin, 12, and Educational Change and Development*, **1**(2).

Mulford, B. (1979). *Andragogy and some implications for teacher education*. ACT Papers on Education. Canberra: Canberra College of Advanced Education [and Canberra Papers in Continuing Education, New Series No. 2, Australian National University, Centre for Continuing Education, 1982].

360   *Mulford*

Mulford, B. (1982). Consulting with education systems is about the facilitation of coordinated effort. In H. Gray (Ed.), *The management of educational institutions: Theory, research and consultancy.* Lewes, Sussex: Falmer Press.
Mulford, B. (1994). *Shaping tomorrow's schools.* Melbourne: Australian Council for Educational Administration Monograph No. 15.
Mulford, B., Conabere, A., & Keller, J. (1977). Organisational development in schools: Early data on the Australian experience. *The Journal of Educational Administration,* 15(2).
Mulford, B., Fisher, D., & Grady, N. (1991). Educational leadership for quality teaching and learning. In R. Glatter, T. Simkins, & L. Watson (Eds.), *Developing educational leaders.* London: Longman.
Mulford, B., Watson, H., & Vallee, J. (1980). *Structured experiences and group development.* Canberra: Curriculum Development Centre.
Murninghan, K., & Conlon, E. (1991). The dynamics of intense work groups: A study of British string quartets. *Administrative Science Quarterly,* 36, 165–186.
Murphy, J. & Beck, L. (1995). *School-based management as school reform: Taking stock.* Thousand Oaks, California: Corwin Press.
Murphy, J., & Louis, K. (1994). The evolving role of the principal: Some concluding thoughts (Chapter 12). In J. Murphy & K. Seashore-Louis (Eds.), *Reshaping the principalship: Insights from transformational reform efforts.* Thousand Oaks, California: Corwin Press, Inc.
Ontario Royal Commission on Learning. (1994). *For the love of learning.* Toronto, Ontario: Publications Ontario.
Ogilvie, D. (1977). Survey feedback in four high schools. *ACEA Bulletin,* 8, 7–52.
Pentland, B., & Rueter, H. (1994). Organizational routines as grammar of action. *Administrative Science Quarterly,* 39(3), 484–510.
Peters, T. (1987). *Thriving on chaos.* London: Macmillan.
Pusey, M. (1976). *Dynamics of bureaucracy: A case study in education.* Sydney: Angus and Robertson.
Quinn, R., & Cameron, J. (1983). Organizational life cycles and shifting criteria of effectiveness. *Management Science,* 29(1), 33–51.
Redding, J., & Catalanello, R. (1994). *Strategic readiness.* San Francisco, CA.: Jossey-Bass.
Russ, J. (1995). *The learning institution: A pathway to real school improvement?* Unpublished paper, Centre for School Improvement, University of Bath.
Sackney, L., Walker, K., & Hajnal, V. (1 April, 1995). *Organizational learning, leadership, and selected factors relating to the institutionalization of school improvement initiatives.* A paper for AERA, San Francisco.
Schein, E. (1996). *Three cultures of management: The key to organizational learning in the 21st century.* Working paper #10.011, The Massachusetts Institute of Technology Centre for Organizational Learning.
Senge, P. (1990). *The fifth discipline: The art and practice of organizational learning.* NY: Doubleday.
Senge, P., Roberts, C., Ross, R., Smith, B., & Kleiner, A. (1994). *The fifth discipline fieldbook: Strategies and tools for building a learning organization.* NY: Doubleday.
Sergiovanni, T. (1990). *Value-added leadership: How to get extraordinary performance in schools.* London: Harcourt Brace Jovanovich.
Sergiovanni, T. (1994). *Building community in schools.* San Francisco: Jossey-Bass.
Shakeshaft, C. (1989). *Women in educational administration.* Newbury Park, CA: Sage.
Sheehy, G. (1976). *Passages.* NY: E. P. Dulton & Co.
Sheehy, G. (1995). *New passages: Mapping our lives across time.* NY: Random House.
Sizer, T. (1984). *Horace's compromise.* Boston: Houghton-Mifflin.
Stoll, L., & Fink, D. (1994). School effectiveness and school improvement: Voices from the field. *School Effectiveness and School Improvement,* 5(2), 149–177.
Stoll, L., & Mortimore, P. (June, 1995). School effectiveness and school improvement. *Viewpoint,* 2, 1–8. London: Institute of Education, University of London.
Thomas, F., & Caldwell, B. (1994). *Leading Victoria's Schools of the Future: Some findings from the early stages of reform.* Paper presented at the Annual Conference of the Australian Council for Educational Administration, Melbourne, Victoria, September.
Tyack, D., & Tobin, W. (1994). The "grammar" of schooling: Why has it been so hard to change? *American Educational Research Journal,* 31(3), 453–479.
Tyack, D., & Cuban, L. (1995). *Tinkering towards utopia: Reflections on a century of public school reform.* Cambridge, Massachusetts: Harvard University Press.

Watkins, K., & Marsick, V. (1993). *Sculpting the learning organization: Lessons in the art and science of systematic change.* San Francisco: Jossey Bass.

Weiss, C., & Cambone, J. (1994). Principals, shared decision making, and school reform. *Educational Evaluation and Policy Analysis, 16*(3), 287–301.

Wheelan, S. (1994). *Group processes: A developmental perspective.* Boston: Allyn and Bacon.

Policy and Change: Getting Beyond Bureaucracy

LINDA DARLING-HAMMOND[1]

Teachers College, Columbia University

One of the toughest nuts to crack in educational change is policy itself – not this policy or that policy, but the basic ways in which policy is conceived, developed and put into practice.
In this chapter, Linda Darling-Hammond outlines a new paradigm for educational policy better suited to the complexities of our times. In place of top-down, linear approaches to educational policy and its implementation, Darling-Hammond argues for a more inclusive approach to policy that combines and integrates bottom-up and top-down approaches in a framework that will be more empowering for all. Darling-Hammond argues for policy processes that create political consensus, ensure equity, develop and enforce standards and build local capacity, school-by-school for people who work in the front lines of our classrooms. Policies she says, should be more concerned with learning than compliance, as much about support as pressures and demands. She closes her chapter with specific instances of where such new paradigm policy processes in education are already beginning to emerge.

Change is a constant for educational systems. As every society's frontline institutions for social coherence, cultural continuity, and economic progress, schools must always cope simultaneously with provocations to change and conservative forces to preserve tradition. Creating school systems that can balance these forces and continually respond to their students' and societies' ever-evolving needs is always a challenge. In times of great social ferment and transformation, like the one in which we currently find ourselves, the challenge is even greater.

Three circumstances facing contemporary schools make the tasks of educational change particularly fascinating and particularly problematic. These are, first, the growing importance of educational success to individuals and societies around the world which provokes a corresponding need to create much more productive schools quickly. Second, the explosion of knowledge and the rapid pace of technological change suggest that what students will need to learn – and what schools might be expected to transmit – is both more complex and more difficult to codify in easily managed policy tools like curriculum guides, textbooks, and tests. The knowledge and capacities of frontline educators, and the responsiveness of the organizations they work in, become much more important in this situation. Third, much of the task of preparing many more citizens for more complex kinds of learning is contingent upon dealing well with diversity, a task that twentieth century bureaucracies are ill-equipped to handle.

As societies increasingly require the full range of human abilities potentially available to it, developmental strategies that build the capacities of individuals

A. Hargreaves (ed.), Extending Educational Change, 362-387.
© 2005 Springer. Printed in the Netherlands.

and institutions are ever more necessary. Glaser (1990) describes how 21st century demands require that schools shift from a selective mode, "characterized by minimal variation in the conditions for learning" in which "a narrow range of instructional options and a limited number of ways to succeed are available," to an adaptive mode in which "the educational environment can provide for a range of opportunities for success. Conceptions of learning and modes of teaching are adjusted to individuals – their backgrounds, talents, interest, and the nature of past performance." From a societal perspective, Glaser explains:

> This adaptive mode is especially relevant to today's aspirations for school-
> ing. . . . As we move toward the 21st century, we are becoming more
> pluralistic and diverse than at any time in our history, and aspects of school-
> ing that may make sense in relatively homogeneous societies are probably
> less workable in our country. In adaptive education. . . the intent is to focus
> on the needs and potential of each individual and to develop these to a high
> extent.

An eleven-nation study of teaching conducted by the Organisation for Economic Co-operation and Development (OECD) (1994) characterized new cross-national expectations this way:

> The new challenges and demands for schools and teachers emerge from new
> and heightened expectations of schools, advances in research on teaching
> and learning and the need to manage classrooms that are increasingly diverse
> in terms of ethnic, linguistic, and cultural backgrounds. These new chal-
> lenges and demands require new capacities and knowledge on the part of
> teachers. The current situation is both dynamic and varied. Schools are now
> being organised in different ways, in terms of both the tasks and the
> responsibilities assigned to teachers and the differentiation of roles among
> teachers and between teachers and other school staff. . . The breadth of the
> challenges and demands and the pace of change make the current situation
> different than in earlier years. Teachers must be able to accommodate
> continuing changes – dramatic in some countries – in the content of what is
> to be taught and how it can be taught best (p. 9).

A NEW PARADIGM FOR EDUCATIONAL POLICY

The changed mission for education rests on a new set of understandings about teaching and learning, and it requires a new framework for school reform, one in which policymakers shift their efforts from *designing controls* intended to direct the system to *developing capacity* that enables schools and teachers to be responsible for student learning and responsive to diverse and changing student and community needs, interests, and concerns. Capacity-building requires different policy tools and different approaches to producing, sharing, and using knowledge than those traditionally used throughout this century.

Competing Theories of Reform

The paradigm for school management developed in many countries at the turn of the twentieth century was grounded in a view of schools as bureaucracies run by carefully specified procedures to produce standard products (students). Based on a faith in rationalistic organizational behavior, the power of rules to direct human behavior, and the ability of researchers to discover the common procedures that would produce desired outcomes, the 20th century school reform paradigm assumed that changing the design specifications for schoolwork would change the nature of education that is delivered in classrooms – and would do so in the ways desired by policymakers.

This approach fits with an older behavioristic view of learning as stimulus-response management, easily controlled from outside the classroom by identifying exactly what is to be learned and breaking it up into small, sequential pieces dictating what should be taught and when. Now, however, we know that, far from being *tabula rasa* waiting to accumulate bits of information, learners actively construct their own knowledge in very different ways depending upon what they already know or understand to be true, what they have experienced, and how they perceive and interpret new information. Furthermore, they construct this knowledge in a much more holistic and experiential fashion than is assumed by the sequenced teaching packages, worksheets, texts, and basal readers produced by the old paradigm approach to teaching and learning (Curtis & Glaser, 1981; Gardner, 1983; Resnick, 1987).

To foster meaningful learning, teachers must construct experiences that allow students to confront powerful ideas whole, creating bridges between learners' very different experiences and common curriculum goals. They must use many different approaches to build upon the conceptions, cultures, interests, motivations, and learning modes of their students. They must understand how their students think as well as what they know. This more complex approach to teaching requires that teachers combine deep knowledge of subject matter and a wide repertoire of teaching strategies with intimate knowledge of students' growth, experience, and development (Piaget, 1970; Berliner, 1986; Shulman, 1987; Carter & Doyle, 1987). Furthermore, if schools are to be responsive to the different needs and talents of diverse learners, they must be organized to allow for variability rather than assuming uniformity. Teachers must diversify their practice so that they can engage each of their students in whatever ways are necessary to encourage their learning.

These tasks suggest a radically different approach to educational improvement. Rather than seeking to make the current system of schooling perform more efficiently by standardizing practice, school reform efforts must focus on building the capacity of schools and teachers to undertake tasks they have never before been called upon to accomplish – i.e. ensuring that *all* students will learn to think critically, invent, produce, and problem-solve. Because this requires responding to students' nonstandardized needs, such a goal far exceeds what teacher-proof curricula or administrator-proof management processes could ever accomplish.

The goal of teaching most or all students for understanding is not one that most nations have undertaken. Lawrence Cremin (1989) argued that curriculum stratification or "tracking" is a direct result of the problem of not knowing how to teach challenging content to students who do not learn it easily on their own:

> . . . There was never enough research on the nature and variety of pedagogical method that might be necessary to teach academic arithmetic, physics, or biology to the newly heterogeneous clientele of the American high school. It proved infinitely easier to juggle the substance of the curriculum than to develop pedagogies for conveying the more intellectually demanding materials to most or all of the students (p. 17).

The same dilemma is confronted in various ways in other countries, which track or stream students earlier or later, but nonetheless ultimately respond to the question of uneven student performance by differentiating curriculum rather than creating more powerful and adaptive teaching. Research on schools that have been able to produce high levels of performance for very diverse learners demonstrates that such success requires dramatically different classroom and school practices than those found in standardized settings that transmit information through rote methods (for a review, see Darling-Hammond, in press). I argue that reforms that rely on the transformative power of individuals to rethink their practice and redesign their institutions can only be accomplished by investing in individual and organizational learning – in the human capital of the educational enterprise: the knowledge, skills, and dispositions of teachers and administrators, as well as parents and community members.

This view, however, is not universally shared. In the international press for improved schooling, there are at least two very different theories of school reform working in parallel and sometimes at cross-purposes within and across nations. One focuses on tightening centralized controls: more prescribed courses, more external tests, more directive curriculum, more standards enforced by more rewards and more sanctions. Some versions of recent national testing programs and accountability schemes follow this model. These approaches essentially assume that the basic problem is a lack of focus, direction, and effort on the part of school people. Teachers are "holding out" on their students, not using their skills and exerting their efforts to produce achievement. In organizational management terms, this is the Theory X of policy thinking, which assumes:

- that the average human has an inherent dislike of work and will avoid it if he can,
- that people, therefore, need to be coerced, controlled, directed, and threatened with punishment to get them to put forward adequate effort toward the organization's ends, and
- that the typical human prefers to be directed, wants to avoid responsibility, has relatively little ambition, and wants security above all (McGregor, 1960, pp. 49–50).

This view is at odds with contemporary research indicating that workers derive satisfaction from doing their jobs effectively; are motivated by opportunities for learning, growth, and responsibility; are more productive when they have opportunities to work with others toward the attainment of shared goals; and are more effective when they receive concrete feedback about the results of their work (Deming, 1988; Senge, 1990). In this view, the task of policy is to provide these conditions for learning, feedback, and responsibility within organizations.

The second view undergirds policy proposals that aim to increase the knowledge of school staff and to redesign schools so they can use more effective practices. They attend more to the development of schools as inquiring, collaborative organizations than to tighter specifications of curricula and management systems. Policies built upon this theory include efforts to strengthen teacher education and certification processes, to create knowledge-building institutions such as professional development schools, to decentralize school decision-making, to support collegial teacher development, to redesign local assessment practices, and to create learning networks among teachers and schools. While this new paradigm of educational improvement emerges, however, the old one often remains in force, pulling educational systems in contradictory directions.

A Top-Down and Bottom-Up Approach

To add to the dilemmas of educational change aimed at developing responsive schooling is the fact that both individual schools and the policy system are deeply implicated in the change process. One lesson of change, according to Michael Fullan, is that neither centralization nor decentralization works: That is, just as systems cannot change schools by mandate, widespread school change cannot occur by school invention alone, without supports and leadership from the policy system.

If school-level reforms occur only where staff are already dynamic, deeply knowledgeable, and well-supported – and, in many systems, on waiver or by exception from standard practice – they will surely evaporate in a very short time, long before good schooling spreads to the communities where it is currently most notable by its absence. And if policies do not address questions of educational goals, system-wide capacity, and equity, the outcomes of bottom-up efforts will be inadequate to the needs of democratic societies. Neither a heavy-handed view of top down reform nor a romantic vision of bottom-up change is plausible. Both local invention and supportive leadership are needed, along with new "horizontal" efforts that support cross-school consultation and learning.

POLICY AND THE REALITIES OF CHANGE

In devising new policies for educational change, policy makers need to understand that policy is not so much implemented as it is re-invented at each level of the system. What ultimately happens in schools and classrooms is less related to the intentions of policymakers than it is to the knowledge, beliefs, resources, leadership, and motivations that operate in local contexts. These are among the factors that produce what Richard Elmore (1983) has called "the power of the bottom over the top."

Telling schools to change has never worked to produce markedly different teaching over many decades of efforts at curriculum reform (Cuban, 1990; Tyack & Tobin, 1994). Studies of change efforts have found that the fate of new programs and ideas rests on teachers' and administrators' opportunities to learn, experiment, and adapt ideas to their local context. Without these opportunities, innovations fade away when the money or enforcement pressures end (Berman & McLaughlin, 1978; Fullan, 1991). Because policies "cannot mandate what matters most" (McLaughlin, 1990), they must alter the conditions for local learning if they want to achieve their goals.

In addition, policy makers need to understand that their intentions will land in an environment already constrained by geological layers of prior policies and local conditions that may be hostile to the desired changes (Darling-Hammond, 1990). They must build capacity for and commitment to the work required, rather than assuming that edicts alone will produce new practice. The more policies impose inflexible constraints, the less possible and likely it is for innovation and learning to occur.

A particularly knotty problem is how to generate and sustain changes aimed at a "pedagogy of understanding,"– that is, teaching so that all students, not just a few, can come to understand ideas deeply enough to apply them to novel situations and to perform proficiently in their own right. This kind of teaching, which reformers claim must become much more widespread to meet today's and tomorrow's educational demands, is much more complex than traditional transmission teaching that seeks to produce straightforward recall and recognition of information.

Howard Gardner (1991) claims that no society has developed an educational system that succeeds fully at teaching most students for understanding, although more and more countries hold this as a goal. Practice that succeeds in developing deep understanding of challenging content for a wide range of learners is highly complex: it maintains a dialectic between students and subjects, allowing neither to overwhelm the other. Because students will necessarily come to any learning experience with different strategies and prior experiences – which provide different starting points for the material to be learned – successful teachers must know how to help students access ideas in a variety of ways, without losing track of the content and while pressing always for more disciplined understanding.

This kind of teaching is purposeful and may be highly structured, but it is also inevitably improvisational. Because real understanding is always hard-won and human beings bring different mixes of abilities and types of insight to the task, there is no pre-packaged set of steps or lessons that will secure it for every learner in the same way. Teachers have to bring a great deal of knowledge and analytic ability to the task of developing understanding with their students.

Transmission teaching is much simpler. Teachers can "get through" texts and workbooks. Classroom routines are straightforward, and controls are easier to enforce. There is a sense of certainty and accomplishment when a lecture has been given, a list of facts covered, or a chapter finished, even if the result is little learning for students. When a teacher has delivered information, it is easy to say "I taught that" even if students did not learn it. Active learning situations infuse more uncertainty in the teaching process. When a student is building her own understanding through a research project, for example, the teacher needs to construct careful scaffolding to guide the learning process and well-designed strategies for eliciting the student's thinking in order to know what is being learned.

Particularly in those nations that have invested least in teacher preparation, many teachers have not been taught how to implement variable, student-based strategies while also teaching for high levels of disciplined understanding in the content areas. Unless teachers know how to create situations in which learners can have real breakthroughs in understanding and know how to evaluate learning and adapt their teaching, it is easy to lose track of either the students or the curriculum goals in the process of breaking with routines. Teachers who are unprepared for the task often try to be more child-centered by letting go of subject matter standards, or more subject-centered by ignoring students while the curriculum marches on ahead.

Given the difficulties of the task ahead, what are policy makers to do?

Lessons from Previous Curriculum Reforms

An examination of recurrent efforts to expand the reach of engaging, intellectually demanding instruction in the United States is instructive in developing an answer to this question. There, neither bottom-up nor top-down reforms of the 1930s, 1960s, and early 1990s have had much reach or staying power. The efforts of progressive educators in the 1930s demonstrated both the success of school-level reforms and their failure to change the system. Conversely, government-sponsored curriculum reforms in the 1960s demonstrated how consensus about learning could be created at the "top" of the system without widely influencing the field.

A major reason for these failures was the process by which changes were sought in schools beyond the initial experimental sites. Early "implementers" who had had the opportunity to become deeply engaged in the process of school invention developed the commitment and capacity to undertake new practices. Others, however, were later expected to enact these complex and different ideas without struggling through a process of questioning and developing their own practices. Reform ideas are often passed on as dicta or mandates, a thin listing of new things to do, conveyed with little discussion or rationale. Thus, many of the practitioners involved in the second and later stages of reform never really understood what the initiatives were about.

Perhaps the most important finding from a major longitudinal study of progressive schools during the 1930s (the Eight Year Study conducted by Ralph Tyler and a team of leading researchers), was that the the most successful schools were distinguished by the process of inquiry they undertook together rather than the content of the particular reforms they developed. Their success came from "their willingness to undertake a search for valid objectives," using these to guide curriculum and organizational decisions and ongoing evaluation (Chamberlin, Chamberlin, Drought, & Scott, 1942). Teachers and administrators reported that it was the collective thinking stimulated by this process that engendered the vitality, willingness to change, and conviction to continue that changed the life of the school (Aikin, 1942).

This commitment and a schoolwide capacity for collective problem solving are essential to any serious change. Because practices that take learning seriously affect all of the core technologies of schooling, they threaten all of the "regularities" of schools (Sarason, 1982). When teachers try to develop more challenging instruction and attend to the individual needs of students, their efforts bump up against traditional schedules, discipline policies, grading and promotion procedures, and virtually everything else that defines the schooling enterprise. When schools are able to recognize the extensive changes needed for this kind of teaching to succeed, new instructional practices can lead to transformation of other existing conditions of schooling. Otherwise, reforms become diluted or pushed off to special programs for small numbers of students. If the whole school does not evolve to support the demands of more challenging instruction and more learner-centered practices, the changes are strangled. Practitioners claim, honestly, that "we tried it and it didn't work."

Similarly, it can be argued that the federal curriculum reforms of the 1960s were successful in articulating the big ideas underlying a curriculum of understanding and enacting them in powerful ways in the schools where teachers worked as partners in invention (Elmore, 1996). Their participation in the inventive process made serious change possible. As the curricula spread to other schools, however, teachers were expected to implement approaches they had had no role in developing. Without deep understanding or commitment to the ideas, they were unable to bring them off successfully, and the reforms died out.

Despite a tremendous investment in development and a massive flurry of adoption activities, the reforms withered on the vine, soured by the inability of most teachers to implement the kind of challenging instruction they envisioned and starved of local support for the kind of teaching and learning they sought. The limited payoff from these enormous investments demonstrates that reliance on top-down curriculum reform alone as a means of changing schools is a strategy with serious flaws. School change is a much more complicated affair, resting on the capacities and willingness of teachers and administrators to comprehend and undertake desired changes, as well as on the support or resistance offered by the community in which they must root if they are to survive.

Analysts who have examined the failure of England's initial foray into a complex national curriculum and assessment system have made similar points (See, for example, Silvernail, in press). As seems to have been true in the recent British experience, the post-mortem analyses of the United States' 1960s reforms found that teachers' curriculum translations were so varied as to negate the concept of a common curriculum (Gallagher, 1967). Students' ultimate achievement and attitudes proved to be less a function of the curriculum than of teachers' values, teaching behaviors, and the social learning climate in classrooms (Rothman, Welch, & Wahlberg, 1969; Walberg & Rothman, 1969). Finally, the processes of curriculum implementation and school change – that is, the ways in which schools and school districts set out to engage these new ideas – strongly influenced outcomes (Carlson, 1965). The manner in which change is introduced and supported influences the attitudes, knowledge, ability, and political will of those attempting implementation (Fullan, 1991). And the dispositive factor in curriculum reform is what teachers know, believe, and are able and willing to do.

U.S. curriculum reforms of the 1990s are meeting a similar fate. For example, with little information or professional development available, teachers striving to use the state of California's new mathematics framework have had difficulty learning to teach in new ways. One teacher commented to a researcher, "My biggest hurdle to doing all these new methods. . . is my knowledge of what I've done all these years." Another asked repeatedly, "Still, how do you teach problem solving? I do not know" (Darling-Hammond, 1990, p. 239).

The flawed belief that reforms can be "replicated" elsewhere once they have been developed in demonstration sites is one key to the unhappy history of curriculum change. The process of change is inherently constructivist. Any reform that is merely implemented will eventually recede rather than taking root. Each school community must struggle with new ideas for itself if it is to develop the deep understanding and commitment needed to engage in the continual problem-solving demanded by major changes in practice. As Michael Fullan notes, it is impossible to achieve ownership in advance of learning something new. "It is only when greater clarity and coherence is achieved in the minds of the majority of teachers that we have any chance of success" (Fullan, 1994, p. 4).

Transformations that stick also require the involvement of parents and students and the commitment of education agency officials who will otherwise continue to develop competing policies. Because many school systems do not know how to manage the intensive engagement with ideas and people required to enact broad policy change, they typically adopt only the superficial trappings of reforms – those features they can absorb with comfort without threatening the status quo. If schools do not have the fiscal resources or curriculum tools to enact reform goals or if community members are suspicious about the goals and tactics of new curricula, they cannot succeed. Furthermore, policies do not land in a vacuum; they land on top of other policies, many of which are not conducive to the strategies needed for enacting the "new" ideas.

In the case of the California mathematics framework, researchers found that teachers' efforts were confounded by the state's multiple choice basic skills testing program, which was at odds with the goals of the new framework, and by many districts' use of direct instruction models for classroom control and teacher evaluation. One teacher noted that:

Teaching for understanding is what we are supposed to be doing. . . (but) the bottom line here is that all they really want to know is how are these kids doing on the tests. . . They want me to teach in a way that they can't test, except that I'm held accountable to the test. It's a Catch 22. . .

(quoted in Wilson, 1990).

Especially in decentralized systems with substantial policy making by lay bodies, educational directives frequently exist in conflict with one another. Teachers sense the contradictions in the way they are being required to teach under old systems and the way they would need to teach to be successful in the new system, but education agencies have not been prepared to deal with the conflicts their policies posed. In the United States, as in other decentralized countries that have been trying to implement reforms, teachers' efforts to learn a difficult new pedagogy have been undermined by curriculum guides, teacher evaluation systems, and testing programs reflecting contradictory images and standards for teaching. Centralized systems can also experience these problems, as well as the problem of moving from a reasonably coherent system aimed at one set of goals to a system with new goals which has not yet changed all of the policies and practices aligned with the older paradigm of teaching and learning. As Brian Rowan (1996) notes:

Misaligned standards can result from an incremental approach to change, in which standards in one area are reformed while others remain unchanged. But misaligned standards can also result from invalid theories of performance. For example, policy makers can hold a faulty theory of teacher performance and design a system of educational standards consistent with this faulty theory.

Getting it Right

Coherence clearly counts. If parts of the policy system conflict with one another, the enterprise lurches about like a carriage pulled by horses dashing off in different directions. When school people are continually asked to work in self-contradictory contexts, they must either become cynical or adopt an Alice-in-Wonderland attitude – "if you don't know where you're going, any road will get you there." After a while, people cease trying to make sense of things.

The obvious need for sensible, reinforcing connections among the influences that guide teaching, learning, curriculum, assessment, evaluation, and funding has led to a set of proposals for "systemic reform" that have informed much policy work in the 1990s, especially in decentralized systems, which appear frustrating fragmented to many reformers (Fuhrman, 1993; O'Day & Smith, 1993; OECD, 1994). Even among those who believe that greater coherence in the cause of more empowering forms of learning is a worthy goal, however, there is substantial disagreement about how best to achieve it. A key area of disagreement is the extent to which systemic reform ought to try, as some reformers did at the beginning of the 20th century, to design and mandate the specifications for schooling from the top of a governmental system and the extent to which it ought to establish key parameters and supports while delegating strategic and technical decisions to schools, communities, and the teaching profession.

The questions of how to find the right balance between top-down and bottom-up decision-making are arising in many contexts. A recent analysis of curriculum reform in seven nations (OECD, 1993) noted efforts in highly centralized systems like France, Spain, and Sweden to allow more institutional autonomy "to allow for greater flexibility of response to the very real different educational needs of students within the system" (p. 39). Meanwhile, more decentralized systems like England, Germany, and the United States were pursuing reforms to create more commonality in education across localities, aiming to "harmonize the provision [of education] made in different parts of the country" (p. 53).

Finding the right role for government. Part of the task of developing more constructive supports for schools is understanding what the best roles are for government and for local practitioners, parents, and professional associations. We now know some things about what governments are good at and where their intervention is likely to be counterproductive. In general, higher level agencies are needed for allocating and reallocating resources in equitable ways, for addressing gross abuses of authority or law, and for supporting learning across institutions and jurisdictions. They can help spread knowledge by funding and disseminating research and demonstration projects; and they can help widely dispersed people and institutions work with one another, thus offsetting parochialism and inefficiences in service delivery. Recently, networks have become another strategy for doing this where bureaucracies have failed.

However, governments are not good at specifying precisely how funds should be spent, how resources should be configured, or how educational "treatments" should be conceived and delivered. As Tom Green (1980) notes:

> Public policy is a crude instrument for securing social ideals. We would not use a dropforge to quarter a pound of butter or an axe to perform heart surgery. Public policy is the dropforge or the axe of social change. It is not the knife or scalpel. That is to say, public policy deals with gross values. It . . . is not the fit instrument to secure all our desires. For example, even if we knew what is needed to make every school excellent and every teacher a paradigm of wisdom in the care of children, it would remain doubtful that we could express this knowledge in public policy and thus secure the good we seek . . . Minimizing evil is a proper aim of public policy. Maximizing good is probably not. The latter assumes that we may shape the axe into a scalpel (pp. 322–323).

It is useful to divide responsibilities between those that must be centrally administered and those that, by their nature, should not be. Wise (1979) offers a useful distinction between equity and productivity concerns. The former generally must be resolved by higher units of governance, since inequalities arise out of the conflicting interests of majorities and minorities and of the powerful and the powerless. Because local institutions are apparently the captives of majoritarian politics, they intentionally and unintentionally discriminate. Consequently, we must rely upon the policymaking system to solve problems of inequity in the operating educational system (p. 206).

However, productivity questions are intrinsically more difficult because they arise not out of a political impasse but from the fact that the appropriate use of teaching knowledge is highly individualized, while policies are necessarily standardized. Varying student circumstances make it impossible to effectively regulate methods of teaching. It is because public policy cannot act as an effective arbiter of such decisions that it is important to ensure professional competence.

This analysis suggests that governments should undertake policies that:

(1) create a political consensus around goals for education and adopt high-quality standards and assessments that evaluate the extent to which they are being met,
(2) ensure adequacy and equity in the allocation of resources,
(3) develop and enforce meaningful standards of competence for professional staff, and
(4) build local school capacity through professional development and the support of organizational learning across schools.

Meanwhile, governments should delegate decisions about teaching and learning processes and specific curriculum strategies to local schools and professional associations that can better account for the needs of individual learners and for advances in knowledge. Professionally-developed standards can create a lens for examining local school practice against norms (Elmore, 1996). This can create the discourse needed to support improvement within schools while also developing an external presence for accountability.

As a non-hierarchical alternative to the top down / bottom up rhetoric which places policy people at the top and school people at the bottom, we might imagine embedded concentric circles beginning with the student, the teacher, and the school and eventually encompassing the community, the school district, and the state. This image allows for an "inside out/outside in" view of schooling influences. Productive tension and learning can occur as faculty interact with one another and with students and families within schools, and as schools interact with community concerns, external standards, and professional networks. These influences are multi-directional; every part of the enterprise informs and affects every other.

For each aspect of the system, accountability is achieved as shared goals, norms, and values are translated into *policies*, organizational *structures* created to make the policies work, *processes* used within these structures, *feedback and assessment* mechanisms established to identify needs and progress, *safeguards* created to ensure that harmful practices do not occur, and *incentives* to promote productive practices. For children to be well-served, these aspects of school, district, and state efforts must work together and focus on both the demands of learning and the needs of learners.

Supporting the work of change. If policymakers want to design policies that can work to change instruction in support of greater understanding, their theories must

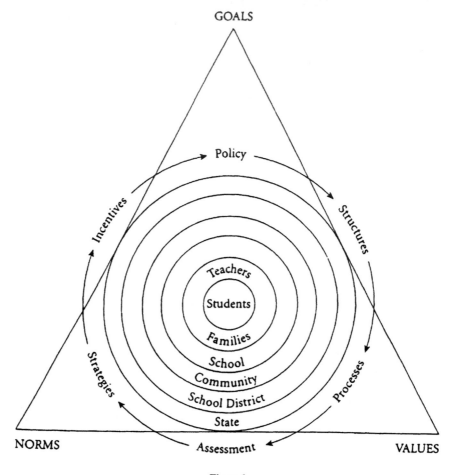

Figure 1

account for the ways in which teacher knowledge, beliefs, and contexts influence their teaching. In particular, they need to understand how human beings learn to do things differently (Elmore, 1996), so that they can structure reforms in ways that are likely to be able to change practice.

What teachers already know and believe about subjects and students, what they have had the opportunity to learn about pedagogy, and what the structures of schools enable them to do are all critical variables. Policymakers who want teachers to succeed at new kinds of teaching must understand that the process of change requires time and opportunities for teachers to reconstruct their practice through intensive study and experimentation.

This means that policies should, first, create extensive *learning opportunities* for teachers, administrators, parents, and community members, so that the complex practices envisioned by ambitious learning goals have a chance to be studied, debated, tried out, analyzed, retried, and refined until they are well-understood and incorporated into the repertoire of those who teach and make decisions in schools. These opportunities must be collaborative rather than individualistic, creating groups of educators, parents, and others inside and across schools who interact regularly around problems of practice, who can engage in joint problem solving, probe the meaning of their experiences, and provide each other with moral support in the difficult process of reform.

Second, policies should allow for widespread *engagement* of a school's constituencies in the process of considering, developing, and enacting changes. For this to occur, communities must have a substantial role in constructing their own reforms rather than trying merely to implement ideas handed down to them by others – ideas which are bound to be poorly understood and mistrusted unless there is an opportunity to create adaptations that are valued and appropriate in the local context. The trick is to provide leadership and direction that enables participation rather than smothering it in precriptions for implementation.

Third, policies should recognize the need for *simultaneous change* in all of the regularities of schooling that influence the possibilities for successful teaching of this kind. This means rethinking the array of policies – from school funding to teacher education to school accreditation to collective bargaining rules – that hold the current regularities of schooling so firmly in place.

Finally, policies should be constructed in ways that maintain the delicate balance between external standards that press for improvement and the school autonomy needed to create an engine for internal change. I argue that this can best be achieved by developing *professional standards* for learning, teaching, and schooling and using them to guide *school inquiry* processes that stimulate engagement, learning, and renewal within schools.

Standards for Student Learning

One area in which the debates about policy are currently most heated, and efforts for change are most pronounced, is in the area of setting curriculum standards and assessments. Some centralizers argue that governments should create a tightly specified curriculum that outlines in great detail what is to be taught each year, in invarying scope and sequence, so that transient students will be able to "pick up" with the curriculum wherever they go (see e.g. Hirsch, 1996). In systems that have previously done so, efforts are moving in the opposite direction (OECD, 1993). The problem with heavy-handed curriculum guidance is that it ignores the role of the learner in the learning process. Even students who stay in one place learn at different rates and in different ways. While general curriculum guidance can be useful in helping teachers build on the work of their predecessors, lockstep curriculum programs hold some back when they are ready to move ahead while proving ineffective for those who do not learn in the manner the curriculum assumes they will.

To be effective, teachers must meet students *where they are,* not where an ideal-ized curriculum guide imagines they should be. This is even more important in nations with high rates of immigration and mobility where students continually enter and exit classrooms at various ages and grade levels from other states and countries. If teachers are to succeed, they must have the flexibility to teach what students need to know based on what they have learned before. Teachers must also be free to use material that allows them to create connections with what students can understand. Curriculum guidance that overly prescribes content and methods prevents teachers from creating the necessary bridges between students' experiences and learning goals.

Standards and frameworks are likely to be most useful when they focus on a relatively small set of truly important core ideas and on preparing students to inquire successfully into new areas of study, to find and use information so that they can analyze and generate ideas, and to produce ideas and products so that they have the tools to continually educate themselves for the world they will live in. It is important for standards to leave room for local choices in how learning opportunities are structured to maximize their chances of making sense to students. One extraordinarily successful teacher in an inner city school in Los Angeles argues that external standards should account for about 50% of curriculum space and teaching time, leaving the other 50% for teachers to create work that builds on students' interests and experiences and addresses their specific learning needs (Guti-errez, 1995). At least some of this work should be jointly developed and assessed by teachers across the school, so that collective goals and norms of practice are established to create a more coherent, reinforcing experience for students.

At their best, curriculum standards can provide a general aim and vision for changes that must still be worked through in more specific terms in the schools. This "working through" is in itself educative and supportive of change as it stimulates inquiry into practice. Local engagement in standard-setting is important for several reasons: first, because contexts vary and hence good practice must also vary; second, because ownership and involvement are critical components of the change process; and finally, because learning how to practice well (or differently) requires active engagement in constructing the intellectual foundations upon which that practice rests. This last reason is why progressive educators have always insisted that teachers must learn to be curriculum developers rather than being trained only as curriculum implementers. Teachers must learn how to look closely at their students and think deeply about curriculum goals and the varieties of pathways to learning if they are to teach in ways that make the connection between students and subjects. They can profitably use curriculum ideas developed by others, but they must construct the curriculum enacted in their classrooms with their own students in mind.

If teachers are to focus on essential goals rather than a cacophony of compet-ing directives, government policy makers will need to restrain themselves from thinking that the only strategy for change is to enact an ever-increasing pile of mandates from the top, leaving regulatory gridlock and intellectual chaos in the schools that must reconcile these conflicting impulses. As Michael Fullan (1994) notes of United States standards-writing efforts to date:

> Current systemic reform initiatives may ironically actually increase (schools') overload and incoherence problem. What looks like clarity at the top may contribute more clutter at the bottom. There is no reason to assume that the systemic reform debate to this point has added one iota of clarity to the confusion faced by the majority of teachers (p. 4).

While coherence is an important goal, it is most important that it be achieved at the local school level where students and teachers must make sense of the educational environment, so that it works toward integrated learning. This kind of local coherence is possible only if educators are encouraged to use resources such as standards and frameworks as tools for informing their own curriculum-building, rather than as mandates to implement unthinkingly.

Multi-Level Standard-Setting. The presumption of hierarchical intelligence – that is, the notion that higher levels of government will always create better ideas to guide local decisions – has been a problem for educational policymaking in systems that have grown more centralized over time. This assumption has created regulatory gridlock in some school systems. It is an assumption that competes with ideals about local control, decentralization, and diversity and that has been increasingly brought into question by the lessons of restructuring businesses which have learned the importance of encouraging front-line inventiveness.

In the U.S., for example, the presumption that national standards would be superior to state and local initiatives has already proved to be unwarranted. Some local work was built upon more serious consensus-building, better-grounded views of teaching and learning, and more sophisticated thinking about teaching and assessment than some of the federally-sponsored standards efforts turned out to be. Many states and localities were concerned that their own efforts would be held hostage to less thoughtful conceptions of teaching, schooling, and the disciplines if they must be certified against national standards, rather than evaluated on their own terms.

At the same time, local work can also be shoddy. It can be poorly informed, unaware of knowledge about teaching and contemporary conceptions of disciplinary knowledge, constructed hurriedly, and developed without adequate input. There is no guarantee that what is invented locally will always be of high quality, and little sense in asking everyone, including practitioners who are already overloaded, to reinvent the wheel on their own.

The trick, then, is figuring out how to value quality throughout the system and to create better vehicles among educational agencies for sharing knowledge. Since the field knows little about how to structure curriculum to support the success of a wide range of learners at much more intellectually ambitious tasks, it is important to encourage different approaches and learn from those that work, Schools that are succeeding at the dual tasks of raising expectations and helping diverse learners to meet them should be studied and understood as grist for ongoing work on standards and school improvement. Their approaches should inform the standard-setting work of states and national organizations, just as their practice may be informed by the efforts of these other bodies.

If systems are to learn how to support successful practice where it exists and grow it in other places, the assumption of hierarchical intelligence must be suspended. Government agencies should take on as their own obligation learning about what allows good schools to succeed and what effects agency actions have on school practices. The policy system must learn to be both appropriately humble and effectively bilateral so that its work is informed by the wisdom of good practice and its efforts do not override those of good schools.

There are ways to construct policy that provide leadership while also developing local capacity to make good decisions and leaving room for those decisions to be made. In some systems, educational policy makers have tended to use only a limited array of tools that are potentially available to them, relying more heavily on mandates or ineffectual inducements for change than on strategies that increase the authority of professional guidance for practice and that transform the incentives that operate within and across schools (Elmore & Fuhrman, 1993).

One way to promote continued healthy debate and experimentation is to encourage multiple versions of standards and have them reviewed by bodies comprised of members with expertise in the discipline(s), curriculum and teaching, assessment, and schooling. (For one example of how this might be done, see Cohen, 1995.) A diverse set of high-quality standards and assessment options might be preferable to a single set of standards as sources of intellectual leavening for states and local districts that are creating curriculum frameworks, so long as these were informed by research and professional knowledge about learning and had in common a focus on students learning to reason, understand, and apply their knowledge.

As many governments seek to use new student standards to improve curriculum, teaching, and assessment, they should seek policy strategies that encourage schools to consider professionally developed standards as touchstones for their development of curriculum and assessments, while focusing national or state frameworks and assessments on a small but powerful set of core knowledge and skills which are at the heart of schools' central purposes: the ability to think, communicate effectively, use mathematical and scientific ideas well, understand social systems, and acquire resources to frame and solve problems. If governments can resist the temptation to prescribe everything, and if they create processes that allow some local participation in standard-setting and assessment development, they will have begun to create the conditions under which schools develop the capacity to set standards wisely and teach more effectively.

Local Participation in Assessment. Ultimately the work of enacting new standards is intensely local and directly tied to the work that teachers and students do together. As David Cohen (1995) notes, the chief use of standards is to help to focus attention on student work, "and it is student work that we want to improve, not standards or scholars' ideas about standards" (p. 755). Real improvements will come about not because standards have been written by committees, but because they begin to come alive as teachers study student work; collaborate with other teachers to improve their understanding of subjects, students' thinking, and learning; and develop new approaches to teaching that are relevant and useful for them and their students.

Teachers' hands-on work with the creation of curriculum and assessments and the setting of standards is part of their own learning process and a major motivator for change.

> Translating an idea into action and experiencing its consequences counts for much more [than simply having a new idea] and constitutes the basis of personal (as opposed to "academic" knowledge and learning. . . If significant change is to occur, it requires a quality of experience that supports personal exploration, experimentation, and reflection (Chittenden, Bussis, & Amarel, 1976, p. 17).

It is for this reason that the locus of assessment development and scoring are as important as the nature of the assessment tools and strategies. An assessment system in support of improved teaching and learning will include both state- and locally-developed assessments that are constructed and evaluated by teachers to inform their teaching as well as to inform their publics. In schools that are developing more authentic assessments of student learning, especially when these are schoolwide exhibitions or portfolios, teachers' engagement in evaluating student work proves to be a powerful vehicle for professional development, because it helps them look at the effects of teaching on learning.

Looking at student work with other teachers and discussing standards in very explicit ways also helps develop shared definitions of quality. Evaluating work collaboratively rather than grading students in isolation helps teachers make their standards explicit, gain multiple perspectives on learning, and think about how they can teach to produce the kinds of student work they want to see. Where teachers do this, changes in teaching and schooling practices almost invariably occur – especially for students who are not as often successful at schoolwork (Darling-Hammond, Ancess, & Falk, 1995; Kornhaber & Gardner, 1993). This also happens in settings where teachers from different schools convene to score assessment tasks together. As one account describes the conversations of some U.S. teachers from Vermont who gather in the summer to evaluate portfolios:

> Often heated, the discussions focused on what constitutes good communication and problem-solving skills, how first rate work differs from less adequate work, and what types of problems elicit the best student work (Murnane & Levy, 1996).

As teachers see how students approach tasks, they learn about their teaching. A 4th grade teacher from rural Vermont, put it this way: "Through the scoring I find my own personal weaknesses in what I am doing with my children. By seeing so many portfolios and listening to Jill (the leader of the 4th grade math scorers) I find lots of avenues that I can bring back to my children" (Murnane & Levy, 1996). The more information teachers obtain about how students perform, the more capacity they have to rethink their pedagogy, and the more opportunities they create for student success.

In addition, when schools wrestle with standard-setting, the collective struggle to define directions, to evaluate progress, and to "map backward" into new curriculum and teaching possibilities can create an engine for schoolwide change that is absent when assessment is entirely externalized. Case studies of schools in many different countries (OECD, 1993) note the importance of teachers assessing learning together to plan their teaching. The use of the new Record of Achievement, a method for teachers to document student performance in Italian schools, provokes conversations about the links between teaching and learning (p. 61). Teachers involved in self-assessment in a Finnish school "talk about the possibility of doing things in a different way so as to attain even better results. Teachers are continually writing a school-level curriculum. Objectives, contents, means and methods of evaluation are the subjects of continuous development" (p. 62). In a U.S. school working on new forms of assessment, when teachers found students unprepared for the demands of the new Senior Project they had developed, they began to integrate research skills into their courses, give students more practice in oral and written communication, and plan professional development days to address the issues that had surfaced, such as integrating mathematics across the curriculum and teaching special education students more effectively (Darling-Hammond, Ancess, & Falk, 1995).

Mixed models that include roles for both states and local schools in developing and implementing standards and assessments that "count" can support local change while also stimulating widespread rethinking of educational goals.

This inside-out, outside-in approach can be supported by school quality reviews, like those recently developed in several states in the United States modifying inspectorate systems from Great Britain and some parts of Europe. In these reviews, expert teams of local practitioners and education agency staff spend a week in individual schools to examine teaching and learning and create an "evidence base" about school practices. This becomes the basis for continuous work on school improvement, linking standards for student learning to standards of teaching practice in a fashion that takes account of local contexts and stimulates local improvements that enrich students' opportunities to learn.

After reviewing the school's goals, reviewers shadow students, sit in dozens of classrooms, sit in faculty meetings, look at students' work, examine school documents, and interview teachers, students, administrators, other school staff, and parents. Following this intensive immersion in the teaching and learning work of the school, the team members aggregate their information, develop a collective perspective on what they have seen, and prepare an oral and written report to the school reflecting back to school members what they have observed. By helping schools look at the consonance and gaps between their visions and current realities, the review process motivates self-generated change as people recognize that there is work to be done to achieve their own goals. The review process helps to generate the kind of tension between ideals and reality that Peter Senge describes as essential for organizational learning:

The juxtaposition of vision (what we want) and a clear picture of current reality (where we are relative to what we want) generates what we call "creative tension": a force to bring them together, caused by the natural tendency of tension to seek resolution. "Learning" in this context does not mean acquiring more information, but expanding the ability to produce the results we truly want . . . . And learning organizations are not possible unless they have people at every level who practice it (Senge, 1990, chap. 9).

The school quality review process differs from many accreditation procedures by directly examining practice rather than reviewing documents and by focusing on the quality of teaching and learning rather than on inputs like the number of library books or the paper credentials of staff. It also differs from accreditation or registration procedures in its affirmatively developmental stance. It is not used for monitoring or decision-making about the school. It is used to provide feedback about how well the school is achieving its goals and enacting professional standards of practice. Its explicit goal is to help stimulate thinking about ongoing school development and improvement. The process has proved an extremely effective strategy for serious change focused on teaching and learning, rather than rules and procedures (Ancess, 1996).

Standards and Supports for Teaching

Finally, educational change in the context of current demands of schools requires substantially more knowledge directly in the hands of educators, rather than organized to influence the top of a hierarchical system from which it is supposed to "trickle down" to teachers in the form of memos, directives, texts, and curriculum guides. Although things like standards, funding, and management are important, the sine qua non of education is whether teachers know how to make complex subjects accessible to diverse learners, and whether they can work in partnership with parents and other educators to support children's development. If only a few teachers have this capacity, most schools will never be able to produce better education for the full range of students who attend them. Furthermore, managing decentralizing decision-making successfully so that responsible decisions are made depends on the development of a professionwide base of knowledge along with a commitment to the success of all students – in short, the development of a stronger education profession.

What do teachers need to know to teach all students for high levels of understanding and performance? First of all, teachers need to understand *subject matter* in ways that allow them to organize it so that students can create useful cognitive maps of the terrain. They need more than formulaic or procedural understanding of the core ideas in a discipline and how these help to structure knowledge, how they relate to one another, and how they can be tested, evaluated, and extended. Teachers also need to be able to use their knowledge of subject matter flexibly to address ideas as they come up in the course of learning. They need to understand how inquiry in a field is conducted and what reasoning entails – such as what counts as "proving" something in mathematics as compared with proving something in history (Ball & Cohen, in press). And they need to see ways that ideas connect across fields, and to everyday life, so that they can select and use examples, problems, and applications well.

Understanding subject matter in this way provides a foundation for *pedagogical content knowledge* (Shulman, 1987), which enables teachers to represent ideas so that they are accessible to others. Knowledge of the domain of study is critical: the teacher needs to understand what ideas can provide important foundations for other ideas and how they can be usefully linked and assembled. The audience is also key: people will understand ideas differently depending on their prior experiences and context. A skillful pedagogue figures out what a particular audience is likely to know and believe about the topic under study, and how learners are likely to "hook into" new ideas, so as to create productive learning experiences. Knowledge of cognition, information processing, and communication are also important so that teachers can shape lectures, materials, learning centers, projects, and discussions in useful ways.

Interpreting learners' statements and actions and framing productive experiences for them requires knowledge of *development* – how children and adolescents think and behave, what they are trying to accomplish, what they find interesting, what they already know and what they are likely to have trouble with in particular domains at particular ages in particular contexts. This knowledge includes an understanding of how to support further growth in a number of domains – social, physical, and emotional, as well as cognitive.

Teaching in ways that connect with students also requires an understanding of *differences* that may arise from culture, language, family, community, gender, prior schooling, or other factors that shape people's experiences, as well as differences that may arise from developed intelligences, preferred approaches to learning, or specific learning difficulties. Teachers need to be able to inquire sensitively and productively into children's experiences and their understandings of subject matter so that they can interpret curriculum through their students' eyes and shape lessons to connect with what students know and how they learn well. To get non-stereotypic information that can help them come to understand their learners, teachers need to know how to listen carefully to students and look at their work as well as to structure situations in which students write and talk about their experiences and what they understand. This builds a foundation of *pedagogical learner knowledge* (Grimmett & Mackinnon, 1992) which grows as teachers examine how particular learners think and reason, where they have problems, how they learn best, and what motivates them.

An understanding of *motivation* is critical in teaching for understanding, because achieving understanding is difficult. Teachers must know how to structure tasks and feedback so as to encourage extensive effort without either relinquishing the press for understanding when the going gets tough or discouraging students so that they give up altogether.

Motivating students not only requires understanding general principles about how to engage young people and sustain their interest at different ages, but also understanding what individual students believe about themselves and their abilities, what they care about, and what tasks are likely to give them enough success to encourage them to continue to work hard to learn.

Teachers need several kinds of knowledge about *learning*. Since there are many kinds of learning – for example, learning for recognition or appreciation vs. learning for various kinds of applications or performances – teachers need to think about what it means to learn different kinds of material for different purposes, how to support different kinds of learning with distinctive teaching strategies, and how to make judgments about which kinds of learning are most necessary in different contexts. Not everything can be learned deeply – that is, with opportunities for extensive application – but some things must be deeply understood as foundations for work that is to follow and as a means for developing specific skills and performances. Other ideas may be understood more superficially to create a map of the domain, but learned so that they connect to concepts that are meaningful.

Teachers need to understand what helps children (or anyone) learn in these different ways. They need to be able to construct and use a variety of means for *assessing* students' knowledge, as well as for evaluating student's approaches to learning. To be effective, they must be able to identify the strengths of different learners while addressing their weaknesses – those who rely more on visual or oral cues; those who tend to reason from the specific to the general or vice-versa; those who use spatial or graphic organizers vs. those who are more text-oriented; those who bring a highly-developed logical/mathematical intelligence and those who bring a strong aesthetic sense.

Using this information well requires a command of *teaching strategies* that address a variety of ways to learn and a variety of purposefully selected goals for learning. Strategies that regularly use multiple pathways to content are one major part of a teacher's repertoire. In addition, more than ever before in the past, all teachers need tools to work with the students in their classrooms who have specific learning disabilities or needs. And, because language is the gateway to learning, teachers need an understanding of how students acquire language, in both their native language and others, so that they can build language skills and create learning experiences that are accessible.

Teachers need to know about *curriculum resources and technologies*. They need to be able to connect their students with sources of information and knowledge that extend beyond textbooks, that allow for the exploration of ideas, the acquisition and synthesis of information, and the development of models, writings, designs, and other work products. The teacher's role will be to help students learn to find and use a wide array of resources for framing and solving problems, rather than to remember only the information contained in one source.

And they need to know about *collaboration*. They need to understand how interactions among students can be structured to allow more powerful shared learning to occur. They need to be able to shape classrooms that sponsor productive discourse that presses for disciplined reasoning on the part of students. They need to understand how to collaborate with other teachers to plan, assess, and improve learning within and across the school, as well as how to work with parents to learn more about their students and to shape supportive experiences at school and home.

Finally, teachers need to be able to *analyze and reflect* on their practice, to assess the effects of their teaching and to refine and improve their instruction. When teaching for understanding, teachers must maintain two intertwining strands of thought at all times: How am I doing at moving the students toward high levels of understanding and proficient performance? and How am I taking into account what students know and care about in the process of moving them toward these curriculum goals and developing their talents and social abilities? Teachers must continuously evaluate what students are thinking and understanding and reshape their plans to take account of what they've discovered as they build curriculum to meet their goals.

These demands that derive from the desire to teach a much wider range of students for much higher standards of performance are new ones for many teachers and teacher educators. However, over the last decade, a quiet revolution in teaching has been underway. In many societies, teaching is evolving from an occupation that was thought to require relatively little skill to a profession that enables its members to become as capable as the real demands of the work require. The profession has begun to engage in serious standard-setting that reflects a growing knowledge base about teaching and a growing consensus about what teachers should be able to do to help all students learn to challenging new standards. Changes are underway in teacher preparation programs around the world; approaches to licensing, certification, and accreditation are being redesigned; and, in the U.S., a new National Board for Professional Teaching Standards has created assessments for certifying accomplished teachers. In some places, a concerted effort has been made to strengthen the knowledge base for teaching and teachers' regular access to that knowledge. In others these efforts remain piecemeal – a good idea here and a thriving innovation there. To support educational change that is responsive to students' real needs and the demands of ever more complex societies, it will be increasingly critical to create systems for teacher development that ensure teachers ongoing access to the knowledge they need to teach.

BUILDING NEW PARTNERSHIPS BETWEEN RESEARCH, POLICY, AND PRACTICE

Creating widespread change will require an infrastructure for adaptive, learning-centered education: policies that develop more intelligent professional preparation; that support appropriate teaching, learning, and assessment practices; that provide educators with continuous opportunities to learn; and with resources to enable them.

Building such knowledge and capacity in schools will require constructivist relationships between research, policy, and practice that allow reciprocal learning to occur. Researchers cannot hand knowledge to policymakers to enact in new mandates anymore than policymakers can hand new practices to teachers to enact in classrooms.

Policymakers and educators must together develop strategies for professional development that will infuse greater knowledge in schools and schools of education to strengthen their ability to transmit and develop knowledge for practice.

In the search for "what works" researchers, educators, and policymakers must also be prepared to deal with the dilemmas of change – to acknowledge that getting there is extremely hard work which requires massive learning from us all. "Schools should" statements will not get us from research to practice. Trying to "mandate what matters most," without building capacity for new practice, leads to certain failure. If we have learned anything about change it is that all of the actors in the system need to develop first-hand deep understanding of new ideas and of the complex kinds of practice needed to carry them off. This is beginning to happen most productively where people are creating hyphenated roles for themselves as researchers, teachers, and policy makers engaged in *doing* policy, school reform, and teaching as well as looking at it (Darling-Hammond, 1996). These activists are helping schools deepen their capacity by moving beyond a world in which those who think and plan are separated from those who teach and do the work; they are working to understand schooling, teaching, and change by engaging in the work as well as by studying it and by creating collaboratives for democratic work and action. This kind of work, at the nexus of policy, research, and practice will be, perhaps, the most productive for provoking 21st century educational change.

ENDNOTES

[1]   This chapter draws substantially on Darling-Hammond, L. (1997). The right to learn. San Francisco: Jossey-Bass.

REFERENCES

Aikin, W. (1942). *Adventure in American Education Vol 1: Story of the Eight Year Study*. NY: Harper and Brothers.

Ancess, J. (1996). *Outside/inside, inside/outside: Developing and implementing the school quality review.* NY: National Center for Restructuring Education, Schools, and Teaching, Teachers College, Columbia University.

Rowan, B. (1996). Standards as incentives for instructional reform. In S. H. Fuhrman & J. A. O'Day (Eds.), *Rewards and reform: Creating educational incentives that work* (pp. 195–225). San Francisco: Jossey-Bass.

Berliner, D. C. (1986, August-September). In pursuit of the expert pedagogue. *Educational Researcher*, 513.

Berman P. & McLaughlin, M. W. (1978). *Federal programs supporting education change: Implementing and sustaining innovations* (Vol. 8). Santa Monica, CA: RAND.

Carlson, R. O. (1965). *Adoption of educational innovations*. Eugene, Oregon: Center for Advanced Sudy of Educational Administration, University of Oregon.

Carter, K. & Doyle, W. (1987). Teachers' knowledge structures and comprehension processes. In J. Calderhead (Ed.), *Exploring teacher thinking* (pp. 147–160). London: Cassell.

Chamberlin, D., E. S. Chamberlin, N., Drought, & W., Scott. (1942). *Adventure in American education, vol. 4: Did They Succeed in College?* NY: Harper and Brothers.

Chittenden, E., Bussis, A., & Amarel, M. (1976) *Beyond surface curriculum*. Boulder, CO: Westview Press.

Cohen, D. (1995, June). What standards for national standards? *Phi Delta Kappan*: 751–757.

Cremin, L. (1989). *Popular education and its discontents.* NY: Harper & Row.

Cuban, L. (1990). Reforming again, again, and again. *Educational Researcher*, **19**, 3–13.

Curtis, M., & Glaser, R. (1981). Changing conceptions of intelligence. In D. Berliner (Ed.), *Review of research in education* (Vol. 9). (pp. 111–150). Washington, D.C.: American Educational Research Association.

Darling-Hammond, L. (1990). Instructional policy into practice: The power of the bottom over the top. *Educational Evaluation and Policy Analysis.*

Darling-Hammond, L. (1996). *The right to learn: A blueprint for creating schools that work.* San Francisco: Jossey Bass.

Darling-Hammond, L., Ancess, J., & Falk, B. (1995). *Authentic assessment in action: Studies of schools and students at work.* NY: Teachers College Press.

Deming, W. E. (1988). *Out of the crisis.* Cambridge, MA: Massachusetts Institute of Technology.

Elmore, R. (1983). Complexity and control: What legislators and administrators can do about implementing policy. In L. S. Shulman & G. Sykes (Eds.), *Handbook of teaching and policy.* NY: Longman.

Elmore, R. (1996). Getting to scale with good educational practice. In S. Fuhrman (Ed.), *Incentives and school reform.* San Francisco: Jossey-Bass.

Elmore, R., & Fuhrman, S. (1993). Opportunity to learn and the state role in education. In *The debate on opportunity-to-learn standards: commissioned papers.* Washington, D.C.: National Governors Association.

Fuhrman, S. H. (1993). The politics of coherence. In S. H. Fuhrman (Ed.), *Designing coherent policy: Improving the system.* San Francisco: Jossey-Bass.

Fullan, M. (1991). *The new meaning of educational change.* NY: Teachers College Press.

Fullan, M. (1994). *Turning systemic thinking on its head.* Paper prepared for the U.S. Department of Education.

Gallagher, J. J. (1967, January). Teacher variation in concept presentation. *BSCS Newsletter* (No. 30).

Gardner, H. (1983). *Frames of Mind: The Theory of Multiple Intelligences.* NY: Basic Books.

Gardner, H. (1991). *The unschooled mind: How children think and how schools should teach.* NY: Basic Books

Glaser, R. (1990). *Testing and Assessment: O Tempora! O Mores!* Pittsburgh, PA: University of Pittsburgh, Learning Research and Development Center.

Green, T. F. (1980). *Predicting the behavior of the educational system.* Syracuse, NY: Syracuse University Press.

Grimmett, P., & MacKinnon, A. (1992). Craft knowledge and the education of teachers. In G. Grant (Ed.), *Review of research in education*, (Vol. 18, pp. 385–456). Washington, D. C.: American Educational Research Association.

Gutierrez, C. (1995). Personal communication.

Hirsch, E. D. (1996). *The schools we need and why we don't have them.* New York: Doubleday.

Hudson Institute. (1987). *Workforce 2000: Work and workers for the 21st century.* Indianapolis, IN: Author.

Kearns, D. (1988). An education recovery plan for America. *Phi Delta Kappan*, **69**, 565–570.

Kornhaber, M., & Gardner, H. (1993). *Varieties of excellence: Identifying and assessing children's talents.* NY: National Center for Restructuring Education, Schools, and Teaching.

McGregor, D. (1960). *The human side of enterprise.* NY: McGraw-Hill.

McLaughlin, M. W. (1990). The RAND change agent study revisited: Macro perspectives and micro realities. *Educational Researcher*, **19** (9), 11–16.

Murnane, R., & Levy, F. (1996). Teaching to new standards. In S. Fuhrman & J. O-Day (Eds.), *Rewards and reform.* San Francisco: Jossey-Bass.

O'Day, J. A., & Smith, M. S. (1993). Systemic school reform and educational opportunity. In Susan Fuhrman (ed.), *Designing coherent education policy: improving the system.* San Francisco: Jossey-Bass.

Organisation for Economic Cooperation and Development (OECD). (1993). *Curriculum reform: Assessment in question.* Paris: Author.

Organisation for Economic Cooperation and Development (OECD). (1994). *Quality in teaching.* Paris: Author.

Piaget, J. (1970). *Science of education and the psychology of the child.* NY: Penguin Books.

Resnick, L. (1987). *Education and learning to think.* Washington, DC: National Academy Press.

Rothman, A. I., Welch, W., & Walberg, H. J. (1969). Physics teacher characteristics and student learning. *Journal of Research in Science Teaching*, **6**, 63.

Rowan, B. (1996). Standards as incentives for instructional reform. In S. H. Fuhrman & J. A. O'Day

(Eds.), *Rewards and reform: Creating educational incentives that work* (pp. 195–225). San Francisco: Jossey-Bass.

Sarason, S. (1982). *The culture of schools and the problem of change* (Rev. ed.). Needham Heights, MA: Allyn & Bacon.

Senge, P. (1990). *The fifth discipline: The art and practice of the learning organization.* NY: Doubleday.

Shulman, L. (1987). Knowledge and teaching: Foundations of the new reform. *Harvard Educational Review,* 57(1), 1–22.

Silvernail, D. (1997). *England's market system of education.* New York: National Center on Restructuring Education, Schools, and Teaching.

Tyack, D., & Tobin, (1994). The "grammar" of schooling: Why has it been so hard to change? *American Educational Research Journal,* 31(3), 453–479.

Walberg, H.J., & Rothman, A. I. (1969). Teacher achievement and student learning. *Science Education,* 53, 256–257.

Wilson, S. (1990, Fall). A conflict of interests: Constraints that affect teaching and change. *Educational Evaluation and Policy Analysis,* 12 (3),

Wise, A. E. (1979). *Legislated learning.* Berkeley, CA: University of California Press.

International Handbook of Educational Change - Table of Contents

Printed in the United States
45623LVS00002BA/23

9 781402 032912